COLLECTED WORKS OF ERASMUS

VOLUMES 23 AND 24

Literary and Educational Writings 1 and 2

Edited by Craig R. Thompson

These volumes are the first in a series containing works by Erasmus 'that concern literature and education': interests which to him were scarcely separable. For centuries the classical curriculum was the core of liberal education, and Erasmus was long regarded as its exemplar. The four works presented here in annotated translations are characteristic expressions of his dedication to learning and his confidence in the values of classical literature for the modern world of his time.

Antibarbari (1520), translated and annotated by Margaret Mann Phillips, is a defence of the humanities against ignorant and misguided critics who question both their supposed worth and the appropriateness of pagan writings for Christian pupils. The reply of Erasmus becomes a manifesto on behalf of reason, scholarship, and literature. As for paganism, he insists that if secular knowledge is used properly it cannot harm but must help Christians.

Parabolae (1514), translated and annotated by R.A.B. Mynors, a work that 'contributes eminently to style,' is a collection of similitudes drawn from observations of men, customs, and nature. Many are culled from Plutarch and Seneca, but for those from Seneca, and from Aristotle, the moral applications are added by Erasmus.

De copia (1512), translated and annotated by Betty I. Knott, is not a plan for the entire curriculum but a treatise on the 'abundant' or rich style in writing and speaking Latin, a guide to attaining fluency and variety in discourse. It was a remarkably successful work, used in schools in many lands for generations. From 1312 to 1600, more than 130 printings are recorded.

De ratione studii (1312), translated and annotated by Brian McGregor, furnishes a concise but clear exposition of the curriculum, text, and methods of Erasmus' programme for liberal studies in grammar schools. Here as in all of his writings on education, language is the heart of the matter.

Each translation is introduced by the translator, and a general introduction by the editor discusses the significance of each of the works, its relation to the others, and its subsequent fortunes. Wallace K. Ferguson provides an introductory essay, 'The Works of Erasmus.'

CRAIG R. THOMPSON Schelling Professor of English Literature, University of Pennsylvania

Erasmus
Hans Holbein the Younger, 1523
Erasmus is shown standing at a table, writing the opening lines of his Paraphrase on
St Mark, which he dedicated to Francis I, king of France (Ep 1400). The Louvre
portrait was once owned by Charles I of England, who traded it to Louis XIII of
France for a picture by Leonardo da Vinci.
Musée du Louvre, Paris (Giraudon)

COLLECTED WORKS OF
ERASMUS

LITERARY AND EDUCATIONAL WRITINGS 1 AND 2

ANTIBARBARI / PARABOLAE

DE COPIA / DE RATIONE STUDII

edited by Craig R. Thompson

University of Toronto Press

Toronto / Buffalo / London

The research and publication costs of the
Collected Works of Erasmus are supported by the
Social Sciences and Humanities Research Council of Canada
(and previously by the Canada Council).
The publication costs are also assisted by
University of Toronto Press.

Library of Congress Cataloging in Publication Data
Erasmus, Desiderius, d. 1536.
Literary and educational writings.
(Collected works of Erasmus; v. 23–24)
Bibliography, v. 2: p.
Includes indexes.
CONTENTS: [1] Antibarbari. Parabolae.–
[2] De copia. De ratione studii.
I. Thompson, Craig Ringwalt, 1911–
II. Title.
PA8502.E5T5 1978   089'.71   78-6904
ISBN 978-0-8020-5395-4 (bound)   ISBN 978-1-4875-2073-1 (pbk.)

Collected Works of Erasmus

The aim of the Collected Works of Erasmus
is to make available an accurate, readable English text
of Erasmus' correspondence and his
other principal writings. The edition is planned
and directed by an Editorial Board, an Executive Committee,
and an Advisory Committee.

Contents

Illustrations

The Works of Erasmus

Although the number of students of the Renaissance who have not read some of Erasmus' works must be small, very much smaller must be the number of those who are acquainted at first hand with the entire *corpus* of his writings. In view of the enormous volume and variety of his published works, it seems indeed unlikely that there have been many since his own day who have read them word for word in their entirety. What is more to the point, however, is the fact that the number of those capable of reading any considerable portion of what Erasmus wrote in its original form has in recent years greatly diminished. His most popular works, it is true, notably *The Praise of Folly* and the *Colloquies*, have been translated frequently, and several others have also been made available in English, although not always in carefully edited and annotated editions. The greater part of his writings, however, can still be read only in Latin and hence remain practically inaccessible even to those who can read some Latin but do not feel sufficiently at home in it to read it easily. It was to rectify this deplorable situation that the present edition of the *Collected Works of Erasmus* (cwe) was undertaken.

The editors hope that cwe will attract readers who are simply members of the educated reading public as well as those who have a profession-

* * * * *

Works cited frequently in these volumes are referred to in the notes in abbreviated form only. A list of the abbreviations and full bibliographical information are given in cwe 24 704–5.

In these volumes references to the correspondence are to the English translation of the letters in cwe, where these have already been published, or to the Latin edition of Allen. Since Allen's numbering of the letters has been adopted in cwe, letters are cited by epistle number and, where applicable, line number (for example Ep 66; Ep 373:5–6). In references to letters not yet published in cwe 'Allen' will be inserted before the letter and line numbers (for example, Allen Ep 1814:23).

References to the works translated in these volumes refer to page and line numbers.

al interest in the Renaissance and Reformation. Even Erasmian specialists, since few can be equally familiar with all parts of the humanist's vast literary production, may find the translation useful if only as a time-saving device, although for passages of special importance they would doubtless check with the original Latin text. Scholars for whom Erasmus' works have only a peripheral relation to the main subject of their research will find it an even greater convenience. Every scholar is familiar with the time-consuming necessity of skimming rapidly through masses of possibly relevant material in the hope of finding something he can use or, conversely, that there is nothing there for him. And anyone, with the possible exception of a few professional classicists, who has attempted to skim through the columns of LB will probably admit that he could have grasped the sense more rapidly had it been in English. Such utilitarian considerations aside, however, it is to be hoped that most readers will read the great humanist's works as they deserve to be read – for their inherent interest.

The varied character of the potential readers of CWE presents certain problems which the editors and annotators can solve only by a series of compromises. At times they may feel constrained to identify classical, biblical, or historical figures and to explain allusions that some readers will think could safely be taken for granted and that possibly could have been a century or so ago. At the same time they will attempt to satisfy the legitimate demands of Erasmian specialists by providing somewhat more critical apparatus than the general reader may feel necessary. They will not, however, annotate simply for the sake of annotating. Nor, while calling attention to recent scholarship bearing directly on the subject, will they load the notes with bibliographical material easily obtainable elsewhere. In general they will attempt, as a minimum requirement, to furnish in notes and introductions such information as a well-educated reader might require in order to understand the text.

A further problem which the editors have had to solve is that of arranging Erasmus' works in some sort of rational order. At first glance a chronological sequence, like that adopted in the volumes of correspondence, would seem the most obvious solution. But closer examination proves it to be in practice unfeasible. Erasmus frequently worked on more than one project at a time. Two at least of his most important works, the *Adages* and the *Colloquies*, were republished in enlarged editions over a period of years. Some of his earlier writings, too, were revised at intervals for as much as two decades before he finally put them into print. Once his fame was firmly established, printers were eager to have anything he wrote. On more than one occasion they published unauthorized editions from early or corrupt manuscripts, thus forcing Erasmus to bring out revised and corrected editions worthy of his mature reputation.[1]

A more practical solution, therefore, seemed to be to follow in general conception the plan for the arrangement of his works for publication set down by Erasmus himself in a letter to Johann von Botzheim, 30 January 1523,[2] and again with additions and some minor alterations in a letter to Hector Boece, 15 March 1530.[3] Here he arranged his shorter works in groups according to subject matter or purpose, while the longer ones, like the *Adages*, the Correspondence, and the New Testament, were left to stand by themselves, all with little concern for chronological sequence.

In the letter to Botzheim Erasmus divided the list of his works into ten volumes, beginning with the volumes into which he would put 'everything that concerns literature and education' and ending with two volumes which were never actually published in any collection of his *opera*. Volume IX was to be dedicated to the *Letters* of Jerome 'on which,' he wrote, 'I have expended so much labour that I can without impudence add this work to my own list,' while the tenth was left open for his Commentaries on the Epistle to the Romans in the hope that Christ would grant him life and strength enough to finish it.

In the letter to Boece the list was brought up to date with the addition of works published since 1523. Apparently Erasmus realized that some of the groups had now grown too large to be published in a single volume, and so he substituted the term *ordo* for *tomus*. Otherwise the second list follows the first fairly closely, with three major exceptions. The New Testament and the *Paraphrases*, to which had been assigned the sixth and seventh volumes respectively, were now put together to form the sixth *ordo*, while the seventh, thus left vacant, was filled with Erasmus' translations of the Greek Fathers, Chrysostom, Athanasius, Origen, and Basil, all published since 1523. Finally Erasmus tacitly abandoned the projected tenth volume while at the same time vastly expanding the ninth *ordo* to include the whole of Jerome, the *Opera omnia* of Augustine, and half a dozen other Latin texts of patristic authors which he had edited and published.

The canon of Erasmus' works thus established was followed in the first edition of the *Opera omnia*, that published by Froben at Basel in 1538–40, except that the Latin editions of the Fathers which had composed the ninth

* * * * *

1 Epp 66; 71 introduction; 130:108n
2 Allen I 38ff
3 Ep 2283. For the lists of Erasmus' works in the letters to Botzheim and Boece see the appendix to CWE 24.

ordo were omitted, the *Paraphrases* were once more separated from the New Testament to make up the seventh *ordo*, while the translations from the Greek Fathers and the *Apologiae* became the eighth and ninth respectively. The omission of what had been the ninth *ordo* in the letter to Boece was doubtless the result of economic considerations rather than wilful disregard of Erasmus' wishes. The reprinting of such massive works would have been prohibitively expensive. Moreover, since they were editions of Latin texts, they lacked the quality of semi-originality that enhanced the value of Erasmus' translations from the Greek. They have never been published in any edition of the *Opera omnia*. Yet Erasmus' desire to add them to the list of his published works is easily understandable. The list, indeed, would have seemed to him sadly incomplete without them. They had cost him years of arduous toil, and he had reason to feel that to make available in print carefully edited and corrected editions of the Fathers was one of his most important contributions to the study of theology. This is a point worth noting, lest the facts that they do not appear in the *Opera omnia* and that they have been superseded by later scholarship lead us to underestimate their importance for their own age.

Although a good deal of new material, especially in the form of letters, poems, or various bits of juvenilia, was brought to light from manuscript sources during the century and a half following the publication of the Froben *Opera omnia*, Jean Leclerc adopted the same arrangement of the works in the great Leiden edition of 1703–6, commonly known from its place of origin (Lugduni Batavorum in the Latin) as LB. The result was a rather awkward variation in the size of the volumes, the division of volume III (the Correspondence, swollen by many newly discovered letters) into two parts, and the addition of a tenth volume, numbered consecutively after volume IX, to take care of the overflow of the *Apologiae*. When listing these in 1523 Erasmus had added to the heading the heartfelt cry: 'These too (alack the day!) will make a whole volume ... and I pray there may be nothing to add!' It was a vain hope.

The editors of the new edition of the *Opera omnia* (ASD), in process of publication in Amsterdam since 1969, have stated their intention to respect the Erasmian *ordines*, but have permitted themselves considerable freedom in number, sequence, and contents of the volumes within each *ordo*. This scholarly edition with its lengthy introductions and its massive substratum of footnotes will eventually replace LB, but, despite its obvious superiority, many scholars will still retain a nostalgic affection for the familiar Leiden edition.

The editors of CWE have allowed themselves still more freedom in their arrangement of the works, while conforming to Erasmus' intention as nearly as seems feasible under the altered conditions imposed by translation and by a different type of potential reader. Certain practical considerations have, however, led them to abandon the constricting scheme of the *ordines,* among them consideration for the convenience of librarians who might find it awkward to catalogue books under both *ordo* and volume numbers. Some alterations in the grouping of the works have also resulted simply from the fact that the modern reader tends to regard them from a different point of view from that of the aging humanist as he looked back over his life's work. For example, it now seems natural to place the *Antibarbari* at the beginning of the first volume of the Works, that devoted to the teaching of letters.[4] Not only was it Erasmus' first major literary undertaking; it was also a kind of revolutionary manifesto proclaiming the need to rescue education from the hands of the barbarians and to restore Good (that is, classical) Letters. It was a theme to which he returned perpetually throughout his life. Erasmus himself, on the other hand, arranging the order of his works at a time when such a call to battle was less needed, seemed to regard the *Antibarbari* as simply one of his innumerable controversial pamphlets and placed it among the *Apologiae.* In the letter to Botzheim it is sandwiched rather incongruously between the *Spongia adversus Ulricum Huttenum* and the *De libero arbitrio.*

In much the same way the modern reader's view of the *Colloquies* may differ in some degree from that of its author. Erasmus seems to have valued it less highly than his more serious writings.[5] In accordance with its ostensible purpose he placed it in the overcrowded first *ordo* among his educational works. It is true that in its early form as *Colloquiorum formulae* it was designed merely to provide examples of colloquial Latin for students. Even in its final form, after it had long outgrown its purely pedagogical purpose, it was widely used as a school text for two centuries or more. But as Erasmus added more and more colloquies in edition after edition from 1522 on, the mature *Colloquies* developed into a literary masterpiece in which he expressed his ideas freely on subjects of every sort, religious and secular. Read for pleasure by every generation since, it has been one of Erasmus' most popular books, second only to *The Praise of Folly.* The editors have therefore thought it fitting to give it an independent position more or less centrally located in the series of Works.

A more striking innovation in the arrangement of the works has been planned for the volumes of CWE devoted to the New Testament. Aside from

* * * * *

4 The editors of ASD, despite their stated intention of maintaining the *ordines,* also placed the *Antibarbari* at the beginning of the first volume.
5 Cf Thompson *Colloquies* xxvii.

the fact that Erasmus printed the Greek text, in itself an offence verging on
heresy in the minds of conservative theologians, it was his annotations on
the text which made his New Testament the most controversial of all his
works. Although ostensibly intended merely to elucidate the text,[6] the
notes became in fact a running commentary, discursive and interpretive,
serving as an effective vehicle for the dissemination of Erasmus' conception
of the *philosophia Christi*. They were very widely read. Even when published separately, they ran through edition after edition. In his *Paraphrases*
on the books of the New Testament, published at intervals from 1517 to
1524,[7] Erasmus found an even more congenial medium for his propaganda
for religious reform in the free interpretation of what he believed to be the
real meaning of the Scriptures. They were in fact a greatly expanded commentary, shorn of all philological apparatus and written in an informal style
designed to appeal to any educated reader. They proved to be immensely
popular, especially in England where they were early translated and where,
thanks to the influence of Catherine Parr, an injunction of Edward vi, 31
July 1547, ordered that copies of the *Paraphrases* on the Gospels in English
should be placed in every church.[8] Hitherto the *Paraphrases* and the *Annotations* have never been published together. The editors of cwe have felt
that a fuller understanding of the development of Erasmus' thought would
be facilitated by placing both, together with the biblical text and the
translator's notes, in close proximity.

As for the Correspondence, vastly increased in size by the great
number of letters to and from Erasmus that has come to light since his
death, it has seemed logical to place it in the opening volumes of cwe and to
treat it as forming a special category, different in kind from the Works, to
which in fact it forms the perfect introduction. In the *Opus epistolarum*, as
the editors of asd have noted, lies the key to the *Opera omnia*.[9] Moreover the
existence of Allen's magisterial edition, for the free use of which we cannot
be too grateful to the Clarendon Press, has made the Correspondence a
tempting place at which to begin this edition.

Aside from the rearrangement of the Works outlined above, the
editors of cwe have departed from the Erasmian canon by omitting a
number of works which were either untranslatable or pointless when
translated. Erasmus was proud of his translations from the Greek of Lucian,

* * * * *

6 Cf Ep 373:5–6.
7 Cf Allen Ep 710 introduction.
8 See E.J. Devereux 'The Publication of the English *Paraphrases* of Erasmus'
   Bulletin of the John Rylands Library 51 (1969) 354ff.
9 Cf asd I–1 xiv.

Galen, Euripides, and Plutarch, and rightly so. At a time when knowledge of Greek was still rare in northern Europe, to make these available in Latin was no mean contribution to his life-long campaign for the revival of classical literature. His own mastery of Greek had been hard won, and he regarded his translations as almost equivalent to original works and worthy of presentation to influential patrons.[10] They have been included in all Latin editions of the *Opera omnia*. But they have little value for modern readers with the exception of those who are sufficiently at home in both the ancient languages to appreciate Erasmus' ability to catch in Latin the nuances of Greek poetry and prose. These nuances, however, must inevitably be lost when translated into English. The editors have therefore seen no point in publishing an English translation of a Latin translation of a well-known Greek classic. There seemed to be even less reason, if possible, for an English translation of Erasmus' translation of Theodorus Gaza's *Greek Grammar*, useful though it was to his contemporaries. It is, in any case, by its very nature almost untranslatable, as are also Erasmus' 'epitome' of Lorenzo Valla's *Elegantiae linguae latinae* and his revision of William Lily's little book on Latin syntax, *De constructione octo partium orationis*, written for St Paul's School and revised by Erasmus at Colet's request.[11]

Of greater interest, because of their role in the revival of patristic studies during the Reformation, were Erasmus' translations of the Greek Fathers, now published in volume VIII of LB, but the same argument for omitting them from CWE applies to these as to Erasmus' translations of the Greek classics. The editors hope, however, that at some convenient place they may publish as much as seems feasible of Erasmus' original contributions in the way of introductions and notes, not only to these but also to the numerous critical editions of the Latin texts of classical and patristic authors which he prepared for the press.

A more difficult problem, although in some respects similar to that presented by Erasmus' translations from the Greek, concerns his poems – some six thousand lines in all. It is difficult to avoid the conviction that these, particularly the long poems written during his apprentice years, were essentially exercises and that their chief reason for existence was to demonstrate their author's ability to write classical metres correctly. This was, it is true, an accomplishment highly prized by the humanists of Erasmus' generation, and to attempt it was almost obligatory for anyone who aspired to the status of a man of letters. Clearly, however, no trace of

* * * * *

10 See Epp 187, 191, 192, 193, 197, 199, 205, 261, 267, 293.
11 Cf Ep 341. It appears in the letters to Botzheim and Boece and in the table of contents of LB I under the title *Syntaxis*.

classical metre would remain in an English prose translation – nor, indeed, in a complete verse translation. Yet they are not without translatable content. The religious poems of his mature years, reprinted scores of times,[12] were almost certainly read for their edifying content as well as for their classical form. There are also interesting fragments of biographical information scattered through occasional poems and epigrams. But of all the poems, their modern editor finds only one that expresses a deep personal emotion and rises to the level of genuine poetry: the meditation on approaching old age written in 1506 while Erasmus, still under forty, was riding across the Alps on his way to Italy.[13] Just what will be the place of the poems in CWE has not yet been determined, but should the editors eventually decide to publish translations of them in whole or in part, their task will be greatly simplified by the existence of Reedijk's meticulous edition, which would serve for the poems a function similar to that of Allen's *Opus epistolarum* for the Correspondence.

In much the same way the Amsterdam edition of the *Opera omnia* has already begun to establish a scholarly textual foundation with accompanying critical apparatus for the volumes of the Works. The editors and translators of CWE do not consider it part of their duty to edit the Latin text before translating it. That task they leave with gratitude to the editors of ASD, from whose labours they expect to draw increasing profit. For those works which have not yet appeared in ASD the translators will in general follow the text in LB. They will, however, collate the LB text with earlier authorized versions where there are significant variants, but will note only substantive changes, additions, or omissions that seriously alter the sense of the text. For each work the translator will supply a brief introduction summarizing its origins and textual history, as well as the general character of such changes as were made in successive editions during Erasmus' lifetime.[14] Such introductions, as well as the editor's general introduction to each volume, will of necessity vary in length and in the amount of detail considered necessary to facilitate the reader's understanding of the text. And while consistency is a virtue – though not beyond price – translators and editors must be left considerable leeway to use their discretion in adapting their contribution to the requirements of the work in hand.

W K F

* * * * *

12 Cf Reedijk 112.
13 *Carmen de senectute*; cf Reedijk 121ff and 280ff.
14 When different editions of Erasmus' works are identified by year dates only, the dates are italicized.

Introduction

I

When Erasmus in 1523–4 and again in 1530 drew up a list of his writings[1] for an edition of his collected works, should one ever appear, he assigned to the first volume those *quae spectant ad institutionem literarum* 'that concern literature and education.'[2] Among them are three of the four works in these first two volumes of a series devoted to translations of Erasmus' literary and educational writings in CWE. *De copia* describes the principles and methods of abundant or 'rich' style in discourse. *De ratione studii* summarizes the Erasmian curriculum in a liberal education. *Parabolae* shows what ethical wisdom and adornment of style lie in metaphors drawn from apposite passages in Greek and Latin authors. The fourth work, *Antibarbari*, because it is argumentative as well as expository, is relegated by Erasmus to a later volume of 'apologies.' As a spirited attack on 'barbarism' and a cogent defence of the classics, however, it is more appropriate to the present volumes than to one reserved for Erasmus' numerous controversies with academic and ecclesiastical adversaries. Its character as an eloquent though uncompleted statement of the case for Good Letters entitles it to stand first in this series. The other three works were included in volume I of the large folio edition of Erasmus' *Opera omnia* published by Froben in 1538–40 and are characteristic treatments of subjects to which he often returned: the value of classical languages and literature, their role in liberal education, and the relations between classical and Christian culture.

Antibarbari was begun as early as 1488 and possibly even earlier, but the manuscript was lost for many years, and no version of what remains was printed until May 1520 (Basel: Froben). *De copia* and *De ratione studii*

* * * * *

1 His letter to Botzheim (Allen I 38ff), in which the list is included, is dated 30 January 1523 and was printed in April 1523, but the list was added in the second edition of the letter, September 1524. For the two lists see the appendix in CWE 24 693–702.
2 Allen I 38:19–20

date from the period in the 1490s when Erasmus was living in Paris. The first edition of *De copia* appeared in July 1512 (Paris: Bade); the same volume contained the first authorized edition of *De ratione studii*, of which an unofficial and partial text had already been printed three times (1511–12). *Parabolae* was printed first in a volume containing a revised edition of *De copia* and other material (Strasbourg: Schürer December 1514). The proximity in dates of publication for three of these four works is a suggestive fact for Erasmus' biographers and at times a challenge to his editors. Of more concern to the non-specialist, who may be reading these writings for the first time, or at any rate has them in the same volumes in English for the first time, is the question of what their purposes were and why for many years they had readers.[3] In one sense the question answers itself. If writings intended for teachers and pupils were often reprinted, as for example *De copia* was, they must have been used; and if that is so, it is evident that they served the needs of education as education was then defined and carried on.

Not all schools were the same in every respect, to be sure, but they had more uniformity in curricula and procedures than ours have. Erasmus laboured to improve schooling, but he was not a radical reformer or visionary. On the question of liberal education for girls he was, like a few other humanists, ahead of his time, though this topic plays no part in the four works under discussion. In his belief in literature as the best instrument of liberal education, and in his immutable commitment to the best writings of the best classical authors as the choicest literature, he was in the true sense of the word conservative. In his opinions on the teaching and use of this literature he differed unmistakably from many of his predecessors and contemporaries. His treatises and essays enunciated principles, described methods, furnished texts and other materials to make schooling more rational and more rewarding. To compare and contrast the old and new in

* * * * *

3 So far as can be determined, this volume and the next contain the first complete English translations of these writings to be printed and published. Portions of *De copia* (chaps 1–33 of book I and all of book II) are translated in Donald B. King and H. David Rix *Desiderius Erasmus of Rotterdam 'On Copia of Words and Ideas'* (Milwaukee 1963). Woodward provides an abbreviated version, much of it paraphrase, of *De ratione studii*. James F. Larkin's unpublished dissertation on *De ratione studii* (University of Illinois 1942) includes a translation. Mrs Lizette Westney's *Erasmus' Parabolae sive similia: An English Translation with a Critical Introduction* (Ohio State University dissertation 1972) is unpublished. All of these works have been useful to the writer of this introduction.

his conceptions of education would require a long account with many quotations of what school texts, grammars, rhetorics, and teaching standards were like before the advent of purified Latin, of Greek, of printing, and their consequences: in short, of everything Erasmus and other humanists thought of as the 'renaissance' or 'revival' or 'restoration' of arts and letters.[4] Such an account cannot be attempted in a volume whose main purpose is to let Erasmus speak for himself, in English. Specialists in Renaissance studies would be the first to acknowledge that 'the Renaissance' (a metaphor, after all) is a term beset with ambiguities, whether used to denote an epoch or to characterize cultural and intellectual activities of that epoch.[5] An inquirer who wishes to satisfy himself as to the nature of what Erasmus and like-minded men deplored when they criticized their predecessors must be familiar with the literature, philosophy, and scholastic curricula of the fifteenth and sixteenth centuries, but from *Antibarbari* and *De ratione studii* he can at least learn what Erasmus says they were like; what inherent defects he found in prevalent texts, tastes, and practices, both literary and scholastic; and what reforms he thought were needed.

Some of Erasmus' moral essays and literary works have as much to do with what he conceived of as education, in the broad sense of the word, as did his specifically pedagogical tractates. They all contain the same presuppositions about life and society, and express the same convictions about learning and teaching. Whether an impassioned defence of humanities in *Antibarbari*, or books used as guides or manuals (*De copia* and *De ratione*

* * * * *

4 'When I was a boy, the humanities had begun to put forth fresh shoots among the Italians; but because the printer's art was either not yet invented or known to very few, nothing in the way of books came through to us, and unbroken slumber graced the universal reign of those who taught ignorance in place of knowledge' (to Botzheim 1523; Allen I 2:20–4). The rebirth or 'renaissance' of arts and letters (cf 'priscae litteraturae renascentis,' 'renascentibus priscis studiis' Allen Epp 541:134; 967:128) is said by Erasmus in 1518 to date from 'about eighty years ago,' and although it extended to various arts the basis was philological: the recovery of sound Latin. See Ep 862, a typical statement of Erasmus' opinion, and Ep 23:49–116, written c 1489.
5 Of making many books on definitions and interpretations of the Renaissance there is no end, but a selection of the best would include the following: Wallace K. Ferguson *The Renaissance in Historical Thought* (Cambridge, Mass 1948); Denys Hay ed *New Cambridge Modern History* I: *The Renaissance 1493–1520* (paperbound edition Cambridge 1975); Paul Oskar Kristeller *Renaissance Thought* (New York 1961) and *Renaissance Thought* II (New York 1965); Sem Dresden *Humanism in the Renaissance* trans Margaret King (New York and Toronto 1968).

studii, and others not in this volume), or books we would consider literary rather than pedagogical (*Adagia, Parabolae*), or books that began as pedagogical and became literary (*Colloquia*) – in all these his premise was the same: that liberal education was the soundest training for youth who would later serve church and state and the learned professions or, if not, would be among those who also serve because they only stand and wait. Whatever this type of education be called – liberal, literary, humanistic – it meant a classical curriculum. Moreover it meant an education in and for societies professedly Christian, and in schools in which there was no choice of studies, no options. Latin and Greek took up most of the time. One's native language was not altogether neglected but played a minor part in the formal work of school. First things first was the rule: the essential function of a grammar school was the teaching of Latin. A child would learn his native language from infancy, without formal instruction. Latin had to be learnt in school.

The fact that the sort of educational programme we can describe in general terms as Erasmian prevailed for many generations may tempt us today to take it for granted, and so to underestimate the freshness and vigour in Erasmus' writing about it. A reading of *Antibarbari* or *De ratione studii* in the context of European society of the earlier sixteenth century will remind us that acceptance of the humanists' doctrines of education, and specifically of the Erasmian programme or practices, was not immediate or universal. He had to explain and defend his recommendations. Nor did he make concessions to critics. He never thought avoidable ignorance had any privileges which truth was bound to respect, obscurantism any rights which enlightenment need tolerate.

From boyhood, he tells us, he was drawn to literature (*bonae literae*, a favourite phrase) by 'a kind of secret natural force.'[6] 'When naphtha, which is a kind of bitumen, appears even at a distance, a flame will dart across and kindle it, because their natures are allied. Likewise a spirit made for good literature seizes upon it at sight.'[7] In Erasmian usage 'literature' meant works of the imagination such as the Homeric and Virgilian epics, drama, stories; second whatever was written with exceptional grace or emotional force on subjects of general interest or non-technical nature, whether prose or verse, imaginative or not: Cicero's speeches, Plato's dialogues, Lucian's rhetorical compositions, the histories of Tacitus. But one difference from the modern point of view or emphasis is worth notice: the assumption by

* * * * *

6 Allen 12:30, and see Epp 23:37–42, 1110:1–9
7 *Parabolae* below 246:29–31

sixteenth-century writers that literature has, and ought to have, moral purposes and effects.[8] This expectation was as normal for works of imagination as for other types of literature. Poets and scholars alike, and certainly Erasmian humanists, had no doubt that the function of literature was, through art, to serve moral truth. An Erasmus, a Spenser (see his explicit language in the prefatory letter to Raleigh about the ethical purpose of *The Faerie Queene*, or Milton's phrase about *Paradise Lost*, 'to justify the ways of God to men') exemplifies this common conviction. Sir Philip Sidney in his *Defence of Poesy* charges us to 'believe, with Scaliger, that no philosopher's precepts can sooner make you an honest man than the reading of Virgil.' Many other passages could be quoted from major and minor writers to illustrate this habitual judgment that literary art did not exist for its own sake alone but for what Sidney calls 'delightful teaching.' The argument for liberal education in *Antibarbari* rests on Erasmus' confidence in the combined ethical and artistic power of ancient literature and eloquence; they delight and therefore move us. When read critically, with an understanding of what sixteenth-century readers took for granted about the nature of literature, his own *Moriae encomium* and many pages of *Adagia* and *Colloquia* will be found to satisfy both the aesthetic and ethical assumptions of his age.

As a glance at articles about him in encyclopaedias or histories will confirm, Erasmus is not easy to label. His interests and writings were too various for that. Perhaps the phrase that sums him up best is the inclusive one 'Christian scholar and man of letters.' He cannot be called philosopher in a technical sense. He had little time for formal logic, no patience with metaphysics. The only sort of philosophy he cared for was moral philosophy, which, as Bacon says, was to the heathen as theology to us.[9] 'What I call philosophy is not a method of analysing first principles, matter, time, motion, infinity, but that wisdom which Solomon deemed more precious than all riches and on that account prayed God to grant him above all else.'[10] He was a grammarian, both in the ordinary sense of an expert on the structure and functions of words and also a 'Christian grammarian' who, distrusting dialectic as a method of reaching and teaching theological truth, applied linguistic knowledge in order to clarify biblical and patristic texts and contexts, interpreting them by the aid of all the arts and all the

* * * * *

8 *Parabolae* includes some of Plutarch's dicta on the moral aspects of poetry; below 181:1 ff.

9 *Novum organum* 1 79

10 Allen Ep 2533:109–13; cf Ep 393:18–28.

ancient testimony.[11] Such a conception of the true significance of grammar for Christian scholars is precisely what is claimed for Erasmus by the man who for many years knew and understood him best, Thomas More.[12] In recent years Erasmus has been much studied as a theologian,[13] and this attention is a salutary redress of long neglect; but to regard him as primarily or essentially a theologian[14] is going too far.

He was a tireless critic of men and manners, a moralist who tried by satire, irony, and exhortation to reform social, political, and ecclesiastical abuses or corruption. The famous epigram[15] that Erasmus laid the egg which Luther hatched is provocative but begs some questions. Erasmus was a shrewd and persistent advocate of reforms rather than a reformer who actually brought about rapid or drastic changes. Luther was a reformer in the latter and more obvious sense: he caused something to happen, and in a fairly short time; Erasmus and the More of *Utopia* did not. Nevertheless the ideas and writings of Erasmus can be shown to have been influential both in his lifetime and in the long run.[16] This is particularly true of some of his religious writings,[17] most of all *Enchiridion*, his edition and translation of

* * * * *

11 See James K. McConica 'Erasmus and the Grammar of Consent' *Scrinium Erasmianum* II 77–99.
12 Rogers 27–74 (More's letter to Dorp); see especially 32–3:141–77. For translation see Miss Rogers' *St Thomas More: Selected Letters* (New Haven and London 1961) 6–64, especially 13–14.
13 For example by Kohls; J. Coppens 'Où en est le portrait d'Erasme théologien?' *Scrinium Erasmianum* II 569–93; C.J. de Vogel 'Erasmus and His Attitude towards Church Dogma' *Scrinium Erasmianum* II 101–32; John B. Payne *Erasmus: His Theology of the Sacraments* (Richmond, Va 1970); G. Chantraine 'Mystère' et 'Philosophie du Christ' selon Erasme (Namur 1971); E.J.M. van Eyl 'Erasmus en de hervorming van de theologie' *Archief voor de Geschiedenis van de Katholieke Kerk in Nederland* 5 (1963) 129–219; C. Augustijn *Erasmus: Vernieuwer van Kerk en theologie* (Baarn 1967); Manfred Hoffman *Erkenntnis und Verwirklichung der wahren Theologie nach Erasmus von Rotterdam* (Tübingen 1972); Marjorie O'Rourke Boyle *Erasmus on Language and Method in Theology* (Toronto 1977).
14 See de Vogel *Scrinium Erasmianum* II 103; Etienne Gilson 'Erasmus and the Continuity of Classical Culture' *Erasmus in English* 1 (1970) 4.
15 According to Erasmus it originated with the Franciscans of Cologne (Allen Epp 1528:11–12; 2956:39–40).
16 Some examples from England are given in Craig R. Thompson 'Erasmus and Tudor England' *Actes du Congrès Erasme, Rotterdam 1969* (Amsterdam and London 1971) 29–68.
17 Including some unknown to modern readers. Zwingli dated his conviction that Christ is the only mediator between God and man from the day he read Erasmus' poem *Expostulatio Iesu cum homine suapte culpa pereunte*: B.J. Kidd *Documents of the Continental Reformation* (Oxford 1911) 378–9; for the poem see Reedijk 255, 291–6.

the New Testament, his *Paraphrases*, and his editions of patristic texts. Beyond question these affected currents of scholarship and thereby the course of religious controversy during the remainder of the century.

To these religious, theological, philological, literary, moral, and social concerns evident in the stream of his books and essays that poured from the press year after year, we must add as his other major interest the one with which we started: education. Except for a residence of two years and more at Cambridge (1511–14), where for a time he lectured on Greek and divinity, he never taught formally at a university. In his Paris years he tutored private pupils, an experience which we can thank for the origins of *De copia*, *De ratione studii*, and the early parts of *Colloquia*. For most of his later years, especially after his return to the Continent in 1514, he had a succession of servant-pupils who acted as secretaries and amanuenses in return for tuition.[18] When Dean Colet wrote to acknowledge Erasmus' still unprinted version of *De ratione studii* in September 1511, he added that he longed to have Erasmus as a teacher in his school, but failing that, 'I am hopeful that you may lend me some assistance, if only in training my teachers ...'[19] To be a teacher of teachers was often the role of Erasmus. His learning and eloquence enabled him to express a set of convictions, a point of view, lucidly and persuasively, with the result that his principal writings tended to become identified with or typify those attitudes towards learning and life known as Renaissance humanism.

Still another fact to be kept in mind about his contributions to learning is that he could reach the educated public promptly not only because of his gifts as a writer but because he and they had inherited a technological innovation responsible for far-reaching changes in European culture, intellectual habits, and educational practices: printing. That our reliance on printing is so customary must not allow us to underestimate its profound effects in the lifetime of Erasmus. Without the rapid production and circulation of books in numerous copies, and at prices that put them within reach of the general public, including students, he could not have done most of the work on which he spent his life. Few men of his time were more

* * * * *

18 On these servant-pupils, several of whom became men of distinction in later years, see Allen *Lectures* 99–108; and Bierlaire. One, Gilbert Cousin (Cognatus), wrote while he was still with Erasmus (1535) a tractate on the duties of a servant, *De officiis famulorum*, which draws upon his experience in Erasmus' household. This was translated into English by Thomas Chaloner (1543), who also made the first English translation of *Moriae encomium* (1549). On Cousin see Ep 2381 introduction.

19 Ep 230:10–16

perceptive of the differences printing made to scholarship and education.[20]
He might not have concurred uncritically with John Foxe's remark that
'When Erasmus wrote, and Frobenius printed, what a blow thereby was
given to all friars and monks in the world,'[21] had he known the rest of Foxe's
opinions; but about the power of print, for better for worse, there could be
no dispute. 'Printing, gunpowder, and the magnet ... these three have
changed the whole face and state of things throughout the world.'[22]

II

In her introduction to *Antibarbari* Margaret Mann Phillips calls attention to
its character as a manifesto. As originally planned it was to be an oration,
but Erasmus later recast it as a dialogue, the favourite literary form of so
many Renaissance writers. He continued to think of it as a declamation,[23]
however, since it contains long speeches whose purpose is persuasion.
These speeches by Jacob Batt, Erasmus' friend and *persona*, have the manner and tone of both common types of classical declamation, the deliberative *suasoria* and the forensic *controversia*.

   Antibarbari is a defence of the humanities, explicitly of classical literature, against their professed enemies and others who questioned their
value in education. To understand why Batt's indignation becomes so
intense and his language so fervid we must accept as wholly sincere the
antipathy of Erasmus and other humanists of his time to the ignorance,
obscurantism, and conceit of men (whether within or without religious
orders) who cared too little for good teaching and good Latin; failed to
recognized the importance of Greek ('to know Greek is heresy'),[24] which is
essential to the theologian; and, in their hostility to pagan literature simply
because it was pagan, assumed it must be injurious to Christians.
Humanists made common cause against 'barbarians' before Erasmus came
on the scene, but in his lifetime no one did more to advance the intelligent
study of classical languages and literatures and to explain their value for
Christians.

   What literature is good or bad and ought to be included in the cur-

* * * * *

20 See his tributes to Aldo Manuzio and Johann Froben in LB II 402B–6A, and his
   comments in Allen Epp 919:1–41, 1390:94–100. See Allen *Lectures* 109–37.
21 *Acts and Monuments* 2nd ed (London 1570) I 837–8
22 Bacon *Novum organum* I 129
23 He describes it as such in 1523; Allen I 19:15–17. At one time he apparently
   thought of making More a speaker in the dialogue (Allen Ep 706:32n).
24 See translation below 32:22; cf Allen Epp 1033:239, 1062:82, 2468:76–9. Yet
   without Greek, Latin scholarship is seriously crippled (Ep 149:16–79, and see
   Ep 337:719ff).

riculum or excluded from it, what methods of teaching it are most beneficial, what standards of work ought to be maintained in schools, are questions inviting debate in every generation, not least our own. When viewed
in perspective, such questions are more than merely occasions for academic
quarrels. They are indicators of cultural standards, or shifts of taste, or new
knowledge. To anyone interested in the history of literature and education
the issues raised and discussed in *Antibarbari* will accordingly seem intelligible enough, and genuine, if he makes proper allowance for the
sixteenth-century setting and the rhetorical organization and colouring of
the dialogue. This last is a matter of some importance, for we have nearly
lost touch with a world in which rhetoric permeated education to the degree
it did in the sixteenth century. Questions of diction and style could have
strong and sometimes emotional appeal to those well-educated persons
who shared a common experience in studies and strong convictions about
the authority and value of humanities. Among the educated, sound Latinity
implied respectability and status; gross faults of grammar or idiom in the
writing of one who should know better could draw contempt and scorn. For
the humanists these matters came close at times to being moral issues. God
is not offended by solecisms, says Erasmus – but neither is he pleased by
them.[25]

If it was nature, as Erasmus tells us, that drew him to literature, wide
and critical reading made him a sensitive judge of style, constant practice a
fluent writer. His abhorrence of barbarism was the result both of temperament and of rational choice. Possibly we can come closer to the deeper
meaning of this aversion by thinking of it as a reaction to the inherent
tension between style and substance, form and idea, in discourse; from one
standpoint, at any rate, as an echo of the ancient quarrel between rhetoric
and philosophy. Erasmus was too accomplished a rhetorician and too
sincere a moralist to consider form and substance as separable or unrelated
parts of expression and communication. 'Speak, that I may see thee,' the
saying attributed to Socrates,[26] implies that the style is the man, that the
speaker's or writer's language discloses the quality of his mind. 'Style is the
dress of thoughts'[27] is an observation at least as old as Quintilian,[28] and

* * * * *

25 LB VI **3
26 Apuleius *Florida* 2. Used by Erasmus more than once: Allen Ep 3141:16–18; LB
   IV 162D, 698C; and see *Adagia* II vi 54 (LB II 602C). In *Adagia* I vi 50 (LB II 243B) it
   is attributed also to Plato *Charmides*, but it is not there (157) in the form quoted
   by Erasmus.
27 'Style is the dress of thoughts, and a well-dressed thought, like a well-dressed
   man, appears to great advantage' (Chesterfield *Letters to His Son* 21 January
   O.S. 1751).
28 *Institutio oratoria* 8 preface 20

Erasmus himself uses it in *De copia*.[29] If matter and expression are parts of one, and style a 'thinking out into language,'[30] then the shaping of discourse and control of diction are matters of personal and sometimes public consequence. And if that is so, grammar and rhetoric must be fundamental concerns of education. Erasmus and his partisans accepted this conclusion as axiomatic.

With these propositions in mind, it is not hard to understand why a reader as responsive as Erasmus to the virtues of clarity, coherence, and grace in writing should find the density and jargon of academic writers repellent. He thought their addiction to Aristotelian philosophy and dialectic related to their arid style and distrust of humanities as cause to effect. In a letter of 1515 he speaks of 'the portentous filth' of this 'barbarous and artificial style, its ignorance of all sound learning, and its lack of any knowledge of the tongues,' its contamination by Aristotle. 'What can Christ have in common with Aristotle?'[31] Whether representative theologians and philosophers were so steeped in pedantry and ignorance as their critics liked to think is something else. The permanent contributions of Scholastic philosophy to European thought cannot be brushed aside by epigrams about style. Nor can the humanists be accepted as unbiased judges, for they sometimes oversimplified and overstated their case. None the less the rigour, excessive formalism, and want of appeal to imagination and feeling in Scholastic writing offered irresistible targets. For Erasmus the beauty of holiness was lost in what were to him dreary logic-chopping and disputes over questions which were anyhow insoluble by human reason and beyond the grasp of language. This is why, after telling in another book of his veneration for Cicero's moral essays, he adds: 'But when, on the other hand, I read these modern writers on government, economics, or ethics – good Lord, how dull they are by comparison! And what lack of feeling they seem to have for what they write! So that I would much rather let all of Scotus and others of his sort perish than the books of a single Cicero or Plutarch. Not that I condemn the former entirely; but I perceive I am helped by reading the latter, whereas I rise from the reading of those others somehow less enthusiastic about true virtue, but more contentious.'[32] Comparable expressions of feeling occur in *Antibarbari*, which is a vehe-

* * * * *

29 CWE 24 306:3–10
30 J.H. Newman 'Literature' *The Idea of a University* II ed C.F. Harrold (New York, London, Toronto 1947) 241
31 From his defence of *Moriae encomium*, Ep 337:424–6, 435
32 Thompson *Colloquies* 65. Milton, in *Areopagitica*, praises Spenser as 'a better teacher than Scotus or Aquinas.'

ment protest on behalf of imagination and art, as well as reason and learning, against barbarism.

Antibarbari was a popular book for some years, printed at least ten times in Erasmus' lifetime, though how many of its readers were the friars and monks Erasmus criticizes so severely we can only guess.[33] If those enemies of sweetness and light disliked what was said about their deficiencies in scholarship and style, they must have been equally resentful of Erasmus' treatment of another subject which fills a large part of the book, the immorality and licentiousness in pagan literature. Was this so common that classical literature must be thought dangerous to Christian youth? On this question what we may call the Erasmian view gradually prevailed, but the arguments and eloquence devoted to the subject in *Antibarbari* show that in 1520 it was still deemed necessary, or expedient, to prove that (with some exceptions) classical literature and learning were of great value to Christians and Christian schools.

The problem of paganism in literature was nearly as old as Christian society itself, involving as it did the complex question of the relations of early Christians and Christian institutions to Greek and Roman culture, and in later centuries to the legacies of ancient civilization. In the arts and education, as such devout humanists as More and Erasmus were always mindful, the debt of modern Christians to the ancients was almost incalculable. In law, philosophy, and many other facets and interests of civilization much was kept or adapted and assimilated; in religion what was pagan had to be rejected. These distinctions seemed clear and decisive to an Erasmus, not always so clear or manageable to others. With respect to secular knowledge, at no time in post-classical civilization did the indebtedness to Greece and Rome receive more animated and grateful acknowledgment than in the era we know as the Renaissance. Erasmus observes, with the air of uttering a truism, that 'almost everything worth learning' is set forth in Greek or Latin,[34] and that traditionally 'almost all knowledge of things is to be sought in the Greek authors.'[35] These claims, large as they are, must command respect: first because in 1512 they were credible; second be-

* * * * *

33 A Frisian Dominican, Laurentius Laurentii (also a critic of *Moriae encomium*), must have read it soon after publication, because he attacked it publicly before the end of 1529. Yes, retorts Erasmus, Batt in *Antibarbari* denounces certain monks who rail against languages and letters, and they richly deserve reproach (Allen Epp 1164:1–45, 1166:26n). Erasmus' relations with the Dominicans were consistently hostile.

34 *De ratione studii* CWE 24 667:3–4

35 *De ratione studii* CWE 24 669:25–6

cause, if credible and accepted, as they were, the logical inference was that Greek and Latin ought to play the principal role in liberal education.

Christian educators had always taken for granted that at every level schooling had moral as well as intellectual purposes, that implicitly and ultimately education was religious in nature. In Erasmian writings these postulates were accompanied by careful distinctions between what the liberal arts could do of themselves and what they could do under Christian auspices. These arts do not 'bestow virtue but ... prepare the soul for the reception of virtue ... do not conduct the soul all the way to virtue, but merely set it going in that direction.'[36] Thus one of Erasmus' favourite authors, the philosopher Seneca. How much more striking is Erasmus' own affirmation, in *Antibarbari*, that 'None of the liberal disciplines is Christian, because they neither treat of Christ nor were invented by Christians; but they all concern Christ.'[37] They 'concern Christ' both because they are activities of the human intellect, which is a divine gift, and because they enlarge our knowledge of the world and our understanding of ourselves. Knowledge is not faith, but it can be the handmaiden of faith. To refuse or belittle secular learning is to reject divinely provided means of improving our lives, of making them more satisfying and more useful. This is the typically Erasmian doctrine found in *Antibarbari* as elsewhere. It is a key to the meaning of his life's work.

We must not suppose that the use of pagan literature in Christian schools gave trouble only to those whom Erasmus calls barbarians and whom more recent generations term Philistines. Take the example of Colet, whose moral character and friendship were an inspiration to Erasmus, and for whose school of St Paul's he wrote *De copia*.[38] In his statutes for St Paul's Colet wrote under 'What Shall Be Taught': 'As touching in this school what shall be taught of the masters and learned of the scholars, it passeth my wit to devise and determine in particular, but in general to speak and somewhat to say my mind: I would they were taught always in good literature both Latin and Greek, and good authors such as have the very Roman eloquence joined with wisdom, specially Christian authors that wrote their wisdom with clean and chaste Latin either in verse or in prose, for my intent is by this school specially to increase knowledge and worshiping of God

* * * * *

36 Seneca *Epistles* 88:20 (Loeb Classical Library translation). One would expect to meet this passage in *Antibarbari*, but it does not seem to be there.

37 Below 90:10–12; and see *Enchiridion* LB V 7C–8D

38 In addition he revised *De constructione* (Ep 341), which had been prepared by William Lily, Colet's first high master; wrote a *Concio de puero Iesu* for the school; and versified, under the title *Christiani hominis institutum*, a catechism for youth written by Colet.

and Our Lord Christ Jesu and good Christian life and manners in the
children.'[39] As acceptable Christian authors he names Lactantius, Prudentius, Proba, Sedulius, Juvencus, and the popular modern poet Batista
Mantuanus, Shakespeare's 'good old Mantuan.' He wants 'true Latin
speech,' uncorrupted by barbarism, but he intends that much of this true
Latin be read in Christian texts which will promote the Christian aims of
the school. Erasmus endorsed Colet's moral and religious purposes but
must have had reservations about the literary qualities of certain of Colet's
Christian authors. With few exceptions Christian Latin writers were not so
instructive, on purely literary grounds, as the classics. There seems to be no
proof that the Christian writers named by Colet were read at St Paul's.
Nevertheless the passage quoted above illustrates the concern of an exem-
plary Christian on the question of religious values in literature and the
safeguarding of young pupils against what would be unfit for them to read
in classical authors.[40] A literary curriculum must be selective. In *Antibarbari*
one of Erasmus' friends, though inclined to favour the liberal arts, voices
serious misgivings about obscenity and licentiousness in pagan writings.[41]
He is answered in some of Erasmus' most interesting pages.

On this and all other topics in *Antibarbari* Erasmus devises arguments
and cites evidence from many sources. For the general line of his defence of
the liberal arts he has Augustine and Jerome on his side, and his strategy
leads to more and more use of both patristic and later precedents. He makes
much of the scriptural injunction about 'spoiling the Egyptians' (Exodus
3:22), always a favourite proof-text with Christian humanists. The counsel
of Augustine is to be followed: if philosophers, particularly the Platonists,
spoke truth and what was consonant with Christianity, 'we should claim
[these utterances] for our own, taking them over from their unlawful possessors.'[42] The intellectual and artistic achievements of antiquity were
intended, though the ancients knew it not, for the adornment and support
of the Christian religion. 'Everything in the pagan world that was valiantly
done, brilliantly said, ingeniously thought, diligently transmitted, had
been prepared by Christ for his society.'[43] Erasmus interprets a passage in a
famous letter by Jerome[44] to mean that 'we should not run away from any
heathen literature but should hand it over, cleansed, to Christian learn-

* * * * *

39 Lupton 279
40 See *De ratione studii* Introductory Note cwe 24 663–4.
41 Below 38:12ff
42 Below 97:5–6, quoting Augustine *De doctrina christiana* 2.40.60
43 Below 60:21–3
44 Ep 70.2 on Hosea 1:2–4; see below 92:1–31.

ing.'[45] These are the sentiments of a Christian scholar who valued all knowledge and arts, confident that to the pure all things are pure and delighting to plunder Egypt *ad maiorem Dei gloriam*. Erasmus would not, like monks in the desert, turn his back on all secular wisdom and art. Heaven was his destination, but he believed that human learning, rightly used, was intended to help and not hinder the pilgrim's progress.

In one passage, a remarkable one on the value of learning and literature, he dares to suggest that in the long run humanity owes more to the labours of scholars than to the blood of the martyrs.

> The man who lives an upright life is indeed doing a great thing, but it is useful only to himself, or at most to the few with whom he passes his days ... Worth without learning will die with its possessor, unless it be commended to posterity in written works. But where there is learned scholarship, nothing stops it from spreading out to all humanity, neither land nor sea nor the long succession of the centuries. I would not like here to bring up an invidious comparison as to which has been of most value to our religion, the blood of the martyrs or the pens of the learned writers, I am not disparaging the glory of the martyrs ... but to speak simply of usefulness to us, we owe more to some heretics[46] than to some martyrs. There was indeed a plentiful supply of martyrs, but very few doctors. The martyrs died, and so diminished the number of Christians; the scholars persuaded others and so increased it. In short, the martyrs would have shed their blood in vain for the teaching of Christ unless the others had defended it against the heretics by their writings.[47]

To some readers these words may have seemed audacious, or worse, but they are deliberate and characteristic utterances which, when taken in context, make *Antibarbari* more provocative than the opening pages may have led us to expect.

III

When thinking about the projected edition of his works Erasmus decided that volume I should open with *De copia*. In these volumes, for reasons already explained, it seems better to print *Antibarbari* first. Of the other works *De copia* ought to be emphasized because of its importance and

* * * * *

45 Below 92:33–93:2
46 Probably he has Origen in mind.
47 Below 82:23ff

originality as a manual on how to vary vocabulary and how to present material in different ways: the two basic methods of achieving the abundant style. Of additional interest are its later effects, unintended, indirect, and seldom recognized, on vernacular writing. When writers of French, English, and other languages practised the varying, 'dilating,' and amplifying *De copia* describes for Latin, they were paying the book a compliment Erasmus could not have foreseen in 1512. With good reason *De copia* is said to provide us 'in a sense with a clue to the whole of humanism.'[48]

In scholarship Erasmus ranged as widely in Greek as in Latin, but for the purposes of *De copia* his subject was Latin. In fertility of ideas Greek literature had more to offer than Latin,[49] but despite the enthusiasm of early students of the language in Italy it was known to comparatively few northern scholars until the later years of the fifteenth century. Erasmus and More began to study it in the 1490s, though Erasmus did not make much progress until after his return from England in 1500. One of his best services to learning thereafter was his incessant preaching of the gospel that Greek was necessary for all theologians and biblical scholars.[50] Colet sought for St Paul's School a master learned in Latin 'and also in Greek if such may be gotten'; they were not easy to find. Colet himself began to study Greek only in his last years. Whatever the school statutes might say, and however highly regarded it was by Erasmus and all other humanists, Greek did not become a standard study in more than a few English grammar schools before the middle of the century. The basis of grammar-school training was

* * * * *

48 Bolgar 274; a book important not only for its estimate of Erasmus but for its history of Renaissance humanism. On *De copia* see also Baldwin; Rix; George J. Engelhardt 'Mediaeval Vestiges in the Rhetoric of Erasmus' PMLA 63 (1948) 739–44; E.V. Telle 'Le "De copia verborum" d'Erasme et le "Julius exclusus e coelis"' *Revue de littérature comparée* 22 (1948) 439–47; J.K. Sowards 'Erasmus and the Apologetic Textbook' *Studies in Philology* 55 (1958) 122–35; James D. Tracy 'On the Composition Dates of Seven of Erasmus' Writings' *Bibliothèque d'humanisme et renaissance* 31 (1969) 355–64; G. Vallese 'Erasme et le *De duplici copia verborum ac rerum*' *Colloquia Erasmiana Turonensia* 233–9; Margaret Mann Phillips 'Erasmus and the Art of Writing' *Scrinium Erasmianum* I 335–50; 'From the *Ciceronianus* to Montaigne' in R.R. Bolgar ed *Classical Influences on European Culture A.D. 1500–1700* (Cambridge 1976) 191–7; Terence Cave 'Copia and Cornucopia' *French Renaissance Studies 1540–70* ed Peter Sharratt (Edinburgh 1976) 52–69. An article on *De copia* by Virginia W. Callahan is forthcoming in a volume of essays on the works of Erasmus (Yale University Press).
49 See *De ratione studii* CWE 24 669:21–7.
50 Much as Erasmus respected Thomas Aquinas, the best of the Scholastic doctors, he never ceased to regret Thomas's lack of Greek. See LB V 78E–F; VI **3, 554E, 707E–F, 777E, 791C, 890D, 933C–D, 1017D–E, 1020F; IX 86E–F.

and continued to be, necessarily, Latin because educated men were expected to read and write Latin. Veneration of Latin and sensitivity about
classical correctness in the use of it were common characteristics of the
humanists. That forthright Elizabethan schoolmaster Richard Mulcaster
declared that 'I honour the Latin but I worship the English';[51] pardonable
patriotism but dubious pedagogy from the standpoint of conservative
educators. As for schoolboys, we can only conjecture that most of them
looked upon the Latin curriculum as something ordained in the nature of
things, beyond good and evil. What they were supposed to think is expressed in a *vulgaria* (c 1500 but unprinted until 1956) by a grammar master at
Magdalen School, Oxford: 'Here we may drink of the pure well of Latin
tongue and eloquence, [than] which is nothing fairer. O gracious children
that wetteth their lips therein!' And: 'Trust ye me, all language well nigh is
but rude beside Latin tongue. In this is property, in this is shift, in this all
sweetness.'[52]

The supreme exemplar of Latin prose was Cicero, 'the great father of
all eloquence.' 'Your Cicero should be always in your hands, for from this
writer alone will you learn Latin.' In Roman eloquence no further development was possible after Cicero. For *copia* he had no equal.[53] As in earlier
centuries it had not been necessary to name Aristotle but simply refer to 'the
Philosopher' because there was no one comparable, so in the sixteenth 'the
Orator' designated Cicero; a good example of the contrast between the
medieval academicians' devotion to philosophy and the Renaissance humanists' preference for rhetoric and eloquence.[54] The implications for education are clear. When eloquence (defined by Cicero as *copiose loquens
sapientia*) is more attractive than metaphysics, and rhetoric than philosophy, *copia* will be valued above dialectic. Men owe more to language than
to logic.[55] Yet one mark of Erasmus' critical judgment is that, although he

* * * * *

51 E.T. Campagnac ed *Mulcaster's Elementarie* (Oxford 1925) 269
52 William Nelson ed *A Fifteenth Century School Book* (Oxford 1956) 18 (No. 73),
    19 (No. 74). The indispensable *vulgaria* by John Stanbridge and Robert Whit-
    tinton (ed Beatrice White for Early English Text Society o.s. 187, Oxford 1932)
    and by William Horman (ed M.R. James for the Roxburghe Club, Oxford 1926)
    have long been valued by students of sixteenth-century humanism. The
    Magdalen School text easily bears comparison with them.
53 CWE 24 297:28ff, 415:26–31, 313:11–13, 496:10–11
54 Cf E. Gilson 'Le message de l'Humanisme' in Franco Simone ed *Culture et
    politique en France à l'époque de l'humanisme de la Renaissance* (Torino 1974) 1–9.
55 On discourse, eloquence, and the blessings and abuses of speech see Eras-
    mus' *Lingua* (1525) LB IV 657–754, ASD IV-1 223–370. Cf Hanna H. Gray
    'Renaissance Humanism: The Pursuit of Eloquence' *Journal of the History of
    Ideas* 24 (1963) 497–514.

emphasized in *De copia* the unique merits of Ciceronian diction and style, and the profit of close study of it by those who are in certain stages of apprenticeship as writers of Latin, he was likewise the author of *Ciceronianus*, the most exquisite and entertaining satire of Cicero-idolatry ever penned.

Copia, a fairly common Latin word, is used by Cicero and Quintilian in discussions of rhetoric and eloquence; Erasmus found the phrase *copia rerum ac verborum* in Quintilian (10.1.5; cf 10.1.61).[56] *Copia* signifies 'abundance,' 'richness,' 'fullness,' though none of these English words is quite satisfactory. Some sixteenth-century English writers 'naturalized' *copia* as 'copie' but this went out of use long ago.

The term itself, then, like much else in this treatise, Erasmus owed to Cicero and Quintilian, but the enhancement of *copia* in his book was original. He insists on this in his prefatory letter to Colet, printed below. 'What I can really claim is that I have been the first to envisage the subject and give an account of it.' Earlier scholars had produced lists of names and synonyms, but none wrote an account having the substance and scope of this one.[57] *Copia verborum* (book I), abundance of expression, 'involves synonyms, heterosis or enallage, metaphor, variation in word-form, equivalence, and other similar methods of diversifying diction.'[58] It shows the aspiring writer how to express himself fluently but with propriety and precision, taking into account the connotations of words as well as their basic meanings and aiming at that harmonious marriage of meaning and language which will enlighten and move the reader. *Copia rerum* (book II), abundance or richness of subject-matter, 'involves the assembling, explaining, and amplifying of arguments' by the use of examples, comparisons and contrasts, and other like procedures.[59] It illustrates the uses and effects of different kinds of material such as examples from history, allegory, fables, or legends. When the writer decides how his subject should be presented, he is free to employ whatever rhetorical devices will produce *copia*. What Erasmus did in this work was to enlarge and diversify the idea of *copia*, making it a major strategy of composition. By means of a vast number of illustrations he demonstrated how many opportunities for effective expres-

* * * * *

56 *Rerum copia*: Quintilian 7 preface 1; *copiam verborum*: Quintilian 1.8.8 and Cicero *De oratore* 3.125; *copiam sermonis*: Quintilian 8.6.5; *copiosam verborum supellectilem*: Quintilian 8 preface 28; *dicendi copiam*: Quintilian 10.6.6 (cf Cicero *De oratore* 1.50). Erasmus also met such phrases in Jerome, for example *verborum copia* in *Praef in Pent* (Migne PL vol 28: col 151A).

57 Ep 260:51–62; printed in CWE 24 285:51–62

58 CWE 24 301:17–19

59 CWE 24 301:19–22

sion, vivid description, and elaboration of argument were available through variety and amplification of words and ideas imaginatively used.

His instructions are meant for speakers as well as writers of Latin. 'All men covet to have their children speak Latin,' Roger Ascham tells us in one of the classics of sixteenth-century pedagogy, *The Schoolmaster* (1570). Statutes make plain that practice in speaking Latin and avoidance of lapses into the vulgar tongue were expected. 'What wilt thou learn?' a new boy is asked. 'To speak Latin,' he replies; 'to write right, and understand all such things as be written already.' 'If I had not used my English tongue so greatly, the which the master hath rebuked me ofttimes, I should have been far more lighter (or cunning) in grammar. Wise men say that nothing may be more profitable to them that learns grammar than to speak Latin.'[60] 'He speaketh well in his mother tongue,' remarks one schoolboy of another (1519),[61] as though this were a noteworthy accomplishment. In some schools boys were punished for speaking the vernacular.[62]

When merely described, *De copia* may seem technical and dull, even though instructive. Admittedly it is not a book to draw children from play, old men from the chimney corner. That some parts are technical was unavoidable; and, as Miss Knott notes, it is hard to see what the principle of arrangement is for some chapters.[63] But on the whole the book is logical and lucid when taken on its own terms. Erasmus assured Colet that it was suitable for boys to read.[64] It was not made for beginners but for students who had been at grammar and elements of rhetoric for some years.[65] Quintilian says the young man studying to become an orator must accumulate *copia rerum ac verborum* after he has been training for some time and has mastered the preliminary work.[66] Erasmus may have expected his readers to remember that passage. In any event he intended *De copia* to be intelligible to serious readers who had had sufficient preparation for it. The evidence we have suggests that it was. One reason for this, in addition to its

* * * * *

60 Nelson *A Fifteenth Century School Book* 28 (No. 114), 22 (No. 87)

61 Horman *Vulgaria* 139

62 'Whatever they are doing, in earnest or in play, they shall never use any language but Latin or Greek' say the Canterbury School rules 1541; text in A.F. Leach ed *Educational Charters and Documents 598 to 1909* (Cambridge 1911) 469.

63 *De copia* Introductory Note CWE 24 281

64 Ep 260:48–9; CWE 24 285. For a pleasant if idealized portrait of a St Paul's pupil, possibly Thomas Lupset, see Erasmus' *Confabulatio pia* (sometimes called *Pietas puerilis*) in Thompson *Colloquies* 30–41.

65 In Ep 296:159–60 he says it is 'a useful handbook for future preachers.' Erasmus' last major publication, *Ecclesiastes* (1535; LB V 767–1100), was a treatise, in preparation for many years, on preaching.

66 10.1.4

intrinsic merits, must have been the author's manner. He is often informal
and never condescending. We get glimpses of his love of literature and
good writing. Clearly this is the book of an author happy with his subject
and sympathetic with the needs of those for whom he writes.

As a manual of instruction it was meant above all else to be practical.
Erasmus' endeavour, he says, was to 'point to certain fixed types of *copia* as
the primary sources, the method being to progress by stages from the
general to the particular.'[67] He supplies plenty of examples, usually stating
first the fact or principle – it cannot always be called a rule – and then giving
a variety of illustrations from classical sources or of his own invention, or
both. Probably the best-known passages are those in chapter 33 where he
shows what can be done to vary two short sentences, *tuae literae me magnopere delectarunt* and *semper dum vivam tui meminero*. The first he expresses in
141 different ways; the second (which is about Thomas More) in 200. This
remarkable display of *copia* was much admired.

Colet was convinced that there were too many rules. Study the best
authors, he advises, and follow them. 'Latin speech was before the rules,
not the rules before the Latin speech.'[68] However, there must be a standard
of usage. We should not overdo archaisms, Erasmus warns, nor on the other
hand should we be afraid of making 'bold use of forms already in authors of
the right sort, nor should we consider harsh or obsolete any word that
occurs in a reputable writer.'[69] Common usage is a dangerous guide. 'At
one time common usage had a great deal of authority ... But nowadays we
acquire our way of speaking not from the community at large but from the
writings of learned men, so usage does not have the same prescriptive
power.'[70] This advice is for modern users of Latin; about vernacular languages he says nothing, since they have no place in *De copia*.

The way to become a good reader, says Epictetus, is by reading; a
good writer, by writing.[71] Erasmus leaves students in no uncertainty about
the work ahead of them. Anyone who wishes to be thought educated must
cover the whole field of literature, in his reading, at least once in his

* * * * *

67 Ep 260:63–5; CWE 24 285
68 Lupton 291–2. 'For reading of good books, diligent information of taught
   masters, studious advertence and taking heed of learners, hearing eloquent
   men speak, and finally busy imitation with tongue and pen, more availeth
   shortly to get the true eloquent speech than all the traditions, rules, and
   precepts of masters' (292).
69 CWE 24 338:23–5
70 CWE 24 309:26–310:3
71 *Discourses* 2.18.2

lifetime.[72] What is more, he should keep notebooks or commonplace books
for recording, classifying, and afterwards recovering whatever information
or wisdom he comes across in his reading. Erasmus has an interesting
section in book II, with examples, on this essential technique. Develop the
habit of entering in the proper places whatever phrases, *sententiae*, maxims,
proverbs, or curious pieces of information may some day be useful. Such
collections, filled with topics under headings and subheadings, will be an
invaluable source of *copia*,[73] for, as the greatest collector of his day observes, reading maketh a full man. Keeping notebooks in this fashion
seems such an obvious everyday tactic that we may wonder why Erasmus
takes the trouble to dwell on it. The reason is that, although identification of
commonplaces and 'topics' was as old as Aristotle, these could now be used
in a new and fruitful way: in 'paper books' or notebooks. The availability of
paper and the vastly increased number of books made possible by printing
made note-keeping an innovation, prized accordingly as a means of storing
up the memorable things one found in reading. Erasmus was not the first to
urge the use of notebooks but he emphasized it. Thanks to the humanists,
note-taking became a habit with students and many other readers. When
Hamlet is shaken by the horrid discovery that 'one may smile, and smile,
and be a villain,' he exclaims 'My tables! – meet it is I set it down.'[74]

Though *De copia* was generally praised, it had a cool reception from
one scholar Erasmus could not ignore: Guillaume Budé,[75] whose only rival
in erudition and influence as a humanist was Erasmus himself. Erasmus
summed up their different approaches to scholarship by saying that while
Budé wrote for men of learning, he himself wrote for the public.[76] In a letter
of 1 May 1516 Budé referred to some writings by Erasmus as 'trivialities.'
Later he admitted that *De copia* was one of the works he had in mind,
though he now excused 'trivialities' as a slip of the pen.[77] In a polite and
sometimes ironic reply Erasmus defends the originality of *De copia*. His sole

* * * * *

72 CWE 24 635:31–3
73 CWE 24 635:19ff, 672:24–7; and see Bolgar 269–75.
74 *Hamlet* I v 107; cf II ii 136–7. 'Tables' are tablets.
75 Author of a celebrated commentary on Roman law (1508). His other principal
   works were not yet published in 1512: *De asse*, on Roman coinage (1514);
   Commentarii linguae Graecae (1529), and *De transitu Hellenismi ad Christianis-
   mum* (1535). Budé persuaded Francis I to establish the institute (1530) that
   became the Collège de France.
76 Ep 531:504–12. On Erasmus and Budé see Pierre Mesnard 'Erasme et
   Budé' *Bulletin de l'Association Guillaume Budé* 4 (1965) 307–31; A. Stegman in
   Colloquium Erasmianum (Mons 1968) 280–2.
77 Epp 403:134–6, 435:74–92.

object was to help others, not to advertise himself. 'The title seems to you to hold out great hopes; but for the rest, you do not approve of my drawing the material from common sources, feeling I suppose that it is taken from common and widely accessible authors. But if no one else ever laid down any principles for abundance of style, what would you do then?' If anyone else wants to write a book on *copia* he is welcome to do so. 'It is sufficient credit for me to have done so either for the first time or more carefully and accurately than anyone else.'[78]

Assessment of *De copia*, even with the advantages of hindsight, is not easy. We need to notice, for instance, that while the purpose of the book is to demonstrate elaborately the sources and potentialities of *copia*, Erasmus does not encourage readers to think that the abundant style is the only good style. He warns at the outset that 'I am not prescribing how one ought to write or speak, but merely indicating what is useful for practice.' Some persons prefer Laconic brevity to eloquence. Nothing wrong with that, but knowledge of *copia* is still needed, because 'the craftsman in words who will be best at narrowing down his speech and compressing it will be the one who is skilled in expanding and enriching it with ornament of every kind.' Laconic or copious or still other styles may be appropriate sometimes; hence, he says, the purpose of his instructions is 'to enable you so to include the essential in the fewest possible words that nothing is lacking, or so to enlarge and enrich your expression of it that even so nothing is redundant.'[79] Once he understands the principles and methods, the speaker or writer can decide for himself which style best suits his purposes and the occasion.

The pupils for whom *De copia* was published in 1512 spent their years at grammar school mainly on Latin. So did their descendants in 1612, but by that time the dominance of the vernacular as the literary language was far more evident. Latin of course remained the basic subject in grammar school. Works of many kinds continued to appear in Latin throughout the seventeenth century;[80] poets – for example Herbert, Milton, Marvell, and many others in England – wrote polished Latin verse; but vernacular literature counted for far more than it did in the early sixteenth century.

* * * * *

78 Ep 480:94–122. The exchange with Budé is continued, rather tiresomely, in Allen Epp 778:190–7, 810:56–69, 906:222–55.

79 CWE 24 299:19–20, 300:17–19, 301:4–7

80 Bacon intended that the final enlarged edition (1625) of his *Essays* be translated into Latin: 'For I do conceive that the Latin volume of them (being in the universal language) may last as long as books last': Sidney Warhaft ed *Francis Bacon: A Selection of His Works* (Toronto, London, New York 1967) 46.

Needless to say, a native literature had always existed side by side with Latin. But it was different in form, social antecedents, and other respects besides language. It had no academic standing, since it was not read or taught formally in school or university. That may not have mattered much. What surely mattered more was that by 1612 a society that could boast of Spenser, Sidney, Shakespeare, Marlowe, Jonson, and the English Bible; or Rabelais, Montaigne, Ronsard, Marot, and du Bellay could not have quite the same attitudes towards vernacular languages that its ancestors had. 'I honour the Latin but I worship the English.' Elizabethan defence of the English language and its capacities for literary expression, and the efforts of the Pléiade to cultivate French at the expense of Latin, were signs of the times. Of English Sidney wrote (c 1583) that 'for the uttering sweetly and properly the conceits of the mind, which is the end of speech, that hath it equally with any other tongue in the world.' 'All our understandings are not to be built by the square of Greece and Italy,' adds Daniel (1603). 'We are the children of Nature as well as they.'[81]

The question for historians of literature and education is, what happened to the kind of training represented by Erasmus' manual when most new literature of worth was in the vernacular languages and not in Latin? One answer seems to be that many of its principles and methods passed over into vernacular writing; in some cases through writers who had known *De copia* in school, in others through writers who may never have seen the book but inherited or borrowed those of its doctrines which were now common property. The teachings of *De copia* on varying are present in the exuberant vocabulary of *Gargantua and Pantagruel* and in the pages of Thomas Nashe, Gabriel Harvey, and other Englishmen.[82] Finding the springs and following the currents of style and vocabulary is a notoriously

* * * * *

81 The *Defence of Poesy* was published in 1595. Texts of Sidney and Daniel are available in Hyder E. Rollins and Herschel Baker eds *The Renaissance in England* (Boston 1954) 623, 659.
82 On Rabelais see Bolgar 320–1. There is other evidence besides his style that Nashe was acquainted with *De copia* (*Works* ed. R.B. McKerrow [London 1904–10] III 6; cf v 116). Walter J. Ong 'Oral Residue in Tudor Prose Style' PMLA 80 (1965) 145–54 considers some relationships between (1) *copia* as taught by Erasmus, rhetoric, and oral expression and (2) vernacular expression. He argues that 'Renaissance works proposing expressly to develop *copia* are often curiously elementary. The *copia* which they assure is often that which would come in great part from normal nonacademic oral activity in the case of the vernaculars ... Latin sustained the rhetorical – which is basically oratorical and thus oral – cast of mind. The stress on *copia* ... favored exploitation of commonplaces' (147, 153).

tricky business, but an investigator who after studying *De copia* and the education of sixteenth-century writers compares the precepts of Erasmus' book with the manner of the writers just named (and others could be added) is left with a conviction that the devices for *copia* they used were learned directly or indirectly from Erasmus and his successors.

The classicism of Erasmus, which transcended quarrels over Ciceronianism, could have been, and for some must have been, a liberating doctrine when correctly understood. This was possible because Erasmus did not believe in servile imitation of Cicero or any other writer. Imitation ought to support and not hinder nature. It should endeavour to catch the spirit of a writer, not collect and repeat his very words. What is worth imitating in Cicero is 'not his words or what is on the surface of a speech' but the truth, judgment, insight, genius.[83] Now this kind of imitation was that which served those authors and critics, Jonson for instance, who were engaged in their own generations' discussions about imitation and the comparative merits of ancient and modern languages or authors. They were not much exercised about the paganism of ancient literature, a topic Erasmus had to confront in *Antibarbari*, nor did the imitation of classical models mean for them Cicero alone. They were concerned, however, about the resources of their own language. For these reasons Erasmus' contribution to the quarrel over Ciceronianism was a useful legacy to those literatures which meant little to him but would one day take their places beside Greek and Latin even in the schools. Of *De copia* something of the same sort may be suggested: for though the book itself finally disappeared after a long and honourable career, its ideas affected vernacular as well as Latin composition; *copia* was a source of creative energy.

The latter part of the sixteenth century and the first part of the seventeenth witnessed a reaction against eloquence, specifically against Ciceronian style as a model for writers, both in Latin and in vernacular literature (Montaigne, for example).[84] This shift in taste has particular importance in English literary history, since it brings us to that era, the first half of the seventeenth century, which was the greatest in English prose. The anti-Ciceronians distrusted eloquence as something speciously ornamental,

* * * * *

83 *Ciceronianus* LB I 1022C, 1026B; for translation see Izora Scott *Ciceronianus* (New York 1908) 123, 129.
84 See Morris W. Croll's collected papers *Style, Rhetoric, and Rhythm* ed. J. Max Patrick et al (Princeton 1966); George Williamson *The Senecan Amble* (Chicago 1951); Brian Vickers *Francis Bacon and Renaissance Prose* (Cambridge 1968). On Montaigne and *De copia* see Margaret Mann Phillips in *Colloquia Erasmiana Turonensia* I 491–501.

therefore insincere, self-conscious, unsuited for expressing private or adventurous reflections or disclosures of the self. They valued substance above style and preferred Tacitus or Seneca to Cicero. Ascham in *The Schoolmaster* had rebuked persons who undervalue style: 'They be not wise, therefore, that say, "What care I for a man's words and utterance if his matter and reasons be good?" ... Ye know not what hurt ye do to learning, that care not for words but for matter and so make a divorce betwixt the tongue and the heart.'[85] This is sound sense by Erasmian principles,[86] but when we pass from Ascham's reproach of 1570 to Bacon's writings we meet dogmatic pronouncements that reach the opposite conclusions. It was Bacon, not inappropriately, who wrote the epitaph of *copia* in that famous passage of his *Advancement of Learning* (1605) where he describes 'the first distemper of learning, when men study words and not matter.' According to Bacon the mischief began with Luther, who in his contest with the Roman Church 'was enforced to awake all antiquity' and to resuscitate ancient authors. This effort required, and then promoted, more study of the ancient languages, 'and thereof grew again a delight in their manner of style and phrase ... there grew of necessity in chief price and request eloquence and variety of discourse, as the fittest and forciblest access into the capacity of the vulgar sort ... the admiration of ancient authors, the hate of the schoolmen, the exact study of languages, and the efficacy of preaching did bring in an affectionate study of eloquence and copie of speech, which then began to flourish. This grew speedily to an excess, for men began to hunt more after words than matter, and more after the choiceness of the phrase, and the round and clean composition of the sentence, and the sweet falling of the clauses, and the varying and illustration of their works with tropes and figures than after the weight of matter, worth of subject, soundness of argument, life of invention, or depth of judgment.' He quotes a gibe at the Ciceronians from one of Erasmus' colloquies[87] and concludes, 'In sum, the whole inclination and bent of those times was rather towards copie than weight.'[88]

When thus identifying *copia* with preference for words over matter, Bacon ignores Erasmus' cardinal distinctions between good and bad or true and false imitation, book II of *De copia*, and the reminder that knowledge of

* * * * *

85 *The English Works of Roger Ascham* ed. W.A. Wright (Cambridge 1904; repr 1970) 265

86 Though Ascham was a stricter Ciceronian than Erasmus

87 *Echo* (Thompson *Colloquies* 376)

88 Ed Warhaft (above n80) 222–3. For an intemperate denunciation of Ciceronian rhetoric by another early English essayist, Sir William Cornwallis (1601), see the excerpt in F.P. Wilson *Elizabethan and Jacobean* (Oxford 1946) 31.

copia is valuable for making a reasonable choice of whatever manner of writing one adopts. It is ironical that in later years Bacon came to dislike the excesses of Senecan style nearly as much as those of 'copie.' It is likewise ironical that the man who deplored the former popularity of *copia* was, of all writers in his time, most responsive to the advice in *De copia* about collecting notes. Bacon's obsessive fondness in his writings for *sententiae*, aphorisms, maxims, *formulae*, apophthegms, his 'promptuary' and his habit of keeping commonplace-books were a tribute to the methods taught by Erasmus and the other humanists. Bacon was more indebted to prescriptions for *copia* than he allowed, and his prose leaves little doubt that he was studious of words as well as matter.

IV

The earliest authorized text of *De ratione studii*, Erasmus' concise exposition of the curriculum, texts, and methods for his programme of liberal studies, appeared with *De copia* in the first official edition of that work (Paris: Bade July 1512). When Erasmus gives advice in *De ratione studii* on making lists of material encountered in reading, he refers to what he has already written in *De copia*. Of the two works *De copia* is the more specialized; *De ratione studii*, despite its brevity, is wider in scope. Though not written for Colet's school, as *De copia* was, it often accompanied reprints of *De copia*. For the better understanding of the St Paul's curriculum and that of many other English schools thereafter, *De ratione studii* is even more necessary than *De copia*.

Erasmus describes the nurture of young children and their first instruction in letters in a later work, *De pueris instituendis*,[89] which was at first intended for inclusion in *De copia*. In *De ratione studii* the pupils he has in mind are older. They are ready for studies in grammar. (We may note in passing that 'grammar' was a term less narrow than is sometimes supposed; 'grammar and rhetoric,' for the main studies in grammar school, was a phrase almost as inclusive as 'language and literature' today.) The underlying principles in *De pueris instituendis* and *De ratione studii* are much the same, but the aims and materials of the latter are more advanced. We learn which grammarians are esteemed, what the levels and complexities of reading and writing are, what good teaching is and does. Erasmus prescribes sustained work in carefully chosen texts. There is no freedom of choice by pupils; wanton permissiveness of that sort had not yet been

* * * * *

89 Published in 1529 but drafted many years earlier. Text in LB I 489–516, ASD I–2 2–78.

thought of. For learning Greek the recommended authors are Lucian, Demosthenes, and Herodotus, in that order, for prose; Aristophanes, Homer, and Euripides for verse. In Latin Terence (and Plautus may be added) stands highest, followed by Virgil, Horace, Cicero, and Caesar. These will be standard authors in sixteenth-century schools. The Greek ones were recent additions to curricula, because Greek itself was fairly new. The Latin ones had been used time out of mind; their appropriateness in the Erasmian programme confirms their traditional status.

Selections from these authors will supply the reading for pupils who in the next half-dozen years will be expected to attain some measure of competence in reading and writing Latin and Greek and in speaking Latin, though probably very few become as competent in Greek as in Latin. In this curriculum language was the heart of the matter: absorbing grammar and learning how to use it correctly, how to read and construe texts, write compositions.[90] As he grew in grace and grammar and later proceeded to rhetoric, the boy would learn something about the meaning of diction and tone, about synonymy, about context. He would be encouraged to look for the moral implications as well as literary characteristics in Terence and Virgil – for instance in the second *Eclogue*, which Erasmus interprets in interesting fashion. The pupil would be expected to memorize, recognize, and utilize the principal techniques, modes, and figures of rhetoric. If diligent, and lucky enough to be taught by a master as learned, thorough, patient, and sympathetic as Erasmus demands, he would presumably acquire a sound knowledge of these subjects and skill in applying them. There is plenty of evidence that the system produced such pupils. If on the other hand nature did not intend the boy for study or for languages, or if his master were like Holofernes in *Love's Labour's Lost* rather than the one Erasmus hopes for, results must have been less fortunate.[91]

* * * * *

90 Translating Greek and Latin into one's native language, and vice versa, gave practice in vernacular composition also, but the work was done for the sake of Greek and Latin. Compositions in schools had been mainly oral, but written ones were emphasized by the humanists. When More sends his children directions for writing Latin letters he advises them to draft these in English first (Rogers 256:32ff; translation in *Selected Letters* 151). Cf J.A. Gee 'Margaret Roper's English Version of Erasmus' *Precatio dominica* and the Apprenticeship Behind Early Tudor Translation' *Review of English Studies* 13 (1937) 257–71. Ascham's chapter on 'double translation' in *The Schoolmaster* is well known.

91 The preface to Colet's catechism for St Paul's School warns parents: 'If your child after reasonable season proved be found here unapt and unable to learning, then ye, warned thereof, shall take him away, that he occupy not here room in vain' (Lupton 285).

The course of study outlined by Erasmus looks formidable and, at first, far removed from those now in favour. It was both; yet the differences, though undeniable, need not be exaggerated. Probably the main difference is that between the overwhelming dominance and prestige of the classical languages in sixteenth-century formal education and their diminishing role today. Methods of teaching and learning a 'dead' language (Greek was so but Latin was still a living language for educated Europeans in that century), and of reading texts, have not changed all that much. Making games of lessons, making texts interesting and 'relevant' (not the sacred word then it is now, but its meaning was well understood), bringing into the lesson allusions and references to other texts and other subjects were tactics familiar to Erasmus and enlightened pedagogues of his era. The proof of these assertions is that we recognize immediately what is going on when we read sixteenth-century curricula and descriptions – many of which survive – of teaching, study, and classroom exercises. Erasmus set high standards, and indeed some of his recommendations sound like counsels of perfection. Nevertheless his writings show that he was familiar with the nature of schoolboys, aware of their need for recreation as well as work, and insistent on the importance of finding the exceptional man as master. He is ruthless only when writing about ignorant, callous, pretentious teachers.

All this work at grammar, rhetoric, and composition furnished a training which, though undoubtedly acceptable to society and useful to that minority of males who received it, must strike most readers today as curiously narrow. This criticism would have surprised Erasmus. He expected much besides literature to be learned through literature, as *De ratione studii* itself makes clear. Yet it is true that his principles of education, like those of nearly all his contemporaries, assumed the cultural authority of classical civilization. In practice this meant that school at the secondary level was dominated by Latin, with as much Greek as could be added. Without question, and without regard to what present preferences may be, an education based on classical languages and literatures was a factor we must treat as fundamental in any effort to understand the intellectual and cultural history of European society. To learn how one of the most erudite and articulate writers on education in the Renaissance would organize such an education, we can hardly do better than turn to *De ratione studii*. Other important Renaissance contributions to this subject exist but few surpass those of Erasmus in clarity, sanity, and humaneness.

De ratione studii describes succinctly and coherently the Erasmian scheme of humanistic learning in secondary schools. Readers will find in it the same reliance on Cicero and Quintilian, the same allusiveness to the larger problems of pedagogy and concern for the moral aspects of education, as in *Antibarbari*, *De copia*, and other writings by Erasmus. Likewise present is the question, so often troublesome to sensitive minds in the early sixteenth century, of justifying pagan authors in Christian schools. As we have seen, this matter gave Colet some anxiety. Erasmus supplies no new answers in *De ratione studii*, but in *Antibarbari* he clarifies the question, arguing cogently that despite its paganism and secularism the best (but not all) of classical literature contains so much that is illuminating, beautiful, and morally instructive that to reject it would be utter folly. As literary art it furnished permanent models of excellence, and as the source of a vast amount of secular knowledge it was indispensable. Modern readers could enjoy the riches of the ancients without being injured by their paganism. They could do this, for example, through tropological (moral) and allegorical interpretation of texts or passages which, if taken literally and at face value, would be offensive to Christian ears; the letter killeth. So Erasmus finds the Virgilian Eclogue both instructive and beautiful. All the poetry of Homer and Virgil is allegorical, he says.[92] In this attitude he follows a convention of long standing.

Likewise conventional but sincere, and seldom emphasized more than it was by Erasmus, is the need for superior teachers. Pupils must have guidance from a master who is morally and religiously sound, knows literature, understands boys, makes them work, takes trouble to explain points of grammar and rhetoric adequately, analyses texts, corrects compositions. As Erasmus reminds us in a hundred maxims and proverbs, learning is rewarding but laborious. He is sure that if the teacher is both competent and conscientious, even a mediocre pupil can reach the goal and 'may then with confidence turn his attention to higher studies.'[93] He will be able to do more by himself. That is the test: 'For what other purpose have we in teaching them, than that they should not always need to be taught?'[94]

V

What has been said of *Antibarbari*, *De copia*, and *De ratione studii* invites the inference, which a reading of those treatises confirms, that while each has its own theme and method, all share certain assumptions and purposes. *Parabolae* has close ties with *De copia* and with several works by Erasmus published between 1512 and 1515. Much of the material in *Parabolae*, as

* * * * *

92 *Enchiridion* LB V 7F; cf *De copia* CWE 24 611:4ff.
93 CWE 24 691:15–16
94 Quintilian 2.5.13

Professor Mynors points out, was a by-product of Erasmus' labours on a
revision of *Adagia* (1515) and on Seneca (1515). 'In re-reading a number of
authors in order to enrich my Adages, I noted down many parallels on the
side, more pointing the way and setting others an example of a work to
come than finishing a book with the necessary care. This makes one book of
Parabolae or *Parallels*, addressed to Pieter Gillis, lawyer and citizen of
Antwerp, who was once the companion of my studies.'[95] Not only has
Parabolae much in common with *Adagia*; it may also be considered, Erasmus tells us, a kind of supplement to *De copia*, since it 'contributes eminently to abundance of style.'[96] But it has its own distinctive character.

The dedicatory letter to Gillis defines *parabolê* as 'a sort of comparison
... nothing more than a metaphor writ large.'[97] It is essentially aphoristic,
not (like an adage) proverbial. As an ornament of style metaphor is unexcel-
led in power and variety of effects; it can do anything other ornaments of
style can do, and more besides. Good metaphors are not to be had for the
asking, however. They must be sought by those who know how and where
to search: 'Such things must be unearthed in the innermost secrets of
nature, in the inner shrines of the arts and sciences, in the recondite
narratives of the best poets or the record of eminent historians.' 'I have
brought forth precious stones from the inner treasure-house of the
Muses.'[98] Equally difficult and important is the mounting of the gem after
its discovery. A fact or event needs to be clarified and applied or moralized
before we get a 'parallel' or simile[99] whose truth will strike us at once as
self-evident, illuminating experience or corroborating moral wisdom and
bringing it home to men's business and bosoms.

Aphorisms in *Parabolae* are arranged only by author, with little regard
to classification by subject. Modern editors would arrange things differently, but this miscellaneous character of the work is no real hindrance to
using it if there is a good index. Nearly all the material comes from Plutarch,
Seneca,[100] Lucian, Xenophon, Aristotle, and Pliny; a few items are from
other sources, for example, Theophrastus. Plutarch's *Moralia* supplies almost half the aphorisms. It is no surprise that Erasmus borrowed so much
from an author always congenial to him, one to whom he was heavily

* * * * *

95 Allen I 17:18–23, to Botzheim
96 134:90–3 below
97 130:28–9; cf *De copia* CWE 24 621:1ff and (on metaphor) 333:1ff
98 131:55–8, 52–3
99 Simile is defined in *De copia* CWE 24 337:16–17 as 'a metaphor that is made
    explicit and specifically related to the subject.' See also *De copia* CWE 24 641:5ff.
100 Several parallels are from Seneca the Elder (cf CWE 24 214:34n and 215:25n),
    father of the philosopher. See *De copia* CWE 24 299:3n.

indebted in *Adagia*. A few months before *Parabolae* came out Erasmus had
published some translations from *Moralia*.[101] In sixteenth-century literary
history Plutarch's *Lives* has a definite place, thanks to Amyot, North, and
Montaigne; Shakespeare's debt to it is obvious. But *Moralia* too was popular; one of Montaigne's favourite books; prized by Erasmus for moral
wisdom applicable to so many social, political, and educational topics, as
we see for instance in *Institutio principis christiani* (1516). Excepting Plato
and possibly Seneca, no pagan writer attracted him more when he looked to
the ancients for instruction. Of Greek writers none is more venerable or
worth the reading.[102] He is 'of all authors particularly worthy of respect'
because one finds in him philosophy, historical knowledge, and eloquent
style combined.[103] When the host in the colloquy *Convivium religiosum*
presents a guest with a Greek text of *Moralia*, he adds that 'so much piety do
I find in them that I think it marvelous such Christian-like notions could
have come into a pagan mind.'[104] Erasmus advises a young student that his
studies should be chiefly history and ethics, and that for ethics he must go
to Cicero and Plutarch's *Moralia*.[105] For *Parabolae*, *Moralia* was indispensable, because in metaphor Plutarch 'is possibly more prolific than anyone.'[106]

Pliny's *Naturalis historia* was an inexhaustible mine of information,
authoritative for many centuries: 'Mundum docet Plinius.'[107] Aristotle was
still the master of them that know, the mòst learned of philosophers.[108]
Seneca was preferred to Cicero by the young Erasmus,[109] who later modified this judgment but never lost his admiration for Seneca's earnestness

* * * * *

101 *Plutarchi opuscula* (Basel 1514); text in LB IV 1–84 and ASD IV-2 119–322. When
    praising the printers Aldo Manuzio and Johann Froben for their services to
    learning, Erasmus recalls (LB II 405D) that when working on the 1508 revision
    of *Adagia* in Venice he was furnished with manuscripts of Plutarch's *Lives* and
    Moralia. The Aldine edition of *Moralia* was published in 1509.
102 Allen Ep 2431:89–91
103 *De copia* CWE 24 608:26–31
104 Thompson *Colloquies* 76
105 Allen Ep 1798:5–10. The Ciceronian works are *De officiis*, *De amicitia*, *De
    senectute*, and the *Tusculan Disputations*.
106 *De copia* CWE 24 335:21
107 From Erasmus' preface to a 1525 edition, Allen Ep 1544:91
108 So Erasmus in his preface (addressed to Thomas More's son John) to an edition
    of Aristotle (1531); Allen Ep 2432:2
109 Allen Ep 1390:103–6

and eloquence as a guide to virtue. He had no patience with those who thought Seneca may have been a Christian, but valued him for what he was, a highminded pagan. If read as a pagan, Seneca wrote like a Christian; if read as a Christian, he wrote like a pagan.[110] Lucian scorned all religions, but Erasmus liked his wit and rhetoric and thought there was much in him which was useful for students as well as entertaining. Not everyone agreed, but Lucian was a popular and often imitated writer in the sixteenth century. A volume of translations from Lucian by Erasmus and More appeared in 1506.[111]

Pliny's huge work on natural history, a mixture of careful observation and traditional or legendary lore, is not 'science' by our standard but it has historical and literary value for the very reason that it was so long one of the main sources of inherited knowledge about the natural world. If often uncritical, it is nevertheless readable. The lion, we learn, 'spares simple folk and those who lie down before him.'[112] We do not inquire how lions identify simple folk but we can draw a political moral from the statement. A stag bitten by a tarantula can cure itself by eating crabs;[113] no use inquiring where a stag will find crabs. The lore and the implied sententiousness, we must surmise, were equally acceptable to sixteenth-century readers. A modern reader who lingers longer over the curiosities of natural history in *Parabolae* than over Erasmus' moralizings of them does injustice to the order of emphasis intended, but he can hardly be blamed.

In *Parabolae* the moral application of images in material from Plutarch and Seneca is theirs, as Erasmus is careful to state in his prefatory letter. In anything from Aristotle and Pliny the application is added by Erasmus. Whatever the source, more than one lesson can be learned from the excerpt. A reader may test his wits by trying to guess what moral Plutarch will provide, or Erasmus educe from Pliny, but Erasmus never implies that his is the only interpretation possible. He tells us how the passage strikes him; if we are clever enough to see it from another angle, we are welcome to do so. Sometimes he feels free to change or adapt a Plutarchan comparison, or suppress part of it, for the sake of clarity or emphasis. Or he may adjust the text to suit his own rhetorical or moral purposes better.[114] He permits

* * * * *

110 Allen Ep 2091:221–2
111 On these translations see *De copia* CWE 24 603:17n.
112 249:12–13
113 251:1
114 See 164:3n.

himself to change slightly the application of a text in different parts of his book, or in different books, as his theme and the context require.[115]

Now and then in the second half of *Parabolae* he adds allusions or observations from personal experience to make an idea more vivid or convincing. Thus after remarking that we are astonished when people do something of whom we expect nothing of the kind, he adds, 'for instance, if we were to see a Dutchman who knew how to ride a horse, a frugal Englishman, or a theologian who is eloquent.'[116] He tells us that in England kites (birds of prey) are protected; he knows this because he had lived there. In Italy everyone is avaricious; he had lived there too.[117] A sentence in Pliny to the effect that 'the wind normally blows more strongly shortly before it drops' leads him to remark: 'so with mortals; when they exalt themselves to the highest point, like Pope Julius, they are then often close to their destruction.' Since Julius, whose pontificate had been busy with so many diplomatic and military manoeuvres, had died less than two years before *Parabolae* was published, this allusion would not be lost on Erasmus' readers. We have also a few dicta on scholars. Here is one, prompted by a passage in Pliny: 'Trees that do not bear fruit are more robust than those that do. So is it with writing: those who publish nothing are more robust physically than those who wear themselves out with the labours of composition.'[118] It is pleasant to learn of a gem (chalazias) so cold by nature that it retains its chill even when thrown on the fire; or that elephants, though unable to swim, like to be near rivers; but could we have guessed what moral Erasmus would draw from those facts? Some men are like that gem: 'education and virtue leave them so cold that neither example nor precept can fire them with a wish to do better.' Those elephants remind him of men who, though without book-learning, enjoy the company of scholars.[119]

The 'parallels' that give *Parabolae* its name are similitudes elicited from observations of nature, men, and customs. The book therefore is an exercise in the rhetoric of moral philosophy. For us it is likewise a reminder

* * * * *

115 For an example see 156:12–15 and 224:38–225:4. In *Parabolae* 265:30–6 the terror snakes have of the ash tree provides the reflection that 'there is nothing common between vice and the pursuit of wisdom, but whoever shelters in the shade of wisdom will be safe from the poisonous contagion of this life.' In the colloquy *Amicitia* the enmity between snakes and the ash is mentioned simply as an example of antipathies in nature (Thompson *Colloquies* 524); no moral is drawn.

116 224:14–16

117 257:1–2, 262:13–15

118 On Julius 274:1–3; on scholars 263:17–20, 265:10–13, 269:1–3

119 220:26–9, 248:41–249:2

of how central the discipline of moral philosophy was in Erasmus' life and work. Because the proper study of mankind is man, we must study history and learn what man's past has to teach us. In addition, the world of nature, in which man is placed, furnishes countless phenomena from which a reflective observer or reader can draw instructive comparisons, analogies, images, metaphors. The moral philosopher studies history and nature not merely because they are interesting in themselves but for their usefulness to mankind. The abiding commonplaces of moral experience are truths as well as truisms, and when elegantly expressed in apposite and memorable images or metaphors, imagination being called to the help of reason, they become persuasive enthymemes. We meet examples in many of Erasmus' pages; how many in *Parabolae* the reader must decide for himself, but he will certainly encounter comparisons whose lucidity and persuasiveness are impressive. Here is one: 'The Indians also have a thorn-bush, the sap of which, if dropped into the eyes, causes blindness in all living creatures. But men are blinded more severely if you put in their eyes a little gold-dust.'[120]

Only in the second half of the work do we find parallels between ancient and contemporary matters. There are not many, but contemporary readers could not have missed them. A few refer to princes and governance, most to religious topics. Christ's power of calming the soul or rousing it comes to Erasmus' mind when he reads of Jupiter's spring in Dodona. As Alexander the Great would permit no one but Apelles to paint him, 'so it is not proper that Christ should be preached by the first comer.'[121] Other parallels touch on Christian piety and the Scriptures.[122] Some comment on the shortcomings of priests, prelates, and theologians.[123] Even Pliny can be co-opted for a gibe at the Scotists.[124]

Parabolae was designed for readers who could be expected to value ethical wisdom available in this convenient form. Like the *Adagia* it would give them food for thought and provide for writers a collection of useful source material. If they in turn wished to communicate or persuade, command of metaphor (as Erasmus assures Gillis) would be one of their most effective advantages. *Parabolae* shows the possibilities. Here Erasmus uses not the poet's eye, in a fine frenzy rolling, but the vision of the moralist who

* * * * *

120 268:27–9
121 246:13–17, 220:30–3
122 222:21–5,   223:15–18,   227:8–11,   228:11–13,   236:37–237:4,   238:13–15,
     246:36–247:2, 258:24–7, 259:41–260:3
123 220:8–14, 225:15–16, 226:16–19, 233:3–7, 241:11–16, 258:4–7, 262:19–24,
     275:26–9, 276:33–277:2
124 272:36–273:6

Prelum Ascensianum
Detail from the title-page of Guillaume Budé *Commentarii linguae Graecae*
Paris: Bade 1529
The central figure pulling the bar of the press is believed to be
Josse Bade (Ascensius), the scholarly printer of Paris,
who was a friend, correspondent, and publisher of Erasmus.
Reproduced by permission of the Thomas Fisher Rare Book Library,
University of Toronto

finds tongues in trees[125] and sermons in stones,[126] and whose scrutiny includes both the spacious firmament on high and the little busy bee.[127] From the pen of a mere compiler this book could have been as uninspired and dull as many sixteenth-century works of edification were. Erasmus avoids that – by being Erasmus. The compactness of his observations and the addition of wit and imagination make the book readable. This is not to say as readable now as it was for his contemporaries. It is a book for browsing rather than for going through from beginning to end, except for a special purpose. 'Many jewels in one small book,' as its author tells Gillis. The sixteenth century, which took pleasure in ornamentation of language, as of dress, evidently agreed. But fashions change. Dictionaries of proverbs and quotations continue to be compiled, but moralization is seldom offered. If any such application is wanted, it must be supplied by the reader himself.

The scholarly printer Josse Bade,[128] who published many books by Erasmus, issued a revised edition of *Parabolae* in late 1516,[129] dedicated like the first edition to Pieter Gillis. Bade's letter to Gillis pays such a generous tribute to Erasmus and *Parabolae* that part of it should be quoted: 'Nothing in him that is not wisdom, nothing not theology; such integrity, such fairness of mind, such a high moral standard! Not a parallel in the book that does not contain a pair of corresponding ideas, and those of no ordinary kind; they are worked out most precisely against the false-seemer and the pretender to learning, the illiterate purveyor of nonsense, the ignoramus, the parasite, the toady, and all who have no grace and no charm. Seeing therefore that this work would be of the greatest use to all inquiring minds, I have reduced it to a handy form, that it might be no burden even on a poor man's pocket or cheat him of his coin ...'[130]

VI

In following the fortunes of books by Erasmus we soon discover how much more we know about some than about others. His major publications were reprinted frequently and read steadily for several generations after his death. Enumerative bibliography can tell us this much, but not what

* * * * *

125 As in 236:37–237:4
126 220:15–20, 220:35–8, 222:1–5, 223:15–18
127 242:6–243:34, 259:38–261:4
128 See Ep 183 introduction.
129 Bade added a vocabulary to it. This is printed in ASD 1–5 328–32.
130 Text in Ph. Renouard *Bibliographie des impressions et des œuvres de Josse Badius Ascensius* (Paris 1908) II 425; translated by R.A.B. Mynors

difference the books made, or whether their ideas and precepts lived on
through adoption or absorption by later writers or, having done their work,
disappeared. Which ones had a life beyond the last reprint, and of what
kind?

The reputation of Erasmus declined in the seventeenth century, but
his name and some of his books were still known to educated people. In
the eighteenth century his name was honoured but his books read less,
though we are well aware that it was that century which gave us the great
Leiden edition (LB) of his writings, the edition that remained standard until
very recently. He had both strong defenders and severe critics in the
nineteenth century, when for various reasons there was recurrent interest
in his religious thought and his place in history. It was impossible for
serious students of the Renaissance and Reformation to ignore Erasmus,
but they were mostly concerned with political and ecclesiastical conflicts,
not with education or literature. They cared much more about Luther than
about Latinity.[131]

When considering his reputation in the sixteenth century we have to
treat the printing record of his books with a certain caution, despite its
impressiveness. A book may be a best-seller, a popular success, and forgotten in a few years. It may be a standard work for a long time, as *De copia* was,
and then either superseded by other manuals or abandoned because the
subject itself goes out of fashion or is approached in new ways. Influence is
harder to judge than popularity. When influence is discussed, the word
may prove to mean simply being the source of passages or scenes or plots;
in this sense Rabelais was an early instance of Erasmian influence. Or
influence may refer to a memory of, respect for, affinity with, one writer by
a later writer; in this sense Lucian was influential on Erasmus' *Moriae
encomium* and More's *Utopia*. Influence has many nuances, such as half-
conscious recollections, indirect or mingled borrowings, or adopted techniques which a well-read writer may use for his own purposes without
knowing or caring whence he derived them. Influence of ideas is easy to
suspect, notoriously difficult to prove. We can scarcely avoid talking about
influence, but, bearing in mind that its importance is more qualitative than
quantitative, we must not expect the term to be more than suggestive unless
accompanied by the sort of detailed analysis of text which belongs to

* * * * *

131 On his reputation to the eighteenth century see Andreas Flitner *Erasmus im
Urteil seiner Nachwelt* (Tübingen 1952). Two articles by Bruce Mansfield clarify
nineteenth-century attitudes towards him: 'Erasmus and the Mediating
School' *Journal of Religious History* 4 (1967) 302–16; 'Erasmus in the Nineteenth
Century: The Liberal Tradition' *Studies in the Renaissance* 15 (1968) 193–219.

specialized studies. In the paragraphs that follow, only some fairly obvious facts are assembled and a few clues to further investigation indicated.

Hundreds of substantial articles and books on Erasmus exist, in many languages, but despite this abundance work remains to be done. We have no comprehensive history of his fame and influence. Marcel Bataillon's *Erasme et l'Espagne* (1937) is admirable, the best book of its kind, but none of comparable scope or depth for other countries exists, though many partial contributions towards these are available. One principal source of knowledge for the history of Erasmus' writings is the learned notes in the Allen edition of his correspondence. The most ambitious bibliography of the writings yet attempted, the Ghent series[132] which commenced in 1897 but has languished for many years, did not reach the four works included in these volumes of cwe. Here our interest is limited to those works. Portions of *Parabolae* and *De copia* were borrowed, adapted, or revised, but no English translation of them was published in the sixteenth century. Nor is it easy to imagine why anyone would have wanted *De copia* translated when it was made for speakers and writers of Latin and had nothing then of the historical interest it possesses today. Similarly *Antibarbari* and *De ratione studii* were addressed to Latin readers, for their themes concerned classical and not vernacular literatures. Readers curious about these writings but unable to read them did not exist in sufficient numbers to tempt printers, who knew their market, to print translations. Erasmus' religious writings, especially *Enchiridion*, and *Adagia, Colloquia, Moriae encomium* were issued in various languages from time to time, but his strictly scholarly and pedagogical works appealed, for good reason, only to readers of Latin.

* * * * *

132 F. Vander Haeghen et al eds *Bibliotheca Erasmiana, extrait de la Bibliotheca Belgica* (Ghent 1897–1936). E.J. Devereux ed *English Translations of Erasmus to 1700*, Oxford Bibliographical Society Occasional Publications 3 (Oxford 1968) is a useful checklist. Printed catalogues of the great national libraries such as the British Library and Bibliothèque nationale list many editions but must be supplemented by the collections in the City Library of Rotterdam and the libraries at Basel, Oxford, and elsewhere. Recent and current lists of work on Erasmus appear in annual bibliographies in *Studies in Philology* (to 1970), the Modern Language Association's *International Bibliography, Bibliographie internationale de l'Humanisme et de la Renaissance* (Geneva) since 1965, *Erasmus in English* (occasional publication of University of Toronto Press). Three volumes edited by J.C. Margolin, *Quatorze années de bibliographie érasmienne (1936–1949), Douze années de bibliographie érasmienne (1950–1961)*, and *Neuf années de bibliographie érasmienne (1962–1970)* give detailed information for those years. A good selective bibliography 1531–1969 appears in *Scrinium Erasmianum* II 621–78. Introductions to editions in asd, particularly those by J.C. Margolin, include surveys of the diffusion and use of Erasmus' writings.

Reprints of a book tell us nothing about its merits but are irrefutable evidence of its success when success is measured, as it is by publishers, by sales. If we know *De copia* was printed approximately 160 times between 1512 and 1600,[133] we can be certain that it was widely used. Another kind of evidence that is valid but rather scarce is booksellers' records. One well-known example is the ledger of an Oxford bookseller, John Dorne, for ten months of the year 1520.[134] These records testify to the stature of Erasmus in a university town in that year. Of the Latin books Dorne sold in ten months, most were primers and breviaries, works of theology, classics, and handbooks of grammar and syntax. But his most popular author was Erasmus, nearly all of whose writings to 1520 are represented. At least 175 of the 2114 books sold by Dorne were written or edited by Erasmus.[135] Of these *Colloquia* did best (at least forty-seven copies); then come *De constructione* (thirty-one) and *De copia* (seventeen).[136] Seventeen is not many, but in proportion to the number of other works sold it is a respectable showing.

Sometimes the impact of a book can be inferred not only from its popularity but from the hostility it aroused; this is true of *Colloquia*, for instance. Erasmus' prolonged controversies with the theologians of Paris and Louvain and with critics in the religious orders involved his writings on the Bible and religion but had little to do directly with his treatises on education. Still, his reputation in certain ecclesiastical circles was such that any book by him was suspect. The sixteenth-century indexes of forbidden books show several examples. In the index of Pope Paul IV (1559) all of Erasmus' works were expressly prohibited. The index of Pius IV (1564, the so-called Tridentine index) banned only some of them and included none on education. In the index of Sixtus V (1590) all the writings were again forbidden.[137] At that date churchmen would have had slight interest in *De*

* * * * *

133 Rix lists 150 but more are known.
134 Dorne 71–177; supplementary data in *Collectanea* II ed Montagu Burrows (Oxford 1890) 453–78
135 Bennett 22 says 'over 150,' but this count apparently fails to include works by Erasmus not listed under his name in Dorne; when those are added the count is at least 175. Cf James K. McConica *English Humanists and Reformation Politics* (Oxford 1965) 88ff.
136 Possibly more, but abbreviations of titles make a few identifications uncertain.
137 See F.H. Reusch *Der Index der verbotenen Bücher* (Bonn 1883–5) I 347–55; *Die Indices librorum prohibitorum des sechzehnten Jahrhunderts* (Tübingen 1886) 183, 259, 477.

copia,[138] but prohibiting all books by an author because of strong disapproval of some was easier and safer than discriminating among them. It is only fair to add, however, that some indexes did attempt to classify books according to degree of pravity.

Of *Antibarbari* we hear little after Erasmus' death,[139] but while he lived it sold well: five editions in 1520 and other editions in 1521, 1522, 1524, 1527, 1535.[140] When replying to Pierre Cousturier (Sutor), a Carthusian who had attacked (1525) his translation of the New Testament, Erasmus declines to answer Sutor's accusations at length because, he says, he has already dealt with them in *Antibarbari*. He found the troublesome Sutor a typical specimen of those clerics who tried obstinately to deny the advantages of 'languages and good letters' to theologians.[141]

Defence of the humanities was Erasmus' main purpose in *Antibarbari*. If his theme and arguments interested enough readers to encourage printers in Basel, Strasbourg, Deventer, and Cologne to issue the work ten times, we must conclude that the book struck a responsive chord. By the date of the last edition, 1535, the cause of humanities had improved. His edition and translation of the New Testament had survived attacks. In *Paraclesis* (1516), *Ratio verae theologiae* (1518), a new edition of *Enchiridion* (1518), editions of the Fathers, even in *Colloquia* he had often and at times forcefully expressed his opinions on current religious questions. When commenting on attempts by opponents to link him with Luther he charged more than once in the early 1520s that many of the attacks on Luther were motivated by hatred of liberal studies.[142] By 1535 the controversies of 1520 had subsided; with respect to Luther at any rate lines had long since been clearly drawn, and

* * * * *

138 In 1533 Erasmus writes that some Paris theologians raided a bookshop and confiscated copies of his books, including *De copia* (Allen Ep 2868:12–32). *De copia* was probably an innocent victim; the culprits were *Colloquia, Moriae encomium*, and the translation of the New Testament.

139 Roger Ascham, in a letter to Hieronymus Froben 10 June 1551, says that the long-sought manuscript which had been kept by Richard Pace (Ep 30:17n) is in England and that he himself has used it in Cambridge (J.A. Giles ed *The Whole Works of Roger Ascham* [London 1864–5] I pt 2 288–9), but it appears that this manuscript contained only the printed part of *Antibarbari* (see Rudolf Pfeiffer *Ausgewählte Schriften* [Munich 1960] 198).

140 See ASD I-1 26–34. Erasmus presented a copy of the May 1520 edition, inscribed in his own hand, to Ferdinand Columbus, son of the explorer, October 1520 (Allen Ep 1147 introduction).

141 *Apologia adversus Petrum Sutorem* LB IX 777C–82B

142 For example Allen Ep 1141:25–6; and see the colloquy *Inquisitio de fide* ed Craig R. Thompson 2nd ed (Hamden, Conn 1975) 12.

events had taken courses which Erasmus deeply deplored. Despite all that, languages and letters were better off than they had been in 1520. The eloquence of *Antibarbari* was not needed so urgently now. Humanities always need defending, to be sure, but not always in the same idiom or tone.

The history of *De copia* differed from that of *Antibarbari* because it was a different sort of book, not a defence of humanities but a guide for students. This distinction need not imply that *De copia* had no relevance for literature; on the contrary. But since it was primarily a textbook for those willing to practise its precepts, it lacked the eloquence and contentiousness of *Antibarbari*. It had other qualities to recommend it, plus a wealth of examples. How many students were stimulated by it – some of them in spite of themselves, perhaps – we cannot know, because not one student in a thousand leaves a record of what he thought of a textbook. We know, however, that this book was taught in many schools for many years. Published with St Paul's School in mind, it was written for pupils everywhere and was used in many lands.

For these reasons both the printing record and the pedagogical history of *De copia* are of interest. No bibliography of Erasmus' publications can be safely called complete; all are tentative; but the checklist provided by Rix[143] gives the approximate record of *De copia*. It added some fifty editions to previous lists.[144]

* * * * *

143 'The Editions of Erasmus' *De copia*'
144 'Edition' is a distinctive technical term in later printing, but with respect to sixteenth-century books it is usually interchangeable with 'impression.' If an early printer, who normally distributed his type after printing a pamphlet or a portion of a book, decided later to re-issue the work, he had to reset the type; and this resetting is regarded as constituting a new edition. Printers (who were often publishers as well) reprinted successful books as often as the market made it profitable to do so. Because *De copia* was in demand many printers reprinted it. After the author's death there could not be a new 'authorized' edition, but an important revision or rearrangement of material, no matter who was responsible for it, might be an excellent publishing risk.
Various forms of privilege or copyright were known in the sixteenth century, but these were civic or regional, not international, and enforcement was erratic at best. More often than not the printers had a free hand to reprint anything, or acted as if they did. On the early history of privilege and copyright see Rudolf Hirsch *Printing, Selling, and Reading 1450–1550* (Wiesbaden 1967). For some notes on Erasmus and copyright, including troubles over *De copia*, Allen *Lectures* 133–7; Peter G. Bietenholz 'Ethics and Early Printing: Erasmus' Rules for the Proper Conduct of Authors' *Humanities Association Review* 26 (1975) 180–95.

De copia was successful from the first edition (July 1512). It was printed four, perhaps five, times in 1512–13. From 1514 to 1536, the year of Erasmus' death, there were at least seventy-four printings, and approximately the same number from 1536 to 1600. The numbers fall off sharply after 1551: about thirty between 1552 and 1600. At least fourteen printings appeared in the next century between 1600 and 1690, three in the eighteenth century, two in the nineteenth. Allowing for the menaces of duplicates and 'ghosts' lurking in the Rix list, its total of 180 printings (a figure that may be too low) shows that *De copia* enjoyed a far longer life than most books have a right to expect. In the sixteenth century it was printed in at least twenty-one cities by sixty-five printers.

'Standard work on the subject,' the highest praise for any work of learning, fits *De copia* during the sixteenth century. Like other school texts, it was more than once revised for particular needs. In 1526 Georgius Major compressed chapters 11 to 32 of book I and all of book II to tables for rapid memorizing. These tables, which filled only twelve or fifteen pages, were often appended to the *Tabulae de schematibus et tropis* of Peter Schade (Mosellanus), 1529, a compilation long popular. In some and no doubt many schools chapters 11–32 of book I, on varying, were the parts of *De copia* most used.[145] Editions of 1528[146] included scholia, added by Christian Hegendorff, identifying quotations in the text.[147] Joannes Veltkirchius produced an edition (Hagenau 1534), publication of which was arranged by Philip Melanchthon after Veltkirchius' death. This, we are told, 'became the school type, and is the form printed in England.'[148]

Four years after the first publication of *De copia*, John Watson of Cambridge, who became master of Christ's College a year later, reported

* * * * *

145 Rix 600–1; on Mosellanus Allen Ep 560 introduction. Chapter 32 is misnumbered in early editions of *De copia*; it is correctly numbered 33 in later editions.
146 Antwerp: Hillen; Hagenau: Secer; London: Wynkyn de Worde; Paris: S de Colines. See Rix 599.
147 On Hegendorff Allen Ep 1168 introduction
148 Baldwin II 176–9. Melanchthon advised teachers always to have *De copia* and *Adagia* at hand. Veltkirchius agreed that the essential part of *De copia* for schools was book I chapters 11–32 (Baldwin II 32, 179). Another standard handbook on tropes and schemes was Joannes Susenbrotus *Epitome troporum ac schematum* (1541), which was based on the usual classical sources but also (like Mosellanus' work) relied heavily on *De copia* and other Erasmian writings. The *Epitome* was printed twenty-five times between 1541 and 1635, eight times in England. On Susenbrotus see Joseph X. Brennan in *Quarterly Journal of Speech* 46 (1960) 59–71; PMLA 75 (1960) 485–96; Baldwin II 138–75.

the enthusiasm of his Italian friends for the book.[149] Leonard Cox, an
Englishman resident in Poland, wrote to Erasmus from Cracow (March
1527) that he had lectured on it in Cracow and twice in Hungary.[150] Cox
was author of an *Art or Craft of Rhetoric* (London 1532).

With few exceptions the English literature of the sixteenth and seventeenth centuries we read and remember is vernacular, not Latin, written by
men whose main concerns in mature life were the English language and
English poetry. Yet consider the nature of Spenser's or Marlowe's or Jonson's grammar-school education. Six or seven formative years spent on
Latin and Greek literature and rhetoric could not have left them untouched,
responsive as they must have been to language. When we read *The Faerie
Queene* or *Volpone* or *Hero and Leander* we do not, or should not, worry
about sources and influences; we read a poem as a poem. Nevertheless a
writer's background is worth knowing if it can throw any light on his art or,
if nothing else, evoke the society or milieu in which he lived and worked.
Knowledge of Spenser's studies under Mulcaster at Merchant Taylors'
School would not affect our response to his verse but might help scholars to
trace the growth of his mind. Jonson's famous tribute to Camden of
Westminster School surely tells us something about Jonson. If an investigator of Marlowe's poetry asks[151] whether he learnt anything from *De
copia* at Canterbury School, the question may be valid even if it cannot be
answered satisfactorily.

T.W. Baldwin's formidable 1525-page treatise *William Shakspere's
Small Latine and Lesse Greeke*, a study of curricula, texts, and rhetorical
training in sixteenth-century grammar schools, is not a critique of Shakespeare's art. It may, however, sharpen our perceptions of argument, diction, and style in the plays. To a large extent Baldwin's volumes are devoted
to Erasmus's writings on education and the influence of his programme in
the grammar schools. *De copia* receives generous attention, for with the
exception of *Colloquia*, none of Erasmus' books was more common in the
schools. Of the 115 or more printings of *De copia* to 1550, only one is known

* * * * *

149 The passage is quoted in introduction to *De copia* CWE 24 282–3. On *De copia* in
Elizabethan Cambridge cf Lisa Jardine 'The Place of Dialectic Teaching in
Sixteenth-Century Cambridge' *Studies in the Renaissance* 21 (1974) 50, 61.
150 Allen Ep 1803:83–8. Cox's translation of Erasmus' paraphrase of the Epistle to
Titus was published in London 1534 and later revised for the great 1548–9
edition of the complete *Paraphrases* in English.
151 As Eric Jacobsen does in his *Translation: A Traditional Craft* (Copenhagen 1958)
114–16

to have been made in England, Wynkyn de Worde's of 1528.[152] All the same this was a peculiarly English book because of its connections with Colet, St Paul's School, and subsequently with so many other English schools whose statutes or curricula copied those of St Paul's. By revising a Latin syntax, *De constructione*, Erasmus furnished a book for instruction in grammar at St Paul's; by writing *De copia* he furnished a book on rhetoric.[153] When we speak of the Erasmian character of the curriculum in the grammar schools we have specific evidence for doing so. It is spelled out in school statutes and school histories. In the Eton timetable of 1530 *De copia* was used as an alternate to Mosellanus' *Tabulae* by the sixth or seventh form.[154] Similarly at Canterbury School (1541) it was used by the sixth.[155] The boys were to study varying and so to learn to speak Latin suitably 'so far as is possible for boys'; likewise at Winchester and numerous other schools.[156]

Two of Erasmus' contemporaries whose writings on education are of continuing interest to historians echo the almost universal approval of *De copia*. One was Sir Thomas Elyot, whose scheme in *The Governour* (1531) for the bringing up of youths who will be members of the ruling class combines the bookish training we would expect from this English Erasmian with training in moral virtue and attention to sports, drawing, and dancing. He would have boys begin Greek and Latin at the same time – when they are seven – or else begin Greek first, but a remark about *De copia* shows that common sense was always breaking in. For after prescribing as an introduction to rhetoric Cicero, Hermogenes, and Quintilian, he decides that after all *De copia* will serve instead: 'And in good faith to speak boldly that I think, for him that nedeth not or doth not desire to be an exquisite orator, the little book made by the famous Erasmus (whom all gentle wits are bounden to thank and support) which he calleth *Copiam verborum et rerum*, that is to say plenty of words and matter, shall be sufficient.'[157]

* * * * *

152 Rix 617 lists one before 1520 by this printer, but no satisfactory evidence for it is available. In the printed text of Dorne (93 No. 449) the entry is transcribed as 'copia rerum wen[ken].' If the ledger and transcription are accurate, and if Wynkyn de Worde did print *De copia* before 1520, no copy seems to have survived.

153 For his other services to St Paul's School see Thompson *Colloquies* 32. *De copia* was still in use at St Paul's School in the 1830s: Michael F.J. McDonnell *A History of St Paul's School* (London 1909) 398.

154 Leach 451

155 Leach 468

156 For some examples see Baldwin I 298, 305, 310, 314, 328, 348, 361, 378, 402, 417, 431, 490, 728; II 176–96; cf I 317, II 37.

157 H.H.S. Crofts ed *The Book Named The Governour* (London 1883) I 54, 72–4

Page from the ledger of an Oxford bookseller, 1520

This ledger records titles of books, many of them by Erasmus, which were sold in the shop of John Dorne in ten months of the year 1520. The arrows indicate Erasmian works: '1 copia rerum paris li[gata] in pergameno'; '1 colloquia erasmi'; '1 erasmus de construction e lo[uanii] li[gatus] in pergameno'; '1 erasmus de construction e'; '1 adagia erasmi parua pa[ris] in qua[ternis].'

By permission of the President and Fellows of Corpus Christi College, Oxford; now deposited in the Bodleian Library, MS 131, f 14[r]

Juan Luis Vives, whose name ranks close to Erasmus' as a writer on
education in those times,[158] stresses, as Erasmus had done earlier, the
importance of keeping notebooks for recording information of all kinds met
in reading and for material dictated by the teacher. He follows the lead of
Erasmus in the choice of classical texts and on the question of reading pagan
authors. For rhetoric he recommends *De copia*, both parts to be expounded
by the master. On another topic Vives is emphatic where Erasmus is silent.
He insists on the importance of the vernacular tongue. Though Latin is the
universal language and the business of the grammar school, teachers of
Latin must pay strict attention to the native language of their charges and
they themselves must speak it aptly and exactly.[159]

We return to Shakespeare. He knew all there was to know about *copia*,
but whether he learnt any of it from Erasmus must remain unanswered
until further evidence turns up, if it ever does. No record of his attending
grammar school survives, but it is very difficult to believe he did not do so.
His Latin tags, allusions to many classical names and stories, and adroit-
ness in using structural and stylistic techniques taught in school rhetoric
would be even harder to account for if he had not experienced the kind of
curriculum Baldwin describes so elaborately. As readers we can catch
nuances better in

> Conceit, more rich in matter than in words,
> Brags of his substance, not of ornament[160]

if we have known about the distinctions between *copia rerum* and *copia
verborum*. Or in 'more matter, with less art,'[161] the most familiar phrase in
English literature for this idea. We can say that Shakespeare may have used
and remembered parts of *De copia*. On this question, as on so many about
him, the rest is silence.

Dorne sold no copies of *De ratione studii* in 1520. Was this because it
was more pertinent to masters than to pupils? There were schoolboys as
well as university students in Oxford, and even the university students

* * * * *

158 He lived in England from 1523 to 1528, lectured at Oxford, and was tutor to the
     princess Mary. Both More and Erasmus praise him, and many letters between
     him and Erasmus survive. See Ep 927 introduction. On Elyot and Vives see
     W.H. Woodward *Studies in Education during the Age of the Renaissance
     1400–1600* (Cambridge 1906; repr New York 1967).
159 *De tradendis disciplinis*. See the translation by Foster Watson *Vives: On Educa-
     tion* (Cambridge 1913) 100–6, 108, 134–5.
160 *Romeo and Juliet* II vi 30–1
161 *Hamlet* II ii 95. See the collection of passages in Baldwin II 183–92.

were younger, on the average, than they are now. The number of books on
grammar and syntax Dorne sold is noticeable, and most of the books by
Erasmus he sold were school texts. We know that *De ratione studii* did well
elsewhere. The full text was published twice in 1512, then in 1513, twice in
1514, again in 1526 and 1530. Vander Haeghen's checklist of editions and
reprintings of Erasmus' works[162] contains seventy-odd entries for *De
ratione studii* to 1576, none between 1576 and 1622, seven in the rest of the
century.[163] This seems convincing evidence that it was highly regarded
long after Erasmus' death. It remains a valuable document for the understanding of humanistic ideas on education.

   We may surmise that its brevity and incisiveness recommended it to
readers. It offered specific suggestions based on sound general principles. It
had close associations with *De copia* (and was often printed with it) and
hence with the St Paul's curriculum. Both works had a career of continuous
use from publication to the 1570s; in fact longer than that, but the number of
reprints after the 1570s does not compare with what we find earlier. Their
popularity coincided with an era when many new schools were founded in
England. H.S. Bennett is undoubtedly right in emphasizing the connection: 'Under the powerful influence of Erasmus, and in particular of his *De
ratione studii*, the new principles which were to underlie the grammar-
school teaching for many generations to come were set forth.'[164]

   Parabolae was another work for which we have ample evidence of
popularity and use: thirty-eight printings in Erasmus' lifetime, twenty-two
more by 1600.[165] Budé was critical of it, as of *De copia*.[166] After many
editions had appeared a correspondent reported that the faculty of theology
at Paris condemned *Parabolae* along with *Colloquia* and *Moriae encomium* as
dangerous to faith and morals.[167] Censure of those books was no novelty; if
Parabolae was added to the list the reason must have been its unfavourable
remarks about theologians and prelates. Expressions of disapproval were

* * * * *

162 Vander Haeghen ser 1 169–72. (This *Repertoire* is not the same as the *Bib-
    liotheca Erasmiana* in n 132 above.)
163 The count for the sixteenth century is probably too low. Cf ASD I-2 96. All totals
    in Vander Haeghen are provisional.
164 Bennett 87
165 Vander Haeghen 137–9, gives a partial list. Dorne sold a single copy in 1520.
    The vice-provost of King's College, Cambridge, Bryan Rowe, who died in
    1521, owned a copy of *Parabolae* and six other works by Erasmus in addition to
    editions, translations, and commentaries. See F.J. Norton in *Transactions of
    the Cambridge Bibliographical Society* 2 (1954–8) 339–51.
166 Ep 435:85–92
167 Allen Ep 1784:5–8. Whether Erasmus' informant was correct is uncertain.

few and futile, and *Parabolae* quickly made its way as an instructive book for the general reader and a convenient source of material for writers. More than once it was adapted or edited for scholastic purposes. Of adaptations the most widely circulated seems to have been that of Conradus Wolfhart (Lycosthenes), Basel 1557, who rearranged the contents under general heads or topics. This method of revision enabled teachers and pupils to find quickly whatever classical material on a subject *Parabolae* contained.

Whether in its original form or in a revision by Lycosthenes or someone else, *Parabolae* was known and used for a long time in schools and universities. An admirer in Bologna assured Erasmus in 1535 that *Parabolae* and *De copia* were among the texts used and liked by Italian teachers.[168] Alexander Nowell, the future dean of St Paul's Cathedral and author of one of the most common catechisms taught in Elizabethan schools, owned this and other books by Erasmus at Oxford in the 1530s.[169] It is on a list of grammar-school texts published in 1581.[170] Gabriel Harvey, the learned and cranky scholar in Elizabethan Cambridge (of whom more in a moment), describes *Parabolae*, *Adagia*, and *Apophthegmata* as Erasmus' three principal 'paper books' or collections.[171] *Parabolae* complemented the other two by furnishing a stock of similes. With these three works a writer had a ready supply of metaphors, images, and lore to which he could turn, much as his modern counterpart might turn to Bartlett, a dictionary of proverbs, or the *Oxford Companion* to this or that. Similes were favoured by rhetoricians because they were ornamental and were thought to contain substantial truth, concisely expressed. Similitude of course can be misleading, because it is only analogy. Erasmus is fond of suggesting or affirming that as *a* is to *b*, *c* is to *d*. The relation of *a* to *b* may be a fact, but in the relation of *c* to *d* there's many a slip. Rhetorically, though, if not always logically, the device can be pleasing and persuasive; sometimes it has powerful emotional effect in a particular context:

> As flies to wanton boys are we to th' gods:
> They kill us for their sport.[172]

* * * * *

168 Allen Ep 3002:625–9
169 Baldwin I 174
170 Baldwin I 436
171 G.C. Moore Smith ed *Gabriel Harvey's Marginalia* (Stratford-upon-Avon 1913) 141
172 *King Lear* IV i 36–7. On whether Shakespeare knew *Parabolae* see Baldwin II 352.

'As well to a good maker and poet as to an excellent persuader in prose, the figure of *similitude* is very necessary, by which we not only beautify our tale but also very much enforce and enlarge it. I say enforce because no one thing more prevaileth with all ordinary judgments than persuasion by *similitude*.'[173]

In sixteenth-century England readers liked popularized moral philosophy, and many were addicted to sermons and to improving books of every sort.[174] Their acceptance of *Parabolae* and similar books reflected this taste, and they read other collections which were equally weighty in moral wisdom but far less attractive in style; for example, William Baldwin's *Treatise of Moral Philosophy* (1547–8), a pastiche whose popularity is confirmed by at least eighteen printings to 1640. It has obvious Erasmian affinities (*Parabolae* and *De copia* among them) but nothing of Erasmian wit or style.

Lyly's *Euphues* (1578), which had an extraordinary vogue for a generation, illustrates another side of Elizabethan taste, the enjoyment of tropes and patterned prose in narrative fiction and dramatic comedy. For his sententiousness and examples Lyly owed much to *Adagia* and *Parabolae*, to the latter especially for his illustrations from natural history. These were a feature of *Euphues* which attracted attention and at times ridicule.[175]

Chapman's poems and plays are thought by some to show traces of Erasmian passages.[176] The resemblances are there, but whether the lines echo Erasmus or are common property is open to question. Renaissance dictionaries, compendia, translations, or simple plagiarism sometimes account for supposedly direct borrowings.[177] It is seldom safe to assume that an Elizabethan writer had a certain text in front of him, especially if he is

* * * * *

173 George Puttenham *The Arte of English Poesie* ed Gladys Doidge Willcock and Alice Walker (Cambridge 1936) 240. On similitude, including specific reference to *Parabolae*, see William G. Crane *Wit and Rhetoric in the Renaissance* (New York 1937) passim; Baldwin passim; Brian Vickers *Francis Bacon and Renaissance Prose* 143–54; Lizette Westney (n 3 above); Margolin's introduction to the ASD edition.

174 See Louis B. Wright *Middle-Class Culture in Elizabethan England* (Chapel Hill 1935; repr Ithaca 1958).

175 Cf Morris P. Tilley *Proverb Lore in Lyly's Euphues and in Pettie's Palace of Pleasure* (New York 1926). Shakespeare occasionally parodies the Euphuistic style, for example in *I Henry IV* II iv 440ff: 'for though the camomile, the more it is trodden on, the faster it grows, yet youth, the more it is wasted, the sooner it wears.' Lyly uses sentences of this kind to excess.

176 See ASD I-5 56–9.

177 On dictionaries see DeWitt T. Starnes and Ernest W. Talbert *Classical Myth and Legend in Renaissance Dictionaries* (Chapel Hill 1955).

quoting from a classical author. He may have been using a commonplace book, his own or somebody else's, instead.

Thomas Nashe's works, both satires and prose fiction, show familiarity with some of Erasmus' books, though how much of this was at first-hand is uncertain. In *The Unfortunate Traveller* (1594) the hero encounters Erasmus, 'aged learning's chief ornament,' in Rotterdam; Thomas More happens to be there at the same time. In his *Anatomy of Absurdity* (1589) Nashe borrows more from *Parabolae* than from any other single source.[178]

Nashe's *bête noire* Gabriel Harvey, the friend and correspondent of Spenser, owned and annotated a copy of the 1565 (Basel: Episcopius) reprint of *Parabolae*.[179] Harvey read this in 1566 and again in 1577. He valued Erasmus but privately preferred men of action to men of ideas or preachments. He compares Erasmus' *Institutio principis christiani* unfavourably with Machiavelli's *The Prince*.[180] But he has high praise for *Parabolae*, a really useful book: 'An excellent and most necessary storehouse for all discourses, written or spoken.'[181]

Parabolae was well suited to the sixteenth century's bias for rhetoric, its respect for authority, its attention to classical precedents. These characteristics produced excess or pedantry at times, as in *Euphues*: the same weakness that in Latinity lured the injudicious down the primrose path of Ciceronianism. Sir Philip Sidney reproaches over-zealous imitators of Cicero (and Demosthenes) who, he says, 'cast sugar and spice upon every dish that is served to the table, like those Indians not content to wear earrings at the fit and natural place of the ears, but they will thrust jewels through their nose and lips, because they will be sure to be fine.' With Lyly evidently in mind he adds: 'Now for similitudes in certain printed discourses, I think all herbarists, all stories of beasts, fowls, and fishes are rifled up, that they may come in multitudes to wait upon any of our conceits; which certainly is as absurd a surfeit to the ears as is possible; for the force of a similitude not being to prove anything to a contrary disputer, but only to explain to a willing hearer, when that is done, the rest is a most tedious prattling, rather overswaying the memory from the purpose whereto they were applied than any whit enforming[182] the judgment already either satisfied, or by similitudes not to be satisfied.'[183]

* * * * *

178 McKerrow ed *Works of Thomas Nashe* v 117
179 Now in the Folger Shakespeare Library, Washington, DC
180 *Marginalia* 149:10–13
181 *Marginalia* 140:17ff
182 In the older sense of 'shaping,' 'moulding'
183 Rollins and Baker eds *The Renaissance in England* 622, 623

Erasmus, it is scarcely necessary to add, was no more responsible for the excesses of Lyly than for the absurdities of extreme Ciceronianism. His sense of decorum and mastery of style did not allow such extravagance. Rightly conceived and practised, imitation should be a liberating rather than servile doctrine. As Professor Mynors remarks, 'Immense as is Erasmus' respect for the ancient authors whom he knew so well, he never lets them limit his independence; and this is one reason why he could do so much with them.'[184] In their admiration of classical antiquity the best Renaissance writers and scholars studied its achievements gratefully and often looked to its literatures for models, as they were trained to do. But they believed also that what is past is prologue: 'We are the children of Nature as well as they.'

Readers of this volume who meet Mr Bolgar's assertion, in his deservedly respected book *The Classical Heritage and Its Beneficiaries*,[185] that Erasmus 'is the greatest man we come across in the history of education' may think that a bold claim requiring a willing suspension of disbelief. It is bold because education is an activity as old as civilization; and as there were many brave men before Agamemnon, so there were many other educators of importance besides Erasmus. He himself would probably have nominated Plato for the highest honour.

If by education is meant liberal-arts education as known in the West during the past five centuries, a training whose basis was grammatical, rhetorical, and literary, the primacy of Erasmus can be accepted without demur. Assessment of his work as an educator cannot be made only by the four treatises in the present volumes, however. Everything he wrote on education and much that he wrote on religion and ethics must be taken into account if we want to understand his conception of education and estimate his contributions to it. One thing at a time: the works translated in these two volumes show only four pieces in a variegated pattern. All the pieces are needed before we can pronounce judgment. Meanwhile what should be kept in mind, in reading these and other volumes of the series, is the controlling idea set forth in *Antibarbari*, that the best pagan wisdom and culture were not only good in themselves but good for the Christian society that inherited the wealth of antiquity. If we can see what Erasmus means by the relationship between learning, Good Letters, education, and religion we are on the road to understanding him and his purposes.

CRT

* * * * *

184 Introductory Note *Parabolae* below 124
185 Bolgar 336

ACKNOWLEDGMENTS
The editor wishes to thank Professors James Hutton, Elaine Fantham, and
Charles Mitchell for their generous assistance. He is indebted likewise to
his colleagues on the Editorial Board, to the staff of University of Toronto
Press, and to the various libraries which provided the illustrations. Like all
editors and readers of the Collected Works of Erasmus, he is most grateful to
the Social Sciences and Humanities Research Council of Canada for continuing support of the series.

THE ANTIBARBARIANS

Antibarbarorum liber

translated and annotated by
MARGARET MANN PHILLIPS

The book which was hopefully called *The Four Books of the Antibarbarians* was among the first of Erasmus' works. He tells us that he began it before he was twenty, and if recent attempts to decide his birth year are correct, this would indicate the year 1487–8.[1] He had already written poetry, 'to which study,' he says, 'I was much inclined as a boy – so much so that I had great difficulty in turning towards prose.'[2] He is rather sardonic about his earliest attempts. He had also by this time written an essay on the monastic life, *De contemptu mundi*, but he was not proud of this in later years; he said it was written *alieno stomacho*,[3] or with reluctance, but that could never be said of the other serious prose work of those years, the *Antibarbari*.

This book has had its full share of critical examination in the first volume of *Erasmi opera omnia* (ASD), published in Amsterdam in 1969, where it figures first; the present translator is much indebted to this edition. The introduction contains a wealth of information and a good summary. For light on textual problems the reader is referred to ASD. It is chiefly necessary here to explain the character of the book and its curious history.

Only book I of the projected four exists, for reasons which will soon appear. The work is a spirited defence of the study of the classics, in the form of a dialogue between Erasmus and his friends: Willem Hermans, a monk like himself from the monastery of Steyn; an energetic character named Jacob Batt, town clerk of Bergen; the burgomaster of Bergen, Willem Conrad; and the town doctor Jodocus.[4] They meet and talk, and their conversation develops into a debate on the reasons for the stiff resistance they find among the traditionalists to the introduction of classical studies. Three of them are young enthusiasts, regarded by the older generation as revolutionary and subversive because they want to substitute the 'abominable monsters of paganism,' Horace, Virgil, and Ovid, for the accepted reading of the schools, Alexander's and Eberhard of Béthune's Latin grammars for instance. The two other men are in agreement, and together they discuss the motives for this resistance and for the decline of true learning. The doctor says it is because of the stars (he is addicted to astrology); the burgomaster says it is because of Christianity; Willem Hermans says it is a result of the ageing of the world. Batt, however, puts it all down to the terrible teachers who reign undisputed in the field of education. The others beg him to make this clear, and he explains himself in a long speech, punctuated by a few remarks from his hearers. He sketches the

* * * * *

1 A.C.F. Koch *The Year of Erasmus' Birth* (Utrecht 1969); M.M. Phillips in *Erasmus in English* 3 (1971) 24; 6 (1973) 14–15
2 For Erasmus' early inclination to poetry see Allen I 3:16–18 and Ep 1581:524–5.
3 Allen Ep 1194:13
4 Jooste van Schoonhoven; see below 20:23n.

battlefield, divides the enemy into three camps – the ignorant, the narrow-minded, and those who wish to use learning for their own ends – and starts on an eloquent attack on the first group, who know nothing about the classics and therefore regard them as harmful ('beware, he's a poet, he's no Christian') or who take their stand on apostolic simplicity.

Eventually the burgomaster's wife sends a servant from their country house nearby to say that dinner is spoiling, and they decide to adjourn and take up the discussion in the afternoon. That afternoon, for us, has not arrived.

The history of the book is remarkable. It must have been an obsessive thought with Erasmus. If he did indeed begin it before he was twenty, he went on tinkering with it for a long time. It had started as a speech pure and simple, put into the mouth of his childhood friend Cornelis Gerard, but he changed it into dialogue form during his stay at a country house at Halsteren near Bergen, as the guest of the bishop of Cambrai, who had taken him out of the monastery to be his secretary. This stay can be dated to the spring of 1494 or 1495.[5] The immediate circumstances gave the *dramatis personae* and the setting, which is realistic and paints the garden of a country house in Holland instead of the shade of a plane tree by the Ilissus; the Platonic inspiration is expressly stated but the model is also Cicero.

The stage being set, Erasmus intended to develop the theme in three more books. After the refutation of the enemies of humanism the second book was to provide an answer to this, in which a fictitious character used all the powers of eloquence to pour scorn on eloquence; the third book was to be a refutation of the second, and the fourth a defence of poetry.

After the bishop's projected visit to Rome had fallen through, it appears to have been Batt who suggested that Erasmus, disappointed by this change of plan, should ask the bishop to send him to continue his studies in Paris. He left Bergen for Paris, probably in September 1495, and soon after his arrival submitted the first book of his *Antibarbari* to the historian Robert Gaguin.

In 1499 Erasmus went to England and it was probably then that he showed the draft of books I and II to John Colet.[6] During the penurious years in Paris which followed he apparently went on with it during the time he could spare from his teaching. He took it with him to Italy in 1506, and revised books I and II at Bologna. But when in 1509 he received an urgent invitation to come to England and share in the golden age that was opening with the reign of Henry

* * * * *

5 Allen I appendix V and Ep 1110 introduction. Probably the dates of Epp 30 and 37, which Allen gives as c 1489 and c spring 1494, should be reversed. See Roland H. Bainton *Erasmus of Christendom* (New York 1969) 29 n34; Tracy 82 n7.

6 On Colet and Erasmus see Ep 106 introduction.

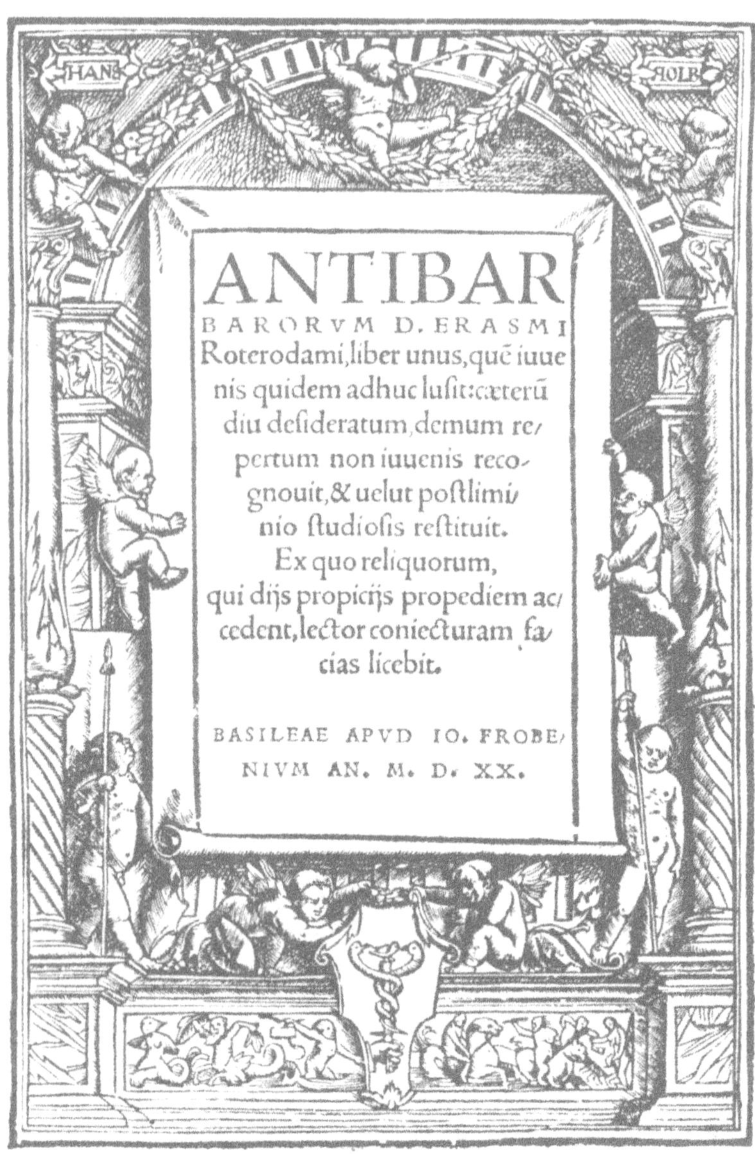

Title page of the first edition of the *Antibarbari*,
with decorative border by Hans Holbein
Basel: Froben May 1520
A copy of this edition, inscribed in Erasmus' hand, was owned by Ferdinand
Columbus (son of the navigator), who called on Erasmus in Louvain in October
1520. See Allen Ep 1147 introduction.
Beinecke Library, Yale University

VIII, he left Italy in a hurry and consigned his papers to the care of an English friend, Richard Pace, at Ferrara. Soon Pace had to leave too, and the papers went to another Englishman, less conscientious, who sold what he could and gave away the rest.[7]

Erasmus asked over and over again for the return of his brainchild. But he never saw most of it again. He got hold of book I when he was in Louvain many years later, revised it again, and sent it to Froben, who published it in May (and again in December) 1520. The reason given for this was that Erasmus had found the manuscript circulating from hand to hand, and he was conscious of its juvenile mistakes; the only way to deal with this was to produce a new and revised edition. There was also perhaps, as we shall see, a new reason for reviving his old work. A year or two later he had the beginning of book II sent from England and found the end of the same book at Bruges. But nothing more ever emerged, and he never fulfilled his intention of rewriting it.

In spite of this loss we know a surprising amount about the development of the project, because we possess a copy of the first (or second) draft of book I as well as Froben's revised edition. A manuscript found at Gouda by P.S. Allen is without doubt this early draft; it had been copied for the Brethren of the Common Life and bound up with their Jerome – in the ninth volume of the *Opera*. It was published in 1930 by Albert Hyma in his book *The Youth of Erasmus*. Hyma printed the early text beside the later version, and the ASD edition also gives a parallel arrangement. A comparative study of the two states was published by R. Pfeiffer in 1936.[8] Out of these studies come some large deductions: the fact that the attacks on the religious orders were largely added in the 1520 version, the signs of careful stylistic amendment and greater erudition, wider reference to the Fathers, and freer use of amusing asides and irony.

Further light on the development of the text as we have it now is given by James D. Tracy,[9] who shows that it is possible by internal evidence to distinguish between the earliest state of the work (as a speech by Cornelis Gerard) and the later draft of 1494–5 in which it was already in dialogue form. He separates the text of the Gouda manuscript into three categories: the original

* * * * *

7 See Ep 30:17n.
8 Rudolf Pfeiffer 'Die Wandlungen der "Antibarbari"' *Gedenkschrift zum 400. Todestage des Erasmus von Rotterdam* (Basel 1936) 50–68; reprinted in his *Ausgewählte Schriften* (Munich 1960) 188–207. On the date of the text copied in the Gouda MS see Silvano Cavazza 'La cronologia degli "Antibarbari" e le origini del pensiero religioso di Erasmo' *Rinascimento* 25 (1975) 141–79.
9 Tracy 81–120

oratio (see Tracy's appendix I), the additions of uncertain date (appendix II), and additions of 1494 (appendix III). This analysis suggests to him a development in Erasmus' attitude, summarized by Tracy as follows: 'In the original *oratio* he was primarily a student of Valla's *Elegantiae*. In the 1494/5 version he became Erasmus.'[10] That is to say that the early version is an attack on idleness and ignorance and a lively defence of humanism, while the additions show an extension of the attack to the protagonists of Scholastic theology and a wider recognition of the positive values of classical studies. Tracy regards the 1494 *Antibarbari* as a watershed: Erasmus refused 'any longer to regard the world primarily as a source of temptation.'

We may further ask, what is the significance of the additions to the text in the edition of 1520, and is it possible to build up a general picture of the development and aims of the book?

It is noticeable that the process of its coming to light is shared by almost all the works of Erasmus' youth. The exception is the *Adagia*, which never got lost and which was printed by Erasmus himself in all its stages. But the *Colloquies*, written for his Paris pupils in the first place, remained in the hands of his agent Augustin Vincent (Caminade) until the latter published them in November 1518, which roused Erasmus to print an authenticated edition in March 1519. With them were some notes on style entitled *Brevis de copia praeceptio*, which were really out of date since Erasmus had published the *De copia* in full in 1512 for Colet's school. The *De ratione studii* was included and published later by Erasmus in the same way. The book on letter-writing, *De conscribendis epistolis*, was printed without his knowledge in Cambridge in 1521 and called out an author's edition in 1522.[11] It was certainly the custom for an author to disclaim his work or to ascribe its publication to the urging of his friends, but the fact that Erasmus so often immediately published a better version suggests that his indignation was genuine. At the end of his life he wrote a letter[12] mentioning that he knew people had kept manuscripts of his and that he was doing his best to see that nothing further would be printed without his supervision.

This history suggests that he was careless about his papers. He was a quick writer and hated revising, though there is evidence that he did a good deal of it.

Why should all these early works be included in a wave of publishing which brought them all out into the open between 1512 and 1522? The answer is

* * * * *

10 Tracy 94
11 Ep 71 introduction. *De copia* and *De ratione studii* are translated in CWE 24. For *Brevis de copia praeceptio* see Thompson *Colloquies* 614ff.
12 Allen Ep 3100:29–48

probably to be found in the leap into public notice which resulted from the publications of 1515–17: the two new editions of the *Adagia* which turned it into a topical work, and above all the publication of the Greek New Testament. It was not the *Praise of Folly* but the New Testament which had made Erasmus a *succès de scandale*, and anyone who possessed a manuscript of his even dating from twenty years before was bound to rush into print.

When we consider the *Antibarbari* in its relation to the better known works of Erasmus, this history becomes important. We have here two (or three) states of the work, the first expressing the views of an enthusiastic young man before the close of the fifteenth century, the other those of a mature and celebrated man in 1520. We should expect some changes, but one thing is obvious: the basic attitude is unchanged. Erasmus still considered the ideas about learning expressed through Batt and his friends to be applicable to the situation at the later date. Even more applicable in fact. He was no less convinced of the value of the classics, though the opponents before him changed.

To take first the early version, which was not altered basically in shape and intention: it has many characteristics which are those of his later work. As we have seen, he was feeling his way, transforming a speech into a dialogue, but the purpose is the same, to avoid direct statement; the writer himself is in the background, and of all Renaissance writers Erasmus is the one who prefers the dialogue, with its avoidance of dogmatism, its balance and swing of debate, its insistence on friendship and communication. It was not here, as in later dialogues like the *Ciceronianus*, a satiric delineation of a crank. The speakers are all real people under their own names, equally respectful of each other. The opening, where the friends meet and chaff each other and decide to accept Erasmus' invitation to talk in the delectable surroundings of the garden, has all his later tones, half humorous, half earnest, witty and civilized. He himself is present only as a reporter. This is carefully developed in the later version, when Batt teases his friend about his watchfulness and his long memory, but it was in the first draft that Batt accused Erasmus of wanting to get them all into print.[13]

The circle of friends was established once for all in 1495. Two of them, the burgomaster and the doctor, are there for the sake of argument and on the whole take the joint office of *advocatus diaboli*. Willem Hermans and Batt had played a large part in Erasmus' life up to this date. Willem, the faithful friend who helped to make life possible in the monastery, had written poems which Erasmus published, with one of his own, on his return to Paris in 1497 after a visit to Steyn. Batt was a new friend, and whereas Willem's part in the

* * * * *

13 ASD I-1 66:9–16, 121:4–13

introduction was diminished in the published version, the memory of Batt was vivid enough for Erasmus to add a phrase in 1520: 'I have never yet seen any human being who was so lost in admiration before learned men, who so venerated and loved them, especially in the field of what are, not without reason, termed Good Letters.'[14]

Although he ascribes to himself a minimal part in the debate, Erasmus is the link which binds these people together. He attributes this shared enthusiasm, in his own case, to a mysterious inward urge, a natural inclination which carried him onwards in spite of all the obstacles of his boyhood; this is what he states in the preface to the *Antibarbari*,[15] and indeed the only source of encouragement we can discern in his schooldays is the reverence of his teachers for Rodolphus Agricola, unless we regard the legend of his father's transcription of classical texts as being significant for him.

What we do know is that the *Antibarbari* is a manifesto, like the *Deffence et illustration* of du Bellay, asserting the conviction of the humanists that they were inaugurating a mighty revolution, whatever later historians may say to the contrary. Erasmus' manifesto was fundamentally just as serious, though he lightened it by adopting the dialogue form, feeling the artistic need to bring into relief the impassioned oratory of Batt by inserting the conversation of others, and ironic quips put into his own mouth. This was to be the characteristic Erasmian procedure. The *Antibarbari* was the passport which Erasmus was going to show to the leaders of thought in the circles he frequented in France and England. We have already seen that in Paris it was Robert Gaguin to whom he submitted his manuscript. The ageing historian was an important person in Paris: General of the Maturin order, former ambassador, forward-looking patron of printers, several times dean of the law faculty. Erasmus attempted to take him by storm, and one of the earliest letters preserved from Gaguin is a warning against too blatant flattery.[16] Gaguin was not given to flattery himself, and his letter about the *Antibarbari*,[17] while warmly supporting the general theme of the essay, suggests changes. Batt's speech is too long, he says; a dialogue should be a dialogue. Have a look at Plato and Cicero and more recent dialogue-writers, and take your cue from them.

Very different was the reception of the dialogue by Colet. By the time Erasmus reached England in 1499 he had apparently completed the second book, which put the case against eloquence. This was characteristically the

* * * * *

14 ASD I-1 40:18–20; see below 20:10–13.
15 Ep 1110 (for translation see below 16–17)
16 Ep 43
17 Ep 46

part which Colet preferred. He said to Erasmus in all seriousness, 'Your book
has quite persuaded me to abandon eloquence.' When Erasmus protested that
this was merely a rhetorical device and Colet should wait to see the arguments
which were to be arrayed against this view in book III, Colet said: 'You could
not possibly refute the arguments you have already put forward.'[18] This is
recalled by Erasmus himself, and it is a loophole which allows us to peep into
their relationship and perhaps adds a factor to the question which has been
much discussed, the extent of Colet's influence. Taken in conjunction with the
deeply serious letter[19] which Erasmus wrote to Colet before leaving England,
it suggests that Colet had not entirely seen eye to eye with him on the subject
of rhetoric and poetry, and had tried to call him away from purely literary
studies to the new theology, based on the text of Scripture. The words in
which Erasmus declares he is not ready for such a vocation, not worthy of it,
not strong enough to face the violent resistance it would arouse, have a ring of
truth.

Dr Ernst Kohls, in his book on the theology of Erasmus,[20] and in an article
for the *Colloquium Erasmianum* of 1967,[21] studies the early works and finds
especially in the *Antibarbari* many of the basic principles of Erasmus' later
writings. He shows how the concept of 'spoiling the Egyptians' could be
found by Erasmus in Jerome and Augustine,[22] how the attitude to grace and
free will typical of Erasmus' reply to Luther is already present in this work of
his youth, how close Erasmus is to Thomas Aquinas. All this being said,
however, it remains true that his main preoccupation here is with the classics.
The guiding principle of the book is stated early in a passage about the divine
plan for humanity; Erasmus never stated his case better, even in the famous
colloquy where he wrote in the margin, 'I am tempted to say, *Sancte Socrates
ora pro nobis!*'[23] The central passage of the *Antibarbari* seems to be this paragraph beginning: 'Everything in the pagan world that was valiantly done,
brilliantly said, ingeniously thought, diligently transmitted, had been prepared by Christ for his society.'[24] Later on he says, 'None of the liberal
disciplines is Christian, because they neither treat of Christ nor were invented
by Christians; but they all concern Christ.'[25] The belief that all that is good

* * * * *

18 Allen Ep 1110:25–33; for translation see below 16:27–34.
19 Ep 108:89–96
20 Kohls I 35–68
21 E. W. Kohls 'La position théologique d'Erasme et la tradition dans le 'De libero
    arbitrio' *Colloquium Erasmianum* (Mons 1968) 69–88
22 Augustine *De doctrina christiana* 2.40.60–1. See below 96–8.
23 *The Godly Feast*, Thompson *Colloquies* 68
24 ASD I-1 83:17–18; below 60:21–3
25 ASD I-1 110:14–16; below 90:10–12

comes from God, and that the pre-Christian ages were inspired by the Holy
Spirit for his own purposes, is the basis of Christian humanism and it was a
sine qua non in the whole of Erasmus' work; here at the outset it is stated
clearly.

There are signs in this book, which Erasmus later deleted or transformed, of
the mental suffering which the monastery, in its aloofness from this position,
had inflicted on him. At the beginning, where the burgomaster puts down the
decline in learning to the advent of Christianity, the later version has a
reasoned account of the conflict between the pagan world and the Christian
pioneers. 'Possibly,' he says, 'they had some perception that there is an
incompatibility between pure religion and consummate learning. Piety rests
on faith, erudition uses arguments for investigation, and calls the facts in
question.' This passage is not in the early version, and the sentence which
was suppressed for it perhaps gives us a glimpse of the author's impatience
with the community of Steyn: 'Unlettered religion has something of stupidity, which is violently distasteful to those who know letters.'[26]

This evidence seems to illustrate the state of mind in which Erasmus went to
England and met Colet. He was already out of sympathy with the monastic life
and, as his letters show, hostile to the methods of recent Scholastic theology,
which he was to describe in the later version of the *Antibarbari* as 'a kind of
uneducated erudition, which corrupted not only humane studies, but, in
distressing ways, theology itself.'[27] It is worth noticing perhaps that in
1494–5, before he had had a taste of the methods of the Paris faculty of
theology, he was ready to make fun of them (with a joke on talking Oaks);[28]
Batt had just come back from Paris and may have described the egregious
Duchesne. The painful rift in Erasmus' life at this time seemed difficult to heal,
because he was apparently condemned by his profession to both the monastery and Scholastic studies. The 1495 text of the *Antibarbari* shows us Erasmus
just before the impact of two of the deepest influences of his life: that of Colet,
providing a bridge between learning and religion, and that of the Franciscan
of Saint-Omer, Jean Vitrier, who released in him the deeper strain of devotional feeling which was to have its expression in the *Enchiridion militis
christiani*. (It was not until 1520 that he included in the list of the Fathers the
name of Origen, whom Vitrier had taught him to love.[29])

When we turn to the other aspect of the history of the *Antibarbari*, the
publication of 1520, we find that it has not been as much investigated; scholars

* * * * *

26 ASD I-1 47:22–4; below 25:26–9. For the suppressed sentence see ASD 47:3–5.
27 ASD I-1 47:35–7; below 26:9–11
28 See 119:10n.
29 See 108:16n.

who have compared the versions have concentrated on the recently discovered Gouda text. Indeed Albert Hyma turns this research into a series of assumptions about Erasmus' attitude. He found that all the violently anti-monastic passages were *1520* insertions into the original text. As we have seen, it would not be quite true, even so, to say that there was no trace in the first version of Erasmus' discontent with his surroundings at Steyn. Hyma neglects these small indications, and accuses Erasmus of two contradictory faults: first, that he later, when it suited his advantage, represented himself as having hated monasticism from the beginning, when he had really been a submissive monk in the first place; and second, that he was immune to the devotional mysticism of the Brethren of the Common Life, the beauty of which passed over his head.[30]

We will not stop to inquire why anyone should note the absence of the mysticism of Thomas à Kempis in a book in favour of the classics. But it is strange that no investigation was made as to the real reason for the attacks on monks in the 1520 text. The explanation given by Hyma is that Erasmus in later years wished to be free from his obligations to his order, and so made it appear that in this early book he was already prone to vilify monks in general. But when we look at the state of his affairs in 1519, when he must have been preparing the text published in 1520, the reason for the additions is abundantly clear. He was using his old dialogue as a pamphlet against the theologians of Louvain.

Hostility to him among the theologians, especially monastic, in Louvain and Cologne, had been violent for some years. There was the scandal over Johann Reuchlin, the eminent Hebraist persecuted by the Dominicans and tried for heresy. The inquisitor Hoogstraten who had condemned Reuchlin was an ally of Nicolaas Egmondanus (Baechem), the head of the Carmelites in Louvain, an inveterate enemy of Erasmus. The great opposition began after the publication of the New Testament (1516) and increased after the appearance of Luther. The establishment of the Collège Trilingue on 1 September 1518 roused determined antagonism in the university among both professors and students. Erasmus was known to have been much concerned with this, and, as he was now living in Louvain, that town became the centre of a concerted attack on him, on his reinterpretation of Scripture, and on the humanist enterprise in general.

We are concerned here only with the traces of this controversy which were occupying Erasmus in 1519. One of the chief protagonists was Jacobus Latomus, who published a dialogue on the subject of whether the three

* * * * *

30 Hyma 190

languages, Latin, Greek, and Hebrew, are necessary to the theologian.[31] This called forth a defence by Erasmus, dated 28 March 1519.[32] On 1 March 1519 he had dated a short defence of his views expressed in the *Encomium matrimonii* and addressed this to the University of Louvain.[33] The revision of the *Antibarbari* must have come in the middle of this conflict, in which the monks were accusing him of heresy (i.e., writing in contempt of celibacy) and of Lutheranism. He retorted both seriously and with ridicule. There is a letter[34] in which he describes a sermon preached against him at Antwerp by a Carmelite, a man who had a title and a purple bonnet and who therefore seemed to be a doctor of theology. Erasmus remarks that he has consulted the astrologers to know why there should be such a tumult going on at Louvain, and they gave him an explanation involving an eclipse, the Ram, and Mercury badly aspected by Saturn – the *Lovanienses* being under Mercury. He goes on: 'The astrologers may make their own guesses. For my part I think the thing is being managed by a conspiracy of fanatics; it is so clear that when the signal was given the uproar broke out all over the place, against the study of languages and Good Letters.' This letter is dated 22 April 1519.

Traces of this quarrel and the pain it inflicted are clearly to be seen in the new passages of the *Antibarbari*. As Hyma has pointed out, the decline in culture is now pinpointed to the failure of the monastic orders. They were left in charge of 'the care and profession of letters' and at first did not acquit themselves too badly, but as time went on ambition, luxurious living, and neglect of languages and of antiquity set in, and in place of true learning there was only *inerudita eruditio*. Where in the early version a stricture is addressed to churchmen, *ecclesiastici*, in the later Erasmus adds 'even some cowled ones,' *quidem etiam cucullati*.[35] There are several references to camels (Carmelites), and the abbot who prefers to rule over sheep rather than monks reminds one of a famous colloquy.[36] The most violent attack on the monks is an extension of a passage in the original about persons who wear the mask of religion, and are asked by parents about the education of children – and use all their authority to prevent the reading of the poets. Here the addition is virulent, and the Franciscans and Dominicans and Carmelites are mentioned by name.[37]

That the Louvain attacks are in Erasmus' mind is proved by a curious small point which is important in translation. Batt is being persuaded to speak; he

* * * * *

31 *De trium linguarum et studii theologici ratione* (Antwerp 1519)
32 LB IX 79ff
33 LX IX 105F–112A
34 Allen Ep 948:110ff; on astrologers lines 18–30
35 ASD I-1 123:13; below 104:7
36 *The Abbot and the Learned Lady*, Thompson *Colloquies* 217–23
37 ASD I-1 57:16–17; below 33:14–15

says, 'Well, you are promising a much greater reward than I ask for. It will be enough execution for me if Ate alone, the scourge of studies, is dragged along by a hook like a criminal and thrown straight into the public sewer.'[38] This is one of the *1520* additions. Why should Ate, the spirit of strife, be an enemy of studies? Should the reading be *a te*, 'by you' (singular)?[39] This rings oddly when addressed to a group. The goddess Ate crops up in other places at this time: there is an allusion to her earlier in the book ('Homer's Ate'[40]) and in the letter just quoted about the Louvain attacks her name recurs: 'you would think some Ate was throwing the affairs of the studious into confusion.' To Erasmus, Ate therefore, was the spirit of turmoil, and connected with the Louvain troubles.

There is a simple explanation: the vice-chancellor of the University of Louvain from c 1507 to 1520 was Jan Briart, known as Atensis from his birthplace in the district of Ath. P.S. Allen has a short biography of him and states that his relations with Erasmus were usually cordial, the only breach occurring in early 1519.[41] But in early 1517 Erasmus was talking about a conspiracy under the leadership of Atensis, 'all the more dangerous because he was an emeny disguised as a friend.'[42] Atensis was the ally of Edward Lee, later archbishop of York, who was one of the fiercest critics. Erasmus was not sure which of them had egged on the other. In a letter to Lee, in July 1519, he speaks of a person who is appropriately a close friend of Lee's, and calls him D. Joannes Briareus Ateus.[43] Allen's note asks if this is a series of misprints or a clumsy attempt at disguise. Neither; it is a joke. For Erasmus, for the moment, Atensis had become the spirit of discord, Ate, humorously turned masculine; and Briardus had become Briareus, the giant with fifty heads and a hundred hands, pursuing Erasmus like a nightmare.

What entirely clinches this argument is a dialogue[44] published by Wallace K. Ferguson, which makes the whole passage clear. This *Dialogus Nastadiensis* or *Dialogus bilinguium ac trilinguium* came out anonymously in the late spring or early summer of 1519. It was attributed to the friend of Erasmus, Konrad

* * * * *

38 ASD I-1 64:16–17; below 39:8–10
39 This reading is adopted by ASD I-1 64:16 as an emendation, but in all the editions the word 'Ate' appears, and this is clearly Erasmus' intention. The play on names is a good example of Erasmian irony. For Ate see *Iliad* 9.504ff; Erasmus uses her name in *Spongia* LB X 1634A. See *Adagia* I vii 13.
40 See below 27:28.
41 Allen Ep 670 introduction
42 Ep 539:5–6
43 Allen Ep 998:4
44 *Opuscula* 191–224; see lines 141ff. The mention of Ate in this dialogue was pointed out to me by Mrs Sheila Porrer.

Nesen, but possibly it was a collaboration; Ferguson suggests it might have been a school exercise which Erasmus rewrote in parts. Contemporary friends like Beatus Rhenanus and Richard Pace did not attribute it to Erasmus. There are strong resemblances between this dialogue, especially in its third edition in 1520, and the inserted passages of the *Antibarbari*. What is quite clear is that the identification of Ate with Atensis was no mystery to the reading public. All the enemies of Erasmus – Atensis, Egmondanus, Lee, Latomus, and others – are figures of fun as they proceed on their way to bury the muse Calliope, followed by a crowd of students of the *Collegium porci* at Louvain, a 'herd of pigs,' *grex porcorum*, singing a *chorus porcorum* in a style of Latin which reminds one forcibly of the chorus at the end of Molière's *Le Malade imaginaire*.

Briart died in 1520 and the quarrel faded, but Erasmus was still sore about it in 1523 when he wrote his *Catalogus lucubrationum*.[45] He thought then, however, that others (whom he darkly calls *artifices*) had pushed Atensis into the battle. But there is no doubt that the *Antibarbari* was published at the touchiest moment of this episode. In fact, he had good reason for bringing it to light: the situation as regards the classics was no different in 1520 from what it had been in 1495, except that the resistance was more acrimonious, more informed perhaps, more localized, and infinitely more dangerous. The defence had to be on a different plane. In the earliest version it was stupidity and ignorance which were the chief targets, the blind dislike of anything new which he had observed to prevail since boyhood in his native Holland; in the later version he is faced with powerful enemies who intend to destroy him and his cause. There is little need to wonder at the increased bitterness of tone in the version of 1520.

The *Antibarbari* is thus an attack in two stages on the opponents of the revival of learning. But its main importance did not lie in being a successful piece of propaganda. In it, from the outset, Erasmus was trying to embody the very thing he was defending. The brilliant beginning, with its insistence on friendship, the humorous backchat and shared enthusiasm for a cultural ideal, the beauty and calm of the surroundings, all lend themselves to the creation of what he had in mind, the actual and living flavour of the classics. It was a picture of civilization, and the eloquence and good Latin and cogent argument were not the only means of persuasion. Perhaps the author was endangering this more serene atmosphere by his pugnacious insertions. But he would have said that by adding passages aimed at his own enemies and critics he was not destroying the first intention but amplifying it. He was doing just what he had done with the *Adagia*, when he extended a book of classical learning to make it a commentary on the times. So in the *Antibarbari*

* * * * *

45 Allen I 22–3

he added his own later experience, emphasizing and darkening the lines of
the picture, giving it a contemporary slant but preserving intact its youthful
charm and fire.

The translation of the *Antibarbari* is based on LB X 1691–1744, a reprint of the
1540 text, and has been checked against ASD I-1 38–138, edited by K.
Kumaniecki, with occasional reference to the 1520 and other editions.

                                                                    M M P

ERASMUS OF ROTTERDAM TO HIS FRIEND JOHANN WITZ

There is a strange power and active force, as it were, in nature, my dear
Witz; which I infer from this fact among others that, though in my boyhood
the humanities were banished from our schools and there was no supply of
books and teachers, and they had no prestige to spur on a gifted student –
quite the reverse: discouragement of them was universal, and drove one
into other subjects – in spite of this, a sort of inspiration fired me with
devotion to the Muses, sprung not from judgment (for I was then too young
to judge) but from a kind of natural feeling. I developed a hatred for anyone
I knew to be an enemy of humane studies and a love for those who delighted
in them; and those who had acquired any reputation in that field I looked
up to and admired as more than human. For this spirit even now, as an old
man, I have no regrets. It is not that I condemn the interests of other men,
for which I felt no such sympathy; but I see clearly how cold, how maimed
and blind a thing is learning when deprived of the patronage of the Muses.
In any case it is a shameful story, the stupidity with which some men reject
what is far the most excellent province of knowledge, dismissing as 'poetry'
all that belongs to an ancient and more civilized culture. These were the
men who, when I was a boy, spitefully enough put obstacles in my path and
kept me away from my first love; and I had planned to take my revenge with
pen and ink, with this one proviso, that I would attack no man by name.

I had not yet reached my twentieth year when I set to work. Then, a
few years later, I had the idea of refashioning the same matter as a dialogue
to make it easier reading. I had arranged the whole work in four books. The
first was to refute the objections habitually raised against us by the
superstitious or by those who have the form of religion rather than its
substance. In the second a fictitious character like Glaucon in Plato railed
against eloquence with all the force eloquence can wield, and robbed the
inmost arsenal of rhetoric of all its panoply in order to deploy it against
rhetoric itself – with such success that John Colet of blessed memory, when
he read the book, said to me seriously in familiar conversation, 'Your book
has quite persuaded me to abandon eloquence.' And when I advised him
to suspend judgment until he had heard the character who championed
eloquence, he assured me that my attacks could not be weakened. Book III
was a refutation of the arguments in the second book; but I had not yet
finished it. The fourth was a separate apology for poetry, the poetry I had

* * * * *

1 Witz] Schoolmaster in Sélestat; see Ep 323 introduction. This dedicatory
preface to the *Antibarbari* is Ep 1110 (c June 1520).
17 'poetry'] See 33:23n.
27 Glaucon] In the *Republic*

loved so tenderly as a boy. This I had not yet set in order, and had only a
great pile of material for future use.

The first book I had supplemented in Bologna, with publication already in mind; the second I had revised. When I was about to leave Italy, I deposited them with Richard Pace, a man endowed with virtues and accomplishments of every kind, and while they were in his keeping both were lost, by the fault of others whose honesty that most honourable man assumed to be equal to his own. The loss of the first book hurt me little, to be sure, for there was too much immaturity about it, and I had piled up in it all my crudest arguments. As for the others, I could wish they had survived; but those drones thought otherwise who, while attempting nothing of any note themselves, undermine the work of others.

After my removal to Louvain I learnt that book I, in the form I had set down long since, enjoyed too wide a circulation for me to suppress it; it had in fact already come near to being published by certain supporters of my humble self whose zeal outruns their discretion. To prevent that happening I myself revised the book and sent it to the printers, though in other respects I would rather it had been suppressed entirely; especially since a book on this subject has now been published by Hermann von dem Busche called *The Bulwark of the Humanities*, which is scholarly and trenchant and well written. But I thought it had better face the world with such revision as I could give it than in the form taken by the manuscript copies, which were badly corrupted. Book II shall join it if I can secure a text. The rest of the work shall be added out of my own head, unless the persons who are keeping my own drafts secret prefer to behave like honourable men, and not like petty thieves of other men's midnight oil.

Those who do not wholly reject this portion, the worst of the whole work, must please keep their eyes open in hopes of tracing the remainder. This will make me the readier to publish other things too which I now have in my desk, roughed out, such as a work on letter-writing. In the meantime this fragment shall be dedicated to you, my dear scholarly Witz, who in educating the young of your town show such devotion to high character no less than to sound learning. Keep it up! Continue as you have begun, and do not rest until, so far as one man can, you have driven all barbarism out of our native Germany. It is time we learnt to know ourselves, after so long being treated almost as animals by men who credit themselves with every virtue. Farewell.

From Louvain

* * * * *

55 Busche] See Allen Ep 830 introduction.
66 letter-writing] See Ep 71 introduction.
71 Germany] See Epp 305:221n, 307:14n, 321:16n, 334:9n.

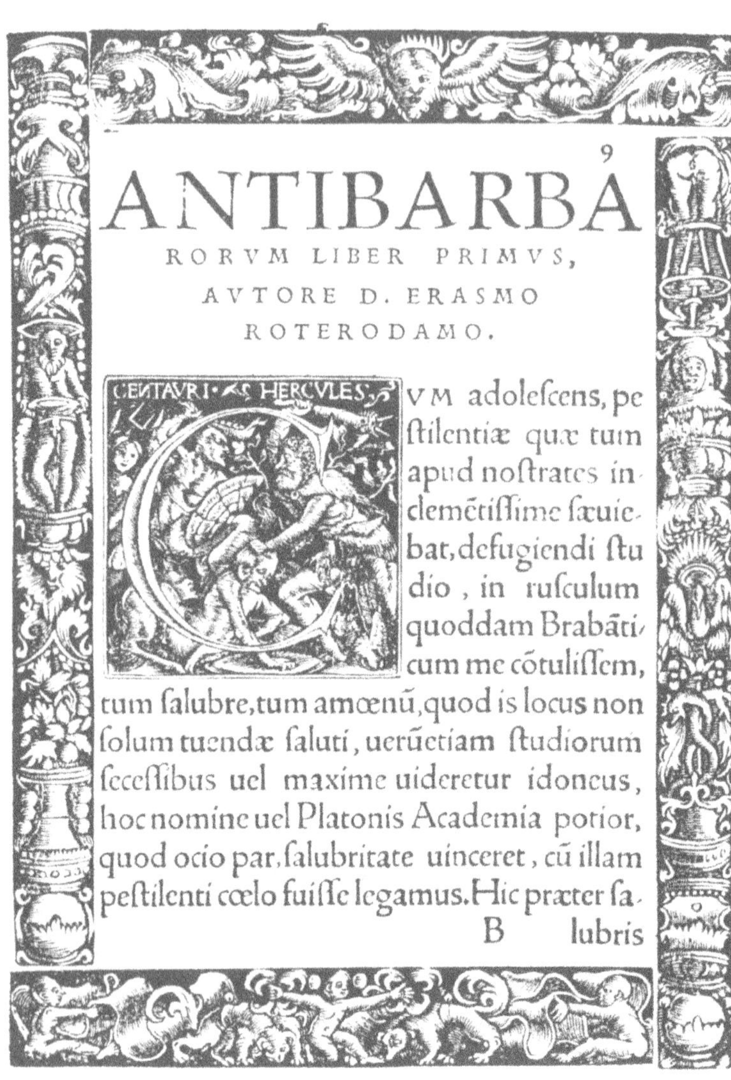

ANTIBARBA
RORVM LIBER PRIMVS,
AVTORE D. ERASMO
ROTERODAMO.

VM adolescens, pe
stilentiæ quæ tum
apud nostrates in-
clemétissime sæuie-
bat, defugiendi stu
dio, in rusculum
quoddam Brabāti-
cum me cōtulissem,
tum salubre, tum amœnū, quod is locus non
solum tuendæ saluti, uerū etiam studiorum
secessibus uel maxime uideretur idoneus,
hoc nomine uel Platonis Academia potior,
quod ocio par, salubritate uinceret, cū illam
pestilenti cœlo fuisse legamus. Hic præter sa-
B   lubris

Opening page of the text of the first edition of the *Antibarbari*
The drawing around the initial letter shows Hercules clashing with Centaurs.
In Greek legend the Centaurs were typical examples of wildness and barbarism; in
Erasmus' *Antibarbari* the main speaker, Jacob Batt, compares his own labours to
defeat modern 'barbarians' with those of Hercules.
Beinecke Library, Yale University

When I was a youth I took refuge from the plague, which was then furiously
raging in our country, and went to stay in a rural corner of Brabant, so
salubrious and charming a place that it seemed highly suitable not only for
preserving health but for a studious retreat. It was even better than the
Academy of Plato (we read that this was set in an unhealthy climate)
because it provided as much leisure but more health; here, as well as fresh
air and quietude, there was as much beauty as a philosopher could desire,
or perhaps even the Muses, who are said to delight in clear springs, green
grassy banks, and the thick shade of the woods. While I was lying hidden
here and enjoying country life, I had a surprise visit from Willem Hermans,
at that time the one among my contemporaries who was much the dearest to
me: a special affection dating from the cradle, as they say, together with the
pleasant association of our studies, had increased as we grew up, and by
those links we were bound with such loyalty and friendship that I cannot
believe any closer existed between Orestes and Pylades, Pirithous and
Theseus, Patroclus and Achilles, Damon and Pythias, or Euryalus and
Nisus. So true it is that a comradeship based on the shared studies of

* * * * *

5 corner of Brabant] Halsteren near Bergen op Zoom

13 Hermans] Willem Hermans of Gouda (1461?–1510), an Augustinian canon of
Steyn, and the closest friend of Erasmus' youth. His poems, *Sylva odarum*,
were seen through the press in Paris by Erasmus in 1497. See Epp 33 and 49
introductions.

The Gouda manuscript has less description of the place and more in praise of
Hermans. The following passage was omitted in the 1520 version: 'Willem
Hermans, the best and most learned of my contemporaries; you might wonder
which to admire most, his charming character or his brilliant mind, for
nothing could be more frank than the one or more sublime than the other. But I
must temper my praise of so close a friend, lest I should do my friend harm by
very warmth of friendship. It would be wrong if my mention of him were to
detract from his fine qualities. Things spoken by a lover, even though they
may be less than the truth, are usually attributed to love rather than judgment
and considered either false or trivial. Anything I said about Willem would not
satisfy me. I leave it to unbiased judges, to more learned men than I am, who
love less and see more, and are yet bolder in their praise and admiration.'

15 from the cradle] A proverb ('from tender fingernails') which came into Latin
from Greek: see *Adagia* I vii 52. On *Adagia* see Phillips 'Adages.'

18 Orestes ... Nisus] These examples of friendship in classical literature also
appear in Erasmus' early letters, for example, Epp 17, 83. All these pairs of
friends could be said to have risked their lives for each other: Achilles, who
died in combat to avenge the death of Patroclus; Orestes and Pylades, who

boyhood is a stronger bond between men than any tie of blood or family relationship.

The arrival of this friend was all the more welcome for being unexpected and it gave me incredible pleasure. So as not to keep such a good thing to myself, like a miser, I sent a message immediately to our mutual friend Jacob Batt, who was then town clerk of the nearest city, Bergen – a man, heaven knows, of the greatest simplicity, sweetness of character, learning, and charm of speech. He was burning with an incredible desire to see Willem, partly because I had praised the old friend to the new, partly because of Willem's own letters. I have never yet seen any human being who was so lost in admiration before learned men, who so venerated and loved them, especially in the field of what are, not without reason, termed Good Letters. As soon as he had heard the news, he took just one of his jolly companions and came; I will not say he ran, rather he flew, and late at night at that, because it was difficult for him to be absent during the day, particularly as he had only recently been appointed to public office and had to attend to business with all the more zeal and devotion to the people's interests. Very little of that night was given to sleep! As soon as day had broken, we rose and returned to our literary story-telling, and then the fine weather invited us out for a walk. As we strolled, I pointed out to my guest the local landmarks and the characteristics of the region.

There, as luck would have it, as we stood on a bridge over a canal, Jodocus the doctor appeared, coming along the road quite unexpectedly. He is among the most cordial and learned of men. With him there was

* * * * *

faced death with and for each other in Euripides' *Orestes* and *Iphigenia in Tauris*; Theseus, who went down to Hades to help Pirithous. Damon and Phintias (not Pythias) were two friends from the Pythagorean brotherhood; when the tyrant Dionysius had one condemned to death, the other stood bail for him and convinced the tyrant of the greatness of friendship (Cicero *De officiis* 3.45; *Tusculan Disputations* 5.63; Diodorus Siculus 10.4). Nisus and Euryalus are the young heroes of Virgil *Aeneid* 9.176ff.

3 unexpected] A change from the *expectatissimo* of the manuscript
6 Batt] Jacob Batt (1465?–1502) studied in Paris but returned to Bergen c 1492 and became master of the public school; he was later appointed secretary of the town council. See Ep 35 introduction. He was a close friend of Erasmus from this time onwards, giving him much help during the penurious years in Paris.
9 I ... Letters] This grateful sentence was added in 1520. In the manuscript Batt is described as *non indocto tum candidissimo*.
13 just one] There is no further trace of this person.
23 Jodocus] Jooste van Schoonhoven (d 1502 or earlier), town physician of Bergen; first identified by C. Slootmans 'Erasmus en zijn vrienden uit Bergen op Zoom' *Taxandria* 35 (1928) 121

Willem Conrad, a foremost citizen of that town. Not far away from where
we were there was a small country house belonging to this man, where he
very sensibly used to betake himself whenever he had enough of the
business affairs of the town and the townspeople (for he was always having
to act as chief magistrate in his district), whenever he wanted to escape for a   5
while from civil lawsuits with their clamour, whenever he had a mind to
relax a little more freely and play, as Horace says, in carefree fashion. In fact
at this time, while he was staying in the country, either he was always with
us or we were with him, whether because of the pleasure I took in his
company and his learning, or because I had business matters to go over   10
with him.

When he saw us, he gave us his usual cheerful smile. Then I said,
'Where are you running off to, so early in the morning? It's a bad lookout,
I'll take my oath, for the public welfare committed to you, when you prefer
the woods to anything else, like a nightingale, and hate the town as if it   15
were a cage. What has a burgomaster to do with the country, what have you
to do with this leisured retreat, you, the busiest man alive?'

He laughed at this. 'Why,' he said, 'I am envious of your delightful
life, you happiest of all men alive! While we poor wretches are tossed hither
and thither by the raging sea of public affairs, you are strolling about all the   20
time with your Muses, entirely at leisure and unoccupied, now chatting on
whatever topic you like with a friend, now holding a conversation with one
of the ancient writers, at times beating out the rhythm of some ditty, or at
others committing to paper, as to faithful companions, whatever you are
turning over in your mind. It does not surprise me at all that, however often   25
we invite you, you can never be dragged away from your woods to go to
town.'

'You, in fact,' said I, 'are not a bit less foolish than your colleagues,
since you are of this mind. If those Sirens of yours – money-making and
ambition – would allow you, I have no doubt that you would find it easy to   30
despise that raging sea and all the towns as well. But you are ashamed to
appear inadequate as an important citizen, and so you choose the wrong
kind of life to lead to happiness.'

'Your observation is not very far from the mark,' he answered, 'and I
wish I could deny what you say! But perhaps one day I shall shake myself   35

* * * * *

  1 Conrad] Willem Colgheenes; see Slootmans 121–3,
  7 Horace] *Discincti ludere: Satires* 2.1.73
24 faithful companions] Horace *Satires* 2.1.30
31 are ashamed] Cf Caelius to Cicero, *Ad familiares* 8.16; *Ad Atticum* 10.9.
34 from the mark] *Adagia* I x 30

free, and imitate that Scipio of yours whom you are always preaching to me
about. Meanwhile, since I knew I should have a few days' holiday from
affairs, and yesterday's sunset seemed to promise fine weather, I was off at
dawn with my whole family into the country.'

At this point he looked at Batt, who was quietly coming forward. 'And   5
where have you come from?' said he, 'and pray how so early, since you were
drinking with us last night into the small hours?'

To this Batt the joker retorted: 'You need not be surprised to find your
last night's boon companion turning up early in the morning in the country. Don't you know what a night-owl I am? There is someone here who has   10
turned me into a Daedalus. In Ovid "fear adds wings to the feet," but love
sewed onto me better wings than Daedalus had.'

And he indicated Willem with a wink. 'Do you think Batt could be
prevented from setting eyes on "so dear a head" by those shades of darkness which he often manfully despised for less important reasons?'   15

The burgomaster smiled, knowing that Batt had in early youth been
given to surreptitious affairs with girls, from which however he had soon
been recalled by the study of letters. Now that he had become aware of
Willem's presence, the burgomaster immediately stepped down from the
carriage with the doctor, and sent on his wife with all her train (as he put it) 20
to the house.

At this I said to him, 'Have you got such a very low opinion of our rural
retreat that you bring along with you such a troop of girls?'

'Why?' he asked.

'Because it is clear that in your view our glades are not haunted by any   25
of the nymphs and graces, no Dryad nor Naiad,' said I.

'On the contrary, I wanted to complete the chorus,' he said, 'and
combine your semi-goddesses with nymphs of the human kind.'

Then taking Batt a little aside he said to him privately in his ear, 'You
wretch, why did you not let me fly with you here as your Icarus, especially 30

* * * * *

1 Scipio] Scipio Aemilianus (second century BC), after his victories for Rome
  against Carthage, was attacked by political enemies and retired to his country
  estate. Cicero (*De oratore* 2.22) speaks of the amusements on which the
  intellectual Scipio Aemilianus spent his leisure. As a result of Cicero's portrayal of him in *De republica* and *De amicitia* Aemilianus was renowned for his
  cultured circle of friends and patronage of Greek philosophers.
11 Ovid] Erasmus made a slip of the pen: the quotation is not from Ovid but from
  Virgil (*Aeneid* 8.224). Daedalus made wings for himself and his son Icarus to
  escape from Crete; cf *Adagia* III i 65.
14 "so dear a head"] Horace *Odes* 1.24.2

when you knew I had as much desire to see this man as you had yourself, and you knew how much this was your own doing?'

'To begin with,' said Batt, 'I was frightened by the omen; and then, frankly speaking, I begrudged you such a magnificent pleasure while I was starved myself; as soon as I had been satisfied I would have summoned my friends. To tell the truth, it is rather a nuisance that you have come now. I am afraid that a man as busy as you are, who not only attract to yourself like a sort of Caecias a multitude of concerns, but must forever carry round with you business that pursues you of its own accord when you run away – such a man, I am afraid, will be a disturbance in some degree to our peace. Then there is Jodocus, whom you bring with you, and we hate his harsh philosophy. We had arranged to spend all these three days in pure amusement, in the freest of murmured talk. What have we to do with the rod of office, or with the arrogance of the philosophers?'

The burgomaster answered: 'Nay, we have arrived at the right time; we will all amuse ourselves together. For Jodocus has left the stricter bit of his philosophy at home with his wife (he has a rather peevish one) and I have left the burgomaster at home.'

We laughed at this, and Batt said, 'All right, if you will vouch for that, we accept you in our fellowship.'

Then, when Willem had had a proper greeting, we began to walk along, not without the usual varied talk about the landscape, the nature of the soil, the healthiness of the climate, and the sad state of affairs in our Holland. Finally, as always happens in these conversations when one subject follows another, we fell to discussing that prime topic of complaint in our times, long-standing indeed but absolutely justified: we tried to discover, and not without sharp wonder, what the disaster was that had swept away the rich, flourishing, joyful fruits of the finest culture, and why a tragic and terrible deluge had shamefully overwhelmed all the literature of the ancients which used to be so pure. How did it happen that there is such an enormous distance between ourselves and the writers of antiquity; that

* * * * *

3 omen] Batt means that Icarus was a bad model to propose, as his wings melted when he flew too near the sun and he fell into the sea.

8 Caecias] Name of a northeast wind, according to Pliny, which attracted the clouds instead of driving them away. See *Adagia* I v 62.

13 rod of office] The *fasces* in the text are the Roman symbol of government; for the arrogance of the philosophers see *Adagia* I viii 49.

17 peevish] The sentence in parentheses is not in the manuscript.

23 sad state of affairs] A reference to the civil strife and popular revolt in Holland during the years 1488–92. See Epp 20:106n; 35:51–3. Willem Hermans mentions this subject in ode 3 of his *Sylva odarum*.

men who are now at the summit of learning, a few only excepted, hardly
seem worthy to enter the literary arena against women and children, mere
beginners, of the ancient world; and that the present generals of our army
would not deserve enrolment among their common soldiers, nor would
those who now steer the ship of learning find a place in the hold?   5

The doctor was a man of ready eloquence, but remarkably addicted to
astrology, which he regarded as the answer to everything; in all other
respects he was a religious-minded and excellent man. He tried to trace the
whole cause of this trouble to the stars, and he produced a number of
arguments which showed much penetration and had a good deal of proba-   10
bility. He explained that the vicissitudes of human affairs were due to the
stars, which were the origin of the rise and fall of empires, the transfer of
kingdoms from one hand to another, the continual flux of change in the
minds, principles, character and appearance, studies and fortunes of men.
He said there were changes in the stars, and their power was not always   15
equal or the same, some being friendly to study and some hostile. And so it
happened that, as alternate forces held sway, studies also must undergo
change: now in chilly disregard, now in full bloom, now neglected, now
considered highly valuable; and he went back to the beginning of the world
to collect instances of change in different conditions, with a remarkable   20
exercise of memory.

The burgomaster, while not disagreeing wholly with what the doctor
said, produced many hypotheses by which he attempted to prove that the
death of letters was to be laid at the door of the Christian religion. Not that
he was ill-disposed towards Christianity – indeed, he was as devout as any   25
other man – but he believed it was this religion which had given a handle
(to the enemies of learning). They saw that the beginnings of our religion
did not come from the philosophers, orators, dialecticians, or mathematicians, but from the deep simplicity of Christ, and that it was spread abroad
by uneducated apostles. Hence the earliest supporters of the faith had a   30
horror of worldly learning, as of a thing inimical to Christ, and it was held a
noble thing to be ignorant of profane literature; it was in fact no less
praiseworthy to neglect Aristotle and Plato than to despise kingdoms, tread
riches underfoot, spurn pleasures. Anything which the world held in
honour, religion disdained, and it was from devotion to this, more ardent   35

* * * * *

7 astrology] Erasmus had a sceptical attitude to astrology. See Allen Ep
1005:1–14; Kohls I 43–5.

12 empires] The theory of the transfer of empire, *translatio imperii*, was a preoccupation of the time.

26 handle] *Adagia* I iv 4. The following paragraph, with its historical approach,
was a new addition in 1520 and took the place of a few lines in the manuscript.

than wise, and from a violent hatred of the adversaries that liberal disciplines were neglected. They were so resolved to have nothing in common
with the enemy that they gave up the best things as well, acting no more
sensibly than a Frenchman who out of hatred for the English would rather
go naked than be clothed in English cloth, or an Englishman who would
rather come to bursting with thirst than drink a French wine. Some there
were, no doubt, who made the mistake of neglecting literary studies in all
simplicity. There were also those who shunned work and used the honourable name of religion to cloak their indolence; there could be no better
screen for lazy dawdling and sluggish idleness. Some, maybe, and I dare
say the majority, had no other reason for hating Good Letters than the fact
that they had not learnt anything, and were both ashamed and unwilling to
learn. A further contribution was made by certain despots who closed the
schools to Christians, thinking that when the faith was deprived of the
support of teaching and eloquence it would fade away of its own accord and
finally die out. But what happened was that when they felt themselves
pressed by the learning and oratory of their adversaries they began to
protect themselves with the very same arms and weapons, so as to cut the
enemy's throat with his own sword, as they say. Then other men followed,
violently zealous men, who understood that something of paganism was
imbibed from the books of the pre-Christian writers, ardently loved for
their dazzling erudition and alluring eloquence; and now that Christianity
had spread everywhere and the use of these books was not greatly needed
for the confutation of opponents, they were inclined to think that, the
superstition of the Jews and pagans having been destroyed, their literature
and language should also be abolished. Possibly they had some perception
that there is an incompatibility between pure religion and consummate
learning. Piety rests on faith, erudition uses arguments for investigation,
and calls the facts in question. Lastly it happens, I do not know why, that
the educated are less tractable than the ignorant. Thus for the ordinary run
of abbots, in our own day, there is nothing more objectionable than that
their monks should penetrate at all deeply into good learning. They would
rather rule over sheep than men, and the only reason for this preference is
that it is easier.

    As a result of all these things studies were not held in their due esteem,
and all the best books, the only guardians of culture, were either deliber-

* * * * *

19 own sword] *Adagia* 1 i 51
32 learning] The manuscript has a telling phrase: 'Unlettered religion has something of stupidity, which is violently distasteful to those who know letters'
   (ASD I-1 47:3–5).

5

10

15

20

25

30

35

ately destroyed or perished through neglect. Soon, as a further consequence, princes and bishops considered it dishonouring to themselves to
have a knowledge of letters. However, so that the life of men should not be
absolutely blind, as it would be if no learning were to survive, the whole
care and professional responsibility for letters were relegated to the monks,   5
and for a time they managed the business not too badly. Later, when
through some kind of swollen pride the monks turned to luxurious living,
when languages were neglected and antiquity was neglected too, there
grew up a confused sort of teaching, a kind of uneducated erudition, which
corrupted not only humane studies but, in distressing ways, theology   10
itself.

When the burgomaster had voiced these and other similar opinions,
Willem said that he was influenced by many theories and by the authority
of the most serious writers, to believe that there was a season of old age for
everything. He thought that the entire world, and whatever this world   15
produces, grows with its own youth, and when it has come to full strength
through its stages of growth it turns at last towards old age and gradually
falls into decay. Cybele, that great mother of the gods, had now lost her
fertility, and she who used to give birth to youthful gods was now worn out
with child-bearing and scarcely produced men; for this was the meaning of   20
the riddling fable. He adduced not a few proofs of this out of theologians of
the early days (though from our own country), but these observations were
not so germane to the matter as to make me repeat his lengthy speech here.
To put it shortly, he arrived at this: the men of our time, according to him,
were intellectually inferior to the great men of the past, and Nature, now   25
ageing as it were, who used to bring forth not only finer bodies but more
virile and gifted minds, now engendered pygmies whose mental equipment was no less poor than their bodies were puny. And so in the end it
came about that what the ancients had the power to discover, we could not
even perceive when it was discovered; where they combined marvellous   30
powers of knowledge with equal forces of eloquence, we were unsuccessful
in our efforts to attain either.

As I listened to these things in wonder – and it seemed to me that every
point had been discussed by each person in good oratorical style so that no
one had said anything improbable – I noticed that my friend Batt was   35
longing to speak, and was in travail with something. He had a freedom of
speech which was truly frank, not without wit and emphasis, and he was as

* * * * *

18 decay] The idea of the ageing of the world was a common one. Cf Kohls I 46. Is
    this an echo of Lucretius 2.1150?
18 Cybele] See Hesiod *Theogony* 453ff. Cybele was identified with Rhea.

much an enemy of the barbarians as they were hostile to letters; in fact
meeting with them often made him vomit or go hot with rage, and sometimes he would change his route to get out of their way as if at a bad omen. I
looked at him, with the others standing expectantly round. 'You are asleep,
Batt,' said I, 'and you are not like Batt any longer. Do you see how the horse   5
is being put on his mettle in his own training-ground?' He smiled and
nodded. Then to challenge him further I asked him whether these things
received his approval.

With his usual comic expression he said, 'You have all spoken quite
splendidly, but really you have not kept your promises. It was agreed that   10
we should do nothing but amuse ourselves, and here we are falling straight
into the midst of philosophy. All the same, although I was irritated, I rather
enjoyed those remarks of yours. But why do you entangle our brief moment
of idleness with such questions as even Chrysippus himself or Carneades,
fasting and purged with hellebore, could hardly settle? You, Jodocus, did   15
indeed leave the philosopher at home, only to bring us the astrologer; and
you, burgomaster, laid down your office only to put on the mantle of the
philosopher (God save the mark!) on the model of that old Dionysius of
Syracuse! As to your opinions, I cannot agree with any of you. I certainly
admired your cleverness and eloquence, but not your judgment. One of you   20
put the blame on the harmless stars; another stood the best religion in the
dock; another pleaded some imaginary ageing of Nature. All quite unfairly,
to my way of thinking. What kind of attitude is it, I ask you, which throws
on circumstances the blame for the faults of men, and would rather make
anything else responsible for the wrong we do than confess our fault? If our   25
object is to shield ourselves from being the cause of evils which patently
exist, why not heap everything which goes wrong in the lives of mortals on
the head of Homer's Ate, just as Agamemnon does, in the same poet, and

* * * * *

  1 in fact ... omen] These sentences elaborating Batt's reactions are an addition of
       1520.
  6 training-ground] *Adagia* I viii 82: 'When someone is being urged to do the
       thing for which he is most fitted or most enjoys'
 14 Chrysippus] Stoic philosopher (third century BC)
 14 Carneades] A distinguished philosopher of Cyrene (second century BC),
       founder of the New Academy in Athens
 15 hellebore] Hellebore was used as a purge in the ancient world, and Carneades
       is said to have used it before writing a refutation of the books of Zeno the
       Stoic: *Adagia* I viii 51.
 18 Dionysius] Dionysius the younger, tyrant of Syracuse (fourth century BC),
       invited Plato to his court and studied under him.
 25 If ... folly?] This passage is not in the manuscript.
 28 Ate] See *Antibarbari* Introductory Note 13.

Jupiter, and just as the common run of Christians do when they blame the devil as the author and instigator of anything they contrive by their own folly? Once we have allowed the opening of a window like this, what is to prevent the rake blaming his youthfulness, the miserly niggard his age, the climber the ways of Fortune, the irascible man his physical constitution?

'To go straight to the point, I myself will indicate to you, if you like, the person you are searching heaven and earth for, the man who is the cause of it all: I can lay my finger on him.'

We begged him to do so. Pointing his finger at the burgomaster, he said: 'You, little as you know it, are the instigator of this evil; the whole blame for it falls on you. To your hands the community has committed all its fortunes, its safety, honour, prosperity, and lastly what is dearest to it, its children – and you allow a set of blackguards to dwell in the city – did I say dwell? I mean rule, unchecked.'

When the burgomaster in amazement interrupted, 'Who are you calling blackguards?' Batt went on, 'Those Arcadian asses, or Antroniuses if you like it better, whom you can hear all over the public schools not speaking but hee-hawing with more than asinine impudence, when they ought to be handing on genuine knowledge of literature; the men who with all confidence and full authority, as Quintilian says, teach their own fatuity, and think themselves fitted by that to be in charge of a school, in fact born for the sole purpose of unteaching everything which concerns Good Letters, so that they can foist their ignorance upon us and make us like themselves.' At the same time he gave the names of a number of people who were notorious at that time for exceptional stupidity; with these monsters Batt had waged an irreconcilable war as long as he had the management of the town school, for it was from that post that he was appointed secretary. I am prudently suppressing these names for several reasons: for one thing I should be sorry to give them that amount of fame, since they deserve to be buried in the darkness of eternal oblivion, and for another I would rather not dirty my paper with their filthy names, especially since there is such a large number of these people about – an ill weed grows apace.

'Look,' said Batt, 'are the wretched citizens handing over their hearts' dearest to brutes like these? Is it to these that the highest princes entrust

* * * * *

1 Jupiter] *Iliad* 19.86–138
8 finger] *Adagia* I x 43
16 Antroniuses] *Adagia* II v 68. Arcadia, in the Peloponnese, was a land of shepherds and considered rustic; Antron, a town of Thessaly, was famous for the large size of its asses.
20 Quintilian] 1.1.8

their children? Are these men to have charge of young people endowed
with the finest minds, eager for good knowledge, so that these fellows can
make boors out of the well-born, unteachables out of the untaught, and
raving madmen out of the stupid? This is what is happening in your
community, I say, under you as citizen, as councillor, as burgomaster! 5
Private business of the least important kind is looked after with extraordinary care; and this plague, which is a public concern and so important that
nothing more so can exist in the state, is neglected or even encouraged?
Criminals of another sort, even those who cause a little private loss, are
extremely severely dealt with: one is fined, the other flogged, another 10
thrown into prison for an unpaid debt, another sent into exile, others
hanged for a stolen cup or a tiny sum of money. Against these and their like
customary rigour is enforced, laws operate, the magistrates are vigilant; but
those who shamefully corrupt your children, sweeter and dearer to you,
and rightly so, than anything else, your children who are the single hope of 15
the state – you do not throw them out or consider they deserve punishment?
There is the death-penalty for stealing a horse, but for betraying, no,
destroying, all those dear pledges of our society, you do not cut the man's
throat? Legal proceedings may be taken against anyone who has maltreated
a hired horse, but there is no prosecution possible for a son badly treated? If 20
your bailiff here, and this man's neighbour, were to sow a fine wheat-
bearing field with weeds and rushes, tell me, what would you do? You
would turn him out, have the law on him, sue for damages – but there is no
condign punishment for the man who fills the promising, unspoilt minds of
children with the thorns and brambles of ignorance, so that neither hoeing 25
nor burning off will ever make them clean again. Anyone who commits a
small fraud, only a little one, by clipping coin, is forced in terrible ways to
pay the penalty laid down by law; but anyone who gives the children
committed to his charge nothing but sheer nonsense instead of liberal and
wholesome teaching seems worthy of a reward! In no other matter are 30
people so careless, so ineffectual, even the highest princes. They employ
many servants to taste their food; they do not employ people to discern
what is poured into their minds and hearts. A doctor or surgeon would be
ruined if he made a mistake in his treatment of the prince's body; but there
is no risk for those who do the same to the mind of one who is to rule over so 35
many. You do not thoughtlessly hand over a horse to be doctored or trained,

* * * * *

21 sow a ... field] Is he thinking of the parable of the wheat and the tares, Matt
13:24–30? Or of Plato's *Apology* 20A–B, 25B (horses and sons)?
30 In no other] The text from this point to the allusion to Camillus is an addition
of *1520*. Compare the argument that follows with Plato *Protagoras* 313Aff.

but you never take a good look at the man you trust to train your son, as if
you had carried out the function of a father by merely begetting, when by
far the greater part of fatherhood is to educate rightly what you have
begotten! What is the use of being well born, unless nature is backed up by
a worthy upbringing? You do not entrust the farming of your lands to just   5
anyone – you consult well-tried husbandmen with long-standing experience of the job; but when you are going to choose a tutor for your son, you
ask advice from one of those petty tyrants, and though he is a blind man
showing you the way you follow it! You choose a headmaster for your
public school on the advice of people you should not ask to help you choose   10
a stable-boy. There is nothing more like ruling a kingdom than being the
master of a school; and you let your children be bullied by people who (if
you knew what they were like) you would not allow to command your dogs?
There is good pay for a man who teaches the young – tormented by
whippings and abuse – to know nothing and yet to think they know   15
everything; and it often happens that the morals of those fellows are no
better than their literacy. What a crime it is to imbue that first happiest age
given by nature for good lessons with things we must either unlearn
afterwards with still greater effort or retain to our great damage! It seems to
me that there are three things above all on which hang the safety or sickness   20
of the state: the good or bad education of the prince, the preachers in public
places, and the schoolmasters. But it would be right to take the greatest care
with these last, because the schoolmaster deals with the earliest age, innocent and inexperienced, which cannot yet take care of itself, and with the
years of greatest promise, which fly swiftest away and never return again.   25

  'Among the Romans execution with savage tortures awaited one who
had exercised command without turning it to the good of the people. I wish
that such a law were in force today, which would act as a salutary deterrent
against these pernicious rulers of youth! Now such beasts are held in
honour, and a man with such deserts is paid out of the public funds! Why is   30
such a pest not torn to pieces by public hands? Why is he not deported to
some desert land? Why do you, burgomaster, not follow the example of the

* * * * *

3 educate rightly] This idea is amplified in the opening passages of Erasmus' *De
    pueris instituendis*: 'To be truly a father you must take care of the whole of your
    son' (ASD I-2 26:29).
8 petty tyrants] The Greek word means beggars who rule. Erasmus means the
    friars, and his warning here recalls the comment in *Adagia* I iv 39 on 'the dog in
    the bath,' where among his praises of Rodolphus Agricola he mentions the
    advice to the council of Antwerp, not to put a theologian or doctor in charge of
    the school.
8 blind man] *Adagia* III iii 78, but also Luke 6:39

military tribune Camillus? He handed over that notorious dishonest schoolmaster, with hands bound and bare back, to be driven back with blows into the town of the Falisci by the very boys he had betrayed, and you might use the same ceremony to drive these corrupters of youth out of your city. You wonder at the death of letters, when even labourers and block-heads run schools! We wonder why the old learning went to pieces, even in the past, but since nothing could be less doctoral than the doctors them-selves, I should be still more surprised if this did not happen. I ask you, what can you expect from a brutish teacher but a more brutish pupil? Or, as the old proverb says, what can you get from a bad raven but a bad egg? What Horace wrote on this subject, is it not true?

> In calves, in horses there is found
> The valour of their sires;
> Fierce eagles bring not forth the timorous dove;
> Brave sons are born from fathers that are brave.

True, we do see it happen that sons do not always repeat the physical defects of their parents. I myself knew a number of brothers who were born of a blind father and a lame mother, and none of them was blind or lame. But when mind is poured into mind, and one intelligence formed by another, it is not possible for the pupil not to resemble his teacher, who is like the parent of his mind. Why should we arraign the stars and the innocent sky for this? Why accuse unoffending Nature? What has religion, with its saving grace, done to deserve such odium? If only you take care that suitable teachers are supplied, and the princes look to it that honour is paid to Good Letters, you will see soon enough that neither stars nor intellects are lacking in our century or even our country; though I must confess that one could hardly find any country more gross than ours, at least in what concerns letters. If we ourselves fail in our duty, as we do, the whole sky may smile in vain; it is in ourselves that those fatal comets are, which breathe their destroying influence over our best studies. So I cannot won-der at the extinction of letters, when everybody competes to extinguish them, and only a tiny few offer their support. It is a true saying, "Honour

* * * * *

1 Camillus] Livy 5.27.9
10 proverb] *Adagia* I ix 25
11 Horace] *Odes* 4.4.30–2, 29
31 comets] Cf *Julius Caesar* I ii 140: 'The fault, dear Brutus, is not in our stars.' This was a view often expressed by Erasmus; cf Epp 948, 1005.
34 Honour] *Adagia* I viii 92, where Erasmus quotes Cicero *Tusculan Disputations* 1.2.4.

nourishes the arts." And that other one, "While there are patrons like
Maecenas, there will be Virgils, my dear Flaccus." Where can you find now
the honour due to letters? Where is the place worthy of a really polished
mind? Where is the fruit which should rightly result from long and excellent
toil? Those who cry their wares by claiming to be men of religion think it the   5
height of piety to know nothing, and for the most part they look either to
gain or to their bellies; the rulers of the church prefer to emulate Epicurus
rather than Cicero. Literary studies are usually both called into being and
fostered by the generosity of princes, but *they* gather round them not Platos
but Gnathos. Their gifts go to jesters, flatterers, the architects of their   10
pleasures. More respect is paid to the man who leads in a fine dog than to
the one who presents a learned book. The large incomes of the priests are
either a matter of bargaining or the reward of being a toady. It is nearly
always the very dullest who burst into the role of abbot or some other high
office. The satirist complains that rich men "merely marvel at fluent speak-   15
ers, and praise them like boys looking at Juno's bird." But nowadays it is
discreditable to know more about literature. Here, more than anyone else,
this pestilential type of man is at the top, the kind you would be right in
calling a petty tyrant; these people arrogate to themselves the right of
censorship in everything, especially with foolish women, even immodest   20
ones, and with the uneducated crowd; these latter are persuaded by the
successful tricksters that to know Greek is heresy, and to speak like Cicero is
heresy too. And whoever in his sane mind wants to go through the harass-
ment of such lengthy labours, without which not even a mediocre knowledge of literature can be obtained, just to win enmity and jealous ill will   25
instead of a reward? Even suppose erudition came to one while asleep, with
no effort, who would not rather flee into the farthest solitudes of India than
put up with these apes of culture? For my part I would far rather live my life
among the animals, like those early men antiquity imagined made out of
tree-trunks, than live among this kind of brute, the most brutish of all.   30

* * * * *

  1 other one] Martial 8.56.5, quoted in *Adagia* I viii 92

  7 Epicurus] In this reference to Epicurus, which dates from the manuscript,
    Erasmus is using 'Epicurean' in the ordinary pejorative sense. But later he was
    to give a very different meaning to the word (see his colloquy *The Epicurean*,
    1533).

10 Gnathos] Gnatho, a parasite and flatterer in Terence's *Eunuchus*, was often
    used to typify these qualities by Erasmus. Gnatho actually boasts of founding
    a new school of *Gnathonici* and making a discipline out of parasitism
    (*Eunuchus* 264).

15 satirist] *Adagia* IV i 84; Juvenal 7.31. Juno's bird is the peacock.

19 tyrant] See 30:8n.

30 tree-trunks] Virgil *Aeneid* 8.314 and other poets, including Homer

Everything here seems to be swarming with them, these people who
worship their own uncouthness as placidly as they despise other men's
teaching.

'But among these beasts rather than men there is nothing more detest-
able or more dangerous or more inimical to the Muses than the ones who   5
dress up in the mask of religion, those of whom I began to speak just now;
they manage by dignified dress and the false semblance of holiness to
acquire no little authority among the ignorant crowd, especially with women, whose folly they exploit and whose appetites they energetically assist
– being select fat bulls, uncommonly well provided, genitally speaking; and   10
these are they whom the aforesaid brutes call in for consultation, and if they
do not, these people have enough impudence to thrust themselves into
council whether welcome or no. You might as well ask a camel's advice on
dancing or a donkey's about song. What else are you doing when you
consult a Friar Minor, a Dominican, or a Carmelite as if he were an oracle,   15
asking him who should be put in charge of a boy destined for the best
education to form his mind; what methods, which authors should be used
for his instruction – just as Demodocus in Plato consulted Socrates? There
he is, my dull-witted, vain consultant, unlike Socrates in anything but his
face (they both have a bovine look), issuing a terribly severe warning   20
especially against reading the poets. To these idiots Quintilian is a poet,
and Pliny, and Aulus Gellius, and Livy – in short everyone who wrote in
good Latin. They are so far from understanding the nature of poetics, for
which their name is *poetria*, that they do not even recognize who the poets
are or who can be given that name. The footsteps in which they are   25
following show them up as men born and bred in unrelieved barbarism.
One orders you to learn the psalter by heart, another thinks that the Latin

* * * * *

  6 mask of religion] Although the following passage is an interpolation of *1520*, it
     is worth noting that the germ of the idea ('those who dress up in the mask of
     religion') is in the manuscript.
10 genitally] This translates an adjective from Martial 3.73.1.
13 You ... song] Several adages are embedded here: *Adagia* I iv 35; II vii 66; IV i 47.
15 Dominican] 'Jacobite' in the text, a name taken from the Paris house of the
     Dominicans in the rue St Jacques
18 Demodocus] In the pseudo-Platonic dialogue *Demodocus* (380A)
23 poetics] Batt uses the Greek term *poetice* and sneers at the medieval *poetria*
     (which he knows means only 'poetess' in good Latin). Here he means 'the art
     of poetry'; otherwise he would use the correct Latin *poesis*. Petrarch and
     Boccaccio use *poetria*, but Boccaccio's epitaph has *poesis*. English has kept
     'poetry'; the more correct 'poesy' has remained a learned innovation. See
     Allen Ep 1153:215n; E. Faral *Les arts poétiques du xiie et du xiiie siècles* (Paris
     1924).

language can be learnt from the Proverbs of Solomon, another calls you to
that silliest of authors, Michael Modista, another to the *Mammetrectus*,
another to the *Catholicon*, – in fact being corrupted oneself gives the right to
advise others. Then if they have got to know about some teacher as peculiarly asinine, as they are peculiarly hypocritical, they order the wretched   5
children to be sent to him. It is not difficult for them to get their way,
because they are dealing with the uneducated, and because they are the
craftiest master hands at simulating virtue, and lastly because the general
mob nearly always agrees more readily with the views of the worse people.
On the other hand, if they smell out someone with learning of a more   10
polished kind, they hold him in abhorrence. "Beware," they say, "he's a
poet, he's no Christian." Everywhere they are dropping these ideas into
people's ears, in their sermons (which are their kingdom, trusting as they
do to the folly of the people), in private conversation, in those secret
confessions of theirs in which they think themselves gods. Who would not   15
get tired of living among monsters like these? Who would not wish to fly
"beyond the Sauromates and the icy ocean," if only he were to set the
humility and learning of the great men of old against the pride and ignorance of this century of ours?

'But why should I start on a long and useless lament? It is on you, as I   20
said, that the whole blame rests, and if you were to sack these undoctoral
doctors and counselless counsellors, or if – which would suit them better –
you were to throw them into that sea over there, sewn up in bags full of bugs
and fleas – why then if you did not see a fine crop bursting into bloom, I
would willingly submit to whatever penalty you might exact from me.'   25

Batt was really on fire as he issued these recommendations, for although he was otherwise a mild and quiet man, he could not temper his

* * * * *

2 authors] This attack on medieval grammarians is an interpolation of *1520*, and
very characteristic of Erasmus. See Allen *Age of Erasmus* 36–46. The term
modistae was applied generically to authors of treatises *de modis significandi*,
which were speculative restatements of Priscian's grammar. See G.L. Bursill-
Hall *Speculative Grammars of the Middle Ages: The Doctrine of Partes Orationis of
the Modistae* (The Hague 1971). The translator is indebted for this reference to
Dr Marjorie O'Rourke Boyle.

2 *Mammetrectus*] A medieval biblical dictionary, first printed 1470; the *Catholicon* is a Latin grammar c 1286. The title of the book here called *Mammetrectus*
was uncertain. A current form was *Mammothreptus*, 'which was interpreted as
"brought up by one's grandmother"' (Allen *Age of Erasmus* 53). See Ep
337:330n.

17 Sauromates] Juvenal 2.1. The Sauromatae inhabited the Ukraine and NE Bal-
kans.

words on this subject – he had so great a love for Good Letters. The burgomaster smiled.

'We'll decide later, Batt,' said he, 'which form of execution is to put an end to them. If I were Jupiter, I would turn them all into asses and camels. Meanwhile you seem to be quite clear that I am here in my private capacity, since you have dared to take so much liberty in speaking to me, as if it were Conrad and not the burgomaster you had to do with. I; in my turn, by your leave, will bring an accusation against you: you have neglected your duty too. It was your business, since you have a public appointment, to bring these abominable things to the notice of the burgomaster and council, unless by any chance you are a councillor to no purpose: certainly it was your province to sound a warning.'

The burgomaster said this to inflame the heated man still further.

'What impudence!' cried Batt. 'Are you talking to me about warnings, when I undertook the labours of Hercules for this – even beating him at it? You may pretend to forget and be facetious about it, but I know you remember how about two years ago I came back from Paris and took up the job of running the school, and what an Augean stable I found there. Ye gods! what nonsense, what inanities, what mockery, what barbarism, what thorns and brambles, what dregs had been forced upon the unhappy schoolboys by those before me who had taught them to know nothing. I proved then by experience the truth of that saying of Quintilian's, that unlearning is much more trouble than learning. For as soon as I had decided to tear up these weeds – which had to be done – it was amazing how those masters of unlearning rose up against me with their bitter hatred, their dedicated band of supporters, their gladiatorial fury. Come now, when did you ever see an outbreak in your community more violent than that one? They stirred up against me men tainted with the same madness among the clergy – of whom there are a great many – and also the chief men of the city, whose minds still smacked of their ancestral farms; they appealed to the

*　*　*　*　*

15 Hercules] The labours of Hercules included the cleansing of the Augean stables, the destruction of the man-eating storks of the lake of Stymphalus, and the conquests of the giant Antaeus, of the threefold monster Geryon, of Diomedes king of Thrace, and of the centaur Nessus. Hercules mastered Cerberus, the many-headed watch-dog of the underworld, and destroyed the Hydra, whose hundred heads grew again as soon as they were cut off. In *Adagia* III i 1 Erasmus compares his own efforts to the labours of Hercules, and this comparison was taken up by others (Allen Epp 2424:261; 2466:58).
22 that saying] Quintilian 2.3.2
26 gladiatorial fury] *Adagia* I iii 76
30 ancestral farms] Juvenal 16.36

piety of the young people's parents by awaking a religious fear, and urging
them to look to their children's morals in good time. They set on fire the
carpenters, fullers, cobblers, druggists, beggars, players, buffoons, fowlers, fishermen, coachmen, fishmongers, cooks, sausage-makers, porters,
from whom they differed much less in intelligence than in social position.   5
Add to these the barbers, pimps, bawds, and little old gossips: whom did
they leave out? This included by far the greater part of the lowest order of
people, and it was not at all difficult, for several reasons: the common herd
is naturally easy to rouse; they have an inborn stupidity which makes them
dislike letters; they are as unthinking in their wonder at the silliest things as   10
in their willingness to defend them. But let us follow up the valiant conduct
of the generals.

    'These men, confident in their vast resources, were everywhere fling-
ing harsh and terrible accusations against me, in the open street, in their
drinking-places, in the shops, at the barber's, in the brothels, in public and   15
in private, drunk or sober, repeating that some nonentity of an outsider was
spreading a new heresy, that those first-rate authors through whom their
grandfathers and great-grandfathers had become immensely learned,
Alexander, Ebrardus Graecista, Modista, *Breviloquus, Mammetrectus,
Catholicon*, were being shamefully pushed out for the introduction of some   20
unheard of and abominable monsters of paganism – Horace, Virgil, and
Ovid; that the young were being taught about nothing but love, and things
were being inculcated in children that it would be wrong for even adults to
know. If they did not take immediate steps, Christianity would come to an
end, the century of Antichrist would already be here or at any rate immi-   25
nent. There had come teachers, they said, who pleased those whose ears
were always itching for something new, the sort whom Paul prophesied
about, turning people from the truth and leading the young to nonsensical
fiction. You were a witness of that fight; you saw for yourself how I acted
Hercules, how many lions and boars and bulls and Stymphalian birds I   30
slew, how many versions of Antaeus or Geryon or Diomedes or Nessus,
how I dragged Cerberus out of his den where he was terrifying the pallid
shades, and held him up to the sky; you saw how my Greek fire only just
managed to wipe out the Lernaean Hydra, fertile with its own deaths, and I
rather think that worst of all plagues is still alive and breathing. The   35

                    * * * * *

  17 authors] The list of medieval grammarians was extended in the 1520 edition.
      Alexander de Villa Dei wrote a Latin grammar in verse, c 1200; *Graecista* was
      the nickname of Eberhard of Béthune, called Ebrardus (twelfth century);
      Breviloquus is probably *Brachilogus* by Johannes de Mera.
  27 Paul] 2 Tim 4:3
  34 Hydra] Ovid *Metamorphoses* 9.70

Pompey of our town, more like Midas than Pompey, and what he is plotting, does not escape me. Alone I faced all those monsters, but I did not give way; no, I won through, and convinced the saner intelligences, confuted the others with clear reasoning, and held some up to scorn.'

When Batt had finished, Willem said, 'Well, on my life, my dear Batt, you deserve not only a public thanksgiving, but a triumphal procession. That rhapsodist in Plato, Ion, was loud in the praise of Homer alone, and boasted that he himself deserved to be crowned with gold by the admirers of Homer; but you have defended almost the whole of literature against so many monsters, with such energy, that surely you have more claim to be endowed with the triumphal wreath by the Muses, nay by Apollo himself, or at any rate to have a golden statue in every one of their shrines.'

The others laughed at this joke, and Batt capped it by saying, 'Get along, you are laughing at me as Hercules, and for you I cut the figure of a Pyrgopolinices; but I did what I could as far as I was able; and if you, Willem, were to join this energy of purpose with your skill in language and your learning, the cause of Good Letters might perhaps come off better.'

'Come, Hercules,' said the burgomaster, 'what if we arrange a triumph for you, in recognition of great deeds, and a more splendid one than ever Paulus Aemilius or Pompey had? Tomorrow, drawn by horses white as snow, you shall enter the town wearing a laurel wreath, between cheering rows of the lovers of literature assembled together; the barbarian leaders conquered by your valour shall march before your triumphal chariot, hands pinioned as they deserve, and shall stretch out beseeching hands to the victorious nation. Behind them the conquering warrior shall sing the praises of his general, booty shall be distributed, trophies set up for Apollo, the *opima spolia* dedicated to the Nine Sisters. In a word, we will make you a god, so that you will not be a second Hercules, as the proverb says, but Hercules himself; when did he ever deserve so much? But on the

* * * * *

1 Pompey of our town] Pompey is chosen for his ambition as dictator, Midas as an example of bad judgment.

7 Ion] *Ion* 530D

15 Pyrgopolinices] A strutting braggart in Plautus *Miles gloriosus*

20 Aemilius or Pompey] Aemilius Paulus, victor over Macedon in 168 BC. His triumph was of unprecedented luxury. Pompey celebrated three triumphs in 79, 71, and 61 BC.

24 pinioned] After this word 1520 adds 'behind them' (*post tergum*).

27 opima spolia] Erasmus is here voicing the interest of his time in the Roman triumph, often copied in the festivals and art of the Renaissance. *Opima spolia* are the arms taken on the field of battle by the victors. The Nine Sisters are the Muses.

28 proverb] *Adagia* I vii 41

LB X 1701E / ASD I-1 62

understanding that you do first what victors usually do, that is expound in a brilliant speech the whole course of the struggle and of your deeds on land or sea. Even if you scorn such a triumph, you should not refuse to do this, both for our sakes who beg it of you, and for the sake of letters which I know to be dearest to your heart, or for the sake of the city to which you have recently been admitted; you have begun to care for it, and you owe it a certain loyalty. Just now you were blaming me, but what do you think I can do all by myself, one among so many who have quite different views? Do you want me to kick against the pricks, as they say, especially as this way of thinking is not yet fully fixed in my mind, and I am sometimes defeated by their arguments, so that I can hardly defend your case adequately?

'And now, this must be said in all seriousness, Batt: what you say as you argue learnedly with me about the proper, the improper, the indeterminate, may all be true; but a good deal of obloquy does seem to cling to your cause, not only with the uneducated but among people who are prepared to judge letters more justly. For your authors are – let's face it – first heathen, which may admit of a defence; and second very difficult to know, which certainly makes them disliked by many people; and lastly, most important of all, licentious, even obscene. Now admit the facts: you are rejecting Christian writers and bringing in heathen ones; you are throwing out the well-known and importing the unknown; you are ousting the old to admit the new; you are taking away the easy and pushing at us what is difficult; and finally – here is the chief point – you are forbidding the young to read chaste authors and offering them lascivious ones. What face do you think I can put on it, when my citizens ask me as burgomaster whether it is really the object of a public school that the young should learn all about shady love affairs (as if they were not inclined to these studies by a natural bent) or get used to the idea of cunning tricks and skilful deception of their parents, of shamelessness and lying, of putting off one face and putting on another – for this is what they learn from your comedies, and they bring the lesson home with them? How serious do you think this sounds in a parent's ears? Are we sending our children to school, they say, or to the brothel? For those three letters which the old man in Plautus was so proud of knowing, we can easily learn at home. Besides, when people who have a little more learning sing over and over again the same song about the papal decrees and the opinions of the theologians, which they know by heart, it is then that I hesitate; but truly because I am defeated, not a traitor. You are easily

* * * * *

9 kick] Acts 26:14; *Adagia* I iii 46
13 proper] Erasmus uses three Greek technical terms. Cf Quintilian 4.1.40.
33 three letters] *Mercator* 303 (*amo*, 'I love')

the most experienced of all in this field; you must have read and thought
many things which would serve to rebut this sort of accusation; and so
really it would be doing something truly great if you would explain this
whole controversy from beginning to end, not because your cause seems
doubtful to me, but just to make me a more informed defender of it.'   5

Each one of us for his own part joined in this request to Batt, and he
could find no way of escape. 'Well,' he said, 'you are promising a much
greater reward than I ask for. It will be enough execution for me if Ate alone,
the scourge of studies, is dragged along by a hook like a criminal and
thrown straight into the public sewer, and then I only ask for the tongues of   10
some of the leading supporters, not their heads.'

'What do you want those for?' I asked.

'For nothing but lavatory use,' said he, 'or for wiping out chamber
pots, or at least for wiping dirty dishes.'

'Nothing would do better,' said I. 'But seriously, my friends, since we   15
have happened by chance on such a splendid subject, why should we not
set up an academy here on the model of Plato's? No matter if we have not a
plane tree like the Platonic or Ciceronian ones, which were planted and
grew by favour of the writings of the most eloquent of philosophers and the
wisest of orators, rather than being watered in the ordinary way. I am   20
offering you real trees instead of imaginary ones, and in the place of one
poor tree a whole orchard, which you can see near our house on the left,
bordered by noble oaks and the clearest of streams. What if we water this
place too with our discussions, so that it will never dry up at any future
time? And under that great pear tree, practically in the middle of the   25
garden, there are some very comfortable seats, and I will order cushions to
be brought, if you wish. I am not sorry to have such personages present, fit
for the school of Hiarcas and not only for an Academy: a burgomaster, a
doctor in public practice, a town clerk, a theologian and orator combined,
and I myself as the master of this splendid estate. Not to mention Plato   30
(though he makes everyone talkative), when did Cicero, brazen as he was,
ever dare to collect together a more distinguished gathering? If so weighty a
philosopher as Socrates could be allured (as in the *Phaedrus*) by the pleas-

* * * * *

  4 beginning to end] 'From top to toe' *Adagia* I ii 37

  9 scourge of studies] This passage (to 'since we have happened by chance') is an
     addition of 1520 and directly concerns the controversy with the theologians of
     Louvain. See *Antibarbari* Introductory Note 12–14.

18 Platonic or Ciceronian] In *Phaedrus* and *De oratore*; on *Phaedrus* see 119:22n.

28 Hiarcas] The letters of Jerome (for example 53:1) had introduced Erasmus to
     this philosopher and his school.

31 brazen] *Adagia* I viii 47

antness of the place to lie down on the grass and converse beside the little
spring, why should we not be tempted to sit down here, by these gardens
which Epicurus himself might praise? There is everything here which
Socrates admired there; the pear-tree in the middle, as you see, serves our
pleasure in three different ways: it is tall enough and has spreading   5
branches which will protect us from the heat, and as it is now springtime it
will not only gladden our eyes with blossom but refresh our nostrils with
the sweetest scent. Socrates will not outdo us with his little fountain of
ice-cold water; instead of a spring we have a murmuring stream which
flows round all the gardens and irrigates them. What could be better to   10
breathe than this fresh air or, as the doctor will tell you, more health-
giving?'
    At this point Batt, who had a clear recollection of that description in
Plato, interrupted my speech: 'We may be better off in other ways, Erasmus, but we certainly have to own ourselves beaten by Socrates in Plato in   15
one particular. You may add the tuneful chirping of crickets and cicadas to
the rustle of blossoming plants and grasses spangled with many-coloured
flowers, but there is one thing in which we are unable to compete.'
    'What is that?' I asked.
    'The statues of the nymphs,' he replied, 'which I see Socrates did not   20
fail to mention.'
    The burgomaster and the doctor laughed at this.
    'By the Dog,' they said, 'and the Socratic Goose, that is just the remark
one would expect of Batt – except that he does not usually take much delight
in sculptured nymphs; he would rather have flesh-and-blood ones, given   25
the choice. Anyway this is hardly an obstacle to our discussion – come
along.'
    We agreed that the place was charming and sat down, all telling Batt
with equal energy that he must start. He looked straight at the burgomaster.
    'It is quite right,' he said, 'that I should have my throat cut with my   30
own sword; I ordered you just now to do some magnificent fooling and here
I am being compelled by you to be the greatest fool and clown of all. Well, I
see I have got to obey a burgomaster, a doctor, and close friends, in such
numbers too; but first shut the orchard gate, so that no one will see us. I am
not afraid of one of you giving me away, if only Erasmus can be got to give   35
his pen a rest. Whatever he even dreams at night he blackens his paper with
in the daytime.'

　　* * * * *

23 Dog ... Goose] Favourite oaths of Socrates
31 own sword] See 25:19n.
36 Whatever ... begin] This exchange of quips is an addition of 1520.

'Look,' I said, 'I have neither pen nor paper.'

'Quite so,' said he, 'but I know what a memory you have – it is as good
as a notebook to you. Even if you missed something you would easily fill the
gap out of your own head. However I will trust you all, and begin.'

He stood up and arranged himself to speak – dress, expression, gesture all composed; and for a short time he paused to think, with eyes fixed
on the ground. His pallor and rising agitation were signs to us that the
intending speaker was no thick-headed and self-confident orator but a man
of judgment, who, as Quintilian says, knew the danger he was in. When he
had worked out and settled the various parts of his speech (I inferred that he
had done this as he counted on his fingers), he gave a little cough and spat,
as his custom was. Then, lifting up a cheerful face he looked eagerly at each
of us in turn and, with everyone giving him the greatest attention, he
began.

Opening of Batt's speech

'If I did not know that I was to speak before most cultivated judges, and was
not largely assisted by the very soundness of my cause, I should be afraid
that, in the face of such hatred on the part of the stupidest people, literature
was not going to have a very good advocate today. But, as it is, I am so far
from any apprehension of not being able to refute all the objections that the
anti-rhetoricians can ever raise that I do not think it necessary in such an
easily won cause even to use an introduction. It is not only in front of you,
my good friends, with all your learning, you who have begged me for this
speech and who cannot, I know, be anything but kind, willing, attentive
hearers, but even among the Sauromates or whatever may be more barbarous, provided they are human beings, I can promise myself certain victory;
human beings, I say, who follow the lead of reason and not the dictates of
passion. For as to these brawlers who go on obstinately defending their
obvious idiocy, I look on them as Diogenes looked on his public assembly.
When several thousand men had come together there, he still declared he
had not yet seen a man. They say that learning is deadly to mortals, and the
thing to wish for is ignorance,

* * * * *

9 Quintilian] 12.5.4
28 hearers] See the description of the mood of an audience in Cicero *De oratore*
2.19.80, and the *Rhetorica ad Herennium* 1.4.6.
28 Sauromates] See 34:17n.
32 Diogenes] Anecdote from Diogenes Laertius 6.32

Olive no stone shall have nor nut no shell.

Sure as I am already of making my point, this one thing I ask: do not expect
magnificent oratory on such a thorny and intractable subject; even on the
most favourable topics you should not require this of a Batt. You will not
even demand to be amused, except when the crass stupidity of the barbarians' reasoning makes you laugh.'

Beginning with an apology, I said, 'Is it permissible to interrupt you
sometimes as you speak?'

·'Certainly,' replied Batt, 'interrupt me as often as you like; we are not
speaking by the clock, and the cause will not be lost if a little time is spent on
the way.'

'You seem to me,' I said, 'to have dispensed with an introduction in
such a way that not to have one is in itself an introduction. But go on, I beg,
do not let us hold you up in your first stage any longer.'

'That's just like you,' retorted Batt; 'it isn't my way; you have got by
heart all those subtleties and rhetorical tricks, but it is enough for me, I
think, to set forth the thing as it is in the fewest possible words. And so I
shall not go back further to inquire how it happened that the learning of
antiquity fell from such a pinnacle of honour into this pit of darkness, or try
to find out what fate caused this, when it came about, by what stages, as you
were trying to do just now.· That could be better done at another time
perhaps. It is not really important to decide how someone fell into a well;
the main thing is how to get him out. We shall therefore plead the cause of
the old learning against its new opponents, and I see that the trouble comes
mainly from three types of enemy.

'There are those who want the Republic of Letters to be destroyed root
and branch. Others are doing their best to get its power not exactly extinguished, but restricted within narrower limits. Lastly there are those who
want to see the republic preserved but utterly ruined, by themselves becoming tyrants, abrogating the laws of our fathers, and introducing foreign
magistrates and behaviour.

'The first-named of these, as I see it, are those quite uncouth people
who detest the whole of literature (which they call poetry) on some vague
religious pretext, whether from jealousy or stupidity I cannot say. The
second lot I understand to be the educated who are really uneducated, the
people who somehow find other studies acceptable (that is, their own), but

* * * * *

1 Olive] Horace *Epistles* 2.1.31
11 by the clock] 'By the waterclocks,' an allusion to the method of timing cases in
    the Roman courts. See *Adagia* I iv 73.

as for the humanities, without which all learning is blind, they hate them
worse than a snake. Then there are the last, and who else are they but the
people who admire and approve of every kind of literature, especially
poetry and rhetoric, but on condition that they themselves are considered
the finest poets and orators – which is far from the case.   5

'It would not be easy to say which of these enemies does the most
grievous and dreadful harm to the Republic of Letters, or which of them is
to be credited with the largest share of its disasters. For the first (do not let
us underestimate them) may have nothing in the way of weapons and
knowledge of warfare, but, as a savage horde massed together from the   10
fields and hills, I wonder whether any kind of enemy could be more
dangerous. They do not march into battle; they throw themselves into it like
ravening wild beasts, mistaking fury for fortitude. They have four strong
points: fury (like the Andabatae), noise (like Stentor in Homer), numbers
(in which they exceed even the army of Xerxes), and lastly a kind of shield   15
which is the pretence of religion; and under that they are always sheltering
– it is all they can put up against all kinds of missiles. These people are
entirely outside the world of literature, and have a burning hatred of the
glory attached to men of letters; they think it proper and pious to carp at the
finest studies of others, and it is amazing how cunningly they mask their   20
sluggishness, their envy, and their pride under the attractive names of
simplicity and religion.

'The second lot are rather better educated than these, and they attack
us from far and near: from a distance with missiles, but quite laughable
ones (they hurl at us tow, smoke, and dung); in hand-to-hand fighting they   25
go for us with daggers, but leaden ones. They offer peace, but on obviously
arrogant terms, on condition that we should get our learning without the
humanities – though without these no literature can exist. They ban all
culture, and whatever they themselves have not learnt. They are difficult to
get hold of, and most troublesome on this account. They never make a   30
stand; they are more elusive than the Parthians, now saying yes and then
no; they are always shuffling, getting away with a quibble, and like Proteus,

Into all kinds of wondrous shapes they change.

* * * * *

14 Andabatae] The Andabatae bashed about with closed eyes; see *Adagia* II iv 33.
14 Stentor] *Iliad* 5.785; *Adagia* II iii 37
15 Xerxes] The size of Xerxes' army became proverbial: see Herodotus 7.60.
31 Parthians] The Parthians were noted for deceptive manoeuvres in war; see
     Virgil *Georgics* 3.31, etc.
35 change] Virgil *Georgics* 4.441

'The last group might perhaps be judged not very bitter enemies, because their offence comes from zeal, not hatred; but I find them far and away the most harmful. The others attack under hostile banners and can be driven from the ramparts, but these are living inside the walls, in our very strongholds, and by their weapons and badges look like our friends, but all the time they are planning for the eternal ruin of the republic under a deceptive appearance of devotion, and the more they strive to deliver their country, the more they entangle it in shameful slavery. One might almost warm to the first group of opponents, because their hatred of letters means that they never touched them. The second group are the less harmful for having kept away from the best writers, that is, the poets and orators, being content with their own state. The last want to know everything and meanwhile they have mixed up, corrupted, and ruined everything. It is said, and how truly, that there is nothing less kind than a mistimed kindness. Just so, these people have tried to come to the rescue of literature in distress, and they have entirely wiped it out by their disastrous zeal. The thing to do was to measure their powers, to determine the range of their intellect, before taking up so strenuous a task. What they did was to prefer to imitate Phaethon, the inexperienced driver who tried to manage his father's chariot, and upset it to his own downfall. And as they are like Phaethon in their folly, they deserve a similar calamity or even worse. It is by their rashness that philosophy, the great, old, and true, has been reduced to sheer nonsense, mere fantasy. Through them we have lost innumerable works of the early writers; the fact that corrupt textual readings abound, and abound the more the more learned the author, is something we owe to them; if the fine theology of the old days has so much degenerated, this is their doing and no one else's; if the grammarians write and teach nothing but sheer barbarism, we have them to thank. And to bring this to a close: it is their doing that in both verse and prose mute and inarticulate authors are prized above the most learned; one among them writes on grammar, another on rhetoric, another on dialectic, another on natural philosophy, another on theology; while this one writes commentaries on the best authors, shedding darkness on them, not light, not adorning but corrupting, and another one tries to emend what he does not understand, and a third turns into bad Latin what was in good Greek, though he knows practically nothing of either language; and so, I say, while they are vying

* * * * *

14 less kind] *Adagia* III x 35
19 Phaethon] Ovid *Metamorphoses* 2.1–340. Phaethon borrowed the chariot of the sun, and by his loss of control brought drought and destruction upon the earth before he was finally burnt to death.

with each other to make an uproar, they have managed to confuse, corrupt,
and overturn everything with their futile efforts; and the more industri-
ously each of them tries to do his part, the more ruin he causes. It is like
someone trying to wipe a speck of dust off a purple robe with hands
smeared with ordure – the harder he tries to help the more harm he does.   5

'But, leaving them aside (for to discuss the subject one would have to
go on for ever), I shall fall on the other two lines in two separate offensives;
and here I shall acquit myself so that you will swear I am more expert than
Pyrrhus.

'As to the army of yokels, I shall be content to have dispersed them   10
with a hastily raised force, and put them to flight stripped of their shields of
religious pretence; this will not need much doing. For they are an unwarlike
crowd made up of old men, who, realizing that their time has been passed
in self-indulgence and run out, are futilely jealous of the young who are
advancing to better things. I shall first force them to turn tail, using the most   15
cogent arguments as javelins, and then, when they turn again to fight, I
shall stab them with swords – the testimony of Holy Writ. When they are
stunned by this barrage of instances, I shall drive them from their strongholds, and once these have been reduced I shall drive on in the same flush of
battle to attack the stragglers, and, stripping them of all their arms, carry off   20
the victory in every kind of warfare.

'But now the first lot are to be challenged, and we will suppose that the
chief of the Fetial priests has completed the ceremonies; for them, I think,
the following declamation would be suitable, if the matter were carried out
seriously.   25

Speech of the Fetial priests

' "Hear, ye Goths! By what right have you crossed your frontiers and not   30
only occupied the domains of the Latins – I mean liberal studies – but dared
to invade the city which rules all, Latinity itself? What injury has been done
to you, what are your demands? If you want war, decide the matter in open
fight; give us the opportunity to do battle with you. If you shrink from the
fray, cease to be troublesome, withdraw from the land, clear the country of   35
your presence, remain within your own boundaries. If you would rather be

* * * * *

  9 Pyrrhus] King of Epirus, famous for his talents as a general
17 Holy Writ] Eph 6:17: 'The sword of the Spirit, which is the word of God'
23 Fetial priests] The *Fetiales* were a body of priests in Rome whose duty it was to
    declare war and make peace.

called foes than brigands, come out of your lairs, join battle with us, and
these feuds shall find a conclusion in open fight; either you will be defeated
and quiet, or we shall admit that the victory is yours.''

If literature appears objectionable to many people,
the cause lies merely in their ignorance

'Now the Fetial priests, their plea unheard, have declared war by casting a
spear; now the enemy must be challenged to battle.'

Here I interrupted: 'Take care you don't go too fast! You have not
completed all the formalities – you have to kill a pig with a stone before you
rush to arms.'

'Quite right,' said he; 'I wish I were allowed to choose a fine specimen
out of those sties where so many fat healthy porkers idle away and are
stuffed with the food of the people. I would rather sacrifice a biped than any
four-footed pig. But come on, let us take it as done, the thing we so ardently
wish done, and go on with good auguries to attack the enemy. For at
present I am going to behave exactly as if I had them face to face. You sit and
watch, as the spectators of our skirmish. And as it would not do for my
friend Erasmus to complain that we had no trumpet – I see he is a fastidious
observer of ceremonies – let this blast of abuse take the trumpet's place.

'Tell me, I say, you loutish fellows, race of Midas, senseless blocks of
marble, what have letters done (''profane'' letters as you call anything you
have not learnt) to deserve that you should attack them with such obstinate
virulence, as if men were born for one thing only, to hate learning? It
annoys you that you learnt nothing, and cannot learn now, but must you
choose to hate? If you have sunk into hopeless sloth, do you think it a fine
thing to look on others with envy? Why not rather set vigorously to work,
and wrest from us this glory which you envy? But you are afraid we shall
poke the ancient jests at you, ''a donkey learning the fiddle, a bull in the
wrestling ring; what has a jackdaw to do with a harp, or a pig with
amaranth?'' But there is nothing remarkable in your hating – the wonder
would be if you were to love. What the greatest of Peripatetic philosophers

* * * * *

12 kill a pig] A ceremony described by Livy 1.24.8
20 And ... place] This quip is an addition of *1520*.
23 Midas] *Adagia* I iii 67
24 marble] *Adagia* IV iii 99
31 donkey ... amaranth] Ancient jokes; see *Adagia* I iv 35, 37, 38, 62.
34 greatest] Aristotle

wrote is true, as usual – "only the ignorant is an enemy to knowledge." "A cock does not appreciate a bit of jasper, nor do pigs delight in roses; no picture pleases an ape, no light the purblind; for Midas there is no pleasure in the song of Apollo." Why do you foolishly show off your asses' ears; you are even sillier than your father Midas who did try to keep them hidden. Why not rather bury the shame of your ignorance in the ground? Why not imitate the artfulness of some people who praise letters, to give themselves the air of knowing? Why not at least keep your mouths shut and look like philosophers? Now you are caught in your own accusation like squeaking mice. But maybe you are so far advanced in your madness as to think it a clever thing to do to hate and envy and carp at the best things of all, which the wisest men think worth obtaining with many labours. That bit of glory, in case you don't know, you share with porters, cobblers, sailors, and grave-diggers; they hate cultivated studies too, and despise and curse them, but they are better than you for two reasons; their hate is less violent, and they despise our studies for love of their own skills. You detest the refined arts and have none of your own. They prefer one skill to another, one kind of study to another; you put ignorance before knowledge, madness before a sane mind, animals before men. You slavish herd of sneerers, even the asses laugh at you!

'Now just look and see how unfair it is to hate without knowing what you hate or why you hate it. You condemn rhetoric, but what that might be you have not the foggiest idea. You hate poetry, without understanding what it is or what kind of thing. You hate antiquity, but the ancients mean nothing to you. In short, you pour scorn on the whole of what learned scholars toil for far into the night, and the whole of its greatness is unknown to you. For if you ever did learn these things yourselves why rebuke those who want to learn, and if you never learnt them (and this you not only admit but glory in) why pronounce judgment so ponderously on matters you know nothing about? You have heard, I think, that there is something bad in these studies. Of course you have, but from people like yourselves, envious, ignorant, and hostile; it is like pig teaching pig, or the blind leading the blind. But show me, if you can, one person who has found fault with this literature when he has thoroughly understood it, one person who

* * * * *

2 cock] The fable of the cock comes from Phaedrus; for pigs and roses see *Adagia* III vii 23. The story of Midas is told by Ovid (*Metamorphoses* 11.146–93).
10 mice] *Adagia* I iii 65. The allusion is to the shrew, supposed to be shriller than the ordinary mouse and therefore prone to give itself away.
19 sneerers] Horace *Epistles* 1.19.19
32 blind] *Adagia* I viii 40; Matt 15:14

has said that he regretted the time spent on it. Why should a dolt be
believed, jabbering about things he does not understand, and a learned
man disbelieved when he talks about what he knows? Do you think your
jealousy is concealed from anybody? Do you think you are deceiving us
with your pretences? or that we cannot see what disease is eating you up?   5
Suppose we now give things their proper names: stop posing as devout and
religious men instead of the jealous, sluggish creatures you are!'

It is malice and not piety to hate literary studies   10
of which you are ignorant

The doctor said then: 'As you have given leave, I will make use of it and
interrupt you. You have shown yourself a valiant skirmisher, and I think
you are rightly called Batt!'   15
When the other asked him why he thought so, he went on: 'These are
no riddles to you who know the fables so well. You have shown up the tricks
of the barbarians so well that I could almost believe that a second metamorphosis had transformed you back from that legendary stone into Batt again;
and then your challenge to these fellows provoking them to fight was clever   20
too. There is nothing which can so rouse their rage as to charge them as you
do with stupidity, ignorance, envy – in fact, hearing some truths about
themselves.'
'You are right,' said Batt, 'and it really is no wonder if scabby fellows
jump when you touch their sore places. You may see the arrogant men   25
giving proof of their soul's rage by their flashing eyes and the savagery
written all over their faces; even though in the midst of this they do not
yield a step in their fake religious fervour – like characters in a play they act
out their tragic parts. For religion, while it is the best of all things, is also,
the famous historian tells us, the most convenient cloak for any vice you like   30
to name, because if anyone tries to draw attention to the vices themselves
he appears to many people to be attacking religion, by which they are
masked; and so it often happens that "evil oft lurks, masked by its
neighbour, good."

     * * * * *

19 stone] The Battus of legend was a shepherd of Pylos, turned to stone by
    Mercury (Ovid *Metamorphoses* 2.687–707).
30 historian] Probably Livy 39.16.6–7
33 evil ... good] This was an opportune moment for Erasmus to insert the attack
    on the monastic orders which expresses his feeling about the situation at
    Louvain. The following paragraph is an insertion of *1520*.

'These people are soaked in vice – in much worse vices than any other
mortals, whom they, demigods as they are, regard as the common herd; yet
they make attacks on others' lives with their impudent tongues and spare
nobody, neither age nor sex nor nationality nor order, neither a man's
person nor his good fame. But whenever anyone finds them drunk, or
whoring, or committing some deed even worse than these, they put up
excuses, they cover up, they will have it hushed up for the honour of their
order, as they say – as if other mortals were outside all orders. When they
bawl about the vices of the secular clergy, and preach revolt, and incite the
ignorant mob to stone them, they never think of the risk of rousing the
anger of Christ, the Founder of *that* order – for he was a priest, but not a
Dominican. If anyone dares to divulge any of their secrets and disturb the
Augean stable, they announce that he is in danger of destruction from an
irate Francis, or Dominic, or Elijah, so help me! One of this flock recently
gave high praise to a colleague of his order, because he shouted all manner
of things in a public sermon against priests with concubines, and tried to
persuade the people and the magistrates that priests' concubines should be
compelled to wear a red cross on the left shoulder. As he was enjoying
himself mightily over this story, someone asked him – with compliments
about the other man's speech – what colour would he wish the cross to be
for the Dominicans, the Carmelites, and the rest. Would he like the concubines of the Friars Minor to wear grey crosses, those of the Carmelites
white, of the Dominicans black? At this the pious man crossed himself
vigorously against the evil omen. The second man continued, "You will
never succeed, however big a sign of the cross you make, in hiding from
many people what shameful things are sometimes perpetrated by your
colleagues. It could not possibly be otherwise, given such a heap of
offscourings of men and races. But perhaps it is not right to make all this
public, for the sake of the order." The first speaker agreed heartily with this.
Then the other asked, "And the priesthood, is not that an order?" As he
could not deny it, the second man asked why he should think the wrongdo-
ings of priests ought to be howled out in front of the people with such
inflammatory uproar. Not to digress further from our subject, we may say
that they use the same cloak for their crass ignorance as for the other
shameful things in their lives.
    'They hold out false piety everywhere as their shield, and they do it

* * * * *

11 a priest] Heb 6:20; 7:1–8:7
13 Augean stable] See 35:15n.
14 Elijah] Because the Carmelites took their name from Mount Carmel, where
    Elijah vanquished the prophets of Baal (1 Kings 18)

with such art and cunning that they manage to deceive not only other
people, but themselves as well, clever fellows that they are! Not that they
are moved by any real religious fervour – they have no wish to appear
religious in anything but this one particular – but, as Quintilian puts it,
they want to "skulk in the shadow of a great name." This is the religion of   5
evildoers, of robbers and murderers, who have a habit of flying to the altar
and the temple as soon as they have perpetrated any crime, like the wicked
slave in Plautus. Why do they do this? Because they are charmed with the
religious feeling of the place? Not in the least – they do it to escape the cross,
to go unpunished for their evil deeds. In the same way our severe critics –   10
who may be Dionysius or Clodius in other things – want to appear like
Numa whenever it comes to discussing good studies; it is then that they
remember they are Christians; it is then that they begin to chant the bits out
of the Gospel, and wrap up ugly things in attractive words, and say they are
inspired by zeal, not envy, and do not hate our studies but despise them –   15
that being the special duty and honour of a Christian. They hold up before
us the rustic simplicity of the apostles. They say that there is a high reward
among the blessed which awaits those who for religion's sake can despise
these heathen teachings, invented for ostentation and pride; ignorant piety, they say, is most pleasing to heaven; as if heaven were in any way   20
gratified by our being boorish – in that case why do we not cherish
stupidity more than anything? – or as if ignorance were useful to any aspect
of the management of life; when the truth is that to despise in others the
splendid thing which you have not got and never hope to have is utterly
absurd and a mark of insanity. They are wildly wrong if they think a   25
contempt for any kind of thing will redound to their own credit. Take
Thersites, the least of the Greeks: supposing that he in his utter cowardice
were to declare that he despised the glory of Achilles, and the arms by
which it was won (those arms which Ajax and Ulysses quarrelled about),
would he not provoke a universal shout of laughter? Who would not smile if   30
a snail despised the speed of the horse? or an owl mocked at the eagle's eyes,
or a mole at a roebuck's? if a raven scorned the colours of a parrot? or a

* * * * *

4 Quintilian] 12.10.15
8 Plautus] *Mostellaria* 1094
11 Dionysius or Clodius] Dionysius II, tyrant of Syracuse, and P. Clodius
Pulcher, the enemy of Cicero, exemplify the dissolute life. Numa Pompilius,
the early ruler of Rome (seventh century BC), typifies beneficient and wise
government.
27 Thersites] Thersites (*Iliad* 2.211–77) is used as a symbol of baseness. In post-
Homeric tradition (as reflected in Sophocles *Ajax*) Achilles' arms were made a
prize after his death.

donkey belittled the intelligence of an elephant? or if a doltish fool despised
the prudence of a wise man? That will never win him praise. And so I shall
be doing the barbarians a good turn if I explain the rational basis of scorn,
and thus prevent their using scorn as a means of self-glorification.

Things which may be rightly despised, and others which may not

'In human affairs there are certain things which attract the minds of mortal
men with a special ingrafted longing, whether because they look honourable and beautiful, or sweet, or useful, and in this category are wealth,
fame, rank, pleasure; if you possess these, or if they are easily within your
reach, to hold them lightly is an act worthy of a strong and upright man – at
least in so far as they turn him away from virtue. It is equally praiseworthy
to disdain the sad things and the sweet; that is, to be able to renounce the
latter and go to meet the former. Plato does not altogether approve of the
Spartan way of life, because while they made nothing of the hardest toil,
they seemed less practised in the contempt of pleasure. But these Catos of
ours are weaker than any woman on both counts; they only show themselves men when it comes to the contempt of literature. To make it even
funnier, they pour scorn not only on the most admirable things, but on
things entirely outside their knowledge. They scorn Ciceronian eloquence,
being themselves as dumb as fish; they scorn the acuteness of Chrysippus,
and they themselves are as dull as a pounded pestle. They scorn poetry,
being uninitiated and, as Plato says, foreign to the Muses. They scorn the
refined literary style of the old theologians, which they cannot hope to
follow, and if they were to hope for this they would be all the crazier. What a
doltish herd of scorners! Just tell me, what new greatness of soul is this?
What is this extraordinary type of contemptuousness? You cannot despise
money, but you bask in the glory of despising erudition? For kissing and
cuddling a whore you beat Hercules, silly childish lust is your master, any
kind of adulation ravishes you, the least opposition dismays you, and you
think you will cut the figure of a strong man if you manage to pour scorn on

* * * * *

16 Plato] *Laws* 1.633B ff
18 Catos] Cato the Censor (second century BC), famous for his temperate way of
life
23 Chrysippus] Stoic philosopher; cf 27:14n.
24 pestle] Dumb fish and beaten pestles are proverbial: *Adagia* prolegomena xiii
(LB II 12E) and III vi 21.
25 Plato] For example, *Republic* 8.546D; *Adagia* II vi 18

Map of Bergen-op-Zoom, c 1560
The town is in Brabant, a few miles from
Halsteren where Erasmus evidently revised
the earlier version of the *Antibarbari*. Three of
the five characters in the dialogue are residents
of Bergen: Jodocus (Jooste van Schoonhoven),
town physician; Willem Conrad (Colgheenes),
burgomaster; and Jacob Batt, secretary of the
town council.
Copyright, Bibliothèque royale Albert Ier,
Bruxelles
Manuscrit HS 22090

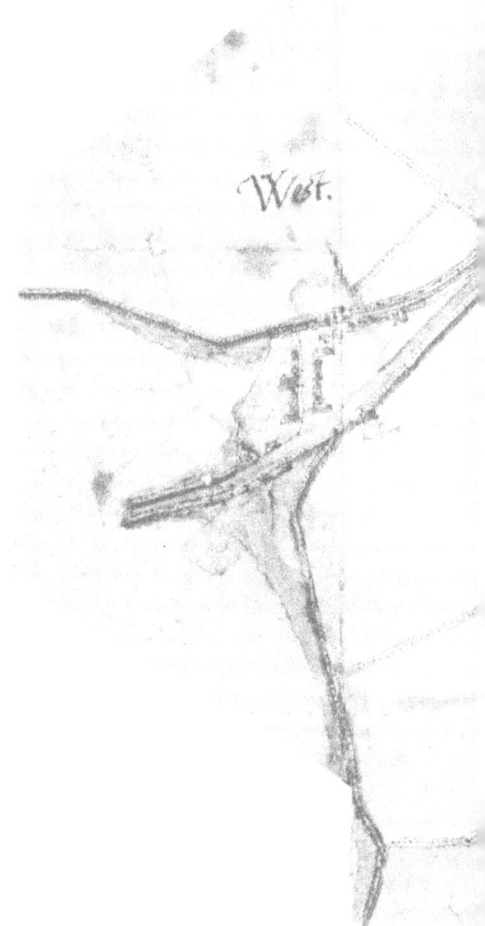

Oost.
Berghen op Zoom

things more important than you could possibly understand? To take pride
in a well-turned speech is not permitted, but you sell yourself to the
womenkind with your well-cut gown; you prefer your speech to be empty
and squalid but your skin is well filled and shining. You turn away in
disgust from the mention of girls in the stories of the poets, but meanwhile   5
you have no disgust at all about forcing other men's wives, even Vestal
virgins. The pen must not be sleek and shining, but the purse can. Listen,
proud scorner, you must get learning first and then despise it; if you want to
play the strong man, first acquire the object of your scorn; unless perhaps
your boast is that you are imitating the apostles in this also, that your   10
reputation of virtue rests on the relinquishment of desire, and not on the
kind of thing relinquished. Come now, suppose there were no difference
between wealth and learning: the apostles were indifferent to poverty or to
the hope of greater wealth, and that without envy; stripped bare themselves, they did not envy the riches of others. You have not even a little   15
learning, which you could claim to despise, but a great hopelessness,
because learning is a matter of great difficulty and needs infinite toil, and
your brains are heavier than lead.

'Finally, supposing you were right to despise learning, why should
you envy others? If you envy, that means you wish for something; and if   20
you wish, why do you not come down with us into the arena, and try to be
happy with us instead of being wretched because of us? Strive, win,
triumph. But lazy men see how our learning is hedged in on all sides by
hard labour and nightly vigils; if they were equal to making light of it, they
would not talk so boastfully and stupidly about despising erudition. When   25
I have mastered the whole of literature, that will be the time when I shall be
right in despising it, not that I shall lose interest in it, but so as to avoid
arrogance; and I will see to it that, though I excel all others in learning, I shall
not put myself before anyone, not even the stupidest. I shall frankly encourage modest efforts; I shall congratulate the victor and not envy him. The   30
greater I am, the greater will be my humility – the more I know, the more
gently I shall tolerate the ignorance of others, and bearing with all I shall
take care that no one has anything to bear from me. I shall vie with the
studious in learning, and with all men in gentleness, courtesy, modesty; I
shall conduct myself so that it is clear that I am better for being wiser. The   35
more others look up to me, the more I shall look down on myself. Finally,
when I have tried my best to learn everything, I shall not seem to myself to
know anything.

* * * * *

6 Vestal virgins] Nuns
18 heavier than lead] *Adagia* prolegomena xiii (LB II 12D)

'This is the way in which our scorn may be praiseworthy, if we are scorning not others' learning but our own. Looking at it this way, not erudition only but virtue itself is to be despised, and the thing above all to be scorned is scorn. Augustine "despised" heathen culture in this way, but only after becoming a prince of learning in this field. Jerome's "contempt" for the writings of Cicero and Plato did not debar him from an excellent mastery of them, and he used them continuously. Basil and Chrysostom were so neglectful of the orators' and philosophers' talents that you have only to look at the documents to see that they knew all about them!

'To sum up, why on earth should these fellows glory in their scorn? Is it because, like the fox in the fable, they have vain longings? The fox began to be disgusted by the ass's testicles only when it had stopped hoping; "what vile food," it said, "I could never have eaten that!" But if we are to call things by their right names, this is sheer envy, not scorn. Or perhaps the reason is that they are weaklings, frightened by the difficulty of work, without which there is no approach either to virtue or to learning. Anyone can see that this is the attitude of a lazy man, and a spiteful one too. Or perhaps they have an innate uncouthness which makes them hate the elegance of literary studies? This seems to me not the attitude of a pious Christian (as they say), but of a clodhopping and actually brutish mind. Now let us have a little modesty, please; let them give way to those who are trying for better things. Let it be enough for them to acknowledge their own ignorance to themselves, and not go on making unnecessary trouble for us, and looking down on people they should respect and admire; and if they find nothing better or sweeter than sleep and idleness, let them show more justice as regards others; they can just leave the gloomy night-watchings and crazy toil to us, seeing that we have not the slightest envy of their delights. It is a worse kind of envy to be galled by other people's hard work.

**It is absurd to disapprove of anything simply because
it was discovered by the ancients**

'With this vinegar running through them, it is amazing how noisily they attack us, saying we are not Christians but heathens, idolaters, and more noxious than the heathens themselves. They ask if a person can really be considered Christian when he takes so much trouble and finds so much

* * * * *

5 Jerome's ... them] The irony of this passage is increased in the 1520 version.
13 vile food] A variant of the fox and the grapes? Cf Stith Thompson *Motif-Index of Folk-Literature* (Helsinki 1932–6) J 2066.1.

LB X 1710A / ASD I-1 78

delight in irreligious exercises invented by wicked men to satisfy their
pride, when he finds all his repose in these things and makes them into his
leisure occupation, his business, his one solace? And is it not obvious to
everyone that this is sacrilege, if a man who has once enrolled himself in the
ranks of Christ's soldiers, once been admitted and pledged himself to the   5
service of Christ as his leader, should desert to the enemy, the spirits of evil,
and have dealing with the worshippers of idols? Surely those people deal
with idols, they say, who delight to be called Ciceronian as speakers,
Virgilian or Horatian as poets, or as philosophers Aristotelian, Academic,
Stoic, Epicurean? This is the Chrysippean argument that you have heard,   10
the two-horned syllogism. You see how they go about to tie you up all
unawares in this sophistical trap. I see there is some need of that famous
hellebore of Carneades. What are you saying, you anti-Chrysippeans? Is
everything which came out of the heathen world always to be bad, and
forbidden to Christians? So we are not to be allowed to take over anything   15
discovered by the pagans unless we cease forthwith to be Christian?

'In that case you had better preach to the carpenters and warn them not
to dare to use any of their saws, axes, adzes, gimlets, nor their wedges,
rules, plumblines, centring, nor straight edges. Should you ask why, I'll tell
you: this carpenter's art and its tools were invented by Daedalus, a heathen.   20
The blacksmiths had better stop – it was the Cyclops, men-monsters, who
discovered how to work iron. Let no one work in bronze – they say this was
first taught by the Chalybes; and pottery by Choroebus, so the potters can
have a holiday. A certain Boethus was the first cobbler, so let no Christian
sew together a shoe; Niceas was the first fuller, so no one must wash the dirt   25
out of his clothes. The Egyptians invented weaving: back we go to dressing
in skins. The Lydians invented dyeing, so let no one tint the wool shorn
from the sheep. Cadmus the Phoenician found out how to cast metal, so the
furnaces had better cool off. As for sailors, we must get them to vow, if
possible, that they will not use their customary tackle, and coachmen must   30
be warned not to imitate Erichthonius. Painters, carvers, glaziers, every
kind of craftsman, in short, must find some other way of earning their living
if they can, to avoid defilement of themselves and their families by these
heathen arts; and if they cannot they must starve, rather than give up being
Christians. Suppose we inspire the soldiers too – very pious fellows – with a   35

* * * * *

11 syllogism ... Carneades] See Jerome Ep 69.2; above 27:14–15nn; *Adagia* I viii 51.
17 carpenters ...] The catalogue of ancient inventors in this paragraph comes
from Pliny *Naturalis historia* 7.56.196–202.
31 Erichthonius] The fourth king of Athens, said to have invented chariots and
harnessed horses to draw them

religious scruple against using shields, breastplates, helmets, swords, greaves, crests, bows, arrows, lances, and spears? They ascribe the invention of all these things to the wicked. But who could bear to take away from the girls their devotion to Minerva and their tools at the same time – their bundles of wool, their distaffs, spindles, shuttles, and looms – none of these having been invented by Christians? And then the tillers of the soil – I see that you must put them out of work even if you starve for it: the plough was invented by Osiris; from now on let no one dare to turn the soil, or sow it when turned, or reap it when sown, for they say all this was due to Saturn. No one may cultivate the vine, for that was devised by Bacchus. No one may drink wine neat, or even watered down – it was Staphylus who demonstrated this. Sick people must not send for the doctor: medicine is an invention of Apollo. And these were not merely wicked men but, according to popular belief, demons.

'So for you it is permissible to use things invented by evil spirits, but for us it will be forbidden to use the works of studious men? The fact is that those people are not ashamed (even those who want to figure as dialecticians and theologians) to throw up against the studious a kind of reproach which, if tried with diggers and reapers in the field, would bring the yokels out to finish them off with mattocks and scythes. If we are to be forbidden to use the inventions of the pagan world, what shall we have left I ask you, in the fields, in the towns, in churches and houses and workshops, at home, at war, in private and in public? To such an extent is it true that we Christians have nothing we have not inherited from the pagans. The fact that we write in Latin, speak it in one way or another, comes to us from the pagans; they discovered writing, they invented the use of speech.

'These people say, "Am I to carry books by damned men in my hand and in my bosom, and read them over again and reverence them? Virgil is burning in hell, and is a Christian to sing his poems?" As if many a Christian were not burning there too, whose writings – if any good ones survive – would not be shunned for that reason by anybody. Really, who can bear this capricious way of sitting in judgment, waving a Mercurial wand and sending off whoever they wish to hell, and calling up whom they wish to heaven? I will not enter here on that quarrelsome discussion about the pagans, which is unworthy even of women; it is not for us to discuss the damnation of the heathen, those, I mean, who lived before our faith. If we wished to indulge in guesswork, I could easily prove that the great men

* * * * *

11 Staphylus] A son of Silenus
32 Mercurial wand] A reference to Hermes Psychopompus, escort of the dead in Greek mythology

LB X 1711B / ASD I-1 80

among the pagans are saved, or else no one is; let us concern ourselves with
the fineness of their teaching, rather than ask ourselves how well they lived.
The judge orders stage-actors to be heard as witnesses, even though anyone
who knows their manner of life condemns it. The books of Origen, censured as heretical in many passages, are read by the Christian church with   5
profit to scholarship; and yet we shun the divine writings of men on whose
moral character we cannot pass judgment without the greatest impertinence. Or, to put it better, one may judge them favourably with credit, but
one could not criticize them without great fault.

'"Be off!" they say. "Am I to let myself be called a Ciceronian or a   10
Platonist, when I have once and for all chosen to be called a Christian?"
Why not call yourself a monster of a man? If you can truly be called a
Sardanapalus when you copy his abandoned luxury, or a Gnatho because
you are a flatterer, or a Thraso when you are a stupid boaster, why should
not someone who imitates Cicero's language be called a Ciceronian, or   15
why, if I try to emulate something of Virgil's should I not be called Virgilian? You arrogate to yourself those barbarous titles and love to be called
Albertist, Thomist, Scotist, Occamist, Durandist as long as you take these
names from Christians. For my part, I will allow myself to be called after
any pagan so long as he was deeply learned or supremely eloquent; nor   20
shall I go back on this declaration, if only the pagan teaches me more
excellent things than a Christian.

'To bring this discussion to an end at last: if our opponents were not
made blinder than moles by their own envy, they would see what is clear
even to the blind – they would see that among the inventions of the pagans   25
there are distinctions to be made; some of them are useless, doubtful,
unwholesome, while others are extremely useful, health-giving, and even
necessary. Let us leave the bad things to them; why should we not take over
the good for ourselves? This is what a Christian man should do, a prudent
and studious man. But what we do, heaven help us, is just the opposite: we   30
imitate the vices of the heathen all the time, in fact we beat them at lust,
avarice, ambition, superstition: but the one thing it would be right to
imitate, their learning, is the one thing we reject, whether from stupidity or
pride I cannot yet tell. For if we have inherited from them, without doing
wrong, things which were to be of general usefulness to us, what is there to   35

* * * * *

13 Sardanapalus] King of Assyria, notorious for effeminate luxury
13 Gnatho ... Thraso] Thraso is a braggart soldier in Terence's *Ennuchus*, and
   Gnatho (see 32:10n) his flattering parasite.
19 names] Followers of the medieval Schoolmen Albertus Magnus, Thomas
   Aquinas, Duns Scotus, William of Occam, Durandus

hinder us from doing the same in the case of their arts? Nothing more useful
or more excellent than these exists in the affairs of men, if we are to believe
Jerome.

The pagans perfected systems of knowledge according to the divine plan, not for us to scorn them, but for our use

'When I look a little more closely at the wonderful arrangement, the harmony
as they call it, of things, it always seems to me – and not to me only: many of
the weightiest authors have thought the same – that it was not without
divine guidance that the business of discovering systems of knowledge was
given to the pagans. For the great and eternal Disposer, who is wisdom
itself, establishes all things with consummate skill, differentiates them
with beautiful play of interchange, and orders them with perfect rightness,
so that each balances another in a marvellous way; nor does he allow
anything to move at random in all the immense variety of the world. It was
he who willed that the Golden Age in which he had chosen to be born was
to be sovereign over all epochs which came before or followed after; it
pleased him that whatever existed in nature should be put to use for
increasing the happiness and glory of that time. He himself promised that
this should be done: "I, if I be lifted up from the earth," he says, "will draw
all unto me." Here it seems to me that he most aptly uses the word *traho*, "I
draw," so that one may understand that all things, whether hostile or
heathen or in any other way far removed from him, must be drawn, even if
they do not follow, even against their will, to the service of Christ. What of
that great universal harmony, which in the eyes of St Augustine meant that
not even bad things were created without intention? All those allegories,
signs, and mysteries existing from the beginning of the world – in which
direction did they point? Why, to the century of Christ. What about the
whole Mosaic law, all those rites and ceremonies, those forms of worship,
those promises and prophecies? Is not Paul the witness that all these things
happened to them for examples? Not to speak of the transfer of empires,
what was the purpose of "founding the Roman nation with such vast
effort," and through such great disasters and bloodstained victories sub-

* * * * *

3 Jerome] Cf Jerome Ep 53.5–6.
18 Golden Age] The fourth *Eclogue* of Virgil, prophesying the return of the
  primeval Age of Gold, was applied by Christian writers to the birth of Christ.
22 he says] John 12:32
32 Paul] 1 Cor 10:11
34 founding] Virgil *Aeneid* 1.33

jugating the entire world to the City which held sway? Was it not according
to the divine plan, so that when the Christian religion was born, it might
spread abroad the more easily into different parts of the world, diffused as it
were from one head into the separate members? And again, what was his
intention in allowing almost the whole earth to be entangled with such   5
lunatic, scandalous religions? Why, so that when the One arose, it would
overturn all the others with the utmost glory. Nothing fine is ever done
without struggle.

'It was Greece, devoted to study, which discovered the arts; then
Latium entered into rivalry with her, and was the victor as far as concerns   10
war, but barely equalled her achievements in literature and oratory. Some
concerned themselves with searching out the hidden causes of things;
others, bound by the fetters of Prometheus, observed the regular revolu-
tions of the heavenly lights. There were those who tried to explore divine
mysteries; one discovered methods of argument and another laws of ora-   15
tory; some portrayed the customs of men with great sagacity, and for some
their great concern was to hand on to posterity the memory of past deeds. In
law, in philosophy, how the ancients laboured! Why did all this happen? So
that we on our arrival could hold them in contempt? Was it not rather that
the best religion should be adorned and supported by the finest studies?   20

'Everything in the pagan world that was valiantly done, brilliantly
said, ingeniously thought, diligently transmitted, had been prepared by
Christ for his society. He it was who supplied the intellect, who added the
zest for inquiry, and it was through him alone that they found what they
sought. Their age produced this harvest of creative work, not so much for   25
them as for us; just as every region cannot supply every commodity, nor (as
Virgil says) does every land grow everything, so it seems to me that every
century is allotted its own gifts. Many of the philosophers wore out their
lives and their brains in seeking the highest good; but the real highest
good, the perfect gift, was reserved by Christ for his own time. However he   30
did not intend all the rest to be useless and done to no purpose. We see with
our own eyes how in material things nature takes care that no portion of
time shall slip away uselessly. Look at the trees (the sight of them suggests
this example to me): in early spring they supply sap to nourish the leaves,
and now you see the leaves are joined by flowers, and how much pleasure it   35
gives us to look at them. As summer comes, these little flowers swell out
gradually into the pulp of the fruit; in autumn, the trees will stand weighed

* * * * *

10 Latium] Italy
27 Virgil] *Eclogues* 4.39 prophesies that in the Golden Age every land will bear all
   fruits.

down with ripe apples, and, as soon as they let them fall, once again that
season which passes from autumn into winter is spent in making new
shoots for the coming summer. Even winter itself is not idle, but re-
establishes things in an interval of quiet; the same effect is produced by the
revolving of the heavenly bodies, disposed in such varying ways. There is a
great discord in nature which is the completest concord. All things, both
particular and universal, are carried in the same direction; they all face the
same way, tend towards one thing. So while Christ, the greatest and best of
disposers, allocated to his own century in a special way the recognition of
the highest good, he gave the centuries immediately preceding a privilege
of their own: they were to reach the thing nearest to the highest good, that
is, the summit of learning. What could man acquire, by virtuous striving,
that is more valuable than knowledge? Indeed, on this point God was
willing to consult the laziness or the leisure of the Christians, by taking
away a great deal of the hard work from us, who were likely to have much to
do elsewhere. It is much easier to master a thing which is already worked
out to the last detail than to invent it. If they had not sown the seed of letters,
perhaps we should have had nothing to reap; what should we have discovered by ourselves, we who have never added anything to their inventions,
but have damaged many of them and thrown them all into confusion? This
makes it all the more ungracious, in fact spiteful, that we should not be
willing to accept things freely offered, which were to be of so much use to
us, and which cost them so dearly; and we not only refuse a splendid gift,
but treat the giver of the gift with contempt, instead of the gratitude we owe
him.'

It is ignorance rather than erudition which makes men insolent

Here I said: 'You speak most learnedly and truly, my dear Batt; and yet I
could hardly believe that there was anybody so bereft of human reason as to
think that the whole of literature should be separated from religion, provided it be Christian.'

'As if there were any Christian erudition,' said Batt, 'which is not the
very reverse of erudition! I am not speaking of the mysteries of our religion,
but of invented systems of learning. If we are willing to admit the truth, can
we say that since the time of those great pagans we have invented anything
new, which was not at the same time crude? How could we be good at
discovering anything when we are so bad at preserving the discoveries of

* * * * *

17 detail] *Adagia* I v 91

others? In my opinion there is no erudition in existence except what is
secular (this is their name for the learning of the ancients) or at least
founded on and informed by secular literature; I would allow this to be
called Christian (if we rule out perverse and wicked prejudice), although I
meet a number of people who are religious in such a doltish fashion that   5
they think little even of that so-called Christian, that is, ecclesiastical,
learning. ''What does it matter,'' they say, ''if we are not theologians? If you
know Christ well it is enough; you need not know anything else. Eternal life
is promised to the innocent, not to the learned. Am I to be condemned for it
if I have no very lofty understanding of the writings of Paul? if I don't grasp 10
Jerome's style of composition? if I have never even read Augustine and
Ambrose, and don't even understand the Gospel?'' You dunderhead, does
it matter if you don't understand yourself, and whether you are a camel or a
man? ''Don't worry, even the beasts will go to heaven.'' What a race of men,
to be sure – not only stupid, but irreligious. If only they did know Christ,   15
those who congratulate themselves on knowing nothing of letters! But it
often happens that people who wish to be credited with simplicity in this
line are the knowingest of rogues in worldly affairs; however my business
is not with them at present. I introduced this aside so that it will not
surprise you if those people detest our kind of learning, which I have just   20
described, when they also despise the Gospel. As I have just said, I am not
dealing with these, but with people who want to appear learned in matters
relating to the church, and yet abstain from all secular learning, like a Jew
shunning unclean food. They have forgotten what Paul said, ''To the pure
all things are pure.'' For my part, I consider the learning of these people so   25
narrow that it is not learning at all, and worse than any sort of ignorance.
These are the ones who detest our whole body of knowledge, and call it bad,
pagan, and irreligious; what *they* know, they claim to have received not
from the studies of men but from heaven. I am even told it is commonly
remarked that if anyone is particularly well versed in literature he must be   30
particularly immoral. And this is an insult which touches not only poets
and orators but theologians, lawyers, dialecticians, and other studious
men, and should be confuted by them all.

   'If learning is bad, is it bad in itself or because of something else? If
because of something else, why do we confine our reproaches solely to   35
erudition? If it is bad in itself, why do the most serious authors judge it to be
among the most honourable and valuable things? Why is it ranked above
wealth, which is not in itself bad? Furthermore, truth can never be bad in
itself, and since the liberal disciplines are truths, they must be good. If

* * * * *

24 Paul] Titus 1:15

knowledge is good in itself, ignorance is bad; if knowledge is bad, it should
be avoided, although if we listen to the voice of Nature, who would not
rather be entirely knowledgeable than entirely ignorant? This is where our
dialecticians begin to be barbarians. We do not rebuke learning, they say,
as learning, but because it makes people wily, conceited, unmanageable,   5
arrogant, and supercilious. They ask, ''What are you aiming at, if not to get
away from the common herd, to stand out from the rest, to be lauded and
celebrated and to treat us and our like as mere animals?'' This tells you what
is really biting these sanctimonious people: they are unwilling to be despised. They want to rule and lead, not to be led, not to obey, and so they   10
come to think it is essential for keeping the peace that no one shall exist who
can correct the ignorance of others. I think you can see that slander against
learning proceeds from nothing else than pride. But it would be most unfair
if a purblind man were to accuse the sun because its light irritated him.
''Knowledge puffs up,'' they say, ''charity builds.'' Arrogance is a defect,   15
but is it a defect of knowledge or of ourselves? They will not dare, I think, to
say it is a defect of knowledge, because in that case no one would ever have
been erudite who was not arrogant, and the more learned anyone became,
the haughtier it would make him. Such a statement is not only absurd, it is
manifestly slanderous. Against whom? Against Augustine, against Jerome,   20
against many others – it would be wicked to accuse them of pride because
they were great authors. ''But I am talking of profane learning,'' you say.
That is what we accept, what we admire and reverence as we find it in these
princes of the Christian religion whom I have just named – a kind of
learning very different from yours, you who profess to have the teaching of   25
the church. Another point: if it is through our own fault that we grow
haughty and not because of the fault of things round us, which is right: to
correct our own character or to blame our environment, with no justification? Would you not be behaving more modestly, you who teach modesty
to others, if you were to admit your ignorance frankly and not work up a   30
slander against the most valuable things, merely in order to protect your
own vice? In everything else you are clumsy, but this slander finds you
eloquent. ''Secular learning,'' you say, ''supplies the material for arrogance.'' Who denies that? But that material can be procured from anywhere
– even from the best and holiest things. So is it the things themselves which   35
are to be blamed, or you yourself and your wretched misuse of the best? A
mind which is inherently arrogant seizes every opportunity to swagger.
How many vices are encouraged by money? Yet no one accuses it of being
bad; it is the spirit of those who use it badly which is reproved. What can

* * * * *

15 charity] 1 Cor 8:1

there be which is so good that it does not sometimes provide an occasion for evil? Not fasting, nor alms, nor chastity, nor virtue itself. The philosophers have their pride, the poets are pleased with themselves. Tell me, you, are there no proud theologians? Is there any haughtiness anywhere more arrogant than theirs? But who would dare to bring an accusation against sacred theology! Plenty of them are proud on this account, yet the fault is not theology's but theirs. Are there no cases of illiterate insolence? What makes such people overweening? Why, their own ignorance. What would they do then, if they had learnt letters?

Ignorance is the mother of pride; it is from learning, on the contrary, that modesty is born

'What could be more untrue than to say that literature makes men wily, conceited, and supercilious? If by wiliness you mean prudence, I do not disagree, since we are commanded by the advice of the Gospel to imitate the wisdom of serpents. As to superciliousness, anyone can see the absurdity there. What is it that leads those hard and boorish men towards a more humane type of life, towards a kinder outlook and gentler ways? Is it not letters? It is they which mould our character, quiet our passions, check our uncontrolled impulses, give mildness to our minds in place of savagery. When they talk of superciliousness, do they mean that we refuse to admire their barbarism? Or that we are unable to enjoy the silly nonsense of utter blockheads, and that we do not treasure dung as if it were diamonds? Is this the behaviour of a supercilious man, or is it not rather that of a sane one, able to distinguish the worst from the best? As to modesty, I think just as St Jerome does when he quotes the opinion of some Greek writer or other (and to me he seems to have thought rightly and written elegantly) – that inexperience produces self-confidence, but knowledge is accompanied by fear. I perceive that Quintilian saw this clearly: "the less a person's mind is worth," he says, "the more he tries to aggrandize himself and increase his importance." We see many people who seem to themselves consummate scholars before they have any idea of what they know or do not know. By the time they have persuaded themselves, and through their folly made a bid for a certain reputation for erudition among the common herd, it is inevitable that they should have no little esteem for themselves and should

* * * * *

18 serpents] Matt 10:16
28 Jerome] Jerome Ep 73.10
31 Quintilian] 2.3.8

despise others. They boldly teach what they do not know; they write, they
speak, they explain; there is nothing they leave unattempted, nothing they
do not dare; relying on the applause of their supporters, they pour scorn on
the judgment of the learned and on their fewness in number; they are a
pestilential race of men, and their mental outlook is in keeping with their
stupidity.'

Willem said, 'You will excuse me, Batt, according to our agreement, if I
delay the course of your argument by a few words. If I am not mistaken, the
things you are saying cancel each other out. You say these people are
pleased with themselves and despise others for the very reason that they
think themselves learned; but that is in itself a proof that erudition produces pride. What other reason have they for self-conceit than knowledge, a
very little knowledge, almost none?'

'None is the word,' replied Batt; 'it is ignorance, not knowledge,
which puffs them up. That conviction of being competent carries with it a
certain self-assurance which is the very acme of incompetence. Socrates
spoke truly when he said, "There can be no greater ignorance than to think
you know what you don't know." If they were really learned, as they think
they are, they would at once begin to admire others and think less of
themselves. It is no wonder if what they conceive is mostly wind, since they
are quite empty. Solid worth is self-contained, and is measured by its own
value and not 'by the opinion of others. So if those people were more
learned, they would be more modest too. I would not ask you to take my
word for this, were it not that we ourselves experience the same thing. It is
exactly what happens at the beginning of our studies, when we have stood
on the threshold, as they say, and made our bow to the liberal arts, and then
we are at once carried away and are much more pleased with ourselves at
that rudimentary stage than later on, when much experience has given us
some exact knowledge of many things. So it is with young people – the less
prudence they have, the more confident they are. Why is this? Because we
do not yet know this one thing – how much we do not know; and it may be
that Nature has deliberately implanted this vacuity in us, to make us
attempt great labours, spurred on by a touch of vainglory. Who would settle
down to such unending nightly toil, if he did not promise himself great
achievements? I am far from thinking like the Stoics on this subject: they
consider all emotional impulses to be not only superfluous but actively
harmful, whereas I should see them as tutors, attached to souls striving

* * * * *

16 Socrates] Plato *Apology* 29B
26 threshold] *Adagia* I ix 91
35 this subject] Cf Erasmus *Enchiridion* chaps 4–5.

towards virtue. This confidence, this ambition, if it is not immoderate, can be seen to have its uses in the case of beginners, by applying a spur, a goad to our minds; you will hardly find anyone who needs a curb! But when we have learnt more sense, we laugh at that wish for glory and condemn it. As far as I am concerned, I confess that as a boy I was a proper smatterer, and thought highly of myself when I had scarcely taken a sip, as they say, of these studies. Now after so many years – for I am entering on my twenty-ninth – I am less and less satisfied with myself every day, and I embrace that saying of Socrates', "One thing only I know, that I know nothing." In those days I thought I had gained the heart of the fortress; now I think I have not got beyond the outer court or, in the words of the Greek proverb, pro-gressed beyond the parsley stage. Then nothing pleased me, however ac-curate, polished, and perfect; now there is hardly anything I do not admire. Then I did not wait for provocation to challenge everyone; now I am like the ageing Milo, I venture less and I tremble more. From this I easily deduce that, when my erudition becomes greater than it is now, I shall be even less satisfied with it. If it is like this with me, who am a bit of a windbag anyway (among friends one can speak plainly), what do you think is likely to happen to people with better minds?'

'I agree with you about this, Jacob,' said Willem; 'you have learnedly expressed something I recognize in myself, and I declare there are many instances of it to be seen. Minds are ripened by erudition, and it makes them mellower and gentler.'

'Yes, indeed,' said Batt, 'and countless examples are to be found everywhere, whether we look at our own times or at those of the ancients. What could one mention or imagine more arrogant than the idea of teaching others, with supreme confidence, what one does not know? This is what our anti-academicians do all the time – they know nothing and teach everything. Lord love me! It makes me quite sick when I look at the titles of some people's books and discover what affectation and self-glorification they represent. Although they may have vomited up nothing but crass barbarism, listen, I beg you, to the splendid titles they adorn their nonsense with: you will easily gauge how affectionately these apes love their off-

* * * * *

6 a sip] 'Touched them with my lips': *Adagia* I ix 92, 93
11 proverb] *Adagia* I x 89, where it is explained that in antiquity it was customary to plant parsley at the entrance to a garden
15 Milo] The text reads 'Milium senescentem,' which is evidently an error for 'Milonem senescentem.' See Cicero *De senectute* 9.27, where Milo in old age (*senex*) mourns his lost strength.

spring. One calls his ravings the *Little Jewel*, another *Pearl*; this one chooses
the title *Flower-Garden*, that one *Rose-Bower*, yet in the middle of it, good
God, you will not find anything but thistles and tares. There was one who
gave his book the title of *Mirror* and one who dares to call a complete
collection of errors the *Catholicon*. It was sillier still to choose *Mammetrectus*,   5
as if holding out a promise of hen's milk. Some call their books *Summa* and
Summarum summa, as if the reader were not in need of another writer after
procuring himself such expanses of nothing. You can observe the same
impudence in the titles the authors attribute to themselves, so magnificent
that it would seem they had something remarkable and superhuman to say.   10
They do not quote Basil, Origen, Chrysostom, and men like them, or if they
do it is with contempt, censoriously; but when they jingle those names of
theirs, Holy Doctors, Irrefragable Doctors, Most Subtle Doctors, Seraphic
Doctors, they think they are announcing something which should take
precedence over even the majesty of the Gospel. If scholars refused to   15
tolerate this leaning for fancy titles among the ancients and the truly
learned, who can stand it among these barbarians, who seem to be born for
the purpose of polluting literature? Who would not, as the proverb says,
find a beam to hang himself from, when he sees the libraries stuffed with
books like these and the schools ringing with them, and finds that these are   20
the books from which sermons are made, from which are extracted the
doctrines that rule the world, the books by which we are rated as Christians
or not? What is more, they never hesitate a moment as they hand out these
things; they have no doubts; they settle everything; they dispense instruction wholesale. You would think they were not teaching but legislating.   25
There is modesty for you – the sort which is acquired by slothful ignorance!

* * * * *

 1 ravings] These titles of devotional handbooks are also parodied by Rabelais in
the 'library of St Victor,' *Pantagruel* 7. The *Floretus* was a poem of John of
Garland, often attacked by Erasmus.
 4 *Mirror*] The famous one was the *Speculum mundi* of Vincent of Beauvais
(thirteenth century), but there were many other books with this name.
 5 *Catholicon*] See 34:2n.
 6 hen's milk] *Adagia* I vi 3: 'a rare discovery.' From this point to 'the majesty of
the Gospel' is an addition of 1520.
 6 *Summa*] Erasmus can hardly be referring to Thomas Aquinas, whom he
admired as far as he could admire a 'modern' theologian without Greek, but to
the many subsequent books called *Summa*.
14 Doctors] The 'Irrefragable Doctor' is Alexander of Hales (fifteenth century),
author of a *Summa universae theologiae*; the 'Most Subtle' is Duns Scotus
(thirteenth-fourteenth centuries); the 'Seraphic' St Bonaventure (thirteenth
century).
19 hang himself] *Adagia* I x 21

LB X 1716E / ASD I-1 89

How much better it would be to imitate the humility of the Academic
philosophers; these people are not worthy to be compared to them, and yet
the philosophers, who professed to know nothing, preferred to argue about
everything with modesty rather than confidently assert. I am not unaware
that some people disapprove of this class of philosopher, but to me it seems   5
preferable to any other, for reasons which may perhaps appear elsewhere.

'If we turn to early times, what could be further from arrogance than
the learned and eloquent mind of Socrates, who was never ashamed of
being taught, even as an old man? He thought it no shame to be taught
rhetoric – a masculine art too – by a woman, Aspasia. He was well on in   10
years when he took to learning lyre-playing from a teacher called Conus, if I
am not mistaken. And then there is that noble saying, "Only this I know,
that I know nothing," and I ask you, does that seem to come from a
conceited man or a most modest one? It was because of this modesty that he
deserved to be judged wise by Apollo, he and he alone, because while   15
others imagined they knew what they did not know, this man was not only
wiser but more modest. This is clearly borne out by his discourses (as they
are given in the dialogues of Plato): they all reflect the speech of a studious
and penetrating mind, but more that of an inquirer than a teacher. If only
the philosophasters of our time, who complain of our haughtiness, would   20
choose to take as a model the modesty of that father of philosophy, rather
than the rash garrulity of a Gorgias! They do not even understand the words
they themselves use, but they have the utmost assurance in deciding every
case, approving and disapproving, instructing and prescribing. But let us
follow up the example of some others.   25

'Was there ever anyone of more penetration or more learning than

* * * * *

  1 Academic philosophers] Followers of Carneades the Sceptic
  6 elsewhere] This view of the young Erasmus links him with Montaigne
(*Apologie de Raimond Sebond, Essais* 2.12). If the remark foreshadows a work on
scepticism, it was never to be written. However Erasmus did correspond with
Melanchthon on the subject of Academic scepticism. See Allen Ep 3120 introduction; and Charles B. Schmitt *Cicero Scepticus* (Leiden 1972) 59, who also
quotes the *Praise of Folly*, where Folly calls the Academic philosophers 'her
own' and 'the least insolent of philosophers' (LB IV 450C).
  9 old man] Plato *Menexenus* 235E
11 Conus] Plato *Menexenus* 253E; see also Cicero *Ad familiares* 9.22.3.
15 judged wise] Plato *Apology* 21A–E
20 philosophasters] St Augustine uses this word in *De civitate Dei* 2.27.
22 Gorgias] This comparison comes from Cicero *De finibus* 2.1, and the following
passage about Pythagoras is from Cicero *Tusculan Disputations* 5.3.7–9. Gorgias was a Greek sophist (c 485–375 BC); one of Plato's dialogues bears his
name.

Pythagoras? He surpassed earlier philosophers in modesty as he conquered
them in learning. Before that time they used to be called *sophi*, that is, "wise
men," and he was the first to refuse this overweening title, preferring to call
himself *philosopher*, that is, "lover of wisdom," rather than wise. Plato was
charged by some people with pride, because of a certain divine sublimity of
mind; but how modest he was! We read that when he had drunk in all that
his preceptor had to teach him, he set out as if this had not happened to
range over land and sea in quest of what he might learn. "A master in
Athens, and a powerful one" (I am glad to quote from Jerome), "when his
teaching was ringing through the schools of the Academy, he became a
pilgrim and a pupil, preferring to learn humbly what others taught rather
than imperiously obtrude his own teaching." What about Solon and
Herodotus, whom we see already old, wandering to all the corners of the
earth, on journeys that were certainly laborious, like busy merchants of
wisdom? Theophrastus, easily foremost among philosophers, is said to
have envied stags and ravens when he was dying, because nature granted
them so long a life and man so short. And he, who by common consent was
held to have reached consummate wisdom, mourned that his life was
ending just when he had begun to see what it was to be wise. Where did
these great minds get this great modesty – from inexperience, as those
people make out, or from some distinctive learning? Who ever disagreed
with giving Virgil the palm among the poets? But did not his modesty
contrive that while he lived he was held inferior to many less learned? Virgil
was disturbed by the censures and witticisms of Philiscus, a mediocre
orator, and attacked by the silly Pero, in slanderous verses, and praised by
the greatest of orators, Cicero; and he accepted the gibes of the one and the
praise of the other with equal modesty. What shall I say about the
churchmen? Jerome is far and away the greatest of these, and with his
incredible eagerness for learning when did he ever reject a teacher? A Jew?
A heretic? Latin? Greek? Hebrew? He was immensely learned but thought
it finer to learn than to teach. Who was more scholarly than Augustine? But
who could be more modest? When he had been for many years a bishop and
a doctor, he not only declared himself ready to be taught by a churchman of

*   *   *   *   *

9 Jerome] Jerome Ep 53.1
15 Theophrastus] Cicero *Tusculan Disputations* 3.28.69
24 Philiscus] Philistus. See next note.
26 Cicero] It appears that Erasmus was mistaken here. This information came to
   him from Donatus 61 and 77, where the names are given as Philistus and Paro.
   Cicero died before Virgil's earliest works were known. See ASD I-1 92n.

LB X 1717C / ASD I-1 91

lower rank, but was not ashamed to confess his own errors and to write a
retractation of his own books. Who among the critics of our time has ever
imitated this humility? Are they more wary or more learned than Augustine? Or are they not more impudent the more ignorant they are? Whatever
they write, they expect it to be taken as true because they have written it;   5
they wish their mere fancies to be accepted as divine oracles. I am speaking
here of those who have a little learning, for I never yet met a truly learned
man in whom I did not observe a singular modesty. ''The proud and
arrogant shall be called unlearned,'' according to the saying of the Hebrew
sage, and not learned; and ''the fool is wiser in his own conceit than seven   10
men who can render a reason.''

'Beware then, whoever you are, who put on a pious face and charge
me with immodesty; that modesty of yours might turn out to be immodesty
in the highest degree. I ask you, by the Muses, which is the prouder, the
rich man who invites others to partake of his wealth, or you, who are so   15
proud of your beggarliness that you seem to yourself to be a princeling, for
the very reason that you have nothing? Which is the prouder, he who uses
his knowledge for the glory of Christ, or you who condemn the teaching of
others and scorn your neighbour, in case the ignorant folk you sell your
wares to should think you less than a demigod? Finally, granted that both   20
parties are satisfied with themselves, which is the more arrogant – the man
who is exalted by his own learning or you who congratulate yourself
impudently on your ignorance? The former raises no objections if people
are unwilling to learn better things, but you raise a great storm if anyone
dares to teach what you and your companions have not learnt. He is given   25
confidence by his eloquence; you are in high feather because you are
tongue-tied. Which is the prouder? He makes his way through all the
systems of learning so as to become truly learned, but you, after a hurried
taste of grammar, and poor grammar at that, with the hasty addition of
three syllogisms and a few Thomist or Scotist questions, you leap at once   30
into the arena, ready to do battle with anyone about anything. You pattern
of modesty, do you censure others for their arrogance? But while I argue

* * * * *

1 lower rank] Literally 'by a bishop of one year' (*anniculo episcopo*; see Valla
  Elegantiae ASD I-4 222). He means Jerome; see Augustine Ep 67.2. Jerome was
  not a bishop. Erasmus says Augustine was Jerome's superior in nothing but
  the honour of the episcopate (*Opuscula* 167:905–7).
8 The proud] Prov 21:24
10 the fool] Prov 26:16
14 I ask you] The text from here to the end of the paragraph is an addition of *1520*.
24 raise a great storm] *Adagia* I iii 81: 'to mix heaven and earth'
26 high feather] *Adagia* I viii 69: 'it adds a crest'

about immodesty I am forgetting to be modest myself; I see I have been
pushing my argument further than necessary on so obvious a subject. To
conclude, I am so fully convinced that, when I see an arrogant and self-
conceited man, I cannot believe that he has deep learning. And so the thing
which they think productive of pride seems to me simply in the nature of a
preventive lest we should be proud.

How we are to understand the saying of Paul: 'Knowledge puffs up'

'They return to the charge, however, in their accustomed manner, and
constantly repeat from St Paul "Knowledge puffs up; charity builds." "The
apostle was not lying," they say; "knowledge puffs up." No one denies
that, but ignorance puffs up too. What do you say, you who are theologians
and ignorant all the same? You have selected just a single sentence out of
Paul, and it does not enter your heads that in another place he says,
"Though I be rude in speech, yet not in knowledge." Have you not heard
his boast that he learnt the Law at the feet of Gamaliel? Or his request for
books written on vellum? Whatever did Paul mean then, Paul who was the
most learned in every way among the apostles, and often stimulates us to
imitate him – why should he in this one passage wish to warn us against
knowledge? Deprived of knowledge, what is charity? A ship without a
rudder. Who ever loved anything he did not know? When indeed was
ignorance useful for anything? Paul did not lie, but he was imperfectly
understood; we shall take his meaning rightly at least if we compare what
goes before and what comes after this passage. (Look out, Batt is going to
play the theologian.) A question had been put before Paul about food
offered to idols, from which some Christians used to abstain owing to a lack
of strength in their conscience; others, more experienced, who understood
that "offered to idols" meant nothing, and that to the pure all things are
pure, ate without making any distinction. And they were quite right in
their opinion, but meanwhile this strength of theirs was an occasion of
stumbling to the weaker and more superstitious. So there was disagree-

* * * * *

12 Knowledge] 1 Cor 8:1. See Kohls I 62ff; and Erasmus' annotations to the New
   Testament in LB VI.
17 rude in speech] 2 Cor 11:6: 'I may be no speaker, but knowledge I have' (*New
   English Bible*).
18 Gamaliel] Acts 22:3
19 books] 2 Tim 4:13
27 question] 1 Cor 8:1–13; 10:23–33
30 pure] Titus 1:15

LB X 1718D / ASD I-1 93

ment among brethren. Paul replied; "As far as our conscience is concerned,
it does not matter whether we eat food offered to idols or the contrary; it
does matter in terms of brotherly charity." I have offended my weaker
brother, who had not yet come to the point of despising food offered to
idols, by giving him an uncomfortable conscience, when he sees his
brother bowing down before heathen gods; for this reason the apostle
considers it better to comply with a brother's weakness, rather than disregard him and act on our knowledge. The charity which makes concessions
is more pleasing to heaven than proud knowledge which cannot give way.
It is in this way that he says knowledge puffs up, if you deliberately offend
your brother; and that charity builds up, if with no harm to yourself you
concede something to your brother's weakness. Not to mention the fact that
this situation was peculiar to those times. Superstition was too deeply
rooted from past generations to be suddenly discarded, and for the establishment of the Gospel teaching it was necessary to be considerate in every
way. Finally, let me say, this stumbling-block was found, not supplied, by
us. It was a matter of Christian charity to accommodate ourselves for a time
to our brother's weakness, but with the hope that he would later grow
wiser.

'What has all this to do with us? with philosophy, or oratory, or
poetry? Nothing; but if you like let us force it to apply to secular learning,
since Holy Scripture has learnt to put up with anything. However you may
twist the phrase, Paul does not mean that knowledge should be non-
existent, but that it should not exist alone, that is, without charity. If one
has to do without one or the other, it would be more bearable to be without
knowledge than without charity; this interpretation is supported by St
Augustine. "Knowledge by itself," he says, "is useless; but with charity it
is useful." Who would be crazy enough to reject silver because he knew
gold was more valuable? Are stones to be put to no use because jewels are
finer? In the same way, is not knowledge a good thing, even if charity is a
better? In another passage, where Paul is singing the praises of charity, he
puts knowledge among the greatest gifts, along with prophecy, faith,
working of miracles, the gift of tongues, and the like. Would he do this if he
considered knowledge a thing to be shunned like the plague? "Well," you
say, "why does he say knowledge puffs people up?" When he became the

* * * * *

3 charity] 1 Cor 8:4–13
26 St Augustine] In many places: see ASD I-1 95n. Erasmus himself refers to
   Contra Faustum 15:8 (LB VI 703D).
31 charity] 1 Cor 13:8
35 When] Reading *cum* for *cur* (manuscript and *1520*)

most knowledgeable of men, did this make him straightaway the most
conceited? He wished to point out the danger, so as to make people more
cautious, but not to discourage them: charity is safer; knowledge is necessary but has its dangerous side; in fact it is a thing which can be disastrous if
it does not conform with charity. It would be more becoming if the person
without learning were to defer to and obey the one with knowledge, but, as
it is, the more learned man yields of his own accord to the uneducated.

'Why are you so pleased with yourself, you with your charity? Why do
you decry knowledge? The charity which wins praise is not yours, but that
of the one who excels you in knowledge. For as far as you were concerned,
your ignorance would have cancelled out your charity because you thought
you were something when you were nothing, but the fact was that the other
man's wisdom gave way willingly to your stupidity. You are tolerated; the
first place is not yours. Which of you is the more arrogant, you who refuse in
your ignorance to submit yourself to a more learned man, or the well-
instructed person who indulgently yields to the ignorant? Is it really right
always to give way to the unschooled? No, or at least only in matters where
insistence would mean a violation of charity, and where this indulgence
can be seen to be likely to have no ill effects. Paul did not wish us to be
discouraged from learning – in fact he encouraged us in it by his example –
but he wished us not to fall into danger by our rashness, and like a careful
pilot he pointed out the reefs and rocks. Why should we drag pure and
unsullied Scripture into line with our shortcomings? Why do we preen
ourselves on our ignorance? Why do we seek to turn away from sound
studies those who are fit for them and dedicated to them? Instead, why do
we not, when we see someone hastening towards them with might and
main (with sails and oars, as Plautus says), give him this kind of encouragement: "Go where your valour calls you, go and prosper!" You are swept
along at full sail towards humane studies, but see you navigate with care.
That sea has rocks; that grove has gold and emeralds, but for heaven's sake
beware of the poisonous roots. You will learn excellent arts, and useful
ones, only if you add to them an equal proportion of moral worth, for
without that they will hardly be useful at all – they may even be destructive.
Take care not to apply yourself to them in such a way that "your sense of
right diminishes"; study to become better no less than cleverer; knowledge
is good, charity is better. If you see that the one is combined with the other,
you will achieve a perfect result.'

* * * * *

27 with sails and oars] *Adagia* I iv 18; Plautus *Asinaria* 157
28 prosper] Horace *Epistles* 2.2.37
34 sense of right] Virgil *Aeneid* 2.595

When Batt had spoken like this, the doctor, who had been smiling for some time (he is one of the merriest of men, full of jests), remarked, 'Why, Batt, whoever would have believed that a poetic fellow like you would have so much theology in him? I swear by the favour of your Muses, you seem to me to have explained Paul's meaning most accurately, and as far as I can see no theological term escapes you; from what I have heard I should think you would make a beautiful preacher. If those Dominicans of ours hear about it, I am rather afraid they will eagerly snatch you up and put you into a cowl.'

Batt laughed and said, 'That had better be the fate of the Muses' enemies; but you won't get away easily if you challenge Batt. What an impudent fellow you are, to be surprised at theological knowledge in me, a poet, when you, a doctor, are more theological than anybody! If I were a theologian, that would not mean that I was straying from the domain of the poet. In ancient times poets and theologians were held to be the same people, and I frankly admit that the writings of eloquent authors on theology delight me no less than Cicero. The modern ones – well, I often try them and force myself to read, but nausea overcomes me as I go on, I am so disgusted by the barbarous style and confusion of thought. You, however, are stepping outside your own field, and by doing so you wrong the theologians; the care of souls is committed to them and of bodies to you, and here you are arrogating to yourself the whole man. But if you will allow me, I shall go on talking theology – even in front of you who are the ablest theologian of all medical men – and I will make you swear I have never looked at a book except on a theological subject.'

'Come on then,' said the doctor, 'I am eagerly waiting. But I will set you back into the path from which I turned you aside. The final term of your argument was that you said charity must be combined with knowledge. My opinion is the same as I see expressed by St Augustine in his dialogues, that is to say, I believe that knowledge can hardly be divorced from virtue; but,

* * * * *

4 theology] R. Pfeiffer and James D. Tracy have shown that Batt's speech was originally put into the mouth of Cornelis Gerard, himself a theologian. This bantering exchange provides an excuse for the alteration of plan. See *Antibarbari* Introductory Note 5.

14 same people] Identification of ancient poets with theologians seems to derive from a loose interpretation of a sentence in Aristotle (*Metaphysics* 1000a8–10) linking Hesiod with writers of cosmogonies. Medieval writers such as Boccaccio and Petrarch could have found the idea in Augustine *De civitate Dei* 18.14. It was well known to Renaissance apologists for poetry. See Boccaccio *Genealogia deorum gentilium* 14.8, 15.8; and E.R. Curtius *European Literature and the Latin Middle Ages* trans Willard R. Trask (New York 1935) 218.

28 dialogues] See ASD I-1 96n.

as you know, my profession leads me to deal with all kinds of people, and I
often meet with certain monks who are steadfastly persuaded that there is
no way in which what they call secular literature can be combined with
Christian piety.'

'They are right there,' said Batt; 'in their case it can't, because they lack   5
both, but it can in the case of Jerome, Cyprian, Augustine, and a thousand
others; and who would dare to put on the same footing the piety of these
men and the sluggishness of the monks?'

'Come now,' said the doctor, 'I know you dislike everyone who wears
a cowl; and although I have a predestined love for the monastic life (for I was   10
born under kindly Jove, and Venus too) and both admire and reverence it,
all the same I do not exempt them from all reproach. I see some of them
getting close to the Epicurean way of life, taking incredible care to escape
work, embracing sloth and a sheltered life. They believe themselves safe if
they hide away like snails in their shells, fretfully concerned with the   15
smallest detail of bodily comfort; they think themselves quite religious
enough if they never touch anything in the way of literary culture; they
imagine they are consulting the interest of their own people if they forget
what they have learned in the schools. Never do they cease to urge the
citizens to stop sending their children to the secular schools they call   20
universities. According to them people who go down into these places, as
into the underworld, have perished, never to return, or only to return the
worse. They preach simplicity, whatever they mean by that; literature, they
say, distracts the mind from right living, and does not improve the intelligence but destroys it. It is a stupid thing, they say, to have an elegant   25
tongue and disordered morals; no one can deceive death by the quibbles of
dialectic (they dare not even mention rhetoric and poetry); they call geome-
tricians mad, because they measure fields cleverly and do not know the
measure of their own mind. Astrologers are raving when they keenly scan
what is above them; scientists are accused of impiety, because they pry into   30
the works of God and neglect the artificer who made them. They do not even
spare the revered teachers of theology, whom they tax with preaching
virtue in imperious style but never living it themselves. So these Cynics of
ours despise the whole race of men, and pass judgment on everybody. "All
must die," they say; "what good will it do you then to be wiser than   35
Solomon? What use are the intricacies of dialectic, or the periods of
rhetoric? We must all die."'

* * * * *

13 Epicurean] See 32:7n.
15 like snails] *Adagia* IV iv 57

'By the Goose,' returned Batt, 'those fellows are fit for the treadmill.
Everybody knows we must all die; are we to do nothing in the meantime?
I would rather die wiser than I was born. They talk exactly as if it were
inevitable that anyone who is learned must be bad. If a man has a disorderly
tongue, does it follow that he must have well-ordered morals? Will the man   5
who despises dialectic straightway escape the snares of death? To have had
no acquaintance with the poets, does that at once make one a Hippolytus?
Does a man instantly know himself because he does not know geometry?
What is the advantage of not having philosophized among the stars, if
meanwhile you have been philosophizing among the sauce-boats? Do you   10
think it finer to scrutinize the smells of cookshops rather than the hidden
causes of things? To speak more generally, is the least educated of men to be
esteemed forthwith the most religious? Learning does not exalt us to
heaven; does ignorance? Proficiency in literature does not produce a well-
disposed mind; are we to take it that ignorance will? Letters do not produce 15
a good mind, that we can admit, but neither do they make it into a bad one.

'Is not the shoemaker's craft accepted, and those of the weaver, build-
er, tailor, fuller? as for cookery, that is positively held in honour. Which of
these arts confers morality on men? We praise the skilful painter, the expert
carpenter, the clever weaver, and we praise him even if he is a wicked man.   20
We do not call an art bad if it happens that it is a bad man who practises it.
Yet we condemn literature which, even though it may not produce a good
mind, contributes not a little to that end. If we see someone misusing
literary skill, we must not recommend him to abandon learning, but not
to twist it to evil purposes. How much better was the advice of that   25
philosopher, wise although without Christ, who said: "Live as if you were
to die tomorrow, study as if you were to live for ever." Death will take over,
but I would rather it took me studying than idling. However I will concede
one thing to my opponents: that for people born with little intelligence, or
very slow, it may be as well to warn them off difficult subjects of study;   30
otherwise when the ass is led to the lyre both the teacher and the taught will
lose their labour. But with people whose intelligence promises to be good,
what is it but "quenching the spirit," as Paul says, if you deter them from

* * * * *

1 Goose] See 40:23n.
7 Hippolytus] Hippolytus, son of Theseus, vowed himself to Artemis and was
    wrongly accused by Phaedra, his stepmother, of attempting to seduce her. He
    is taken here as an example of chastity.
26 Live ... idling] This quotation and comment are an addition of *1520*. The
    philosopher has not been identified.
31 ass ... lyre] See 33:13n.
33 Paul] 1 Thess 5:19

valuable efforts? If that had been done in the case of the great doctors whom
I have often named, the church would have been deprived of a notable
protection and support. I might say however that you who uphold the cause
of the barbarians make your replies more learnedly and modestly for them
than they usually talk themselves; for generally men of that sort do not even   5
know what the disciplines are that they are raging against. They think
poetry a meretricious art; rhetoric for them is nothing but flattery; geography and astrology they believe to be prying and blameworthy arts, like
necromancy.'

'You speak with probability, Batt,' said the doctor, 'truly like a   10
rhetorician. Now I will state the case against you for these admirers of
ignorance, who incite the ignorant mob to bitter animosity with such
speeches as these: "Well, what is going to happen in the end? Are the
well-educated the only ones who will take heaven by storm? Are you people
who swell with windy doctrines the only ones who are going to occupy   15
heaven as the Giants did, casting out the gods and shutting out hell? What
will happen to the ignorant multitude? Or to the simple brethren who have
walked in the steps of the apostles and never learnt the tangles of Aristotle
or the thorny ways of Chrysippus, or Attic wit or the eloquence of Plautus?
Is not this the very simplicity which God manifestly chose for himself,   20
when he wished to enter Jerusalem riding on a donkey, and whose exhortation is 'Learn of me, for I am meek and lowly of heart'? He did not say learn
a well-composed speech, measure the sky, construct a syllogism – but learn
humility." There are many other sayings they have for us, about lambs and
doves, which they take to mean the docile simplicity of the untutored mind;   25
but I am advising someone who has long known all this; you hear these
things prated about every day by these people in the presence of the
untaught common herd.'

'Marvellous,' said Batt. 'You are calling me into the thick of theology,
you a doctor and I a poet! They may say they are modelling themselves on   30
the donkey, and that seems to me to fit quite well, except that while they
identify themselves with its sloth and slowness, they seem to have mixed
up with that no small share of lion, tiger, and scorpion – just like a Chimaera, made up of various monstrous shapes. If we had time just now to
follow up the mystic meaning of that donkey, that dove, that lamb, it would   35

* * * * *

16 Giants] The sons of Ouranos (Sky) and Ge (Earth) in Greek mythology, who
tried to dispossess the Olympian gods
21 on a donkey] Matt 21:1–7; Luke 19:29–35; John 12:14
22 lowly of heart] Matt 11:29
33 Chimaera] A mythical monster with lion's head, goat's body, and dragon's
tail, described in *Iliad* 6.181

easily be clear that such a kind of man has no place in that order of things. I
think it will be enough rebuttal to say that these mystic expressions refer
not to knowledge but to conduct, that is, to speak more theologically, not to
the intellect but to the emotive life. What could be more asinine, if I may say
so, than the kind of mind which can cover up and let pass the troublesome   5
trivialities of these men? What could be more dovelike, or lamblike? As for
them, it is true they have one thing in common with the donkey, their
stupidity, but what else? They do not let themselves be led by more sensible
people, and they shun work like the plague. What likeness have they to the
dove, when they put such bitterness into their hatred of their brother's   10
virtue? What have they in common with the lamb, when they have nothing
that is of any use to others? Jerome, who got through such a vast amount of
work for the increase of the Christian religion, was a donkey all right; so
was Augustine, who spent unending labour on the Christians – and these
are the donkeys we must imitate. Why do lazy individuals, born to be mere   15
ciphers, flatter their idleness with this sort of reflection? They call themselves plain and simple brethren, when they would be quite capable of
starting a struggle with anyone, and craftily too, if something cropped up
which concerned their bellies or their reputation. May my name be inscribed among those of the great liars, if what I say is not admitted by all   20
who have come to close quarters with these simple souls.

'But in order to deal gently with the grievance of those who think they
have been rejected for ignorance, we accept them, we conciliate and embrace them; I will show how, if your ears will put up with me a little longer,
while I explain this in a few words.   25

'It seems to me reasonable that many authors have agreed with that
celebrated opinion of Hesiod, that there are three kinds of men. First, there
are those who know of themselves what is right and follow it. Then there are
those who have small wisdom of their own, but obey the advice of the wise.
The third class he calls good for nothing, that is the people who neither have   30
wisdom of their own nor believe the adviser who tells them right. The first
are good, and also full of learning. The second are good also, though
untaught. The third are not endowed with either knowledge or worth. The
first of these classes, being the most excellent, is the one to be most sought
after; the second is to be tolerated only in so far as these people defer to the   35
learned body; but if they start to be intractable, as they usually do, they
already start to merge into the third class. And so I say that learning is

* * * * *

16 ciphers] *Adagia* II iii 23
16 They ... souls] These two sentences are an addition of *1520*.
27 Hesiod] *Works and Days* 293

necessary, but where will you send the unlearned? To the gallows-tree, as
the writers of comedy say, if they refuse to be taught. If they are unteachable, I accept that, but there must be some people in whose hands scholarship will go on. If we are all to be illiterate, who is to correct the mistakes of
the ignorant? In a painter's studio there are those who are unskilled in the   5
art but do merely what they are told; they do the grinding, mixing, and
cleaning. The work of these people is useful in its way, but only if the
instructor is there; otherwise it is useless. And I do not think we should
listen to those who say that education need not be a general thing, that there
is no need for such a crowd of learned men, that the majority can be led by a   10
few. If a thing is fine for the few, why should it not be all the finer in the
possession of many? Why should anyone prohibit efforts to be made
towards something which everybody hails as excellent? The wise general
uses the services of the ordinary ruck of the army, allows the lazy ones to
mingle with the active, and does not even throw out the camp-followers   15
and drudges, but he would much rather they were all Scaevolae or Sicinii or
Decii. It would be a shocking thing if the common soldier were to be jealous
of the valiant deeds of a distinguished comrade and say, "Well, if we are all
to distinguish ourselves, what is to happen to the rank and file?" If we are all
educated, where are we to banish the uneducated? As if there were any   20
need for the uneducated anywhere! There may be those who have been
hindered from learning, or it has just not come their way: it is for them to
keep quiet and stop obstructing people who are trying to achieve something good. There is the man who will lead the way: let him do so, and
follow his lead, and you will reach the same place in the end. The common   25
people are not praised for their ignorance, but if they are tractable with it
they are not scorned. Something that is tolerated can even be pleasing when
it is compared with something worse; but it will please a great deal more if it
is changed into something better. If we are untaught, and listen to wiser
people, that is indeed good; but we shall be better if we ourselves come to   30

* * * * *

  1 gallows-tree] The solution jocosely accepted by Montaigne in *De l'institution
     des enfants, Essais* 1.26: 'Je n'y trouve autre remede, sinon que de bonne heure
     son gouverneur l'estrangle, s'il est sans temoins, ou qu'on le mette patissier
     dans quelque bonne ville, fust-il fils d'un duc ...' The reference is to Plautus,
     in many plays: see ASD I-1 100n.
  2 unteachable] Reading *indociles* for *dociles*
  5 there are those] A reminiscence perhaps of time passed with painters; in his
     youth Erasmus had some knowledge of the art (Ep 16:10–13).
 12 many] The constant opinion of Erasmus
 17 Decii] C. Mucius Cordus Scaevola, L. Sicinius Dentatus, and the three Decii
     were military heroes in the history of Rome.

be able to teach the untaught. So here they may have the thing in a few
words: the man who is both untaught and unteachable, whether from
laziness or because he is engaged in that kind of life which demands a man
of learning, is a bad man simply because he is ignorant. You profess to teach
sound learning in a public school, and you boast of your ignorance of it? As   5
for you, you dare to write books in which you discourage us from literature?
And you, you are in high public office and you do not want to learn what
you teach? A private citizen, who has not altogether neglected his education but has not really learnt much, may seek satisfaction for himself alone;
born for himself, let him live for himself, not to be despised by the more   10
learned if only he admits his lack of skill. But a man who adds learning to his
uprightness will be a finer person, more useful and more valuable, the more
he goes on doing this. At present no one wields a worse despotism than
those fellows who caricature apostolic simplicity. Ignorant abbots refuse to
allow any of their monks to put a finger on Good Letters, the better to   15
impose on them whatever commands they wish; they would much rather
have command over animals than men. Petty tyrants want the people to be
stupid, the more easily to impose what they want and get anything accepted, and to frighten people through superstition; for superstition is a
thing from which erudition usually sets one free.'   20
   'What you say has some truth in it,' said the doctor, 'but having once
undertaken to defend the cause of these simple souls, I am not going to be
made out a liar. You are excellent, Batt, at explaining the arguments on your
own side, but if anything damages your cause you hide it. I am returning to
your classification: suppose you are both educated and bad, in what class   25
shall we put you?'
   'Rather suppose I am not educated and am bad,' returned Batt, 'what
class do I go in then? But I was coming to that. Come, we will add a fourth
class to Hesiod's three, if you like: it may happen that a man who can see
what is right refuses to act on what he sees, so that while he knows the best   30
he does the worst. But wait a minute, I see exactly what argument you will
have got ready: "so learning is not good, since it can belong to bad people."
It should rightly follow that what makes people bad is bad itself; but
learning is one thing, virtue another; a man who is good is not necessarily
learned, nor a learned man necessarily good. To explain this more fully let   35
us postulate four classes of men. I am talking to you, doctor, as the defender
of the ignorant – uphold your clients' cause now, as you began to do. Let us

* * * * *

13 At ... superstition] This passage was added in 1520. 'Petty tyrants'
   (ptochotyranni) is a term Erasmus often directs at the mendicant orders. See
   30:8n.

place two men on each hand, and from this side take two, one learned and
bad, the other unlearned and bad – which do you prefer?'

The doctor replied, 'The first of the two will be much the worse. And
this makes a clear case: literature cannot be good when it makes a man more
worthless. I am cutting your throat with your own sword.'

'Whether one is more worthless than the other,' said Batt, 'I would
hardly take it upon me to decide. Certainly both seem to me to stand
accused, the one because he is misusing the best things, the other perhaps
all the more seriously because he has not even taken the trouble to know
them. The first is open to the rebuke of the prophet: "they are wise to do
evil, but to do good they have no knowledge." The other meets that saying
of David: "He hath left off to be wise, and to do good." Nothing useful can
be hoped for from ignorant wickedness, but when the wickedness has an
element of education, even if it is ruinous to itself, it can contribute something useful to others. If an evil disposition goes with ignorance, there is
more confidence in sinning and less shame. The ignoramus thinks that
everything he strongly desires is right to do. But cultivation of mind, even if
it does not altogether exclude base desires, must needs temper them. When
a man clearly understands the difference between right and wrong, it is
impossible for him not to recoil with horror sometimes from a disgraceful
course, or not to look with admiration sometimes on the fair face of virtue.
The educated man perhaps makes a pretence of honourable conduct, which
is next to being virtuous; the boor will expect to gain credit from his very
vices. The one is aware of his disease, and so nearer to being cured; the
other's condition is desperate because he believes himself in good health.
The one has weapons at the ready, which could be used for virtue, the other
has nothing which would be of any use to it. But this is not really the subject
of our discussion.

'Suppose we concede that wickedness of an unpolished kind is less
harmful than educated wickedness, does that make education bad? By this
very token it is excellent, if I may turn the dart against you that you were
going to slay me with. To begin with, letters do not bring wickedness with
them, but, when present, they are like a torch carried in front of it and
showing it up more clearly. For instance, I imagine two adulterers, one
single, the other married: although they confess to the same act, their guilt
will not be equal, since it is greater in the married man. Why is this –
because marriage is a bad thing? Certainly not, but just because marriage is

* * * * *

10 prophet] Jer 4:22
12 David] Ps 36:3 (35:4 Vulg)
25 health] The same argument as in *Adagia* IV v 4

LB X 1723E / ASD I-1 102

holy, the desecration of it by adultery is all the worse. To filch church
property is worse than ordinary stealing, since it is sacrilege: therefore is a
profane thing to be preferred? Debauchery in a priest is worse than in a
layman; is priesthood therefore a bad thing? Naturally, it has made the man
more guilty; but, on the other hand, if priesthood were not a better thing it   5
would not have made him more guilty in this way. The holier a thing is, the
more shameful the misuse of it will be.

'Now let us imagine two other people, both worthy men, one uncouth, the other educated: which is to be preferred to the other? (They
shuffle and stammer: just find a man, they say, who has both worth and   10
learning.) I admit that there is a great scarcity of this kind of person, for
there are plenty of unlearned and unworthy people everywhere. But why
should they stammer when Jerome never did? He freely and at the top of his
voice, as they say, put saintly learning above saintly simplicity. "Daniel,"
he says, "at the end of his most holy vision, says that the righteous shall   15
shine like stars, and the wise" – that is the learned – "like the firmament."
Do you see what difference there is between righteous simplicity and
learned righteousness? The first is compared to stars, the last to heaven. A
little before this he says: "Holy simplicity is profitable only to itself, and
however much it builds up the church by the merit of the life lived, it does   20
an equal amount of harm if it does not resist the destroyers." Jerome is right
here as in everything; for the more widely a good thing is known, the more
influential for good it must be. The man who lives an upright life is indeed
doing a great thing, but it is useful only to himself, or at most to the few with
whom he passes his days. If learning is added to his upright life, how much   25
the power of his virtue will be increased, more brilliantly and more widely
known as if a torch had been set before it! And if he is one of those who can
put down in writing the most beautiful meditations of his heart, that is if he
is eloquent as well as learned, the usefulness of this man must necessarily
be widespread and pervasive, not only among his friends, his equals, his   30
neighbours, but for strangers, for posterity, for the people at the uttermost
ends of the earth. Worth without learning will die with its possessor, unless
it be commended to posterity in written works. But where there is learned
scholarship, nothing stops it from spreading out to all humanity, neither
land nor sea nor the long succession of the centuries. I would not like here to   35
bring up an invidious comparison as to which has been of most value to our

* * * * *

13 Jerome] Ep 53.3; Dan 12:3: 'They that be wise shall shine as the brightness of the
firmament, and they that turn many to righteousness as the stars for ever and
ever.'
21 Jerome] Jerome Ep 53.3

religion, the blood of the martyrs or the pens of the learned writers. I am not
disparaging the glory of the martyrs, which a man could not attain to even
by unlimited eloquence; but to speak simply of usefulness to us, we owe
more to some heretics than to some martyrs. There was indeed a plentiful
supply of martyrs, but very few doctors. The martyrs died, and so di-   5
minished the number of Christians; the scholars persuaded others and so
increased it. In short, the martyrs would have shed their blood in vain for
the teaching of Christ unless the others had defended it against the heretics
by their writings. The Christian religion found Good Letters a valuable
safeguard in times of stress, and it will not be so ungrateful now, when it   10
has peace and prosperity, as to thrust them into exile – for it was through
them that it attained peace and happiness.

'I cannot help being amazed at some people who quite deliberately
admit that they shun literature; we have already shown how idiotic it is to
say they are abstaining from the inventions of the heathen. Is there any-   15
thing in what they say about wishing to avoid pride? Surely it is not so
much because their weak minds tremble as because they want a cover for
their indolence that they invent a sin where no sin is. I could believe these
people were simply mistaken if they altered their ways when admonished
and rebuked; but what kind of religion will that be which for fear of some   20
trifling trouble falls into utter ruin? So while these silly fools, trembling like
women, do their stupid best to flee from naughty curiosity, they fall into a
different but much more dangerous vice. "It is in vain that you have
avoided one vice, if you have been turned to wrong ways by another," says
Horace. You have escaped from Scylla to no purpose if you fall into Charyb- 25
dis; it is no good avoiding the storm only to break up your ship on the rocks.
The childish, not to say perverse, timorousness of these people is what
David was talking about (that holiest of kings and prophets): "They were
afraid where no fear was." For the man who superstitiously observes the
wind will never trust himself to the sea; and one who anxiously watches the 30
clouds will never reap. What could be more disastrous than to raise up
imaginary fears where the most distinguished work is to be done, and
snore idly away where there is acute and certain danger? With their idiotic
solicitude they want to remove the mote of curiosity from our eyes, and do
not feel the beam of laziness in theirs. They reproach us with always   35

* * * * *

4 heretics] He may mean Origen.
25 Horace] *Satires* 2.2.54
25 Charybdis] *Adagia* i v 4
28 David] Ps 53:5 (52:6 Vulg)
34 mote ... beam] Matt 7:2–5; Luke 6:41–2

wanting to learn more when we know more than enough already; but they take no interest in learning the things without which we are not human, or even alive. Supposing we have overstepped the limits, which is the way of honour where honourable things are concerned – to go too far or not far enough? Is it better to exceed or fall short? They are afraid that somewhere in the pagan books they might find something that sounded not quite strict enough to crabbed ears, but they are not afraid of that terrifying word of the Lord, "Thou wicked servant, wherefore gavest thou not my money into the bank, that at my coming I might have required mine own with usury?" So true it is that there is nothing so unpleasing to God as sloth! The prodigal son, who had spent all his substance on harlots, pimps, and cookshops, he joyfully welcomed back; but the servant who returned to him even an undiminished talent was bitterly reproached. God, our parent, imparted to us, as seeds of fine skills, intellect, understanding, memory, and other gifts of the mind, which are talents put out to usury, and if we double them by practice and study, our Lord on his return will praise us as industrious servants and give them to us for our inheritance; but if we bury the talent we have received in the ground, how shall we bear the eyes, the face, the voice of our returning Lord, when others are counting out the profit they have made from what they were given, and we in our indolence present our useless talents? This is where these timorous people should rightly be afraid, not where there is so much profit and so little danger.'

Authorities confuted by authorities

Here Batt closed his eyes and was silent for a while. Then he said, 'Great heavens, what a field of discussion I see opening out before me – but enough is enough. The right flank we have conquered, I think, or at least turned it; but the enemy presses on, brings up the left flank with furious hostility, and menaces us from far and near with the weapons of Holy Scripture. The first thing to do is to snatch the darts from the enemy, and then cut their throats, as the comedy-writer says, with their own sword. Forced by reasoning to give ground, they fly for help to the writings of the church, and din into our ears what they themselves do not understand. I have a kind of Cato in mind, with chin tucked in, protruding lips, glazed eyes, contracted brows, right hand extended, left hand thrust into his belt,

* * * * *

7 word] Luke 19:22–3
11 son] Luke 15:11–32
33 comedy-writer] Terence *Adelphi* 958

saying: "Silence to human carpings, let us hear what is commanded by Holy Scripture. Let us hear Paul: 'Mind not high things, but condescend to men of low estate.' The same Paul commands us to be wise 'but think soberly.' And again: 'Be not high-minded, but fear.' Again in another place: 'If any man think that he knoweth anything, he knoweth not yet as he ought to know,' and 'if any man seemeth to be wise, let him become a fool, that he may be wise.' And Isaiah says the same: 'I will destroy the wisdom of the wise, and will bring to nothing the understanding of the prudent.' Also St James: 'This wisdom descendeth not from above, but is earthly, sensual, devilish.' 'But the wisdom that is from above is first pure, then peaceable, gentle and easy to be intreated, agreeing with the good, full of mercy and good fruits, without partiality and without hypocrisy.'"

'These stupid men throw in our faces a few little extracts of this sort. It would be tedious and unprofitable to go through them all, especially as they all tend the same way and can all be answered by the same reasoning, although every one of them was rightly and justly written. But we twist and distort for other purposes things which were rightly said; the reason being that we turn them round to make a covering for our indolence, when it is so clear that you can put your finger on it, as they say, that it is not erudition at all which is being attacked by these remarks, but we who are being warned not to be inflated by worldly successes but to remember Christian modesty. Wealth raises a man's crest; and this is where we must look with fear on the warning given by Paul; indeed, these are words which apply even to those who have made progress in the virtuous life. Nor would I deny that they may apply also to the learned, not to all, but at least to those who pride themselves on a little more learning, or are found to be immoderate in these studies or untimely in their zeal, or dare to hold on to their opinions and disagree with those of the church, or in one way and another make bad use of Good Letters. Impious, arrogant, immodest literature is abhorrent to

* * * * *

3 estate] Rom 12:16
4 soberly] Rom 12:3
4 fear] Rom 11:20
6 know] 1 Cor 8:2
7 wise] 1 Cor 3:18
8 prudent] 1 Cor 1:19, quoting Isa 29:14
12 hypocrisy] James 3:15, 17. In quoting the Latin text Erasmus includes *bonis consentiens*, 'agreeing with the good,' after 'intreated,' but in his version of the New Testament he omitted the phrase and appended a note saying that he did not find it in the Greek codices nor in the oldest Latin codex at the College of St Donatian in Bruges, 'although Bede reads thus and expounds it' (LB VI 1033F).
22 crest] See 70:26n.

LB X 1726A / ASD I-1 105

heaven, we know this; yes, and odious to mortals too – it deserves the thunderbolts hurled at it by Scripture. Those who acknowledge their offence must look on it with horror and mend their ways; the blameless may rejoice. What has all this to do with the ignorant, who have learnt hardly anything? I suppose they are triumphant because they have succeeded perfectly in not having any of these things said about them! No one can be blamed for mismanaging a property, who never had any property at all. It is really ridiculous to suppose that these observations are aimed at the skilled in learning rather than the unskilled. That phrase about minding high things, does it fall only on the learned, and not much more onto any blockhead? What is "minding high things" – being deeply learned, or being conceited? This song is better sung, not to the truly learned, but to those who have learnt nothing and yet try to lay down the law to people better informed. Paul was talking to the wealthy, not to the studious, when he spoke of minding high things. These remarks are not suited to the erudite; let them be droned out to the stupid, who despise the learning of others and admire their own uncouthness.

'And what is that knowledge which is "sensual, devilish"? The kind which keeps a jealous bitterness, which gives birth to strife and contention, which fights against the truth; the feeling of the apostle was directed to this, the very sequence of the passage points to it. Why do we twist the meaning of plain Scripture? Why force it, unwilling and reluctant to be forced? It is not a question here of liberal studies but of the quibbles of theologians, which they often squabble about among themselves with considerable obstinacy in spite of their irrelevance, and thus manage to seem sublimely learned to the senseless rabble – though Christian erudition knows nothing of pride. What could be more contentious than these fellows who will confound heaven and earth sooner than give way? and raise a shout immediately about heresy if you disagree with them?

'The passages just quoted they take from the writings they designate as canonical. Now I will mention a few which they borrow as weapons from other writers, but to avoid counting the sands (as the Greek proverb has it) by recalling a great many, it will be enough to mention only Gratian, who could strike terror into us above all others, if not by his authority, at least by his huge output. Just lately, when I had returned home from the University of Paris, I fell into dispute with a man who was a mortal enemy of our studies: otherwise an amiable fellow, obliging, not without distinction,

* * * * *

32 sands] *Adagia* i iv 44
33 Gratian] Franciscus Gratianus (twelfth century), founder of the science of canon law

LB X 1726C / ASD I-1 106

handsome, agreeable, humorous, and, as befits these virtues, an active
lover, a peerless drinker, an assiduous table-companion, a mighty gambler,
in fact adorned with many virtues of that kind. This Sardanapalus and I had
been intimate friends from childhood, and even now, for the sake of old
acquaintance, I will forbear to mention the name of my old comrade.   5

'He had a habit of boasting to me (as soldiers in comedy do) about his
great deeds, how many sweethearts he had in one single town, how often
and by what means he managed to meet other men's wives, how many
rivals he had conquered, how often in one night he could prove himself a
man, what glorious victories he had pulled off in drinking against other   10
topers. These were the fellow's studies – on these he lavished his toil, his
care; in these he placed his pleasure, his leisure, his business, his happiness. When he had warmed my ears with this sort of nonsense for two days
running, it so happened that while we were at dinner I made some allusion
to a delightful bit out of the poets. At this the man suddenly changed   15
character and began to talk in quite a new tone of moral strictness, to curse
me for reading those heathen pornographic writers, and to exhort me
seriously to repent and go back to the study of ecclesiastical writers. I was
amazed at the sudden transformation of the man; my Epicurean had become a Zeno.   20

'I asked him why he thought like this, and whether he had read these
authors himself. "Heaven forbid," said he piously. "Never in my life have I
touched such things, nor ever will, so help me God." "No need to swear it, I
can easily believe you," I said. "But why do you recoil from them like this?
If they are chaste, there is no need to avoid them; if they are unchaste, why   25
run away from those who write down the very things you yourself do? Why
not clasp them to your heart, for giving publicity to your virtues? You can
see the very image of your own behaviour portrayed in them. You Sardanapalus, are you not ashamed to show me at one and the same time those
deeds and that pious face? Are you really telling me to imitate your piety,   30
when you think it a worse crime to touch a pagan book than to grind away at
other men's wives? You think it a game, a bit of boyish fun, to drink and
make love and ravish maidens, but reading a poet is in your eyes a mortal
sin! It is all right for you to plan heathen crimes, but not for me to learn from
heathen writings!"   35

'The man concealed his anger, saying that it was a shame to spoil a
good dinner with squabbles of this kind. In the afternoon he led me, by way
of being obliging, to the public library; and there, when he saw me deeply

* * * * *

20 Zeno] See 56:10. Zeno (335–263 BC) was the founder of the Stoic school of
philosophy.

interested in some Ciceronian dialogues I had happened to pick up, he was
much annoyed and brought me Gratian, the only author he had read.
"Now," said he, "I will competely confute you."

'He pointed out section thirty-eight, where some point about liberal
disciplines is treated, but treated in such a way that everything is equally   5
called in question. Who cannot see how ridiculous this is? I tell him to speak
out. He could hardly read the passage, so far was he from understanding it
rightly: "A bishop may not read the works of the heathens, but he may scan
those of the heretics when time and necessity call for it." I asked the man
what he understood by "time and necessity." He said it meant when there   10
was need to dispute or write against a heretic. "And what if the same need
arises about a pagan writer?" I asked. "What if you cannot understand the
books of the theologians? Do you not see how the necessity would arise?"
He did not like this reasoning; I told him to go on reading. "The man who
spends days and nights struggling with the art of dialectic, the watchful   15
scientist who lifts his eyes to pierce the heavens, is he not obviously
applying himself to vanity of the senses and confusion of mind," and so
forth. And then that bit, "They are intoxicated with strong wine, who
misuse secular knowledge and the snares of the dialecticians." "And do
you not see," said I, "that the word is *misuse* and not *possess*? If you did you   20
would understand that secular learning is certainly to be used, and is
neither forbidden nor unprofitable!"

'After collecting a lot of stuff together, Gratian in his own learned style
sums up thus: "From all this the conclusion is that it is not for ecclesiastics
to seek for expertise in secular literature."   25

'At this point, exactly as if he had won his battle, the silly fellow began
to get ready for his triumph; but I begged him to listen to a few words from
me.

'"Do you really not understand," I said, "how this very conclusion
tells against you? In the first place it would not have been surprising if a   30
person who was ignorant of secular literature had condemned it, especially
in this passage where he is combating it expressly for the sake of investigation. However he does not dare to conclude that pagan literature is forbidden to Christians, but only that it should not be sought out – not that it is
any good looking for it where it hardly exists, but, joking apart, 'seeking   35
out' here means requiring. The point in question here is not whether

* * * * *

7   passage] Gratian 1 dist 37 c 1
14 The man] Gratian 1 dist 37 c 3
18 that bit] Gratian 1 dist 37 c 4 (quoting Jerome on Isa 28; Migne PL 24:328c)
24 sums up thus] Gratian 1 dist 37 c 7

churchmen should be allowed to read secular literature but whether it should be required of them, not whether they should have access to it but whether they may be allowed to leave it alone. He adds *ecclesiastics* so that you should have no doubt that it is required of students. You may be forgiven for lacking it, but if we lack it we stand condemned. So you see 5 how your little conclusion works in our favour; but wait a moment, we have heard the accusation, let us hear the defence.

'"You are not yet thoroughly versed in Gratian's eloquence. He argues about each subject, not on one side or the other, but on both sides, with equal abundance and facility, as we read that Gorgias and Carneades used 10 to do in old times. Now listen to his recantation." I ordered the page to be turned, for those well-known words follow: "But on the contrary we read that Moses and Daniel were learned with all the knowledge of the Egyptians and Chaldeans." And a few lines further on that it is clouding the perception of the readers, and forcing limitations on them, to think that they must 15 be totally prohibited from reading secular books; if anything useful is found in these, it can be adopted as one's own, "otherwise Moses and Daniel would not have allowed themselves to become learned with all the wisdom of the Egyptians and Chaldeans," and so on. Again a little later, quoting Ambrose: "If anyone has learnt the art of grammar, or of dialectic, 20 so that he knows the right way of speaking and can distinguish between false and true, we do not disapprove." Soon after, on the same subject: "... who refused to partake of the king's food and wine, lest they should be polluted; just as, if they had known Babylonian learning to be sinful, they would never have agreed to learn what was not permitted." A little further 25 on there is a reference to the Synod of Pope Eugenius: "It is reported to us that in certain places no teachers can be found, nor is care taken for the study of letters; therefore great care and diligence must be applied by all the bishops for the people under their authority, and for other places where the need occurs, to see that masters and doctors are established to teach 30 literary studies and the principles of the liberal arts, because it is in these most of all that the divine commands are shown forth and made known."

* * * * *

10 Gorgias] See 68:22n.
10 Carneades] See 27:14n.
14 Chaldeans] Gratian 1 dist 37 c 7
17 otherwise] Gratian 1 dist 37 c 8
20 Ambrose] Actually Jerome; Gratian 1 dist 37 c 10
25 permitted] Gratian 1 dist 37 c 11, again from Jerome
26 Pope Eugenius] Eugenius II. For the decree (826) see *Monumenta Germaniae historica* Legum sectio III, tom. II 2 page 581.
32 known] Gratian 1 dist 37 c 12

'When I had shown him these passages, I asked him whether he regretted now having set up Gratian against a mere rhetorician?

'"I never noticed these before," he said.

'"No wonder," said I, "if you do not catch what you are not really hunting! You select the passages which tell on your side, you read the bits which seem to support your cause, but you do not read them thoroughly nor understand what you read; and that would not happen to you if you did not so zealously keep away from the literature of the heathens. You have heard how a most venerable council provided that people should be appointed to teach liberal subjects, and do it assiduously. None of the liberal disciplines is Christian, because they neither treat of Christ nor were invented by Christians; but they all concern Christ. You need not boggle about it: no art is excepted, not even rhetoric nor poetry, all are included in the decree, unless you object that poetry is not liberal, being something which is not numbered among them in elementary schools. For my part I scorn this ruling, and judge poetry to be not only liberal but the most liberal of all arts, if only because it used to be presented to children [*liberi*] not as one art among them all, but before all the rest."

'My learned counsel was silent. I asked him to show me his other authors: he refused. I went on from the Decretals to the Decretal Letters, and pointed out the chapter about masters, where great care is taken about providing teachers of languages; when those opponents of ours think no one Christian unless he is bereft of language. From there I turned to the *Summa* of Antoninus, and the Pisanian, Astesanian, and Angelican ones, and to others, not authors alone but compilers: they nearly all sing the same song, "cuckoo calls to cuckoo." For it is the habit for writers of this kind to put down nothing of their own, but to collect the sayings of others picked out here and there, not only different but often at variance with each other. It is enough for them to have piled up heaps of stuff; the remaining trouble is left to the reader's judgment. And he, when his head has started going round and his eyesight is failing from long reading, rises from his studies

* * * * *

10 None ... Christ] This sentence appears to sum up the whole argument of the book.

20 Decretal Letters] That is, from the collection of Gratian to that issued by Pope Gregory ix (1234). Decretals were papal decisions in response to questions and had the force of canon law.

24 *Summa*] These medieval writers of general books on theology are the archbishop of Florence, Antoninus (fifteenth century); the Dominican Bartolomeo Pisano and the Franciscan Astesanus (fourteenth century); the Franciscan Angelus Carletus (fifteenth century).

26 cuckoo] *Adagia* ii v 76

with no more certitude than that Demipho in Terence, who consulted three
advisers: one spoke in favour, one against, and the third said "we must
think it over"; and Demipho remarked, "You have all done well; I am now
much more undecided than I was before."

'When we had read through a number of these boring arguments,   5
what came out of it all was that pagan literature was never a reproach to
anyone, but could rather be considered a matter for praise; the misuse of it,
however, was dangerous and therefore forbidden, as every child knows.
He was subdued now, and it was fair to have a little fun with him; I asked
whether he had read anything in Gratian where churchmen were au-   10
thorized to make love, drink, go whoring, and commit adultery? He said
no. "But these are the things they do every day, and the Decretals slumber
on; it is we, who read the pagan orators and historians, who get them
thrown in our faces. But now since I have humoured your wishes, I beg you
to do the same for me in return, and let us consult my theologians for a little   15
while."

'I open Jerome and point out a passage taken at random, where he
discusses the case of the captive woman. The great scholar takes this to
mean profane learning, and discusses it most pertinently and charmingly:
"Is there any wonder," he says, "if I long to turn secular wisdom, with its   20
beauty of speech and loveliness of proportions, from a captive slave into a
daughter of Israel, and if I trim away whatever is dead in her – idolatry,
sensuality, error, lust – and unite with her in heart's purity to raise up
trueborn children to the Lord of Hosts? My work is of value to the family of
Christ: adultery serves another's, increasing the number of slaves."   25

'He did not understand the metaphor used in this speech, nor even the
words; he thought *ancilla* meant a household servant, and as for *vernaculos*,
which Jerome uses with great discrimination, he could not imagine what it
meant. "Now here," said I, "is the revenge of secular literature against
those who scorn it. There was a passage in that particularly noble letter   30
dedicated to Magnus the orator (I am not sure whether Jerome wrote it) in
which that great saint spoke out quite clearly, though in other places he
deftly masked his opinion, to placate hostility. Let us go back to the
beginning," I said, "the letter is not very long:

* * * * *

 1 Terence] *Phormio* 446–59
17 Jerome] Ep 70.2
21 captive slave] *ancilla atque captiva*
24 trueborn children] *vernaculos*
30 letter] Ep 70
34 letter] Ep 70.2

At the end of your letter you ask why in our writings we sometimes take
examples from secular literature, and pollute the purity of the church with the
filth of the heathen. Here is a brief answer: you would never ask this, if you
were not entirely possessed by Cicero, if you read the Holy Scriptures and
scanned the commentators (putting aside Vulcatius). Who does not know that   5
in Moses and in the prophetic books there are things which come from the
literature of the Gentiles, and that Solomon proposed subjects of debate to the
philosophers of Tyre, and also responded to them? Thus in the introduction to
the Book of Proverbs he admonishes us to understand words of prudence,
subtleties of language, parables and dark speeches, sayings of the sages, and   10
riddles, which properly belong to the dialecticians and philosophers.

A little further on, writing in praise of Paul:

As if this were not enough [he says], the leader of the Christian army, the
matchless orator pleading the cause of Christ, turns round a chance inscrip-   15
tion to make it into an argument of faith. He had learnt from the true David to
seize the sword out of the hands of the enemy, and cut off the arrogant head of
Goliath with his own blade. He had read in Deuteronomy the command
delivered by the voice of the Lord, that the captive woman should have her
head and eyebrows shaved, all the hair and nails of her body cut off, and thus   20
she should be taken to wife.

Then after those words which we quoted a little earlier,

Hosea [he says] accepted as his wife the adulterous Gomer, daughter of
Debelaim (that is, sweetness); and there was born to him from the harlot a son,   25
Israel, who is called the seed of God. Isaiah took a sharp razor and shaved the
beard and shanks of sinners. And Ezekiel, to symbolize the fornication of
Jerusalem, shaves off the hair, and whatever is without life and feeling in her
is taken away.''

30

'As I read these things and he understood nothing, he asked me what
all that was about. "It means," I said, "that we should not run away from
any heathen literature, but should hand it over, cleansed, to Christian

* * * * *

 5 Vulcatius] A commentator on Cicero
16 argument of faith] Acts 17:23
18 blade] 1 Sam 17:51
21 wife] Deut 21:10–13
25 a son] Hos 1:2–4
26 razor] Isa 7:20
27 Ezekiel] Ezek 5:1

learning; and if you had done this, you would not be standing there like a
post. When I said cleansed, I was not referring to knowledge but to
standpoint. The perilous thing is not to read the errors of heathen
philosophers but to mix them in with ecclesiastical arguments, not for the
sake of confuting but of approving, which was never allowable.''

'Then Jerome constructs a catalogue of illustrious writers, both Greek
and Latin, and ends the Greek section with this note of praise: "They all
filled their books to such an extent with the teachings and knowledge of the
philosophers, that you do not know what to admire first, their worldly
learning or their knowledge of the Scriptures." The Latin section he ends
thus: "I am not speaking of others, both living and dead, whose writings
express both power and purpose." Then, to reject the sly misrepresentation
of the ignorant, he adds, "Do not be deceived hastily by perverse opinion,
to think that what must be concealed in other disputes can be allowed
against the heathen; because all books of all authors, except those who with
Epicurus have never learnt letters, are full of learning and doctrine." The
closing passage of the letter is biting, but quite deserved by the stupidity of
the barbarians: "Do persuade him, I beg, in case the toothless should envy
those who have teeth to eat with, and the mole despise the eyesight of the
goat."

'I pointed out also that preface which Jerome prefixed to *Exodus*, in
which he is so far from concealing anything that he mentions the liberal arts
by name: "I am not speaking," he says, "of grammarians, rhetoricians,
philosophers, geometers, dialecticians, writers on music, astrology, and
medicine, whose learning is for the human race" (what do you think Jerome
is going to say? pestilential?) "most useful," he says.

'I asked my man if these things pleased him. "We have an author of
such magnitude and quality, and you must rise up against us and taunt
liberal studies with goodness knows what futile comment out of your
barbarous authors? Your decrees condemn astrology, but Jerome approves
of this study both for curiosity's sake and as useful in a limited way. So what
do you think he thought of rhetoric and poetry?" I showed the man Jerome's
Catalogue of Illustrious Authors, in which he marvels at the eloquence of

* * * * *

7 this note] Ep 70.4
10 he ends] Ep 70.5
13 he adds] Ep 70.6
18 Do ... goat] This passage is used as an adage in *Adagia* III i 7.
21 preface] He means Ep 53.6.
33 *Catalogue*] Not the list in Ep 70 (above 93:7n) but a separate work, *De viris
   illustribus* (Migne *PL* 23:631–760), containing brief accounts of Christian writers from St Peter to Jerome himself; a few non-Christian authors are included.

many writers, advises acquaintance with the poets and philosophers, and
extols secular literature. If the latter were really pernicious, such a devout
man would not be continually dwelling on its occurrence in ecclesiastical
writers. In the preface to the same treatise he is so far from disapproval that
he makes bold to voice the splendid boast against the heretics and heathens
that Christians excel them in secular literature: "Let them learn," he says,
"Celsus, Porphyry, and Julian, those mad dogs against Christ, and their
followers, who think the church never had philosophers, and eloquent ones
too, and doctors – let them learn how many distinguished men founded
her, taught her, adorned her, and let them stop taxing our faith with rustic
simplicity; they had better recognize their own lack of skill."

'"Are you not ashamed," I said, "being a Christian yourself, to accuse
a Christian, and a layman at that, of the very thing Jerome was ready to
boast about in the face of the enemy? And he was a churchman, whose
sanctity was well known, and a monk as well, a lover of the hermit's life, at
that time especially when the Christian religion was as yet in conflict with
pagans. If secular learning is bad, nothing could be stupider than Jerome,
who boasts before his opponents about the very thing which they could
have turned back against him as a supreme accusation." But that is enough
about my drinking companion.

'We will hasten on to the rest of the subject when we have quoted one
other testimony. I have decided now to be content with two, but they are
both weighty. Augustine, a man who was equally outstanding in erudition
and holiness, and also of such a strict conscience – not to say hypercritical –
that he often seems to me (I say it with apologies to so great a man) to
tremble without cause, a thing which is easy to deduce from his life and
from his *Confessions* and *Retractations* – Augustine, I say, being the great
man he was, would certainly have dissuaded people from secular literature,
as they call it, if he had thought it harmful, or useless, or suspect. It is he
who, in those books he entitles *On Christian Doctrine*, suggests two kinds of
teaching, "which are practised even in Gentile, that is to say pagan, morals," he says (or secular as those people call it). "Of these kinds of teaching,
one is concerned with those principles which have been instituted by men,
the other with those which have come to their notice either as already
established or as divinely instituted. That one," he goes on, "which is
established by men is partly a matter of superstition and partly not." To

* * * * *

6 Let them learn] Migne *PL* 23:634B. Celsus, a pagan philosopher of the second
century AD; Porphyry, a Platonic philosopher of Tyre, third century AD; Julian
the Apostate, elected emperor AD 361.
32 kinds of teaching] Augustine *De doctrina christiana* 2.19.29

avoid repeating the whole argument, which is a most prolix one, I will omit
his actual words and sum up the whole thing briefly.

'In the last category, which he calls superstitious, he includes sorcery,
incantations, enchantments, spells, divination by sacrifices or bird-flight,
soothsaying, necromancy, pyromancy, alphitomancy, hydromancy,
geomancy, chiromancy, and other things of the same kind. These belong to
the soothsayers and wizards and can only be practised by the aid of wicked
spirits, and so he rightly judges them to be what the Christian should shun.
Certain types of observations he also assigns to this category because they
are most productive of worry and futility: for instance, the interpretation of
visions and dreams, inspection of entrails, the flight and song of birds,
observation of monsters, thunderstorms, lightning, stars, casting lots,
sneezing, weasels or mice running to meet one or squeaking or nibbling at
anything, ears ringing or eyes popping, leaves rustling, names and appari-
tions, and suchlike rubbish.

'Under the other heading, of things instituted by men and yet free
from superstition, he ranges these: writing, names of things, manner of
speech, laws, public decrees, and many other things of this nature. These
he not only does not reprove, but thinks they closely concern a Christian
man, and he should do his best to learn them.

'In the first class, that of notation, he places almost all the liberal
disciplines, logic, rhetoric, physics, arithmetic, geometry, music, finally
histories and the knowledge of antiquity. I should even be ready to cite the
opinion of St Augustine about each one of these, but you must also be
willing to hear. On grammar his views are plain enough not to need
discussion, and, as to what pertains to dialectic, he argues lengthily and
meticulously as usual (*On Christian Doctrine*, book II, chapter 20, if I remember rightly) about dialectical methods, truth and falsity of connections,
the consequent and the inconsequent, opposition and definition and parti-
tion. He even goes to St Paul for the forms of connections, as he puts it, so
that he seems to have wished to teach us if we are ignorant of dialectic. This
discipline is commended by him in that same chapter of the treatise (I think
I can give the wording, since I have just read it): "But in all kinds of
questions which must be examined and solved in theological study, the
skilled knowledge of disputation is of the greatest value, so essential is it
here to avoid the inclination to quarrel." A little further on: "There are steps
in the reasoning process," he says, "carrying with them false opinions,

* * * * *

27 chapter 20] Actually chapters 31–5
33 wording] *De doctrina christiana* 2.31.48
36 further on] *De doctrina christiana* 2.31.49

which follow on the error of the person engaged in debate, and may be used
as inferences by a learned and good man, so that the one who has produced
them will be covered with confusion and abandon his error, because if he
insisted on retaining it he would be obliged to stick to the very things he
condemns.''

'So much for dialectics. As for the poets and orators, on whom he has
said a great deal, I am purposely omitting them here, intending to return to
them in the right place. The other arts, less important certainly, but exact-
ing, Augustine thought likely to be of no little advantage to a theologian, as
Quintilian·thought they were to an orator; and on the subject of music we
have this: ''We find metre and music honourably mentioned in many places
in Scripture. The errors of Gentile superstition, however, are not to be
listened to: they said the nine Muses were the daughters of Jove and
Memory.'' Then, quoting Varro, he explains how the fable began, adding:
''But whether it was as Varro narrated or not, we have no need to abandon
music because of the superstitions of the unenlightened, if there is anything useful we can take from it for the understanding of Scripture.''

'The discussion on arithmetic opens as follows: ''Even the ignorance
of numbers results in inability to understand many things which are sym-
bolically and mystically expressed in the Scriptures.'' All the complications
of the discussions he enters into in the same way about geometry and
astronomy it is scarcely profitable to recall. Again he judges the knowledge
of natural history particularly necessary to the study of Holy Scripture,
because it is scattered all over with the names of animals, plants, stones,
and unless you have some idea of the importance and nature of these from
the instruction of natural history, you will look pretty rash if you try to
explain them. Here is the important point of this passage: ''Ignorance of
objects makes figurative expressions obscure when we do not know the
nature of animals, plants, or stones or other things which occur in Scripture
and are used for the sake of some similitude.'' He continues the subject with
pertinence and erudition.

'When it comes to the philosophers, who particularly profess to teach
the way to happiness, what does he say? It will be a marvel if he does not
forbid them to be read. They have dared to proclaim themselves masters of
truth, full of universal knowledge, and have thus shown themselves to be
the originators of universal error, whose teachings produced almost all our

* * * * *

8   right place] in book II of the *Antibarbari*, which was never published
14 Memory] *De doctrina christiana* 2.16.26–17.27
17 Scripture] *De doctrina christiana* 2.18.28
20 Scriptures] *De doctrina christiana* 2.16.25
30 similitude] *De doctrina christiana* 2.16.24

heresies, whose intricate deductions, like so many battering-rams, have
been used to beat against the walls of Christian faith. Listen to what this
justest of men says about them: "If those who are called philosophers,
especially the Platonists, have chanced to say things that are true, and in
agreement with our faith, far from fearing these utterances we should claim   5
them for our own, taking them over from their unlawful possessors." I wish
I could give you the exact words of what follows, a charming passage about
the household goods of the Egyptians, but nevertheless I will give a faithful
account of it: we read in Exodus, he says, that when the Hebrews were
secretly preparing to fly under their leader Moses from their servitude in   10
Egypt, each took from his obliging neighbour all sorts of household goods,
an immense amount of rings, clothes, and vessels, and, having spoiled the
Egyptians, they departed secretly. As we know that this flight, this theft,
was done with the sanction of God, we may take it that there is a significance here: that divine providence was acting in consideration for the   15
timidity of some people who would have been frightened to spoil the
Egyptians, that is to take over the wisdom of the heathen, unless they had
such an example of this very thing, such a commander, such a leader. To
come out of Egypt is to leave behind heathen superstition and be converted
to the Christian religion. To take away the wealth of Egypt is to transfer   20
heathen literature to the adornment and use of our faith. The barbarians
will perhaps make fun of the interpreter, and they would be right, if I were
not putting forward Augustine's interpretation, not mine. For just as the
Hebrews, he says, in old days seized whatever they judged would be useful
to them, leaving behind what they thought harmful, or useless, or unhal-   25
lowed, so it behooves us to leave to the heathen their vices, superstitions,
lusts, desires – these, I say, are to be left to their owners. But if there is
among them any gold of wisdom, any silver of speech, any furniture of
good learning, we should pack up all that baggage and turn it to our own
use, never fearing to be accused of thieving, but rather venturing to hope   30
for reward and praise for the finest of deeds. Here again we must avoid the
imputation of making difficulties on the question of what is to be left to the
heathen as pernicious or adopted as useful; Augustine excepts nothing
from his classification but those things he names as superstitious. Otherwise he does not withdraw from that arrangement of his, and this is   35
characteristic of him: he wrote that those disciplines which were discov-

* * * * *

  6 possessors] *De doctrina christiana* 2.40.60
13 departed] Exod 12:35–6. On spoiling the Egyptians cf Kohls I 35–7.
21 use of our faith] Augustine *De doctrina christiana* 2.40.60
31 finest of deeds] Augustine *De doctrina christiana* 2.40.60
32 difficulties] 'Looking for the knot in the bulrush': *Adagia* II iv 76

ered by human minds, like dialectic, rhetoric, natural science, history, and so on, seemed to him marked out with gold and silver, because men themselves did not produce them but dug them out like gold and silver from what might be called the ore of divine providence, which runs through all things. By the clothes of the Egyptians he understands disciplines which were certainly instituted by mortal men, but fitted like garments to human society, such as the rules of oratory, ordinances of the people, pontifical decrees, which indeed are all of the greatest use and in his opinion should by all means be snatched from the heathen. Lastly he confirms and enriches the statement with a happy illustration: "This was done by many of our good and faithful people. Do we not see how Cyprian came out of Egypt with his bags stuffed with silver and clothing, sweetest of scholars and blessed martyr as he was? How much did Lactantius bring? and Victorinus, Optatus, Hilary? To say nothing of the living, how much more was brought by innumerable Greeks? Moses himself had done this first, that most faithful servant of God, of whom it is written that he was learned in all the wisdom of the Egyptians. The prevailing heathen superstition would never have allowed such men as these to take over the disciplines it considered useful (especially in times when it was trying to shake off the yoke of Christ and persecuting the Christians) if it had ever suspected that these studies would be used for worshipping the one God, in order that the false cult of idols might be destroyed."

'I thought it sufficient to give a short account of these things, as briefly as I could, choosing a little out of so much. I could in fact quote any number of witnesses, if I did not wish to spare your ears, and if the authority of two such holy and learned men were not sufficient to make it impiety to disagree with them. But the barbarians' abstinence from the heathen is such that they do not touch even the saintly ones, or if they touch they spoil. What is even more disgraceful is that they do not count Jerome among the theologians but among the practitioners of eloquence, barring him from their own sacrosanct assembly to number him among the grammarians, while they themselves grow old over a stack of jumbled anthologies and digests, thinking nothing learned unless it is barbarous. And since we follow these great leaders everywhere, they may come and sing that apos-

* * * * *

4 providence] *De doctrina christiana* 2.40.60

10 illustration] *De doctrina christiana* 2.40.61

33 barbarous] In the manuscript this general criticism was more specifically directed: 'and for no other reason than because they do not understand, they grow old over the notes of Duns Scotus and the glosses of Acursius, in which they admire nothing but what is barbarous.'

tolic song to us, "mind not high things, knowledge puffs up." If they really
want to look like theologians, why do they not instead bring out that other
saying: "Be ye wise as serpents and harmless as doves" – not like donkeys,
slow, apathetic, lazy. Or that other, "In malice be ye children, but in
understanding be men." Or again, "Wisdom conquers malice" and "fools   5
despise wisdom." Why do they not produce those words of David: "Teach
me goodness and judgment and knowledge, O Lord." Or of the wise
Ecclesiasticus: "The wise man will seek out the wisdom of all the ancients,
and will be occupied with the prophets. He will keep the discourse of men
of renown, and will enter in among the subtleties of parables. He will seek   10
out the hidden meaning of proverbs, and be conversant in the dark sayings
of parables. He will serve among great men, and appear before him that
ruleth. He will travel through the land of strange nations; he will try good
and evil in all things."

   'In that book which, in uncertainty as to its author, is called Wisdom,   15
how much praise of learning is to be found! Just as Plato profoundly writes
that wisdom is of such incredible beauty that if it could be seen by our eyes
it would arouse wonderful feelings of love, so this writer (eloquent whoever
he was) seems to have depicted the very image of wisdom, so as to fire us
with love for it. Some may argue that it is not earthly wisdom which is   20
praised here, but another kind, heavenly and divine; that wisdom in fact
which is the most difficult part of the philosophy of our time, which has ·
joined together the knowledge of all things human and divine. I am much
deceived if this is not what these very words mean: "God," he says, "gave
me knowledge of the things which are: to know the constitution of the   25
world, and the operation of the elements, the beginning and end and
middle of times, their alternations and the division of seasons, the circuits
of years and the position of stars, the natures of living creatures and the
ragings of wild beasts, the violences of winds and the thoughts of men, the
diversities of plants and the virtues of roots. All things that are either secret   30
or manifest I learned." In these words is described, it seems to me, no
confused or barren erudition, but one which is polished and rich, and

* * * * *

 1 puffs up] Rom 12:16; 1 Cor 8:1
 3 doves] Matt 10:16
 5 be men] 1 Cor 14:20
 5 malice] Wisd 7:30
 5 fools] Prov 1:7
 7 Lord] Ps 119:66 (118:66 Vulg); Erasmus added the word *Domine*.
14 all things] Ecclus 39:1–5
16 Plato] *Phaedrus* 250D; cf Cicero *De officiis* 1.15.
31 learned] Wisd 7:17–21

founded in high antiquity, more than the knowledge of any special disciplines. In the following chapter he expresses much more clearly how it is
virtue allied to liberal learning which can be called wisdom: "If a man
loveth righteousness," he says, "the fruits of Wisdom's labour are great
virtues: for she teacheth soberness and understanding, righteousness and   5
courage, and there is nothing in life for men more profitable than these.
And if a man longeth even for such experience, she knoweth the things of
old, and divineth the things to come; she understandeth subtleties of
speech and interpretations of dark sayings; she foreseeth signs and wonders, and the issue of seasons and times."   10

'But in a subject as clear as this – abundantly clear indeed in itself,
though not clear enough for their obstinacy – why should I go on in vain *ad
infinitum*, when a host of quotations can be produced from any author? I will
not deny that these authors sometimes argue just as if they were trying to
discourage us from secular learning, and become so heated in their rhetori- 15
cal contention against inquisitive, arrogant, windy, stubborn erudition
that they seem to be attacking not the crime of those who misuse learning
but the thing itself. But it does not enter the heads of these opponents that
the very things which seem to be used in argument against learning are
argued not only by most learned men but in a most learned fashion. With   20
what face would they be exhorting us against secular studies when they
themselves in this very exhortation are exhibiting the knowledge of secular
learning, so that we would have the right to quote against them the saying:
"we willingly flatter our own vices."

'Tell me, you block of marble, you "born fruit-eater," do you really   25
believe that these outstanding men, with the whole of literature at their
fingertips, were simply devoted to commending your yawning indolence
and apathy? It was right to say that dabblers should be discouraged from
over-study, or from study that was futile or inopportune; it was said for the
purpose of curbing pride, possibly for comforting the possessors of dove-   30
like simplicity, but not so that asinine stupidity should be encouraged.
What are you exulting about? Why this idiotic triumph? Why do you twist
what is said from its real meaning? Have you heard someone remark that
expertise is wicked? Why do you preen yourself, as if being inexpert were
being holy? If God rebukes and destroys the sagacity of this world, does   35
that mean that he will love its folly? Not at all – he will hate it even more.
There is condemnation for the learned man who despises the ignorant; but
you are pleased with yourself because being ignorant you despise learned

* * * * *

10 times] Wisd 8:7–8
25 fruit-eater] Horace *Epistles* 1.2.27

men and pass judgment on them. The scholar is rejected because he is
misusing his knowledge, careless of moral standards; but are you, adorned
with the same vices and possibly more, to be absolved simply because you
lack knowledge? One man is censured for spending all his time over
Aristotle and never looking at the Gospels, but you are free from blame –
you cannot understand the Gospels but you never even read them! He,
knowing the will of God, shall be beaten with many stripes, but will you,
who neither do it nor care to know about it, be beaten with few stripes? He
is punished because a kind of zeal has made him overstep the limits of his
duty, but you, not content with your own inertia, do you want to be praised
for hindering the industry of others? But I must make an end of my spate of
words and control my seething anger; only this I say – these numbskulls
would never taunt us like this, if they were to stop pottering about and turn
their attention to reading the Scriptures.'

At this point Batt was silent for a little, and then threw us a more
friendly glance and said, 'Good Heavens! I nearly forgot whom I was talking
to; I was so carried away by some sort of frenzy that I thought I had the
enemy in front of me to rage at. The truth is that I am amazed at the patience
of your well-trained ears, which can bear to listen to me for so long, as I pour
out words in this childish manner.'

'I have been marvelling for a long time,' said I, 'though I did not want
to interrupt the flow of your speech – I am amazed at your ability to quote so
many lines from so many ecclesiastical writers, so exactly to the point, word
for word. I would hardly have believed such a thing could be done, and so
well done, by a practised theologian. I am beginning not to wonder any
more, as the doctor did just now, at the fact that in spite of your deep
devotion to the Muses you have read the theologians' books; what I do find
remarkable is that you can keep all that in the memory.'

'As for us,' said Willem, 'We were carried away by the remarkable
force of your argument. So go on quickly and make a test to find out whether
you can beat us by talking or we beat you by listening.'

Batt smiled at me and said, 'It was not without reason that I was afraid
of your pen. I have an idea of what is in your mind. You want to publish our
nonsense, and you are worried about the stamp of truth. You are afraid that
when you write down this talk of ours (and I know you mean to) someone
will come along thinking that you have imagined a dialogue on the lines of
Plato or Cicero, and will cavil at it, saying that it has taken no heed of
appropriateness or probability, since you have made me, a poet and still

* * * * *

21 said I] That is, Erasmus
23 word for word] See 74:4n.

very young, cite from memory so much of the writings of the church. But it
is not very surprising, as I have a decent, not a prodigious, memory, that I
should retain a little of what I have read – with interest increased by
irritation – or what I have selected and used so often against the barbarians.
And now to take up Willem's challenge.   5

'Since we have routed our opponents first by reasoning and then by
witnesses, there is one sole refuge left to them, the example of certain
individuals of virtuous life, whom they bring forward against us either
because they were considered learned without erudition, or because they
despised learning for the sake of virtue. If we can evict them from this   10
stronghold, it remains for them either to surrender or to take to their heels
ignominiously and confess themselves beaten. Come on, let us get ready to
finish off the last remains of the conflict.

'"You are aware," they say, "that the Christian faith did not arise from
the natural scientists, the dialecticians, the poets, or from the writers on   15
rhetoric, but from rustic men, untaught, unpolished, in short fishermen;
not from the Academy of Plato nor from the Porch of the Stoics, nor from the
Peripatetic schools, were the apostles called, as well we know, but from
ship and net; and it was not classes in rhetoric or dialectic that Christ threw
open – the only precepts he taught were on how to live."   20

'O sacrilegious impudence! They dare to call the apostles rustic so as to
defend their own rusticity; they do indeed deserve the apostles' love,
piously devoted to their service as they are! It matters nothing to them
where the defence for their idleness comes from, even if it means an insult
to a sacred order. Speak, you of the scabrous face, fit for the branding iron, 25
do you say the apostles were rustic? "Yes," he says; "if not, in what school
could they have learnt, when they were suddenly sent off from their fishing
to the apostolate? Were they not swept off from steering a skiff to governing
the world?" What purpose did it then serve when they followed – not Plato
nor Chrysippus nor any other philosopher – but the very father of   30
philosophy, having him as a teacher for so long, hearing him dispute,
watching him work miracles, living and talking with him day by day?
Seneca wrote that philosophy has such power that it benefits not only those
who study it but the chance listener, "just as anyone who comes into the
sunshine," he says, "takes on a tan although that was not his intention.   35
Those who have been sitting in a perfume shop, and have stayed there a
little while, take away with them the fragrance of the place." The apostles,

* * * * *

30 father of philosophy] Erasmus often speaks thus of Christ in the preface to the
   New Testament (*Paraclesis*) and in the *Adagia*, e.g., I i 36, 'Christ, our teacher.'
33 Seneca] *Epistles* 108.4

though, who stayed so long with the very fount of knowledge, lived in close and eager companionship with him: did they remain as ignorant as they were rustic? were there no results from the assiduous work of such a teacher? It is a waste of trouble to take a bull to the wrestling-ring. When Christ had risen from the dead, he stayed on earth forty days; he often appeared to his disciples, instructed them, taught them; and this is not all. When he himself went back to heaven, he sent the Paraclete, so that nothing should be unknown to them. And after all this some little manikins dare to throw up against the apostles the objection that they were rustic and they fished for their living? Why not go on and call them anglers, beachcombers, pirates?

'Even if it were allowable to taunt the apostles like this, can Paul be called rustic? He is the single one, they say, who carried liberal learning with him into the apostolate; and if he stands out among the rest, what is the cause of this but learning? For I think all of them were equal in piety. This man is called a chosen vessel; why he rather than the others? Obviously because he in particular, being so learned and so eloquent, was seen to be fitted to bear arms against the cultured schools of Athens, able to bear the haughtiness of the philosophers, and to range Roman eloquence under the sway of Christ.

'Is John rustic? Where did he get that sublime utterance, "In the beginning was the Word, and the Word was with God, and the Word was God"? Is Peter rustic? The Epistles are certainly his, and may be unpolished in speech but not in wisdom. Was James rustic? Then that Epistle must be falsely attributed to him – it seems to come from a writer who was not only wise but eloquent.

'But suppose we imagine the apostles *were* rustic. Is there nothing in the conduct of the apostles that these people can see worthy of imitation, except just their rusticity? I really cannot help saying what I feel, such a mighty roar of laughter rises up in me every time I think of the profligate lives of these people who throw up against us the apostolic lack of refinement. Who could bear to hear Aesop giving hints about frugality or Sardanapalus discussing harshness? If my anger breaks out too bitterly, remember I am attacking not the man but the thing, though according to

* * * * *

4 bull] *Adagia* i iv 62
16 vessel] Acts 9:15
18 Athens] Acts 17:18–34
22 Word] John 1:1
32 Aesop] Not the fabulist but M. Clodius Aesopus, son of Clodius Aesopus, a celebrated actor. Cf Horace *Satires* 2.3.239ff.

Plautus "what is ill said about those who deserve it is well said." If the
people who never stop yelping at us about apostolic rusticity were to
possess the virtues of the apostles, there might be some way of putting up
with them; but as it is, the corrupt life of some of them is such that I am
ashamed to contemplate it even in thought. They have been ordained in the
church, they live on church stipends, they are old, white-haired, shrivelled,
some even wear the cowl – and yet they seem to have entered into competition with Sardanapalus himself. Here am I, a young man and a layman,
engaged in public affairs, and with a declared interest in literature which is
itself secular, and they arraign me, they put me on trial as guilty of a
nefarious crime, because I freely spend my time reading ancient
philosophy, early history, the writings of the poets and orators. Their duty
is to be occupied night and day in reading the law of the Lord and the Holy
Scriptures, but they carefully avoid any study at all, I suppose guided by a
religious scruple, because they fear that if they began to open a book they
might be unwary enough to fall in with some heathen author. They think
they are really imitating the apostles, if they are uneducated to the point of
not understanding the prayers they mumble over every day. Tell me, you
stupid imitator, is this how you reproduce the apostles for us? Do you say
the apostles were ignorant and rude? Very well, we will grant you that; you
have something to boast about, you have outdone the fishermen in ignorance; we will not envy you that glory (which ploughboys share with you);
but where is apostolic simplicity? Where is their way of life? When did you
ever read that the apostles were given to hunting? or that they adopted your
kind of luxurious attire? Did the apostles keep a troop of concubines at
home? Did the apostles sink so much wealth in one bottomless pit? As for
you, please heaven, in your zeal for imitating the apostles you use church
funds to build yourselves palaces high as the sky. In the vast mansion
shines furniture worthy of Attalus; the whole place is loud with soldier-
servants; banquets are prepared with Persian splendour; you may see
Sybaritic parties going on there all the time; for waste of money Cleopatra is
far outshone, or Aesop with his son, so like his father. There sturgeon are

* * * * *

1 well said] Plautus *Curculio* 513
25 concubines] *Pellacarum gregem.* The usual Latin word is *pellex* or *paelex*, and
here Erasmus is no doubt reflecting Valla (*Elegantiae* ASD I-4 293). The idea of
the apostles keeping a harem is the kind of startling thought that comes to
Erasmus.
29 Attalus] Attalus III of Pergamum (d133 BC) left his wealth to the people of Rome.
31 Sybaritic] *Adagia* II ii 65
31 Cleopatra] An allusion to Cleopatra's pearl, which she dissolved and drank
32 Aesop] See 103:32n.

despised, the murena has no flavour, grouse make you feel sick. For days
and nights there is eating and drinking, play and dancing and prurience,
and when the wine makes them begin to stutter I imagine they think
themselves to be copying the unpolished speech of the apostles. Together
with this behaviour, of which Nero would be ashamed, they dare to talk to   5
us about the necessity of imitating the apostles!

'Recently I went on a mission in your name to Flanders, and I happened to come upon a banquet run by one of these monsters. While we sat
drinking, as usually happens, he boasted to us of his hospitality, and to
enliven the feast with rather more entertaining talk I told the tale of Tantalus   10
and Lycaon and various other stories of the kind. He asked me where these
could be read. I said in the poets. He at once begged me not to mention
those heathens at his board, as he did not want the sacred feast corrupted by
filthy names. I complied with the wishes of my host.

'There was present a certain theologian, a young man but really   15
learned, not like the run of present-day theologians who have mostly learnt
nothing but sophisms, but in a way that made him no less a rhetorician than
a theologian. With him I had a conversation (he was sitting next me) about
church writers and their eloquence. We talked about Augustine, and said
that he certainly spoke with penetration, but his style was rather obscure   20
and involved, and very much his own, and yet this was his peculiar charm,
owing to the figures of speech he liked to use. Jerome, we said, had an
urgent style, varied, subtle, sharp and rich. Lactantius Firmianus flowed
along with Ciceronian smoothness, and was not quite free from the exercises in declamation on which he had spent many years. The pen of   25
Ambrose had more obscurity and less penetration, but pleased all the same
by the sharp sting of his allusions. Bernard's style of writing was choice, not
unpolished, but with an ecclesiastical ring; Hilary's was not quite abundant
enough, but superior in elegance, and flowery too. Bede's we found even-
toned and dull, but learned, considering his century. Gregory's we found   30
musical and rhythmical rather than pithy, because he was forced to repeat
the same phrases so as to fill out his periods. Present-day theologians, we
said, do not even speak; they are so far from illuminating the truth with
the resources of style that they deface matter which is in itself excellent.

'As we were amusing ourselves with these and other subjects, the   35
former severe critic laughed at us and called us idle dabblers, who took

* * * * *

10 Tantalus and Lycaon] The reference is to mythical feasts: Tantalus in Homer
   Odyssey 11.582–92; Lycaon in Ovid *Metamorphoses* 1.196–243.
20 style] With this passage on the style of Christian writers cf Allen Ep 2157:1–29.
27 Bernard's] Of Clairvaux
30 century] AD 675–735

pains over futile and useless things. Realizing the man's worthlessness, I
thought it best to take a hard wedge to split a hard knot, and I deliberately
introduced a topic on which I knew he was very strong: that is, on varieties
of wine, the art of cookery, and hunt suppers. At this he became animated
as if it were a very important matter, and in a general hush discoursed for a   5
long time with great authority and with much acuteness, abundance, and
polish. You would have said he was Plato in person. He enumerated from
memory I don't know how many kinds of wine. In addition, he gave their
prices, qualities, differences, vineyards, and character, and was particularly proud of having learnt all this by means of his own experienced palate,   10
and not from any books of the naturalists. He said that Pliny (whom I
mentioned) was out of his mind to have trusted other peoples' books on
such an important subject, rather than his own palate. If you had heard him
discussing cookery, how to prepare banquets and season them, you would
have despised any other cook, whether he were Catius, or Philoxenus, or   15
Apicius, or Platyna. These are indeed awe-inspiring arts, deserving a
solemn priest; these are what the apostles learnt and handed down to us –
not instructions about how to tie up a network of syllogisms, or to turn over
the pages of Cicero and Virgil, or to be a judge of others' brains and style in
speaking. These, you understand, are not learnt in the fables of the poets,   20
but in Holy Scripture!

'Even this would be bearable if it were not that in the course of these
dinners the old men, weak in everything but desire, vie with each other in
recalling their past feats, and make a boast of the base things they have
done, which age forbids them to do now. These are the people whose ears   25
religiously shun the fables of the poets, and who encourage us to follow
apostolic example; it was their vicious rusticity and fraudulent simplicity
that Jerome was referring to in a shrewd passage: "What always awoke
veneration in me," he says, "was not wordy uncouthness, but holy simplicity. If anyone says he imitates the apostles in speech, let him first copy their   30
virtues in his life. Great holiness will provide an excuse for their simplicity

* * * * *

2 hard knot] *Adagia* i ii 5
15 Catius ... Platyna] These are gourmands and cookery experts: for Catius see
    Horace *Satires* 2.4; Philoxenus, a Greek dithyrambic poet, appears as a gour-
    mand in Athenaeus *Deipnosophistae* 1.6E; Apicius was a Roman gourmand
    whose cookery book is lost, that which is extant in his name being spurious;
    Bartolomeo Platina, a librarian of the Vatican and historian of the popes,
    composed a Latin cookbook (1470) which went through many editions and
    was translated into many languages.
23 dinners] There is another reminiscence of a dinner in *Adagia* iv vii 60.
28 Jerome] Ep 57.12

of language, and the Aristotelian syllogism or involved points of Chrysippus will be confuted by him who was dead and is alive again. But it would be ridiculous anyway if one of us, living amid the wealth of Croesus and the pleasures of Sardanapalus, were to boast solely about his rusticity, as if all robbers and people accused of various crimes were eloquent, and hid their gory swords behind the tomes of the philosophers, not behind trunks of trees.''

'I wanted to touch on this subject by way of digression, so as to make it clear that those who press upon us the notion of apostolic ignorance do not do it for the sake of emulating the apostles, but, as they are proud, they seek a defence from the apostles for their own rusticity. In any case, if it is right to do something because many have given the example, how many and how great are the precursors whom we may imitate! We may go back to Moses: what leader could be holier? And he, as we read, was learned from boyhood in all the skills of the Egyptians. This secular knowledge, as they call it, was no disadvantage to him, who of all mortal men was the one who deserved to be admitted to walk closely with the Lord. Who could be chaster than Daniel? And he did not refuse to be instructed in the disciplines of the Chaldeans. We have heard that Solomon was the wiser son of a wise father. and that Job, and all the prophets, were not illiterate is not only affirmed by the testimony of Jerome and Augustine, but is clear also from their own writings. To forestall the carping objection that this ceased to be right with the ending of the Mosaic law, I will set before them Paul the apostle, Paul's disciple Dionysius; how great was the learning of both, how great their eloquence; they are their own witnesses. Quadratus, who was a hearer of the apostles, did not lose his marvellous erudition with such men as teachers. When he was head of the church in Athens, he is said to have presented to the emperor Hadrian a book of such erudition that he succeeded in stemming a fierce persecution of the Christians by the sheer force of his mind. The same thing was done by his contemporary Aristides, most serious of philosophers, and a consummate orator. Justin, who was a philosopher even in his dress, and in the liberal disciplines a fine craftsman, not only turned his most learned mind to the defence of the

* * * * *

  1 Chrysippus] See 27:14n.

17 with the Lord] Deut 34:10

19 Chaldeans] Dan 1:4, 17

24 Dionysius] 'Erasmus does not yet express any doubt that the theological treatises attributed to Dionysius are the works of Paul's disciple' (ASD I-1 126n). But see LB VI 503C–F.

25 Quadratus ... Clement] Quadratus, Aristides, Justin, and Clement of Alexandria are all mentioned by Jerome in Ep 70.4.

LB X 1737C / ASD I-1 126

Christian religion, but spent his very soul upon it. Clement, the teacher of
Origen, priest of the Alexandrian church, was a man of surpassing learning, and judged to be so by another man of surpassing learning, Jerome;
and he, at a time when the holy faith was in great danger because of the
active opposition of the heathen, brought to its defence no little support   5
through his eloquence and his books full of learning.

'But it would be numbering the sands if I tried here to go through the
whole catalogue of learned men. I could count two thousand whose outstanding erudition came to the aid of the faith in its peril; otherwise we
should not have had a faith so wide-sweeping nor so strongly founded –   10
perhaps we should not have had a faith at all. And then these opponents of
ours are alarmed at the idea of learning human disciplines, as if there were a
dearth of examples to follow! If they would turn away their gaze for a while
from examples near at hand and look through the chronicles of old writers,
if they would examine those who have written about illustrious writers,   15
they would find that Origen, Gregory Nazianzen, Didymus, John Chrysostom, and, to come to the Latin writers, Lactantius, Hilary, Severus, in a
word all of them to a man, who laboured in defence of the faith and in
expounding the mysteries of the Scriptures, were most highly proficient in
scholastic disciplines; and their pagan learning, nay rather their Christian   20
learning, as Jerome says with admiration, we must be careful not to despise.

'But so strict are we that nothing can move us by erudition, however
polished it be, unless it be also pious. Look at Origen – he did not escape the
imputation of heresy! That is their pretext. But look, there are plenty of   25
examples of this too. Hilary is numbered among the saints; let us take him
for an example. Cyprian was as notable for his martyrdom as for being
versed in secular literature; let us follow him. Who could be holier than
Ambrose? let us imitate him. Who could be more pious or more cultured
than Jerome or Augustine? let us try to be like them. In the works of all these   30
men how much there is in the way of literary art, of languages, philosophy,
history, antiquity, Latin and Greek style, how much familiarity with authors! And all this up to that time was pagan. Let us compare these men, I
beg, with the scholastics and theologians of our own day: we shall see that
in both domains they are so inferior that one would call them shadows   35

* * * * *

7 sands] *Adagia* I iv 44
16 Origen] In this list of early Christian writers the name of Origen was not
      present until the edition of 1520. When the manuscript was composed Eras-
      mus had apparently not yet read Origen, for whom he was inspired with
      enthusiasm by the Franciscan Jean Vitrier of Saint Omer in 1501. His interest
      never failed and he was working on Origen when he died.

rather than men; and among such a multitude of weighty scholars the only ones we think of are the apostles, whom we can believe we are imitating only if we stay untaught! In fact, we are as far from the way of life of the apostles as India is distant from here. If we are so keen on imitating the rusticity of the apostles, I wonder we don't turn to fishing.

'But joking apart, need we be afraid of imitating Ambrose? Is there a moral objection against imitating Jerome? Our opponents say, "Those people were imbued with literary studies when they were still children, and not yet Christian." But Jerome was born of Christian parents, and was himself Christian from childhood, and yet admits that he was educated among the grammarians and rhetoricians, and is even proud of it. Not that the argument carries anyway, since these men used the things which they had learnt before baptism, not only when they had become Christians, but when they were bishops and old men. Why did they all sprinkle their books with references to pagan literature? Why do they uphold this as the right thing to do? If they did it without comment, it might seem that it was a thing to be excused rather than imitated, but as it is they bear witness that they acted rightly and after the example of the best authors. Augustine himself, at a time when he was no longer pagan, wrote a separate volume on each of the liberal arts. "But he wrote," they say, "as a catechumen and not as a Christian." You have quite a point there! Then if ever, surely, he should not have been thinking about pagan literature, when as a new recruit he was undergoing training in the Christian religion! But suppose it was really a sin, that he was in error, acting in ignorance – why did he not point out this error when he was older and wiser? Why did he confess that he had done it deliberately, so that walking in these footsteps, as it were, he might come gradually to the knowledge of the fullness of truth? He says, in fact, that these disciplines are like so many sparks glittering forth from that eternal light, and led by them we may approach the source of light itself. How much more religious he is than we are! We with our uncouth minds do not go step by step towards the divine mysteries but suddenly crash in on them; we do not climb towards them but fly at them, as if we were like the Giants, building up great outworks against heaven and trying to occupy Jove's stronghold against his will. So it comes about that the one who climbed gradually was accepted, but we are repulsed, thrown down, and dashed to the ground. Bede the monk was actually English, or more likely a Scot, but upright in his life and no mean teacher; and he was so far from despising the disciplines of the schools that he was willing to write about rules of grammar and prosody. After these writers the lustre and polish of

* * * * *

39 rules] Bede wrote *De schematis et tropis sacrae scripturae* and *De metrica arte*.

St Peter
Marco Zoppo, 1433–78
'Take Peter and Jerome, one the first among the apostles, the other first among the
doctors. In Peter there was the ardour of faith at its highest; in Jerome there was
learning at its best. It is for you to imitate the spirit of the one and the scholarship of
the other' (*Antibarbari* 113:7–10).
National Gallery of Art, Washington

RIGHT St Jerome in His Study
Albrecht Dürer, 1514
Nelson Gallery-Atkins Museum, Kansas City, Missouri
(Gift of Mr Robert B. Fizzell)

theology declined, and degenerated little by little, and it began to collect a
good deal of rust. For several centuries scholars were fewer, and of an
inferior stamp, although they were never altogether lacking; there was
never a time without plenty of plodding workers. That most noble writer
Thomas Aquinas brought out commentaries on the pagan philosopher   5
Aristotle, and even in his theological *Questions*, where he is reflecting about
the first principle and about the Trinity, he offers evidence from Cicero and
the poets. Scotus, who seems to have been far removed from the Muses, is
yet a Schoolman, and even in the middle of his puzzles and deep problems
of theology cannot forget his philosophers. There is little need to mention   10
more recent writers, or those still living, except to say that, although their
erudition is much inferior, even among them that man stands out who is
the most highly educated in secular learning. To put it shortly, many even
of the most outstanding men do not possess secular learning, but among
those who have it not one has not used it, not one has been afraid to adorn   15
the temple of the Christians with the wealth of the pagan world.'

Here Batt paused briefly, and the burgomaster interrupted him.
'Great heavens!' said he, 'what if I stop being a burgomaster and become a
philosopher?'

'You have my permission,' said Batt.   20

The burgomaster went on: 'You seem to me to have gone a long way
round – and I think it was clever of you – so that forgetfulness of the
simplicity of the apostles should steal insensibly upon us; but the most
important point should not have been passed over. We will agree that many
pious men have used secular literature in a creditable way, but still it was   25
not for nothing, I think, that we were given the apostles as founders of our
religion, and leaders and princes in it, the rough and unlettered apostles
whom you are forbidding me to imitate. In my opinion, the way to the
highest and finest praise is to emulate the finest and foremost men.'

Batt smiled. 'Look what a mighty imitator of the apostles is throwing   30
these objections up at me! Am I forbidding you to imitate the apostles?
What I do recommend is that you should reflect the moral virtues of the
apostles and at the same time the learning of Jerome. What happens is that
everybody imitates the roughness of the apostles and no one imitates their

* * * * *

6 *Questions*] Which works by Thomas Erasmus has in mind is uncertain. He
may mean, for the 'first principle,' Thomas' commentaries on Aristotle,
Quaestiones disputatae, or *De principiis naturae*. The Trinity is discussed in
Thomas' *Tractatus de trinitate* (*Summa theologica* I, q xxvii, aa 1–5), *De mysterio
trinitatis*, and the commentary on Boethius *De trinitate*.
8 Scotus] Duns Scotus (c 1265–1308)

lives. You say the way to the finest praise is to emulate the finest men; I am
not against this; but you are mistaken in choosing to set before yourself as
an example the last and lowest characteristics of the first and highest men.
The truly attentive imitator is he who not only chooses for himself, uner-
ringly, the right example, but picks out in it what he thinks finest, and
passes over some things and disapproves of others. He will only try to
imitate the highest qualities. Take Peter and Jerome, one the first among the
apostles, the other first among the doctors. In Peter there was the ardour of
faith at its highest; in Jerome there was learning at its best. It is for you to
imitate the spirit of the one and the scholarship of the other.

'But you prefer to set before yourself the order of apostles rather than
that of doctors, so I will set before you two of the greatest of the first order,
Peter and Paul. Paul was most highly instructed in all branches of literature.
Peter, whose authority was greater than that of Paul, was rebuked by Paul,
and he had confidence in the more learned man and obeyed him. We
imitate these men, yes, but in a topsy-turvy way. Ignorant as we are, we not
only refuse to obey the learned, but take it upon ourselves to reproach them.
But it was not for nothing that it was arranged for the Christian religion to
take its beginnings from untutored founders. That indeed was right, and its
purpose was that the glory of such an event should not appertain to human
effort but be attributed entirely to divine power. This was appropriate to
those times, but what about our own? These times demand another kind of
life, other ways of living. The apostles were not versed in secular learning,
but surely they never reproved it? When do we read that they ever excluded
educated men from their companionship? The apostles were inexperienced
in literary studies; what has that to do with you, who make a profession of
these studies? For what we are discussing concerns less the apostles than
the schoolmasters. What lover of Christian piety could bear the way these
rogues are always heaping blame on holy men, the very authors of our
salvation? Come then, if you like, we will compare *their* rusticity with *our*
erudition. We read for instance that they knew all kinds of languages; we
can scarcely stammer in one. They were so powerful in speaking that they
moved tyrants and fierce and barbarous peoples; we are dumber than the
animals themselves. They held in their memory the mysteries of both
Testaments. We have hardly perceived the first elements of literary study,
and then we dare – we who are cruder than crudity itself – to call the apostles
uneducated men.'

'But you seem to me, Batt,' said the burgomaster, 'to make two mistakes in your argument, which is more impassioned than accurate. The

* * * * *

14 rebuked] Gal 2:11–21

discussion was about secular literature, not about Holy Scripture, which the apostles had received, as we all agree; and they mastered it not through human study, but by the gift of heaven.'

'You know all about their mental equipment, evidently,' returned Batt; 'that is the very argument a stupid theologian would have used in reply. They take refuge in that every time they are confronted with Jerome's eloquence or Augustine's learning and the writings of the Fathers. To all of these, they say, the Holy Spirit was the source. It amazes me to see in people who think themselves particularly sharp – dialecticians in fact – such dull wits, unless they are simply making a mistake. What do they mean by that kind of phrase? Is no knowledge to be sought for by us, except what falls from heaven? Then it is vain that we vex ourselves with daily and nightly study. What are the schools for (and publicly owned ones too), and all those costly libraries? Why do we spend our best years, the whole of them, on crazy efforts of learning? Why do we uselessly grow wan and old over our books? Let us mend our ways – even though rather late – and "try for better things, now we have been told." Let us give up these useless labours; this astute type of individual is showing us a short cut to living. Let us take care of our skins, and "be generous with wine and sleep," as Horace puts it, while we wait for celestial inspiration to descend on us between yawns; and then as if we had drunk from the Aonian spring we shall suddenly emerge as theologians, unless we prefer to await the moment of being carried away like Paul into paradise or the third heaven, to hear things which no man may reveal to another. But we must first get it clear whether we are asking for everything to be revealed to us at once or whether we want the Spirit to be on hand every time we have need of him. My opinion is that the second alternative is by far the most convenient, because if he inspired us only once, we should have a job to remember it all. So as to relieve our memory of such a load, it will be better to leave everything to the Holy Spirit, and let him be ready to suggest to us just enough and no more, whether we call on him or not, as circumstances require. There is a book to be written – let him fly to our side and control our pen, with no effort of ours. A speech is to be given – then let him sit by our ear in the shape of a dove and himself guide our tongue – all we have to do is to remember to open our mouth, as one might sing with the psalmist, "I opened my mouth, and drew in my breath."

* * * * *

17 told] Virgil *Aeneid* 3.188
19 Horace] Horace *Epistles* 1.2.29 and *Satires* 2.3.3
21 Aonian spring] The fountain of Mount Helicon, sacred to the Muses
30 call] *Vocatus et invocatus: Adagia* II iii 32; Horace *Odes* 2.18.40
35 psalmist] Ps 119:131 (118:131 Vulg). There is a pun here, *spiritus* meaning both breath and Spirit.

'There will perhaps be some who think these remarks too harsh. But nothing could be harsh when said against such arrogant people, who despise the excellent labours of others and know nothing themselves, but want to appear inspired by heaven; and I, a mere poet, would not dare to attack these godlike creatures if St Augustine himself had not made fun of their mindlessness, with a good deal of wit, in the preface to his books on *Christian Doctrine*. Where, he asks, would that error finally lead, if once it became supreme in the minds of men? No one would have allowed himself to be taught by a wiser person. No one would have hastened to hear a sermon in church, nor would anyone have lent an ear to the reading of the Gospel, for all these would have been vain, if they had thought they must wait for tuition from heaven. He goes on to say that there was a rumour going around among the people about someone who had had knowledge of letters conferred on him without human aid, and he does not entirely refuse to believe it; however he thinks it of little importance, because, even if it were quite true, it would not be a thing to be hoped for by everyone. He does not think the blessing conferred on that one person should deter us from diligent effort, for to expect from heavenly inspiration what one could suitably be taught by a man is the attitude of a fool or, what is nastier, of an insolent man.'

The burgomaster retorted, 'You can go on arguing with yourself in the manner of the Schoolmen with quibbles like these. What does it mean, when he himself tells his disciples not to be anxious about what they shall say before kings and judges: "It shall be given you," he says, "in that same hour what ye shall speak, for it is not ye that speak, but the Spirit of your Father which speaketh in you." What did it mean when Peter wrote about holy men of God who spoke as they were moved by the Holy Spirit? What of that saying of James: "If any of you lack wisdom, let him ask of God, that giveth to all men liberally and upbraideth not." Unless I am much mistaken, these have quite a different ring from your speech.'

'Your admonition is right and opportune,' said Batt, 'but these questions can easily be resolved. Pray, does it seem to you that Christ, when he spoke those words you have just quoted, was deterring his disciples from thinking over what they would say before princes, which no one but a lunatic would omit to do, when Christ himself in so far as he was a man did not speak without reflection? He did not wish to deprive the apostles of what any sensible man would do, but to take away fear, lest they should

* * * * *

6 preface] *De doctrina christiana* prologue 3–8
24 he says] Matt 10:19–20
26 Peter] 2 Peter 1:21
29 upbraideth not] James 1:5

tremble to speak in their lowliness and ignorance before princes and
learned men, in whose presence the greatest and most accomplished
orators would turn pale; he would have them know that he would not desert
his advocates, if only they would be of good courage. Thus he did not mean
to forbid diligence and carefulness, but to increase their valour. I would go
so far as to say that the other apostles and Paul too sometimes spoke from a
premeditated or even a written text, which one may guess fairly conclu-
sively from the speeches in his defence which are in the Acts of the
Apostles; and that neither the Epistles of Peter, nor of James, nor of John,
are of the kind that could appear to have been written without forethought.

'But you bring up the objection to me that "holy men of God spoke as
they were taught by the Holy Spirit." In what kind of way do you suppose
they spoke? Like the soothsayers and sibyls, carried away by some frenzy
so that they did not understand what they were saying? But it will be more
convenient to deal with this a little later. That passage of James about asking
wisdom from God – they make that into an absurdity. Wisdom is indeed to
be sought from God, I agree, and sought in what way? Why, just like food
and clothing and the other things necessary for human life. We are commanded by God to ask daily for our daily bread, and he gives it to us every
day, but does he give it to the yawners? We ask for clothing and he gives it,
but to those who work. On the same lines we ask for wisdom, but on the
understanding that we do not relax our human effort. Truly, the things you
need for the body are not obtained without your working for them, and do
you think what you need for the mind is to be received gratis? Bread is to be
earned by the sweat of one's brow; is wisdom to be poured in while one is
asleep? It would be deemed a desperate and suicidal act to prefer to die of
hunger while waiting for sustenance from heaven, rather than to escape
death by eating bread gained by human effort; but it is a religious act, is it,
to choose a shameful ignorance rather than accept life-giving doctrine from
men?

'But, you say, wisdom was conferred on the apostles without the aid of
mortal man. Agreed; and we read that food fell from heaven on the Israelites
in the wilderness. But just as it is wicked to want to stand waiting for that
manna from heaven, so it would be equally wicked or more so for people
idly to await wisdom to descend on them from heaven as if they were
apostles! We are forbidden by the word of the Gospel to be anxious about
our food and clothing for the morrow, but nowhere are we prohibited from
seeking wisdom. It is not considered a subject for reproach, you notice, if

* * * * *

32 we read] Exod 16:4, 14–15
36 Gospel] Matt 6:25–34

we scrape, and search, and sow, and build, not only for the morrow but for
many years to come, not for the sake of our own life alone but for posterity;
and is it to be made a reproach if one does the same thing in the search for
wisdom, a far better fruit? We adopt the sensible interpretation that it is not
diligence in seeking our bread which is forbidden, but vain and anxious   5
worry; and why should we not do the same in the other case? Wisdom was
promised to Solomon by the heavenly oracle, as the kingdom of Israel was
promised to his father, but neither of them relied on the oracle to the extent
of bypassing any human efforts by which he could prove himself worthy
(that is, David) or of making only a languid search for wisdom (in the case of   10
Solomon). They evidently understood the weighty word which someone
wrote: "The gods sell everything to us for the price of work." They will give,
but to the man who works; they will add wisdom, but to the man who
strives; they will grant continence to those who endeavour; they will teach,
but it will be the studious; they will help, but help will be for those who put   15
up a good fight. They will forsake no one, always supposing that he does
not fail himself. Otherwise why should the apostles have written at all? Or
the evangelists? Or Jerome? Or Augustine? Why should the rest have left us
records of their minds – illustrious records, if wisdom is to be gained by
attentive work, but useless if it is something we have to wait for in our   20
sleep. We agreed just now that the apostles were endowed with wisdom.
Apart from the fact that both before and after the Resurrection they were
trained by Christ, the best of all teachers, with continuous instruction,
apart from the fact that they read for themselves continually and compared
their views on the Scriptures, why did he not give an equal part to each?   25
Why was Paul wiser than Peter? Why does James surpass Peter in eloquence? Why does John write more divinely than the other evangelists?
Why among the holy doctors is one more learned, another more eloquent?
They certainly all wrote under the inspiration of the same divine power.
The answer is obviously that the Spirit whom we worship does not find the   30
same learning in all. For he increases what our industry has produced, he
promotes our studies, he sustains our efforts. If it be right to bring in the
fables of the poets at this point, we ought to imitate Prometheus, who when
he wanted life for his clay image dared to seek it from the stars, but only
when he had already applied every means available to human skill. We   35

     * * * * *

  7 Solomon] 1 Kings 3:12
  8 promised] 2 Sam 7:8–9; 1 Chron 17:7
20 work] The thought comes from Epicharmus, quoted by Xenophon
     Memorabilia 2.1.20, and is found in many poets.
33 Prometheus] This form of the Prometheus myth is found in the Latin tradi-
     tion. Cf Horace *Odes* 1.16.13; Ovid *Metamorphoses* 1.81ff.

offer an unformed lump, and hope that the Spirit will shape it for us as we
sleep! We have forgotten that Paul himself, who had the experience of being
carried up to the third heaven, sent for his books written on parchment, and
later conferred with Peter and the other apostles about the teaching of the
faith; that the apostles themselves more than once communicated with each   5
other about the new religion, and that Peter was rebuked by the voice of
Paul. What was the Holy Spirit doing then? Why did he allow Paul to read,
Peter to err, all of them to flounder? You see that the gift of the Holy Spirit
does not exclude human work, but comes to its aid. There were times
however when he was present in a marvellous fashion, but only when the   10
occasion demanded a miracle, or when human endeavour was superseded.
And from among those who endeavoured came forth many learned men,
we read, by the help of the Holy Spirit. But did anyone ever hear or read of
an ass being suddenly turned into a theologian? I am not influenced at all by
the instances current among the common people, about a dove being seen   15
at the ear of a speaker or writer, or a book sent down from heaven in a
dream. These may be fictions, invented in good faith for the sake of giving
authenticity to documents, or they may be true – some may argue about it, I
do not. Nevertheless we see that any given person has become an effective
scholar just in so far as he had possessed intellectual ability and striven in   20
his studies. Many people possess brains and talents without effort, for they
are the gift of nature, but no one gets virtue and learning that way.'

'You have nearly removed one of my two objections,' said the burgomaster; 'there is just one thing you must settle for me: the barbarians, to a
man, bring up the case of St Bernard, who was one of a more recent   25
generation and both learned and eloquent as well as having a reputation for
sanctity. According to them he confesses, somewhere or other, that he had
oaks and beeches for his schoolmasters.'

'What wise trees they must have been,' said Batt, 'which produced
such a pupil for us! They deserved better than to grow old on the hills or   30
provide food for swine; they ought to have been occupying the chair of
lecturers in theology, or at least turned into nymphs like Aeneas' ships in
Virgil! Great heavens! They have no shame; these people are stupider than
the oaks themselves – they might seem to be born from the trunks of trees,
as the poets tell. What, are trees to teach men?'   35

* * * * *

3 books] 2 Cor 12:2; 2 Tim 4:13
5 communicated] Gal 1:18–19; 2:1–10
6 rebuked] Gal 2:11–14
25 St Bernard] From an early life of St Bernard: Migne *PL* 185:240
33 Virgil] *Aeneid* 9.107–22

Batt was getting hot with anger, and here my dear Willem intervened,
with his Socratic subtlety – not caustic however, but good-humoured.

'Excuse me, Batt,' he said, 'but it might happen. Quite possibly some
of these trees were seedlings from that tree in the garden of paradise, which
not only possessed the knowledge of good and evil, as we read, but could   5
transmit it. Or if that will not do, since the species does not fit (although to
be sure we have no name for the species and the tree may have degenerated
through frequent replanting), they are surely derived from those trees
which are said to have admired and followed Orpheus as he sang; among
these it is well known that the Oak held first place. Then, as you know, it is   10
common knowledge that in old times men used to be turned into trees.
What if these Oaks and beeches were once great philosophers, whom the
gods, in pity for their long drawn out hardships, ordered to become these
trees? But be that as it may, there is one thing I really do wish: that Erasmus
had a few cuttings from these most knowledgeable trees, which he could   15
plant in the new orchards he is constructing; then he would have something
at home to learn from, as the comedy-writer says.'

Batt hardly smiled at this; he was too wrought up.

'You are right to laugh,' he said, 'the thing is more to be laughed at
than refuted by argument. But joking apart, I am astonished at Bernard; if   20
he wanted to be taught, why betake himself to trees rather than to men,
instead of imitating the Socrates of Plato? When Phaedrus showed him a
particularly attractive place in the country and knew that Socrates was
greatly taken with its beauty, he remarked that he did not know why he had
not left the town and settled in the country long before. Socrates wisely   25
replied: "Forgive me, my dear Phaedrus, for I am anxious to learn, and it is
not fields and trees which can teach me, but men who live in towns." So
why did Bernard prefer to live among the oaks, unless perhaps (pardon the
joke) there are more learned trees in France than there were of old in Greece?
He is speaking figuratively; he used to pray under the shade of the trees,   30
and he read, and thought over what he had read, and wrote and debated
within himself what he should write; thus it was not so much a desire for
learning as for teaching that made him take refuge under the oaks – he

* * * * *

10 Oak] Capitalized here because it indicates a play on the name of Guillaume
   Duchesne (*a Quercu*), a professor in the University of Paris and representative
   (in the minds of Erasmus and Batt) of narrow scholastic learning. He later
   became a critic of Erasmus (see Allen Ep 1188:29n) and was heavily satirized
   by Rabelais.
17 comedy-writer] Terence *Adelphi* 413
22 Plato] *Phaedrus* 230C–D

obtained in that way the solitude and silence that writers need. In this he
was not acting like a superstitious man but imitating the ways of the poets;
when they are going to write a song they usually seek after woods and
streams.

'If our opponents object here that the holy writers achieved their
learning through prayer, they are holding out to us themselves the very
noose to catch them with. For since St Bernard was highly instructed not
only in philosophic writings but in the poets too, at any rate the secular
ones, how dare you reprove us for attempting to gain by our own labours
the very thing which the Holy Spirit has imparted to some blessed souls? If
heathen learning is the gift of the Holy Spirit, it is good and to be sought for;
God is not the author of evil things. But if you deny that heathen literature is
included in this, I will deny that you have eyes in your head; if you say that
divine wisdom was infused into them as they prayed, but human wisdom
was a matter of their own achievement, I shall laugh at this as a fabrication,
and turn the charge against you, since you burst so stupidly into the field of
divine learning by leaving aside human learning, despite the precedents of
such great men.'

Here Batt seemed to be intending to stop, but the burgomaster said,
'Go on, please, and rid me of my other difficulty: just now you touched on
the central problem of your own accord. The Holy Spirit did not inspire any
apostle with secular learning, which is what we are discussing – not with
dialectics or rhetoric or poetry – and there is no doubt that he would have
done so, if these things were to be of use anywhere.'

To this Batt returned: 'He inspired no one with these things, all right,
but did he ever take them away from anyone? He did not breathe them into
Peter; why did he not take them away from Paul? Why did he not forbid
their use? He would undoubtedly have forbidden them if he had wished it
to appear that they were harmful. But what is the point of asking whether he
filled the apostles with pagan learning? What he did fill them with was what
is needed for acquiring pagan learning. If it were simply a gift to speak a
language well and understand what is spoken, there would be no reason for
the teachers of grammar to torment poor schoolboys; or if the human mind
were so constituted that it could immediately perceive and demonstrate the
truth with nothing to cloud its vision, there would be no purpose in our
practising reasoned argument and dialectical subtleties. If we had ready at a
touch all those emotions we wish to assume for ourselves or awake in
others, we should learn the precepts of rhetoric for no reason. But since

* * * * *

1 solitude] Quintilian 10.3.22, 28
7 noose] *Adagia* I i 53

things are very different, and we are not to expect the visitation of the
Spirit, there is need for liberal disciplines, so that we may arrive at last by a
long circuitous route at the place to which the Spirit led the apostles in a
very short time. Peter did not feel the need of our studies; Paul was helped
by them. But we have spent long enough discussing a childish subject; for   5
those who customarily bring up these objections about divine wisdom are
so far removed from any wisdom, either human or divine, that they need to
be tied up like lunatics rather than coaxed by rational argument. They
preach simplicity, but just so as to appear learned; they confess they have
learnt nothing, but just so as to look like know-alls. Let us leave these   10
people to their madness, and spend the rest of our time discussing poetry
and eloquence.'

   Batt was silent for a minute, then went on: 'We have routed one line of
battle, I think, which it did not take much trouble to defeat, as it was neither
sufficiently armed nor very dangerous. It remains for us to refute those who   15
say that it is not for a Christian to pay attention to eloquence, but in this
more difficult campaign I think it would be as well to appoint a different
general, and a better one. Just as in lawsuits that are none of the best one
must have the best defence, so in the hardest war one must look for the most
experienced leader. Those who condemn the study of eloquence are many   20
in number, and they have perhaps something to say, if not true at least
plausible. And by this time I am aware of having said so much that I am
amazed at the endurance of your ears, which have borne with me as I
jabbered for so many hours. So I beg that a successor may be found who can
argue the case more fluently on the remaining points.'   25

   Willem answered with a modest laugh, 'Why, Batt – are you retiring
from your assigned province without leave of the Senate, and before the
business is settled? And when the war has been virtually brought to an end,
are you asking for a successor (this is most unusual) who will take over all
the glory of the fighting you have done? As to what you say about choosing   30
a better general, your wish is not to appear ambitious; but the fact is that up
to now you have proved yourself to be the kind of leader whose term of
office might be extended, far from a successor being needed before the
time. So by the will of the Senate, go on, and discharge yourself of your duty
as energetically as you began. Your speech has not seemed too long to any of 35
us, quite the contrary – everybody was listening with extraordinary attention and pleasure.'

   While they were quipping with each other, we saw the burgomaster's

* * * * *

8 tied up] 'Bound with the fetters of Hippocrates,' a phrase borrowed from
   Jerome *Adversus Jovinianum* 1.3 (Migne *PL* 23:222c)

servant running back from his house. He brought word that everything was in readiness there, that the meal was getting spoiled, and the burgomaster's wife had been waiting for us for a long time.

'Come along,' said the burgomaster, 'let us all go. I invite you to a philosophical, not an official, repast. The rest of the discussion we can 5 finish this afternoon sitting together in my garden.'

'Is that how you treat me?' said I. 'If you were not such a good lawyer I would take you to court and sue you for carrying off these guests of mine, just because you have a more luxurious kitchen – as if they would not be received at my house in proper style, if frugally.' 10

'Be a good friend,' returned the burgomaster. 'I should like to give my little house the honour of this afternoon's discussion. If you don't mind sharing the glory with me, please give your willing consent. And then it is my wife who commands, and in this kind of thing you know her will is law.'

PARALLELS

Parabolae sive similia

translated and annotated by
R.A.B. MYNORS

Of the genesis of the *Parabolae* we learn much from the prefatory letter[1] in which the work is dedicated to Erasmus' dear friend Pieter Gillis. It was a by-product of the work Erasmus put into the 1515 revision of the *Adagiorum chiliades* (first published in 1508), and into the collected works of Seneca, of which the first edition was published in 1515. For the *Adagia* he was collecting only proverbs and words or phrases having a quasi-proverbial currency; but ancient moralists like Plutarch and Seneca contain much wisdom in the form, not of proverbs but of aphorisms, illustrated by comparison with some fact drawn from history, from our experience of life, or from the world of nature. And beside these authors in whom the moral is already drawn, recorders of natural and social phenomena such as Aristotle and the Elder Pliny provided a great store of facts from which a compiler could draw his own morals; and it soon became almost second nature in Erasmus to collect these too. It is this element of comparison, this parallelism, that is the mark of the *Parabolae*, and Erasmus at first refers to his collections as *Similia, Parallels* (in Greek *homoioseis*). It was all potentially material for the man who wished to learn from the ancients to live wisely, but also to think clearly and to write compellingly, the destined beneficiary of *De copia* and *De conscribendis epistolis*.

The resulting collection differs in several ways from the *Adagiorum chiliades*. Each item from an ancient source is independent of its neighbours, and provided with no supplementary material from elsewhere. The emphasis is all on content, not on form, and much is left out; if Plutarch, for instance, quotes an illustrative line of Greek poetry, in the *Adagia* it would have been rendered into Latin verse, but here it is ignored. The source itself is treated with great freedom: sometimes (if Latin) it is repeated verbatim, sometimes it seems to have done little more than start a brief reaction in Erasmus' mind. Unlike the *Adagia*, the book contains little more reference to contemporary society than that other collection whose name it has taken over, the *Parabolae* or Proverbs of Solomon. And there is no visible attempt at arrangement. Aphorisms are set down apparently in the order in which they were collected, sometimes following for a space the order of the ancient source (in Plutarch, for instance, the first complete edition of the *Moralia* in Greek, published by Aldus in 1509); more often not, as though the compiler had returned to his work again and again for short snatches, once or twice inadvertently repeating material that has already been used and drawing a different moral from it. Immense as is Erasmus' respect for the ancient authors whom he knew so well, he never lets them limit his independence; and this is one reason why he could do so much with them.

In the nature of things such a work could hardly be finished, as Erasmus

* * * * *

1 Ep 312, translated below 130–4

himself recognizes;[2] but by April 1514 he had taken it as far as he meant to take it, and it awaited a transcriber.[3] When it was ready to be printed, he sent it to Matthias Schürer in Strasbourg, who published it in December 1514 in a small quarto volume containing also *De copia* and letters and verses relating to the author's successful visit to the humanistic societies of Strasbourg and Sélestat in the preceding August. Schürer was a devoted supporter of Erasmus (from 1509 onwards he published nearly sixty editions of Erasmus' works in ten years), but he was not normally given the privilege of a first edition, and probably owed the *Parabolae* to his position as an active member of the *sodalitas literaria* of Strasbourg. The printing was neither elegant nor free from error, but the book sold out within the year and was in steady demand, as we learn from a letter in which Nikolaus Gerbel, who was then working as an editor for Schürer's press, urges Erasmus to let them have a corrected text from which to reprint. Gerbel wrote again[4] on 21 January 1516, but corrections were still not forthcoming; and the book reappeared without them in February, followed by a page-for-page reprint in November 1516, and another reprint (perhaps with some corrections) in July 1518. After Matthias' death his nephew Lazarus Schürer produced a *Parabolae* at Sélestat in August 1520 (he calls it *ex secunda recognitione*; it looks like a page-for-page reprint of the 1518 book), and the Schürer firm another in February 1521, before they handed over the primacy in Erasmus-publishing in Strasbourg to Johann Knoblauch.

Meanwhile Erasmus had after all done some revision, but for the benefit of another devoted publisher, Thierry Martens of Aalst, who put out a *Parabolae*, much better printed, in Louvain in June 1515 under the supervision of Gerard Geldenhouwer[5] of Nijmegen, who had edited the *De constructione* for him twice in the previous year. The basis for this was a copy of Schürer's first edition, for, though many of its mistakes are rectified, some still remain; but it was corrected in many details. Some of this correction could have been the work of Geldenhouwer, for it would be within his capacity, and also within the degree of freedom which a scholar of those days would have allowed himself in reprinting another man's work. But that it was revised by the author, as the title-page claims, is certain. At LB I 606F Martens' text adds a slighting reference to two Paris theologians, one of them a contemporary, which no one but Erasmus himself would have done. And at LB I 609B is a

* * * * *

2 In the account of his works which he sent to Johann von Botzheim on 30 January 1523; Allen I 17:14–23. (This letter will be printed in CWE as Ep 1341A.)
3 Ep 292 to William Gonnell from London, 28 April [1514]
4 Gerbel's letters are Epp 369 (assigned by Allen to November 1515) and 383.
5 W. Nijhoff and M.E. Kronenberg eds *Nederlandsche Bibliographie van 1500 tot 1540* (The Hague 1919–) 838; and see Ep 487 introduction.

sentence which, in the first edition and in our modern texts, does not make sense; it requires five more words, which are present in Martens' text, and could only have been added by Erasmus, who knew the passage in the *Digest* to which he was referring. They do not appear again, for Erasmus' revision was characteristically unmethodical; no doubt he kept no record of what he had sent to Louvain, and unfortunately the improved text seems to have had no effect on subsequent editions.[6]

He was still not satisfied, and within a twelvemonth had revised the text again, and sent it to Josse Bade in Paris, who acknowledges its receipt in Epp 434 and 472 of 6 July and 29 September 1516. In both letters Bade expresses misgivings, which do him credit, about the effect which publication by himself might have on Martens' sales; but in September he says he will do an edition to match the type and paper of his *De copia*, as soon as he shall have a press free. Actually he 'reduced it to a handy form' (*in enchiridii modulum compressi*), for it was an octavo and not a quarto; appended a vocabulary made by himself of less common words, most of them Greek in origin; prefixed a letter dated 29 November to Pieter Gillis,[7] to whom the book had been dedicated; and published it without date, but probably in December 1516.[8] It is notable that Erasmus says, in a letter[9] to Bade dated 16 January 1518, that he has not yet seen a copy, for in Basel Johann Froben must already have been engaged on what was apparently a reprint of the Schürer text, with Bade's at his elbow; his edition of February 1518 takes over without acknowledgment Bade's expression 'reduced it to a handy form' and Bade's vocabulary. He repeated this in February 1519 (a page-for-page reprint as far as page 167, and thereafter more closely set, in order to save paper and presswork by bringing the last quire down from ten leaves to the standard eight); and of this there was a page-for-page reprint in July 1521.

In 1522 Erasmus again took some interest in the text. Froben published in quarto that August the first authorized edition of *De conscribendis epistolis*, revised by Erasmus himself who was in Basel at the time, and to this he added the *Parabolae*; the way in which that work appears on the title-page suggests that it was an afterthought, but the overlapping signatures and the absence of pagination in the second half indicate that the setting-up of it was begun

* * * * *

6 For the two additions see below 239:24 and 244:31. Some thirty-five of the corrections and additions in the Louvain text are not reported in ASD, where it is said to offer no notable differences from the first edition.

7 The Latin is reprinted in ASD I-5 19–20.

8 For details of Bade's edition I rely on ASD. Margolin's researches have shown to be untenable Allen's suggestion (in the introduction to Ep 312 and a note to Ep 434) that what Bade was sent was a copy of the Louvain edition.

9 Ep 764; his comment would seem more timely in January 1517.

before the first half was finished. Again there was some revision by the author; Bade's name was restored to the vocabulary, to which a few additions were made; and (what is more significant for the translator) Erasmus added at the end[10] sixteen more *similia*, described in the colophon as 'no mean addition' (*auctarium non mediocre*). Contrary to what might have been expected, it was not until 1534 that Froben reprinted either of these works, and then they appeared separately. The text chosen for the printer's-copy of the *Parabolae* was not that of August 1522 but, for reasons unknown to us, an earlier printing, probably that of 1519 or 1521, as the 1534 reprint has the same number of pages that they have. It was no doubt this reprint of 1534 that supplied the printer's-copy for the Froben *Opera omnia* of 1540, the source of Leclerc's Leiden text of 1703, which we call LB. Thus it came about that the additions of August 1522, though they appear in a few reprints published elsewhere, are ignored in LB; the credit of restoring them to the canon belongs to J.C. Margolin, who prints them as an appendix to his edition for ASD I-5 (Amsterdam 1975). We have placed them at the end of the main text and as part of it, in the place where Erasmus himself saw them in print; for the suggestion[11] that he decided deliberately to suppress them lacks all plausibility.

The book was now finally launched on its course, and later editions do not concern us here. Over fifty in all are known. The wide circulation begins in 1520 and runs for nearly half a century, embracing most of the publishers, from Venice to Cracow, who were normally interested in Erasmus' work; while in 1557 the *Parabolae* was incorporated in the great corpus of such material edited by Conrad Lycosthenes. A useful survey of all this, and an introduction to the impact of the work on Tudor England, will be found in the introduction to the text in ASD.

It follows from what has been said that, if the translator is to be true to the author's intentions, he should follow the text of the first edition but incorporate later corrections, many of which were no doubt due to Erasmus himself and some of which are essential to the sense. Erasmus' additions are not numerous and they are rarely of much interest; but he presumably intended them to remain in the text, and they are therefore included in the translation, but identified by square brackets. A rather free and sententious rendering was suggested by the nature of the work; and it seemed impossible to provide much in the way of commentary without losing one's way in superfluities or commenting not on Erasmus but on his originals, on Plutarch or Pliny. The

* * * * *

10 Margolin's suggestion (ASD I-5 27), that Froben asked the author for material to fill a couple of leaves that would otherwise have been blank at the end of the volume, seems very likely.

11 ASD I-5 28 n99

PARABOLAE SIVE

SIMILIA DES. ERASMI RO/

TERODAMI, cum uocabulo/

rum aliquot non ita uulga/

rium explicatione.

BASILEAE, IN OFFICINA

FROBENIANA

ANNO M. D. XXXIIII

Title page of the *Parabolae sive similia* (Basel 1534)
The last Froben edition published in Erasmus' lifetime. Evidently this was the text
used in the Basel *Desiderii Erasmi opera omnia* (1540).
Folger Shakespeare Library

notes therefore attempt to identify the sources,[12] to explain allusions, and occasionally to throw light on the author's methods of work. If here and there they seem to point out a flaw in Erasmus' knowledge of Greek, nothing is further from my thoughts than criticism; that knowledge is of such immense historical importance, and can be so well documented, that the smallest light upon it may prove worth having. To illustrate the past history and future use of the ideas transcends alike my purpose and my capacity.

Translation and notes were already in draft when the edition of the Latin text by Margolin appeared in ASD. His text follows the first edition too closely to be acceptable as a basis for translation; but to his researches on the significant early editions I owe an immense debt, and I have taken from him half a dozen identifications of sources which I was still in search of. Of the imperfections of my own work I am well aware; there would be more, but for the help of Professor Elaine Fantham, and especially of the long-suffering editor of this volume, Professor Craig R. Thompson.

RABM

* * * * *

12 The reader should be warned not to place implicit trust in the identifications of sources in ASD, of which about a hundred are erroneous.

ERASMUS OF ROTTERDAM TO PIETER GILLIS, SECRETARY OF THE
FAMOUS CITY OF ANTWERP

Friends of the commonplace and homespun sort, my open-hearted Pieter,
have their idea of relationship, like their whole lives, attached to material
things; and if ever they have to face a separation, they favour a frequent
exchange of rings, knives, caps, and other tokens of the kind, for fear that
their affection may cool when intercourse is interrupted or actually die
away through the interposition of long tracts of time and space. But you and
I, whose idea of friendship rests wholly in a meeting of minds and the
enjoyment of studies in common, might well greet one another from time to
time with presents for the mind and keepsakes of a literary description. Not
that there is any risk that when our life together is interrupted we may
slowly grow cold, or that the great distance which separates our bodies may
loosen the close tie between our minds. Minds can develop an even closer
link, the greater the space that comes between them. Our aim would be that
any loss due to separation in the actual enjoyment of our friendship should
be made good, not without interest, by tokens of this literary kind.

     And so I send a present – no common present, for you are no common
friend, but many jewels in one small book. Jewels I well may call them,
these parallels selected from the richly furnished world of the greatest
authors of antiquity. Of late, as I reread Aristotle, Pliny, and Plutarch for the
enrichment of my *Adagiorum chiliades*, and cleared Annaeus Seneca of the
corruptions by which he was not so much disfigured as done away with
altogether, I noted down by the way these passages, to make an offering for
you which I knew would not be unwelcome. This I foresaw, knowing as I
did your natural bent towards elegance of expression, and perceiving that
not polish alone but almost all the dignity of language stems from its
metaphors. For the Greek *parabolê*, which Cicero latinizes as *collatio*, a sort
of comparison, is nothing more than a metaphor writ large. Of the other
ornaments of style, each makes its own peculiar contribution to its charm
and flexibility; metaphor taken alone adds everything in fuller measure,
while all the other kinds of ornament add one thing each. Do you wish to
entertain? nothing adds more sparkle. Are you concerned to convey information? nothing else makes your point so convincingly, so clearly. Do you
intend to persuade? nothing gives you greater penetration. Have you a
mind to expatiate? nowhere is plenty readier to your hand. Or to be brief?

* * * * *

    1 Gillis] A close friend of Erasmus; see Ep 184 introduction. This letter to him is
      Ep 312.
   22 *Adagiorum chiliades*] Cf Ep 269 introduction.
   22 Seneca] Cf Ep 325 introduction.
   28 Cicero] *De inventione* 1.30.49

nothing leaves more to the understanding. Have you a fancy to be grand?
metaphor can exalt anything, and to any height you please. Is there something you wish to play down? nothing is more effective for bringing things
down to earth. Would you be vivid and picturesque? metaphor brings it   40
before one's eyes better than anything else. What gives their spice to
adages, their charm to fables, their point to historical anecdotes? metaphor,
which doubles the native riches of a pithy saying, so that Solomon himself,
an inspired author, chose to recommend his wise sayings to the world by
calling them *Parabolae*. Deprive the orators of their arsenal of metaphor,   45
and all will be thin and dull. Take metaphor and parable, *parabolê*, away
from the Prophets and the Gospels, and you will find that a great part of
their charm has gone.

Someone will say, perhaps, 'This man has a pretty knack of making his
work sound important, as though it were really difficult to produce paral-   50
lels, when they lie to hand everywhere.' But I have not chosen what was
ready to hand, nor picked up pebbles on the beach; I have brought forth
precious stones from the inner treasure-house of the Muses. The barber's
shop, the tawdry conversation of the marketplace are no source for what is
to be worth the attention of the ears and eyes of educated men. Such things   55
must be unearthed in the innermost secrets of nature, in the inner shrine of
the arts and sciences, in the recondite narratives of the best poets or the
record of eminent historians. In this field there is a twofold difficulty, and
double praise is to be won. That first task is already something, to have
tracked down what is really good. But it is no less labour to arrange neatly   60
what you have discovered, just as it is something to have found a precious
jewel in the first place, but there is credit to be won from its skilful
mounting on a sceptre or in a ring. I will add an example to make my point
clear. Hemlock is poisonous to man, and wine neutralises hemlock; but if
you put an admixture of wine into your hemlock, you make its venom much   65
more immediate and quite beyond treatment, because the force and energy
of the wine carries the effect of the poison more rapidly to the vital centres.
Now merely to know such a rare fact in nature is surely both elegant and
interesting as information. Suppose then one were to adapt this by saying
that adulation poisons friendship instantly, and that what neutralises that   70
poison is the habit of speaking one's mind, which Greek calls *parrhesia*,
outspokenness. Now, if you first contaminate this freedom of speech and

* * * * *

45 *Parabolae*] Cf 1 Kings 4:32.
72 outspokenness] This information about hemlock and wine and the analogy
with *parrhesia* come from Plutarch *Moralia* 61B and are developed by Erasmus
in *Parabolae*; see below 146:12ff.

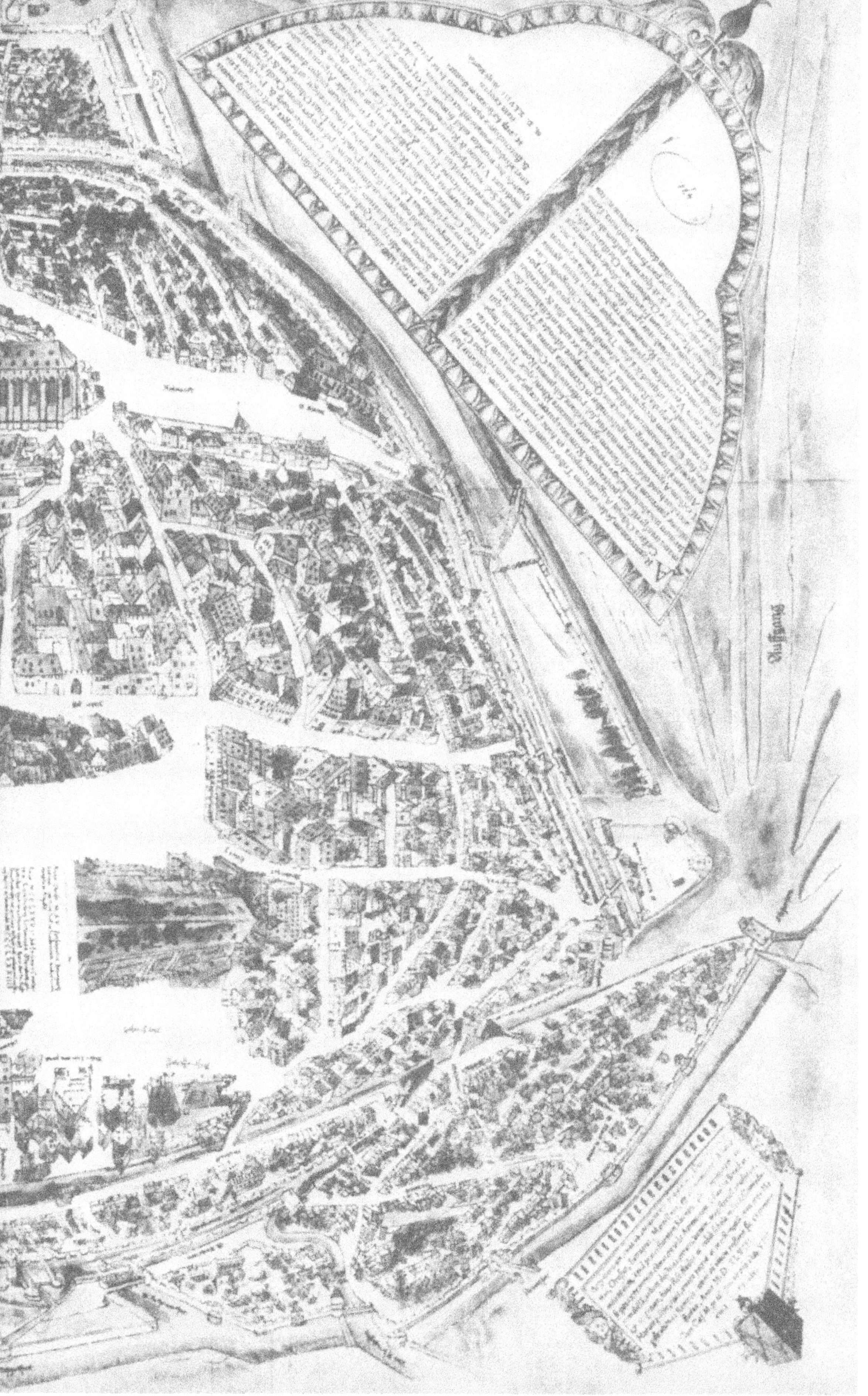

put a touch of it into your adulation, so that you are flattering your friend
most insidiously while you most give the impression of perfect frankness,
the damage is by now incurable. Would this not win credit as an ingenious   75
application of the parallel? I think it would.

Yet I do not mean to fish for gratitude where I deserve none. In
anything under the heading 'From Aristotle and Pliny' the application of
the image is my own invention. For anything taken according to the rubric
from Plutarch and Seneca I claim no credit, except for the labour of collec-   80
tion and exposition and such praise as is due to brevity and convenience. I
as well aware what an ocean of parallels could be got together from the
whole realm of nature, from all the fields of knowledge, all the poets, the
historians, the orators. But an attempt to pursue the infinite would be mere
madness. I wished to give at least a taste, and thus to arouse young men's   85
minds to find such things for themselves. Of Plutarch I have made a very full
survey, partly because he wrote in Greek, partly because in this field he is
such a leader as to defy comparison even with the greatest authors. From
Seneca, since my work on him at the time had a different purpose, I have
not gathered so much. It will not be found out of the way to attach this book   90
to my *Adagia* or, if so preferred, to my *Copia* as a kind of supplement, since
it has so much in common with the former and contributes eminently to
abundance of style. If your epithalamium is not yet finished and published,
the fault lies with my servant, who left the text in Louvain, of which I was
unaware. Farewell.   95

Basel, 15 October 1514

* * * * *

78 heading] Erasmus refers to the cross-headings which name the classical
 sources of his material, Plutarch, Seneca, and the writers on natural history.
93 epithalamium] A work to mark the occasion of Pieter Gillis' marriage to his
 first wife Cornelia Sandria, about this time. Erasmus was often a guest in their
 house in Antwerp. See Ep 184, and Reedijk appendix I.2 for the text of the
 epithalamium. The verses were printed in the colloquy *Epithalamium P. Aegidii*
 in the September 1524 edition of the *Colloquia* (translation in Thompson
 Colloquies 229).

PARALLELS

From Plutarch's *Moralia*

5

Those who arouse one and urge one to study philosophy, and give one no
teaching or instruction, act like those who snuff a lamp and then pour in no
oil. (798B)

They who have no comforts at home spend most of their time in the
marketplace, walking to and fro; so some people, having no private business of their own, devote themselves to public affairs. (798C)

A man may board a ship for amusement, in order to inspect it or walk
up and down in it, and then, when it is cast off suddenly and bears out to
sea, he is queasy and sea-sick, and gazes vainly overboard; even such are
they who take up public business lightly and almost as a pastime, but once
they are entered into it, cannot extricate themselves, but are borne away
even against their wishes by the tide of affairs. (798D)

Like an actor who comes on the stage all made up for his part is he who
enters public life not to improve the lot of his fellow-citizens but to win
reputation for himself. (799A)

Those who descend into a well slowly and on purpose come to no
harm, those who fall in by accident suffer serious hurt; so a man who enters
public life with some definite purpose finds it tolerable, he who rashly hurls
himself into it is sorry afterwards. (799A)

As wine is at first the obedient servant of the man who drinks it, but as
it gradually creeps into his veins carries him away and makes him behave in
its own fashion, so does the ruler of a polity adapt himself at the outset to
the traditions of its people, and then by degrees bring it over to his own way
of thinking. (799B–C)

The bird-catcher imitates the call of birds to entice them into his nets;

* * * * *

4 Plutarch's *Moralia*] Almost exactly half of the *Parabolae* is drawn from the
Moralia, of which the first complete Greek text was published in Venice by
Aldus in 1509. In order to identify the sources without distracting the reader
by continual footnotes the reference by column and letter given in the margin
of all modern texts of Plutarch has been added in parentheses at the end of
each aphorism.

6 Those who] The first thirty-five aphorisms are derived (save for one intruder)
from *Moralia* 798A–825F *Praecepta gerendae reipublicae* 'Precepts of Statecraft.'

12 walk up and down] Plutarch says 'to enjoy the rocking motion' as a form of
passive exercise; it may be that Erasmus did not know this very uncongenial
practice.

even so, to bring the multitude to your opinion, you must encourage and be
subservient to its natural disposition. (800A)

A mole or wart on a man's face offends us more than great blotches or
scars on the rest of his body; and small faults seem great in a prince who
lives in the eye of the world. (800E)

As women with the cravings of pregnancy, or sufferers from nausea,
stuff themselves with unwholesome food and soon vomit it up again, so the
multitude through folly or the lack of better men choose the first comer as a
magistrate and very soon reject him. (801A)

The best wine, poured into a foul and dirty glass, loses its attractions;
so does good policy proceeding from a bad man, or learning that has fallen
to a bad man's lot. (801C)

Rudder and rein are not enough unless there is someone with the skill
to use them; and eloquence does not suffice to govern a people unless
reason be there too, to govern what is said. (801C–D)

The master of a ship works through the voice and orders of other men;
but he who would be master of a polity must have wisdom of his own, so
that he needs no other to speak for him. (801F)

As the man who uses a smooth bit to break in a horse is thrown off
because the horse thinks nothing of it, so he who tries to tame a multitude
without sufficient power is thrown down from the seat of government. (802D)

They who govern the mob by pageants, largesse, and free dinners are
like those who herd brute beasts, or hunt them. (802D–E)

Musicians win our hearts with a light touch on the strings, not heavy
pounding; even so an equable speaker moves the people sooner than a
harsh one. (802F)

As it is better to take the longer route, if it be safer, instead of one that
is shorter but perilous, so when wealth and glory are our aim, we should
strive to achieve them late but safely, rather than at once and with great
risk. (804C–D)

A fire makes no smoke if from the outset it breaks into flame, and no
one is jealous of glory the brilliance of which is clear from the start; ill will
attends on those who grow by stages. (804E)

As ivy clinging to the branches of trees is raised high on borrowed
strength, so do men rise from obscurity through acquaintance with the
great, and then strangle those by whom they have been promoted. (805E–F)

*****

6 cravings of pregnancy] The Greek word *kittan*, which Erasmus would have
known from Aristophanes, he renders with a transliteration, *citta*, unknown
to classical Latin.

Some surfaces, when the sun's light falls on them, increase its brightness in exchange by their own brilliance; even so, some men who owe their fame to the favour of others, make them in turn more famous by their genius. (806A)

Not every tree will tolerate a vine clinging to it; some of them stifle it and kill it. So some ambitious people keep down younger men from jealousy, for fear they may one day reach the top. (806C)

The ship's captain aims at the best sailors, the master mason looks for the most skilled workmen; so the prince will acquire such friends as are best fitted for the business of the state. (807B–C)

The musician whose strings are out of tune does not throw them away forthwith and cut them to pieces; he tightens or slackens them bit by bit, until he has got them in tune. So too a prince should gradually correct evil-doers, not destroy them all at once. (809E)

A javelin, if it strikes on something solid, rebounds sometimes against the thrower; so scandal aimed at a brave and upright man rebounds on him who started it. (810E–F)

As the ruler of the world cares only for the big things and leaves small things to the care of fortune (to quote Euripides), so a prince will confine his exertions to difficult and important business. (811D)

Alexander used to have Bucephalus in his old age carried by other horses until contact should be made with the enemy, that he might be fresh when he entered the fray. That is how we should use the powers of elder statesmen: spare them all the labour we can, and keep them fresh for the time when they are needed. (793E)

The skipper of a ship does some things with his own hands, some things by means of others, and sometimes lets others take the tiller while he makes a trip to the bows. So in the body politic one man should not monopolize all tasks; he should in turn give place to others, knowing that things are better done in which many have a share. (812C)

An actor may add character and colour to his part of his own invention, but on condition that he respects his author's prescribed intentions

* * * * *

19 Euripides] Plutarch quotes, and Erasmus paraphrases, fragment 974 from an
   unidentified play.
21 Alexander] This is an intrusion from the preceding essay in the *Moralia, An
   seni respublica gerenda sit* (793E), other material from which is used at 140:27.
   What Plutarch says is that, in order to spare his famous charger, Alexander
   rode other horses himself until the moment of combat; Erasmus almost certainly misunderstood a not very common Greek word.

and his metre; so a man who holds office in the state should so exercise it as
not to go beyond what the law prescribes. (813F)

The hand is not made weaker by its division into fingers, but more
versatile in use; so business shared among many men in the state is
despatched more adequately. (812D–E)

As those who have acquired the habit neither to dine nor to take a bath
except on doctor's orders are never well, so he who refers everything to the
prince for an opinion makes him more completely master than is good for
the community, so that no step can any longer be taken, even in the right
direction, without his leave. (814F)

Physicians, when faced with diseases which they cannot entirely
remove, summon them out into the open, to the surface of the body; so does
a ruler, if he cannot heal the distempers of a polity unobserved, that he may
have as little need as possible of doctors and medicines, I mean punishments. (815B)

The physician who has drawn off much infected blood gives the
patient a little food that can do no hurt; so the prince, having eliminated
much that is evil and hurtful, will soften the resulting discontent by kind
and liberal treatment. (818D–E)

Like the man who, having sailed safely past the Syrtes only to
wreck his vessel close to harbour, has achieved nothing very great, is he
who, after holding two or three offices of state successfully, comes to grief in
the highest of all. (820C)

As [colossal figures or] statues that are badly balanced often fall over,
so overmuch promotion overturns many men through ill will. (820F)

The noise and bustle of a beehive tells men that the bees are in good
health; but in a commonwealth, if things are quiet, all is well. (823F)

A spark on the thatch or a lamp neglected in the home sometimes

* * * * *

2 the law] So (*legis*) in the Froben edition of August 1522; previously *regis*, the
king. The correction is probably Erasmus' own: he would think of the civil
power as answerable in the first instance to law rather than to a monarch.

13 that he may have] In the second edition (Louvain June 1515) Erasmus altered
this to *id agit* 'make it his business to have.' Neither version does justice to .
Plutarch's point, that the ruler, unlike the physician, will try to prevent an
obstinate distemper in the body politic from breaking surface (and so attracting would-be physicians from outside).

20 Syrtes] Sandbanks, proverbially dangerous, off the coast of North Africa

24 colossal figures or] These words were added in the Paris edition of 1516. In the
vocabulary which he provided Bade explained the word by reference to the
famous Colossus of Rhodes, 'whence' says he 'the Colossians get their name,'
forgetting that Colossae is a city in Phrygia.

burns a whole city to the ground; thus private hatred and differences are a source of public mischief. (824F)

The air inside our ears, if it is not at rest and free from any sound of its own, but is full of buzzing and confusion, receives what is said inaccurately. In the same way that faculty which assesses the pronouncements of philosophy will not make a right judgment of what is submitted to it from without, if there is any noise or interference from within. (1000B)

Diseases of the body are detected by pulse and colour, and their approach is foretold by fever and lassitude; but diseases of the spirit are not recognized by most people as diseases. (500E)

As the first step towards health is to feel that you are ill, so the first step towards amendment is to confess that you were wrong. (500F)

The most difficult patients to cure are those whose illness makes them lose awareness of themselves, like men in coma or delirium; and the most difficult to restore to a right mind are those who do not recognize their faults. (501A)

As the storm which does not allow one to put into harbour is more dangerous than that which forbids one to set sail, even so those tempests of the mind are more severe which allow a man no rest once his reason is in turmoil, but bear him away headlong into stormy seas. (501D)

A sufferer from bodily sickness takes to his bed and rests, sends for the doctor, fasts; but they who suffer from sickness of the spirit, the more ill they are, the less can they stomach rest or physician. (501C)

As the world is composed, according to Plato, of fire and earth as its essential elements, earth giving solidity and fire giving heat and form, even so great empires cannot be achieved without a mixture of valour and good fortune, such that each supports the other. (316E)

Just as the world was as yet no world while its smaller elements were still whirling and flying everywhere and its more solid parts fighting among themselves, but all was full of tumult, tempest, and confusion until the earth out of those parts grew to full size, took root, and offered in itself a stable resting-place for the remainder; so are great empires full of tumult

* * * * *

3 The air] From *Moralia* 999C–1011E *Quaestiones Platonicae* 'Problems in Plato'
8 Diseases] Five aphorisms derived from *Moralia* 500B–2A *Animine an corporis affectiones sint peiores* 'Whether the Affections of the Soul Are Worse than Those of the Body,' of which Erasmus published a version in 1514
24 As the world] Three from *Moralia* 316C–26C *De fortuna Romanorum* 'On the Fortune of the Romans.' The reference to Plato in the first of them is to the cosmogony in his *Timaeus*.

LB I 562D / ASD I-5 104

until their growing authority confers stability even on neighbouring
monarchies, as the earth does on the other elements that whirl around
her. (317A–B)

It takes many blows to fasten a ship together with nails and dowels,
and then she is left for some time until fastenings and joints grow together
into one, after which she can safely sail the seas; so too it needs much toil to
found a commonwealth, until with time it grows and offers a safe and
peaceful life to its citizens. (321D)

They who hunt wild beasts wear the skin of a stag; fowlers put on
jackets quilted with feathers; men take care not to be seen wearing scarlet
by a bull, red or white by an elephant, because these colours irritate the
animals. Similarly he who would break in and domesticate an untamed
nation must for a time adapt himself to it in habits and in costume. (330B)

A kindly temper in the circumambient air brings out the fertility of the
soil, which a harsh or corrupted climate represses and snuffs out: even so do
the favour and generosity of a prince encourage the liberal arts, which a
niggardly and hostile prince represses. (333E)

Stags get no benefit from their great antlers, lacking the spirit to use
them. To be rich is not enough: you must be brave as well. (336A)

As the Cyclops with his eye put out reached forth his hands at random
with no certain target, so a great king who lacks wisdom embarks on any
undertaking with much sound and fury, and no judgment. (336F)

Unskilful craftsmen, setting diminutive statues on great pedestals,
make their small size more conspicuous; and in the same way, if fortune
confers great resources on a man of feeble character, she demonstrates and
makes more obvious his poverty of spirit. (337C)

Iron, unless you use it, rusts; so does your mind [grow slack], unless
by using it on business you maintain its vigour. (783F)

He who is engaged in public business and at the same time practices
some sedentary craft acts like a man who would strip a well-born and
virtuous woman of her proper dress, give her an apron, and keep her busy
in a workshop. (785D)

It ill became Hercules to lay aside his lion's skin and don a Milesian

* * * * *

9 They who hunt] Five from *Moralia* 326D–45B *De Alexandri Magni fortuna* 'On
the Fortune of Alexander'

27 Iron] Twenty-one aphorisms inspired by *Moralia* 783B–97F *An seni respublica
gerenda sit* 'Whether an Old Man Should Engage in Public Affairs,' which has
already contributed one at 137:21. *relanguescit* 'grow slack' was inserted in the
second edition (Louvain June 1515).

LB I 563A / ASD I-5 104

robe when Omphale made him her slave; and it is unbecoming for a public man to give up the part he has played and devote himself to a life of idleness and pleasure. (785E)

Fire once kindled is easily kept alight; when extinguished, it is rekindled with difficulty. Even so it is easy to preserve a reputation, but not easy to re-establish it, once lost. (787A)

The sacred Delian ship by continual patching and refitting is made almost indestructible for many centuries; similarly a man should be always adding to his reputation for fear it crumbles. (786F)

A dog barks at strangers and is friendly towards those he knows, as Heraclitus says; just so, the favourite target of ill will is new men lately risen in the world, and it grows kinder towards a familiar face. (787C)

When a flame first breaks out, much smoke comes with it, which thins out as the flame grows more fierce and spreads; in the same way, a man engaged on some great enterprise meets much ill will at first, until that ill will is dissipated like smoke by his growing reputation. Jealousy is to fame as smoke to fire. (787C–D)

A fool sails on [for a long time] with winds and waves against him, and makes for harbour when the weather clears. Such is the man who abandons an enterprise just when, after prolonged struggles against ill will, he can live free from it in future. (787D–E)

Just as it is both difficult and hazardous to dig up ancient trees, which already have widespread roots, and transplant them to another site, so a nation that has long grown old in its own traditions cannot be translated to another way of life without great upheavals. (787F)

Iron or bronze gleams from hard use, and powers of mind are polished by the conduct of business. (788B)

As men rejoice who have escaped from demented tyrants, so should the aged, whose years protect them from attack by the passions. (788E)

* * * * *

1 Omphale] Queen of Lydia, to whom Hercules, as part of his purification from blood-guilt, was sold as a slave. She set him to do women's work, wearing women's dress. Miletus was famous for luxurious fabrics.

7 Delian ship] The *Paralos*, a state galley despatched officially every year by the Athenians to the festival in the isle of Delos. It had been patched so often that perhaps, as with Nelson's *Victory*, none of the original remained; but it was of course the same ship.

11 Heraclitus] Greek philosopher of the sixth/fifth centuries BC; Plutarch cites fragment 97.

18 A fool] The first sentence was altered in the second edition (June 1515).

28 demented tyrants] Based on a remark put by Plato in the mouth of Sophocles the dramatist, a character in the opening scene of his *Republic*.

They say that the ibis, when it has grown old and has by now breathed out all that was disordered in it, has a sweeter smell; even so the reputation of old men is more settled, and their ideas are more equable. (791B)

As water mixed with the wine makes it less powerful, and sober nymphs restrain the tipsy god, so in affairs of state an admixture of old men makes the headstrong ambitions of younger men less violent by evoking their respect. (791B–C)

Like a stage army, which appears only for show and neither speaks nor acts, is a prince who plays his part with titles and uniforms, and takes no thought for the real duties of a prince. (791E)

The overstrung bow snaps; the spirit that relaxes is broken. (792C)

An ageing singer does not abandon his art or cast his instrument away, but looks for easier music and avoids notes that would strain his voice and are more suited to the young; similarly in old age one should not abandon public affairs, but choose the lighter business that suits one's years. (793A)

Athletes refrain from necessary work to conserve their strength for what is unnecessary; we must do the opposite. (793F)

Horse-breakers use endearments at first, and treat their animals very gently until they are used to the bit; even so the multitude must be approached with discretion. (795C)

The Vestal virgins had a fixed programme: first, time for learning, then for practice, thirdly for teaching. It was the same for the priests of Diana of the Ephesians. It should be the same for those who take up politics. (795D)

Trees as they age grow selfish, and oppress with their shade the young growth underneath them, not suffering it to grow and flourish. This is no pattern for elder statesmen; rather should they encourage and assist the young. (796A–B)

* * * * *

1 ibis] Modern editors, following A. Coraes (1748–1833), emend *ibis*, the Egyptian bird, to *iris*, the flower.

2 reputation] Plutarch has not *doxa* 'reputation' but *dogma* 'opinions.' Both are common words; Erasmus has probably made the change deliberately.

11 The overstrung bow] Erasmus uses the same sentence from Plutarch in *Adagia* IV v 77 'Arcus tensus rumpitur,' added in 1523. But this is more than the familiar 'Too much bending breaketh the bow'; the emphasis lies in the second half. The spirit of Erasmus never relaxed.

19 Horse-breakers] Erasmus has somewhat deserted Plutarch here, who speaks not of breaking in a horse, but of teaching a young man to mount while his horse is tractable, and when entering politics to learn to master the multitude while it is obedient.

Physic, when first administered, hurts or is nasty, but later it brings
health and comfort. Good advice sometimes, like that, is bitter at the start,
but brings delight later, when you stand corrected. (796B)

The mad passion to keep horses does not go with little oil-bottles but
with rich corn-land; even so adulation does not trouble the poor and lowly,   5
but is the disease and ruin of great family and fortune. (49C)

As lice abandon dead bodies which are deserted by the blood on
which they fed, so do flatterers wait upon prosperity and promise of gain,
and leave alone what is barren and unpromising. (49C)

As you examine a coin to see if it is counterfeit before you need to   10
spend it, so you should test a friend before you need him. (49D)

Like those who bring heedless destruction on themselves by tasting in
advance some deadly poison is he who makes a friend of some man he does
not know, and learns that man's true nature to his own hurt. (49E)

The best of sauces, says Euenus, is the kitchen fire; likewise an   15
admixture of friendship makes the whole of life taste good. (50A)

As imitation gold reproduces only the brilliant sheen of the original,
so does the flatterer copy the readiness to oblige and gay complaisance of
the friend. (50A)

Weed-seeds which in size and shape resemble wheat are not easily   20
screened out, for they do not pass through a small mesh, and a large mesh
lets through the wheat as well. In the same way, flattery, the ape of friendship, is not easily distinguished from it and rejected. (51A)

Your truly expert sauce-cook mixes a touch of something bitter with
his confections to take away a sweetness that might cloy; and in the same   25
way flatterers mix in an air of free speech and severity so that their flattery is
never more skilful than when they seem to criticize and freely speak their
minds. (51C)

As animals which change colour to match the ground beneath them

* * * * *

4 The mad passion] Sixty-three aphorisms derived from *Moralia* 48E–74E
  Quomodo adulator ab amico internoscatur 'How to Tell a Flatterer from a Friend'

4 little oil-bottles] Plutarch quotes the early Greek poet Simonides (fragment 86;
  D.L. Page ed *Poetae melici graeci* [Oxford 1962] 302), who said that horse-
  breeding does not suit Zakynthos, which is a rugged and tree-covered island
  in the Ionian Sea, and no place for brood-mares. In the manuscripts, and
  consequently in the Aldine Plutarch of 1509, *Zakunthos* had been corrupted to
  lakuthos, a small oil-flask, for which Erasmus' *lenticula* is a recognized Latin
  equivalent. It seems to be a mere coincidence that *lenticula* in its commoner
  sense 'lentils' is a symbol of poverty (*Adagia* II viii 36 'Dives factus iam desiit
  gaudere lente').

15 Euenus] Greek elegiac poet of the fifth century BC; Plutarch quotes fragment 10
  (M.L. West ed *Iambi et elegi graeci* [Oxford 1971–2] II 67).

are hard to detect, so you will not find it easy to detect a toady who adapts
himself to every habit and every mood. (51D)

They who keep a wild beast in captivity first of all adapt themselves to
its natural ways and observe what things annoy it or placate it, until it feels
at home and can be handled; the flatterer likewise adapts himself to every   5
mood and interest of a friend. (51F)

As flowing water has no definite colour, but always takes its colour
from the ground over which it flows, so the flatterer is never his true self,
but adapts himself to circumstances. (52B)

The ape is often captured while he tries to imitate a man; but a toady   10
by the same imitation captures and wins the confidence of other men. (52B)

Circe's potions changed men suddenly into wild beasts; likewise the
passions suddenly make a man different. (52E)

A flatterer, like a mirror, reproduces whatever is set before him. (53A)

Your shadow, whatever you may do, responds and is always there;   15
like that, the flatterer follows wherever you may turn. (53B)

The chameleon imitates every colour except white. The toady imitates
everything discreditable; it is only what is honourable that he cannot
copy. (53D)

Unskilful painters, unable to attain something beautiful, achieve the   20
effect of a likeness by warts and wrinkles; even so does a flatterer reproduce
the intemperance or anger of his friend. (53D)

A perfume smells sweet, and so does a drug; but one serves no
purpose except to give pleasure, while the other besides its sweetness
renders valuable service. Similarly a flatterer is merely agreeable; a friend is   25
also serviceable and necessary. (54E)

There are delightful colours in a picture, and some drugs are agreeable
in colour too; like them, a friend gives pleasure that he may be of service, a
flatterer merely gives pleasure. (54E)

The physician sometimes, if the case calls for it, applies saffron and   30
spikenard, he prescribes soothing baths and appetizing diet; so too a friend
can sometimes flatter. (55A)

Some men put a gadfly in a bull's ear or a tick in a dog's; so too a

* * * * *

7 As flowing water] It looks as though Erasmus had slightly misunderstood
   Plutarch, whose text is not entirely clear; he speaks of water poured from one
   receptacle into another, and taking the shape of each.

17 The chameleon] This image recurs at 252:6 and (without reference to Plutarch)
   in *Adagia* III iv 1.

33 Some men] Who ever implanted a gadfly or a tick? In Plutarch 'they say that
   the gadfly makes its way into an ox, and the tick into a dog, close by the ear';
   Erasmus has rendered a Greek verb in the middle voice, *enduesthai* 'to find an
   entrance,' as though it were active, 'to insert.'

flatterer who has the ear of his patron is not easily shaken off, but drives him astray whither he pleases. (55E)

Painters make their highlights more brilliant by juxtaposition of shadows and dark colours; likewise the flatterer by praising different faults in others feeds and encourages those that are present in his friend. (57C)

A man speaking in public sometimes puts words in some other person's mouth, either to gain credence or to avoid giving offence. In the same way the flatterer quotes what he has heard others say about his friend, even if he has heard nothing of the sort. (57B)

Wrestlers prostrate their own bodies in order to overthrow others; so do some people speak harshly of themselves, to give the impression that they think highly of the company they are in. (57D)

Painting is silent poetry; and a flatterer too can praise in silence, by facial expression and gestures and attitudes. (58B)

As those who hunt wild beasts more easily escape the notice of their quarry if they do something else at the same time, such as pass along a road or plough a field, even so the flatterer is most fully active when he is not seen to be bestowing praise. (58B)

If praise made a field more productive, it should be praised no less than it should be ploughed or manured. In the same way, if praising a friend makes him better, it is well to praise him sometimes; but if not, what is the point of useless adulation? (59A)

As Patroclus when going into battle took the rest of Achilles' armour, but did not touch the spear, which was too strong and heavy, so the flatterer imitates all the characteristics of a true friend, except the freedom with which he points out a mistake. (59B)

In Menander's comedy the sham Hercules enters carrying a light and useless club with no strength in it; similarly a toady's frankness is gentle and designed to please. (59C)

A lady's cushion may seem to offer resistance and to withstand her head, but really it gives way and takes the right shape; so may a flatterer's frankness have an air of substance, but it gives way beneath those who lean on it. (59C)

Just as honey makes sore places pain while it cleans them up, though it is wholesome and pleasant elsewhere, so there is no hurt in the frank speech of a friend, except when there is something wrong that must be put right. (59D)

* * * * *

23 Patroclus] The friend of Achilles who borrows his armour in Homer *Iliad* 16.130–44

27 Menander's] Plutarch refers to his comedy *Pseuderakles* 'The Sham Hercules' (fragment 523).

The man who complains of his friend over some trifle, and in
weightier matters holds his tongue, acts like the trainer who allows an
athlete freedom with the wine and the women, and then is tiresome and full
of objections over the way he rubs himself down. (59F)

Or like a teacher who complains about a boy's pencil or his slate, but
overlooks some barbarous expression or gross fault of syntax. (59F)

Or like an incompetent speaker, who answers none of the points at
issue, and says he has lost his voice or cannot read his notes. (59F)

Just like the man who, when someone suffers from a boil or an ulcer,
uses the doctor's lancet only to cut the patient's hair and nails, is the flatterer
who uses frankness when there is no call for it. (60B)

If a man takes neat wine, which is normally valuable against hemlock
poisoning, and mixes it with the hemlock, he makes the poison invincible,
because the heat of the wine carries the force of the poison straight to the
heart. Similarly the toady, who knows that freedom to speak out is a specific
against flattery, mixes freedom and flattery together, and so makes his
flattery more dangerous. (61B–C)

A physician devotes his efforts to preserve and increase good health; a
friend does the same; but a toady excites the inflamed parts. (61D)

There are foods which contribute nothing to blood or spirits, sinews
or marrow, but only rouse the privy parts, fill the belly with wind, and make
the whole body swollen. Such are the words of a flatterer; they merely
increase and stir up what is unhealthy, but in other respects do no good at
all. (61E)

Where the body is swollen by peccant humours, boils must form; just
so, it is on the points where his friend is affected by anger, love, or hatred
that the flatterer concentrates. (61F)

As actors in a tragedy feel the need of a chorus and sympathetic friends
and the applause of the theatre, those likewise who enjoy adulation refuse
to do anything without an audience ready to applaud. (63A)

Mathematicians tell us that plane surfaces and lines neither bend nor
lengthen nor move independently, being objects of the understanding, but
bend, lengthen, and change position together with the bodies to which
they belong. In the same way the flatterer is never moved by feelings of his
own, but is angry when his friend is angry and smiles when his friend is
pleased. (63C)

* * * * *

7 incompetent speaker] Erasmus seems to have missed Plutarch's point without
making one of his own. Plutarch has the patron make a bad speech or write
something unreadable; and all the toady says, instead of telling him the
unpalatable truth, is 'You ought to take more care of your voice' or 'You need
better paper' (papyrus) or 'a new secretary.'

A living creature holds deep within itself those faculties which are most truly its own; just so a friend makes no show, but conceals what he does at the moment when he is being most helpful. (63c)

As a physician cures a patient even if he is unaware of it, so a friend is helpful even if his help is undetected. (63D)

Like a bad painting, that apes reality with rags and wrinkles and ugly angles, is a flatterer who imitates his friend with labour and noise, but has nothing genuine to offer. (64A)

A monkey, which cannot guard the house like a watchdog nor carry burdens like a packhorse nor plough like oxen, plays the parasite and amuses the company. Similarly, since the flatterer can be of no use in real and serious business, he is a mere servant of pleasure. (64E)

A man once made a most incompetent picture of fighting-cocks, and told his servant to keep real cocks well away from the painting, for fear that the comparison might show him up. In the same way a flatterer does all he can to keep true friends away [for fear that he may be shown up as a false friend by comparison with them]. (65c)

Like medicine unseasonably taken, which hurts and does no good, is a reproof administered in the wrong way. A friend causes pain in doing what the flatterer does agreeably; both hurt. (66B)

Men who for lack of skill do not know how to straighten a piece of wood bend it in the opposite way; and some people in their attempt to escape from one vice fall into another, and a worse one. (66D)

As a surgeon performing an operation maintains a sort of neatness and elegance of movement but avoids the gestures of the dancer, so does frankness admit of courtesy while remaining serious. (67F)

The flatterer sweetens his frankness with jests and scurrilities, like some sauce gone sour. (68c)

A dog of no spirit is bold at dinner and cowardly in the field: similarly it betrays a mean nature to be frank in one's cups and not dare speak out when sober. (68D)

Water flows downhill wherever it finds hollow sloping ground; so does a flatterer bear hardly on his friend if he once falls. (66B)

* * * * *

16 for fear that] The words in brackets replace *etc* in the first edition; in the second edition (Louvain June 1515) *ne cum illis collatus deprehendatur non esse verus amicus*; in the Paris revision of 1516 the same sense in other words *ne ex illorum comparatione deprehendatur fictus amicus*.

27 The flatterer] This aphorism appears in all editions as part of the preceding, but it has a different source, and something different to say.

Just as rheum, when it has accumulated gradually, comes out into the open and overcomes a man at the very moment when it is itself overcome by process of nature, so some men dare not warn their powerful friends until they have come to grief; but as soon as fortune's favouring breeze veers round and their friend is brought low, they choose that moment to preach him a sermon. (68E)

A healthy man takes it in good part if you tell him he lacks self-control and is lascivious or intemperate, but would not endure this if he were ill; in the same way you should wait to correct a friend until he has recovered from anger or infatuation. (69B)

When a child has fallen down, the nurse does not upbraid or punish it; she runs to it and picks it up, and upbraids it afterwards. Similarly a friend should be given aid and support in his affliction, and be upbraided and admonished after that, if the calamity that befell him was his own fault. (69C)

As ruptures and dislocations do not really move until the body falls victim to some other trouble, so do false friends flatter men in prosperity, and, when they fall, upbraid them and profit by their misfortune. (69E)

Sore eyes should not be exposed to a strong light; and a spirit in trouble should not be exposed to severe reproof, but praise should be intermingled, and this is the way to obtain a cure. (72B)

He who reproves a friend severely for some trivial cause acts like the physician who habitually prescribes a bitter, powerful, and expensive drug for the most trifling complaints. (73A)

As a man suffering from a disease of the liver, who showed his doctor a sore finger-nail, would act like a fool, so would he who, though suffering from serious troubles, consulted a friend about some trivial thing. (73B)

Iron that first was made malleable and softened by heat is afterwards hardened and toughened by cold water; even so a friend who has first been softened by kind words will soon endure reproof freely. (73D)

As a good physician would rather use sleep and dieting to cure an illness than scammony or castor, so a friend, a father, or a teacher does his best to use praise rather than reproof as a corrective if he can. (73E)

A surgeon, when he has used the knife, does not immediately abandon the site of the operation, but bathes it and gives it soothing treatment;

* * * * *

1 rheum] Plutarch's flatterer looses on his patron, who has now met with misfortune, a flood of frank criticism which has hitherto been like a stream (*rheuma*) unnaturally pent up. Erasmus takes him to mean *rheuma* in the medical sense, rheum or phlegm, and has some difficulty in extracting sense from the passage.

so ought a man who has administered some severe rebuke to soothe the
pain of it by his conduct in other respects. (74D)

As stone-carvers [first] cut into the marble with hammer-blows and
thereafter smooth and polish it, even so a friend will soften a reproof with
kindly words. (74E)

Like a tutor keeping watch over a young man, who guards him and
counsels him to keep him from doing wrong, is reason, which, if always
present in the mind, keeps it from lapses into wrongdoing. (779F)

As unskilful sculptors think every statue beautiful which is very large,
even so some kings suppose that pride and ruthlessness give them the air of
famous princes. (779F)

Like colossal statues splendid in appearance, which represent some
deity, but are full within of clay and nails and rubbish – such is a king who
is glorious with purple and with horses, with gold and retainers, but in his
heart has nothing but base passions and ignorance. (780A)

Statues are held steady by their size and weight, and so stand firm;
foolish kings by the same causes are overthrown. (780A)

A carpenter's rule must first itself be straight, and then let it correct the
vagaries of what it measures; even so a prince must first be without faults
himself, and then let him lay down the law for others. (780B)

When two men have fallen, one cannot help up the other; nor can a
bad and foolish prince correct the errors of his people. (780B)

As God has set the sun in heaven for a most beautiful and delightful
image of himself, even so has he set up the prince in a commonwealth to
represent him towards all men in respect of wisdom, justice, and benevolence. (780F)

As God is angry with those who imitate his lightning and thunder and
plunges them into hell like Salmoneus, so is he angry with the proud and
overweening, who emulate his greatness and do not reproduce his good
will. (780F–1A)

Sheepdogs keep watch in concern for their sheep and not themselves;
and a king ought to be anxious not so much for himself as for his
people. (781C)

* * * * *

3 As stone-carvers] 'first' was added in the Paris revision of 1516.
6 Like a tutor] Seventeen aphorisms inspired by *Moralia* 779D–82F *Ad principem
   ineruditum* 'To an Uneducated Ruler,' one of the essays of which Erasmus
   published a translation in 1514.
28 Salmoneus] Mythical king of Elis, who imitated lightning and thunder, and
   was hurled by an authentic thunderbolt into Tartarus (Virgil *Aeneid* 6.585–94).
   He is not mentioned here by Plutarch.

LB I 567A / ASD I-5 120

The sun gives most delight to those who are able to look at him; a
prince to those who love justice. (781F)

Just as in a great storm a ship needs a strong rudder, a skilful
helmsman, and plenty of undergirding, so he who would govern a great
and turbulent state needs the highest wisdom. (782B)

Bad dreams, in which the spirit is troubled by some degree of uneasi-
ness with no further effects, are like evil but powerless men who cannot do
much hurt. (782B)

Like lightning that has flashed before we hear the thunder, because
our ears must wait for the sound while the eye goes out to meet the flash,
and like blood which appears before the wound is visible – such is the
prince who sometimes passes sentence before the man who laid the
information can be contradicted. (782D)

In great waves a ship does not stay in the same place, unless she is held
by all the weight of an anchor firmly fixed deep in the sea-bed; and similarly
in a great tempest of human affairs it takes reason in all its force to restrain
the intelligence from being swept away by the emotions. (782D)

When the sun reaches its greatest elevation, high up towards the
northern pole, its movement is the least; and similarly the greater a man's
power, the more he should restrain a headstrong disposition. (782D)

Men subject to the falling-sickness are detected by cold weather, for at
once they suffer from giddiness; and uneducated men who are raised a step
by fortune are at once shown up for what they are. (782E)

You cannot tell whether a vessel is sound or no until you fill it with
liquid; it is the same with a man, until you entrust him with power. (782E)

As a physician takes more pleasure in curing an eye that sees on behalf
of many men and keeps watch over many, so a philosopher will take more
pleasure in training the mind of a prince who is concerned for many men's
welfare. (776D)

Wells are not dug by men who possess springs or know where to find

* * * * *

1 to look at him] Plutarch (who was perhaps read rather hastily) speaks of those
who can see the sun as an image of God.

12 before the man] The revision of July 1521 changes this to 'before the accused
man can be convicted'; Plutarch has simply 'conviction precedes proof,'
which might be represented by either.

21 cold weather] Plutarch wrote *hupsei* 'high places'; but in the Aldine edition of
1509 this has become *psuchei* 'cold.'

26 As a physician] Three aphorisms derived from *Moralia* 776B–9C *Maxime cum
principibus philosopho esse disserendum* 'That a Philosopher Ought to Converse
Especially with Men in Power'; eight more from the same source will be found
at 193:15.

LB I 567C / ASD I-5 122

them; and no man seeks counsel from some outside source who has himself
been taught philosophy. (776D–E)

Ixion in pursuit of Juno fell upon a cloud; even so some people, while
desiring true friendship, accept something trivial and false. (777E)

Between the titmouse and the siskin there is such hostility that, if the
blood of the two is forcibly mixed, it will separate at once and spring apart.
In the same way between patricians and common people a natural hostility
still endures, even though they may join sometimes in a common purpose. (537B)

As beetles breed most readily in a flourishing wheat-crop and in roses
in full bloom, so does ill will chiefly keep company with those who are in
the full flower of virtue. (537F)

When the sun stands right overhead, it either gives a man no shadow
or makes it very short; so does great fame extinguish envy. (538A–B)

Where there is no light, there is no shadow; and where there is no
prosperity, there is no jealousy. (538B)

Those who envy a friend his success do not wish to see him utterly
brought low, but yet take it amiss that he should excel them, like men who
would not wish their neighbour's house demolished, but are satisfied if
that part is pulled down which darkens the house next door. (538E)

As perfume not only smells sweet but is also a remedy against bad
smells, so the memory of past prosperity is some consolation in evil
days. (610F)

A guest once admitted to your house is not easily got rid of, and grief
to which you have voluntarily given way cannot be thrown off whenever
you please. (609F)

They who have sore eyes or some other trouble with their vision do
not allow another person to touch their eyes; while sufferers from grief
expose themselves to treatment by the first comer and so make their trouble
worse. (610C–D)

As melancholics feel a benefit if they go into a well-lighted place out of

* * * * *

3 Ixion] A mythical king of the Lapithae, who attempted to ravish the goddess
Juno, but fell instead upon a cloud which Jupiter had caused to take her shape,
and was punished in Tartarus by being bound to an ever-turning wheel.
Repeated by inadvertence at 193:19

5 Between the titmouse] Five aphorisms derived from *Moralia* 536E–8E *De
invidia et odio* 'On Envy and Hate.' For the supposed hostility between these
two little creatures see D'Arcy W. Thompson *A Glossary of Greek Birds* (Oxford
1936) 23, 32.

21 As perfume] Eight aphorisms from *Moralia* 608A–12B *Consolatio ad uxorem*
'Consolation Addressed to His Wife'

the darkness, so it is good for mourners if they transfer their attention to
cheerful things instead of sad. (610E)

Some men pick out Homer's 'headless' and 'tapering' lines (those, that
is, which are less than normal at the beginning or the end), while passing
over so many which are complete and splendid: those do the same who
complain of the few evils of life and forget all their advantages. (611B)

Misers pile up a great hoard and never enjoy it while it is there, but
lament bitterly if they lose it; men are like that who mourn for their dead
friends and do not appreciate the living. (611C)

As a caged bird, if kept long in captivity, tries even when set free to
return to the familiar spot, so the soul which has spent a long time in the
body is not easily torn from it, while the souls of children take wing quite
readily. (611E)

Like a torch which, if you hold it to the fire when it has only just gone
out, relights at once, a soul that flies immediately out of the body returns
easily into its own nature. (611F)

As clothes seem to give a man more warmth, though cold themselves,
yet really give him no more but only protect the bodily heat he already has,
so does wealth appear to confer happiness, while this proceeds from a
man's spirit, not from external things. (100B)

As men in high fever derive from different sources different effects –
they are cooled by hot things, and cold things make them hot – so too riches
bring trouble on the unwise, and poverty brings a wise man cause to
rejoice. (100C)

A spring is never short of water, which pours from it continually; and
a good man always has cause to rejoice, even if his circumstances alter. (100C)

As a house is more honourable when a fire burns on the hearth (so
Homer says), even so the blessings of fortune bring more honour and more
pleasure if graced by a cheerful heart. (100D)

Spices can impart their fragrance to clouts and ragged clothes, while
silk itself stinks if stale with sweat. In the same way any station in life is
enjoyable if virtue be added, while vice makes tedious and intolerable even
what seems most splendid. (100D)

* * * * *

3 'headless' and 'tapering' lines] Those which begin with a short syllable instead of the normal long one, or have the first syllable of one of the last two feet
short instead of long. The image recurs at 202:15.

17 As clothes] Ten aphorisms from *Moralia* 100B–1E *De virtute et vitio* 'Virtue and
Vice.' Two more from the end apparently became detached, and have found a
home at 172:18.

29 Homer] Plutarch cites the apocryphal *Contest of Homer and Hesiod* 284.

Some men seem happy in public while tormented at home by the behaviour of their wives; so do rich men outwardly seem happy who within are tormented by ill-nature night and day. (100E)

From a vicious wife you can easily obtain a divorce; but vice lodges in the marrow of your bones, and you cannot apply for a separation. (100E)

Men who are grieving when they fall asleep have gloomy dreams, and it is the same with sufferers from envy, superstition, and avarice. (100F)

A wicked wife is shamed into behaving better in public, but at home she shows her true colours. Similarly vice keeps a hold on itself when in company, but reveals itself in sleep; for in dreams a man commits incest with his mother or sister or poisons his friend. (100F–1A)

As the body cannot support pleasures unless it is in good health, so the mind is not capable of true happiness unless free from fear and the other emotions. (101B)

A countryman applies axe or fire to forest trees and has them out by the roots, but his vines and olives he prunes with care and caution, for fear that while he cuts away what is not wanted he may hurt at the same time what is sound. In the same way a philosopher in charge of young men will entirely root out lust and avarice and malice from their hearts, but excessive bashfulness he will correct with due caution, for fear lest at one stroke he remove all modesty. (529B–C)

Nurses by frequently wiping away the mess made by small children sometimes abrade the flesh; and similarly, when we try too earnestly to correct certain faults, we can do harm. (529C)

As men pulling down a house next door to a temple leave alone what stands touching it, for fear they may pull down something consecrated at the same time, so some vices are to be corrected with great caution, which hang together closely with virtues. (529C)

Low-lying and soft ground does not throw off what falls upon it and cannot turn it to one side; similarly a mind infected with the wrong sort of complaisance admits no emotions save those which are degrading. (530A)

As men who cannot tolerate lamplight would find the sun far worse, so

* * * * *

8 A wicked wife] Plutarch has the abstract noun 'vice.'

15 A countryman] Seven aphorisms from *Moralia* 528c–36D *De vitioso pudore* 'On compliancy.' This is shame of the wrong sort, for example, the embarrassment that makes one say 'yes' when 'no' is the right answer, for which Greek (unlike Latin and English) has a word, *dysôpia*. One maxim from the first sentence of the essay will be found at 208:16.

21 modesty] The first edition had 'indignation' (*iracundiam* for *verecundiam*), which was corrected in the revisions of 1516 and 1522, and is revived in ASD.

those who are upset when ordinary things happen are much worse
dumbfounded by great things. (531A)

Wine-jars are easily lugged about by their ears; and some men can be
turned in what direction you please by anything you say. (536A)

A traveller who has once stumbled over a stone and a helmsman who
has struck a rock are fearful not only of the same obstacles but of others like
them. In the same way a man who recognizes his fault will be on his guard
against similar faults as well. (536C–D)

One and the same hand divided into different fingers recalls the
mutual affection of many individuals, which makes them one while they
remain distinct. (478D)

As in the body the nice adjustment of moist and cold, hot and dry
makes the best constitution, so a family flourishes most when brothers
agree. (479A)

Disease in a body that rejects the food proper to it provokes a desire
for many things that are hurtful or even absurd; and similarly slanders and a
suspicious attitude towards one's family and kinsfolk give rise to evil and
noxious relationships with others. (479B)

The man who rejects his own kinsfolk and acquires foreign friends
acts like one who cuts off a leg of flesh and blood to wear a wooden leg.
(479B)

A man who adores his brother's picture but beats his brother's body
black and blue would be insane; and only a fool would love adopted
brothers for the sake of the name and cast off or detest a natural brother.
(479D)

Things stuck together with glue are easily joined again if they come
apart; but if the body is cleft, it joins with difficulty. In the same way,
friendship with other men, if broken, is easily mended; but between
brothers, if broken once, either it never joins, or it joins but leaves a scar.
(481C)

Lose your weapons or other tackle, and you can get new; a new body
you cannot get. So too you will find new friends, yes; new brothers, never.
(481E)

The four elements, so very unlike, so very hostile one to another, are

* * * * *

5 stumbled] Erasmus might have been expected to add this passage in *1515* to
Adagia I v 8 'Iterum ad eundem lapidem offendere'; but his normal practice
seems to have been not to use the same material in both works.

9 One and the same] Twenty-one aphorisms derived from *Moralia* 478A–92D *De
fraterno amore* 'On Brotherly Love'

34 are formed out of] So (*nata sunt*) the Louvain revision of June 1515, better sense
and better Latin; *natura sunt* 'are by nature out of' in the other editions

formed out of the same primal matter; similarly the same parents sometimes produce brothers entirely different. (484F)

Take away the fuel and the fire will go out; take away the occasion for it
and hatred or ill will subsides. (485B)

As we more properly turn the passions of civil strife against the
common enemy, so we are jealous more properly of strangers than of our
own brothers – though it is best of all to be jealous of no one at all. (485E)

As in a balance, when one pan rises, the other must yield and go
down, so one brother should give way to another if he is promoted,
yielding place to him without reluctance. (485E)

In arithmetic a lesser number added to a greater augments it and in
return is itself augmented. It is the same with brothers: if one is exalted to a
post of honour, the other by subservience to him both adds to his dignity
and himself in return shares his distinction. (485F)

Those of one's fingers which have no skill to hold the pen or pluck the
strings yet move in sympathy with those that have it and follow their lead.
So with brothers: if one holds office in the state, the others ought to support
him. (485F)

As wild animals are at war with other kinds that eat the same food, and
live at peace with the rest, so there is envy and competition between men
who practise the same skill; a boxer and a runner get on well together.
(486B)

Men who pursue different mistresses agree together, while those who
have a passion for the same girl are at arm's length; men who seek reputation from the same source are at variance. (486C)

Those who set out on different roads cannot give each other any help;
but those who follow different ways of life escape rivalry and are more
prone to help each other. (486C–D)

As a stain should be washed out forthwith to prevent it from sinking
in and becoming more difficult to remove, so disagreement between
brothers should be settled at once before it can breed hatred. (488B)

If fever follows on swollen glands, this is nothing sinister; but if when
the swelling has subsided the trouble persists, it has clearly struck deeper
roots. In the same way a disagreement between brothers which ceases once
the question is settled was a property of the dispute and not of the parties to
it; but if it continues even when the business is finished, we now see that
the business was a pretext and not a reason, and sore feelings were the
cause. (488C)

As water flows into places where it finds an open gap, and widens the

* * * * *

8 As in a balance] Erasmus' moral is the opposite of Plutarch's.

gap it finds, so some people embitter disputes between brothers. (490B)

As friends treat as a bad omen a rock, or some dog rushing headlong, that comes between them, so they ought to abominate men who behave like curs, who by their scandalous talk break up alliances and mutual good will. (490D)

White metal – tin, that is, and what they call white lead – solders fractured bronze when it touches the two ends, on account of its affinity with both; similarly a friend ought to repair a break in friendship and good will, adapting himself fairly to both sides. (491A)

A vessel that pours out constantly and receives nothing is never full, and no man gets wisdom who always talks and never listens. (502D)

There was a colonnade in Olympia called [Heptaphonos, which means] Seven Voices, because for every sound made it returned many. Some garrulous people are like that: a single word sets them off, and they talk for ever. (502D)

The empty vessel makes the greatest sound, and empty-headed people talk most. (502E)

They say that an immediate ejaculation of seed has no generative power; similarly a garrulous man's talk serves no useful purpose. (503B)

A house with no door and a purse with no fastening are alike useless; much more the mouth of a man who does not know how to keep it shut. (503C)

Grain that has been shut up in a store-jar is found to be greater in bulk, but spoilt; similarly a talkative man always adds to what he has been told and magnifies it, but by now it lacks credibility. (503D)

One who with the girdle of Venus kept men at a distance would seem out of sympathy with Venus; and a man who irritates others by what he says and sets them against him is out of sympathy with the Muses and knows not how to use them, seeing that speech was invented for the purpose of winning men's good will. (504E)

The monad never passes beyond its own boundaries, but remains always in isolation; hence its name. Duality introduces a difference to

* * * * *

10 A vessel] Twenty-four aphorisms from *Moralia* 502B–15A *De garrulitate* 'Concerning Talkativeness'

12 Heptaphonos] The name was added in Greek characters in the second edition (Louvain June 1515), presumably by Erasmus himself. Used again at 224:38

16 The empty vessel] Our English for this phrase is taken from Shakespeare *Henry V* iv.iv.73.

26 the girdle of Venus] The phrase, which derives from Homer *Iliad* 14.214–17, became proverbial for irresistible charm; *Adagia* iii ii 36.

which no limits can be set, for it can without hesitation be multiplied by itself and make a large number. It is the same with language: while it remains inside one man, it is a secret truly kept, but if it once pass to a second man, it is already spreading into rumour. (507A)

It is no simple matter, once you have let a bird out of your hand, to recapture or restrain it; nor can you recapture words that have once passed your lips, for they fly from one group of people to another. (507A)

A ship caught by the waves can be held fast with an anchor; not so a word once despatched out of harbour, as it were, into the deep. (507A)

To test a jar we pour in water and not wine; and in the same way we should sometimes trust our friends with a secret of no importance, to test the value of their silence in such a way that we run no risk if they are leaky. (507F)

A child cannot hold ice in his hand, and yet will not let it go; a talkative person can neither keep to himself what he has heard nor forget it. (508C)

The pipe-fish and the viper are burst by their own offspring; even so a talkative person divulges a secret, even to his own hurt. (508D)

A sick man so hates a bitter and foul-smelling medicine that he hates even the cup he drinks it out of; even so the bringers of bad news get themselves personally disliked. (509C)

As a part of the body which suffers from some distemper attracts distempered humours from neighbouring parts as well, so the gossip's tongue, which is always burning with inflammation, gathers secrets from all directions. (510A)

Rocks are placed as obstacles to a river to prevent floods; and reason must be set in the way of the tongue to keep it from indiscriminate utterance. (510A)

Cranes flying south from Cilicia take up pebbles in their bills, and thus fly safely over Mount Taurus, which is full of eagles, doing this by night, so that their cries may not betray them. So everywhere there is safety in silence. (510A–B)

* * * * *

14 A child] This was proverbial, and Erasmus admitted it to the *Adagia* (II ii 41 'Puer glaciem') in *1508*, with a reference to this passage of Plutarch, which is not quoted.

16 pipe-fish] So Plutarch; his word is *belonê*. This probably suggested to Erasmus the word *belos* 'javelin,' the Latin for which is *iaculum*, and he rendered it by *iaculus*, forgetting that the Latin *iaculus* is a darting serpent, not a kind of fish.

28 Cranes] Other reasons for this supposed habit of cranes on migration are given in the *Adagia* (III vi 68 'Grues lapidem deglutientes'), but Erasmus does not add this from Plutarch. Cilicia was a province in Asia Minor.

A good shot goes straight to the mark; likewise that man [shows sense]
who says little, but to the point. (510E)

The Celtiberians temper and harden iron in such a way that, when it is
buried in the ground, the earthy element is lost and purged away; similarly
Laconic speech, from the purging of everything superfluous, becomes more   5
penetrating. (510F)

As you may easily break sticks one at a time, but a bundle you cannot
break, so men who disagree are easily overcome, not those who are of one
mind. (511C)

Speaking and running serve different purposes, as Sophocles tells us.   10
In a race the winner is he who gets there first; in speaking he who talks not
fastest but most to the point. Indeed he often wins who speaks last. (511F)

They who, when someone asks a man a question, straightway answer
it themselves, are like those who see someone wishing to be kissed by a
third party, and kiss him first. (512B)   15

We keep a hand on the place that hurts, and we keep our tongue on
anything that delights us; I mean, we like to talk about it. (513E)

As dogs which have spent their fury on some rock or stone are gentler
thereafter towards people, so a man who has vented his spleen on strangers
is milder towards his own kindred. (514D)   20

He who complains of Nature that she has produced some things
harmful to man, forgetting all her benefits, acts like someone who would
accuse the Nile, to which after all Egypt owes its crops, for bearing the
crocodile or the asp, and refuses after that to enjoy the harvest it produces,
but merely complains of the poisonous creatures which it breeds; or some-   25
one who in an eloquent speech overflowing with good qualities would find
fault with a few unimportant words that slipped out unnoticed. (994B–C)

Plato says that one ought not to ask a neighbour for water unless one
has first dug down in one's own ground as far as what they call the potter's
clay, and found that there is no hope of a spring. In the same way one   30
should first examine whether one can meet one's needs by economies or in
some other fashion, before one borrows money from the bank. (827E)

* * * * *

1 shows sense] Added in the Paris revision of 1516
10 Sophocles] Plutarch quotes, and Erasmus paraphrases, fragment 772.
16 We keep a hand] Plutarch quotes a Greek line of unknown authorship, which
   Erasmus had used already in the 1508 *Adagia* (II ii 44 'Ubi quis dolet, ibi
   manum habet').
21 He who complains] The source of this is *Moralia* 993A–9B *De esu carnium* 'On
   the Eating of Meat.'
28 Plato says] Nine aphorisms derived from *Moralia* 827D–32A *De vitando aere
   alieno* 'That We Ought Not to Borrow.' The reference is to Plato *Laws* 8.844B.

The temple of Diana at Ephesus gave debtors asylum from their creditors; much better protection is afforded by saving and good husbandry. (828D)

The hare at the same time brings forth young, suckles an earlier offspring, and conceives a third. Money-lenders are like that: borrowed money brings forth before it has conceived. As they give it you, they ask for something back; they put it on the counter and pick up part of it; and what they get back by way of interest is part of the loan for which you pay. (829B)

Usury is like fire; as it grows, it gobbles up one thing after another. (829E)

Like a horse which, once it has had the bit put upon it, carries one rider after another, is the man who has once fallen into debt and never gets free. (830E)

He who has fallen into the mire must either get up or lie there, for if he turns over, he gets muddier still; so it is with a man in the hands of money-lenders. (831A)

Choleric temperaments which refuse to purge their bile in good time gather more day by day, and later on suffer severely. In the same way those who allow interest to pile up are in great trouble for the capital when the term arrives. (831B)

He who says 'What? Shall I give up my house and my servants in order to keep out of debt?' is like a man with a dropsy saying to his physician 'Must I of all people grow thin and go hungry?' It matters nothing how thin he is, provided he is healthy. (831B–C)

If a foot or a hand mortifies, we pay a man to cut it off; and one should cast away house and household to clear oneself of debt, that is, to regain one's freedom. (831D)

In the day of disaster it is our most resolute and wisest friends whose presence can help; so it is with the spoken word. (599A)

People who cannot swim, trying to help others who are drowning and going under, go under with them, and do more harm than good; so do friends who in misfortune merely share a friend's tears. (599B)

Stage tragedies are different: in real disasters we do not need a character to grieve with us and join his tears with ours. (599B)

* * * * *

5 Money-lenders] Plutarch's point is that interest on a loan becomes due and payable the moment the loan is taken up, and the first interest-payment is collected there and then and added to the principal, so that the sum owed includes from the start money which the borrower has never had in his hands. Erasmus refers to the supposed multiple conception (superfetation) of the hare in *Adagia* i vi 6, but does not cite this passage.

28 In the day] Ten aphorisms from *Moralia* 599A–607F *De exilio* 'On Exile'

The body is borne down by the weight of a burden, but the mind often
adds weight to circumstances out of itself. (599C–D)

Things which are naturally bitter we make palatable by the admixture
of sweet things; so what is sad in itself must be relieved by reason. (599F)

Some people have a horror of foreign parts, like snails always carrying
their own homes around with them. (600B)

When children are frightened by masks, we give them the masks to
hold and turn them over to show that they are hollow, so that the children
may learn not to be afraid of them. In the same way it will be a good plan to
call reason to our aid and examine things that frighten us by their appearance, so that when we see that they are not what they seem, we may think
nothing of them. (600E)

As ants, if by some chance they are cast out of the nest, or bees out of
the hive, are all at sea, so some people feel themselves exiled if they once set
foot outside their native country. (601C)

A ship with an anchor well fixed can ride at peace in any harbour, and
a mind equipped with right reason will live in tranquillity anywhere. (601E–F)

A man who counts those people happy who are free to wander at will
over sea and land is like a man who should think the planets more fortunate
than the fixed stars, though they too have each its own orbit in which it
must roll, nor may the sun overstep his allotted course. (604A)

They who introduce a decree into the popular assembly head it with
the words 'May it please Fortune,' for fear they might seem to have added
nothing of their own; and some people add stuff of their own to other men's
books which is quite off the point. (1035B)

A man who has wine that is acid and flat can produce it neither as wine
nor as vinegar; even so to Zeno what he calls *proëgmena* are neither good nor
bad. (1047E)

In the beginning men moved against dangerous animals, later against
sheep and cattle, and ended by keeping their hands off no animal of any
kind. In Athens first of all some retailer of calumnies was punished, and
rightly so; after him two or three more, until finally even respectable people

* * * * *

23 They who introduce] Two from *Moralia* 1033A–57C *De Stoicorum repugnantiis*
'On the Contradictions of the Stoics'

28 *proëgmena*] The term used by Zeno, the great Stoic philosopher, for things
which are neither good nor bad, but 'advanced' above the zero-point of
indifference. 'produce' is an attempt to render *reddere*; Erasmus seems not to
have recognized that the Greek verb *apodosthai* here means 'sell.'

30 In the beginning] Three aphorisms derived from *Moralia* 959B–85C *De sollertia
animalium* 'On the Cleverness of Animals'; there is another at 195:22.

were not spared. When the law finds an opening to attack an evil-doer, it must be watched, or it will fall later on the well-behaved as well. (959D–E)

Boys throw stones at frogs in fun, and if the frogs are hit they die in earnest. In the same way, we hunt for our amusement, but death is a serious matter for our quarry. (965B)

The cricket is not sharp-sighted like the hawk, nor does the partridge fly high like the eagle; even so, all reasonable creatures have not the same strong reasoning powers. (962D)

Bone cannot be cut with a thread unless it has previously been softened with ash and vinegar, nor can ivory be bent unless it has first been relaxed in beer. In the same way fortune cannot wound the spirit of man unless there is an element of wrongdoing. (499E)

As the ground retards the seeds of lucern because they are so prickly, so that they are slow to germinate, so do the causes of sickness and pain in men sometimes lie hid for a long time, until indulgence breaks out in fever. (1088A)

The wise helmsman in fair weather is ready for a storm; and while things go well, one should school one's mind to bear some grief. (1090A)

There is a risk, according to Hippocrates, in absolutely perfect health; and in high prosperity one should fear a change of fortune. (1090C)

As shooting stars at once go out, so do men raised suddenly by fortune to the summit often fall sheer down. (1090C)

Dung-beetles and vultures cannot abide sweet scents, and the Scythian in the story swore that he would rather hear a horse whinnying than a man playing the lyre. The best things do not please everyone. (1096A, 1095F)

As geometers define every circle by centre and radius, so do some men delimit all happiness by their stomachs. (1098D)

The polyp does not reach out its tentacles except to something it can eat; even so there are men who measure all felicity by food and drink. (1098E)

Great pain overshadows small, and happiness of the mind does the same to pleasure of the body. (1099D)

* * * * *

9 Bone] One from *Moralia* 498A–500A *An vitiositas ad infelicitatem sufficiat* 'Whether Vice is Sufficient to Cause Unhappiness'

13 As the ground] Sixteen aphorisms derived from *Moralia* 1086C–1107C *Non posse suaviter vivere secundum Epicurum* 'That It Is Impossible to Live Happily by the Precepts of Epicurus'

19 Hippocrates] Plutarch cites *Aphorisms* 1.3, where it applies to trained athletes.

23 the Scythian] Ateas, a Scythian king who fought against Philip of Macedon. Plutarch tells this anecdote of him three times.

LB I 572A / ASD I-5 140

Men who are starving and have nothing to eat are forced to gnaw their own limbs; and some men from a hunger for reputation are forced to praise themselves if there is no one to do it for them. (1100B)

As from the fish in Hyrcania one expects neither good nor bad, so the Epicureans would have us neither disturbed by fear of the gods nor delighted by their goodness to us. (1101A)

If possible, we relieve an inflammation of the eyes; but if we cannot, we do not remove the eye. Similarly, if superstition cannot be entirely overcome, we need not immediately believe that the gods do not exist. (1101C)

As we both fear and love a prince at the same time, because he is the enemy of the wicked and kindly to the good, so it is with God. (1101C–D)

When we have to do with a savage tyrant, we are anxious at heart; but in the sacred Mysteries there is no call to be anxious and ill at ease. (1101E)

The shipwrecked sailor is borne up none the less by hope, for it may be that by swimming he can reach the shore; but the man who has made shipwreck of his philosophy is lost. (1103E)

An athlete does not wear a garland unless he has won; and good men do not receive the felicity which is their reward until the contest of this life is over. (1105C)

Severe but necessary medicine cures the sick, but upsets those who are in good health and makes them ill; so does a sharp reproof cure a fault, but upset honest men. (1106C)

The Stoics, who maintain they are undefeated, unhindered, and so forth, though their experience is quite the contrary, are like ships with such names as *Swiftsure* and *Providence my shield* and *Safety in service* and other noble and splendid words; in spite of which they are tossed by the waves and wrecked and sunk no less than all the rest. (1057E)

* * * * *

1 Men who are starving] The same idea, drawn from another passage of Plutarch (who repeats himself from time to time), recurs at 197:19.

4 Hyrcania] A region south of the Caspian Sea. Plutarch wrote that the Epicureans no more expect to receive good or evil from the gods, remote as they believe them to be, than we do from the faraway Hyrcanians or (probably) Scythians. The latter word (*Skuthas*) was corrupted in the manuscripts of Plutarch to *ichthus* 'fish'; and hence Erasmus' bizarre statement about the fish in Hyrcania.

8 superstition] The Epicureans were so horrified by its effects that they thought virtual atheism the only cure. Plutarch's point is that there is a middle course between superstition and complete unbelief.

24 The Stoics] Two from *Moralia* 1057C–8D *Stoicos absurdiora poetis dicere* 'That the Stoics Talk More Nonsense Than the Poets'

Dung-beetles run from perfumes and delight in bad smells; some men, like that, choose worst, not best. (1058A)

As poor men sometimes make presents to the rich in hope of favours to come, so we men of little learning sometimes challenge others, in hopes of receiving from them a better-informed reply.

No one is sorry to see a lamp lit, and everyone regrets it when it is put out; so birth is cheerful, death regrettable. (419F)

Good soil is not enough without the proper husbandman and the right seed; and gifts of intellect do not suffice unless there is an excellent instructor to teach and proper principles. (2B)

Constant dropping hollows out a stone, and iron rubs away with handling; the hardest things give way, if you never stop. (2D)

No waggon-wheel, no actor's staff, once bent by force, can ever be restored to its original truth; similarly some men's minds are so much warped by custom and instruction that they can never be straightened. (2D)

The better a soil by nature, the worse it is spoiled by neglect; and the mind that is not properly cultivated is infested with more faults, the more gifted it is. (2E)

Some harsh and stubborn soils are quickly rendered fertile by cultivation; and a mind that is somewhat stubborn by nature can be tamed by instruction. (2E)

There is scarcely a tree that does not grow barren and crooked for want of attention; and no mind is so gifted that it does not deteriorate without the right education. (2E)

No horse obeys its rider as it should unless it has been skilfully broken in; and the mind is always rebellious unless domesticated by the right principles and by instruction. (2F)

No animal so fierce but it is tamed by care; no mind so rustic but it is civilized by instruction. (2F)

As a seal can easily be impressed on soft material, but not once it has set, so children's minds accept any teaching easily, but not once they grow up and start to set. (3F)

As a husbandman stakes trees to make them grow straight, so an
* * * * *

3   As poor men] The source of this has not yet been identified.
6   No one is sorry] One from *Moralia* 409E–38E *De defectu oraculorum* 'The Obsolescence of Oracles'
8   Good soil] Twenty-three aphorisms derived from *Moralia* 1A–14C *De liberis educandis* 'The Education of Children'
11 Constant dropping] This appears as a proverb in *Adagia* III iii 3 'Assidua stilla saxum excavat,' but without reference to Plutarch.

instructor equips the mind with good advice and salutary principles, that it may not grow crooked into evil ways. (4C)

Men who have been long in irons still limp when they are set free, and cannot walk; so those who have lived long with faults retain some trace of them even when they disappear. (6F)

It is not enough to keep one's body in good health, it ought to be fit and strong; so the reasoning faculty should be not only clear and free from faults, but vigorous also. (7B)

To pass through many cities on a voyage is a good thing, but one city should be chosen to live in, and that the best; likewise one should learn many things, but retain what is best and follow that. (7D)

As Penelope's suitors, when they could not obtain her, debauched her maidservants, so those who cannot attain to philosophy demean themselves to a smattering of other subjects. (7D)

Nurses give babies the breast again when they cry; and a pupil who has been hurt by a reproof should be restored again with commendation, lest he lose heart. (9A)

Plants flourish on a moderate supply of water, and drown if it is excessive; likewise the mind profits from moderate exertions, and by immoderate is overwhelmed. (9B)

Sleeping and waking, night and day, storm and calm, war and peace take their turn; so too should labour be relieved by pastime and repose. (9C)

We relax lyre and bow in order to tighten them more effectively, and similarly the mind should be refreshed by repose to make its response to toil more lively. (9C)

The sacred ministers reveal the Mysteries so far as is permitted to them; in the same way we should be careful and circumspect in passing judgment on things that are too high for us. (10F)

* * * * *

3 long in irons] Erasmus applies this image from Plutarch to faults (*vitia*), and the following one to the reasoning faculty (*ratio*); in the original both are applied to style in speech. This is a good example of the freedom he feels entitled to use sometimes in the application of what his source provides; it helps here that Greek should use the same word (*logos*) for both speech and reason.

13 demean themselves] The Greek philosopher Bion, to whom Plutarch ascribes this parallel derived from the *Odyssey*, said that those who cannot achieve philosophy 'wear themselves to a skeleton' on other subjects; 'demean' or 'contaminate' themselves seems to be Erasmus' choice of words.

15 a pupil] So all reported editions; but in the second, of June 1515, *discipulus* became *populus* 'the public'; a change presumably due to Erasmus, which was not repeated.

Spectators watch the Mysteries and say nothing; some things are better praised by silence than in words. (10F)

A doubtful mind is like the tongue of a balance, disposed equally towards either side and tilted towards neither. (11D)

Physicians add something sweet to nasty medicines to make them attractive; and parents likewise ought to soften harsh correction with gentleness. (13D)

A chariot-driver does not always pull at the reins, but sometimes lets them go; and one should give way to children sometimes. (13E)

The thorny asparagus bears delicious fruit; and great happiness springs from initial hardships. (138D)

They who cannot endure for a time the wayward temper of young girls resemble those who dislike unripe grapes, and leave the ripe clusters for others. (138E)

A bride who at the outset takes offence at her husband's ways and leaves him acts like a man who gives up eating honey because he has been stung by a bee. (138E)

Pots, to begin with, come apart at every opportunity, but with time their joints set fast, and they can scarcely be broken up with fire and tools. Similarly the unity of a married couple can at first be broken apart by some minor force; once established, it is stronger by far. (138E–F)

Fire kindles easily in straw and hare's fur, but soon goes out again unless you give it further fuel. Such are the quarrels of lovers or the newly married, provided no one interferes. (138F)

The fisherman who uses poison easily kills and takes his fish, but it is unfit for use and spoilt; in the same way she who entraps a husband with a love-philtre gets one who is stupefied and no good at all. (139A)

As Circe got no profit from the men she had turned into pigs or lions, but loved above all others Ulysses who had kept his wits, so women who have used witchcraft to secure their husbands [lead a sorry life with them, for their wits are touched]. (139A)

* * * * *

4 neither] The revision of June 1515 added *minimo momento huc aut illuc impellitur* 'and is moved by the smallest weight to one or the other.'

10 The thorny asparagus] Thirty-five aphorisms derived from *Moralia* 138B–46A *Coniugalia praecepta* 'Advice to Bride and Groom.' *Asparagus acutifolius* is a small Mediterranean shrub, said by Plutarch to reward with delicious fruit those who face its formidable spines; it comes again at 196:17.

18 Pots] The common meaning of Erasmus' word *vasa*; but it represents *skeue* in Plutarch, which probably means (wooden) furniture.

28 As Circe] *Odyssey* 10.239–43. The words in brackets were added in Erasmus' Paris revision of 1516. In the first edition the sentence ended at 'husbands' and the second (Louvain June 1515) added *nec amant eos* 'nor do they love them.'

LB I 573E / ASD I-5 146

A woman who would rather lord it over a witless husband than obey
one who is sound and sensible behaves like a man on a journey who would
rather have a blind man follow him than follow a man himself who can see
and knows the way. (139A)

As Pasiphaë preferred carnal connection with a bull, although she was   5
Minos' wife, so some women married to sober and strict husbands sink to a
passion for some debauchee. (139B)

Men who are too weak to vault upon a horse's back teach the horse to
kneel instead; and in the same way some men blessed with well-born
influential wives make no effort to improve themselves, but drag their   10
wives down to their own level. (139B)

According to the size of a horse we adapt his bit; and the management
of a wife should be suitable to her position. (139B)

It is when the moon is near the sun that she is darkened and put out;
when she is at a distance, she shines. Not so a virtuous wife: she ought to be   15
most noticeable in her husband's presence, and in his absence especially to
be retiring and withdrawn. (139C)

When two notes sound together, their harmony has a new depth; and
similarly, whatever happens in a household is done by agreement between
both partners, but the husband has the final choice. (139C–D)   20

When the north wind blows, it tries to tear away a man's coat by main
force, and he wraps it the more tightly round him; but if the sun cockers him
with a warm breeze, of his own accord he throws off coat and waistcoat too.
In the same way a wife who tries to recall her spouse from extravagance by
abusing him makes him worse, and if she takes it calmly and asks him   25
civilly, she does more good. (139D)

A mirror set in gold and jewels is useless unless it returns a true
reflection; and a wife is useless, however rich she may be, if she is cheerful
when her husband is sad and sad when he is cheerful. (139F)

* * * * *

5 Pasiphaë] Wife of Minos king of Crete, who developed a passion for a bull,
   and became the mother of a bull-headed monster, the Minotaur.
18 When two notes] This appears to be Erasmus' meaning, somewhat varying
   Plutarch's 'When two notes are sounded in harmony, it is the bass part' – the
   husband in a married couple – 'that carries the tune.' His revisions of Louvain
   June 1515 and Paris 1516 read *gratior* 'charm' for *gravior* 'depth'; but even
   though this may be his own correction (made without looking again at
   Plutarch), the other reading, which is much nearer his source, seems to give
   his true sense better.
21 When the north wind] Plutarch applies the familiar fable (Aesop 82, Babrius
   18) to husbands who try, by reason if possible rather than by force, to restrain
   the extravagance of their wives; in Erasmus it is the other way round.

Geometry lays it down that lines and surfaces cannot move independently of body, but move together with the bodies to which they belong: and similarly a wife, in serious business and in gaiety and laughter, in joy and sorrow, will take her cue from her husband. (140A)

As men who do not allow their wives to eat or drink with them teach them to guzzle when their husbands are from home, so those who do not share with their wives their pleasures and amusements encourage them to look elsewhere without their husbands' knowledge. (140A)

A king who is fond of music makes many men musical; if fond of learning, he makes many scholars; a gamester produces gamesters and an extortioner extortioners. It is the same with husbands: a dandy makes his wife like himself, a voluptuary makes her licentious, a virtuous and sober man gives her virtue and sobriety. (140C)

Blows on the left side of the body affect the right side; and similarly a husband should be moved by the good and bad fortune that befalls his wife, and the wife by his. (140E)

The strength of a chain is in its joints; and the stability of a household in the agreement of husband and wife. (140E)

As the body can do nothing without the mind, nor can the mind be really sound unless the body is well, so between wife and husband all things are in common. (140F)

We still call it wine, even if more than half water is mixed with it; and a household will take its name from the husband, even if the wife has contributed more than he. (140F)

Just as no one except the wearer feels where the shoe pinches, so no one knows a woman's character except the man who has married her. (141A)

As fever contracted gradually and from an unknown cause is more feared than one whose origins are obvious and serious, so secret, small, daily causes of offence do most dissolve the attachment of a married couple. (141B)

When doing sacrifice to Juno, goddess of marriage, they used to pick out the victim's gall-bladder and throw it down beside the altar, to signify that gall and bitterness should be kept far from matrimony. (141F)

The mistress of a household should be like a dry wine which, for all its dryness, is drinkable and pleasant, not bitter like aloes. (141F)

The woman who dare not laugh in front of her husband for fear he may think her skittish, or take any action for fear she may seem managing, might

* * * * *

28 more feared] In the second edition, of June 1515, Erasmus added *medici* 'by physicians,' which is in Plutarch; but the correction did not survive.

as well use no oil on her hair for fear she may seem steeped in scent, and not
wash her face lest she be thought a martyr to make-up. (142A)

As an orator who abandons all tricks and theatrical ornament moves
his hearers more powerfully by unvarnished fact, so does a wife endear
herself more to her husband by her character than by the time she spends,   5
like a woman of the town, on her toilette. (142B)

A flute-player produces sounds that are not his; and I know a wife who
will not be sorry to have her husband speak for her. (142D)

Philosophers paying their respects to a prince add honour to themselves, not him. In the same way wives who submit to their husbands win   10
praise, but if they try to rule the roost they are worse thought of than the
submissive kind. (142D–E)

The power of a husband over his wife will not be that of an owner over
his chattel, but like what the mind exercises over the body. (142E)

As two liquids form a perfect mixture, so between spouses all should   15
be shared. (142F)

A cat is maddened and driven wild by perfumes; and some wives, if
they find perfume on their husbands, lose their reason. (144C–D)

An elephant's keeper does not wear bright clothes, and the man who
is in charge of a bull does not wear red, because these colours drive the   20
creatures wild; a tigress cannot endure the roll of drums. Likewise a wife
should avoid things which she knows will greatly irritate her husband.
(144D–E)

The bee flies everywhere, and carries home what she can use; and a
studious man extracts from his reading what will make him better. (145B)   25

As those distempers of the body are more serious which leave a scar,
so some distempers of the mind are worse than others, because they cause a
more serious disturbance; for the torment is less if a man does not believe
the gods exist, than if he superstitiously fears that they do. (164F)

A comic poet said neatly of those who cover their bedsteads with gold   30

* * * * *

7 flute-player] So Plutarch; and therefore when he becomes in the second
   edition a trumpeter (*tubicen* for *tibicen*), we may suspect a misprint, rather
   than an author's correction.

24 The bee] Plutarch makes the husband bring home what may contribute to his
   wife's education; Erasmus has made the advice more general and more banal.

26 As those distempers] Eleven aphorisms derived from *Moralia* 164E–71F *De
   superstitione* 'On Superstition'; thirteen more, some of which overlap with
   these, have found a place at 173:11–175:23 and one at 176:1.

30 A comic poet] Plutarch quotes two anonymous lines, probably from the New
   Comedy (anon. fragment 150).

and silver plating, 'The gods have given us nothing free except sleep; why need people make it so expensive?' Worse, while the gods have given us sleep to be the remedy for toil and cares, the superstitious man makes it his place of torment. (166B)

Heraclitus says that men in waking life share the same world, but when they sleep they go off into worlds of their own. But the superstitious man does not enjoy a world shared with others even when awake, for his reason is always in a dream. (166C)

Polycrates the tyrant was formidable only in Samos, and Periander similarly in Corinth. The man who had escaped from their rule into some free city had nothing more to fear; but the superstitious man can take refuge nowhere and be free from fear. (166C–D)

Slaves, who have no hope of freedom, can take sanctuary at a statue of the emperor, or demand to be sold, or get a new master, if they are treated more harshly than they can bear; to the superstitious man even this much is impossible. (166D)

If it is pitiful to be a slave, by far the most pitiful fate is to be the slave of masters whom you cannot escape. (166E)

Robbers or runaways are safe if they can clasp an altar or a statue; but this is just the place where the superstitious man is most frightened. (166E)

The tigress is driven mad by the roll of drums all round her; in the same way what soothes a sound mind provokes and maddens a wild, uncivilized one. (167C)

Some men have found it less disastrous not to see at all than to see all awry, like Hercules who espied his sons, thought they were enemies, and killed them; likewise it is a lighter evil not to believe in gods at all than to believe them wicked. (167D)

As a peg on a wall, says Bion, takes whatever you hang on it and bears the weight, so do some people accept whatever you put up to them and bear whatever imposition you lay upon them. (168E)

The skipper who foresees a storm implores the gods for help, but none the less he minds his helm the while and lowers his yard-arm; but the superstitious man just loses heart. (169B)

* * * * *

5 Heraclitus] Plutarch quotes fragment 89.
9 Polycrates] He and Periander are Greek tyrants of the sixth century BC.
13 of the emperor] Added in the Froben edition of February 1519
25 Hercules] He killed his sons when under the influence of madness inflicted on him by Juno.
28 Bion] Of Borysthenes, a philosopher of the third century BC
31 skipper] See 175:7.

LB I 575B / ASD I-5 150

The digits in arithmetic stand sometimes for many thousands, sometimes for nothing. So it is with the friends of kings: now they can do what
they please, anon they fall into disgrace, and then they are powerless.
(174B)

A spectacle accompanied by some largesse draws a larger crowd; and
those subjects attract more students which promise not only happiness and
social position but profit and advantage. (122D–E)

In fair weather the body is trained to face the impending storm;
similarly one should live [with moderation and] on a low diet, [as the
physicians call it,] so that if a rich banquet comes one's way, one can ride
the waves. (123E)

As at a dinner-party we go slow on the dishes in front of us to keep
room for the delicacies we look forward to, so daily economy should be our
protection against the future. (123F–4A)

Like men who offer a sacrifice and do not taste of it themselves are
those who provide an entertainment and themselves do not partake. (124C)

Those who eat and drink only to satisfy their needs are like men who
convert temple funds to warlike uses, sacrificing pleasure to meet necessity. (124E)

There are men who scorn their own wives, comely and loving though
they are, and pay money to an expensive mistress for her favours, to satisfy
their pride more than their love of pleasure. In the same way some enjoy a
dish for the sole reason that it is scarce or very expensive. (125A)

As the tickling of the armpits makes one laugh, but disagreeably and
convulsively, so there is little enjoyment in those pleasures which the
body feels as a result of some stimulus from the mind, and not of its own
accord. (125C)

We abhor women who use black arts against us, and welcome cooks
who deploy their arts on what we eat. (126A)

Like a sore place on a limb that demands to be rubbed continually, so
desire in the mind is never satisfied. (126B)

Demades observed that the Athenians never deliberated whether to

* * * * *

1 The digits] One aphorism from *Moralia* 172B–94E *Apophthegmata regum* 'Sayings of Kings,' which is not used elsewhere in the *Parabolae* but is a principal
source for Erasmus' *Apophthegmata*. The remark is attributed to Orontes,
son-in-law of king Artaxerxes, when he fell into disgrace.

5 A spectacle] Twenty-seven aphorisms derived from *Moralia* 122B–37E *De
tuenda sanitate* 'How to Keep Well,' of which Erasmus published a version.

9 with moderation] The words in brackets were added in the Paris revision of
1516.

32 Demades] Attic orator of the fourth century BC, opponent of Demosthenes

make peace until they were wearing black; and in the same way we never
think of reducing our style of living unless we are already in a high fever
and taking physic. (126D–E)

Lysimachus, who had been driven by thirst to surrender to the Scythians, said after a draught of cold water 'In heaven's name, how brief is the
pleasure for which I have sacrificed so much felicity!' We too should make
the same reflection, when some short bout of drinking or venery ill-timed
has run us into a long sickness. (126E–F)

A scar reminds us to avoid injury, and the memory of past evils makes
us more wary. (126F)

Children's grievances quickly blow over; and casual appetites quickly
pass off if the object is removed. (127A)

The scent of flowers is not strong in itself, but gains in force when
mixed with oil; so do the causes of disease, if they light on a body that is
already full of peccant humours. (127B)

Those with a morbid tendency by nature, who encourage illness by
their manner of life, are like men who stir up mud. (127C)

Like sailors who overload their ship, and then must toil at baling out
the bilges, are they who load their bodies with over-eating and then
disburden them with clysters. (127C)

The man who drags a sickly body to the baths and a life of pleasure is
putting out in a rotten and broken boat. (128B)

If drunken revellers break into a house of mourning, not merely will
they bring no rejoicing with them – they will rouse more bitter lamentation.
Similarly a life of pleasure makes a sick man actually worse. (128D)

Sailors under a clear sky shake out more sail, perhaps, but when they
suspect a storm they take it in. Likewise one's body, when in good case, can
be allowed some liberties, but if there is any reason to fear sickness one
must proceed with caution. (128F)

Men who are stout and strong and tough and nothing else, said
Ariston, are like the columns of their own gymnasium. (133D)

Ships that are full of bilge-water must jettison their load; and a body
over-burdened must be deprived of food and drink. (134C)

Men who reduce their bodies with purging drugs, in order to fill them
up with outlandish delicacies that will make them worse, act as a man
would who should drive out Greeks from a city and install Persians or
Scythians. (134D)

* * * * *

4 Lysimachus] One of the generals of Alexander the Great, afterwards king of
  Thrace, who surrendered to the Getae in 292 BC.

30 Ariston] Ariston of Chios, a Stoic philosopher who flourished in the mid-
   third century BC

Clothes suffer more damage if washed with nitre or other such substances; and vomiting is more unpleasant if brought on by emetics. (134E)

Women of ill fame bring on an abortion in order that they may enjoy
the pleasures of conception all over again; and some men reduce their
bodies with drugs and clysters for the sole purpose of renewed guz-   5
zling. (134F)

Those who dare not diverge a hairsbreadth from their prescribed
regimen live more the life of a barnacle or a tree-stump [than of a human
being]. (135B)

As iron is worn away through frequent tempering in water, so is the   10
body damaged by frequent alternations – I mean, if it is overstrained one
moment with excessive toil, and the next softened and relaxed by luxury. (136A)

Sailors have a shocking habit of plunging into debauchery after the
hardships of a voyage, and then returning from pleasure to seamanship;   15
some men likewise change with supreme inconstancy from labour to luxury
and back again. (136C)

He who confers wealth and high station on a bad man is giving wine
to one in high fever, honey to a bilious man, or rich food to one with a
stomach-ulcer; for they are things that aggravate mental sickness, by which   20
I mean folly. (101C)

A sick man will dislike the purest and most delicious food, and reject it
if he is forced to eat, but once restored to health he will contentedly eat
cheese or onions; likewise a splendid fortune brings no pleasure to a fool,
while the wise man enjoys life even in humble circumstances. (101D)   25

Those who go to a dinner-party merely for the food bring a sort of
container with them to be filled up. (147F)

Passengers in the same ship and soldiers who share a tent must bear
each other's vagaries; and so must those who work together in public
affairs. In social life this is not so necessary: there there is common danger   30
[, not so here]. (148A)

The men who ask what we should find to do if we did not eat and drink

* * * * *

8 than of a human being] Added in the second edition of June 1515
18 He who confers] Two further aphorisms from the *De virtute et vitio*, to add to
those at 152:17–24
26 Those who go] Five aphorisms from *Moralia* 146B–64D *Septem sapientium
convivium* 'The Dinner of the Seven Wise Men'
31 not so here] These words were absent from the first edition; the second edition
(Louvain June 1515) supplied *hic quod aliis conducit, aliis noxium est* 'here what
is good for some is bad for others.'

and so on act as the daughters of Danaus would, if they were anxious what
they should do, once their great jar is full. (160B–C)

Those who have been freed from slavery now do for themselves and at
their own discretion and responsibility what they used to do for their
masters when they were slaves. In the same way the soul now supports the   5
body with much labour and anxiety; but later, when it has obtained its
freedom, it will be self-supporting in contemplation of the truth, and will
never be torn away from that. (160C)

As the body is the instrument of the soul, so the soul is God's instrument. (163E)   10

Those distempers of the body are more serious which break out in
sores and swellings, and those affections of the mind are more serious
which make life a burden from anxiety. Thus it is a fault to think that
everything is made of atoms, but it does not torment the mind as avarice
does. (164F)   15

The sea holds no terrors for him who is never in a ship, nor war for him
who never fights, bandits for him who stays at home, blackmail for the poor
man, unpopularity for the private citizen, earthquakes for the man in Gaul,
thunderbolts for him in Ethiopia. But the superstitious man fears them
all, land and sea and air and sky, darkness and light, noise, silence, dreams.   20
(165D)

Slaves when they are asleep do not fear their masters, captives forget
their gyves; in sleep sores and cancers and the severest pains are at rest.
Superstition alone still plagues a man while he sleeps. (165E)

One can escape a despot by flight to another country; he who is afraid   25
of God has nowhere he can escape to, for God is everywhere. (166D)

Slaves can demand to be sold and to change their masters; the same
privilege is not granted to the superstitious, for they fear all the gods
alike. (166D)

If slaves are in sorry case who have harsh masters, how much more   30
unfortunate are men who are the slaves of their own vices, from which they
cannot run away. (166E)

Slaves have altars and statues, bandits have sanctuaries, where they

* * * * *

 1 Danaus] The mythical founder of Argos; forty-nine of his fifty daughters
   murdered their husbands on his instructions, and were punished in Hades by
   the eternal attempt to fill a great vessel with a hole in it, using leaky pitchers.
11 Those distempers] Thirteen aphorisms derived from the *De superstitione*, to be
   compared with those already placed at 168:26, with which there is some
   overlap
18 Gaul] That France is free from earthquakes and that lightning does not strike
   in Ethiopia were known facts in antiquity.

LB I 577A / ASD I-5 158

Title page of Plutarch *Moralia* (Venice: Aldo Manuzio 1509)
This *editio princeps* of the *Moralia* was being printed at the Aldine press while
Erasmus lived in Venice in 1508, revising and enlarging his *Adagia*. In later years he
recalled with gratitude the opportunity of using manuscripts of Plutarch there
(LB II 405D). He published some translations from the *Moralia* in 1514. Nearly half
of the aphorisms in the *Parabolae* come from that source.
Courtesy of The Newberry Library, Chicago

can take refuge and be safe; but these are the places where the superstitious man is most frightened. (166E)

They say that the tigress, if she hears the roll of drums all round her, is driven mad, and ends by tearing herself in pieces; even so, some people cannot stand what raises the spirits of others, as music, eloquence, and so forth. (167C)

When a mariner espies an impending storm, first of all he prays to the gods that he may be allowed to reach harbour in safety; but none the less he then furls his sails, and takes every other step that is necessary. Likewise we ought to trust to divine assistance, but not so as to prevent us from using our own efforts. (169B)

Similarly the ploughman in Hesiod is told to sacrifice to the gods and then set to work, and the soldier first says his prayers but then girds on his armour. (169B–C)

Like men trembling as they approach the haunts of bears or serpents are the superstitious when they have anything to do with the gods, whom they suppose to be always ready to hurt. (169E)

They who worship the gods for fear of suffering harm act like men who reverence despots in self-protection, though hating them inwardly. (170E)

Some men while fleeing heedlessly from bandits or wild beasts find themselves in some pathless jungle or among chasms and precipices. Likewise some men are so anxious to escape from superstition that they fall into impiety, while piety lies between the two. (171F)

Men released from prison are more given to aimless wandering than those who have never been in chains; and so it is with children released from the control of their pastors and masters. (37D)

Those who are given freedom from their tutors and left to their own devices do not throw off all control: they change masters, for instead of their tutors they now obey the dictates of reason. (37D–E)

Naturalized citizens and strangers find many things to condemn and criticize which are acceptable to those who have been brought up in the community from childhood and have grown used to them. It is the same with those who have imbibed philosophy in early youth. (37E–F)

Athletes wear earpads to protect them from blows; children need even more some sort of muffler to protect them against the vile things they hear. (38B)

* * * * *

12 Hesiod] Plutarch alludes to *Works and Days* 465–7.
24 Men released] Fifty-four aphorisms (with one straggler from the *De super-stitione*) from *Moralia* 37C–48D *De recta ratione audiendi* 'On Listening to Lectures'

They form a lower opinion of a man who declare that he is bad-tempered and vicious than they who deny he is alive; and in the same way it shows a higher opinion of the gods to deny their existence than to say they are resentful, malicious, and irritable, as superstitious people do. (169F–70A)

As a field, if it is not cultivated, not merely remains unfertile but grows a heavy crop of weeds, so a young man capable of rational behaviour, unless he is practised in the use of sound principles, not merely will not turn out well, but will be led astray into many vices. (38C)

In a ball game they learn at the same time to deliver the ball and to catch it properly; but in education to receive properly is an earlier stage than to deliver, just as conception must precede birth. (38E)

Like the wind-eggs laid by birds is a foolish remark; heard but not listened to, it is scattered at once to the four winds. (38E)

Vessels intended to receive something poured into them are suitably disposed and tilted forward; even so the learner should dispose himself so that nothing that is said to the point may be spilt. (38F)

The ears of bad and decaying vessels are filled with anything rather than what is necessary; some people likewise learn immediately the most foolish things. (39A)

Those who train horses properly teach them to obey the bit; and he who would teach children must first give them the habit of obedience. (39B)

If you wish to pour something good into a leather bottle, you must first get the wind and air out of it; and similarly you must remove conceit from the swelled head of anyone you propose to teach. (39D)

An unwise counsellor sits at your elbow, spoiling everything; in the same way ill will is most severely critical of the best things in a book. (39D)

Words are like light: they do no one any good unless he is willing to receive them. (39E)

A wise householder profits, as Xenophon says, by both friends and enemies; and similarly an attentive and intelligent listener learns from the errors of others as well as from what is well expressed. (40C)

* * * * *

1 They form] One aphorism derived from Plutarch's *De superstitione*, the main contributions of which are placed elsewhere

18 The ears] Plutarch says that foolish young men 'fill their ears, like worthless and decaying vessels, with superfluities.' Erasmus would not have misunderstood a simple participle *empiplantes* 'filling' nor would he have spoken of filling the ears of a vessel. It looks as though what he wrote must somehow have been misread by copyist or printer.

31 Xenophon] Plutarch quotes his *Oeconomicus* 1.15.

As we see ourselves reflected in other people's eyes, so we should
keep watch, in the style of other men, for things that will suit us, or the
reverse. (40D)

One should go to a recitation as one goes to a ceremonial dinner, with
a heart full of peace and good will, ready to approve with open mind what is   5
well put; or, if anything is put less well, to note in silence the cause of the
mistakes, while at least approving the speaker's intentions. (40B)

As it is easy to demolish what someone else has built, but most
difficult to build the same thing or something better, so it is child's play to
find fault with another man's speech, but to speak oneself to the same effect,   10
or better, is not so easy. (40E)

The illusions of war are proverbial; and this applies equally to a
recitation, with the speaker's superior bearing, the applause, the clamour,
and the rest. (41C)

When a singer has a flute accompaniment, he can make many mis-   15
takes which his audience does not detect; in an ornate speech many fallacies
escape the hearer's notice under the deceptive ornaments of style. (41C)

People making garlands seek out the prettiest, not the most serviceable plants; bees settle even on thyme, that very pungent herb, and gather
nectar from it. In the same way a listener should not look out for flowers of   20
speech to give him pleasure, but for vigorous and useful ideas. (41F)

One should not go to hear an author reading in the same frame of mind
as to the circus, purely to enjoy oneself, but in search of self-improvement. (42A)

It is inconsistent to look at yourself in the mirror as you leave the   25
barber's to see if he has done you properly, and not to weigh up, as you
leave a public reading, whether you have been made better or worse by
what you have heard. (42B)

A speech is like a bath: if it does not leave you fresher, it is no good.
(42B)   30

You should not attend a public reading in the mood of one who wishes
to be done over with perfumes and cosmetics until he looks smart; you
should be grateful if the words have an edge to them, which purges and

* * * * *

12 The illusions of war] *Adagia* II x 19, where Erasmus added a reference to this
   passage of Plutarch in 1515. He uses the phrase himself, for example, in 1518 at
   the end of Ep 855.
29 A speech] In the second edition (Louvain June 1515) this was changed to *Ut*
   balnei non purgantis nulla est utilitas, ita nec sermonis qui non reddat meliorem 'As
   a bath that does not leave you fresher is no good, so is a speech that does not
   make you better.'

freshens your mind as a beehive is purged by acrid smoke, for it is all
purblind and full of cobwebs. (42C)

Give a man a drink, and he will slake his thirst before he admires the
embossing on the tankard. It is the same with a speech: first you should
notice whether it makes sound sense, and then, if you have time, you may
consider what part of it is elegant and polished. (42D)

The man who goes straight for ornament in a speech acts as one might
who should refuse to drink a life-saving medicine unless the cup came from
some potter of fine Attic quality, or wear a coat in winter unless the wool
came from Attic sheep. (42D)

When a man arrives at a dinner-party, he eats what is set before him
and does not call for something else; so should a learner sit in silence until
the speaker has wound up, and then, if he wishes, ask some relevant
question. (42F)

Ulysses in Homer is laughed at by the suitors, because he asked for a
piece of bread and not for swords or cauldrons; even more so do men
deserve mockery who bombard a speaker with minute and frivolous questions. (42F–3A)

Anyone who tries to cleave his firewood with a key and open his door
with an axe deprives himself of the use of both. Similarly those who disturb
a man while he is speaking with irrelevant and frivolous questions not
merely get no benefit from what is said, but gain the reputation of being
tiresome fellows, and are disliked for their pains. (43C)

An illness should not be kept dark, but brought out into the open that
it may be cured. As Heraclitus said, ignorance likewise ought not to be
hid. (43D)

A philosopher in the lecture-room, like a tragic poet in the theatre,
must be listened to until he has finished. (43F)

Give another man money, and you have as much less yourself as you
have given him. It is not so with praise; and yet some selfish people seem to
think so, and grudge praise more than money. (44B)

They who give grudgingly to others appear to have less than they want
themselves; and similarly those who praise other men sparingly and grudgingly seem to be still hungry and thirsty for praise themselves. (44C)

A judge trying a case gives no weight to his affections, he considers
nothing but the facts, and gives judgment accordingly; but in listening to
philosophers one should have an open mind and look kindly on many

* * * * *

15 Homer] *Odyssey* 17.222
25 Heraclitus] Plutarch quotes fragment 95.

mistakes. That is why the ancients used to set up statues of the Graces next
to the statue of Mercury. (44E)

Along a rough and rugged road one sometimes finds violets and
other flowers; and likewise in a prosaic speech one can meet with ideas and
expressions which deserve praise. (44E)

Ivy left to itself can find everywhere something to cling to; and fondness can attach itself even to things that offend him who is not fond. (45A)

Lovers put a favourable interpretation on certain faults; those who
listen to a speaker should do the same. (45A)

A satisfactory guest does not think that he has played his part when he
is agreeably entertained by someone else's forethought and expense; it is
his business in return to be an agreeable guest. In the same way a good
listener does not merely listen at his ease, while the speaker is under stress;
he ought to aid the speaker by his expression, his glance, his applause, and
general support. (45E)

As in a game of ball one party has to throw the ball correctly and the
other to catch it with skill, so at a public reading [both sides have a duty to
perform, the listener no less than the speaker]. (45E)

Those who greet a disciplined and fully argued speech with tawdry
and clever-seeming words of praise are like men who would crown a
victorious athlete with lilies or roses instead of bay or wild olive. (46A–B)

The same crown, be it what it may, does not suit every victor; nor the
same praise or honour every man. (46A–B)

The composer who would set a serious subject to soft Lydian airs
would be absurd; and he would be absurd who, having to speak about the
gods or the right rule of life, would play the mountebank with tinsel
rhetoric. (46B)

A servile dependant, abused by those at whose table he sits, grins and
remains unmoved. Not so the man who is rebuked by a philosopher: he
[ought to be touched by it, but] should neither take offence nor brazenly
ignore it. (46C)

Flesh which has grown insensible under a horny callus does not show
any bruise after a blow; and a spirit that has the habit of wrong-doing is
unmoved by rebuke however severe. (46D)

* * * * *

9 do the same] Erasmus substituted for these words in June 1515 *ita et auditores
   dicentium errata commode debent accipere* 'give his errors a kindly reception.'
20 crown] Bay formed the victor's crown at the Pythian games at Delphi, wild
   olive at Olympia. The allusion is Plutarch's.
30 ought to be touched by it] These words were added in the Paris revision of
   1516.

He who when rebuked at once detests his corrector and gives him a
wide berth is like a man who after an operation instantly dashes off full of
resentment, not waiting for the wound to be bandaged up and given
soothing dressings: he has survived the painful part, and will not try the
part that will do him good. (46E)

Telephus' wound was healed by the same spear that inflicted it, and
the wound of reproof will be healed by him that gave it. (46F)

They who are initiated into the Mysteries endure all that preliminary
ill-treatment in hopes of the sweetness and light that is to follow; when you
are rebuked by a philosopher, you should do the same. (47A)

Before we have got to know a man, many things in him annoy us
which afterwards, when we are familiar with him, may actually delight us.
It is like that in scholarship and in philosophy: that initial tedium must be
endured, until by familiarity all becomes easy and delightful. (47B)

Vessels with a narrow neck are more difficult to fill, but retain their
contents more reliably; likewise a mind which learns slowly often remembers longer. (47E)

Like nestlings not yet fledged, which lie with ever-gaping beaks,
waiting for another mouth to feed them, some students are a burden to their
teacher, because he must put everything into their mouths bit by bit, and
they get nothing for themselves. (48A)

Some men by frequent deviations make a short journey long; so there
are those who interrupt a teacher with frequent questions trivial and off the
point, and break up the steady flow of teaching. (48B)

Like idle and greedy dogs, which in the house gnaw the pelts of wild
beasts and worry their fur but in the hunting-field give the beasts themselves a wide berth, so do some students get things the wrong way round:
they are active over trifles and never touch the heart of the subject. (48B)

The mind does not ask to be filled up, like a container; a kindling spark
suffices, like setting fire to wood, to rouse the faculty of discovery and the
desire for truth. (48C)

Like a man who goes to ask his neighbour for a light, and finding a
good fire burning there sits down and goes no further, is he who sits for
ever at his teacher's feet, and never kindles his own mind, that he may
warm himself at home by his own fire. (48C)

* * * * *

6 Telephus' wound] Telephus, king of Mysia, was wounded in the Trojan war
by the spear of Achilles, and afterwards healed by rust from the same weapon;
cf 190:7.

Just as (to quote Philoxenus) the most delicious meat is that which is not meat and the best fish what is not fish, so the greatest delight is to be found in poetry that is mingled with philosophy or philosophy with an admixture of poetry. (14E)

Hearing and reading authors is like eating: our aim is not pleasure only but well-being. (14F)

The city-gates are closed in vain, if one is left open through which the enemy may force an entrance; and similarly it is not enough to be well governed in all other respects, if your ears are open to language that corrupts. (14F)

A special guard must be set on the gate that gives access to the royal palace, and a special watch must be kept on the ear, because of its close connexion with the reasoning part of the soul; what enters by that gate has great power for good or ill. (15A)

Some men wear an amethyst at a drinking-party to preserve them from intoxication; much more should one bring principles with one to hear a poet read his works, for fear they have a bad effect on one. (15B)

Places where many plants grow which are valuable as antidotes produce also many that are lethal. Poets are like that – many splendid things, many noxious. (15C)

Simonides said the Thessalians were too stupid to be taken in by him; it is the clever people who are the first to be corrupted by poetry. (15D)

As Ulysses stopped his ears with wax, and so sailed safely past the Sirens, so should we pass by anything in an author that is attractive but obscene. (15D)

If many people drink wine until they are intoxicated, this is no reason for cutting down all the vines, as Lycurgus did: spring water should be made more accessible. In the same way, if many make a wrong use of

* * * * *

1 Just as] Twenty-nine aphorisms derived from *Moralia* 14D–37B *Quomodo adolescens poetas audire debeat* 'How a Young Man Should Study Poetry.' The first is based on a quotation in Plutarch from Philoxenus of Leucas, a poet of the fourth century BC: fragment 836f; D.L. Page ed *Poetae melici graeci* (Oxford 1962) 441.

21 Simonides] Of Ceos, famous writer of lyric and elegiac poetry, who died in 467 BC. Many anecdotes about him, true or false, were in circulation.

23 Ulysses] It was Ulysses' crew, not the hero himself, whose ears were stopped with wax that they might not hear the Sirens' fatal song (*Odyssey* 12.177); the slip (a venial one) is not Plutarch's but is found in Lucian *Nigrinus* 19.

27 Lycurgus] A mythical king of Thrace, so hostile to Bacchic revelry that he cut down all the vines in his dominions

poetry, it should not be banned, but care should be taken to make it more beneficial. (15E)

As mandragora growing near vines makes the wine less potent, so when philosophical principles are combined with poetry, it makes the risk of learning lighter. (15F)

As in pictures we are more affected by colour than line, because it gives a closer representation of the human form and increases the illusion, so falsehood mingled with the semblance of truth attracts and persuades us more than plain writing with no deception about it. (16C)

One can find religious ceremonies with no flutes or dancing; one cannot find poetry without falsehood. (16C)

Like ratsbane in one's food are corrupting principles mingled among what is profitable and pleasant. (17C)

We enjoy disgusting creatures when they are skilfully represented, and in poetry, since it is an image of life, even bad things give pleasure when they are well reported. (18A)

When we see a picture of parricide or incest, we praise only the skill of the artist, and abominate the subject itself; similarly in the poets we shall imitate the style and detest the subject. (18B)

Some things without beauty in themselves are held by some critics to be good because so well adapted to their purpose; similarly some things in poetry are praiseworthy because they are so much in character, though objectionable in other respects. Demonides the cripple, when his shoes were stolen, prayed that the thief might have feet to fit them. (18D)

It would be dangerous if everybody in a boat leant over towards one side, but they tilt it in different directions, and the boat is well trimmed; hostility and disagreement between politicians makes the state more secure. In the same way disagreement among poets means that they have less power to warp the reader's views. (20C)

The cantharid beetle is a deadly poison, but physicians use its legs and wings none the less as an antidote. Likewise one can cull from the same poem a remedy for the harm it does, for poets always put in something to show that they disapprove of the story they tell. (22B)

Those who try hard to express everything represent many bad things

* * * * *

23 Demonides] Nothing seems to be known of this proverbial Damonidas (as Plutarch calls him). His shoes were hideous, but they did fit his hideously deformed feet.

without noticing them, just as their associates used to imitate Aristotle's
lisp and Plato's bowed shoulders. (26B)

In divine service we may be full of religious awe and reverence; but in
our reading we ought not to respect everything, but use our judgment
keenly to approve of some things and disapprove of others. (26B)

We ought not to bow before poets or philosophers as children obey
their tutors, but be like Cato who, when he was a boy, did what his tutor
told him, but asked him why. Likewise we should put ourselves in the
hands of our author, if he has given us good reasons. (28B)

As the fruit on a vine is often hidden by the luxuriance of leaves and
shoots, so in poetry which is over-luxuriant in metaphor and myth many
useful lessons are concealed from a young man. (28E)

As in the same pastures the bee seeks flowers, the goat foliage, the hog
seeks for roots, and larger animals for fruit, so in the poets people look for
different things, one for history, another for ornaments of style, another for
apt quotations, another for maxims of the good life. (30D)

We do not make a horse feel the bit as we gallop along, but before
we start; and similarly those who are inclined to anger or lust should be bri-
dled beforehand by argument and warning, before they come in reach of
danger. (31D)

As the bee gathers from bitter flowers and prickly thorns the sweetest
smoothest honey, so in stories of lechery and crime some profit can somehow be found. (32E)

The horse is turned by the bit, the ship by the rudder; and men are
steered by words. (33F)

As physicians, when a specific has been discovered for one particular
disease, adapt it to all diseases that are related and similar, so it is reasonable to adapt an author's words to various purposes. (34C)

Flog a man's clothes, and you do not touch his body; criticize him for
low birth or poverty, and you do not really touch the man himself at all, but
find fault wrongly with external things. (35E)

A man brought suddenly out of pitch darkness into daylight is badly
dazzled, unless he has gradually grown accustomed to the light; similarly in
reading the poets with a class one should now and then introduce argu-

* * * * *

2 shoulders] *Sic in autoribus optima dumtaxat sequi conveniet* 'Likewise in reading
it will be right to follow only what is best' added in the second edition
(Louvain June 1515), presumably by Erasmus
7 Cato] The younger Cato, called 'of Utica' (d 46 BC)

ments from the philosophers into the boys' minds, that they may not be
upset later, when they meet such a different method of approach. (36E)

In vain are corks fixed on a net to make it float if lead is added to drag it
down and keep it in equipoise; likewise it is vain to educate us in the
maxims of the good life, if added vice does not allow us to rise above our   5
folly. (75B)

In the curing of a malady no relief is felt until a state of health is
re-established; and similarly in philosophy no progress is made unless
there is a gradual reduction in one's original folly, until one achieves a new
habit of mind. (75B–C)   10

Caeneus suddenly became a man instead of a woman merely by
wishing; but no bad man on the instant becomes good, any more than you
can go to bed foolish and wake up wise. (75E–F)

The marble must be made to fit the measuring-line, not the line to fit
the marble; life likewise must be directed by the precepts of the philos-   15
ophers, which must not be distorted to fit our behaviour. (75F)

As when a shadow is relaxed in stages we feel ourselves more and
more in the light, so, as our folly is gradually lessened, we make progress in
wisdom. (76B)

Men sailing far out at sea estimate that they must have progressed   20
from the mere force of the wind and the time they have run before it, even if
there is still no sign of harbour; but nowhere do they pause until they have
reached the haven where they would be. Likewise there must be no resting
in philosophy until we have reached that perfect state that belongs to the
wise man. (76C)   25

As he who adds little to little, and does so often, piles up a great heap
[as Hesiod says], so diligence is of 'great value in acquiring sound sense.
(76C–D)

He who stands still on his way from time to time makes little progress;
but in philosophy we actually slip back into evil if we relax our pursuit of   30
the good, like a boat carried back by the tide. (76D)

* * * * *

3 In vain] Forty-three aphorisms derived from *Moralia* 75B–86A *Quomodo quis
suos in virtute sentiat profectus* 'How a Man May Become Aware of His Progress
in Virtue'

11 Caeneus] A Thessalian maiden ravished by Neptune, who promised her
whatever she wished, and she instantly became a man (Ovid *Metamorphoses*
12.119–209).

14 The marble] Proverbial; inserted by Erasmus in the *Adagia* of 1508 (II v 36)
with a reference to this passage of Plutarch

27 as Hesiod says] *Works and Days* 361–2; the reference was added in the second
edition (June 1515), but not maintained in the text.

Astronomers tell us that the planets, when they cease to advance, stand fast; but in philosophy you cannot stand still – you must go [steadily] forward. (76D)

As a balance cannot stand stationary, but must always be tilting one way or the other, so in philosophy he who makes no progress towards wisdom slips back into folly. (76E)

In war the night-watch can never be relaxed, and against the vices we must always be under arms. (76E)

A cornstalk shoots up vigorously at first, then is divided frequently by joints, and ends in the ear as the sport of the winds. So some begin with enthusiasm, then stop from time to time and find things difficult, and in the end collapse exhausted. (77A)

Those who like a person superficially enjoy his company and forget him easily when he is not there; a true lover cannot bear to be parted from the object of his affections. Likewise some are easily called away by business from the pursuit of philosophy; but those who really love her forget all beside her, and to them nothing without her can taste sweet. (77B)

We enjoy perfumes when they are in the air, and do not suffer severely when they are not. That is no way to treat philosophy. (77c)

The sufferer from severe hunger or thirst cannot be distracted until he has satisfied his appetite; so too a man with a thirst for wisdom must put that before all else. (77c)

It is a serious moment for passengers in a ship when the land which they recognize disappears and the land for which they are bound is not yet in sight. So it is with students of philosophy: at first it is painful to abandon their familiar comforts, while they do not yet behold the happiness to which philosophy will lead them. (77D–E)

In the study of philosophy [there is a kind of metamorphosis:] some men become like birds and devote themselves to the contemplation of nature, and some like puppy-dogs turn to wrangling and worrying their sophistries and quibbling questions. (78E–F)

Anacharsis said that the Athenians used money merely as something

* * * * *

2 steadily] Added in June 1515 and in the 1516 editions.
10 sport of the winds] Plutarch speaks of the 'breath' (*pneuma*) or life-giving spirit of the plant as exposed to buffeting. It is hard to be sure whether Erasmus has misunderstood or deliberately improved his original.
28 In the study] The words in brackets are an addition, perhaps of the Froben edition of February 1519.
32 Anacharsis] A half-legendary Scythian traveller of philosophical tastes, who visited Athens early in the sixth century BC

to count; and some people use the principles of philosophy merely for
show. (78F)

As the bee gathers from flowers the nectar for her honey, where other
creatures get only the pleasures of colour and scent, so too the student of
philosophy finds even in poetry things that can contribute to the good life,
while others find only pleasure and relaxation. (79C)

Those who look for nothing in Plato and Demosthenes but the purity
of Attic Greek are just like those who appreciate nothing in drugs except
their scent and glistening colour, ignoring their power to purge and restore
good health. (79D)

Apothecaries do not cure the sick, nor are they true philosophers who
get a smattering of philosophy and use it for show. (80A)

Like a bird which carries any food she has picked up straight to her
nestlings, and gets no good from it herself, are those who learn in order to
teach immediately, and themselves are none the better for it. (80A)

As true love for a woman feels no need of witnesses, but is content to
possess the loved one in solitude, so is a wise man content with a good
conscience. It is those whose passion is feigned who advertise it and make a
show. (80E)

The husbandman would rather see his corn-ears bowed over than
standing upright, for he perceives that those are heavy with grain but these
are empty. In the same way young men who have not yet made much
progress in philosophy hold their heads high, but when they develop the
good grain of sound doctrine, they humble themselves. (81B)

As air is driven out of a bottle when it is filled with liquid, so
proficients in philosophy are filled with true good things, and have learnt to
pride themselves less on cloak and beard; they are less critical of others,
more severe judges of themselves. (81C)

In the Mysteries candidates are initiated with shouting and disorder,
but when the sacred rites begin, they listen in silence and awe; so the
beginnings of philosophy are disorderly, but its mysteries are peaceful. (81E)

In a storm, when St Elmo's fire appears, sailors' hopes rise; likewise in

* * * * *

7 Demosthenes] Plutarch has Xenophon, who was probably not regarded by
Erasmus as a sufficiently pure exemplar of Attic style.

33 St Elmo's fire] Continuing from the last aphorism, Plutarch speaks of the great
light seen in the Mysteries, 'as though a shrine (*anaktorôn*) were opened.'
Either Erasmus misunderstands this, or it reminds him of something quite
different – of the Anakes, Castor and Pollux, the twin deities held responsible

philosophy lack of confidence at the outset is familiar, but then the light of truth appears and scatters despondency. (81E)

Menedemus used to say that many men made the journey to Athens who were wise to begin with; then they became philosophers, that is, professional seekers after wisdom; then rhetoricians; and lastly private citizens. Similarly in philosophy, the further you progress, the less you are swollen with self-esteem. (81F)

The man with toothache goes straight to the dentist and shows him his trouble; if he has a fever, he sends for the doctor; the madman neither sends for a physician nor will let him into the house, under the violence of his disorder. Men who conceal their faults and will not suffer correction are like that: there is no hope of cure. (81F)

Men who suffer from sores have no desire to be thought to do so, but they wish to escape from the fact even more than from the appearance. Likewise to seem wicked is not desirable; but to be wicked is more to be shunned than to seem so. (82B)

Diogenes saw a young man in a low tavern, who was ashamed and took refuge further in. 'The further you retreat,' he said, 'the deeper in a tavern you will be.' Men with faults are like that: the further they retreat into themselves, the more they are what they are; they must come out into the open if they wish to escape themselves. (82C–D)

The poor find their poverty greater [and less tolerable] the more they try to conceal it; similarly those who conceal their faults through pride and arrogance make them worse. (82D)

A well-trained horse will continue on the right road of his own accord, though his driver does not use the reins; and if the affections are tamed by reason early and accustomed to it, they never attempt to do wrong, even in dreams or illness, when the reason is asleep. (83A–B)

As the body can learn by experience to stop the eyes winking or running with tears, and the heart from throbbing, so, and much more, can the mind learn not to be carried away by fancies. (83B–C)

The transference of a disease to parts of the body not proper to it is a sign that it is preparing to depart; likewise when we lose the taste for things to which we have become devoted, it is an indication of a return to normality. (84A)

* * * * *

for the ball of light seen on mast or yard-arm in a storm, which was later called a corposant or St Elmo's fire, and which was a good omen; cf below 242:33.
3 Menedemus] A philosopher and statesman of the late fourth century BC
17 Diogenes] The famous Cynic philosopher
22 and less tolerable] Added, perhaps in the edition of February 1519

Love that breeds no jealousy is no true love; and no man is a true devotee of virtue who is not fired with envy of the virtuous deeds of others. (84C)

A high-mettled horse breaks easily into a gallop of his own accord; a man fired with the love of virtue needs no one to spur him on. (84D)

As the lover approves all points in his beloved, so in a man whose virtues we admire we imitate also with pleasure his gestures, his walk, and his appearance. (84E)

True lovers love even a lisp and a pale face in their loved ones; even so an admirer of virtue does not blench at Aristides' exile or Socrates' poverty or the condemnation of Phocion. (84F)

A man combing his hair uses a mirror; a man setting out on an enterprise holds up before himself the examples of great men of old. (85B)

It was an old custom to learn by heart the names of the fingers, and recite them slowly one by one, as a sort of antidote to fear; similarly, as a protection against all disturbance of the mind, it is good to have some examples to hand of great and good men. (85B).

The man who despairs of becoming rich is a generous spender, while he who already hopes he is approaching wealth does not despise small gains and makes little economies. In the same way the man who is confident that he can become virtuous is keen to correct his lightest faults, and overlooks nothing that may contribute in any way to a virtuous frame of mind. (85E)

Those who make a boundary-hedge or bank pile up whatever they can get together – wood, stones, or a column fallen from a tomb; but he who builds a palace puts nothing together at random. Likewise a good man leaves no part of his life in random disorder. (85F)

You may find places where nothing poisonous grows, as they say is

* * * * *

10 Aristides'] Three famous examples of good men condemned unjustly: the politician Aristides surnamed 'the just,' Socrates the philosopher, and Phocion the fourth-century general

14 names of the fingers] Plutarch refers to the *Idaioi Daktyloi* Idaean Daktyls, a mythical race of wizards or craftsmen who lived on Mount Ida in Crete, of whom Erasmus might have known from Pliny's *Natural History* 7.197. But the Aldine *Moralia* of 1509 printed *idiôn daktylôn* 'of their own fingers'; and that was the text he had in front of him.

28 You may find] Twenty-three aphorisms from *Moralia* 86B–92F *De capienda ex inimicis utilitate* 'How to Profit by One's Enemies,' one of the essays which Erasmus translated. For 'nothing poisonous' both Plutarch and Erasmus' version have 'no wild beast.'

true of Crete; you cannot find a body politic that does not encourage envy and strife. (86c)

Our forefathers were content if they were not hurt by wild beasts; later men began to make use of them, wearing their skins, eating their meat, using their gall for medicine. We should do the same – not only avoid being hurt by our enemies, but turn them to our good. (86D)

Not every tree can be domesticated nor every wild animal tamed, yet these too are put to use by men as best they can; so it is with those who will not make friends – we must use their unfriendliness for our own benefit. (86E)

Sea-water is undrinkable, but fish live in it, ships sail on it; likewise in everything we should pick out whatever it contains that may be of use. (86E)

The first time a satyr saw fire, he wanted to embrace it, and Prometheus warned him that it burns you when you touch it, while it gives light to the eyes; it warms you, he said, and is the handmaid of the useful arts. The same thing can help or hinder; all depends on how you use it. (86F)

In illness some men find this much advantage, that they enjoy a holiday from business that oppressed them; some men, made to work hard, have gained in strength. Similarly exile, poverty, and shipwreck have been for some people the stimulus to become philosophers. (87A)

Men of strong stomachs, and living creatures in perfect health, can digest stones, iron, snakes, and scorpions, and get nourishment from them; invalids are upset even by wine and bread. So fools lose their friends, while the wise can make good use even of their enemies. (87A–B)

Lynceus saw through an oak; an enemy watches you through a servant or a friend. (87B–C)

As vultures find their way to dead bodies by the smell but sound bodies they do not notice, so, if you make a mistake, your enemy scents it out at once and hurries to the spot; what you do right leaves him inert. (87D)

A hostile army always threatening the walls makes a city watchful and temperate; and an enemy who watches all you do makes you do and say nothing rash. (87E)

Singers often take little trouble when singing in chorus in the theatre,

* * * * *

27 Lynceus] A fabulous character with superhuman eyesight. Erasmus added to the *Adagia* of 1515 (II i 54) a reference to his power of seeing through rocks and trees, giving Plutarch as his authority; but it was *Moralia* 1083D and not this passage.

but put them into competition with one another and every note is studied.
Likewise a man takes much more trouble who knows that his life is sur-
veyed by hostile eyes. (87F)

It is commonly thought absurd to blame someone for a bodily fault
from which you are not free yourself; but it is much more ridiculous to cast a   5
fault of character in someone's teeth which will recoil on you. (88D)

As Telephus, having no friend, was obliged to seek a remedy for his
wound from an enemy, so those who have no outspoken friend to give them
advice often hear about their faults from an opponent. (89C)

Again, as Telephus did not consider the enemy whose spear it was,   10
but the cure that it effected, so we ought not to take offence at criticism from
an opponent; but if his remarks are true, we should convert them into a
means to improvement. (89C)

The man who wished to kill the Thessalian Prometheus opened a
tumour with his sword and cured him; so it often happens that abuse   15
uttered in anger by an enemy cures some fault in us that was unknown or
neglected. (89C)

Wrestlers do not wipe the dust off themselves, but cover each other
with dirt, expecting to fall together; even so some people when they are
abused do not defend themselves, but bide their time till they find some-   20
thing to hurl back in their turn. (89D)

If you are shown a lump of mud on your clothes even by an enemy,
you do not throw it at him, you wipe it off; similarly, if anyone shows you a
fault in your character, you must not reply in kind, but remove the cause of
offence. (89D)   25

As ingrained habit even if harmful is hard to get rid of, so a quarrel
leaves a deposit of ill will in the mind, and jealousy and a memory of what
you have suffered. (91B)

As we began with beasts, and thence learnt to kill men too, so, if we
become accustomed to hurting our enemies, which is regarded as a fair   30
thing to do, we learn by degrees, unless we are careful, to do the same to
everyone. (91C)

* * * * *

7 Telephus] See 180:6. Plutarch says that he lacked 'a congenial physician';
   Erasmus omits the 'physician,' perhaps in order to bring out the contrast
   between friend and enemy.
14 Thessalian Prometheus] This name must indicate Jason of Pherae, a Thessalian ruler in the fourth century BC. When an enemy tried to kill him in battle,
   his sword missed its mark but accidentally lanced a tumour that had been
   supposed inoperable, and so saved Jason's life. For moralists this was a classic
   example of doing good when you mean to do harm.

No lark without a crest; and no mind without some inborn dislikes. (91E)

Just as we desire to have our drains as far from the house as possible,
so it will be found a good plan to void the offscourings of your faults upon
your enemies. (91F)

Onomademus urged that not all members of the opposing party
should be executed, because (said he) if we remove all our enemies, we shall
start fighting with our friends. In the same way, once we have spent all
feelings of the sort upon our enemies, we are more cordial towards our
friends. (91F)

Gardeners plant their roses next to garlic and onions, so that any
unpleasant smell in the roses may be diverted into them. So an enemy, by
attracting to himself and absorbing any unpleasant feelings we may harbour, makes us more agreeable to our friends. (92B)

Like a cripple or a blind man afraid of becoming hundred-handed
Briareus or Argus with his hundred eyes, some people are afraid of having
too many friends, when they have not yet acquired one real one. (93C)

A man who aims to have many friends is like a shameless woman who
sleeps with many men but has no genuine lover. (93C)

One who starts many friendships, but then soon tires of them and
looks for others, is like a girl in a meadow picking flowers one after the
other, who is always attracted by the charm of some new one and forgets the
old. (93D)

As a river that is divided into many channels flows shallow and slow,
so good will dissipated among many objects grows faint and evaporates. (93F)

Living creatures which produce only one offspring are more passionately devoted to it; and good will is stronger that has a single object. (93F)

Flies do not stay in a cookshop if there is no smell of food; and a rich
man's ordinary friends do not last if they get nothing out of him. (94B)

* * * * *

1 No lark] A proverb incorporated by Erasmus in the *Adagia* (III iii 67), where in
1515 and 1526 he adds references to two other passages in Plutarch, but not to
this one.

6 Onomademus] In *Moralia* 813A, where the same story is told, he is a popular
leader in the island of Chios.

11 Gardeners] Plutarch speaks of diverting from the flowers into the vegetables
any unpleasant element there may be in what both feed on. By leaving out part
of this Erasmus becomes responsible for the suggestion that there may be
something unpleasant in the smell of a rose.

15 Like a cripple] Twenty-two aphorisms derived from *Moralia* 93A–7B *De
amicorum multitudine* 'On Having Many Friends.' Briareus helped Zeus defeat
Cronus. Two of Argus' eyes were always resting; the others kept watch.

One who has a friend he has not tested is like the owner of a counterfeit coin: when he finds the man is no good, he is thankful to be relieved of
him, and while he has him, wishes he could get away. (94D)

As one cannot retain noxious food without injury nor get rid of it
without discomfort, so a bad friend, if you keep him, does you harm, yet
you cannot be quit of him without bad feeling and unpleasantness, like
bile. (94D)

As we fight our way through thorns and brambles that wind round us
until we reach the vines and olives, so we ought not to admit the first comer
to our friendship, but press on till we find the right person and reject the
rest. (94E)

Zeuxis painted slowly the pictures that were to last for centuries; and
we should take time to explore the friend whom we mean to last. (94F)

A ship that will preserve us in a storm, a dyke that will stand against
emergencies of many kinds, need care in the building; and a friend needs to
be tested with care, if he is to stand by you through thick and thin. (94C–D)

Milk is curdled with rennet; men coalesce and are made one by
friendship. (95B)

Fortune is like the wind, favourable to some people and contrary to
others. (95C)

As Briareus, who with his hundred hands had fifty stomachs to feed,
was no better off than we are, who have one pair of hands and one belly to
provide for, so you will get as much good out of the friendship of a few
people as out of many, for the inconvenience is balanced: if few people
consider your wishes, you have few to consider yourself. (95E)

As Creon gave his daughter no help, but died with her in the fire,
holding her in his arms, so some men get no benefit from successful friends,
and share the fate of the unsuccessful. (96C)

Brute beasts, if they are forcibly mated with an animal of another kind,
retire indignant and resentful; on the same principle it is between like-
minded people that friendship grows smoothly and holds fast. (96D)

Harmony in music comes into existence out of unlike notes, it may be
low and high, matched according to some ratio between them; but friendship exists between like and like. (96E)

Let the octopus adapt itself to different backgrounds; we ought not to

* * * * *

12 Zeuxis] Famous Greek painter of the end of the fifth century BC
26 Creon] Medea, deserted by Jason in favour of Creusa, daughter of Creon king
    of Corinth, gave her rival a magic crown and robe, by which she was burnt to
    death; and so was her father when he tried to help her (Euripides *Medea*
    1136ff).

adapt ourselves to the behaviour of different people indiscriminately. (96F)

The octopus changes only its surface texture and colouring; friend should be really close to friend, in character and feelings and interests. (96F)

Proteus turned himself by magic into every shape and had no certain   5
shape of his own; not for us to have no fixed principle of life, to con a book with the studious, wrestle with the gymnast, go ahunting with the passionate sportsman, sink into stupor with the heavy drinker, and join the ambitious man in his pursuit of office. (97A)

A man with no home of his own wanders from house to house; and a   10
person with no certain principle of life to follow apes the habits of one man after another. (97B)

A mind at the mercy of many friendships is like primal matter, ready to take on any form you please, having none of its own. (97B)

Take a single nanny-goat and put a piece of sea-holly in her mouth: 15
she stands stock still and so do all the flock, until the goatherd takes it out again. So does a monarch's character pass with extraordinary force into his people. (776F)

Like Ixion who, in pursuit of Juno, fell upon a cloud, many run headlong into artificial and casual friendships. (777E)   20

As light is more useful to the beholder than to those who are seen, so glory means more to those who contemplate it than to him to whose lot it falls. (777F)

He who puts poison not into a single cup, but into the spring from which all drink, deserves a heavier penalty; so they who corrupt the nature   25
of a prince do a greater wrong than the corrupters of a private citizen. (778D–E)

A city honours its priests because they pray to the gods for the common good of all men. Much more should men honour the tutor of their prince, if he is good, for he makes the prince capable of being a blessing to   30
everyone. (778F)

A craftsman would rather make a lyre with which he knew that Amphion's skill would build the walls of Thebes than the one Thales used

* * * * *

5 Proteus] The old man of the sea, proverbial for changing his shape; *Adagia* II ii 74

15 Take a single] Eight aphorisms from *Moralia* 776B–9C *Maxime cum principibus philosopho esse disserendum,* 'That a Philosopher Ought to Converse Especially with Men in Power,' which has already suggested three at 150:26–151:4. Ixion is a repetition. See above 151:3n.

33 Amphion's] When he played on his lyre, according to the legend, the enchanted stones took place of their own accord to build the walls of Thebes. Of

to quell sedition in Lacedaemon. Likewise a philosopher will prefer to train the mind of a prince who will improve the world. (779A)

A stain that has dried and had time to take root is removed with difficulty; similarly faults ingrained are not easily corrected. (779C)

A mind that often slips back into the same faults is like a book that has been used again after scraping out the writing: it is not easy to get rid of marks because the ink has sunk in. (779C)

As if a blind man were to run into somebody, and call him blind for not getting out of the way, so we call fortune blind, though it is our own blindness that makes us fall foul of her. (98A)

If there were no sun we should live in night, for all the other heavenly bodies could do for us; similarly, for all our other senses, we should be no different from the brutes if we had not reason. (98C)

The painter in the old story accidentally reproduced the foam on a horse, which he had not skill enough to paint, by dashing a sponge filled with various colours on the mouth of the horse in his picture. In the same way there are some things chance can do, which no forethought or care of ours can achieve. (99B)

A man ought not to take up a lyre who does not know how to play it; and a man ought not to take up a command who is not equipped with wisdom. (100A)

Physicians treating a violent flux of phlegm do not immediately have recourse to drugs, but apply externally what will digest the fluid, given time, and then proceed to their remedies. So it is with fresh grief: we should keep silence until time moderates it, and it admits of consolation. (102A)

In a democracy the man to whom authority is given by lot must exercise it, and he who was unlucky must bear it with resignation. So it is in the life of man: we must make the best of what our lot has given us. (102E)

The fruits of the earth are at one time abundant, at another scarce; in animals sometimes breeding goes well, sometimes there is sterility; the sea is now stormy and now calm. So it is in life: fortune will vary. (103B)

To every tree its own fruit; and the fruit of grief is always tears. (106A)

* * * * *

this Thales nothing is known. Plutarch speaks of a lyre to be used by Amphion or Thales, rather than by ordinary people for less admirable purposes. The same word in Greek means both 'or' and 'than.' By contrasting the two benefactors, and making fortification more beneficial than the pacification of civil strife, Erasmus has perhaps adopted a view which surely he would have rejected, had he stopped to think.

8 As if a blind man] Four from *Moralia* 97C–100A *De fortuna* 'On Chance'

22 Physicians] Ten from *Moralia* 101F–22A *Consolatio ad Apollonium* 'A Letter of Condolence to Apollonius'

No one is surprised to see a thing melted that he knew can melt, cleft
that he knew was cleavable, burnt that he knew would burn. In the same
way we should not be surprised at the death of someone who was always
mortal. (106D–E)

Out of the same clay one can make toy animals, then roll them into one
again, and without pausing make one thing out of another. So nature out of
the same material made our forefathers, then us when they died, then [will
produce] more and still more to replace us. (106E–F)

As borrowed money must be repaid with a good grace, so the
privilege of being alive, which has been lent us by the gods, must be given
up without a murmur. (107A)

It is not the man who has sung the most songs or made the longest
speeches or been captain of many ships who is praised [but he who has
shown skill in the doing of it]. So with the man whose life has been not long
but well spent. (111A–B)

According to the fall of the dice you must make the best and most
skilful move you can; and what befalls you in life you must make the best
of. (112F)

As bankers return the security deposited with them without demur,
because they accepted it precisely that it might be returned, so we should
treat what we have received from the gods. (116A)

Some people invent tales and falsehoods out of their own heads, with
no substratum of truth, like a spider spinning webs out of her own entrails. (966E)

As a rainbow is nothing but the sun's radiance refracted in the clouds,
so a story is a sort of reflection of the truth. (894D)

Smoke that made a great cloud to start with soon disappears, and so
does reputation wrongfully gained.

As runaway slaves when torn from altars and temples have no sanctuary left except the tombs of the dead, so men devoid of true glory which is
really theirs pride themselves upon their pedigrees.

We do not use muddy water unless it has had time to stand; much less

* * * * *

7 will produce] Added in the second edition (Louvain June 1515)
13 but he] The words in brackets were added in the Paris revision of 1516.
22 Some people] Apparently from *Moralia* 959B–85C *De sollertia animalium* which
provided three at 160:30–161:8
25 rainbow] Perhaps from *Moralia* 874D–919D *De placitis philosophorum* 'Opinions of the Philosophers'
27 Smoke] Sources of this and the next paragraph are not yet identified.
32 We do not use] Fourteen aphorisms derived from *Moralia* 548B–68A *De sera
numinis vindicta* 'On the Delays of Divine Vengeance.' Why Plutarch should
ascribe the first one to Socrates is not known.

should we use a mind in turmoil before it has settled down. This comes
from Socrates. (550F)

If a piece of ground is beset with thickets, wild animals, and weeds,
and has much marsh, an inexperienced husbandman rejects it at sight; but
the skilled farmer infers from these same signs that the ground is soft and   5
fertile, and works all the harder to clean it. Likewise do gifted natures tend
to breed great faults, which it is advisable not to remove at one stroke, but to
cure gradually; one must wait for the proper time, until the man can be
brought to bear good fruit. (552C)

As the Egyptians were obliged by law, if a woman had been con-   10
demned to death when pregnant, to wait until the child should be born, so,
when men go wrong, we should not be in a hurry to abandon hope. (552D)

A hyena's gall-bladder and the rennet of a seal and other parts of very
unpleasant animals have great curative force in grave disorders; in the same
way God sometimes makes use of savage tyrants to correct our faults.   15
(552F–3A)

As a farmer does not cut his thorns until he has collected the edible
shoots, and the Libyans do not set fire to the scrub before they have
gathered the incense, so God does not extinguish a pestilent dynasty of
kings before some profit has accrued from them. (553C)   20

Cantharid beetles and scorpions carry in themselves the antidote for
their own poison; but in sin itself lies its own penance and punishment.
(554A)

Some children admire the poor wretches who dance on the stage
covered in golden sequins, and think they must be very rich; so fools think   25
men burdened with riches must be happy. (554B)

Those afflicted with a slow wasting disease do not escape death but
die very slowly; likewise those who are not punished immediately do not
escape punishment but have it long drawn out. (554C)

Men who live a life of pleasure, criminals though they are, are like   30
those in a prison from which there is no escape, who sometimes play a game
of checkers. (554D)

* * * * *

10 condemned to death] So Plutarch, and so the first edition. Erasmus employs
an unusual phrase, *morte correpta*, for normally *correpta* would mean 'rebuked' rather than 'punished' or 'condemned.' It looks as though, when
revising the text for Bade (no doubt under pressure and very probably late at
night), he had taken this to be a mistake for the common expression *morbo
correpta* 'seized by illness'; for so it stands in the Paris edition of 1516 and ever
since, although this does not in fact make sense.

17 thorns] This is the thorny asparagus of 165:10.

21 scorpions] Not mentioned here by Plutarch, but Erasmus was familiar from
other sources with their use as an antidote; see 271:20.

Some rivers suddenly dive under the earth, but none the less they reach their destination; so the wrath of the powers above may act in secret, yet at some time it bears off wicked men into the ultimate of calamity. (557E)

Men sweating in a fever are equally hot, whether you put one blanket on them or many more, but to encourage them the mass of blankets is removed. Thus we must try to humour those whom we cannot cure. (557F)

As physicians cauterize the thumb of a man with a gouty hip, and in general apply a remedy to some part other then the place where it hurts, so God sometimes lets fly against the children that he may cure their fathers. (559F)

As a scorpion must not be supposed to have a sting only when it strikes, but must be watched continually, so the offspring of wicked men, even when they do no wrong, yet have the poison in their veins. (562C)

As physicians take steps against some disorders before they appear, so God punishes some things to prevent their happening. (562D)

A winner in the games employs a herald to proclaim his victory; much more should true virtue be praised by others, not itself. (539C)

Some men are driven by hunger, having nothing else to eat, to feed horribly on their own limbs; likewise some people thirsting for glory, in default of anyone to praise them, sing their own praises, not without disgrace. (540A)

Men who hold themselves high and throw out their chests as they walk along are called pompous; those who do the same in the boxing-ring or on the battlefield get credit for it, and are called brave and invincible. So the man who lifts his mind high in adversity is counted brave and hard to defeat. (541A–B)

Those who take refuge from a storm under a tree, when it is fine again, tear branches from it as they leave it; so in adversity we are glad of the help of some people, and then oppress those same men through resentment when we prosper. (541E)

Those who are careful not to be a burden to sufferers from sore eyes mingle some shadow with the daylight. In the same way some people mingle with praise of themselves some element of mistakes or criticism, in hopes of avoiding unpopularity. (543F)

We envy, not those who have paid a high price for house or land, but those to whom they have come for nothing; similarly no one envies men

* * * * *

17 A winner] Nine aphorisms from *Moralia* 539A–47F *De se ipsum citra invidiam laudando* 'On Inoffensive Self-Praise'

19 Some men] The same remark has appeared, from another source, at 162:1.

who have bought their glory dear, but those who owe it to the favour of
fortune. (544D)

We are told either to avoid a fever-ridden place entirely or, if one must
be in it, to take precautions; in the same way you should either avoid
self-praise altogether, or indulge in it with caution and carefully. (546B–C)   5

As hungry men become more sharp-set if they see other people eating,
so those who are greedy for reputation are fired with more ambition when
they hear others praised. (546C–D)

One should not tickle people who by nature start laughing very
easily, and one should not praise those who are naturally very eager for   10
applause. (547A–B)

Painters set their work aside for a time, in order to form a better
judgment of it [after an interval], for continuous attention is a reason why
they find it very difficult to judge. Similarly we form a more accurate
judgment of friends when we see them again after an interval, and we are   15
less good judges of our own selves, because we are never separated. (452F)

A mind disturbed by anger is like those who set fire to themselves and
their houses, filling the whole interior with confusion, so that they cannot
see their way to decide what to do. (453F)

An abandoned ship can take a helmsman on board, if one is willing to   20
bring her to port, but a mind overmastered by anger does not admit reason
from without to govern it; it must be reason from within that seizes the
helm. (454A)

As those who expect a siege get together their money and bury it, and
make all preparations for the enemy's arrival, so it is with the assaults of   25
rage: the mind should be fortified and equipped against it with the precepts
of philosophy. (454A)

In an uproar we cannot hear what is said to us; and just so, when we
are angry, we do not entertain outside advice. It must be the voice of reason
within us that will pacify the uproar of the mind. (454B)   30

As a well-armed despotism cannot be brought down from outside, but
only by domestic enemies, so the excited mind provides out of itself the
means of dissipating anger. (454B)

Iron that is thin and weak, if it is again furrowed [with the graving-
tool], easily breaks; and a mind that has often been roused by anger is   35
roused easily by any cause. (454B–C)

* * * * *

12 Painters] Thirty-one from *Moralia* 452F–64D *De cohibenda ira* 'On the Control
of Anger,' one of the essays translated by Erasmus. 'After an interval' was
added in *1516*.

34 with the graving-tool] *coelo*, added in the second edition, June 1515, but not
later, though it makes Erasmus' meaning much clearer.

It takes little trouble to extinguish a fire kindled in hare's fur or rushes or straw, but not if it has taken hold on something solid. Likewise anger at its first rising is easily repressed with a joke or a laugh, if we catch it while it is still only smouldering; but once it has burst into flame, it can hardly be extinguished by any effort. (454E)

As sailors foreseeing a storm make their ship fast with anchors, so, before the storm of anger breaks, we should make fast our minds with the anchor of reason and fight against it. (455B–C)

Love's pain is lightened by music and garlands and kisses; but anger, given its head, gets worse. (455B–C)

The first and best answer to a despotism is to withstand it, to refuse to obey; and similarly one should withstand anger from the outset. (455B)

In the opinion of Hippocrates an illness is very serious in which the patient's features change from time to time, and he looks quite unlike himself. Similarly no disorder of the mind is more serious than anger, which alters expression, voice, and footstep, until it makes the victim seem a different man. (455E–F)

They hold a mirror up to people leaving the baths; much more should they do so to an angry man. (456B)

A swelling sea, when it throws up seaweed and foam, is said to clear itself, even if it fouls the beach; but when a man swells with anger and pours out bitter and offensive words, they are a blot first and foremost on the man who utters them, and cast a slur on his reputation. (456C)

To have a soft, smooth tongue can be a hopeful sign in other disorders besides fever. (456D)

In fever a rough and dirty tongue is a symptom of the trouble and not a cause; in anger a harsh tongue is a cause of very great evils. (456D–E)

A swollen bruise rises most often from a blow on some soft fleshy part; in the same way it is weak soft minds, as of women and old men, which swell most with anger. (457A–B)

Some barbarians dip their weapons in poison to make them twice as deadly; likewise some people by their remarks spur on a man who has already lost his temper. (458D–E)

A nurse says to a child 'Don't cry, and you shall have it'; similarly we should say to an angry mind 'Don't shout, don't hurry, and you will get what you want all the sooner.' (459A)

A father, seeing his child trying to cut something, seizes the knife and does it himself; so reason, when it takes over from anger the task of retaliation, punishes a man for his good. (459A)

* * * * *

13 Hippocrates] *Prognosticon,* beginning of section 2

A child hurts itself through lack of skill when it tries to harm someone else with a knife; and anger often does itself an injury, while trying to injure others. (459A–B)

The man who taught us to shoot with bow and arrow did not forbid us to throw the javelin, but he did forbid us to miss the target; similarly there is no rule against punishment, but it must be administered at the right time and appropriately. (459D)

We do not believe news instantly, the first time we hear it; did not Phocion the Athenian say, when he heard of the death of Alexander, 'Well, if he's dead to-day, he'll be dead to-morrow and the day after'? In the same way we should not at once believe the voice of anger, when it says 'That man has done me wrong,' but should postpone belief for a day or two. (459E)

Things look bigger through the fumes of anger, like bodies through a mist. (460A)

Lazy rowers sit idle in harbour when the sky is clear, and then have to set forth at some risk when the winds are blowing; so the man who does not punish when his mind is at rest is sometimes compelled to do so when he is angry. (460B)

A hungry man takes food as nature dictates; but the man who takes vengeance should have neither hunger nor thirst for it. (460B)

As continual coughing shakes and convulses the body and makes it sore, so frequent fits of anger make a sore mind. (461B–C)

A dissolute life is betrayed by the music of flutes and the cast-off garlands and other evidence of the kind; and you can detect a hot-tempered man by the brand-marks on the faces of his slaves. (463A–B)

When men walk on thin ice, the harder they press on it the greater their mistake. Such is the self-confidence of selfish people. (463C)

Physicians may cure a fit of bile with bitter medicines; but a hot temper is no cure for a hot temper. (463F)

Minute writing, if one peers at it, strains the eyes; and he who fusses indignantly over small things becomes more surly in dealing with big things. (464B)

As Xenophon says in his *Complete Householder*, there is a place for everything, the sacrificial vessels and the dinner-service, farm tools and weapons of war. Similarly everyone will find bad things in his mind arising from ill will, from jealousy, from idleness, from greed. (515E)

* * * * *

34 As Xenophon] Twenty-one aphorisms inspired by *Moralia* 515B–23B *De curiositate* 'On Being a Busybody,' which Erasmus translated. Plutarch refers to Xenophon *Oeconomicus* 8.19–20.

The fabulous lamia is said to have eyes out-of-doors, but when at home she puts them in a jar and can see nothing. Some people are like that: clear-sighted in other men's business, blind in their own. (515F)

Those who have trouble at home are thankful to visit other people; a bad conscience, fearful of its own business, minds other people's and indulges its malevolence at others' expense. (516C–D)

The domestic fowl, though its food is put ready, often scrapes and scratches in a dusty corner, and would rather produce one barley-corn out of the dirt. So busybodies ignore or interrupt harmless conversation, and if they know of a hidden scandal in anyone's family, they sweep this dirt out into the daylight. (516D)

The busybody's mind is in many places at once and never stays at home, like Cleon in the comedy, who is taken to task for having his hands in one place and his mind in another. (517A)

Cupping-glasses attract to themselves the worst elements in the body, and the ears of a busybody hear with most pleasure what is most vicious in the life of men. (518B)

Cities have certain gates of ill omen, through which criminals are led out to execution and rubbish is removed, but nothing brought in that is holy and clean. The ears of a busybody are like that: they are open to nothing but murder and adultery [and other accusations of the kind]. (518B)

No one would tolerate it if a physician, even Aesculapius himself, went of his own accord to a stranger's bedside and asked him if he had a fistula in his anus or, if it was a woman, whether she had a cancer of the privy parts, however much this inquisitiveness might lead to a cure, because he interfered without being asked. Far more should we reject an inquisitive man who spares no thought to help other people's misfortunes but merely uncovers them, and that too without being sent for. (518D)

We resent customs-officers because they pry into other people's baggage, though the law gives them power to do this and they would suffer loss, did they not; much more should we be indignant with men who neglect their own business and pry into other people's. (518E)

* * * * *

13 Cleon] Athenian demagogue; Plutarch quotes, and Erasmus paraphrases, Aristophanes *Knights* 79, where he is represented as both ubiquitous and light-fingered.
18 Cities] The bracketed words were added in the second edition (June 1515), but did not survive.
31 they would suffer loss] Because customs-dues in Erasmus' day, as in Plutarch's, were collected by contractors, who paid a lump-sum for the privilege and had to recover their outlay and make a profit

Cooks hope for plenty of butcher's meat and fishermen for plenty of
fish; similarly the man who is eager for bad news hopes for change and
confusion, to give him plenty of targets to pursue. (519B)

When a cat runs past, they pick up the food out of its way; and when
an inquisitive man appears, they change the conversation until he has gone   5
away, so that he actually knows less about things than other people. (519D)

Some men, whose desires are topsy-turvy, pass by the very handsome
women who can be had for ready money, and work their way in to some
cloistered and expensive female, who may be quite plain. In the same way
the busybody despises brilliant spectacles and frequent plays to peer into   10
other men's letters, other men's houses, very often at some risk. (519E–F)

Simonides found the thank-you box always empty, the fee box always
full; even so, if a busybody were to open his stores after some lapse of time,
he will find them full of useless and unpleasant things. (520A)

Some critics choose out the worst things in the poets, for example,   15
Homer's 'headless' and 'tapering' lines, syllogisms in the tragedians, and
Archilochus' coarse remarks about women; likewise the busybody collects
the worst and most unpleasant features in anyone's life. (520A)

As Philip gave to a city peopled by the dregs of the population the
name of Roguesborough, so the busybody collects bad things from every   20
source, and stores his memory with a treasure of what is ugly and unpleasant. (520B)

Busybodies, more delighted with what is wrong with other people
than with their good qualities, are like those who pass by beautiful pictures
and stand gaping before representations of prodigies and monsters – men   25
with three eyes, born without legs, or dog-headed. (520C)

Huntsmen do not allow their hounds to smell or bite anything they
please, but keep them intact for the chase; and in the same way one ought
not to let one's eyes and ears have free rein, but reserve them for their
proper objects. (520E)   30

* * * * *

12 Simonides] The poet once told a man who asked him to write an ode, offering
   thanks but no money, that he had a separate box for each; and that when he
   was hard up, there was good stuff in the money-box, but in the thank-you box
   he never found anything. Erasmus included the story in his *Adagia* (II ix 12),
   adding a reference to this passage of Plutarch in 1515.
15 Some critics] See 152:3n. Plutarch here wrote not 'syllogisms' but 'solecisms.'
   Did Erasmus alter this on purpose, or did he (or some secretary to whom he
   was dictating) make a slip? Archilochus of Paros, the lyric poet of the seventh
   century BC, was celebrated for his powers of invective.
19 Philip] Of Macedon; a reference to this passage was added in 1515 to *Adagia*
   II ix 22.

Eagles and lions when they walk turn their claws inwards, that they may not be worn down, and thus they preserve their sharp points for attacking the quarry. Similarly it is not right to use up one's mental vigour on learning about other people's business; one should keep it for things that concern one. (520F)

It is improper to walk into someone else's house or look through the door; but much worse to watch what other people are doing in their own homes. (521A)

Socrates' advice was to be wary of dishes which tempt one to eat even when one is not hungry, and of liquor that makes even those who are not thirsty want to drink. Similarly one should avoid theatrical shows and conversations which lure those who have nothing to do with them into an addiction. (521F)

A scab, if you scratch it, starts bleeding again. Curiosity is like that: it yearns to know what has gone wrong with it, and the passion or itch for knowledge causes pain. (522C)

Xenophon reminds us that in prosperity we should be specially careful to honour the gods so that, if need ever arises, we may be able to appeal boldly to them for help, as being already our friends and well-wishers. In the same way the maxims which can minister to a mind diseased should be stored up long beforehand, so that when the moment comes they may be easily available, being already familiar. (465B)

As fierce dogs are aroused by every voice, and only a known and familiar voice makes them behave, so when disorders of the mind are seething, they cannot be repressed unless known and familiar maxims are ready to hand, by which the passions can be checked. (465C)

Those who are sea-sick on a voyage suppose that they will feel better if they change from a small boat into a clipper or a man o' war; but this does no good, for their timidity and their nausea they carry with them. In vain do they change their way of life, who bring with them disorders of the mind. (466B)

To chronic invalids everything goes awry: they cannot face their food,

* * * * *

9 Socrates'] Plutarch refers to Xenophon *Memorabilia* 1.3.6.

17 Xenophon] Thirty-nine aphorisms derived from *Moralia* 464E–77F *De tranquillitate animi* 'On Tranquillity of Mind.' Plutarch refers to Xenophon *Institutio Cyri* 1.6.3.

22 already familiar] These words (*iam familiaria*) were printed by mistake in the first edition as a heading; a similar blunder was made in one of the early editions of the *De constructione octo partium orationis*. This was corrected in Erasmus' revisions of June 1515 (for Martens) and 1516 (for Bade), but not finally banished from Froben's printings until 1534.

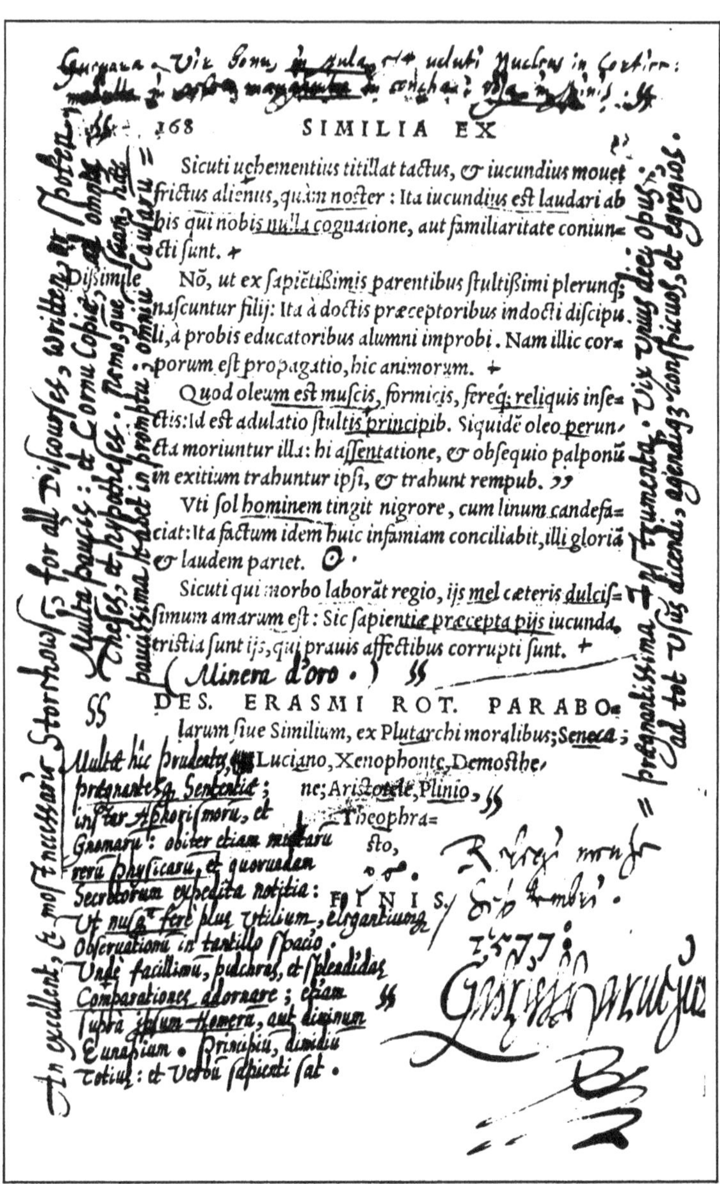

Gabriel Harvey's copy of the *Parabolae*

Harvey owned and annotated a copy of the Basel 1565 (Episcopius) edition of the *Parabolae*, a work which he describes along the left margin of the page reproduced here as 'An excellent, & most necessarie Storehowse, for all Discourses, written, or spoken.'

Folger Shakespeare Library, MS H.a.l, p 168

they complain of the doctor, they lose patience with their friends; but once restore their health, and all goes well. So too a mind diseased finds any way of life unpleasant, and a sound mind enjoys life in any form. (466c–d).

As a shoe twists to suit the foot, and not the other way round, so every man follows the kind of life that suits his disposition. (466F)

It is waste of time to draw water in a clean vessel from a dirty spring; and you cannot be a source of pleasure to other people, or fit yourself for doing business, unless you purge your mind of corrupt affections. (467A)

Plato compares man's life to a game of backgammon: the fall of the dice is outside our control, but how best to move what the dice have given us is in our power. Similarly it is not in us to command success, but to make good use of what befalls us – that is within our scope. (467A)

A man sick in body can bear neither heat nor cold; and a sick mind finds fault alike with prosperity and adversity. (467B)

A wise man gathers something worth having from the saddest events, like a bee collecting honey from the pungent flowers of thyme. (467C)

The man who threw a stone at a dog and hit his stepmother said 'Not so bad after all.' In the same way one should make the best of the unexpected. (467C)

The physician who has to treat a toothache is more disposed to enjoy his own good health than to share the pain of other men's misfortunes, but he must appear gentle to the patient; likewise he who wishes to cure another's hot temper must not be heated himself, but gently treat the mind that is not well. (468c)

When we are in high fever everything tastes bitter, but the sight of other people not rejecting the same food makes us begin to think the fault may not be in the food but in ourselves. In the same way we shall cease to complain of business if we see others cheerfully and willingly performing the same tasks. (468F)

Cupping-glasses attract the worst elements; likewise some people do not enjoy their blessings, but torment themselves by reckoning up their misfortunes. (469B)

Those who run down all their own advantages and get no benefit from their blessings are like the man from Chios in the story, who bought the best wine for his guests and drank vinegar himself. The servant, when asked what his master was doing, replied 'Looking for bad when he has good handy.' (469B)

If you deprive children of one of their games, they refuse to play all the others and burst into tears. Some men are like that: one small setback makes

* * * * *

9 Plato] Plutarch refers to *Republic* 10.604c.

them lose their tempers, and they spoil the taste of all their other blessings. (469D)

As some minutely inspect the paintings, statues, and poems of other men, discussing each at leisure while they neglect their own, so many people more admire other men's fortunes and dislike what is theirs. (470A)

Some men who take more pleasure in other people's possessions and think nothing of what is theirs, or actually neglect it, are like adulterers in love with other men's wives and rejecting their own. (470A)

The prisoner in chains thinks the man let loose is happy, unchained he thinks the same of the man set free, the man set free of the independent citizen, the citizen of the rich man, he of satraps, satraps of kings, kings of the gods, almost wishing they could make thunder and lightning. Thus the man who is always reckoning up how far he is below other men is never content with his lot. (470B)

To win at the Olympic games you are not allowed to choose your opponent; just so in life you must contend with the fortune allotted to you. (470D)

An embroidered coverlet sometimes covers filth, and the glory and bustle of the great hides many disasters. (471A)

Some men who cut a splendid figure in public, in the city or at court, lead a dog's life at home from a shrewish wife; so do monarchy and riches suffer many hidden misfortunes. (471B)

Your sails must match the size of your ship; and your desires must be trimmed to match your resources. (471D)

The man who goes hare-hunting with an ox, hurls his plough at the target, and stalks deer with a dragnet, must blame not bad luck but his own stupidity if he fails. In the same way those who attempt what is beyond their reach should accuse not fortune but their own mad folly. (471D)

Take an ox for the plough, a horse for the chariot, and a dog for the hunt, as Pindar says; similarly, every man should choose the kind of life for which he is fitted. (472C)

He who would strive to be a second Plato in intelligence, to sleep with a rich old woman like Euphorion, to drink with Alexander like Medius, to be as rich as Ismenias and valiant as Epaminondas, and grieves that he cannot be all this at once, behaves like one who should take it hard that he

* * * * *

30 Pindar] Plutarch quotes fragment 234.

33 Euphorion] Of Chalcis, poet of the third century BC. Medius was a friend of Alexander the Great. Ismenias and Epaminondas were Thebans, the latter being the great general of the early fourth century.

cannot be both a lion ranging the mountains and a Maltese spaniel in a rich widow's lap. (472D)

Those who compete on the track are not tormented when they see garlands won in field events; they are satisfied with their own prizes. So one ought not to be tormented by other men's success, but to rejoice in what falls to one's own lot. (472D)

More men are willing to enjoy the bath than to oil themselves for the contest; likewise fewer rally to the more difficult and glorious enterprises. (472E)

Those who resent their inability to excel in all things, however diverse, might as well take it hard that a vineyard does not grow figs or an olive bear bunches of grapes. (472F)

Wild animals find their food in different places, and men have different ways of life, one a philosopher, another a soldier. (473A)

Flies fall off smooth surfaces, mirrors for instance, and settle on rough and hollow places; so some men forget their blessings, but brood over the memory of what goes wrong. (473E)

There is a place at Olynthus in Thrace where, if a beetle alights, he cannot get away, but lies writhing until he dies; so do some people remember their wrongs until death. (473E)

In a painting the brilliant passages should be brought before the eye, and the failures that cannot be done out should be concealed; so it is in life – we should dwell on good things and keep down the memory of bad. (473F)

In music high notes and low are so blended that they form a harmony; and likewise in life we should make such a use of good and evil that our manner of living is a balanced blend of both. (474A)

Life is a mingled web, like language, where the expert must use vowel and consonant, unvoiced and voiced, heavy and long to achieve harmonious sound. (474A)

As musicians obscure the effect of harsher chords by modulating into others, so it is in life: if anything untoward happens, we should play it down by comparison with what goes well. (474B)

A flame blown by the wind is larger and hotter, but not so lasting or so reliable; so also the heat of desire produces uncertain pleasure, because linked with fear. (474C–D)

* * * * *

1 Maltese spaniel] Or Melitaean; the original home of these proverbial lapdogs was a matter for discussion, even in antiquity. Erasmus often refers to them; cf 247:3; *Adagia* III iii 71, IV iv 54.

18 Olynthus] Erasmus refers to this passage of Plutarch in *Adagia* III vii 1, added in 1515.

The steersman cannot still the winds and waves, however much it
pays to do so; but reason and level temperament, besides calming disturbance in the mind, often relieve disorders of the body. (475F)

As those who suffer cold and heat from fever or ague are worse
affected than those who endure the same sensations coming from outside,
so blows of fortune falling upon us from outside hurt less than those which
arise within the mind. (477A)

If the spring itself is muddy, what flows from it cannot be clean;
likewise the mind, if it is poisoned with corrupt affections, spoils everything that enters it; but the reverse, if it is pure and peaceful. (477A–B)

Those who pound incense, however much they clean themselves,
carry the smell round with them for a long time; a mind that has long been
employed in honourable business will long preserve happy memories of it,
in the strength of which it will look down on those who lament that life is a
sad thing. (477B)

Many weeds growing in a field are a bad thing in themselves, but can
be indicators of a kind and fertile soil, if one were to cultivate it. So
affections of the mind, bad in themselves, can serve as signs of a nature far
from bad, if it could meet with the right cultivation. (528C–D)

From Seneca

Those who remember that they are tenants, living in hired lodgings, behave with more restraint and take it less hardly when they have to leave; so
those who understand that a dwelling-place in the body has been lent them
for a short time by nature both live more soberly and are more ready to
die. (70.16)

As the man whom a brisk wind has carried rapidly into harbour is
more fortunate than he whom light airs and lengthy calms have wearied
until he is worn out, so he is more fortunate to whom death comes with
speed and removes him promptly from the evils of this life. (70.3)

Men setting out on a voyage see land and cities growing faint behind

* * * * *

16 Many weeds] From the opening sentence of the *De vitioso pudore*, which has
found a place above at 153:15

22 Seneca] The section of the work derived from Seneca begins with about eighty
aphorisms inspired by his *Epistulae morales* or 'Letters to Lucilius.' These are
divided into short sections as follows, and within each section the material is
presented in reverse order: 70–29, 75–71, 77–76, 81–79, 83, 85–84. As with
Plutarch, in order not to interrupt the reader by continual references to
footnotes, the passages used have been identified in the text in parentheses.

them. So it is with the rapid course of time: first our childhood sinks below the horizon, then our youth, finally even the best years of our old age. (70.2)

He who is slow off the mark must make up for it by running faster, and so put things to rights; and he who has come late in life to virtue or good literature must make up by diligence what he lost by his former slowness. (68.13)

As certain animals confuse the tracks round their lairs to prevent their discovery, so we should conceal the good that is ours, to keep it safe. (68.4)

What is placed in an open and exposed position is neglected and passed by, something concealed is sought out by cunning approaches; even so it is the man who lives in obscurity and far from the world whose life arouses public curiosity. (68.4)

Demetrius called a life of perpetual calm, unbroken by any assaults of fortune, a dead sea. (67.14)

As the sun puts out lesser lights, so other good things are of no account in comparison with virtue. (66.20)

As a storm of rain is of no account if it falls into the sea, so setbacks of fortune have no effect on a wise man. (66.20)

Some fruit has a pleasantly acid taste, and the dryness of very old wine is actually agreeable; so the memory of dead friends vexes us to the heart, but not without a certain pleasure. (63.5)

A man immoderately fond of wine drinks up the dregs as well; such is one with an excessive appetite for life, who will not face death even in extreme old age. (58.32)

As no one can step into the same river twice, so in the swift course of life a man is different from one moment to another. (58.23)

Bandits of the sort called in Egypt 'philistae' greet you with such an embrace they strangle you; so pleasure kills you with a smiling face. (51.13)

Beasts of burden whose feet have grown hard on stony ground can stand a road however rough, but if they have been out to grass in some marshy meadow, their hooves wear down at once; so the mind inured to hardship is less affected by it. (51.10)

As one style of dress suits a philosopher rather than another, while he has no dislike of any, so it is more suitable to live in this place rather than in that. (51.2)

Some medicines are nasty to take but give satisfaction ultimately, when they have made you well; philosophy is equally life-saving and agreeable. (50.9)

* * * * *

14 Demetrius] A Cynic philosopher, who taught in Rome in the first century AD

Oak timbers however much bent can be brought back into the straight; curved beams are relaxed by warmth, and though different by nature can be worked into the shape our purpose needs. How much more does the mind take on another shape, flexible as it is, and more ready to yield than any fluid! (50.6)

That man is foolish who, when he proposes to buy a horse, inspects not the horse itself but its trappings and harness; and he is a great fool who, when he is making a friend, judges him by his wealth or his wardrobe. (47.16)

As hail leaping and rattling on a roof makes a great noise but does no harm, so the assaults of fortune have no power over a wise man. (45.9)

A conjuror's tricks deceive us, and we enjoy it; similarly, if we are taken in by sophistries, this is amusing, not dangerous. (45.8)

In a maze, if you make haste, your very speed confounds you; so those who are devoted to worldly advantage are more likely to be involved in disadvantages. (44.7)

A ship that is large in a river is small on the sea; so men who are ordinary in one place seem distinguished in another. (43.2)

A bird held only by one feather can fly away and suffer little loss; wealth in the same way should not hold us back from the study of philosophy. (42.5)

A serpent, however poisonous, can be handled in safety as long as it is stiff with cold, not because it has no venom but because it cannot produce it; so some men lack the energy, rather than the disposition, to be really vicious. (42.4)

Like the phoenix – one born every five hundred years – distinguished men are in short supply. (42.1)

Gilt harness makes a horse no better; and a man is not improved by the trappings of wealth. (41.6)

The sun's rays fall upon the earth, but they are at home in the source from which they come; and the philosopher's mind, though busy here below, lives in the presence of its great original. (41.5)

A man running too fast cannot stop where he likes, but is carried on further than he would wish; so excessive fluency in speaking is carried away. (40.7)

A very heavy yield lays a cornfield flat, and branches break with the weight of fruit; so excessive prosperity breaks a man's resolution. (39.4)

A flame can neither be repressed nor remain still; likewise the soul is carried by some inborn force towards honourable things. (39.3)

A seed, however small, if it finds a suitable spot, unfolds its native

powers and, from being the least of things, grows and spreads wide; so the
theory of philosophy consists of few words but expands in action. (38.2)

Wine that seemed good in the cask ages badly, and what seemed harsh
and rough when young is good later; thus young people who were rough at
first mature and come to bear good fruit. (36.3)

The man distracted by much business is like a pool to which many
people throng for water, who empty it and leave it muddy. (36.2)

We do not admire one tree, when a whole wood has grown tall; and we
do not notice one epigrammatic remark when a whole piece is full of
epigrams, but only if one is introduced from time to time. (33.1)

A fire which has taken hold of a good supply of material must be put
out with water and, it may be, by pulling down a house, while fire that is
short of fuel goes out of its own accord. In the same way the aged have an
easy death. (30.14)

A gladiator who has shown no spirit all through the fight presents his
throat bravely to his adversary, when the moment comes to die, and guides
his uncertain sword to the fatal place; so the approach of death has been
known to bring courage even to men who have not thought about it, so that
they bear it bravely at the moment, though they feared it from afar. (30.8)

A great ship's-captain sails on with his canvas torn, and if he has lost
his tackle he still puts what is left of his vessel in a state to keep going; just so
the body may meet with mishaps and break down, but the brave spirit is
true to itself. (30.3)

In a leaky ship one can plug one or two holes, but when she starts to
open in several places, the gaping hull is soon past help. An old man's body
is like that: up to a point his weakness can be supported, but when the
whole frame begins to slip, the day of remedies is past. (30.2)

When a building is decayed and threatens to collapse, one does not set
props under it; it is time to look around for the way out. So if your body
fails, you should depart this life. (30.2)

If a man sows seed of every kind, some of it is sure to come up; and a
man who tries everything will succeed somewhere. (29.2)

A single cough does not bring on a consumption, it is the habit of
coughing; and error does not produce an immediate disorder of the
mind. (75.12)

A sick man does not want a physician who writes well, but one who
can cure diseases; in the same way we do not demand ornate prose from a
philosopher. (75.6)

A philosopher who is also eloquent is like a skilled ship's-captain who
happens to be handsome too. (75.6)

LB I 593A / ASD I-5 216

Illness in the body is foretold by fatigue and lassitude; and a weak mind, before it is overtaken by misfortune, is shaken by anticipations. (74.33)

Good seed, if it fall on good ground, comes up true to its kind, while a barren and marshy soil kills it; and it is the same with the principles of philosophy, if they happen on a good spirit or a bad. (73.16)

He is not inevitably the better ship's-captain who has the more handsome or the larger ship; and he is not perforce the better man who has the more splendid position in life. (73.12)

At a dinner given free to the public or a distribution of relief in kind, the more people are given a share, the smaller the share of each individual. It is not the same with the blessings of the mind, which come to the individual in their entirety, and grow no less when they are shared. (73.8)

As that man owes most to Neptune who has brought the most valuable cargo safe to harbour, so he owes most to the prince who employs the tranquillity and peace of daily life not in self-indulgence but in honourable pursuits. (73.5)

Like a dog which promptly devours whatever it gets and has its jaws always open in hopes of more to come, so we swallow without enjoyment whatever fortune puts in our way, as we hoped she would, and are always on the look-out to plunder someone else. (72.8)

Like books that stick together from neglect if you do not read them, memory evaporates if not refreshed from time to time. (72.1)

Wool takes some dyes immediately, while for others it must be pounded frequently and returned to the vat. So there are some studies which the mind can make available as soon as it has imbibed them; but philosophy must sink in and be long established before it will colour the mind all through. (71.31)

Some things which are as straight as can be produce an effect on the eye as of something bent or broken when they are immersed in water; and in the same way, if we make wrong judgments about things, it is our fault, not theirs. (71.24)

We sometimes wonder where people are when they are standing next us; and similarly some men can know a thing without being aware that they know it. (71.4)

As the enemy is a more serious danger to those who run away, so difficulties are greater if you yield and quail before them. (78.17)

Life is like a play: what matters is not how long it lasts, but how well it is acted. (77.20)

When you see a blow coming, you parry it more effectively; and if you have thought over a misfortune beforehand, it hurts less. (76.34)

An actor is no better off because when dressed for the stage he looks like a king or a god; nor is a man who enjoys the gifts of fortune; assessed on his own merits, he is nothing. (76.31)

As a dwarf is tiny even if he stands on a hill, while a giant even in a well is huge, so a wise man is great on his own merits, whatever be his fortune, and a fool even in great estate is of no account. (76.31)

An accused man is acquitted if the votes are equal; and the wise man, where benefits and injuries received are balanced, prefers to remember kindnesses rather than wrongs. (81.26)

The venom which serpents carry without hurt to themselves, they discharge to hurt others; but ill will swallows the greater part of its own venom. (81.22)

To our creditors we make extra payments over and above the principal of the loan, but kindnesses we expect to enjoy without paying anything; yet they too increase by lapse of time, and the longer we delay, the more there is to pay. (81.18)

After a bad harvest we have to sow none the less, the shipwrecked mariner goes to sea again, the tax-collector does not put the banker out of business; and in the same way you must go on doing things for other people, even if you have once struck an ungrateful recipient. (81.2)

A painted face does not impose on many people or for very long; and pretence only deceives a few, and for the moment. (79.18)

As our shadow keeps us company, whether we will or no, so does reputation wait on valour, be it never so unwelcome. (79.13)

Our shadow sometimes walks before us, sometimes follows; and glory comes to some people early, to some when they are dead. In fact, the slower it is in coming, the greater it often is. (79.13)

The world does not grow larger, nor do the sun, the moon, the sea; in the same way, once men are wise, they are all equal. (79.8)

Eyes rendered sensitive by prolonged disease resent any daylight; so do vices acquired by deep and continuous potations still endure when men are sober. (83.26)

As a cask of fermenting wine bursts, and what was at the bottom is forced up to the top, so does intemperance bring up the inmost secrets of the heart. (83.16)

Men far gone in liquor cannot keep down their food, nor secrets either, as their wine spills over. (83.16)

Both are alike dead, the man whose body is embalmed in spices and the corpse dragged on the hook; both are alike unhappy, those who are sunk in pleasures and those who spend their time on business and self-advancement. (82.3)

As a skilful artist makes a statue out of any material you please, so a
wise man will make a wise use of any turn of fortune. (85.40)

The onset of a disease may be slight enough, but it spreads; similarly,
if you once admit even the slightest vice or a touch of passion, it grows and
increases. (85.12)

Some animals even when tame revert without warning to their native
ferocity; you can tame a vice but must never trust it. (85.8)

No animal, tame or wild, is obedient to reason, for it has none; and the
passions are like that. (85.8)

The man who thinks himself virtuous by comparison with others who
are worse is like him who, when confronted by lame men, admires his own
fleetness of foot. (85.4)

Different voices make up a choir; and various disciplines united make
a scholar. (84.9)

He who emulates good authors will take pains to be like them as a son
is like his father, not as a picture is like the sitter. (84.8)

As a single number is made up of the sum of different numbers, which
it contains within itself, so scholarship is an amalgam of different things,
which now belongs to you and no one else. (84.7)

Food floating in the stomach is a burden and no food, but, once
transformed, it passes into energy and lifeblood. So what you read, if it
remains in a lump in your memory, is still the property of others, but, once
absorbed into your mind, it then makes you a well-read man. (84.6)

Bees collect different syrups from different flowers, but they transform
them by a spirit of their own and digest them, for otherwise they would
never make their honey. You in the same way should read all authors, but
convert whatever you have read to your own purposes. (84.5)

Elsewhere a careful reckoning is made not how much property each
man possesses, but how much he possesses that is really his own; in the
same way one ought to gauge a man by the good qualities that are really part
of him.

A brilliant artist displays his art in more than one material, and a wise
man bears himself well whatever may befall. (85.40)

As thieves exchange the handles of the cups they steal that they may
not be recognized, so there are people who make some small change in
other men's discoveries and claim them as their own; they suppose that, if

* * * * *

28 Elsewhere] If this means 'in another author' there may be a reference (perhaps
from memory) to a very similar statement in Cicero's *De officiis* 1.31.113, a
work which Erasmus had edited some years before.

34 As thieves] From the *Controversiae* 10.5.20 (by Seneca the Elder)

they subtract or add a few words, something can be taken for theirs which belongs to someone else.

As the heavenly bodies maintain their course against the motion of the sky, so does the wise man go against the opinions of the commonalty.

Though monarchs of high imperial power, strong in the loyalty of their vassals, aim to do harm, yet will all their attacks fall as far short of the wise man as missiles shot into the air from bowstring or catapult, though they pass out of sight, turn downwards before they reach the sky.

Then there are those who are like men that cannot sleep but turn and toss, lying this way and that, until they arrive at stillness through exhaustion; so, in seeking a pattern for their lives, they set up their rest in the end where they are overtaken, not by dislike for further change, but by old age that lacks the energy to seek anything new.

And so nothing is more to be avoided than to follow like sheep the flock in front of us, proceeding not where we ought to go but where everyone else is going.

As in some great disaster one man drags another to destruction, so when error is dominant, one man carries another away with him to his great hurt.

The members of a team of gladiators live with the same men against whom they fight; likewise the commonalty of men fight among themselves, and a man despoils his neighbour, though it be his best friend.

Wild beasts live by mutual aggression; and among men the stronger grow rich and prosper by the sufferings of the weak.

They who walk through thorny places must step on tip-toe; and in the same way the speaker whose subject is trifling or unpopular must escape as soon as he can into something more fruitful and agreeable.

The man who has a thorn in his foot treads on thorns wherever he goes; and to a barren wit every subject is barren.

Those who live in someone else's house suffer much inconvenience and are always complaining about some aspect of the premises. Even so the

* * * * *

3 As the heavenly bodies] The first of seven aphorisms inspired by the *Dialogues* of the younger Seneca, which are often quoted verbatim. The first two are from the *De constantia* 14.4 and 4.1.

9 Then there are] From the *De tranquillitate animi* 2.6

14 And so nothing] This and the next from the *De vita beata* 1.3, 1.4

20 The members] This and the next from the *De ira* 2.8.2, 3

25 They who walk] This and the next from the *Controversiae* 1 praef 22

30 Those who live] Ten more from the *Epistulae morales* 120–94 in reverse order; a reference has been added to each aphorism. The words in brackets were added in the Paris revision of 1516, replacing 'etcetera' in the first edition.

human spirit, complaining now of the head, now of the feet, now of the
stomach, [now of some other part of the body] shows that it is not in its true
home but will soon have to leave. (120.16–17)

As the height of mountains is less obvious from a distance but, as you
approach, it then becomes clear how steep they are, so no one foresees how
exalted is the spirit of a philosopher and how far it rises above all human
things, unless you look closely and approach him by trying to be like
him. (111.3)

Our breath produces a more brilliant note when it has been passed
through the long narrow passage of a trumpet and finally emitted through
its open mouth; and in the same way our meaning gains in brilliance from
the close restraints of verse: the same matter finds a less attentive reader and
makes less impression on him when expressed in prose. This has another
application: one might say that the glory won by excellence shines all the
brighter if it has long struggled with adversity and won through in the
end. (108.10)

A man who has gone out into the sun is sunburnt, though that was not
his intention, and those who have sat down in a perfumer's shop and
remained there for some time carry the scent of the place away with them.
Similarly those exposed to the conversation of a wise man are made better
thereby, though they have not that in mind. (108.4)

A tempest gives warning before its onset, buildings crack before they
fall, before your house catches fire you smell smoke; but the undoing
contrived by one man for another falls suddenly, and its nearer approach is
the more carefully concealed. (103.2)

In the body the spirit lies hidden, which gives force and motion to the
whole, and the Mysteries – religion's highest form – are open only to the
initiate; likewise the precepts of philosophy are common knowledge, but
the best thing in it is concealed. (95.64)

Some men are tormented by a ·wife whom they took great pains to
acquire; and some devote great labour to the promotion of events that will
do them serious harm. (95.3)

When children are first learning to write, we hold their fingers, which
are guided by the teacher's hand over the shapes of the letters, and later
they are told to copy what is set before them; so too the mind must first be
helped to do what is laid down for it, until it can begin to think for
itself. (94.51)

* * * * *

6 and how far] Reading *quantumque* with LB I 595E, as in the first edition and
Froben's of February 1519. The revisions of Louvain June 1515 and Froben
August 1522 have *quantumcumque*, a good example of the slips one makes
when revising in a hurry and not reading a sentence through properly.

LB I 595D / ASD I-5 226

Some minute creatures are not felt when they sting; only a swelling indicates the bite, and on the swelling no wound is visible. So it is with the society of good men: you do not realize that it does you good, but later that it has done so. (94.41)

One must first purge the melancholy which is the source of madness, and afterwards give the patient good advice; otherwise, he who thinks to advise a madman how he should proceed and how conduct himself in public would be the more mad of the two. So we must begin by freeing the mind from erroneous opinions, and then impart the precepts of philosophy. (94.17)

People who come back into the shade out of bright sunshine can see nothing; it is the same with men who after contemplating heavenly things fall back on earthly.

Physicians say one should not apply remedies while the disorder is on the increase and in the acute phase, but wait for a remission; so with anger or grief one should not apply consolation or precept to their first violent stage, but only when they have begun to grow lighter by lapse of time.

As theatrical properties are given back at once and without complaint, because they are only borrowed, so it is with anything grand that comes our way in life: whether fortune asks for it back early or late, we shall part from it serenely, if we use such things as though they were a loan.

He who has been tossed to and fro by different stormy winds and yet has never reached port has not travelled much; he has been much tossed. Like him the man who has lived a long life and made no progress towards a good character has not lived long; he has long existed.

A thoroughbred horse will carry a burden better than some idle hack, but no one loads him with one. Likewise great talents are suitable for the holding of public office, but too good to be burdened with such sordid tasks.

As the stars of heaven could not stand still even for a moment or wander from their paths without the greatest public mischief, so a prince may not be idle; and if he is, great is the damage that it brings upon the affairs of men.

* * * * *

11 People] From the *Naturales quaestiones* 3 praef 11

14 Physicians] Five more aphorisms inspired by the *Dialogues*, used as before in what appears to be a random order. The first is from the *Ad Helviam de consolatione* 1.2.

18 As theatrical properties] *Ad Marciam de consolatione* 10.1–2

22 He who has been tossed] *De brevitate vitae* 7.10

26 A thoroughbred horse] *De brevitate vitae* 18.4

30 As the stars] *Ad Polybium de consolatione* 7.2

From Lucian, Xenophon, and Demosthenes

An actor will play Hercules on the stage or Agamemnon, wearing a mask, all
cloth of gold and savage frown and great wide mouth – and out comes a poor
little whisper of a voice. Even so some men will write a dialogue in which   5
Plato and other great men speak, the weight of which they have not the
mother-wit to carry.

A good play is sometimes hissed off the stage through the fault of
some clumsy actor; a good speech likewise may fail to please if not properly
delivered.   10

As Momus found fault with God, who designed the bull, for not
putting the eyes in front of the horns, where they would be of most use, so
do men go wrong who put garlands on their heads when they ought rather
to put them under their noses, so as to get the greatest possible pleasure
from their scent.   15

All men do not run mad when they hear the Phrygian flute, but only
those who are possessed by Rhea; and only those are stirred by the praises
of philosophy who are inclined to it by nature.

Riches to a man who knows not how to use them are like a flute in the
hands of one who cannot play.   20

A beginner in music will destroy or damage several lyres; and great is
the public mischief if a man holds office who comes to it without education
and experience.

A balance must tilt towards the pan that has most put into it; similarly
some men favour now one side in a dispute and now the other, considering   25
who has most to give, not who has the best case.

* * * * *

1 From Lucian] Xenophon and Demosthenes were added to the heading in the
   revision of Paris 1516.
3 An actor] These first four aphorisms are derived from Lucian *Nigrinus* 11, 8, 32,
   37.
11 Momus] The patron deity of unsympathetic criticism; see *Adagia* I v 74 (where
   Erasmus refers to several other passages in Lucian, but not this one).
17 Rhea] Otherwise Cybele, the mother-goddess of an ecstatic Phrygian cult
19 Riches] Two aphorisms taken from Xenophon *Oeconomicus* 1.10 and 2.13. In
   June 1515 Erasmus added 'as Xenophon writes' at the end of the second one (*ut
   scripsit Xenophon*), but in 1516 his name appeared in the heading instead.
24 A balance] Similarly he added *iuxta Demosthenem* 'according to Demosthenes'
   after 'put into it' in 1515, but not in 1516. Demosthenes uses this image twice:
   the *De pace* (5.12) is a possible source, the *De corona* (18.298) more likely.

From Aristotle, Pliny, Theophrastus

The inquiring temper of men has collected signs of impending storms of every kind; they would have done better to use this diligence in taking counsel, that from observation and experience they might estimate the harm that flows from every defective institution. (18.340)

As in a sky however clear a cloud however small will precede a storm of wind, so when affairs are at their most peaceful, the least dissension may suddenly give rise to the most severe upheaval. (18.356)

When frogs are more vocal than their wont, they foretell an impending storm; and when bad men's advice weighs heavy with princes, while good men hold their peace, public disorders are at hand. (18.361)

The sea-urchin that feels a coming storm either anchors itself to a rock or ballasts itself with sand; so when an upheaval in his fortunes is impending, a man should confirm his spirit with the precepts of philosophy. (18.361)

As inexperienced men do not observe a storm until too late and suffer for it, while prudent husbandmen foresee it and take precautions, so the imprudent multitude learn to their cost of the evil which the wise man meanwhile sees from afar and can avoid. So Democritus, when his brother was cutting corn on a very hot day, warned him to leave the rest of the crop and get what he had cut quickly under cover; and in a few hours his prophecy was confirmed by heavy rain. (18.340–1)

As it not seldom happens that heavy rain comes on suddenly when the sky has been perfectly clear, so in perfect prosperity and peace great public disorders often befall. (18.341)

When thunder in summer is more violent than lightning, as Pliny says, it threatens wind; similarly, when a man who is not exactly a brilliant example of integrity himself declaims loudly against other people's faults, this is a sign of a mind swollen with the wind of ambition rather than a solid and religious one. (18.354)

* * * * *

1 From Aristotle] The heading took its present form in the revision of Paris 1516; in June 1515 it was 'From Aristotle, Pliny, and the other naturalists' (*physiologi*). The great bulk of the material is from Pliny's *Naturalis historia*, as will appear from the references to book and section added to the text in parentheses. No doubt more Aristotelian material remains to be identified; and the contribution of Theophrastus, Aristotle's greatest follower, remains elusive, whether it came from his botany (*De causis plantarum* and *Historia plantarum*) or his mineralogy (*De lapidibus*). A few items come from other authors, and are identified in the notes; the moralizations are Erasmus' own work.

Dolphins playing in a calm sea threaten wind from the quarter from
which they come; and when the wicked are proud and push themselves
forward, they show that a storm is brewing in the affairs of men. (18.361)

Sun, moon, and stars, land and sea, trees, herbs, and animals (among
them bees, ants, and shellfish), even lamps are aware of the coming storm;
man alone has no presentiment of his misfortunes and does not foresee
them. (18.340 ff)

When the brute beasts desert their natural and normal way of life, it is
a sign of storm; thus, when gulls leave the sea or the marshes, when ants
conceal themselves or carry out their eggs, and worms come up out of the
ground, they foretell foul weather. In the same way, when rascals come out
into the open and good men keep silence, when the common people are
wise and princes foolish, when priests gird on the sword for earthly ends, it
promises disaster for the life of men. (18.362–4)

Just as the stone called pyrites does not reveal its fiery powers unless
you rub it, and then it burns your fingers, so you may not notice some men's
wickedness at first, unless you see much of them or do business with them;
or you may not experience the power of philosophy, unless you put it into
practice. Amber, in the same way, displays its power of attraction and its
smell only when rubbed. (37.189)

The lifelike image of a beetle, a serpent, or a spider produced by
nature in a precious stone (for there are several stones in which we find such
things) does not disgust us; the image gives us pleasure and we value it. In
the same way we take pleasure in the skilful representation of wickedness
in historians and in poetry. (37.187)

The gem chalazias, which is very cold by nature, retains its chill even
if you throw it on the fire. Some men are like that: education and virtue
leave them so cold that neither example nor precept can fire them with a
wish to do better. (37.189)

Just as Alexander the Great gave orders that no one should paint him
except Apelles, or model him in bronze except Lysippus, or engrave his
head on a gem except Pyrgoteles, they being the greatest masters then
living, so it is not proper that Christ should be preached by the first comer
or virtue praised by anyone you please. (7.125)

Like a precious stone which is a very small object, but of more value
than huge rocks, is a man small of stature but greatly gifted. Such are
philosophy and virtue, a very small thing in outward show, but of great
price. (37.1)

As Corinthian bronze was made by accident, and the painters in the

* * * * *

39 the painters] More detail, from Plutarch, at 194:14 above

story, whose art could not capture the foam of horse and hound, achieved
their result by accident, so do many things happen by chance which you
could never bring about by taking thought. (34.7; 35.104)

No one is so crazy that he would rather drink poison, even out of
Nero's goblet (valued by Pliny at three hundred sesterces) than harmless   5
wine out of common Samian earthenware. Likewise a man of sense would
rather imbibe sound advice for the conduct of life set forth in ordinary
language than poisonous views written by the most brilliant pen. (37.20)

Glass is a wonderful imitation of rock-crystal, though one is very
cheap and the other most rare and costly; similarly fawning, a very bad   10
thing, imitates friendship, which is the greatest of blessings. (37.29)

Broken rock-crystal cannot by any means be stuck together; and it is
most difficult to reconcile persons who have come to hate each other after
being intimate friends. (37.29)

As Nature has hidden precious stones deep in the earth, while worth-   15
less things meet one's eye everywhere, so the best things are known to
fewest people and are not to be unearthed without great labour. (37 passim?)

Amber has an attraction for straws, a magnet for iron, malachite for
gold; every man attracts friends whose character suits his own. (37.48,   20
36.127, 33.93)

Adamant can by no force be tamed, and hence its name; fire cannot
heat it, it will not yield to iron, and its reaction to a blow is such that
hammer and anvil split. Like that the wise man's mind is invincible against
the cruellest attacks of fortune. (37.57)   25

As adamant, invincible though it be against all attacks, can yet be
broken with a hammer if steeped in the blood of a he-goat, if it be hot and
fresh, so some men's nature cannot be swayed by any force, and must be
softened with blandishments. (37.59)

One thing alone softens adamant, so that it feels the iron hammer,   30
though it is otherwise indomitable; in the same way no man's nature is so
stubborn that it cannot somehow be overcome. (37.59)

Just as iron, if placed between adamant and a magnet, moves under
opposing forces now this way and now that, so the uncertain mind is
carried by its appetites now towards good, now towards the oppo-   35
site. (37.61)

* * * * *

5 Nero's goblet] Pliny calls it a *capis* worth a million sesterces; Erasmus' *'capedo
worth three hundred sesterces'* is not the result of carelessness – it is the
reading of the editions of Pliny current in his time.
19 malachite] A dubious equivalent for Pliny's *chrysocolla*

Adamant placed near a magnet does not allow iron to be attracted by
it, and if you move the magnet towards the iron until it is attracted, the
adamant pulls in the opposite direction and draws it back. Just so is the love
of money opposed to Christian piety, and it draws a man away by every
means, not letting him remain attached to Christ. (37.61)

Like the emperor Nero watching gladiators fighting through an
emerald are those who would rather devote their minds to the images of the
gods than to the gods themselves. (37.64)

As iron or steel surpasses all other materials in hardness and rigidity,
but is surpassed by adamant, so love of one's children is a very powerful
thing, but even that is outdone by love towards God. (37.57)

Adamant, if broken with a hammer, flies into the most minute chips,
so small that the eye can hardly see them. In the same way a very close
relationship once parted turns into intense hostility; intimate treaties once
broken are a source of the greatest discord. Alternatively patience once
exhausted burns with anger beyond measure. (37.60)

As some living creatures even sacrifice parts of their bodies which
they know land them in danger, for instance the beaver, so it is the part of a
wise man sometimes to take thought for his life by the sacrifice of his
possessions. (8.109)

In an opal we discern the peculiar qualities of many gems: the pale fire
of the carbuncle, the glowing purple of the amethyst, the sea-green of the
emerald, all alike shining together in incredible confusion. Even so the
virtues of many men come to the fore in a single individual; or we find all
together in Holy Writ whatever can attract us in any gentile authors. (37.80)

The Indians make a counterfeit opal, so like that it cannot be distinguished except by trial in the sun; similarly some vices imitate virtues so
closely that it is difficult to separate them, unless they are brought out into
broad daylight. (37.83)

Carbuncles possess the name and the appearance of red-hot coals,
though they are unaffected by fire and hence are called *apyrustae*; so too
some men enjoy the reputation and appearance of piety, when they are very
far removed from the reality. (37.92)

The anthracites, a sort of carbuncle, has the peculiar property that,
when thrown into the fire, it seems to go dead and is extinguished, while, if
water is poured over it, it glows. Some people similarly are moved by
opposites: if encouraged, they lose interest, discouraged they become more
keen; if you are kind to them they hate you, and if you ill-treat them their
opinion of you goes up. (37.99)

The gem called iris does not show the colours of the rainbow except in
shadow, and in such a way that it does not contain them in itself but shoots

them out upon the wall, while in the sun it is colourless. Some men likewise
display the appearance of different virtues, but in a shadowy fashion, and
yet they can, as it were, reproduce and create in other men's minds what
they do not possess themselves. (37.136)

We set the highest value on those gems which not only please our eyes   5
by their diversity of colour and our sense of smell by their fragrance, but are
also valuable as remedies. Similarly the most valuable books are those
which not only possess charm of style, but by their wholesome principles
free us from faults of the mind.

As some men carry jewels round with them everywhere as a protec-   10
tion against sickness, witchcraft, intoxication, lightning, falling buildings,
and other misfortunes, so some of the precepts of philosophy should always
be at hand against attacks by diseases of the mind, lust, anger, ambition,
avarice, and [others like them].

The dragon-stone cannot be polished or worked in any way, though   15
brilliant in other respects and full of light; in the same way Holy Scripture
has a brilliance of its own and cannot be worked over by philosophy or
rhetoric. (37.158)

Certain gem-stones gain in brilliance when pounded in vinegar, and ·
many do so when warmed in honey; likewise some men are made better by   20
severe rebuke, others if they are corrected more gently. (37.195)

One can carve what one pleases on a gem more easily if one's drill is
really hot; and a speaker will move his audience more easily if he not merely
speaks with emphasis but warms to his work, loves what he praises, and
hates what he rejects. (37.200)   25

In Chios there is a statue of Diana, the face of which, being placed well
above the eye, appears gloomy to spectators as they enter and cheerful as
they leave. So some ungenerous people greet a friend on his arrival with
long faces for fear he has some request to make or will prove a source of
expense as a guest; when he takes his leave, they are all smiles. (36.13)   30

As great obelisks are set up and fixed in place with the greatest effort
on account of their massive weight, but once fixed they last for uncounted
centuries, so it is uphill work to earn a reputation for virtue or wisdom, but
once earned it never dies. (36.64–74)

Just as great weights, which no human strength can lift, are raised   35
easily with tackle, so what you cannot do by force you may do easily by
reasoning and skill. (36.64–74)

* * * * *

5 We set] This aphorism and the next one are perhaps general reflections
inspired by the catalogue of gems in Pliny 37.139–85. The bracketed words
replaced 'etcetera' in the revision of Paris 1516.

With very large obelisks almost as much is buried in the ground as projects above it, so that they may stand unshaken; and similarly fame which is to last forever should have great and firm foundations. (36.73)

It was foolish of the kings of Egypt to use up their people's labour and their wealth in building pyramids which had no purpose beyond foolish and idle ostentation, while the same end could have been achieved by something useful. Likewise some men toil away on very difficult but quite unproductive subjects, thinking it a fine thing in itself to be employed on something difficult. (36.75)

As the pyramid built by Rhodope the courtesan, who was a fellow-slave with Aesop, out of the earnings of her profession, was a greater marvel and more famous than the other pyramids that were the work of kings, even so are we more astonished if people do something well of whom we expect nothing of the kind; for instance, if we were to see a Dutchman who knew how to ride a horse, a frugal Englishman, or a theologian who is eloquent. (36.82)

Just as one ought not to enter a maze without a thread by which one can guide one's return without risk, so one should not enter on any piece of business without first considering how one is to disengage oneself from it. (36.91)

In admirable but purely ornamental buildings the designer, whose art achieved the result, wins greater credit than the monarch who paid the bill; and in the same way glory in war belongs for the most part to the hired soldiers whose energy carries on the struggle, and very little of it to the kings who hire troops even with money that is not theirs. (36.93)

The temple of Diana at Ephesus cost the whole of Asia, with the wealth of many kings and the skill of many artists, twenty years to build, yet one Herostratus, a man of no account, could burn it down in a single night; and in a war it is easy enough to destroy famous cities, but to build them up is very hard. (36.95)

As buildings that stand on marshy ground are not shaken by earthquakes nor swallowed up when the earth opens, so a lowly fortune is not exposed to very great disasters. (36.95)

An echo does not answer unless it has received a sound that it can return; and there are people who turn against someone else whatever is said against themselves; or who have nothing to say unless they can repeat what others have said. (36.99)

There is a portico at Olympia which by some device echoes a sound

* * * * *

38 portico at Olympia] The same material, adopted from Plutarch, received a
   different moralization at 156:12.

seven times, whence the local people call it Heptaphonos, the Seven Voices.
In the same way some people when stung by a taunt reply with a stream of
insults, or if you rouse them to speak by uttering a few words, they chatter
without stopping. (36.100)

As a magnet does not attract everything, but only iron, though there
are many substances much lighter, so some men's oratory does not move
everyone, but only those who are already inclined to their way of thinking. (36.127)

As some magnets attract iron, but the theamedes, which is found in
Ethiopia, rejects and repels it, so there is one kind of music that calms the
passions and another that rouses them. (36.130)

The magnet draws iron to itself by some concealed and unknown
power; likewise it is by some secret principle that wisdom draws to itself
the hearts of men. (36.127)

A lean lank horse we blame not on the beast itself but on the stable-
boys; an ill-conditioned people on its bishops [or princes].

As a magnet draws to itself any piece of iron, but the Ethiopian
magnet forcibly attracts another magnet as well, so does a king drive his
people as he pleases, but an outstanding king applies coercion even to other
kings. (36.129)

Agate ignites when water is poured over it and is put out by oil. So it is
with some people: the more you ask of them, the less zeal they show, but
leave them alone and they grow keen of themselves. Or there are some you
estrange by kindness, and you secure their affections by neglect. (36.141)

A stone from Scyros floats in the piece and sinks if broken up; so
things are wrecked by strife and maintained by concord. (36.130)

Siphnian marble hardens when warmed in oil, though it is normally
very soft; and you may make some people worse by kindness. (36.159)

It was said of the Carthaginians that they used pitch for their houses
and lime-wash for their wine; and in the same way there are men who get
things the wrong way round, rude to their friends and fawning on their
enemies. The people of Carthage rendered their walls with pitch, which is
ordinarily used for wine-vessels, and treated their new wine with lime, as
Pliny tells. (36.166)

Quicklime is kindled with water; and some men are roused by their
opposites. (36.174)

* * * * *

15 A lean lank horse] Source not identified. 'or princes' was added in the Paris
edition of 1516.
29 Carthaginians] It looks as though Erasmus had made two independent notes
of this passage in Pliny and later conflated them.

Gypsum must be used promptly, while still wet, because it dries very quickly; in the same way raw youth must be moulded without delay in both education and character, before it sets and will no longer obey the moulder's hand. (36.183)

Gypsum, even if it has set already, can yet be crushed again and reduced to powder; but once the nature of the growing child has set, as years and faults accrue, there is no remaking it. (36.183)

Like glass, which being transparent conceals nothing, are certain persons who do not know how to hide anything or gloss over anything; whatever comes into their heads at once becomes public property. (36.198)

Men with weak sight find every place dark, because they carry darkness round with them in their eyes; so to people of small education every book and writing of every kind are difficult and obscure.

As fire is in every workshop the indispensable tool of all the arts and trades, so without brotherly love nothing goes well. (36.200)

Glass is cheap because it is plentiful; otherwise it would cost no less than gold or silver. Priests likewise lose their value when there are plenty of them, but would be held in high esteem if there were but one in every city, as in the olden time. (36.195)

Just as painting began with silhouettes and outlines, then came monochrome, and after that light and shade and a range of colours, until it reached the perfection of the art; so virtue is not born in us complete all at once, but rises gradually to its summit by improvements day by day. (35.15 and 29)

The best picture is not that which displays by its material the wealth of the man who paid for it or the skill of the artist, but the most faithful likeness of the subject. In the same way the truest eloquence is not what shows off the speaker's gifts but what most fittingly sets off the subject-matter (35.67?)

When Zeuxis set out to paint a Juno, he passed in review all the maidens of Agrigento and chose the five who stood out, so as to reproduce the outstanding quality of each of them. Just so we should set before us the best out of a large field as a pattern of living or of eloquence, and yet even of those we should imitate not every quality, but only the best. (35.64)

All painters are not of equal merit in every branch of the art: this one excels in rendering the gods, that one in drawing faces, one is a master of line, another of the blending of colours, another of design. It is the same in

* * * * *

11 Men with weak sight] Source not identified
30 Zeuxis] See above 192:12n.

the pursuit of virtue: some excel in one gift, some in another, and it is the same in speaking or in writing. (35.112–14)

Those who come hot out of the bath shiver the more violently with cold, and water tends to be colder which has previously been heated. Similarly the ill-feeling is stronger between those who have previously been friends, and those who have exchanged virtue for a life of vice prove the greater criminals.

At midwinter halcyons enjoy a perfectly calm sea, and share this calm with others. In the same way, when fortune is at its stormiest, religious people profit most from tranquillity of mind, and share this tranquillity with others who are within their reach. (10.90)

The donkey is the least musical of animals, but its bones make excellent recorders, as Aesop says in Plutarch; likewise some rich men, who are themselves uneducated, yet use their money to supply inspiration to the learned.

Plutarch declares that he saw crows in Africa piling up pebbles in a water-pot until the level rose to something within their reach; and he also tells of the dog that dropped pebbles into an oil-jar. This is a lesson for us all: what we lose in strength we must make up by cunning. (10.125)

Ants gnaw that part of a grain of wheat from which it begins to sprout, that it may not become useless to them. Magnates who wish to retain their servants in perpetuity repress them, for fear that if they once raise their heads from their tedious bondage, they may quit the court. (11.109)

Bucephalus, the charger of Alexander the Great, would let his groom ride bareback, but the moment the royal harness was put on him, he would carry no one but the king, and met everyone else with ferocity. Likewise some men put up with anyone while they are in modest circumstances, but once they grow rich they despise the crowd. (8.154)

As Timanthes when he painted his Iphigenia rendered the emotions of everyone else but hid Agamemnon's face in his cloak, so some things are better left to the judgment of individuals than set forth in words. (35.73)

Timanthes is praised for leaving more to be understood in all his works than is ever expressed in paint; similarly the best style leaves much to

* * * * *

3 Those who come hot] Plutarch's *De primo frigido* 'On the Principle of Cold' (*Moralia* 949E)

12 The donkey] Its insensitivity to music was proverbial: *Adagia* I iv 35 'Asinus ad lyram.' Erasmus cites a remark made by Aesop in Plutarch's 'Dinner of the Seven Wise Men' (*Moralia* 150E).

16 Plutarch] In his *De sollertia animalium* (*Moralia* 967A). It is a well-known story; see D'Arcy W. Thompson *A Glossary of Greek Birds* (Oxford 1936) 172.

29 Iphigenia] On this painting by Timanthes (c 400 BC) see Quintilian 2.13.13.

LB I 600F / ASD I-5 242

the imagination with only a brief recital of the facts, and contains more
meaning than it does words. (35.74)

Protogenes, who in other respects was in the first rank of painters, was
criticized for not knowing when to leave well alone. Some authors make the
same mistake of overdoing it, and never thinking anything quite
finished. (35.80)

As the painter Protogenes identified Apelles from a single line he
drew, though he had never seen him before, so one who is himself wise can
detect from a single answer whether another man is intelligent and sensible. (35.81–2)

The painter Apelles used to complain that any day was wasted in
which he had not drawn even one line; and a good Christian will be sorry if
on any day he does not end up a more religious man than he began. (35.84)

As certain clay figures were most highly valued for the quality of their
workmanship, so the skill of a speaker sometimes gives value to ordinary
topics of no interest. (35.157)

Like gypsum or clay which, while it is still wet, obeys the hand that
moulds it and takes any shape, uneducated minds are good material for
learning every subject. (35.151)

What you inscribe with additional effort on steel or marble lasts
longer; and what we take special efforts to learn, we never forget.

The object men most admire is one in which the craftsman's skill sets
off the material, and the material sets off the skill; so that book is best in
which the importance of the subject is worthy of the style and the author's
style is worthy of his subject. (34.5)

The poet Accius, who was himself of very short stature, set up a statue
in his own honour in the temple of the Muses, which was very tall. In the
same fashion some men who are lowly and of no account make themselves
big with ambition and pretence. (34.19)

As Perillus, who presented Phalaris with his brazen bull, perished in

* * * * *

4 to leave well alone] Literally 'to take his hand off the picture.' The phrase was
   proverbial (*Adagia* I iii 19 'Manum de tabula,' citing this sentence from Pliny),
   and the whole passage, covering both this paragraph and the next two, is
   quoted in *Adagia* I iv 12 'Nullam hodie lineam duxi.'
20 What you inscribe] Source not identified
26 Accius] Roman tragic poet of the second century BC
30 Phalaris] Tyrant of Acragas (Agrigento) in Sicily, whose cruelty became proverbial (*Adagia* I x 86). The sculptor Perillus presented him with a bronze bull
   in whose hollow interior his victims were to be roasted alive, and was himself
   the first to suffer in it.

his own invention, so bad advice sometimes recoils on the head of the man who gave it. (34.89)

The philosopher who sent the victim's tongue sent at the same time the best of things and the worst. Money likewise is good if you know how to use it, very bad if you do not.

It is not only the magnet itself that attracts; one piece of iron that has been rubbed on a magnet can attract another piece. Similarly, by a kind of infection, the driving force of virtue or the fatal contagion of vice passes from one man to another. (34.147)

Like the Chinese, who export both softest silk and hardest steel, some people produce widely differing effects. (34.145)

Charcoal that has once burnt out and been extinguished gives a more intense heat if it burns up again. Hatred is like that: if it arises again when once lulled to rest, it is more bitter. (36.201)

Land which contains veins of gold or silver is often unproductive of anything else; and those who devote themselves to amassing gold and have reached the stage of dreaming about goldmines, habitually produce nothing of any value. (33.67)

It is rare to discover a vein of gold or silver unless there is another not far off (whence it got its name in Greek); and in the same way no virtue is found in isolation, but one brings another with it. (33.96)

Though silver is a white metal, yet it makes a black line, as it does when alloyed with lead; likewise some men look one thing and act another. (33.98)

On quicksilver everything floats except gold, which is the one substance it draws into itself. In the same way nothing enters the mind of the avaricious man except money; learning and literature and virtue float on the surface and do not make their way down into his bosom. (33.99)

The same object is reflected differently by different mirrors, according as they differ in shape. Thus to the same action a different meaning is given by different people as their temperaments differ; what is large to one man is small to another, and what one thinks beautiful another finds ugly. (33.129)

A mirror returns no image unless you back the glass with silver-lead

* * * * *

3 The philosopher] Pittacus of Mitylene (c 600 BC), instructed by Amasis king of Egypt to send him the best and worst parts of the sacrificial animal, cut out and sent him the tongue. Erasmus (who here may well be writing from memory) added the story in 1526 to *Adagia* III vii 42, perhaps from Plutarch *Moralia* 506C. In *Moralia* 38B and 146F the philosopher is another of the Seven Sages, Bias of Priene.

20 name in Greek] Pliny reports a fanciful Greek derivation of *metalla* 'mines' from *met' alla* 'after other things' one after another.

alloy or bronze or gold, or some such solid substance that keeps the image
from passing through. Likewise it is only in minds that are solid and have a
backing of real virtue that you see reflections of the truth. (39.130)

As there are certain springs which, when drunk by cattle or even by
men, turn skin and hair white or black, so there shines forth from a man's
very face and forehead, as they say, on what principles he was brought up
and on what authorities he draws for his philosophy of life. (31.13–14)

The river Gallus in Phrygia, if you drink its water in moderation, cures
your bodily ills; if you drink to excess, it drives you mad. So it is with
philosophy: a moderate acquaintance with it is good for you, but if you
devote yourself to it entirely, it deprives you of sound judgment and drives
you headlong into a sort of passion for notoriety. (31.9)

In Boeotia, at the shrine of the god Trophonius near the river Or-
chomenos, there are two springs, one of which promotes memory, the other
forgetfulness. Similarly almost every great blessing is neighboured by the
risk of some great evil. (31.15)

Wise men do not drink without hesitation at the first spring they come
across, because some promote health, others mortal sickness, one or two
madness. Nor is it safe to read any book indiscriminately, for out of some
you will imbibe sound sense, and others will infect you with lechery or the
madness of ambition. (31.15)

Those who have drunk of the Clitorian lake develop a distaste for
wine; and those who have once tasted poetry reject the counsels of
philosophy, or the other way round. Equally, those who gorge themselves
with fashionable pleasures reject those satisfactions which are honourable
and genuine. (31.16)

Among the Troglodytes there is a pool which thrice a day turns bitter
or salt and then sweet again, and thrice does the same at night, whence they
call it Madman's Pool. Some unstable people are like that, rude one moment
and fawning the next [now spendthrifts and now mean; sometimes they
love with passion and sometimes hate beyond reason]. (31.18)

Springs are more dangerous if their limpid waters attract the eye while
having disastrous effects, and less to be feared if their appearance declares
that we should not touch them. In the same way it is harder to avoid what is
bad if it deceives us with a mask of goodness. (31.27)

Just as the ground which has water-channels hidden in it exhales a
kind of mist before sunrise if observed from a distance, so men who are

* * * * *

5 a man's very face] A proverbial expression; *Adagia* ii iv 4
27 Troglodytes] The words in brackets were added in the revision of Paris 1516.
The Troglodytes were cave-dwellers in Ethiopia.

really good and well educated, even if they do not show it, always betray
themselves by some indication, from which the observant person can
detect that some power for good lies concealed in them. (31.44)

In the country round Narnia rain makes the ground dry, and it becomes damp in hot weather, which gives rise to Cicero's remark that in
those parts rain causes dust and drought produces mud. In the same way
some men are made worse instead of better if you take them to task. (31.51)

Fish-sauce burnt and applied to a bad place heals it, provided you do
not in the process mention the word sauce. Some kind actions are like that:
they cease to be such if you allude to them. (31.97)

Ground which produces salt grows nothing else; and a mind rich in
literary gifts has not the same power as a rule in other fields. (31.80)

A spring in which nitre forms neither produces nor supports anything
else; like that the pursuit of wisdom claims a man's whole mind. (31.114)

Sponges have such slight indications of feeling that many hesitate
whether to call them living creatures or no. In the same way the costume,
conversation, and behaviour of certain men is such that you might well
wonder whether they are Christians or gentiles. (31.123)

Salt sprinkled over food in moderation seasons it and brings out the
taste. In the same way add to your style a touch of classical allusion or of
humour and it gains in charm; add too much and there is nothing more
unattractive. (31.87)

As the fish called echeneis or remora, tiny though it is (for it resembles
a large slug), can yet suddenly bring to a stop a ship however big under
power from sails and oars, so the love of some worthless wench sometimes
ties down in impotence a powerful impulse of the mind towards noble
deeds. (32.2)

The sting-ray cannot hurt except by contact, but transmits its power in
a wonderful way from the hook through the line and the joints of the rod
into the fisherman's hand. Likewise wicked and pestilent men can do no
harm if you have no dealings with them; but if any business brings them in
contact with you, they infect you with the venom of their ways. (32.7)

The fish called sea-hare is a deadly poison to human beings, as they in

* * * * *

5 Cicero's remark] Pliny cites his lost *Admiranda* (fragment 2).
8 Fish-sauce] Pliny says that *garum*, a familiar Roman sauce, heals fresh burns;
   Erasmus appears to have read him hastily, and inferred a feminine form *garus*,
   which is itself burnt to make the remedy. Such a mistake over a not uncommon Latin word is extremely unlike him.
23 echeneis] Erasmus repeats this at 253:34, prompted by another passage of
   Pliny about the same fish. See D'Arcy W. Thompson *A Glossary of Greek Fishes*
   (Oxford 1947) 68–70.

LB I 602E / ASD I-5 248

turn are to the fish, so much so that if touched with a fingertip it dies on the spot. Similarly enemies inflict and suffer mutual damage. (32.9)

It is simple enough to slip into a fish-trap, but hard to get out; and the road to vice runs downhill, but the way back is not so easy. (32.11)

The lamprey cannot be killed with a cudgel, but is killed instantly with a cane. Even so men will lose heart at some trifling opposition, criticism perhaps, who have endured the most violent storms of fortune with unbroken spirit. (32.14)

Lampreys have their vital principle situated in the tail, not the head. Like them one should not keep one's dearest possession where it is immediately at risk. (32.14)

As fish, though born and bred in the sea, do not taste salt, so some men born and brought up among barbarians are free from all trace of barbarism. (32.18)

As magicians sometimes produce marvellous results without even understanding their own spells, so do some priests, by reciting prayers which they do not understand but repeat in good faith, win God's favour and move him to act. (30.1–18)

Like Apion who, when he had raised Homer from the dead, asked him nothing except the names of his parents, certain people call a council of very important persons, and then consult them about mere trifles. (30.18)

As magicians promise astonishing results and thereby attract the credulous public, so do princes exhibit the most glorious prospects to win men's loyalty.

In the magical arts the public's amazement is greater, the less they perceive why this or that quite absurd rite is ordained; and in the same way some men admire prose or poetry more when they do not understand it.

As physicians to make themselves look more expert compound drugs of different kinds imported from different parts of the world, so some showy orators think a speech sounds uneducated unless they lard it with civil and canon law, poets, orators, philosophers, and logicians all at once, and patch it together out of more authors and more works than there were drugs in the famous concoction of Mithridates, which consisted of fifty-four different substances all at once. (25.3; 29.24)

To call up evil spirits is a dangerous game for, if a mistake is made, the attempt is fraught with great risks to the man who undertakes it; they say that Tullus Hostilius was struck by lightning because he had tried, using Numa's books of magic, to call Jupiter down out of the sky, and had got some things wrong. Similarly it is dangerous to do business with princes

* * * * *

15 As magicians] No precise source for this and the next has been identified.

[or with powerful men who are ill-natured, because they take offence at the
slightest thing and are a man's complete undoing]. (28.14)

As magicians, well aware that their promises are humbug, use a
portentous system of rites and ceremonies to craze and terrify their weaker
victims, so do some of the clergy, who are far from true religion, entangle   5
the ignorant in ceremonies, in order to have the common people more at
their mercy.

Like auguries and signs, which have no force except for those who
seek them and look out for them, the precepts of philosophy change only
those who are keen to become better men, and took to reading it with this in   10
mind.

The crocodile, in other respects such an invincible and destructive
creature, so much fears the people of Tentyra that it is terrified even at the
sound of their voices. Despots equally, great as is their contempt for all
others, have a lurking fear of literary men. (8.92)   15

There are some men whose outward aspect even has a baleful
influence; and likewise some in whom the bad habits of a lifetime stain
their character. (8.92)

The Psylli are not merely themselves immune to snake-bite, but suck
the venom from other victims. In the same way your true philosopher is not   20
only untouched by faults himself, but can cure the defects of others by his
words and his example. (8.93; 28.30)

Those who have once been bitten by a scorpion are never stung
thereafter by wasp, hornet, or bee; and similarly there is nothing untoward
that does not have some advantage connected with it. (28.32)   25

Men bitten by a mad dog go mad themselves also, and pass on the
contagion to others; and, like them, those who from some source or other
have acquired pestilent ideas infect others by their conversation. (29.100)

As the most effective remedies take their rise from the most noxious
diseases, so good laws are bred from bad behaviour. (29.61)   30

The viper, the crocodile, and other most pestilent beasts are valued by
physicians as a source for certain powerful antidotes to poison and disease;
and likewise the punishment of criminals restrains or recalls many men
from crime. (29.69)

* * * * *

1 or with powerful men] The bracketed words were added in the Paris revision
  of 1516.
3 As magicians] This and the following may be inspired by the general remarks
  on magic at the start of Pliny's book 30.
16 aspect] Contemporary Pliny-texts have *uisu* where we read *usu*.
26 pass on the contagion] This is not in Pliny, but may come from Lucian *Nigrinus*
  38.

The crocodile leads a double life, now on land, now in the water; on land it lays its eggs, in the water it hunts its prey and lies in wait. In the same way some men double the parts of courtier and ecclesiastic, and are pestilent in both. (8.89)

The chameleon, being easily frightened, changes its colour from time to time; and men with no strength to back them must of necessity take refuge in various shifts. (8.122)

The lynx has better sight than any living creature, but is amazingly forgetful of anything once it is out of sight. Some men are like that, quick-witted but forgetful. (28.122; 8.84)

Some remedies are more unpleasant than the disease itself, so that it is better to face death than to use them in hopes of a cure: for example, to suck blood from the fresh wounds of gladiators who are at the point of death. Likewise it is sometimes better to suffer wrong in silence than to seek revenge at a still higher price, or to accept terms of peace however damaging or unfair than to enter upon a war with all its measureless evils. (28.4)

The scorpion's venom is fatal, more fatal still is aconite; yet aconite drunk as a medicine is effective against a scorpion sting, and thus the antipathy between one venom and the other saves the patient's life. In the same way the rivalry of two pestilent citizens is sometimes the salvation of the state. (27.5)

Aconite kills by simple contact; and to be in company with certain people can infect one forthwith, or to enter into the very slightest relationship with them. (27.6)

In old days there were chariot races on the Capitol during the Latin festival, and the winner drank wormwood – a reminder that health is more worth having than enjoyment. (27.45)

Fruit from the service-tree that is superficially more attractive can be poisonous. Be more on your guard against friends full of charm than against those who are severe and critical.

The plant called empetron, in Latin saxifrage, has less salt in it the nearer it grows to the sea; the further inland it grows, the more bitter it tastes. Some men are like that, redolent of Germany when in France and of France when in Germany; and the further they are from any nation, the more they bring it to mind. (27.75)

As the best remedies are the most dangerous unless rightly taken, so do Christ's sacraments bring salvation to those who receive them rightly, and death to those who receive them unworthily.

* * * * *

28 service-tree] No source identified
36 As the best remedies] No source identified

Medicinal herbs lose by familiarity their power to heal; and in the same way correction continuously applied does not improve the offender who is already hardened under reproof. (27.144)

Those who take the antidote before the poison do not suffer from the poison; and those who have braced their minds with sound opinions and principles will not be infected by converse with bad men, should they find themselves in such company. (25.6)

Mithridates, who took poison every day, found it lose its effect by familiarity; and similarly the evils with which you have grown familiar do not offend you. (25.6)

Every man thinks his own complaint very serious; and everyone feels his own misfortunes more than other people's. (25.23)

The plant called moly is difficult to dig up, but more effective as a drug than all the rest. In the same way, what is of outstanding merit cannot be secured without great efforts. (25.26)

Books are like medicinal herbs among which poisons grow: one must pick out the good things.

Hellebore stimulates all the inner parts, but is itself the first thing to leave the body; and similarly the brave general, after he has addressed his troops, is the first to advance against the enemy, as Herophilus says, whom Pliny quotes. (25.58)

Hellebore absorbed in moderate quantities is more dangerous, because it establishes itself in the organs and poisons the whole body, but if taken in heavy doses it works its way out more rapidly. Similarly one should not rebuke a friend except with sufficient emphasis to rid him of his fault; more moderate protests cast a shadow over friendship, and do no good. (25.57)

As hellebore, efficient though it is, is forbidden by physicians to the aged, to children, and to patients who are very thin, so reproof should be adjusted to the capacity of him whom you wish to set right. You must consider not only the fault but also the nature of the man whose fault you wish to cure. (25.61)

The ignorant public seek remedies with great trouble and expense from farthest India or Ethiopia, while herbs grow in our own gardens which can cure their complaints. Like them we expend great effort in the search for outward things to buttress a life of ease – power, wealth, and pleasures – while it is the mind that contains what can make us happy. (27.2)

The herb they call climenos cures disease, but at the price of causing

* * * * *

16 Books] No certain source identified

LB I 604E / ASD I-5 256

sterility even in men; similarly some people drive out one evil quality only to make room for a different one. (25.70)

There is less virtue in the roots of medicinal herbs while their seed is ripening; and the powers of mind and body are reduced whenever we devote our energies to getting children. (27.144)

Dogs eat canarywort in such a way that a man cannot detect the plant until it has been eaten, and when bitten by a serpent they look for another plant, but do not eat it while a man is looking. Thus do some conceal subjects they have discovered, for fear that others too may get the benefit of them. (25.91)

The lotus, called by the Romans the Greek bean, has woody twigs which are intensely bitter and a very sweet fruit; in the same way the attempt to scale the highest virtue is hard, but to enjoy it is the most delightful thing there is. (24.6)

The vine has an antipathy to kale, the oak abhors the olive and still more the walnut; for though the vine rambles over everything kale is the only thing it will not touch, an oak planted in the same hole as an olive dies, and placed close to a walnut withers away. Similarly some peoples have a natural antipathy for one another, such that concord between them is unattainable [as can often be seen in those divided by the sea or the Alps]. (24.1)

As Democritus the physician, when treating a woman named Considia who refused all strong measures, prescribed for her the milk of she-goats, which he fed on mastic, so those who at the start reject the more stringent precepts of philosophy must be offered stories with more attraction to them, which all the same have a tincture of philosophy. (24.43)

Fennel is a favourite food of donkeys only, and a powerful poison to other living creatures. [Often] one man enjoys what revolts another. (24.2)

A decoction of ivy damages the muscles, but applied externally it has its value. Philosophy is like that: absorbed in quantity it has a bad effect on your personal piety, applied in small doses and externally, as it were, it makes you a better-educated man. (24.75)

The pounded root of rushes applied externally draws out fern-root from the body, and fern-root does the same for rushes. Likewise the love of money expels the desire for wisdom, and wisdom expels the desire for money. (24.85)

The leaves of a tree called rhododaphne are poisonous to four-footed

* * * * *

20 as can often] The bracketed clause was added in the revision of Paris 1516.
22 Democritus] Early editions have Democrates.
28 Often] Added in 1516.

beasts, but for men are a specific against serpents. In the same way Scripture provides life-giving nourishment to sober prudent minds, but supplies foolish and irreligious men with the occasion for heresy and greater irreligion. (24.90)

What no force will accomplish is sometimes effected by the juice of some herb, if only you apply the right one; so some men are more moved by language that is well chosen rather than forcible.

Wine in moderation is good for the muscles and the eyes; in larger quantities it does them harm. In the same way reading moderately indulged in enhances life, but excessive devotion to it is bad. (23.38)

Wines and fruits with a touch of acidity mature and grow mild with age; and the rashness of youth is tamed by long experience. (23.39)

The plant called chameleon changes the colour of its leaves according to the ground it grows on – black, green, blue, yellow, and many other colours. Likewise a man does well to match his style of living to the place where he lives. (22.45)

Heliotrope is a plant that always faces towards the sun, and when he sets, its flowers close up. So with some men: they watch the monarch's lightest nod, and in whatever direction they see him move, they are quick to follow. (22.57)

As the plant called maidenhair, even if you pour water over it or plunge it in water, always looks dry, so scandal or malicious gossip gets no hold on a good man, even if someone does try to defame him. (22.62)

In nature, plants with showy blooms are the first to fall – roses, lilies, and stocks – while others last; and in human life what seems most flourishing turns most quickly into the opposite. (21.64–9)

As the rose, of all flowers by far the most popular, grows on a thornbush, so does harsh and gloomy toil produce the sweetest fruit. (21.14)

Saffron likes to be trodden on, and grows better when hard-pressed, so that it is most flourishing by footpaths and springs. Virtue shines all the brighter when roused by adversity. (21.34)

As nothing is more insidious than poisonous honey (for such kinds exist), so nothing is more to be guarded against than a soft-spoken enemy. (21.74)

The nettle stings though it has no prickles, and the mere down on its leaves hurts if one does but touch it. Some men are like that: they do harm, not openly by force, but secretly. (21.93)

As the nettle, if you approach it with hesitation and fearfully, will sting you, but if you grasp it with your whole hand does not hurt, so

* * * * *

5 What no force] No source identified

money, if treated with respect and circumspection, will infect you, but if
you despise it and do not worry about it, it cannot hurt you. (21.93)

Like the root which the doctors call rhubarb, which can make you
bilious, yet has a special virtue in driving off bilious attacks, so it sometimes happens that one love drives out another, just as nail is driven out by
nail, resentment by resentment [, and sorrow by sorrow].

There is a sort of contradictory element in poisons, such that often one
poison counteracts another; and in the same way one fault can neutralize
another and villain be matched against villain. (27.5)

As it is perfectly safe to sleep in a clover-field, because they say that in
clover you never see a snake, so one should choose books to read in which
there is no fear of poison. (21.152)

Like the plant called all-heal, which by itself is a remedy for every
sickness, the death of Christ is our one specific against all hurtful desires. (25.30)

Add to the wine men drink the herb nepenthe, of which Homer tells,
and all sadness in the party is dispelled. In the same way good sense once
implanted in us puts an end to anxious care. (21.159)

As vinegar, though sour to the taste, is sovereign against snakebite, so
the principles of philosophy may be unpalatable and uncompromising, but
they provide an instant cure for pernicious cravings in the mind. (23.55–6)

Physicians prohibit the use of halicaccabon, although it helps to fix
loose teeth if they are rinsed in the liquor of it, because if this treatment goes
on too long there is a danger of delirium, and the bad results far outweigh
the good. Likewise we should not read books which improve the style at the
expense of a bad effect on the character, or pursue policies which will
increase one's estate at the expense of one's reputation. (21.180)

Cress makes a man more sluggish sexually, but sharpens the powers
of the mind. Philosophy is like that: it translates training and strength of
body into strength of mind, in such a way as to give a mere man more
discernment in things eternal, the more insensitive he is to these gross
bodily things. (20.127)

* * * * *

3 rhubarb] Erasmus' word *rebarbarum* is found, for instance, in Isidore *Etymologiae* 17.9.40, but his source has not been identified. The words in brackets
were added in 1516.

16 Homer] *Odyssey* 4.221ff, where Helen puts nepenthe into the wine in the
mixing-bowl.

22 halicaccabon] Name given in Greek to several poisonous or narcotic plants

28 Cress] This was one of the paragraphs that ended with 'etcetera' in the first
edition; but Erasmus did not complete it in 1515 or 1516, and we are left to
guess what he originally had in mind.

In Upper Libya, as Aristotle tells us in the *Politics*, since wives are held
in common, the offspring are shared out by their resemblance to their
fathers; and in the same way with works of literature, if the titles are
jumbled up, one should look for resemblances of style and the run of the
language.   5

Like the audience at a comedy, who are not there to learn to act
themselves but for amusement, a great many people now listen to a sermon
with no idea of becoming better men by putting it into practice, but for the
pleasure of listening.

Like the druggist who wraps certain remedies in gold foil to make   10
them more saleable are people who think a proposal is improved when
dressed up in unnecessary words.

Wave chases wave perpetually; and day treads on the heels of day.

Of a flowing stream so much alone is yours as fills your bucket; and of
the years that never stand still you can keep only so much as you have stored   15
up in things that endure.

The worn-out moon is born again, and when she has grown old she is
made new; man is not born again when he is dead, nor do the old grow
young.

When winter passes spring returns afresh; but after old age youth   20
does not return.

The sun that set returns anew; but not so man.

As it is folly to abandon springs and seek out brooks, so it is foolish to
leave the Gospels, and follow the imaginings of Lyra, [Hugo, Bricot,] and
the like.   25

As the greatest physicians show the most skill in curing even minor
complaints, so the most learned teachers teach minor subjects too most
skilfully.

The vampire cannot see in her own house, and sees everything out of
doors; so some people see more than they should in other men's affairs, and   30
too little in their own.

* * * * *

 1 Aristotle] *Politics* 2.3 (1262a20). The next dozen aphorisms have as yet no
    definite source.
24 Lyra] Nicholas of Lyra OFM, who died in Paris in 1349, the most widely read of
    all the scholastic commentators on the Bible. In the second edition (Louvain
    June 1515), but not later, two names were added: Hugo, presumably Hugo
    of Saint-Cher OP, also a leading Paris master, who died in 1263, and Thomas
    Bricot, contemporary logician, who was prominent in the Paris faculty of
    theology, and did not die until 1516. Erasmus has a stinging comment on him
    in the preface (1522) to Arnobius Junior on the Psalms (Allen Ep 1304:61–2).
29 vampire] The fabulous lamia; cf 201:1 above.

LB I 606E / ASD I-5 262

There is a special malevolence in the man who fences off a flowing
spring or blocks the sunshine or refuses another man a light or objects to
showing him the way; and similarly a man would be exceptionally inhu-
man who would refuse to help another with no inconvenience to himself.

Mares who see their own reflection in water are driven mad, says   5
Columella; and some men with an exaggerated idea of themselves are
driven nearly mad by conceit.

The horns of the bonasus are nothing but a burden to it and serve no
useful purpose, so sharply are they bent backwards; and some logicians in
the same way are masters of a dialectic which can convince nobody, so   10
intricate [and thorny] is it. (8.40)

The leopard attracts other wild creatures by its smell, and then attacks
and kills them; similarly some men entrap their victims by flattery, and so
deceive and destroy them. Thus do the courts of princes possess some kind
of attraction that can lure men to their ruin. (8.62)   15

He who has robbed the tigress of her whelps thinks himself lucky if he
saves even one from its mother's pursuit unscathed. In the same way the
man who has seized another's property, even if compelled to give it back,
yet shows a profit if he can keep even a part of it. (8.66)

In the panther, what ought to be the most handsome part must be   20
concealed, in order that the pattern of spots on the rest of the animal may
exercise its attraction; and in some men likewise everything is pleasant
except their way of life, which ought to be the head of the whole business. (8.62)

Like the elk, whose skin no weapon can pierce, some men cannot be   25
hurt by anything you say. (8.124)

The hyena, and also the ichneumon, are male at one time and female at

* * * * *

1 malevolence] Special, because the man would be refusing to a fellow-creature
things of which his own supply would not be reduced if he complied. This
was universally disapproved of in both Greek and Roman society; cf for
instance Seneca *De beneficiis* 4.29.

6 Columella] *Res rustica* 6.35; Erasmus had perhaps been looking at the edition
of the ancient writers on agriculture published by Aldus in May 1514.

11 and thorny] Added in the Louvain revision of June 1515, but not later

20 In the panther] Its fierce-looking head terrified its potential victims, and must
be concealed from them. It was the animal's scent that attracted them; but in
Pliny's text *odore* had been corrupted to *colore*. In this and the next we may
detect the influence of Aelian's *De natura animalium* 5.40, 2.16. This was first
printed by Conrad Gesner in 1556, but circulated in numerous sixteenth-
century and earlier copies.

27 The hyena] Aelian 1.25 (cf Pliny 8.105), 10.47. The words in brackets (replacing
'etcetera') were added in the Paris revision of 1516.

another. So some men are inconsistent with themselves – fierce language one moment, gentle the next; [alternately philosopher and spendthrift, friend and enemy]. (8.105)

The blind-rat lives exclusively in Boeotia, where it is native, and dies if it is moved elsewhere; some men likewise cannot live in a foreign country, lacking the necessary skills.

The chameleon, living as it does on air not food, has its mouth always open; and those who thrive on the tawdry fame of popular approval are always on the lookout for something that may increase their reputation. (8.122)

The amphisbaena is a serpent with a head at each end, and can use either end of its body as a tail. Some men are like that: double-faced, sheltering behind first one way of life and then another; when convenient they take refuge in the independence of the church, and when it suits them they forget the canon law and do their business in the name of princes. (8.85)

The snake they call porphyrius is poisonous but, having no fangs, it keeps its venom to itself. So some men have wicked designs, but for want of opportunity they do no harm.

The palm-tree, having bark with knife-sharp edges, is difficult to climb; but it bears delicious fruit. In the same way learning and goodness are hard to attain, but their fruits are delicious.

As the world is perfectly smooth and round and self-sufficient, so the wise man looks for nothing outside himself, but is content with what he is. (2.5)

How foolish it is, when the nature of this world into which we were born eludes us, to seek innumerable other worlds outside! And it is no less absurd to neglect one's own affairs and be full of anxiety and curiosity about other people's. (2.4)

Just as God, while he sees everything, might be supposed to see nothing, so there is nothing a prince should not know, and many things he should seem not to know. (2.14)

God knows and understands most, and has least to say. The wise man will not speak unless he has to. (2.14)

* * * * *

4 The blind-rat] A small rodent, Spalax typhlus, Greek *aspalax*, proverbial for bad sight (*Adagia* I iii 55). It is said to be confined to Boeotia by Aristotle *Historia animalium* 8.28 (605b31); see also Aelian 17.10.

7 The chameleon] This is repeated at 252:3 below.

17 porphyrius] *prophyrus* in the first edition, properly *porphyrous* the purple snake; from Aelian *De natura animalium* 4.36

20 The palm-tree] Based perhaps on Aelian 10.29

The world is a wonderful harmony made up of discordant elements;
and a true commonwealth is held steady by the differing aims of
men. (2.10)

Just as God, who is the best thing there is, rarely appears, so the best
element in man, the good will, lies very deep. (2.14)

As there is one God who governs the universe, but does so because he
is wisest and best, so a monarch would be a life-giving thing, if one were
granted us who is like God. (2.14)

The momentum of the spheres in contrary directions balances the
motion of the whole; and similarly the slow movement of the aged tempers
the energy and haste of young men in the body politic. (2.11)

As the sun is not one thing to the poor and another to the rich, but is
shared by all alike, so the prince should consider facts, not persons. (2.28)

The same sun softens wax and hardens clay; and the same speech will
make some men better, others worse, as their natures differ.

Like the moon, who has less light the nearer she is to the sun, those
who are outside the orbit of great princes have more profit and greater
dignity. (2.94)

As an eclipse of the sun brings great disasters upon mortal men, so if
the king makes even a small mistake, it causes great disturbance in human
affairs. (2.54)

Mercury recedes but a very small distance from the sun, however
aberrant and irregular in other ways; just so the wise man should not stray
too far from the path of honour. (2.39)

As the appearance of a new comet portends either great blessings or
great disasters for mortal men, so a new prince is the salvation of human
affairs if he is good, and a great plague if he is not. (2.92–3)

Several suns seen at the same time form a prodigy; so do several kings
or emperors. (2.99)

Like the moon, which passes on to the earth the light she gets from the
sun, we should contribute the blessings God has given us to the good of
others. (2.45)

If the fires of Castor and Pollux appear singly, it is a dire presage of ill;
if together, all will be well. Power in the same way should not be found
apart from wisdom, for this is otherwise disastrous. (2.101)

As Saturn, who among the seven planets has the highest station,

* * * * *

14 The same sun] This has not been found in Pliny, and the words are very close
   to Virgil *Eclogues* 8.80, which may well be the source; repeated at 272:1.
33 Castor and Pollux] St Elmo's fire; see above at 186:33.

moves in his orbit more slowly than the rest, so ought those who enjoy supreme power to do nothing in a hurry. (2.32 and 34)

As stars born suddenly go out or fall suddenly, so men raised suddenly to the highest honours often fall headlong soon. (2.89)

The dog-star is a universal plague, and the power of a bad prince does universal harm. (2.107)

The moon has special power to move what lies below her, not because she is more powerful, but because she is nearer; so much more effective is proximity! (2.109)

Like the blank thunderbolts that strike the mountain-tops without effect, so power without wisdom wastes its strength on unnecessary targets. (2.113).

In Africa the south is a fair-weather wind, the north wind cloudy, contrary to the natural habit of other countries; so some men change their mind and character when they change their country. (2.127)

As Egypt is too hot for thunderbolts and Scythia too cold, so very great power or a very lowly station make a man safe from contumely. (2.135)

In autumn and spring lightning is most common, in winter and summer less so. It is the moderately exalted position that is exposed to attack. (2.135–6)

A flash of lightning sometimes melts bronze or iron while leaving wax untouched; and likewise the judgment of God, or the power of kings, lets fly against resistance, but spares what is soft and yielding. (2.137)

As it is not only foolish but dangerous as well to call down the lightning, so it is madness to bring kings into one's country, for they are not aroused without doing us great harm. (2.140–1)

Lightning kills instantly every living creature except man; and in the same way the storms of fortune instantly depress uneducated and stupid men, but not the wise. (2.145)

Men deep in caverns are not struck by lightning; the lowliest station in life is the safest. (2.146)

As it sometimes thunders with no flash, and such thunder is alarming but not dangerous, so some men's threats frighten more than they hurt. (2.142?)

The river Hypanis, the chief river of Scythia, is clear and sweet in itself, but around Callipodes it is adulterated by the Exampeus, the sources of which are brackish, and so is quite untrue to itself when it reaches the sea. Solinus' verdict on it is that those who knew its beginnings speak

* * * * *

38 Solinus'] The third-century geographical compiler; *Collectanea rerum memorabilium* 14

highly of it, and those who have tried its lower reaches quite rightly
abominate it. Some men are like that: you find them friendly and ingratiat-
ing to begin with, and later something quite unlike themselves.

The francolin, though not normally without a voice, is silent in captivity, and in the same way some men lose their voice as slaves, who spoke   5
when they were free men. Alternatively there are people who talk and sing
of their own accord, but are silent if you apply compulsion. (10.133)

Memory is a net which holds large objects and lets small things
through.

Cut a tree down and it will shoot again, grub it up and it does not   10
grow; so evil, if entirely removed, does not reappear.

As we clip a bird's wings to stop it wandering, so some men's wealth
and influence must be clipped before they grow too high.

Clipped pinions grow again in time; and undue influence recovers
unless you constantly suppress it.   15

Those who cannot face the surgeon's knife are treated by regimen;
those who will not take severe correction must be put right by milder
measures.

If Apelles were to see his Venus, or Protogenes his famous Hialysus,
bedaubed with filth, he would be much distressed. Likewise, if a man were   20
to see someone gone to the bad whom he had brought up to a high standard
of conduct, or one whom he had honoured now in disgrace, he would not
take it calmly.

A woman wears the right scent if and when she smells of nothing, and
some women look all the better for a sweet disorder in their toilette. So the   25
style of a theologian gains in eloquence precisely as it eschews ornament.

In medicine treatment which heals the affected parts is better than
cautery; and a judicial system that can amend criminals is better than one
that removes them from the scene.

According to Roman lawyers even the men who sprinkle cold water   30
suffer similar legal disabilities [to those of men who purvey public enter-

* * * * *

4 francolin] *attagen*, the black partridge, a former Greek resident accounted very
good eating
8 Memory] The first of a series of aphorisms, the source of which has not yet
been identified
19 If Apelles] These are masterpieces of two Greek painters, mentioned by Pliny
35.91 and 102.
24 the right scent] A widely held ancient view; Erasmus' words are very close to
Cicero *Ad Atticum* 2.1.1.
30 Roman lawyers] The phrase 'to pour cold water on something,' which to us
conveys discouragement, was thought by Erasmus to have in Latin the opposite effect, the image being derived (he thought) from those who douche

tainment]. In the same way we should blame those who encourage wrong-doing, not only the man who does wrong.

As the man who proposes to carve a statue first makes out a rough sort of figure from the natural log, and then trims it and polishes it; so it is with him who is planning a speech or a book.

Time forms a scab over a wound, and we do not feel it; misfortune long grown familiar is easier to bear.

Nature is never the same everywhere, not winds nor tides nor rainfall, not trees nor living creatures; so a man ought not to be the same everywhere, but to adapt himself to time and place.

The Euripus in Euboea ebbs seven times a day and seven times returns with astonishing speed, while for three days in every month, the seventh, eighth, and ninth of the moon's age, it stands quite still. There are men likewise who show no consistency, either over-hasty or over-cautious, and unduly violent in either direction. (2.219)

As the movement of the tides and the waxing and waning of the moon have more effect on weaker bodies, so adversity affects more forcibly the mind that is less self-consistent, and is damaged by the passions. (2.221)

Shellfish grow larger under the waxing moon and shrink as she wanes. Likewise a foolish man who hangs upon fortune is now great, now small, high one moment and humble the next, as the goddess of Rhamnus turns about. (2.221)

Sea-water is less salt at some depth than on the surface; and the further you penetrate into philosophy, the sweeter you find it. (2.222)

Ancient naturalists tell us that the sun is nourished on salt water and the moon on fresh. So wise men are attracted by unpleasant things if they are of value, while fools pursue only what can give pleasure. (2.223)

* * * * *

race-horses in order to refresh them for yet greater efforts. In the *Adagia* (I x 51) of 1508 he said that the phrase occurred in Roman law, and in 1515 added a quotation from Ulpian (*Digest* 3.2.4), in which it is said to be wrong that those who sprinkle water over the horses, and others engaged on services essential to the races at a festival, should suffer the same loss of status in the eyes of the law as common players. This must be the passage Erasmus has in his mind here. The bracketed words, added in the second edition (Louvain June 1515) but not in later revisions, are essential to the sense.

11 Euripus] We return to the regular use of Pliny with fifteen aphorisms inspired by his book 2, which is geographical. The channel between Euboea and mainland Boeotia was proverbial for its tides and currents, and in *Adagia* I ix 62 Erasmus quotes this passage of Pliny.

21 Rhamnus] In northern Attica; famous for the shrine of Nemesis, the goddess of retribution. Erasmus often uses the phrase with reference to fortune, and gave it the status of a proverb (*Adagia* II vi 38).

There are rivers which force their way right through lakes without mingling with them, and after a traverse of many miles the same river issues at the farther end with the same volume of water with which it entered. Likewise, if you find yourself in a city that is corrupt, use it for a temporary lodging, in such a way that you are the same on leaving that you   5
were when you entered. (2.224)

In the Asphalt Lake in Judaea and in Lake Aritissa in Greater Armenia nothing will sink. Like them some people carry whatever you entrust to them on the surface, and can conceal nothing. (2.226)

Like sea-water, which is undrinkable, but carries a ship much better   10
than river water which is sweet and more fit for drinking, every single thing serves its proper purpose, if you use it as it should be used. (2.224)

Jupiter's spring in Dodona is itself cold, and extinguishes a torch dipped into it; but if you put an extinguished torch down to the water, it relights. Christ is like that: if he touches a soul that is burning with desires,   15
he calms and cools it; the castdown and the spiritless he raises up and gives them new life. (2.228)

The spring among the Lyncestians which they call Acidula intoxicates a man like wine. So with some people: their poverty and ignorance actually make them more obstinate and selfish. For the same effect can arise from   20
opposite causes – arrogance, for example, from knowledge or from ignorance. (2.230)

Tirrhean stone, no matter how large the piece, will float; but break it up small, and it sinks to the bottom. Thus are we buoyed up by concord, and discord is our undoing. (2.233)   25

Oil poured on the sea calms it, and oil is a source of light. Philosophy calms the billows of the mind, and drives away the darkness of ignorance. (2.234)

When naphtha, which is a kind of bitumen, appears even at a distance, a flame will dart across and kindle it, because their natures are allied.   30
Likewise a spirit made for good literature seizes upon it at sight. (2.235)

They say that the fires of Chimaera, a blazing mountain that never goes out, are kindled by water and put out by hay. So it is with some people: the more you entreat them, the less you move them, but discourage them from some course of action, and they adopt it forthwith. (2.236)   35

Like brackish springs, which are less salt than others when rain is

* * * * *

23 Tirrhean stone] Tyrean in the manuscripts of Pliny, Thyrrean in early editions; but it is commonly identified with the Scyrian stone, pumice from the island of Scyros, which Erasmus has already used at 225:25.

falling, those whose lives have been made quite different by an inflow of the grace of God make better men than others, like St Paul. (2.233)

As Maltese spaniels are especially the pets of rich and influential women, so princes who have been enervated by luxury set a high value on those who flatter them and say and do everything simply to please them.   5 (3.152)

Some rivers, while remaining the same, are given different names in different stretches of their course. Some qualities change their name from one man to another: the pride that is called glory in a prince is arrogance in a private person. (3.9–10)   10

The nearer to the vertical the impact of the sun's rays, the shorter is our shadow, and the more aslant they fall, the longer the shadow of our bodies grows. Similarly the more true wisdom a man acquires, the lower his opinion of himself, and the further he is from wisdom, the more he exults in a most foolish conviction that he is wise. (2.182–3)   15

As among so many thousands of mankind no two faces, no two voices are exactly alike, so each man has his own natural gifts, his own acquired way of life. (7.8)

They say that in Albania there are natives with grey-green eyes who like owls can see better at night than they can by day. Likewise some people   20 have a better judgment in shady business than in what is honourable and distinguished, or in commonplace than in unusual things. (7.12)

The Psylli in Africa and the Marsians in Italy not only are themselves immune from attack by serpents, but their touch and their spittle can heal others who are in danger from an attack. Similarly philosophers should not   25 be satisfied if they themselves escape the infection of wrongful desires; their words ought to suppress noxious appetites no less in other people. (7.14–15)

Man always has a remedy at hand against snake-venom – his spittle, contact with which drives away snakes as though boiling water had been   30 poured on them, and kills them outright if it gets between their jaws. In the same way there is a sovereign remedy against all pestiferous desires, which we always carry round with us, did we but know how to use it. This must be sought in the mind. (7.15)

A person who has the evil eye can kill trees, crops, and children by   35 praising them; a flatterer too destroys by praising. (7.16)

As some people cast a spell upon a man with a baneful glance, so the

* * * * *

3 Maltese spaniels] See above 207:1.
11 The nearer] Cf Erasmus' treatment of the same material from another source at 273:14.

eye of envy is the undoing of prosperity; even the eye of kings is fraught with danger, if you possess anything really worth having. (7.16)

Those who can exert the evil eye are said to have eyes with a double pupil. Likewise those who burn with envy at other men's good fortune do not look at it with a single eye: whatever they see, they give a sinister interpretation to it. (7.16–18)

There is a people in India called the Pandorians, who have white hair in childhood which goes black in old age. So some men are restrained and modest in their early years, and when they are already grown-up plunge into time-wasting and foolish pleasures, as if they were becoming children. (7.28)

Women who bear children earlier than usual grow old more rapidly: among the Calingians in India, for example, they give birth when they are five years old and do not live more than eight. So mental gifts that ripen early soon begin to fail. (7.30)

Hermaphrodites follow both sexes so closely that they are neither male nor female; and some men who try to be at the same time both theologians and literary critics are accepted by neither party. (7.34)

A woman carrying a male child has less to endure during pregnancy and in childbirth. So, if we have conceived some honourable purpose, we shall achieve it with less trouble than something foolish only meant to entertain, and those who follow the rewards of the world will find it less painful to acquire for themselves the pearl of which the Gospel speaks. (7.41)

Children who are called by the name Agrippa, because they are born the wrong way round, that is, feet first, are supposed to enter upon life under unhappy omens and to the great detriment of the human race, as happened with Marcus Agrippa and Nero. Similarly those who use criminal methods and simony to force their way to the throne or the episcopate (as they call it) bring with them grievous troubles for themselves and those in their charge. (7.45)

Many women cannot have children by certain men, but if wedded with others they are fertile. In the same way the young may learn nothing from certain teachers, yet when handed over to different instructors they make progress, for minds like bodies have their sympathies and antipathies. (7.57)

You notice when the shadow on the sundial has moved on, but you do not see it move; you observe that a shrub or plant has grown, but the growth is unobserved. Such is also the progress of our mental powers: it consists of minute increases and is detected in process of time. (7.213?)

Though elephants cannot swim, they are very fond of rivers and love to roam in their neighbourhood. Likewise some men without book-learning yet enjoy the society of scholars. (8.28)

Dragons suck the blood of elephants and kill them, but they are intoxicated in their turn, and are caught and die with their victims. So too it often happens in a battle that both sides destroy and are destroyed, both gain and both lose. (8.34)

The bonasus is an animal with useless twisted horns that can do no harm; so, as it runs away, it drops its dung, and the touch of this burns its pursuers like fire. Thus there are some who dare not meet you face to face, but befoul a man with slanders spread behind his back. (8.40)

The lion attacks a man more readily than a woman, and does not touch children except under great stress of hunger; he spares simple folk and those who lie down before him. In the same way powerful men should have pity on those who are weaker than they are, and try their strength on others whose defeat would bring them credit. (8.48)

The playful behaviour of monkeys makes a lion shake off his fever; and slander or abuse from an enemy sometimes shakes off one's sloth and lassitude, and spurs one on to the pursuit of honour. (8.52)

A lioness' whelps are unformed when born; they can scarcely walk at six months, nor move until they are two months old. Thus things with a splendid future often start late and reach completion by slow stages. (8.45)

The lion, the animal of which all others are afraid, fears a cock's crowing and its comb. In the same way great princes sometimes are made to fear the hostile attacks of humble folk. (8.52)

By throwing a blanket over his eyes, a lion can be caught without difficulty, though otherwise invincible. Just so it is very easy to quell even the most powerful person, provided you have learnt to know his nature. (8.54)

The camel does not like to drink until it has first trampled the water and made it muddy; and some men like nothing they read, unless it is disfigured with barbarism. (8.68)

The camelopard or nabis has the neck of a horse, the feet and legs of an ox, the head of a camel, the markings of a tiger or a leopard. Some men, like that, are inconsistent, reproducing different characters at the same time. Look at his dress: you would suppose him some holy man. Hear him talking: you would think it was a satrap. Sample his way of life: you will find a rascal. Glance at what he writes: he is a boor. (8.69)

The rhinoceros has a horn on its nostrils; the humour of some men has teeth and claws. (8.71)

* * * * *

32 camelopard or nabis] Giraffe

The catoblepas and the basilisk can kill just with a look, especially if
you look into their eyes. Likewise some despots merely with a stare drive
men to hang themselves, or a woman lovely but unchaste can undo one
with a glance. (8.77–8)

The hiss of a basilisk puts all other serpents to rout. Thus there are men
so pestilent that others compared with them look virtuous and readily get
out of their way. (8.78)

The wolf-like creatures known as lynxes, even when hungry, forget
their quarry if they look behind them, and immediately seek another
victim. So some people soon forget the story they had begun to tell you, if
you interrupt with a few words, and turn their attention to something
else. (8.84)

That most dangerous pest, the asp, never strays abroad without his
mate, and if he is killed she pursues the killer relentlessly. Even so do
despots associate with themselves a son or some other successor to their
absolute power, that they may have someone to avenge them should things
go wrong. (8.86)

The crocodile allows a bird called the black plover to pick food out of
his jaws, not from love of the bird but for his own comfort; for the bird with
its sharp beak picks his teeth clean. So tyrants, if they make any concession,
do it always with an eye to their own interests. (8.90)

The crocodile is a formidable object to those who run away from him,
but runs away himself if you pursue him. Like that some people are
ferocious if you give way to them and show fear; but if you firmly despise
them and stand up to them, they give way at once. (8.92)

For the asp's bite there is no remedy except to amputate the affected
limb; and there are some vices likewise which only death can cure. (8.85)

The asp would be a danger one could not escape, had not nature given
it very poor sight. In the same way certain persons would be a dangerous
menace if their evil desires were matched by intellectual power, so that they
could equally contrive the means of doing harm. (8.87)

The plant called dittany expels arrows from the body, as stags have
demonstrated. Like that philosophy can charm the darts of fortune out of
the mind. (8.97)

The stag can drive out an arrow fixed in its body by eating dittany, and

* * * * *

8 lynxes] Pliny speaks of 'wolves called *cervarii*,' and these are normally lynxes.
So it runs here (according to ASD) in the Basel edition of 1534 and later; but in
the early editions it is *gregarii,* which should mean 'the wolves called common
or ordinary wolves.' This still awaits explanation.

13 the asp] The hooded cobra. See *Adagia* III i 85 'Morsus aspidis,' to which
Erasmus added this passage from Pliny in *1515*.

if bitten by a tarantula can cure itself by eating crabs; lizards bitten by
snakes recover through eating a certain herb; swallows remedy weak sight
in their young with celandine; the tortoise gains new strength against
snakes from eating savory; the weasel musters its forces for hunting mice
with the use of wild rue; the stork cures itself when sick with marjoram;   5
wild boars use ivy, and also eat crabs; the snake is helped by fennel juice to
cast its slough; the dragon which feels nausea in the spring suppresses it
with the juice of wild lettuce; panthers use human excrement as an antidote
for aconite; the elephant eats chameleon-leaves, which are the same colour
as itself; bears which have eaten mandrake-apples lick up ants; the stag   10
protects itself against poisoned pastures with a kind of artichoke; pigeons,
jackdaws, blackbirds, partridges clear their annual loss of appetite with
bay-leaves; so do stock-doves, turtle-doves, and domestic fowls with a
plant called pellitory, ducks and geese and other water-fowl with ironwort,
storks and similar birds with rushes from the marsh; the crow after killing   15
the chameleon, which is dangerous even in defeat, suppresses the noxious
poison with bay. In a word there is no living creature but knows its proper
remedy; man alone knows not where to seek out remedies either for the
body or for the mind. (8.97–101)

The hyena can imitate the human voice; it learns a man's name, calls to   20
him, and tears him in pieces. Likewise some men ingratiate themselves
with feigned affection until they lure their victim to destruction. (8.106)

The panther has such a passion for human excrement that, if some is
placed in a pot and hung above its reach, it will kill itself by jumping up at
full stretch until it is exhausted. So some people take a great fancy to   25
something absolutely foul. (8.100)

Beavers in Pontus bite off their own genitals when pursued, knowing
that these are the object for which they are hunted; and similarly it is the act
of a wise man sometimes to cast away the thing that exposes him to
danger. (8.109)   30

Stags when they prick up their ears have very keen hearing, but when
they lower them they are deaf. So you may see princes detecting from afar
off something they like, and what they do not like they do not understand
however much you shout at them. (8.114)

Stags when obliged to drop their antlers hide them none the less, the   35
right-hand one especially, that others may not use them as a drug. Like

* * * * *

23 The panther] Pliny has panther, and so does the *Opera omnia* (Basel 1540).
   According to ASD all earlier editions here have *hyena*. Possibly a transcrip-
   tional error, the eye of a copyist or typesetter having jumped from the first
   word of one paragraph to the first word of its neighbour?

them, some rich men, when they cannot use their wealth themselves, yet
allow no one else to enjoy it. (8.115)

Like the chameleon, which lives on nothing but air and so has its
mouth always open, some men live on public applause, and have no object
but empty praise and glory. (8.122)

The chameleon, which from time to time changes its colour, imitates
every colour except red and white. The toady imitates everything in his
patron except what is honourable. (8.122)

The elk, though it has a hairy coat, copies the colouring of every tree
and shrub and all the places where it lurks. Like that a man will be safer who
can imitate the manners and customs of any country in which he may find
himself. (8.124)

The porcupine shoots out its quills only when provoked or tormented;
but a buffoon rains his quips on any target. (8.125)

The she-bear produces her whelps half-formed and licks them into
shape; and the unfinished offspring of the mind needs prolonged care to
polish it. (8.126)

A bitch bears her puppies in haste, and bears them blind; thus work
done in a hurry cannot be well done. (8.151)

A lazy watchdog barks at everyone it does not know; barbarians
criticize and condemn whatever they do not understand. (8.146)

Some dogs are dumb, and bite before they bark; some of this sort I
have seen myself. Similarly there are men I could name who do one an
injury before lodging their protest. (8.147)

The ass breeds throughout life, while man ceases so early to bear
offspring. One sees how things of little worth are more easily produced all
the time, but precious things are hard to come by. (8.168)

No animal is more devoted to its young than are ass and monkey; it is
the uneducated who love their own productions more than anyone. (8.169
and 216)

The mule, sprung from horse and ass, is neither one nor the other, like
some people who try to be both courtiers and churchmen, and are
neither. (8.171)

A kicking mule can be restrained by giving it plenty of wine; but wine
makes a shrewish woman worse. (8.173)

A monkey sometimes hugs its young to death; there are parents like

* * * * *

18 A bitch] This aphorism owes at least as much to a Greek proverb as it does to
Pliny; see *Adagia* II ii 35.

that, whose excessive affection and indulgence spoils their children. (8.216)

There may be places like Crete, without poisonous animals or plants; there is no polity, no court, without jealousy. (8.228)

Crete produces nothing poisonous except the tarantula, a kind of spider. There is no monastery so saintly that it is free from the evils of malice and ill will. (8.228)

The snakes in Syria have no venom effective against the natives and do not attack them, but to foreigners they deal death in torment. Likewise those who live on islands are kindly enough to their neighbours, but pitiless to outsiders. (8.229)

Indian turtles, tempted by the noonday heat, enjoy floating on the calm sea with their whole back exposed, until they forget where they are and their shells are dried by the hot sun, so that they cannot submerge; by now they must needs go on swimming against their will, and are conveniently exposed to those who hunt them. In like manner some men, attracted by the hope of great rewards, plunge into the courts of princes and are so softened by the delights of court-life that without knowing it they reach the stage of being unable to resume their old peaceful existence, even if they want to. (9.35)

The grey mullet supposes that if it conceals its head it is entirely invisible. Some people, like that, conceal their faults from themselves, and suppose that others do not notice them, a habit found in children too. (9.59)

The mud-fish is always followed by one called the sargue, and when it digs in the mud the sargue devours any food it may have turned up. So too there are some who interest themselves in other men's business so that, while the others have all the trouble, they themselves may have first chance at the pickings. (9.65)

The mackerel has a sulphur-yellow colour while in the water; when out of the water, it is the same as other fish. Likewise rich men in their little kingdoms seem equals of the gods and far more distinguished than other men; but in death there is no difference. (9.49)

The sucking-fish or remora is a small creature, but it can bring to a stop a ship under full sail. Even so a mind all set for honourable courses is sometimes called back by some girl or other; she fastens on her man, and holds him down. (9.79)

* * * * *

25 mud-fish] This translates Pliny's *lutarius*; Erasmus' text has *alutarius*.
34 The sucking-fish] See above 231:23.

As the squid holds fast by suction whatever it touches with its arms, and draws it in, so with some people: it is most difficult to get out of their hands anything they have got hold of. (9.85)

The squid, in other respects a stupid animal, shows marvellous cunning in getting shell-fish into its clutches. Similarly some men are intelligent only where their own profit is concerned, and in other things are just sheep. (9.90)

As the squid, while hunting for the meat of a shell-fish, is often caught and held, so oftener than not while we try to harm others we bring ourselves into peril. (9.90)

Like the sea-urchin, which always travels on spines because it carries its spines around with it, some people show bitterness no matter what the business, because they carry this unpleasantness round with them in their minds, even if there is nothing untoward afoot. (9.100)

Like crabs which, when frightened, move in either direction with equal speed, we should be ready to change our habits for something different when need arises. (9.98)

The very small crabs they call pinna-guards hide themselves for their own safety in the empty shells of molluscs, and move into large ones when they grow too big. So some men take refuge in the glories of their ancestors, when they dare not trust their own valour. (9.98)

Pearls grow in the sea, but are more closely related to the sky, whose appearance they reproduce. In like manner the religious and noble mind depends more upon heaven [whence it comes] than upon earth where it lives. (9.107)

The turbot, angel-fish, skate, and sting-ray are the slowest-moving of all fishes, but are often found to have in their stomachs a grey mullet, the fastest fish of all, which they capture by cunning and ingenuity. So some men surpass by their skill those who have far greater wealth and strength than they. (9.144)

Like the fish called trochus, which copulates with itself and conceives offspring of its own begetting, some people blessed with intellectual gifts implant the seeds of literature in their minds with no outside help; the Greeks call them autodidacts, self-taught. (9.166)

The ostrich is the largest of birds and the most stupid, for when it has buried its neck in a bush, it thinks it is hidden. Some men, like the ostrich, have a great heavy body and a minimum of brains. (10.1–2)

* * * * *

24 whence it comes] Added in the revision of Paris 1516

The phoenix is never anything but unique, and hardly anyone believes in it. The best things are supremely rare. (10.3)

The eagle, most rapacious of birds, dies not from disease or old age, but from hunger. A miser is like that: the older he grows, the more he is tormented by the passion for getting, and the less uses he can make of what he gets. (10.15)

Even the feathers of an eagle, if mixed with those of other birds, consume them. Similarly tyrants have a deeply inset urge to plunder the common people, in hopes that they may carry something away with them even in death. (10.15)

Like vultures, which become aware of a carcass three days in advance and fly to the spot, some legacy-hunters await the deathbeds of rich men for years ahead. (10.19)

The vulture kills nothing itself, but seizes on what has been killed by others. Those who live on the fruit of other men's labours are like vultures. (10.19)

The night-hawk carries on a war to the death with the eagle, so much so that they are often taken locked together. Like that it sometimes happens that, while two princes are ruthlessly giving free rein to their mutual hatred, both are overthrown when some third party comes against them. (10.24)

The cuckoo, foisting its eggs on the nests of other birds, is a type of those who get other men's wives with child. (10.26)

The cuckoo-chick when it is grown up, bastard though it is, devours the true offspring, and the mother bird with them. So some people who have been educated with great indulgence and ill-judged affection prove the undoing of their benefactors. (10.27)

The peacock does not display its feathers unless you express admiration for them; and some people cannot believe they possess what is theirs, unless someone is at hand to admire. (10.43)

Fighting-cocks often die together in a fight; and there are men who destroy one another in mutual strife. (10.47)

The winning cock at once asserts his superiority by crowing. Similarly some people vaunt their own criminal achievements, and make themselves ridiculous by blowing their own trumpets. (10.47)

No one sees the storks arrive, one sees they are there; and no one sees them go, only that they have gone, because both movements are carried out by night and secretly. In the same way no man perceives that his youth is passing, only that it is past; and we do not feel old age coming on, only that it has come. (10.61)

In Thessaly it is a capital offence to kill a stork, for no reason except that

IOANNES FROBENIVS LECTORI   S. D.

EN DAMVS

C· PLINII SECVNDI DI

VINVM OPVS CVI TITVLVS, HISTORIA MVNDI,
multo quàm antehac unquam prodijt emaculatius: idç primum ex annota
tionibus eruditorum hominum , præsertim Hermolai Barbari : deinde
ex collatione exemplariorum , quæ hactenus opera doctorum no
bis quàm fieri potuit emendatissime sunt excusa : postremo ex
fide uetustissimorum codicum ,ex quibus non pauca restitui
mus , quæ alioqui nemo , quamlibet eruditus, uel depre
hendit, uel deprehendere poterat. Absit inuidia di
cto. Vicimus superiores omneis. Si quis hanc pal
mam nobis eripuerit , non illi quidé inuide
bimus , sed studijs publicis gratulabi
mur. Bene uale lector, & fruere
Ἀγαθῇ τύχῃ.
Additus est index, in quo nihil desideres.

Basileæ apud Io. Frobenium , Mense
Martio. An. M. D. XXV.

Title page of the Froben Pliny (Basel 1525)
'Not a treatise but a treasure-house, truly a world of everything worth the knowing,'
Erasmus calls Pliny the Elder's *Naturalis historia*. For his *Parabolae* Erasmus
borrowed from it as freely as he did from Plutarch.
Reproduced by courtesy of the Centre for Reformation and Renaissance Studies,
Victoria University, Toronto

it destroys snakes; in England, too, kites are protected because they keep
the city clean by carrying offal away. So some people must be treated with
respect, not because they deserve it, but because we need something from
them. (10.62)

The stork, although a migrant, always makes on its return for the same
nest. Likewise, one ought not to forget one's friends when the association is
interrupted, but always to carry their memory round with one. (10.63)

When the storks gather on a plain called Pythonis kome (it is a place in
Asia), the one which arrives last is torn in pieces by the others, and when all
the laggards have been vicariously punished in the person of one victim,
they go on their way. In like manner the faults of the multitude should be
either cured or prevented by the prominent punishment of one individual. (10.62)

Like the quail, which thrives on the seeds of poisonous plants, some
men take special delight in backbiting and poisonous aspersions. (10.69)

Swallows nest under the roofs of human habitations, and yet never
grow familiar with man or trust him. So some men always keep their friends
under suspicion, especially islanders. (10.70)

The swallow arrives in summer, and at the approach of winter she flies
away. Like that an unfaithful friend is at hand when things go well, and
when fortune changes he deserts you. (10.70)

The rosy pastor is never seen by those who live on Mount Casius,
except when they need the birds' help against the locusts which are ravag-
ing their crops, and it is not known whence they come or whither they go.
Similarly some people never appear except when they need our help, nor do
they visit their friends except under the pressure of some emergency.
(10.75)

Nightingales have such a passion for singing that they compete one
against another to the death; life fails them before they tire of song. Like
them some men destroy their health by an immoderate love of study, and,
being unwilling to face defeat in a contest of erudition, they die in the
effort. (10.83)

Like the halcyon, which calms the sea in midwinter not for its own

* * * * *

1 kites] The kite (now reduced to a few breeding pairs in central Wales) was an
  important scavenger in the London of Erasmus' day, and so bold that, as
  William Turner tells us in his *Avium historia* (Cologne 1544), it would snatch a
  child's food out of his hand.
22 Mount Casius] *Casius* (the reading of the early printed texts of Pliny, though
  most of his manuscripts give *Cadmus*) is the name of two different mountains
  in the Levant (Pliny 5.68, 80). The rosy pastor, Pliny's *Seleucis avis*, is a bird
  like a starling, coloured black and rose-pink.

benefit only but for the general good, the wise man at a time of great public disturbance will not merely preserve his own peace of mind but will calm and pacify excitement in others. (10.89–90)

Halcyons are very rarely seen, but, whenever they appear, they either make calm weather or foretell it. Likewise abbots and bishops ought rarely to come to the fore in the courts of princes, but should be ready to calm civil strife and the storms of war by their authority. (10.90)

The pigeon has an astonishing turn of speed, but when it claps its wings in the air to show off its plumage, its pinions clash together and are caught, so that it can be seized by any hawk that is on the lookout for it. Thus do many men, who display their strength rather than use it, forget their situation, and fall victims to their enemies. (10.108)

Swifts are either suspended in mid-flight, or they are recumbent, for they have no feet. Some men are like that: they swerve with excessive violence first one way and then the other, either overwhelmed with too much business or idle and completely torpid – no half measures. (10.114)

Like the bittern which, though quite a small bird, imitates the lowing of oxen, some men who are really of no account are always talking of kings and satraps. (10.116)

Mice gnaw man's food, they live under the same roof, yet they are never domesticated. So some friends who are not wholly sincere never leave one, in hopes of food and comfort, yet never give one affection or confidence. (10.128)

Magpies have such a passion for mimicking human speech that sometimes they actually die in the attempt. Like them, some men get prayers and psalms by heart, which they intone from time to time, without knowing what they mean. (10.118)

Full eggs settle and empty eggs float. The man filled with true goodness or knowledge makes less of a show on the surface than his opposite. (10.151)

Among fowls if one hen treads another hen, eggs are laid, but nothing hatches from them. In the same way any plans that you make without the aid of common-sense are negligible and worthless. (10.160)

Eggs so produced are called wind-eggs, and another name for them is zephyr-eggs, as being conceived by the wind. Similarly anything is transitory which owes its origin to the fancy and not to the judgment. (10.166)

Creatures which are destined for a longer life take longer to appear;

* * * * *

34 Eggs so produced] This aphorism is given by editions of the Latin text as continuous with the preceding.

and similarly one should spend a long time over work that one hopes will
long find readers. (10.175)

The larger the animal, the fewer its offspring, while minute creatures
are highly prolific, so much that the goldcrest, smallest of birds, produces
twelve young in a brood. What has little weight must be judged by
number. (10.175)

The salamander appears only in very wet weather, and in fine weather
vanishes. Similarly some men make no show unless public affairs are in
turmoil through war or rebellion, and when all is peace, they fade
away. (10.188)

Such is the intense chill of a salamander that if it touches a fire, it puts
it out, as ice does. So there are those who will reduce a man to torpor sooner
than be kindled themselves to any honourable action. (10.188)

Granted that moles can see little or nothing, their hearing is very keen.
Thus does nature strike a balance, denying to some any beauty of form but
conferring on them vigour of the mind. (10.191)

As gnats do not haunt sweet things but make for what is sour, so some
men take an overmastering delight in malicious or dreary conversation. (10.195)

Fish do not enjoy all food equally, some like one and some another; so
fishermen, who know the favourite of each kind, tempt them by the offer of
that in particular. In the same way a toady will sum up a man's nature and
find out what puts him in a good mood and what he does not like; and
whatever he has discovered to be the victim's favourite, he will use to
entrap him. (10.196)

As roe-deer and quails grow fat on poisonous food, so certain people
thrive on calumny and backbiting. (10.197)

Between the different families of living creatures there are some hidden hostilities, of which the reason does not appear: for example, between
the spider and the snake, between ants and shrews, between wren and
eagle, and many others. There are men like that, who hate this or that
nationality, and cannot tell you why. Some men hate rhetoric or Greek,
while perfectly ignorant of the thing they hate. (10.203)

As the gnat displays the power of nature no less than the elephant, so
the wise man shows his measure equally in great things and small. Alternatively mental power makes itself evident even where the subject is ludicrous or mean. (11.2–3)

The bee is but a small insect, yet does wonderful work and rules its
polity with astounding skill. In small bodies sometimes lie hid the greatest
minds. (11.11)

Bees make a rendering for their outer walls with the juice of bitter

herbs, and in the inner hive store up the sweetest thing there is. In like
manner theology conceals her wisdom under layers of tasteless allegory, to
keep outsiders away. (11.15)

Bees do not collect everything indiscriminately from every source, but
bee-glue from one place, pitch-wax from another, from another propolis, 5
from another bee-bread or offspring or honey. In the same way one should
not expect to find everything in the same author, but select from each the
most useful thing he has. From poets and orators one gets splendour of
language, from logicians skill in argument, from philosophers a knowledge
of nature, from theologians the principles of the good life. (11.16) 10

Like bees which, though they fly everywhere, never damage a flower,
virtue and education can be acquired from others in such a way that the
man who has shared them with us loses nothing. (11.18)

As bees avoid withered flowers, so we should steer clear of a book full
of outdated maxims. Alternatively we should touch nothing but what is 15
well written and full of matter. (11.18)

Bees make use of drones as labourers and to keep their brood warm;
then, when the honey has begun to ripen, they turn them out and kill them.
Similarly we should take from our enemies any advantage they can give us,
as opportunity arises. (11.27–8) 20

If you remove the wings from a drone and put him back in the hive, he
removes the wings from all the other drones. This is like people drawn by
monks into their lobster-pots; when they have once lost their freedom, they
attract as many others as they can, that others may not be better off than
they are. (11.28) 25

Bees do their work not on fixed days but whenever they are invited by
suitable weather; every opportunity must be seized as it occurs. (11.29)

The king-bee alone has no sting, or at least does not use it; besides
which, he is larger in body and more showy, but his wings are shorter than
the rest. Like him a prince ought to be greatly disposed to clemency, and 30
never to fly very far away from his own citizen body. (11.52)

The king does no work himself, but walks up and down or flies around
as if exhorting others to work. So a prince should assist his people not by
physical effort but by wisdom and leadership. (11.53)

Like drones, which make no honey themselves but lie in wait for what 35
is made by the bees, there are people who produce nothing themselves but
steal the fruits of others' toil and claim it as their own. (11.57)

A bee when she has lost her sting can no longer hurt, being disarmed,
nor is she any use for making honey. So it is with men: those who know
how to hurt also know how to be helpful. (11.60) 40

When battles of bees among themselves are at their hottest, a handful
of dust or a puff of smoke lulls all to rest. Similarly the most serious
disagreement between princes is resolved by kinship or some other very
trifling consideration. (11.58)

It is thought that twenty-seven hornet stings are enough to kill a man;   5
like that an offence not capital in itself but often repeated breeds enmity that
might well prove fatal. (11.73)

A dress or translucent robe of silk stands condemned because, being
transparent, it does not cover the body, which is the object for which
clothing was invented. Equally absurd is a style which does not explain the   10
meaning but makes it more involved; for men invented speech to convey
what they mean. (11.76)

As crows break through a spider's web while flies are caught fast, so
laws bear hard upon the common folk and are broken by the powerful with
impunity. (11.83)   15

The scorpion carries poison in its tail and strikes obliquely; so some
men save up the voiding of their venom until the last moment and make
mischief undetected. (11.87)

A silent cricket is a marvel in nature, for that kind of creature never
stops chattering; but there are some of the sort in the country round Reggio.   20
In the same way we marvel the more at constancy and silence in a woman,
because the sex is changeable by nature and never stops talking. (11.95)

Like flies and some other insects which live by suction and therefore
have a tube in place of a tongue, you may see some boon-companions who
live on liquor and never touch solid food. (11.100)   25

As glow-worms attract no attention except by night or in a dark place,
so are some men distinguished only in the company of unimportant and
private people; in grander company they are overshadowed. (11.98)

The ant is a hard worker, but toils solely for her own advantage; so
some human beings think of nothing but themselves [and pursue their own   30
interests only]. (11.109)

Indian ants dig gold in caves and store it up, but get no benefit from it.

* * * * *

13 As crows] What Pliny says of spiders' webs is given more content by a
reminiscence of Solon's remark to the same effect about the law, as reported by
Diogenes Laertius 1.58. This does not account for the crows, which appear
again as 'large birds' in *Adagia* I iv 47.

20 Reggio] Erasmus refers to this passage of Pliny in the 1508 *Adagia* (I v 14
'Acanthia cicada').

29 The ant] The words in brackets were added in the revision of Paris 1516

Like them a miserly rich man does not enjoy his wealth himself, and grudges others the use of it. (11.111)

The leech, and a certain kind of louse, which has no vent, since it is never satisfied, sucks blood and swells until it bursts. A miser likewise is suffocated by his own riches. (11.116)

Like the pyraulis, the insect that will fly into a lamp and lose its wings and fall dead, so some men court their own destruction. (11.119)

Snails progress slowly, and never touch anything or move themselves in any direction without first feeling ahead with their horns. In the same way a wise man ought to be slow to move and never precipitate; he should advance step by step, taking samples (as it were) before he moves. (11.125)

Just as baldness carries no slur among the people of Myconos because there they are all born bald, so among the Italians [(to take them as an example)] there is no disgrace in love of money because everyone is overcome by it. (11.130)

Some people cannot see what is near them, but see well enough what is a long way off; and likewise some show more wisdom in other men's business than in their own. (11.142)

Creatures whose hearts are larger than normal are most easily frightened and very stupid, for the donkey has a very large heart, and in Paphlagonia there are partridges with two hearts, though it is the receptacle and origin of intelligence. Some men are like that: the more insignia of rank they wear, the less there really is in them, as for instance in a doctor with a vast bonnet and voluminous hood, who knows no divinity. (11.183)

Creatures with long legs ought to have a long neck; and men who wish to live with great ostentation are obliged to spread their exactions over a wide field, in order to meet their expenses. (11.178)

The chameleon has a very large lung and no other internal organ; and there is nothing in some people except ostentation and conceit and wind. (11.188)

Monkeys, though they closely resemble man, are nevertheless the

* * * * *

6 pyraulis] Erasmus gets the name from Pliny 11.119; but in Pliny it denotes a large fly which lives in the flames of the bronze-foundries in Crete, and dies if it quits them. He applies it to the moth, properly *pyraustes*, which flies into the flame of a lamp and dies there, both in our aphorism and in *Adagia* I ix 51 'Pyraustae interitus,' where he cites our Pliny passage verbatim in *1508*, although it is quite irrelevant to the *pyraustes*.

12 Myconos] An island in the Cyclades, the inhabitants of which were proverbial for their love of free dinners (*Adagia* IV viii 24, added in 1533). The phrase in brackets, which softens the original criticism of Italian avarice, was inserted in the revision of Paris 1516.

ugliest of all living creatures. This is a warning that he who pursues the
best, if he fails to achieve it, falls into the worst. (11.246)

Some families have taken their name from bodily deformities, Varus
from bandy legs [, Chilo from pouting lips, Naso from a huge nose]. Some
men in the same way earn fame by their misdeeds and are enno-
bled. (11.254)

Like children who, if they learn to talk earlier than usual, are slower in
learning to walk, the man who has a glib tongue is less ready to take
action. (11.270)

We recognize a man by his voice without seeing his face, for no two
voices are the same; and similarly we can guess a man's way of life from
what he says. (11.271)

Vultures are driven off by the scent of perfume and collect round
carrion. Some men cannot bear to do what is honourable, and are instantly
attracted by anything foul. (11.279)

Like perfumes and wines, books increase in value with age. (13.19)

Of the larger cedar-trees, those which flower set no fruit, and those
which bear fruit do not flower. So sometimes those who have the gift of
speech lack common sense, and those who have a wide knowledge of useful
subjects want the art of self-expression. (13.53)

Like a palm-branch which, when a burden is hung on it, does not
bend down to the ground as other branches do, but resists and pushes
upwards unbidden against the weight of its load, so the brave man's spirit
is more unbending, the more he is oppressed by business or assailed by
misfortune.

In Campania vines trained up the poplar-trees used to reach their very
summits, so that the vine-dresser was promised a solemn funeral with pyre
and gravestone. Men engaged on hazardous business must not forget the
risks they run. (14.10)

* * * * *

3 Varus] Erasmus selected this example for the first edition from a much longer
list in Pliny of family names derived from physical peculiarities; in the
revision of Paris 1516 he added Chilo (from the dictionary of Festus page 38
Lindsay) and Naso (perhaps from common knowledge).

16 perfumes] So Pliny here; Erasmus perhaps added wines from his own experience. He means that old authors are more rewarding to read than the moderns,
and is not thinking of the rare-book trade.

21 palm-branch] If this refers to a living branch, the source may be Plutarch's
Quaestiones naturales 32 (preserved in Latin only, and first printed by G.
Longolius in 1542); of a beam of palm-tree wood this is said to be true in
Xenophon *Institutio Cyri* 7.5.11; Theophrastus *Historia plantarum* 5.6.1; Pliny
16.223; Plutarch *Moralia* 724E; Gellius 3.6. See also *Adagia* I iii 4.

Like the vine which, though the most distinguished of all trees, yet needs the support of canes or stakes or other trees which bear no fruit, the powerful and the learned need the help of lesser men. (14.13)

As the supporting stake sometimes overwhelms with its leafage the vine that clambers up it, it not seldom happens that men casually brought in to give support undermine and overthrow someone more powerful than they.

As the vine, unless you prune it hard, ranges everywhere and entangles everything in its branches, so an ambitious prince is continually annexing something that belongs to his neighbours, unless he is called to account from time to time. (14.11)

Like Aminean wines, which improve with age, some men are without character or over-harsh in youth, and with time and experience they mature. (14.21)

On the other hand Apian wines and some others are sweet at first, and acquire dryness as the years go by; and some men, like that, grow more hard-hearted as they grow older. (14.24)

The Maronean wine of which Homer speaks can be mixed with twenty times its own volume of water and yet retains its strength; and a wise man, in the same way, is not weakened by any indulgence. (14.53)

Wine is the best thing there is for keeping up one's strength, rightly used, and nothing is more pernicious in excess. Likewise philosophy is life-giving if applied in moderation, and most injurious if you are intoxicated by the study of it and become useless for the ordinary duties of life. (14.58)

As wines without character become vinegar with age, so common talents grow foolish, but great gifts endure until extreme old age. (14.125)

Wine reflects the characteristic aroma, not only of the soil on which it is grown, but even of the trees and shrubs in the vicinity; and in the same way we reproduce not only those from whom we are descended, but those also in whose society we have lived. (14.110)

The substitutes for wine which are made by some people from cereals achieve the strength of wine only to the extent that they intoxicate, but they do not equally restore the vigour of the heart. Similarly, some can achieve what is a fault in poetry, I mean its improprieties; but its expressive force, its grace, its learned skill they cannot reproduce. (14.149)

* * * * *

4 supporting stake] Source not identified. The risk that the stake may itself take root and grow is recognized by Columella 4.12.1.

18 Homer] Maronea, on the coast of Thrace, claimed that its celebrated wine was that which Maron, priest of Apollo, had given to Ulysses, who used it to intoxicate the Cyclops (*Odyssey* 9.196–215).

LB I 617D / ASD I-5 302

The olive takes a long time to come into bearing, but it bears valuable
fruit; the willow quickly makes a tree, and is barren. Precocious talents do
the same. (15.3)

They say that no poisonous creature ever dies of hunger or thirst;
likewise poisonous individuals have their private sources of nourishment   5
and live on their own venom.

Peaches used to fetch a high price, simply because they did not last for
more than two days. We must be quick to seize what quickly passes –
youth, for instance. (15.40)

The fruit of the wild fig never ripens, but it gives birth to worms which   10
fly across to the true fig, pierce the skin of the fruit, and cause the figs to
ripen. In the same way there are people incapable of distinguished work
themselves but somehow able to stimulate others to produce it. (15.79–80)

Just as it is a virtue in water to have no taste, for taste or flavour is a
sign of contamination, so we expect a sense of style in other subjects, but a   15
theologian is given credit precisely if he is inarticulate and has no com-
merce with the Muses. (15.108)

There seems to be some hostility between smell and taste; figs, for
example, a most delicious fruit, have no smell, while quinces have a strong
smell but their taste is very harsh. In the same way you will hardly find   20
obliging manners and generosity and trustworthiness in the same
man. (15.110)

Like the bay-tree, evergreen in every part, the renown of true learning
ages not nor fades. The berries of the bay are bitter, but medicinal; and like
them the precepts of philosophy are not so pleasant and palatable as they   25
are salutary. (15.127)

Wine stored in vessels made from yew-wood is poisonous; likewise,
learning which is life-giving in itself, if it light upon a nasty man, is
rendered noxious by a taint from his character. (16.50)

The common ash is so much dreaded by snakes that they will never   30
enter its shadow, either morning or evening, no matter how long it is, and if
you make a ring of its foliage around a fire and a snake, the creature will take
refuge in the fire rather than in the leafage. Equally there is nothing
common between vice and the pursuit of wisdom, but whoever shelters in
the shade of wisdom will be safe from the poisonous contagion of this   35
life. (16.64)

The lime has pleasant bark and leaves, but no living creature touches
its fruit. In the same way some men's conversation is friendly, agreeable,
and equable, but their remarks bear no fruit. (16.65)

* * * * *

4 They say] No source for this has yet been identified.

Like the box, which is evergreen but apart from that has an unpleasant smell and seeds that all creatures dislike, some men are agreeable to talk to, but in every other respect should be avoided. (16.70–1)

Rhododendron leaves are poisonous to horses, goats, and sheep, but to man they are an antidote against snake-bite. Similarly what bodes destruction to the fool, adversity let us say or education, is turned by the wise man to his own profit. (16.79)

As some trees flourish on mountains, others in valleys, some in dry places, others in wet well-watered ground, so different walks of life suit different men. Some trees grow anywhere; and there are some men for all seasons, who get on well with anybody. (16.97)

Some trees turn their leaves over after midsummer: for instance, elm, lime, olive, white poplar, willow. Likewise the common run of noblemen, the moment the prince changes his style of life, change their looks, their dress, their way of speaking, everything. (16.87)

The service-tree loses its leaves all at once, while with other trees this happens gradually. So some men suddenly cast all their clothes, spend all their money, change their whole way of life, when this ought to be done gradually. (16.92)

The fig-tree has no flowers, but it bears delicious fruit; and men exist who do good without ever making promises. (16.95)

The mulberry breaks into leaf latest of all, and yet bears fruit among the earliest. Likewise those who wait for the right moment to finish a piece of work do so in good time, even if they started late. (16.83)

Some trees have lovely flowers but bear no fruit; and some children show gifts that promise a most fruitful life, but when they grow up they turn to foolish pleasures and belie what everyone hoped. (16.108)

Willow-trees lose their seed before it ripens, whence Homer speaks of 'willows that shed their fruit'; and similarly some precocious minds hurry on to teach or write before they should. (16.110)

The seeds of cypress are so small that some of them are not perceptible to the eye, and yet that great and lofty tree is contained in them. Reason likewise is a small thing and invisible, but can do great things if it comes forward and develops all its powers. (17.72)

If side-shoots are cut off, every part of a tree grows faster, because the nourishment is concentrated into a single stem. Thus too the mind, when relieved of superfluous business, accomplishes more in liberal studies, because all the intellectual force is concentrated on the one object. (17.7)

* * * * *

28 Homer] *Odyssey* 10.510: in the grove of Persephone, goddess of the dead, among whom are so many whose fruit has fallen untimely

LB I 618D / ASD I-5 306

The vine, unless cut back from time to time, grows ragged from its own fertility and dies. Similarly men of promising talents must not work too hard, or they will be worn out with overwork. (17.173)

In the vine whatever growth is removed by pruning is replaced in the form of fruit; and he who cuts back needless anxiety over things of no importance will be all the stronger for the things that really matter. Alternatively the fewer words, the more the weight of meaning. (17.178)

In grafting, the deeper the scion is inserted, the more slowly it comes into bearing, but the longer it retains its vigour. It pays to approach any task so as to secure a reliable and durable result, rather than with an eye to immediate gain. (17.108)

As a tree which of itself is unfertile can yet be taught by grafting to bear fruit, so a cross-grained nature can be transformed by education to give a good account of itself. (17.103, etc.)

A tree of its own nature bears only one kind of fruit, but by grafting it can come to be loaded with fruit of different kinds. Likewise he who follows his natural bent remains the same, while he who is skilfully led on to other things is unlike himself. (17.99)

As owls, which are birds of ill omen, when they complain at night (for complaint is their natural note) grudge human beings their sleep, so a poisonous tongue is ever disseminating something that will disturb the peace of society. (10.34–5)

A field that is fertile, but needs to be tilled at great expense, does not produce much profit for the husbandman; and a man with plenty of means who is also extravagant does not put by much that will benefit his heir. (18.28)

In agriculture it is not enough to be a good husbandman yourself, but it makes a great difference what sort of neighbour you have; and in life it is not enough to be a good man yourself, but it makes a difference whom you associate with. (18.26)

As those who are used to it survive even in a place riddled with fever, so handicaps do less harm to men who are used to them. (18.27)

The healthiness of a place is gauged by the colouring of those who live there, and the sanctity of any office by the lives of those who occupy it. Men whose days are spent in ceremonial, while their lives are disgraceful, show that the ceremonies have little religious value. (18.27)

Nothing pays less well than really careful cultivations; often it is quite useless to take too much trouble over something. (18.36)

* * * * *

18 is unlike himself] 'is like himself' in the Basel edition of 1534 (according to ASD), and hence the *Opera omnia* of 1540; but this destroys the parallel.

Careful husbandmen first inspect their ground and assess it by certain known criteria, before they trust it with their seed; and you should assess a friend before telling him all your secrets. (18.34)

Beans and lupins do not exhaust a field; they fertilize it, where they are grown. Like them a grateful recipient advances the status of his benefactor, and gives back what he has received. (18.120 and 134)

Fenugreek grows the more readily, the worse it is treated. Like that some children turn out worse, the more indulgence you show them, and if neglected and ill-treated make useful citizens. (18.140)

As willow-seed, shed before it ripens, is not only itself barren but when used as a drug causes barrenness in women by preventing conception, so the words of those who teach before they have truly learnt sense not only make them no better in themselves, but corrupt their audience and render it unteachable. (16.110)

A young vine produces more wine, but an old one better wine; young men talk more, old men talk more sense. (16.117)

Among trees, those which bear the heaviest crop grow old all the more quickly; among men, the rarely gifted seldom live long, and [in mortal things] the best is also the most fleeting. (16.118)

Trees have a habit of dying at short notice after an unusually heavy crop of fruit; fortune unusually favourable often indicates that disaster is impending. (16.118)

In India there is a plant with an unusual fragrance which is full of small serpents, the bite of which is instantly fatal. Similarly the courts of [some] princes have their attractions; but they conceal a deadly poison unless you are on your guard. (12.34)

The Indians also have a thorn-bush, the sap of which, if dropped in the eyes, causes blindness in all living creatures. But men are blinded more severely if you put in their eyes a little gold-dust. (12.34)

Just as in trees the parts exposed to the north are more robust than what faces south or west, we are braver and stronger in those fields in which fortune has given us some experience of things going wrong. (16.196)

Cedar-wood and juniper dressed with oil fear neither beetle nor decay. So does the soul once dressed with the elixir of the divine spirit fear no corruption from the world. (16.216–17).

* * * * *

18 in mortal things] Added in the revision of Paris 1516
24 some] Added in the revision of 1516

Trees that do not bear fruit are more robust than those that do. So it is with writing: those who publish nothing are more robust physically than those who wear themselves out with the labours of composition. (16.211)

As oak and some other timbers become harder and more durable if buried in the ground, so men who are long oppressed by bad fortune have a longer flowering-time. (16.218)

Worms do not breed in cypress-wood, which is too bitter, nor yet in box-wood which is too hard. Similarly the plague of flattery avoids severe and sober minds, and likes its victims soft and pliable. (16.221)

Walnut-trees give a loud warning crack before they break, so that one can get out of the way before they come down. In the same way some men do one no hurt without first showing signs of hostility; others hurt one first and protest afterwards. (16.223)

Firwood takes glue so well that the solid wood breaks, rather than part at the glued joint. An image of friendship! After a reconciliation friendship should be all the stronger, and men are more closely united if glued together by mutual good will than if bound by ties of kindred. (16.225)

Ivy strangles trees. So can prosperity, with a winning smile, throttle a man and destroy him. (17.239)

As the ground in some places contains marl, a kind of white paste, which can be used to manure and fertilize it, so does a gifted nature contain within itself materials for self-improvement. (17.42)

Nothing is of less account than animal excrement, and yet it has the highest value for manuring the land. Nothing is so worthless that something cannot be made of it, if you know what to do. (17.50f.)

There is a kind of pulse called cracca, of which pigeons are so fond that, once they have started on it, it is said, they cannot be driven away – like men who have once tasted the honey and the honours of the court, and can never again be induced to leave it. (18.142)

Broomrape is a pest in chickpea and vetches, as darnel is in wheat, the grass-weed they call aegilops in barley, and hatchet-vetch in lentils; and all these destroy the crop by strangling it. Likewise the friendship of some men is more dangerous than their enmity. (18.155)

They say that bath-attendants in Asia and in Greece, when they wish to drive off a crowd of people, throw darnel-seed on their red-hot coals, because it causes giddiness. So when philosophers wish to close their books to the uneducated public, they bring in some mathematical formulae and diagrams, to make a man's head spin so that he throws the book away. (18.156)

'Straight back means crooked furrow' runs the old saying about

ploughmen; and a soldier who is not a godless wretch is a poor sort of
soldier. (18.179)

Like a good husbandman, whose business it is to know the land he
cultivates, the careful tutor must try first of all to learn the character and gifts
of each one of his pupils, for the same treatment does not suit
everyone. (18.163–6)

As a fallow field, though it lies idle every other year, yet makes up for
that idleness in yield, so moderate relaxation for the mind means that when
we return to our studies we are full of energy, and do more in a shorter space
of time. (18.176)

The Nile brings famine to Egypt if it rises either too little, less than
eighteen feet, or too much, more than twenty-seven. In the same way an
equal obstacle to the good life is formed by too much good fortune or too
little, one tormenting a man with poverty and the other tempting him with
luxury away from the path of honour. (18.168)

As heliotrope and lupin follow the sun and, as he moves, they turn
their stems to go with him, so do noblemen at court all turn as the king's
fancy turns. (18.252)

Like some trees which are killed by heavy cropping and luxuriance,
some men are undone when things go too well. (16.118)

A field that gets too much manure is scorched, and if it gets too little it
is cold and hungry. Similarly reading in moderation should refresh the
spirit, for the mind is fed by reading as the field is by manure. (18.194)

Little and often is the rule for manure; and there is more profit in
steady than in greedy reading. (18.194)

As fleabane flowers exactly at midwinter, when everything is withered, so, when things go very badly, bad men rule who are of no account in
peacetime. (18.227)

Change of food, drink, or climate upsets one, even though the change
is to something equal or somewhat better. In the same way it is wiser to bear
with one's original prince or magistrates than to call in new ones, for every
change in government is not free from disturbance. (1.14–15)

* * * * *

1 ploughmen] The ancient ploughman had to bend heavily over his plough-tail
   to keep his furrow on the line and depth it should be; hence this proverb,
   which found a place in 1526 in the *Adagia* (iv v 85). Equally Erasmus regarded
   an upright character as a severe handicap to a military career.
29 Change of food] At this point we turn to an entirely fresh source, the *Problemata* of Aristotle, and the numbers added at the end of each aphorism refer,
   until further notice, to the individual problems in that work.

A man who is very seriously ill can be carried off by an eclipse of the moon or a great storm of wind or a neap tide or some such unimportant change in outside things. So weaker spirits, corrupted by the passions, are upset by the least shock, such as those of stronger character would not notice.

Our bodies are more at risk in spring and autumn from the turning of the year; and similarly all innovation means risk of damage to the commonwealth. (1.27)

As those who have to perform an operation would rather use a bronze knife than a steel one, because the wound then heals more readily, so he who is obliged to administer a reprimand will so choose his language as to convey even at that stage a certain amount of what may silently heal the wound. (1.35)

As chilblains and burns can be treated alike by cold and hot water, so can some faults be dealt with in opposite ways by severity or mildness, by breaking off friendly relations or by increasing generosity. (1.53)

Chilblains are both caused and relieved by cold, and burns are healed by fire; so the language of a reproof from a friend is the best treatment for the pain it has caused. (1.54)

As a scorpion applied to the place it has bitten draws the venom back into itself, so there is nothing so noxious as not to bring with it some remedy for the evil, if only you know how to use it.

Men who drink their wine diluted become intoxicated more rapidly than those who drink it neat. Similarly the mind is more rapidly infected by things which contain an admixture of decency than by obscenity unmixed. From gross obscenity the mind shrinks, while things of the other sort win our confidence by some show of virtue. (3.3)

Men whose sight is affected by wine, or who have some other trouble with their eyes, think they see a thing multiple which they see single. In the same way those who from inexperience do not perceive a writer's true meaning credit him with many different opinions; whence that word 'alternatively,' so much beloved of bad lawyers. (3.10)

As wine makes one man torpid and another man more energetic, one silent and another talkative, according to their habit of body, so the same folly and ignorance of the truth urge some men to pursue money and others to enjoy themselves. (3.16)

* * * * *

1 A man] This is in the style of the *Problemata* (cf *Probl* 1.3); but if it originates from there, Erasmus seems to have added from some other source.
20 As a scorpion] This is from Pliny 29.91, which is used again, with a different moral, in the addenda of *1516* below; see 275:3.

As the sun hardens clay and softens wax, so the same words spoken by
the same person will soften one man until he is ashamed of what he has
done wrong, and rouse another into obstinacy.

Wine heavily diluted makes a man more ready to vomit than either
plain water or unmixed wine; and rascality spiced with sham goodness is
harder to bear than unmixed open wickedness. (3.18)

The stomach is more refreshed and the thirst better quenched by
liquid imbibed slowly than by what is swallowed at one gulp; and requests
are more effectively discouraged by gifts given at intervals and measured
out than by giving everything at once. (3.21)

It is more tiring to swing your arms empty-handed than if you weight
your hand with a stone or a piece of lead; and it is more tedious to expend
effort on things of no account than to cope with difficult business. (5.8)

As walkers on the level grow tired more quickly than those on unlevel
ground, so it is more toilsome to repeat the same or a similar task continually than to be engaged in business of different kinds. (5.10)

As the man who knows not how far he has to go tires all the sooner, so
he will perform his task with less tedium who has learnt the principle of the
business beforehand, and how large it is. (5.25)

Sickness passes to one's neighbours by contagion, health does not
pass like that to the man who is sick. Similarly the society of bad men easily
corrupts the good, but not the other way round. (7.4)

As many people yawn when they see a man yawning, and feel the
need to make water when they see a man doing so, so some are moved to
take up a piece of business not by any definite decision but because they
copy and repeat what they see in others. (7.1)

The scent of perfumes, flowers, and other fragrant things is more
agreeable at a distance than close to; for sometimes we put to our nostrils
something we liked afar off, and it proves offensive. So some things are
pleasant in small doses; but if you examine them more carefully and inspect
them at close quarters, they cease to please. In this class are mythology in
the poets, and gentile history. (12.2 and 9)

As perfumes smell more strongly when they are agitated or ground or
pounded, so does the fame of excellence spread more widely when it is
tested in business or in adversity. (12.5)

Food which smells unpleasant seems to have no smell to those who
have eaten it. The filthy literature of Scotists and sophisters is like that: it
gives great offence to others, who have had a more liberal education, and

* * * * *

1 As the sun] Not Aristotelian; see above 242:14.

makes them feel sick, but to men soaked in that sort of rubbish it gives no offence, and even seems to show neatness and elegance. (13.2)

The panther has a sweet smell, but only for wild animals, which it thereby attracts, and it has no smell for man. Scotus is like that, evil-smelling to enlightened minds, but to those stupid numbskulls more fragrant than any spice. (13.4)

As men who have a goaty smell are more offensive when they wear scent, so the reputation of a scoundrel is a fouler thing if eminent learning makes it more conspicuous and gives it a wider currency on men's lips. (13.9)

Like a diagonal passing from one angle of a figure to another, which divides it in such a way as to leave equal space on either side, a judge ought to incline to neither party. (15.1)

The higher the sun the shorter the shadows it makes, and the nearer it is to the horizon the longer they grow, as at morning and evening. Virtue is like that: the greater and more exalted it is, the less it wishes to be seen and the less show it makes; those who are really worth less do quite the opposite, and make more of a mark by self-advertisement. (15.5)

As there is more pleasure in hearing an old song than a new one, even if it is a better one, so the public derives more enjoyment from the reading-matter it has learnt to like. (19.5)

As in the octave there is such harmony that we seem to hear one and the same note, so do true friends form one mind. Alternatively the toady so closely echoes the remarks of his rich patron that you would think it was one man speaking and not two. (19.14)

Part-singing is more melodious than if everyone sang exactly the same note; and a friend whose agreement with us admits an occasional difference of opinion gives us more pleasure than a toady who never disagrees. (19.16)

As a pair of pots of which one is full and one empty sound the octave when you strike them, so there is close agreement between the generous rich man and a poor man in want. (19.50)

Choice crops need a good gardener to produce them, while onions and garlic and such common things sprout even if you put them on a shelf or hang them up. Likewise what is of real merit can only be achieved by hard work, while bad stuff is found everywhere. (20.28)

It is commonly said that a north wind that gets up in the night never lasts until the third day. In the same way civil commotions which arise, not from deep-seated causes but from something superficial and sudden, are easily quelled, and all is peace in the commonwealth. (26.9)

As the wind normally blows more strongly shortly before it drops, so
with mortals; when they exalt themselves to the highest point, like Pope
Julius, they are then often close to their destruction. (26.25)

The north wind starts rough and ends gentle, while the south is more
gentle to begin with and ends rough. Similarly men who start something
headlong and in a great hurry cool off as they go on; but he who has taken
thought before he starts kindles to his work more and more. (26.39)

As men who wish to see something in sharper focus close one eye, so a
judge will have a clearer perception of what is just if he is not distracted by
any respect for persons. (31.2)

As a short-sighted person sees only things that are close to him, while
an old person sees only things that are further away, so there are people
who suffer from the opposite complaint. One man neglects his friends'
affairs, and attends to nothing except what affects his own interests; others,
on the other hand, neglect their own affairs and are wise only in other
people's. (31.25)

As we can blow either hot or cold by breathing out in different ways,
so the same speech differently delivered will rouse the passions, or fall
flat. (34.7)

As we are more irritated when tickled, and more soothed when rubbed, by another person than by ourselves, so it is more agreeable to be
praised by those who are neither our kin nor our acquaintance. (35.1)

The wisest parents often have the most stupid children, but good
teachers do not often have uneducated pupils, or virtuous tutors vicious
charges. In the one there is an engendering of bodies, in the other of minds.

What oil is to flies, ants, and nearly all other insects, flattery is to
foolish princes. The insects die if touched with oil, and by the flattery and
fawning of their creatures princes are drawn down to their own destruction, and draw the commonwealth down with them.

As sunshine darkens human skin but bleaches linen, so the same
action will bring one man into disgrace and win fame and glory for another.

Sufferers from jaundice find honey bitter, though to all other men it is

* * * * *

2 Pope Julius] Julius II had died on 20 February 1513.

23 The wisest parents] Continuous use of the *Problemata* of Aristotle here seems
to end, and no exact source for this has been identified. It recalls *Adagia* I vi 32
'Heroum filii noxae.'

26 What oil] From Pliny *Naturalis historia* 11.66 and 279; Lucian *Muscae encomium*
4

30 As sunshine] Aristotle *Probl* 38.1 and 11; but he has *elaion* 'oil' where Erasmus
has *linum* 'flax.'

32 Sufferers] Source not yet identified

so sweet; and likewise the precepts of wisdom, which are so pleasant to a
good man, are hateful to those corrupted by evil desires.

[A scorpion, when applied to the bite a second time, draws back into
itself the venom it injected. Not so the tongue of scandal, whose poison is
more deadly.

The sting-ray first inflicts paralysis upon its victim, then devours him.
In the same way tyrants first spread terror among the citizens and paralyze
them; then they despoil and harass them at their own pleasure.

Swallows, for all that they love to share the abodes of men, always
remain untameable, while the parrot imitates the human voice. So some
men are immersed continually in the Scriptures, yet none of this rubs off on
their characters.

If the ink of the cuttle-fish is added to a lamp, and any light which has
not been tampered with is then removed, this makes you think you see
blackamoors standing there, or so Anaxilaus says. Likewise a mind that is
warped by jealousy or hatred detects disgrace in things that are honourable. (32.141)

Leeches applied to the shins do indeed remove the harmful excess of
blood, but once used they leave behind them a longing to use them again,
so that at the same time of the year you are obliged to apply them, however
inconvenient it may be. Some men are like that: they do you a service, but
once you have called them in they operate in such a way that in future, willy
nilly, you are frequently obliged to appeal to them. The same thing happens
to those who, sated with sexual intercourse, try to moderate their appetite;
it always returns. (32.123)

As leeches, once applied to the skin, suck blood to please themselves
and not to suit the man who applied them, so do lay princes, summoned
to their aid by churchmen, stay longer than suits their hosts, and depart
only at their own sweet will. (32.123)

Leeches, when applied to a patient, often leave their heads attached to
him, and thus cause incurable lesions; so that the remedy becomes a
menace, and the man who used them dies – such is said to have been the
death of Messalinus, former consul. In the same way many men seek

* * * * *

3 A scorpion] From here to the end the aphorisms are additions in the revision
   of Paris 1516. The scorpion we have already met at 271:20.
6 sting-ray] Cf 231:28 above.
9 Swallows] 'untameable' is from Pliny 10.128; the parrots from 10.117.
13 cuttle-fish] What follows, except where otherwise indicated, is from Pliny as
   before, and a reference has been added to each aphorism.
15 Anaxilaus] Pythagorean philosopher and naturalist, first century BC
33 Messalinus] Soldier, orator, and one of the custodians of the Sibylline books

LB I 624A / ASD I-5 320

dangerous remedies for moderate ills, and plunge into immediate
peril. (32.123)

As asps kill their quarry by numbness and coma, their venom being
the most incurable of all, so do flatterers inflict inevitable mischief when
they so poison a man's mind that he loses awareness of himself. (29.65)   5

Wasps at a dinner-party sting no one if they are allowed to feed as they
please; but if you drive them off their fury is implacable. Likewise some of
those whose god is their belly, if admitted to your circle of friends and
allowed to follow the dictates of greed and lechery, present themselves as
moderately agreeable friends. If however you fall foul of them and try to   10
drive them off, they will stick at nothing to hurt their benefactor.

In painting the highest praise is won by the deception that consists in
reproducing actual fact; in friendship deception is highly dishonourable,
and yet many men take credit for it nowadays, as though friendship were a
matter of shams and not truth. (35.67)   15

Zeuxis the painter had challenged Parrhasius; and when he had
brought into the market-place a bunch of grapes so brilliantly painted that
the birds were deceived and flocked round the canvas, Parrhasius is said to
have replied with a canvas so skilfully rendered that Zeuxis, full of pride at
his success in deceiving the birds, told him to remove the canvas and let   20
him see the painting. When he found his mistake, he generously yielded
the palm to Parrhasius, on the ground that while he had deceived the birds,
his rival had deceived a fellow-artist. Deceive the deceiver, and you deserve
to win. (35.65)

Ulysses' companions in Homer did not turn to fishing until they had   25
eaten the oxen, and were urged to it by hunger; but men are mad who
pursue the worse when the better is within their grasp.

Persons with larger eyes than average often have weak sight, large
heads can mean small wits, and those whose heart is big in proportion to
their body are more fearful. In the same way we often see less piety and   30
learning in those who more obviously bear their outward semblance. (11.141 and 183)

That famous panel by Protogenes and Apelles, which served to display the skill of two supreme artists in delicacy of line, offers nothing but
dexterity for us to admire, since in other respects it represents nothing   35
worth having. So some men's disputations teach nothing that contributes

* * * * *

6 Wasps] Source not identified
25 Homer] In *Odyssey* 12.327 he says they did not fish until they had finished
   their corn and sweet wine; and when tired of fish they killed and ate, with
   disastrous results, the oxen of the Sun. There is a small slip of memory.

to the good life, and merely display their useless intellectual ingenuity.
(35.81–3)

Famous painters have won renown in different subjects, one repre-
senting the gods with more success, another barbers' shops and cobblers,
one scenes in the theatre and another portraits. So in the other skills, and in
life itself, each man has his peculiar gifts. (35.112–13)

Lepidus the triumvir was once lodged by some local magistrates at an
inn in a wood, and protested next morning, not without threats, that he had
been kept awake by the singing of the birds. They caused a serpent to be
painted on a very long piece of parchment and stretched it round the place;
and this, according to the story, so frightened the birds that they were
silent. Thereafter it was proved that this is the way to restrain them. In the
same way tiresome people who never stop talking when all is safe dare not
open their mouths at the first scent of danger. (35.121)]

Here end the *Parallels* or *Parabolae* of Desiderius Erasmus of Rotterdam,
gathered out of Plutarch's *Moralia*, Seneca, Lucian, Xenophon, Demosthenes, Aristotle, Pliny, and Theophrastus.

Rhetoric
from Cristoforo Giarda *Icones symbolicae* (Milan: Bidellius 1628)
Rhetoric wears a flowered cloak fastened with the jewel of prudence. From her
mouth stream three golden chains (the low, medium, and grand styles of discourse);
speech has power to hold even beasts (lower right). The extended left hand signifies
the gift of words. In her right hand is a caduceus, the token of Mercury who as herald
of the gods is associated with eloquence. As his magic wand once reconciled
opposing serpents (now entwined as figures of concord), so the orator's art
reconciles conflicting arguments. The fiery pot and golden spurs at lower left signify
zeal to guide men's minds and rouse their passions.
Folger Shakespeare Library

COPIA:

FOUNDATIONS OF THE
ABUNDANT STYLE

*De duplici copia verborum ac
rerum commentarii duo*

translated and annotated by
BETTY I. KNOTT

The idea of providing teaching materials to assist schoolboys towards that competence and fluency in the Latin language which was so highly prized at the time was already in Erasmus' mind when he was in Paris in the 1490s. He was working on several topics in Latin grammar and idiom – for example, his epitome of Lorenzo Valla's *Elegantiae linguae latinae* which he made for a schoolmaster (and lent copies of to his friends, though he did not authorize publication until 1531).[1] The first sketch of his ideas on *copia*, the rich oratorical style, and of the means of acquiring it, was in existence at least by 1499, under the title *Brevis de copia praeceptio*.[2] Erasmus did not as yet consider the work ready for the press. The manuscript however came into the possession of Augustin Vincent (Caminade), and the work in this form was later incorporated by him into the *Familiarium colloquiorum formulae* (the ancestor of the *Colloquia*), a volume published without Erasmus' wish or knowledge in 1518.[3]

Meanwhile Erasmus continued to work at the subject of *copia*. He had the manuscript with him during his stay in Italy (1506–9), and by 1508 had some kind of version which, on his return north, was left behind at Ferrara with Richard Pace and apparently never recovered.[4] After he left Italy, he made his third visit to England, and in 1511 took up residence at the University of Cambridge. News reached him that an unauthorized version of his *De copia* based on the manuscript left behind in Italy might appear. About the same time Dean Colet, to whom he was under considerable obligation, asked him to provide some educational work for his new foundation, St Paul's School in London. Erasmus saw in *De copia* something eminently suited to this purpose, and hastily produced a version dedicated to Colet[5] and his school, hoping at the same time to discredit any unofficial version, which would inevitably be both faulty and incomplete. This first official edition, *De duplici copia rerum ac verborum*[6] *commentarii duo*, was published in Paris, in July 1512, by Josse Bade, who had earlier issued other works by Erasmus. In addition to *De copia* the volume contained *De ratione studii*, *Concio de puero Iesu* (a sermon for St Paul's School), and some poems.

The 1512 edition presents a version of *De copia* considerably shorter than the form which the work eventually assumed, as Erasmus, in accordance with

* * * * *

1 See Epp 20:99–103; 23:103–16. On the history of Erasmus' paraphrase or epitome of the *Elegantiae* see ASD I-4 191–205.
2 On *Brevis de copia praeceptio*, introduction to Ep 260; and see introduction to *Antibarbari* CWE 23 6.
3 See Thompson *Colloquies* xxii–iv.
4 Epp 30:17n and 244:7n. James D. Tracy 'On the Composition Dates of Seven of Erasmus' Writings' *Bibliothèque d'humanisme et renaissance* 31 (1969) 360–1 surmises that Erasmus probably did recover the manuscript.
5 The dedicatory letter is printed below.
6 So the title page, but thereafter the order is *verborum ac rerum*.

his usual practice, continued to emend and expand the text throughout his life, though the basic concept and shape of the treatise remained unaltered. After 1512 the principal editions published with Erasmus' authority, each revised and enlarged, appeared in December 1514 (Strasbourg: Schürer, in a volume which included the *Parabolae*), May 1526 (Basel: Froben), and August 1534 (Basel: Froben and Episcopius). A Froben edition of April 1517 had a few slight changes.

The edition published in December 1514 was advertised as one 'which the author himself has carefully revised and corrected, and expanded in numerous places.' Many of the changes made at this stage were minor ones – small omissions and a fair number of brief expansions of the text by a word or two, or at most a line or two. But there were also some more substantial expansions: in book I chapter 52 (LB I 40B), and chapters 76 and 77 (LB I 49F, 50A–B), and, most important, in book II, tenth method of expansion: propositions (LB I 86A–C, 86F, 87B–D), where there is a good deal of additional material.

The most striking feature of this edition is the transfer of whole sections to different positions in the work: the paragraphs giving examples for *plus et plusquam, ad summum, ut minimum* appear in *1512* at the end of chapter 33 *Experientiae* (wrongly numbered 32); they are now moved to chapter 96 (LB I 54D–F). The chapters originally numbered 40–2 (the text from *Dignus et indignus* to the end of *Distribuendi*) become chapters 61–3 (LB I 42D–4E); the final chapters of *1512*, 150–3, are moved to become chapters 54–7 of *1514* (LB I 40F–1D). All this of course entailed considerable renumbering of chapters (though the 1512 edition is not numbered correctly even as it stands because of the accidental attribution to adjacent chapters of the number ix, and the consequent misnumbering of subsequent chapters up to 34). The chapters in book I from 34 onwards each consist (apart from some explanatory material) of a list of idioms and constructions which illustrate the variety of ways in which one basic idea may be expressed in Latin. As these lists do not seem to be arranged according to any principle, apart from some pairs of chapters, the order could be changed without altering the structure of the book in any significant way. The first section moved (chapters 40–2) is probably more satisfactory in its new position, but it is difficult to see the reason for the other changes. Possibly the haste with which the first edition was prepared meant that Erasmus' original intention was not carried out. There are no such transfers in subsequent editions.

The 1526 edition (Basel: Froben), 'freshly revised and enlarged by the author,' shows a detailed revision of the text with dozens of misprints and errors corrected, and small alterations and improvements made to the Latin. Most of the expansions of the text were again of a minor nature – a word or two put in for clarification, the author's name added to an illustrative quotation, the insertion of further illustrative examples. Again there are a few minor omissions. Only in chapter 77 (LB I 50B–C) does an insertion run for more than a very few lines. The most significant development is the addition to book I of chapters 155–71 (LB I 65B–8B), containing further lists of Latin idioms. Little was done to book II at this stage.

The final authorized edition to appear during Erasmus' lifetime (Basel: Froben 1534), 'greatly enlarged with additional material and new examples,' shows the usual type of minor correction and alteration, but these are overshadowed by the very considerable expansion of the text, as promised on the title page. There are over two hundred places where Erasmus has inserted something, ranging from a single word to long sections of additional material. Many of the brief insertions occur where he obviously felt he had been insufficiently explicit; they serve to clarify possible ambiguities in the text or provide additional explanation. The single-word insertions often supply the name of the Latin author from whom an illustrative grammatical or stylistic example had already been drawn, and most of the numerous additional examples now inserted are given with the name of the source. In the earlier editions Erasmus frequently quoted examples without assigning them to an author. He was beginning to change his practice in *1526*, and by *1534* he clearly felt it was more satisfactory to give named examples as far as possible.

In this revision many of book I's chapters[7] were expanded, most notably chapter 11 (*Prima variandi ratio per synonymiam*), which, from being in several of its sections brief and sparingly illustrated, was now made into a substantial collection of examples. Further lists of phrases were added at the end of the book as chapters 172–206.

For the first time book II received considerable additions, the most noteworthy being the examples drawn from Greek tragedy in the section on 'description of things' (LB I 78C–D); towards the end of the work an expansion of the section on 'comparisons in epideictic oratory' (LB I 96B–C); a considerable enlargement of the chapter on 'expanding the formal divisions of a speech' by remarks on dialogue (LB I 106C–D); and a long insertion on the emotions (LB I 108D–9C). The peroration was also added at this stage.

On its first publication the work was received with great acclaim, not only in England but on the Continent, and coming soon after the phenomenal success of the *Adagiorum chiliades*[8] of 1508, it established Erasmus as a leading humanist scholar and educationalist. Already in 1516 John Watson writes to Erasmus reporting his experiences in Italy: 'You are famous everywhere in Italy, especially among the leading scholars. It is incredible with what en-

* * * * *

7 Most notably 10, 11, 12, 13, 19, 24, 34, 35, 37, 42, 45, 56, 60, 64, 65, 71, 72, 75, 96, 122, 130, 149, 150, 152, 169; for details see notes to these chapters.
8 See Phillips '*Adages*' 3–95.

thusiasm they welcome everywhere your *Copia* and the *Moria* too as they would the highest wisdom.'[9] By 1520 his reputation in England was such that John Dorne, bookseller in Oxford, sold in that year quite a substantial number of Erasmus' educational works, including at least seventeen copies of *De copia*, alongside standard classical authors such as Cicero and Terence.[10]

De copia was before long adopted as a textbook of rhetoric in schools and universities throughout northern Europe; so widespread did its use become that it was worth pirating, summarizing, excerpting, turning into a question-and-answer manual, and making the subject of commentaries. Editions, both authorized and unauthorized, of the work in its various forms poured from the presses of Germany, the Netherlands, and Paris.[11] The very frequency of these reprints testifies to the significance of the work and to its influence during the first three-quarters of the sixteenth century in both arousing and ministering to a particular stylistic ideal, which was manifested not only in Latin but in the vernacular literature of the time. Towards the end of that century there was a change of taste. In England at any rate men began to suspect the grand style as meretricious and deceptive, and looked about for a plainer Latin model. Rather surprisingly some chose Tacitus, though this choice was in part a deliberate challenge to the prevailing cult of Ciceronianism and the rich or abundant style.[12]

The translation that follows is made from the fullest version of the text as it appears in Erasmus' edition of 1534. This text is, with some slight variations, also that of LB I. Attention is called in the notes to the main differences in the authorized, enlarged editions. Full textual apparatus is expected in the forthcoming ASD edition. Some spellings have been changed to conform with classical usage.

A reader who checks the sources of Erasmus' Greek and Latin quotations will find in some of them minor disagreements with passages in *De copia*. Occasionally Erasmus paraphrases instead of quoting. When quoting he sometimes depends on memory; and his memory, though prodigious, was not infallible. Or he may be quoting from a text inferior to that used in established modern editions. If differences between his texts and the readings of modern editions are important, the notes will call attention to this fact.

B I K

* * * * *

9 Ep 450:17–19
10 On Dorne and on the use of *De copia* in schools see introduction to CWE 23 lvi, lviii–lxi, lxiii–lxiv.
11 For a checklist see Rix. It was printed infrequently in southern Europe, but see Marcella and Paul Grendler 'The Survival of Erasmus in Italy' *Erasmus in English* 8 (1976) 17.
12 See P. Burke 'Tacitism' in *Tacitus* ed T.A. Dorey (London 1969) 149–71.

FROM DESIDERIUS ERASMUS OF ROTTERDAM TO JOHN COLET,
DEAN OF ST PAUL'S IN LONDON, GREETINGS

I for one am bound to pay warm tribute, dear Colet, to the remarkable and
truly Christian goodness that leads you continually to devote all your efforts
and all your life's endeavours, not to serving your own advantage, but to   5
benefitting your country and your fellow-citizens as far as you possibly can.
Equally do I admire the wisdom you show in having chosen two particular
fields for the greatest possible achievement of this aim. First, you observed
that the richest rewards of charity lie in bringing Christ into the hearts of
one's countrymen by means of continual preaching and by holy instruc-   10
tion. Now you have already been engaged in this for a great many years, I
will not say with great glory, for glory is a commodity you so little regard as
even to refuse it, but at least with great fruitfulness; and it is on this account
that your own Paul, for all his pronounced modesty in other respects,
occasionally turns boastful and vaunts himself with a kind of sanctified   15
insolence. Second, and it was next in importance in your opinion, you
founded a school that far excels the rest in beauty and splendour, so that the
youth of England, under carefully chosen and highly reputed teachers,
might there absorb Christian principles together with an excellent literary
education from their earliest years. For you are profoundly aware both that   20
the hope of the country lies in its youth – the crop in the blade, as it were –
and also how important it is for one's whole life that one should be initiated
into excellence from the very cradle onwards.

Besides, no one could help loving your generous high-mindedness
and, so to call it, your holy arrogance in insisting that both of these services   25
to your country must be unpaid, and your motives above reproach; so much
so that the laborious preaching you undertook for so many years has not
enriched you by a single penny. For though you sowed unto them spiritual
things, you have never reaped any man's carnal things, and you have
resolved to take upon yourself the entire expenses of the school, which were   30
clearly vast enough to appal an oriental potentate. And whereas most
people welcome a partner in this, almost more than in any other kind of
enterprise, you elected to lavish your patrimony, your entire fortune, even
your household possessions, upon it rather than admit anyone on earth to

* * * * *

1 Erasmus ... Colet] This letter dedicating the first version of *De copia* to Colet is
   Ep 260. On Colet see Ep 106 introduction.
14 your own Paul] Cf Ep 181:17n.
23 the very cradle] *Adagia* I vii 53
28 single penny] *Adagia* I viii 9
28 though you sowed ... carnal things] Cf 1 Cor 9:11.

share the honour with you. This means, surely, that you assume the role of a   35
father, indeed more than a father, towards all your fellow-citizens' children
and indeed all your fellow-citizens. You rob yourself to enrich them, strip
yourself in order to equip them, wear yourself out with hard work in order
that your offspring may prosper in the Lord. In short, you devote your
entire energies to winning them for Christ.   40

One would have to be brimfull of ill will not to give enthusiastic
support to efforts such as yours, wicked indeed to cry out against them, and
an enemy of England not to do what one could to lend assistance. For my
part, since I am well aware how much I am indebted both to the English
nation at large and also to you personally, I thought that it would be   45
appropriate for me to make a small literary contribution to the equipment of
your school. So I have chosen to dedicate to the new school these two new
commentaries *De copia*, inasmuch as the work in question is suitable for
boys to read and also, unless I am mistaken, not unlikely to prove helpful to
them, though I leave it to others to judge how well-informed this work of   50
mine is, or how serviceable it will be. What I can really claim is that I have
been the first to envisage the subject and give an account of it. For anyone
may see how different from my purpose was that of the ancient Greek
writer, Julius Pollux, when he classified under topics the names of different
things and made up neat piles, so to speak, of a number of synonyms and   55
related terms. Nor am I disposed to mention authors like Isidore or Marius
or Philiscus, who are at so many removes from *copia* that they are unable to
express their thoughts in good Latin even once. As for the little book
ascribed to Cicero (but I am rather of the opinion that it is a patchwork
collected from the works of Cicero by some devoted follower), it surely   60
contains nothing more than a hurried compilation, covering but few expressions.

My own endeavour has been to point to certain fixed types of *copia* as
the primary sources, the method being to progress by stages from the
general to the particular. Yet I confess with regret that the present work has   65
not received the careful revision it should have had. It is some time since I

* * * * *

54 Julius Pollux] A grammarian of the second century AD whose *Onomasticon*, a
   classified collection of the Greek names for things, had been published by
   Aldus in 1502
56 Isidore] Bishop of Seville, AD 600, compiled, besides his great encyclopaedia
   the *Etymologiae*, a short work called *Synonyma*.
56 Marius] Marius Victorinus was a fourth-century grammarian.
57 Philiscus] Stefano Fieschi of Soncino (fl 1453) was a grammarian whose
   Synonyma was often published in the fifteenth century.
58 little book] The *Synonyma*, attributed to Cicero

Colet's statutes for St Paul's School

ABOVE Colet notes that in June 1518 he presented this copy of the statutes to William Lily, the first high master: 'hunc libellum ego Ioannes Colet tradidi manibus magistrj lilij xviij° die Iunij anno Christi Mcccccxviij vt eum in scola seruet et obseruet' (contractions expanded).

OPPOSITE Prologue, with Colet's signature above. For complete text of the statutes see Lupton, *Life of Dean Colet*, appendix A.

Mercers' Hall, London. Reproduced by kind permission of the Mercers' Company

Prologus

John Colett the sonne of henry Colett Dean
of paulis desyryng nothing more thanne
Educacion and bryngyng vpp Chyldren in
good Maners and litterature in the yere of our
Lorde a ml fyve hundreth and twelff byldeд a
skole in the Esteende of paulis churcħ for Clm
to be taught fre in the same And ordeyned
ther a Maister and a Surmaister and a Chape
lyn with sufficient and perpetuall stipendis
ever to endure And for patrones and defenders
gouernours and Rulers of that same skole the
most honest and faithfull felowshipp of the
mercers of london And for bicause nothing
can contynu long and endure in good ordre
wt oute lawes and statut{es} J the saide John
haue expressid and shewid my mynde what
J wolde shulde be truly and diligently
observid and kept of the Maister and
Surmaister and Chapelyn and of the mercers
gouernours of the skole that in this boke
may apperere to what intent J founde this
skole

unsystematically amassed the raw material for my future work, seeing that I
should require a great deal of time to polish it and must read through a great
many authors. Accordingly I was not particularly anxious to publish it; but
when I discovered that certain persons were laying traps to catch these   70
commentaries and had all but managed to publish them in a thoroughly bad
text, I was obliged to give them such revision as I could, and get them out, as
the lesser evil of the two. Farewell, my dear Colet.
     London, 29 April 1512

ERASMUS OF ROTTERDAM TO MATTHIAS SCHÜRER OF SÉLESTAT
A good proportion of those who print books, Matthias Schürer, either from
ignorance and lack of judgment undertake the worst authors by mistake for
the best, or from greed of gain reckon the best book to be the book from
which they expect the most profit. And so we see the same thing happen in   5
the art of printing that is so familiar in other walks of life, that an invention
designed to be the greatest blessing to learning and education tends
through the errors of those who misuse it to become a serious threat. Now
in this matter you seem to me to deserve credit on two separate grounds:
first, because as an uncommonly well-instructed man and a man of keen   10
discernment you choose works which will contribute to the genuine advancement of knowledge and, second, because you have a natural love of
good literature and are happy to consider these studies of ours and not your
own coffers. Your one purpose is to publish the best books very accurately
printed.   15
     And so I have sent you my *Copia*, which I have most carefully revised
and purged of errors, that a book conceived in England long ago and
published after a fashion in Paris, but now entirely renewed and polished
as though it had cast its slough, may come before the public once again
under happier auspices in your famous city of Strasbourg. Provided you   20
think it not unworthy of your press, this in itself will commend it to lovers
of good letters, when they see it issue from the house of Schürer; for there is
now a general conviction that nothing comes from that address that is not a
finished product of the author's brain, as correct as your expert hand can
make it. I have added a book of *Parallels* hitherto unpublished, which   25
comes to you, as they say, fire-new from the mint.

          * * * * *

     71 all but managed to publish them] See Ep 244:7.
      1 Erasmus ... Schürer] Preface (Ep 311) to the revised edition of *De copia* issued
         by Schürer in December 1514. Schürer, a native of Sélestat, had been printing
         in Strasbourg since 1508.
     25 book of *Parallels*] The *Parabolae*, translated in CWE 23

The works of Rodolphus Agricola, a man of more than human stature, we await with impatience; for whenever I read anything he wrote, I feel fresh admiration and affection for that inspired and soaring mind. Farewell.   30

Basel, 15 October 1514

* * * * *

27 Agricola] The Frisian humanist, highly praised by Erasmus here and elsewhere; see Ep 23:58n.

Index to the commentaries *De copia*: chapters and headings*

BOOK I

ABUNDANCE OF EXPRESSION

*Index] In the first authorized edition (Paris 1512) this index, actually a table of contents, precedes the text; in some later editions it is printed at the end.

End of Book I

In the second book headings do not indicate chapters.

BOOK II
ABUNDANCE OF SUBJECT-MATTER

The End

1 / *Copia*: **Dangers inherent in its pursuit** 5

The speech of man is a magnificent and impressive thing when it surges
along like a golden river, with thoughts and words pouring out in rich
abundance. Yet the pursuit of speech like this involves considerable risk.
As the proverb says, 'Not every man has the means to visit the city of 10
Corinth.' We find that a good many mortal men who make great efforts to
achieve this godlike power of speech fall instead into mere glibness, which
is both silly and offensive. They pile up a meaningless heap of words and
expressions without any discrimination, and thus obscure the subject they
are talking about, as well as belabouring the ears of their unfortunate 15
audience. In fact, quite a few persons of no real education or understanding
have, heaven help us, undertaken to give instruction in this very subject,
and these, while professing a mastery of *copia*, have merely revealed their
own total lack of it.

Such considerations have induced me to put forward some ideas on 20
copia, the abundant style, myself, treating its two aspects of content and
expression, and giving some examples and patterns. Some of my material I
have extracted from works dealing specifically with rhetorical theory. I have
also drawn on my own now considerable experience of the art of speaking
and writing, and on what I have observed in the course of wide reading 25
over a considerable range of authors. It is not my intention to write a book
dealing exhaustively with the whole subject, but rather a short treatise in
which I hope merely to open up the way for teachers and students and
provide the raw material for future work. One of my reasons is that I have
undertaken this task solely out of a desire to be helpful, so I shall be quite 30
content for another to reap the glory, so long as I am ultimately responsible

* * * * *

In the notes a simple reference indicates that Erasmus is quoting an example
in the exact words of the original or with slight divergence; 'cf' indicates a
wider divergence from the original; 'see' means that Erasmus is either using
the subject-matter of the passage identified, or has invented a grammatical
example with the quoted example in mind.

10 proverb] Horace *Epistles* 1.17.36, a favourite line of Erasmus', quoted again in
chaps 50, 154; see *Adagia* I iv i. The proverb refers to the exorbitant price
charged by the famous Corinthian courtesan Lais, who would receive no one,
however distinguished, if he could not pay.

LB I 3A

Aleandri και των φιλ

Title page of an Aldine Cicero (Venice: March 1514)
'The great father of all eloquence,' as Erasmus (echoing Petrarch) calls Cicero, was venerated in the Renaissance for his treatises on rhetoric as well as his orations and philosophical writings.
The implied claim of papal privilege is intended to deter rival printers.
The name at the top of the page may be that of Girolamo Aleandro, whom Erasmus knew in Venice in 1508. Long afterwards, during the Lutheran controversies, they became enemies.
Folger Shakespeare Library

for some benefit reaching the students. Also I am committed to more serious studies which prevent me from expending a great deal of labour on topics which, in spite of their considerable contribution to serious subjects, themselves seem unimportant.

2 / *Copia*: Its invention and practice

Now in case anyone should feel inclined to despise it as some newfangled discovery recently brought into the world within the four walls of my own study, I would have him know that this whole idea of being able to express one's meaning in a variety of ways is in a number of places touched on by that learned and thorough writer Quintilian; further, that a number of famous sophists blazed a trail, showing how to compress and abridge what was being said, and this they could not have done without at the same time demonstrating how to expand it. If their books were extant, or if Quintilian had been prepared to set out his recommendations in full, there would not have been such need of these modest injunctions of mine.

The whole business is further recommended by the fact that men who were the intellectual leaders of their day were by no means averse from constant practice in it. We have a number of marvellous passages where Virgil tried his skill: descriptions of a mirror, a frozen river, a rainbow, a sunrise, the four seasons, the constellations. There is further evidence in Apuleius' treatment of Aesop's fable about the fox and the crow: first he skims over it briefly with a wonderful economy of words, and then he sets it out expansively and in great detail, thus exercising and displaying his talents. But after all, who could possibly regret an enthusiasm for this subject after observing that Cicero, the great father of all eloquence, was so dedicated to this kind of exercise that he used to vie with his friend, the actor Roscius, to see whether Roscius could express the same material more

* * * * *

13 Quintilian] In *Institutio oratoria*, where the importance of *varietas* in every aspect of speaking is mentioned in passing in many places; see 302:4n.

14 sophists] Itinerant teachers who travelled from city to city in Greece in the fifth century BC, giving instruction (for a fee) which purported to enable students to get on in life; the systems of many of them included instruction in the art of speaking. A list is given in Quintilian 3.1.8ff.

22 Virgil] For such descriptions see *Aeneid* 4.700–2, 8.22ff; *Georgics* 1.231ff, 1.441ff, 2.514ff, 3.354–62.

24 Apuleius'] See *Florida* 23 (*De deo Socratis* prologue).

28 great father of all eloquence] Cf Petrarch *Ad familiares* 24.4: *o Romani eloquii summe parens.*

30 Roscius] See Macrobius *Saturnalia* 3.14.12; *Adagia* IV vii 69.

LB I 3C

often using different gestures, or Cicero himself applying the resources of
eloquence and using different language?

3 / *Copia*: Delight taken by ancient authors in demonstrating it   5

Moreover these same writers have quite often taken delight in demonstrating their powers of expression, not only in practice pieces, but in serious
works as well, first compressing the subject to such an extent that you can
subtract nothing, and then enriching and expanding it so that nothing can   10
be added. According to Quintilian, Homer is equally admirable for fullness
and for compression. Although it is not our intention to treat examples in
detail at this point, we will none the less give one or two examples, using
Virgil only. What could be more concisely expressed than his line: 'the
plains where Troy once stood'? As Macrobius says, in a very few words he   15
has here consumed and swallowed up the city without even allowing the
ruins to remain. Now listen to the fullness of expression in this passage:

> Come is the final day, fate's inevitable doom
> Upon Dardanus' city; we Trojans are no more;   20
> Gone is Ilium, gone the mighty fame of Teucer's sons.
> Jove is become our foe and has bestowed
> All that was ours on Argos.
> Greeks now triumph in all the blazing city.
> O my country, O Ilium the dwelling place of gods!   25
> O ramparts of Dardanus' race with all your fame in war!
> Who can unfold in words that murderous night?
> Can any weep the tears those toils deserve?

What fountain, what torrent, what sea so swelled with waters as he with   30
words? But some may think that this example should rather be listed under
wealth of material. Again he revels in verbal luxuriance in the following
lines: 'Lives he still and breathes the air of heaven? / Rests he not yet among
the cruel shades?'

* * * * *

11   be added] *Adagia* IV viii 4
11   Quintilian] See 10.1.46.
15   once stood] Virgil *Aeneid* 3.11
15   Macrobius] *Saturnalia* 5.1.8
17   in this passage] *Aeneid* 2.324ff, 241–2, 361–2
34   cruel shades] As in the previous example, Erasmus has conflated passages:
     here *Aeneid* 1.546–7 and 3.339.

LB I 4B

Ovid makes even more of a feature of this sort of thing; consequently he has been taxed with not knowing when to stop when elaborating an idea; but this criticism came from Seneca, and his style is totally condemned by Quintilian, Suetonius, and Aulus Gellius.

5

4 / *Copia*: **Carried too far by some writers**

It does not worry me that certain writers have been blamed for excessive or misjudged fullness of diction. Quintilian censures Stesichorus for over-abundant and extravagant expression, while at the same time admitting that it is a fault that cannot be absolutely avoided. Aeschylus is assailed in Old Comedy for saying the same thing twice: ἥκω καὶ κατέρχομαι [back I've come and here I am]. There are times when Seneca can hardly put up with Virgil chanting the same sentiment two or three times. So as not to waste time going through a long catalogue, there have even been people who decried Marcus Tullius himself as favouring the florid Asian style and indulging in excessive verbosity. But, as I said, this does not concern me, since I am not prescribing how one ought to write or speak, but merely indicating what is useful for practice, and everybody knows that in practising everything must be exaggerated. Besides, I am giving instructions for

10

15

20

* * * * *

3 Seneca] *Controversiae* 9.5.17. *nescit quod bene cessit relinquere* 'he cannot leave well alone.' This is the Elder Seneca, who wrote on rhetoric, orators, and various literary figures. His more famous son, the Younger Seneca, wrote mainly on philosophy. Erasmus believed the *Controversiae* to be the work of the Younger Seneca. They had been attributed to the father by Rafaelle Maffei of Volterra in *Commentarii rerum urbanarum, Anthropologia*, book XIX, published in Rome in 1506. In conjunction with other scholars Erasmus produced editions of the Younger Seneca's works in 1515 and 1529. In the preface to the 1529 edition (Allen Ep 2091) he gives an extended treatment of Seneca's character and style, but does not there question his authorship of the rhetorical works, though he has doubts about the tragedies.

4 Quintilian] 10.1.125ff

4 Suetonius] See *Caligula* 53; Suetonius is a favourite author whom Erasmus quotes frequently in *De copia*; he published an edition of the *Lives of the Caesars* in 1518.

4 Aulus Gellius] See *Noctes Atticae* 12.2.1.

10 Quintilian] See 10.1.62.

13 Old Comedy] See Aulus Gellius 13.25.7, quoting Aristophanes *Frogs* 1154ff.

14 Seneca] The Elder Seneca (line 3n), *Suasoriae* 2.20, quotes Messala's criticism of Virgil for a line he considered repetitious and otiose. Other criticisms of Virgil by the Younger Seneca are recorded by Aulus Gellius 12.2.10.

16 people who decried] See Quintilian 12.10.12.

the young in whom Quintilian was quite content to see an over-exuberant
style, because the excessive growth can easily be cut back by criticism and
the passing years will wear down other excrescences, while it is quite
impossible to do anything to improve a thin and poverty-stricken style.

5 / Compressed and abundant styles available to the same speaker

There may well be people who admire Homer's Menelaus οὐ πολύμυθος [a
man of few words], and detest Odysseus 'rushing like a river swollen with
winter snows,' and there may well be those who are mightily pleased by
that famous Laconic brevity; yet even these have no right to cry out against
this work of mine, as they too will discover it to be not without profit, for the
reason that the compressed style and the abundant style depend on the
same basic principles. Socrates in Plato's dialogue acutely deduces that the
same man is capable of either lying convincingly or of telling the truth; in
the same way the craftsman in words who will be best at narrowing down
his speech and compressing it will be the one who is skilled in expanding
and enriching it with ornament of every kind. To take compression of
language first, who will speak more succinctly than the man who can
readily and without hesitation pick out from a huge army of words, from
the whole range of figures of speech, the feature that contributes most
effectively to brevity? And as for compression of content, who will show the
greatest mastery in setting out his subject in the fewest possible words if
not the man who has carefully worked out what are the salient points of his
case, the pillars so to speak on which it rests, distinguishing them from the
subsidiary points and things brought in merely for embellishment? No one
in fact will see more swiftly and surely what can be omitted without
disadvantage than the man who can see where and how to make additions.

6 / The wrong way to practise either style

If it is a matter of chance which style we happen to use, we may suffer the
same fate as some fanatics for the Laconic style, who say only a few words,

* * * * *

1 Quintilian] See 2.4.3–4.
9 Menelaus] Homer *Iliad* 3.214
10 Odysseus] Homer *Iliad* 3.222
12 Laconic brevity] *Laconismus*; see Cicero *Ad familiares* 11.25.2; *Adagia* II i 92.
15 Plato's dialogue] *Hippias minor* 367E–8A

LB I 5B

yet those few words are mostly, if not entirely, superfluous. On the other hand, we find that unskilled practitioners of the full style chatter on without restraint, and yet say far too little, omitting a good many of the things that need to be said. The purpose of these instructions is to enable you so to include the essential in the fewest possible words that nothing is lacking, or so to enlarge and enrich your expression of it that even so nothing is redundant; and to give you the choice, once you understand the principles, of emulating the Laconic style if you so fancy, or of imitating the exuberance of Asianism, or of expressing yourself in the intermediate style of Rhodes.

7 / *Copia* is twofold

The abundant style quite obviously has two aspects. Quintilian, for example, among other virtues which he attributes to Pindar, especially admires his magnificently rich style, manifested both in subject-matter and expression. Richness of expression involves synonyms, heterosis or enallage, metaphor, variation in word form, equivalence, and other similar methods of diversifying diction. Richness of subject-matter involves the assembling, explaining, and amplifying of arguments by the use of examples, comparisons, similarities, dissimilarities, opposites, and other like procedures which I shall treat in detail in the appropriate place. It might be thought that these two aspects are so interconnected in reality that one cannot easily separate one from the other, and that they interact so closely that any distinction between them belongs to theory rather than practice. Even so, I intend to separate them as a teaching procedure, doing it in such a way that I lay myself open to the charge neither of drawing hair-splitting distinctions, nor of being careless about details.

8 / Advantages of studying this subject

To encourage students to embark on this study with more enthusiasm I

* * * * *

9 style of Rhodes] The three styles of oratory discussed in Cicero's time were Attic (plain and simple), Asiatic (ornate and exuberant), and Rhodian (intermediate); see Cicero *Brutus* 51; and Quintilian 12.10.18 where the Rhodian style is described as *velut medium ... atque ex utroque mixtum*. Cicero received his main oratorical training from Molon of Rhodes.

14 Quintilian] See 10.1.61.

22 appropriate place] Erasmus deals with the first group in book I chaps 11–32, the second group in book II.

LB I 5E

shall briefly set out the advantages it confers. First of all, exercise in expressing oneself in different ways will be of considerable importance in general for the acquisition of style. In particular however it will help in avoiding ταυτολογία, that is, the repetition of a word or phrase, an ugly and offensive fault. It often happens that we have to say the same thing several times. If in these circumstances we find ourselves destitute of verbal riches and hesitate, or keep singing out the same old phrase like a cuckoo, and are unable to clothe our thought in other colours or other forms, we shall look ridiculous when we show ourselves to be so tongue-tied, and we shall also bore our wretched audience to death. Worse than ταυτολογία is ὁμοιολογία [identical repetition], which, as Quintilian says, has no variety to relieve the tedium and is all of one monotonous colour. Who has got ears patient enough to put up even for a short time with a speech totally monotonous? Variety is so powerful in every sphere that there is absolutely nothing, however brilliant, which is not dimmed if not commended by variety. Nature above all delights in variety; in all this huge concourse of things, she has left nothing anywhere unpainted by her wonderful technique of variety. Just as the eyes fasten themselves on some new spectacle, so the mind is always looking round for some fresh object of interest. If it is offered a monotonous succession of similarities, it very soon wearies and turns its attention elsewhere, and so everything gained by the speech is lost all at once. This disaster can easily be avoided by someone who has it at his fingertips to turn one idea into more shapes than Proteus himself is supposed to have turned into. Also this form of exercise will make no insignificant contribution to the ability to speak or write extempore, and will prevent us from standing there stammering and dumbfounded, or from disgracing ourselves by drying up in the middle. Nor will it be difficult to divert a speech, even when we have embarked upon it rather hastily, into the course we desire when we have so many expressions lined up ready for action. We shall also find it of great assistance in commenting on authors, translating books from foreign languages, and writing verse. Otherwise, if we are not instructed in these techniques, we shall often be found unintelligible, harsh, or even totally unable to express ourselves.

* * * * *

4 ταυτολογία] For this section see Quintilian 8.3.50–2.
11 ὁμοιολογία] Modern texts of Quintilian read ὁμοείδεια.
23 Proteus] A favourite figure of Erasmus; *Adagia* II ii 74; see 388:15n.

9 / Exercises to develop the powers of expression

It remains for me now to give some brief advice on the exercises by which
this faculty may be developed. Once we have carefully committed the
theory to memory, we should frequently take a group of sentences and
deliberately set out to express each of them in as many versions as possible,
as Quintilian advises, using the analogy of a piece of wax which can be
moulded into one shape after another. This exercise will be more profitable
if a group of students competes together orally or in writing on a common
theme; they will all be helped individually by the suggestions made by
other members of the group, and each of them will have his imagination
stimulated by being given a starting-point. Second, we shall treat a connected line of thought in a number of ways. Here it will be best to copy the
expertise of the famous Milo of Croton and develop our powers gradually,
first of all rendering it twice, then three times, and eventually treating it
over and over again, so as to attain such facility in the end that we can vary it
in two or three hundred ways with no trouble at all. In addition we shall add
greatly to our linguistic resources if we translate authors from the Greek, as
that language is particularly rich in subject-matter and vocabulary. It will
also prove quite useful on occasion to compete with these Greek authors by
paraphrasing what they have written. It will be of enormous value to take
apart the fabric of poetry and reweave it in prose, and, vice versa, to bind
the freer language of prose under the rules of metre, and also to pour the
same subject-matter from one form of poetic container into another. It will
also be very helpful to emulate a passage from some author where the
spring of eloquence seems to bubble up particularly richly, and endeavour
in our own strength to equal or even surpass it. We shall find it particularly
useful to 'thumb the great authors by night and day,' especially those who
were outstanding in the rich style, such as Cicero, Aulus Gellius, and
Apuleius. We must keep our eyes open to observe every figure of speech
that they use, store it in our memory once observed, imitate it once remembered, and by constant employment develop an expertise by which we may
call upon it instantly.

* * * * *

7 Quintilian] For this whole section see Quintilian 10.5.
14 Milo of Croton] The famous athlete who lifted a calf every day until it had
   grown into a bull; see Quintilian 1.9.5.
28 night and day] Horace *Ars poetica* 268–9

10 *Copia*: **Preliminary instructions**

Having said all this by way of introduction, I must now tackle the task of
actually setting down my instructions, though what I have said already is
instruction of a sort. I think it will be not inadvisable to launch my remarks   5
with a warning to the candidate for *copia* that his first care must be to see
that his speech is appropriate, is Latin, is elegant, is stylistically uncorrupt.
He should not imagine that the rich style can admit anything which is
abhorrent from the unsullied purity of the language of Rome.

Elegance depends partly on the use of wòrds established in suitable   10
authors, partly on their right application, partly on their right combination
in phrases. An example of the first is the form *piissimus* [as the superlative of
pius], which according to Cicero was never heard by Latin ears – though
even this form is found in quite respectable authors; so it would be better to
use as an example some other barbarous or faulty form, such as *avisare*   15
'advise' instead of *praemonere*. A barbarism is also committed by faulty
writing or pronunciation, such as pronouncing *dócere* with the accent on
the first syllable [instead of the second], or *Christus* as *Cristus* [without the
aspirate], or *perca* as *parca*, or lengthening the first syllable of *lego*.

An example of the second is saying *dedit mihi licentiam abeundi* 'he   20
issued me license to go away,' instead of *fecit mihi potestatem abeundi* 'he
gave me leave to go away.' In the first sentence every word is Latin; the fault
lies in misapplication: *potestas* is a general word for every kind of possibil-

* * * * *

1 *Copia*] In the first (1512) edition chap 10 was numbered 9 in error; subsequent
  chapters were misnumbered until chap 34, where correction was made.
6 candidate for *copia*] *copiae candidatus*, a favourite phrase of Erasmus'; see
  Quintilian 6 preface 13, *eloquentiae candidatum*.
13 Cicero] *Philippics* 13.43
13 though even this form ...] Most of the material from this phrase to 306:2 ('is
  foolish') was added in 1514 and 1534 (LB I 7C–8A).
17 pronunciation] These faults of Latin pronunciation characteristic of the 'ignorant crowd' are discussed in *De recta pronuntiatione* (1528) LB I 940E–1B,
  951C, 935E–F. In this work Erasmus criticizes especially the pronunciations
  employed by the Dutch, Flemish, and French. *dócere* and *lēgo* are typical
  confusions over vowel quantity and the position of the Latin accent; *Cristus*
  exemplifies ignorance as to the correct employment of Greek aspirated stops,
  particularly noticeable among Germanic speakers; the change from *er* to *ar*
  was due to a tendency to use an *e* of too open a quality both in general and
  particularly before *r*. This change was facilitated by the fact that a similar
  development was taking place in Erasmus' time in English, Dutch, and
  French; no doubt speakers carried over this pronunciation from their native
  language into Latin.

ity, *licentia* tends towards a pejorative meaning. So here there is a mistake in the application of a word, as there is in saying *compilare* 'gather up' for *colligere* 'collect.' *compilare* is a good Latin word, but it has acquired a different sense, 'remove by stealth.' Horace uses it when talking about 'slaves on the run filching their masters' stuff,' and in the lines: 'Lest you think that I've been thieving / From runny-eyed Chrysippus' shelves.'

The third type of mistake is very like the second, and consists in wrongly combining words perfectly good in themselves, such as using *iniuriam dedit* as the equivalent of *damnum dedit* 'he inflicted injury.' *dare damnum* is a correct expression, but *dare iniuriam* is not; the phrase is *facere iniuriam*. *dare malum* 'cause misfortune' is a good Latin expression, but not *dare iacturam* or *dare dolorem* 'cause loss or grief.' It is *facere iacturam* that is correct, and it means 'to sustain a loss,' [not 'to cause a loss']; but it is not right to use *facere infamiam* for 'suffer a loss of reputation.' It is good Latin to say *facere iniuriam* for 'inflict an injury,' but Cicero says that Latin speakers did not use the phrase *facere contumeliam* for 'inflict an insult,' although this form of expression is found in Plautus, Terence, and other respectable authors, and it is possible that it had gone out of use in Cicero's time. *accepit iniuriam* is right for 'he received an injury,' but I would not like to risk *accepit contumeliam* for 'he received an insult.' You can say *facere aes alienum* for 'contract debts,' and also *facere vorsuram* for 'raise a second loan,' but you cannot use *facere* like this in the phrases *facere invidiam* or *facere simultatem* to mean 'generate ill will or animosity against oneself.' *aedes vitium fecerunt* 'the building has sustained damage' is all right, meaning that it has disintegrated of its own accord, but I would avoid *rimas facere*, meaning it has developed cracks, because the Latin idiom is *rimas agere*. Likewise *facere stipendium* is right, meaning 'to serve as a soldier for pay,' but not *facere salarium* [which is another word for a soldier's pay]. *fecit sui copiam* is right, meaning 'he granted access to himself,' but again I would hesitate about *dedit sui copiam*, although Virgil with his fine linguistic judgment could write *et coram data copia fandi* 'Granted was leave to speak before her.' *fecit spem* and *dedit spem* are both good Latin for 'he gave hope.'

Sometimes expression is spoiled by an inappropriate word. For

* * * * *

5 masters' stuff] A memory of Horace *Satires* 1.1.78
6 Chrysippus' shelves] Horace *Satires* 1.1.120: Crispinus, not Chrysippus
15 Cicero] *Philippics* 3.22; Quintilian 9.3.13
17 Terence] For example *Eunuchus* 865–6
24 *vitium fecerunt*] See Cicero *Topica* 15.
30 Virgil] *Aeneid* 1.520

LB I 7D

example, *quid sibi vult hic homo*? 'what is this fellow after?' is appropriate, but *quid sibi vult hic mortalis*? 'what is this mortal after?' is foolish.

But to return to the main point, style is to thought as clothes are to the body. Just as dress and outward appearance can enhance or disfigure the beauty and dignity of the body, so words can enhance or disfigure thought. Accordingly a great mistake is made by those who consider that it makes no difference how anything is expressed, provided it can be understood somehow or other. The practice of giving variety to expression is exactly like changing clothes. Our first concern should be to see that the garment is clean, that it fits, and that it is not wrongly made up. It would be a pity to have people put off by a spotty, dirty garment, when the underlying form is itself good. It would be ludicrous to have a man go out in public dressed like a woman, and objectionable to see a person wearing his clothes back to front or upside down. So if anyone sets out to acquire variety of language before equipping himself with a Latinity that is neat and clean, he will be no less ridiculous (in my opinion at any rate) than a beggar who has not got even one garment that he can decently put on, but keeps changing his clothes and coming out in public draped with different sets of rags, ostentatiously displaying not riches but penury. The more often he did it the madder he would be thought. Yet certain persons with aspirations towards the rich style act with equal absurdity; they cannot express what they have to say even once in elegant language, but apparently feeling ashamed if they fail to jabber as well as they can, they display their jabbering in one variation after another, each worse than the last, as if they had entered a competition with themselves to speak just as barbarously as it is possible to speak. Now I would indeed have the furnishings of a wealthy mansion of all sorts and kinds, but I would have it all elegant, not find it everywhere stuffed with things made of willow or figwood, or with cheap pots. I would have all kinds of food served at a splendid banquet, but who could put up with a hundred dishes appearing on the table, every one of them nauseating?

I have deliberately set out these warnings at such length, as I am well acquainted with the headlong presumption that marks most mortal men. As soon as they have passed the lowest stages, they immediately choose to rush on to the heights, all unprepared, 'with unwashed feet' as the proverb says.

* * * * *

2 is foolish] See 308:1n.
20 persons with aspirations] *affectatores*, a word taken from Quintilian
35 proverb] *Adagia* I ix 54

Nearly as bad a sin is committed by those who mix the sordid with the elegant, disfigure their purple with patches, thread together jewels and paste, and add garlic to Greek confections.

And now I will set out the rules for developing variety of expression, confining myself at this stage to the ones involving richness of vocabulary.

11 / Variety of expression (1): Use of synonyms

The first and simplest form of variation depends on using different words which indicate the same thing, so that as far as meaning goes it does not matter which you prefer to employ. The grammarians call these *synonyms*. Opposite to these are words called *homonyms*. These two types have also been called *equivocal* and *univocal*, although according to the logicians these terms are more applicable to the things signified than to the signifying words. It will be more accurate to call different words signifying the same thing ἰσοδυναμοῦσαι [isodynamic] and their opposites πολυσήμοι [polysemantic]. Examples of the first sort are *ensis, gladius* 'sword', *domus, aedes* 'house'; *codex, liber* 'book'; *forma, decor, pulchritudo* 'beauty.'

One should collect a vast supply of words like this from all sides out of good authors, provide oneself with a varied equipment, and, as Quintilian remarks, heap up riches so that we find we have a wealth of words to hand whenever we require it. It will not be sufficient to prepare a copious apparatus or an abundant store of such words unless you have them not only at the ready but in full view, so that they present themselves to the eyes even if you are not looking for them. But here we must take special care not to do what some do and use the first thing that presents itself out of the heap in any context without exercising any choice at all. For in the first place you will hardly find two words anywhere so isodynamic that they are not kept apart by some distinction. What could be more identical in meaning than *men* and *mortals*? Yet the man who on every occasion said *all mortals* for *all*

* * * * *

  3 Greek confections] *Adagia* II iii 100
  8 Variety] Chap 11 was greatly expanded in 1534, the bulk of the text, apart from the introduction, belonging to this date. For the first section see Quintilian 10.1.5–15.
13 These two types ... first sort are] Added 1526 (LB I 8E)
14 *equivocal* and *univocal*] See Aristotle *Categories* 1; the terms *aequivoca* and *univoca* were used to represent ὁμώνυμα and συνώνυμα by Boethius in his Latin translation of this work.

men was stigmatized in the words of the Greek proverb, τὸ ἐν φακῇ μύρον
(sweet oils on lentils). Sometimes *litterae* and *epistola* signify the same thing
[that is, letter], sometimes something different.

Even if we allow that there is absolutely no distinction in meaning, yet
some words are more respectable than others, or more exalted, or more
polished or delightful or powerful or sonorous, or more conducive to
harmonious arrangement. Accordingly the man who is about to speak
should exercise choice and take what is best. Judgment is necessary when
bringing out of stock, whereas industry is necessary when storing away.
You will learn to exercise judgment by carefully observing elegant and
appropriate diction, while the assiduous reading of every type of author
will allow you to fill your store.

There are many things for which the poets use one set of words,
orators another. There are also words peculiar to different ages and centuries, and even the same authors often express the same thing by different
means. So the first thing is to extract the best words one can from every type
of writer, and, whatever they are like, add them to the collection. No word
is to be rejected, provided it occurs in an author who is at all respectable, for
there is no word which would not be the best one in some place or other. So
however vulgar, unusual, poetic, archaic, novel, obsolete, harsh, barbarous, or foreign it may be, lay it up in its proper niche with its fellows, so that
you may summon it if ever a use for it arises. If we are afraid that the
antiquity or novelty of our word may offend the ears of our audience, the
best thing will be to take Quintilian's advice and remember to forestall
criticism by commenting on the word ourselves. Here are some sample
ways of doing this: Cato, a glutton for books, if it is right to use such a word
of such a noble subject; the master's self, to use a phrase of Plautus'; for why
should I not use words employed by Ennius? for I am glad to use a word of
Horace's; for that is how your favourite moderns speak; you will recognize
a barrack-room word; as the poets say; as they used to say long ago; to speak
after the ancient fashion; if I may so express myself; if you allow me to use

* * * * *

1 proverb] English equivalent, 'jewel of gold in a swine's snout'; *Adagia* I vii 23.
  See Aulus Gellius 13.29.5–6 where Fronto warns against overuse of *mortales,*
  quoting the proverb from Varro's *Satires;* Erasmus is quite fond of *mortales*
  himself (see chaps 1, 10, 47), no doubt following the example of Sallust, with
  whose writings he is thoroughly familiar.
7 harmonious arrangement] See Quintilian 8.3.16.
24 Quintilian's] 8.3.37
26 Cato, a glutton for books] Cf Cicero *De finibus* 3.7.
30 barrack-room word] Pliny *Naturalis historia* preface 1

LB I 8F

an everyday turn of phrase; I will say it in Greek, to express my meaning better.

We must do the same with κακέμφατα [cacemphatic words], that is, those that lend themselves to an obscene interpretation.

VULGAR WORDS

Vulgar words are those which will strike the hearer as rather too common for the dignity of the context, like calling one's familiar friend one's 'old hearty,' or an avid reader 'a glutton for literature.' I am surprised that Seneca found the words *acetum, spongia, pulegium* [vinegar, sponge, flea-bane] vulgar. I think one could more properly call vulgar the words he himself used in one of his letters: *pilicrepi, botularii, crustularii* [ball-players, sausage-makers, pastry-cooks]. Words derived from low trades and occupations, like bath-attendant, cook, tanner, and eating-house keeper, are usually vulgar, but we must of necessity use these words if we have to discuss such subjects. Surgeons and doctors often have to use words that are appropriate rather than fine. Pliny jokingly refers to words that originated in the army, and thieves' kitchens have provided us with the word *tuburcinari* 'to guzzle.' Some words are vulgar of themselves, others only in the wrong context, applied to the wrong persons and circumstances. For example, *dung* and the verb *to dung* are not vulgar if you are talking about farming to farmers, but they are if you are making a speech on affairs of state in the presence of the ruler.

UNUSUAL WORDS

At one time common usage had a great deal of authority. Horace says as much in the lines: 'Many words that now are dead will come to life again / Words honoured now will die the death, shall usage so proclaim.' But

* * * * *

3 We must do ... interpretation] Added in 1534 (LB I 9C)
  cacemphatic words] Quintilian 8.3.47
10 Seneca] The Elder Seneca *Controversiae* 7 preface 3, where Albucius is criticized for using words of this sort: *nihil putabat esse quod dici in declamatione non posset.*
11 I think one ... of the ruler] Added in 1534 (LB I 9D–E)
12 letters] *Epistulae morales* 56.1–2 by the Younger Seneca; see 299:3n.
17 Pliny] See 308:30n.
19 *tuburcinari*] Probably gleaned from Nonius Marcellus 179, a lexicographer of the fourth century AD, who quotes many excerpts from early poets illustrating interesting word usages, and whom Erasmus appears to be using extensively in this chapter.
26 At one time ... anyone says] The passage to 310:14 added in 1534 (LB I 9E–10A)
26 Horace] *Ars poetica* 70–1

LB I 9C

nowadays we acquire our way of speaking not from the community at large
but from the writings of learned men, so usage does not have the same
prescriptive power. Even so, words can be considered unusual when they
do not occur with any frequency in those authors which provide the bulk of
scholars' reading. Today we have to take care not to speak in an artificial   5
manner, and to keep a good distance between ourselves and the aspirations
of those who think to speak strangely is to speak well – a mannerism which
Cicero remarked on in Lucius Sisenna, who was in many respects a learned
man. These same people also think themselves clever if one has to be clever
to understand them, as Diomedes wittily remarked, and prefer to write   10
something that will result in amazement rather than comprehension.

    An expression can be unusual in several ways, as will be made clear by
what follows; to give some examples, the form of expression will be unusual
if anyone says *passos senes* 'prune-faced old men' for *rugosi* 'wrinkled'; uses
the [archaic] forms *interduatim* 'somewhile' and *interatim* 'in the mean'   15
instead of *interdum* 'sometimes' and *interim* 'meanwhile'; employs *titivil-*
litium 'jot and tittle' for something of no account; and the [less usual] form
vagor for *vagitus* 'wailing.'

There are also words in the poets which should be used only sparingly,
especially when writing prose. In Horace for example we have *eliminare*
'turn out of doors' used to mean 'carry a confidence to the outside world'
(though Cicero does use it in the sense 'eject'); *iuvenari* 'act the irresponsi-
ble youth,' a word modelled on the Greek verb νεανίζειν or νεανιεύειν [with   25
                * * * * *
     8 Cicero] See *Brutus* 259–60.
    10 Diomedes] Not Diomedes but Quintilian 8 preface 25
    11 comprehension] Suetonius *Augustus* 86.2, where Augustus criticizes Mark
        Antony's style in these terms
    14 *passos*] Used by Lucilius, quoted in Nonius Marcellus 12; *Adagia* II viii 67
    15 *interduatim, interatim*] Festus 234 (*Gloss. Lat.* IV Lindsay); Festus was a gram-
        marian of the second century AD whose lexicon was printed at Milan in 1500.
    16 *titivillitium*] *Adagia* IV viii 3; in medieval fancy a goblin Titivillus gathered up
        in a sack the unconsidered trifles of careless speech let fall by monks.
    18 *vagor*] Nonius Marcellus 184
    21 There are ... poets] Almost all of the material from here to 311:25 was added in
        1534; the original text consisted mainly of lines 311:5–11 (*agmen* ... endure it)
        and 311:18–21 (*vulnificus* ... of the same sort); LB I 10A–C.
    22 Horace] *eliminare*: Epistles 1.5.25; *iuvenari*: Ars poetica 246; *furiare*: Odes
        1.25.14; *clarare*: Odes 4.3.4; *aeternare*: Odes 4.14.5; *inimicare*: Odes 4.15.20;
        pauperare: Satires 2.5.36: *cinctutis*: Ars poetica 50; *invideor*: Ars poetica 56
    24 Cicero] There seems to be no record of Cicero's using this word. Possibly
        Erasmus has confused it with *exterminare* or *expectorare* which have a related

the same meaning]; *furiare* 'furiate'; *clarare* 'luminate'; *aeternare* 'deathlessly memoriate'; *inimicare* 'hostilize'; *pauperare* 'pauperize'; or a form like *cinctutis* 'girthed,' instead of *cinctis* 'girt'; or [the passive form] *invideor* 'I am felt a grudge' instead of *mihi invidetur* 'a grudge is felt against me'; or in Virgil *agmen* [usually 'line' or 'group in motion'] for 'movement' or 'course' in *leni fluit agmine Thybris* 'The Tiber swells with gentle course'; or *indomitum furit* 'he rages a boundless rage' instead of using [the adverb] *indomite* 'boundlessly'; also *acerba tuens* 'glaring savageness' instead of 'glaring savagely'; or *sperare* 'hope' in the sense of 'fear' or 'expect, foresee': 'Could I this mighty grief foresee [*sperare*] / Then, sister dear, can I endure it.' Likewise in Terence: 'Now as for your expectation [*speras*] of keeping at bay ...' Yet Cicero was quite prepared to use this turn of phrase in his letters to friends: 'I had no expectation [*non sperabam*] that your feelings towards myself and my family would be so changeable.'

The Greeks had a wonderful knack for forming compounds, and the Latin poets sometimes achieved a like felicity when imitating them, but the Latin orators never seemed to be quite so successful at it. Examples of such compounds are *vulnificus* 'wound-inflicting,' *tristificus* 'grief-causing,' *tabificus* 'corruption-bearing,' *fatidicus* 'fate-uttering,' *laurigeri* 'laurel-crowned,' *caprigenum pecus* 'goat-natured flock,' *velivolum mare* 'sail-studded sea,' *vitisator* 'vine-planter,' and many more of the same sort. Cato was bold enough to try *vitilitigator* 'fault-picker,' another person *officiperda* 'favour-waster.'

The vocabulary of the historical writers is nearly as bold as that of the poets.

* * * * *

meaning. Nonius Marcellus quotes all three (39, 27, 16), giving quotations from Cicero for *exterminare* and *expectorare*.

5 Virgil] *Thybris*: *Aeneid* 2.782, quoted Macrobius *Saturnalia* 6.4.4; *acerba tuens*: *Aeneid* 9.794; *sperare*: *Aeneid* 4.419; *indomitum furit* appears not to be Virgilian, but see *Georgics* 3.100, *incassum furit*, and cf Prudentius *Psychomachia* 296, *tumet indomitum*.

11 Terence] *Andria* 395

12 Cicero] *Ad familiares* 5.1.2, a letter written by Quintus Metellus Celer

15 compounds] *vulnificus, fatidicus, caprigenum, velivolum, vitisator*, all from Virgil; *tristificus*, from Cicero, in translating verse; *tabificus* from the Younger Seneca, in tragedy; *laurigeri* from Ovid

22 Cato] See Pliny *Naturalis historia* preface 30; *Adagia* II vi 19.

23 *officiperda*] *Disticha Catonis* ed M. Boas (Amsterdam 1952) 4.42; this collection of gnomic sayings in verse was much read in the Middle Ages, and supposed to have been composed by the Elder Cato, though actually belonging to a period several centuries later. It was edited by Erasmus and published at Louvain in 1514; see 628:20n.

ARCHAIC WORDS

Archaic words add charm if they are incorporated in small quantities and in
appropriate places like inlaid decorations: for example, *expectorare* 'dis-
bosom,' meaning to bring out thoughts and feelings with words; *actutum*
'straightway' for *quamprimum* 'at once'; *antigerio, oppido,* both meaning   5
'verily,' in place of *valde* 'very'; *creperum bellum* 'the twilight of war,' for
dubium bellum 'doubtful or undecided war'; *hostire, hostimentum* 'requite,
requital' for *pensare, pensatio* 'compensate, compensation'; *vitulantes* 'joyful' for *gaudentes* 'glad'; *iumentum* 'carriage' for *vehiculum* 'vehicle'; the [old]
words *perduellis* and *perduellio* 'foeman'; *duellum,* an [old] form of *bellum*   10
'war'; *cernere* 'determine the issue' for *pugnare* 'fight'; *temetum* 'mead' for
vinum 'wine'; and *Aemathia* [an old name] for Thessaly.

OBSOLETE WORDS

Unusual words are those which appear only occasionally, archaic ones   15
those culled by later generations from texts discarded because of their
antiquity, such as the Twelve Tables, Ennius, Lucilius, Naevius, Pacuvius.
Obsolete ones have fallen completely out of use and passed into oblivion,
for example, *bovinari,* the equivalent of *tergiversari* 'to shuffle, evade';
apludam edit et floccem bibit 'he eats draff and drinks the lees of wine' (using   20
apluda and *floccem* instead of *furfur* and *faeces* for chaff and dregs) – an
expression that Gellius derides with good reason. The ancients used *hostis,*

* * * * *

2 Archaic words ... *valde*] Comments added to list of words in *1534* (LB I 10C)

3 *expectorare*] See 310:24n; Quintilian 8.3.31.

4 *actutum*] Like *hostire, hostimentum* (below), this occurs several times in early
   dramatists.

5 *antigerio*] Rejected as excessively antique by Quintilian 1.6.40, as is *oppido*
   8.3.25

6 *creperum bellum*] Nonius Marcellus 13

7 *hostimentum*] Festus 224 (Lindsay)

8 *vitulantes*] Nonius Marcellus 13

9 *iumentum*] Aulus Gellius 20.1.28

10 *perduellio*] *Rhetorica ad Herennium* 4.10.15, where this word is given as an
    example of affected archaism.

11 *cernere*] Virgil *Aeneid* 12.709: *cernere ferro*; there are several examples in early
    Latin. The 1514, 1526, 1534 editions read *cluere pro pugnare*; LB has this and a
    note, *lege cernere non cluere.*

11 *temetum*] Festus 452; Aulus Gellius 10.23.1

15 Unusual words ... down to us] Material from here to 313:27 belongs almost
    entirely to *1534* (LB I 10C–11A).

19 *bovinari*] Nonius Marcellus 80; Aulus Gellius 11.7.7

20 *apludam ... bibit*] Nonius Marcellus 70, 114; Aulus Gellius 11.7.3

22 *hostis*] Varro *De lingua latina* 5.3

LB I 10C

now meaning 'enemy,' for 'guest' and 'stranger,' but anyone would look a fool who tried to use it in that sense now.

I cannot see what use could arise for obsolete words, unless by way of joke and irony – if for example one wanted to stigmatize some bungling imitator of antiquity by calling him a fellow who deserves 'to eat draff and drink lees.'

On this question of words we must take into account not only the actual date, but also the predilections and affectations of writers. There is a stage of antiquity already superseded, and one still crude, as we see it at the time of Livius Andronicus; at which period the slow process of refinement began, and continued until the period of Cicero, when Roman eloquence attained such a peak of perfection that there was no possibility of further development, but, as is usual in human affairs, a gradual decline from that brilliance followed; it was inevitable that later generations should speak worse when they tried to speak differently. Yet, although Sallust wrote at the same period as Cicero, his style is more like Cato the Censor's than like Cicero's; and Maecenas lived at much the same time, yet he falls very far short of the pure style of his age. Likewise Valerius Maximus, who belonged to the period of the Emperor Tiberius, when the brilliance of the Ciceronian age had not yet declined, none the less writes more in a style peculiar to himself than in that of his contemporaries. I shall say nothing of Tacitus, Suetonius, the two Plinys, Aelius Lampridius, and other later writers.

While one must applaud the practice of those who set themselves to imitate the felicities of that great age, all the same I cannot approve of those who shudder at anything they find in the later writers as if it were a barbarism, especially as it is possible that the very feature from which they recoil was actually used by Cicero in books which have not come down to us.

HARSH WORDS
Harsh expressions are those used in an uncomfortable metaphorical sense.

* * * * *

10 Livius Andronicus] Fl 240 BC, the earliest literary writer in Latin
13 decline] See Elder Seneca *Controversiae* 1 preface 7.
17 Maecenas] The literary patron of Virgil and Horace; his Latin style was considered extravagant and decadent. See Seneca *Epistles* 114.4–8.
18 Valerius Maximus] See 613:16n.
22 Aelius Lampridius] Historian of the fourth century AD
25 barbarism] A reference to Erasmus' long-standing battle with those who applied strict canons of classical conformity and would have no prose author used as a model but Cicero. See Erasmus *Ciceronianus* (1528).
30 Harsh expressions ... stormy one] Almost all of the passage from here to 314:7 belongs to *1534* (LB I 11A–B).

LB I 10E

One speaker earned censure by saying that Rome was 'castrated' by the death of Camillus, meaning that the strength of the city collapsed at his death. Horace obliquely censures a certain Furius for writing: 'Jove has the Alps with hoary snow bespewed.' Another similar example is: 'He destroyed the plains of peace, and raised the mountains of war.' The metaphor would have been less violent if the writer had used the image of a calm sea and a stormy one.

FOREIGN WORDS

Foreign words also have a charm of their own when introduced in the appropriate place, like using *gazae*, a word meaning 'treasures' taken from the Persians, since the Persians are famous for their opulence and for the luxury that accompanies it. *acinaces* 'scimitar' for *gladium* 'sword' is borrowed from the Medes, and *essedum* 'wagon' for *raeda* 'carriage' from the British. *ungulum* is Oscan for *anulus* 'ring,' *cascus* for *vetulus* 'old' Sabine. *uri* 'wild oxen' is Gallic, as also *merga* 'marle,' the marrow or fat of the land, which is dug out to manure the fields, also *gaesa*, a sort of weapon. *parasang*, a distance of thirty stades, is Persian. *camurus* 'with crumpled horn,' that is, turned in on itself, will also be listed among foreign words.

The early Christians adopted the words *nonnus* and *nonna* 'holy man, holy woman' from Egypt, because it was in Egypt that crowds of male and female recluses were at one time earning their reputation for holiness.

If ever we are forced to use barbaric words, we must always preface their introduction with an apology, as Pliny says. There are many other words which have found their way in, together with the things they name,

* * * * *

1 earned censure] See Cicero *De oratore* 3.164; Quintilian 8.6.15 (death of Africanus, not Camillus).

3 Horace] *Satires* 2.5.41, referred to in Quintilian 8.6.17

5 the mountains of war] See *Ad Herennium* 4.10.15, the passage that criticizes *perduellio* above 312:10

10 Foreign words ... ginger] The passage to 315:2 mostly added in 1534 except lines 13–16 (*acinaces* ... Gallic); LB I 11B–D

13 *acinaces*] Used by Horace *Odes* 1.27.5

15 *ungulum*] Festus 464

15 *cascus*] Varro *De lingua latina* 7.28

16 *uri*] See Macrobius 6.4.23.

16 *merga*] See Pliny *Naturalis historia* 17.42: *alia est ratio quam Britanniae et Galliae invenere alendi [terram] ... genusque quod vocant margam.*

17 *parasang*] Well known from Xenophon's account of the March of the Ten Thousand (*Anabasis*)

18 *camurus*] See Macrobius 6.4.23

20 *nonnus*] See A. Souter ed *Glossary of Later Latin* (Oxford 1949)

24 Pliny] *Naturalis historia* preface 13

from barbarian nations to the Greeks, and from the Greeks to us, such as
sinapi, piper, zinziber [mustard, pepper, ginger], etc.

INDECENT WORDS

Indecent words should be utterly unknown to Christian speech, and no
attention should be paid to the Cynics, who consider no act shameful to
name that is not shameful to perform, and an act that is not shameful to
perform in private not shameful to perform in public, like making water or
evacuating the bowels. On the other hand, it is not automatically shameful
to talk about an act that is shameful to perform. One can name parricide and
incest without loss of modesty, though they would both be utterly shaming
if committed. Again there are certain parts of the body which are not
dishonourable in themselves, yet are kept covered because of a sense of
decency peculiar to civilized man; likewise there are some actions which in
themselves are neither good nor bad which none the less are kept private for
modesty's sake. Yet it is not automatically shameful to use the appropriate
word for an act that it would be indecent to perform openly. One can talk
about giving birth with decency, but it would be shameful for it to happen
in public. 'To piss' is not an indecent word (though 'to make water' is a
more decorous expression), but it is immodest to piss in public. On the
other hand, 'shit' is an improper word, though the action is neutral. The
belly can be named with decency, but it is indecent to show it. The word
'vulva' is respectable, but 'cunt' is highly indecent.

How then do we recognize indecency? Only from usage, and I do not
mean the usage of all and sundry, but of those whose speech is modest. The
poets, in particular the satirists, have allowed themselves too much freedom in the employment of such words.

Sometimes a metaphorical expression is far more indecent than the
direct word, as in 'to grind others' wives' (Horace) and 'piss into an
upper-class hole,' or in Catullus 'he spat down his uncle' and 'take the skin

* * * * *

4 INDECENT WORDS] For this section see Cicero *De officiis* 1.127–8; *Ad familiares*
9.22. The entire section was added in 1534.

29 Horace] *Satires* 1.2.35

30 upper-class hole] Persius 6.73

30 he spat] Catullus 74.3 *patrui perdespuit ipsam / uxorem* 'he spat right down his
uncle's wife.' Erasmus, quoting from memory, has confused this with a later
line in the same poem: *quamvis irrumet ... patruum* 'whatever he makes his
uncle swallow.' (Modern texts of Catullus read *perdepsuit* 'kneaded,' an emendation published in 1566 by Achilles Statius, but claimed by Joseph Scaliger in
an edition of 1577 as one first made by himself years before).

30 take the skin off] Catullus 58.5 *glubit magnanimi Remi nepotes* 'skins the descendants of heroic Remus'

off men.' Some perfectly respectable words have been distorted in the
direction of obscenity, like *dare* 'give, allow' (a modest enough term in *dare
fidem* 'give one's word'), which none the less appears in the Priapeia in an
obscene sense: 'Much simpler would good plain Latin be: Give me – you
know what.' And also in Martial: 'To give way you wish, but not to give   5
away.'

Such obviously obscene words must be totally shunned, but neutral
ones can be accommodated to a decent meaning, like using *exosculari* or
dissuaviari [literally 'to kiss passionately'] to express great pleasure at the
ready wit of some person, or like calling the aspirant after learning 'a wooer   10
of Philology.'

NEW WORDS

Innovations can be taken in three ways: completely new creations, existing
words diverted into a new meaning, and new words made by compound-   15
ing existing forms. An example of the first is Nero's *morari* with a long first
syllable, meaning 'to fool about,' from the Greek word μωρός [stupid]; of
the second, Sallust's *ductare exercitum* 'lead an army,' since *ductare* 'lead
about' has an indecent sense in Terence and other early writers, for example, *ut meam ductes gratis* 'so that you can lead off my girl for nothing.'   20
Likewise *patrare bellum*, equivalent to *gerere bellum* 'wage war,' since *patrare* 'achieve, perform' was earlier used of the endeavour to beget children.
Of the third, *vitilitigator* 'brawler,' compounded from *vitium* 'the fault,'
litigandi 'of picking quarrels,' which I mentioned earlier, and *bubsequa*

* * * * *

3 Priapeia] A collection of obscene verse in honour of Priapus, a fertility god:
  3.9–10 (misremembered); see 388:17.
5 Martial] 7.75.2
8 *exosculari*] See Aulus Gellius 1.23.13: *fidem atque ingenium pueri exosculatur*;
  already in Cicero *Pro Murena* 23 *osculari* occurs in the sense 'make much of.'
14 Innovations ... forms, like] The passage to 317:4 mostly added in 1534 (LB I
   12A–B)
16 Nero's] See Suetonius *Nero* 33, where Nero says of Claudius *morari eum desisse
   inter homines*, punning on the already existing verb *morari* with a short vowel,
   meaning 'stay, hang about'; Erasmus explains this in detail in *De recta pronuntiatione* LB I 945B–C.
18 Sallust's] *Jugurtha* 38.1; See Quintilian 8.3.44, who comments on the change of
   meaning.
19 Terence] *Phormio* 500
21 *patrare bellum*] Sallust *Catilina* 11.5; see 316:18n and Cicero's comment in *Ad
   familiares* 9.22.
24 earlier] 311:22
24 *bubsequa*] Apuleius *Florida* 3

[from *bos* 'ox' and *sequor* 'follow'], equivalent to *bubulcus* 'cowherd,' and Pacuvius' *Nerei repandirostrum incurvicervicum pecus* 'the snout-upturned, neck-arching flock of Nereus,' all examples which Quintilian mentions. To this class belong new words created by derivation from existing forms, like *vituperones* 'vituperists,' *amorabundus* 'love-bound,' *nupturire* 'be wedding-mad,' *verbigerari* 'word-bandy,' the sort of words particularly favoured by Apuleius, Martianus Capella, Sidonius Apollinaris, and those who model themselves on those writers. Such words have their own charm, if they are sprinkled here and there with discretion and in the appropriate place. As Quintilian neatly remarked, in food a touch of sharpness can at times give pleasure.

Not a little charm is added by the judicious mingling of Greek forms with the Latin. This can be when the Greek word is more expressive, like λογομαχία [battle of words] for 'dispute' or 'quarrel'; or shorter, like φίλαυτος [self-lover] for a man who is self-satisfied; or more forceful, like γυναικομανής [mad on women] for a man who is over-fond of women; or more agreeable, like using μετεωρολεσχεῖν [star-gazing] for a man prating on involved but useless topics, or calling μωρόσοφος [fool-wise] a man who is a fool but thinks himself wise.

No Latin expression can approach the charm of a Greek one in which we allude to a passage or remark of some author; if, for example, in reprimanding someone for speaking without thinking, we quote Homer's line ποῖον ἔπος ... ['What a word escaped ...'] or, in pointing out that someone has failed to keep to the point at issue, we say in Greek ἅμας ἀπήτουν [I was needing sickles]. If we were to say in Latin *falces petebam*, all the attractiveness disappears.

There is an allusion also in Horace's lines: 'Anointed, thrice through Tiber's waves shalt pass, / At eve, in liquor soaked *corpus habeas*.' The

* * * * *

2 Pacuvius'] Quoted by Quintilian 1.5.67

5 *vituperones*] Aulus Gellius 19.7.16; *amorabundus*: Aulus Gellius 11.15.1, quoting Laberius; *nupturire*: Apuleius *Apologia* 70; *verbigerare*: Apuleius *Apologia* 73. Cf 338:4n.

7 Martianus Capella] Author (fifth century AD) of a famous allegorical poem on the marriage of Mercury and Philology; it describes the seven liberal arts.

7 Sidonius Apollinaris] Christian Latin poet and bishop (fifth century AD)

10 Quintilian] 9.3.27

13 This can be ... from the Greeks] The passage to 318:20 added in 1534 (LB I 12C–F)

23 escaped ...] That is, 'escaped the fence of your teeth': Homer *Iliad* 4.350, quoted by Aulus Gellius 1.15.4

24 ἅμας ἀπήτουν] *Adagia* II ii 49: 'I was needing sickles and they said they had no mattocks.'

27 Horace's] *Satires* 2.1.9

speaker is Trebatius, a legal expert, and they enjoy words out of the Twelve
Tables, a feature that Cicero imitates in his books on the laws.

Finally we can use Greek words when we wish our meaning not to be
understood by all and sundry; and – not to go through every possibility –
whenever there is a certain convenience, we are justified in mixing Greek
with Latin, especially when writing for the educated public. But to produce
a half-Greek, half-Latin mixture of set purpose when there is no particular
justification for it may possibly be forgiven in the young who are endeavouring to acquire facility in both languages, but in grown men, in my
opinion, such exhibitionism would be quite out of place, and would no
more suggest seriousness of purpose than writing a book in a mixture of
prose and verse – though we observe that some educated men have done
even that, like Petronius Arbiter, whose book however has a certain air of
mad irresponsibility, and Seneca in his mock-encomium of Claudius.
Boethius, more surprisingly, did so in a serious work, though in the poems
he is so different from his usual self that scholars are not inclined to believe
that he wrote them unaided. Boethius was copied by Jean Gerson, who
would be a writer of some standing if his lot had fallen in the present age.

It sometimes happens that we either have to express our meaning by a
circumlocution, or borrow from the Greeks, for example, πολυπραγ-
μοσύνη [officious meddling in many affairs], φιλαυτία [esteem for one-
self], ἀφαμαρτοεπής [talking at random], πολυφιλία [abundance of
friends], δυσωπία [being put out of countenance], περισσολογία [talking
too much], ταυτολογία [saying the same thing again], βαττολογία [talking
gibberish], and thousands more of the same sort, which I shall perhaps
discuss on another occasion.

There are quite a number of Greek words which were given Latin
citizenship in the classical period, and these may be used just like native
Latin ones, for example, *rhetor/orator*; *hypotheca/pignus* 'surety'; *el-
leborum/veratrum* 'hellebore'; *feniculum/marathrum* 'fennel'; *sycophan-*

* * * * *

13 Petronius Arbiter] Nero's famous 'Arbiter of Elegance' in the *Satyricon*, a
   picaresque novel retailing the adventures of three rascals; the *editio princeps*
   (without the section known as *Trimalchio's Feast*) appeared in 1482.
14 mock-encomium of Claudius] *Apocolocyntosis* 'The Pumpkinification,' first
   printed in 1513; included in Erasmus' edition of Seneca (Basel 1515)
15 Boethius] *Consolatio philosophiae*, in which verse and prose alternate
17 Gerson] 1363–1429, a distinguished chancellor of the University of Paris; in
   his *Consolatio theologiae* (1418) he deliberately imitates the form of Boethius'
   work and the metres used.
20 borrow from the Greeks] See Aulus Gellius 11.16.
24 βαττολογία] From Battus, a bad poet whose verses were full of repetitions;
   Adagia II i 92

ta/calumniator 'slanderer'; *praebibo* (used by Apuleius)/*propino* 'drink a health'; *mastigia/verbero* 'scoundrel'. In some cases the borrowed word has become the standard one and there is no native Latin form, for example, *philosophus, theologus, grammatica, dialectica, epigramma*. With these words we can provide variety by declining them sometimes according to the Greek pattern, sometimes according to the Latin, for example, *scorpius/ scorpio; elephantus/elephas; delphinus/delphin; lampas/lampada lampadae; grammatica grammaticae/grammatice grammatices.*

12 / Vocabulary: Chronological considerations

You will need to observe carefully the way usage varied at different periods. The words *beatitudo, beatitas* 'blessedness,' and *mulierosus* 'fond of women,' *mulierositas* 'fondness for women' were bold inventions of Cicero's; and the word *declamare* 'declaim,' meaning 'to do exercises to develop one's powers as a speaker,' was an innovation in his time. In Varro's time *aedituus* 'sacristan' was a new word, replacing earlier *aeditimus* (*aeditimus* being derived from *aedes* 'temple' as *legitimus* is from *lex* 'law'). *interdum* 'on occasion' was replaced by *interim* [which originally meant 'meanwhile'], *interea* 'in the meantime' gave way to *obiter* (which developed the sense 'incidentally'), and *identidem* 'often, repeatedly' gave way to *subinde*, all in the time of Quintilian. Messala was the first to use the word *reatus* 'state of being *reus*, an accused person,' Augustus *munerarius* 'giver of a *munus*, a gladiatorial show.' *favor* 'partiality' and *urbanus* 'urbane' were new words in Cicero's time, and he is of the opinion that Terence first used *obsequium*

* * * * *

1 Apuleius] For example, *Metamorphoses* 10.16

6 *scorpius / scorpio*] See *Adagia* IV x 41: 'Celei supellex.'

15 Cicero's] *beatitudo, beatitas*: *De natura deorum* 1.95, quoted in Quintilian 8.3.32; *mulierosus*: *De fato* 10; *mulierositas*: *Tusculan Disputations* 4.25

16 *declamare*] See Seneca *Controversiae* 1 preface 12: *hoc enim genus materiae quo nos exercemur adeo novum est ut nomen quoque eius novum sit (controversia) ... sicut ipsa declamatio apud nullum antiquum auctorem ante Ciceronem et Calvum inveniri potest.*

17 *aedituus*] See Varro *Res rusticae* 1.2.

23 Quintilian] See 8.3.34–5 for *reatus, munerarius, favor, urbanus, obsequium, cervix, piratica, musica, fabrica.*

26 *obsequium*] Terence *Andria* 68: *obsequium amicos, veritas odium parit*; Cicero *De amicitia* 89 (quoting this line): *Terentiano verbo libenter utimur.* Erasmus here follows Quintilian (see preceding n) and Donatus in his commentary on Terence, who both interpret Cicero's remark to mean that he thought Terence invented the word.

LB I 13A

'indulgence.' It is thought that Hortensius was the first to use *cervix* 'neck' as a singular [instead of a plural]. Quintilian tells us that the words *piratica* 'piracy,' *musica* 'music,' and *fabrica* 'construction' were not yet considered acceptable as nouns by his own teachers.

The accumulation of synonyms, such as I have been discussing, which the Greeks call συναθροισμός, will not only enable us to avoid ὁμοιολογία (that is, a sameness of colour pervading the speech) if we find ourselves having to repeat the same idea several times, but will also contribute to δείνωσις or vehemence: for example, he has gone, he has burst forth, he has escaped, he has fled; you have slain your parent, struck down your father, slaughtered your sire. The rhetoricians count this as one of the ornaments of style and call it interpretation. In my opinion however it is more suitable for exercises than real speeches; it is a very trying form of variation if you get into the habit of expressing the same idea over and over again in different words with the same meaning, without any change in the shape of your sentence, for example, run a risk, be in peril, take a risk, face a peril; he builds a home, he constructs a house; he bought a book, he purchased a volume; he dismissed his man, he sent his servant away; he gave you this recompense, he offered this acknowledgment; I received this reward, I gained this profit; he condoned my guilt, forgave my wickedness, pardoned my offence; whenever I recollect that day, call it to mind, look back on it. There is nothing harder to please than the ears of men, and Horace was right to advise: 'Have your sentence run, / Stagger not with load of words, that dun / Our weary ears.'

It is different when the repetition serves some emotional effect, and variation of some kind avoids the boredom of reiteration, for example, in Virgil's lines: 'Lives he still and breathes the air of heaven? / Rests he not yet among the cruel shades?' Or again in that well-known piece of elaboration in Cicero's speech *Pro Ligario*: 'What marvellous clemency, fit to be glorified by praise on the lips of every citizen, by proclamation abroad, by mention in our literature, by inclusion in our history.' What he has said is similar but

* * * * *

1 Hortensius] Cicero's older contemporary and rival for pre-eminence at the bar; see Cicero *Brutus* 1ff.
10 he has fled] Cicero *Catilinarians* 2.1.1, quoted in Quintilian 9.3.46
12 interpretation] See *Ad Herennium* 4.28.38.
22 There is nothing ... battologia] The passage from here to 321:13 was added in 1534 (LB I 13D–F).
22 Horace] *Satires* 1.10.10
27 Virgil's] *Aeneid* 1.546–7 with 3.339
29 *Pro Ligario*] 6

LB I 13B

not identical. Another passage out of the same speech where Cicero hammers home the same point in one phrase after another, is justly famous: 'What was that sword doing, Tubero, that you drew on the field of Pharsalus ...?' and so on.

I stress these points because I observe that some public speakers of otherwise distinguished reputation, especially among the Italians, actually set out to waste time with strings of synonyms like this, as if that were some splendid achievement. It is just like someone expounding the verse from the psalm, 'Create in me a clean heart, O God' by saying 'Create in me a clean heart, a pure heart, an unsullied heart, a spotless heart, a heart free from stain, a heart untainted by sin, a purified heart, a heart that is washed, a heart white as snow,' and so on, right through the psalm.

'Richness' of this sort is practically battologia.

13 / **Variety (2): Enallage or** ἑτέρωσις

The next type of variation arises when an element of variety is provided by the employment of related forms of words which differ only slightly: for example, *edax* or *edo*, both meaning 'glutton'; *bibax, bibulus, bibosus,* or *bibo* 'tippler'; *loquax* or *locutuleius* 'chattering'; *nugator* or *nugo* 'trifler'; *blaterator* or *blatero* 'prattler'; *fallax* or *falsus* 'deceiver'; *voluptuosus* or *voluptuarius* 'voluptuary.'

We may have an adjective substituted for a noun or vice versa; for example, *iuxta sententiam Homeri* 'according to Homer's view,' *iuxta sententiam Homericam* 'according to the Homeric view'; *vir mire facundus* 'a wonderfully eloquent man,' *vir mira facundia* 'a man of wonderful eloquence'; *insignite impudens* 'strikingly impudent,' *insignita impudentia* 'of striking impudence.' Or an active verb may be changed into a passive and vice versa: *plurimam habeo gratiam* 'I feel great gratitude,' *plurima tibi a me habetur gratia* 'great gratitude is felt by me towards you'; *magna me tenet admiratio* 'great wonder overcomes me,' *magna teneor admiratione* 'I am overcome by great wonder'; *non sic amat filium mater* 'a mother does not so

* * * * *

  1 same speech] *Pro Ligario* 9, quoted in Quintilian 8.4.27; see 594:18.
  9 psalm] 51.10 (50:12 Vulg)
13 battologia] See 318:24.
19 words which differ only slightly] *bibax, bibosus, edax, locutuleius, blatero* from Aulus Gellius 3.12; 1.15.20; *nugo* from Apuleius *Metamorphoses* 5.29
28 *insignite impudens*] Cicero *Philippics* 3.10
33 *non ... filius*] 1512 has here: 'We must be careful not to operate this change wrongly, for the transformation will not work with any and every subject, for

love her son,' *non sic amatur a matre filius* 'a son is not so loved by his mother.'

To sum up in a few words a topic that offers infinite variation, this interchange takes two particular forms: either a different part of speech is substituted, or the part of speech remains the same but a different inherent quality is expressed; and the quality can be varied in as many different ways as there are possibilities available for the word in question.

Examples of the first type: *non confido facturum me* 'I do not believe that I shall achieve this' [verb], *non est fiducia* 'I have no belief' [noun]; *non dubito quin possit* 'I do not doubt but that he can do it' [verbs], *non est mihi dubium quin adsit illi facultas* 'I have no doubt but that he has the ability' [nouns]; *iudicent alii* 'other people may judge of this,' *aliorum esto iudicium* 'let the judgment rest with others'; *quid huc redisti?* 'why have you returned?' *quid huc reditio est?* 'what is the meaning of your return?'; *desine nugari* 'cease to play the fool,' *desine nugas* 'cease your folly'; *id mihi anus indicium fecit* 'of that the old woman gave me indication' (a noun instead of the verb *indicavit* 'indicated'); *est illi mira sitis auri* 'he has an incredible thirst for gold,' *mire sitit aurum* 'he thirsts incredibly for gold'; *non est apud illum discrimen amici et inimici* 'with him there is no distinction between friend and foe,' *non discernit amicum ab inimico* 'he does not distinguish between friend and foe'; *nostrum istud vivere triste* 'this wretched living of ours' (a verbal noun *vivere* instead of the noun *vita* 'life'); *virtus est vitium fugere* 'virtue is fleeing from vice,' *virtus est fuga vitiorum* 'virtue is flight from vice' [again a verbal noun *fugere* instead of the noun *fuga*]. Here verbs and nouns are interchanged.

amantem redama 'return the love of the loving,' *promerenti benefac* 'do good to the deserving,' *redama eum qui te amat* 'return the love of him who loves you,' *benefac ei qui promeretur* 'do good to him who deserves it'; *tui desiderantissimus est* 'he is missing you very much,' *te maxime desiderat* 'he misses you especially'; *nemo tui videndi cupientior* 'no one more desirous of seeing you,' *nemo qui te magis videre cupiat* 'no one who desires more eagerly to see you.' Here verbs and participles are interchanged.

venisti ereptum [supine], *venit eripere* [infinitive], *venit erepturus* [fu-

* * * * *

example, "I have taken food" becoming "I have been taken by food" or "I have taken the province" becoming "I have been taken by the province" ' (LB I 14B).

13 *quid huc reditio est*] Terence *Eunuchus* 671
15 *anus indicium fecit*] Terence *Adelphi* 617
21 *nostrum istud vivere triste*] Persius 1.9
22 *virtus est vitium fugere*] Horace *Epistles* 1.1.41
32 supine] See 323:19n.

LB I 14B

ture participle] 'you have, he has come to seize.' [These are ways of expressing purpose] using the supine or participle in place of a clause with a personal verb: *venit ut eripiat.*

ad congerendas pecunias inhiat, ad congerendum pecunias inhiat 'he is open-mouthed to amass money'; here the so-called gerundive is interchanged with the gerund.

hoc dictum oportuit 'this needed said,' *hoc dicere oportuit* 'this needed saying'; *siquid recte curatum velis* 'if you want anything properly looked after,' *siquid recte curari velis* 'if you want anything to be properly looked after'; participle and infinitive interchanged.

magnum dat ferre talentum [infinitive], *magnum dat talentum ferendum* [gerundive], both meaning 'he gives him a whole talent to carry.'

Sthenelus sciens pugnae 'Sthenelus skilled in fight,' that is, *sciens pugnandi* 'in fighting'; *cupidus litium* 'eager for law-suits,' *cupidus litigandi* 'eager for going to law,' noun for gerund.

libitum est, libuit 'it was agreeable'; *misertum est, misertus sum* 'pity was felt, I felt pity'; *pertaesum est, taeduit* 'boredom was experienced'; *placitum est, placuit* 'assent was expressed'; *puduit, puditum est* 'shame was felt.' Here the supine is an alternative for the personal verb form.

meliuscula est, meliuscule est 'she is a little better'; *plurimum est in foro, plurimus est in foro* 'he is much in the forum'; *rarus est conviva, raro est conviva* 'he rarely goes out to dinner'; *multus est apud mulierem, multum apud mulierem versatur* 'he spends a great deal of time with the woman'; *frequens est in aula* 'he is frequently at court'; *assiduus in litteris* 'applies himself to literature devotedly.' Here adverbs are replaced by the adjectival forms [in agreement with the subject of the sentence], as in these last examples *frequens, assiduus* replace *frequenter, assidue.*

But I shall possibly discuss all this on another occasion when I can deal with it more conveniently and at greater length.

Now I shall give a few examples of the second type of variation, that is, variation in quality, which will show what I mean and point the way as it were to the springs of the usage.

* * * * *

7 *hoc dictum oportuit*] Plautus *Mercator* 724
8 *siquid recte curatum velis*] Terence *Adelphi* 372
11 *magnum dat ferre talentum*] Virgil *Aeneid* 5.248
13 *Sthenelus sciens pugnae*] Horace *Odes* 1.15.24
19 supine] Used by ancient grammarians for various forms of the verb which could not be considered as belonging to either active or passive voice (for example impersonal verbs, especially in the 'impersonal passive,' some participles), and also for the verbal nouns gerund and supine (called 'first supine' 426); for this section see Diomedes *Ars grammatica* 1 in Keil 1 342, 397–8.

NUMBER

Singular and plural may be interchanged, for example, 'the Roman, victorious in battle,' for 'the victorious Romans'; 'even as the Roman, alert his country to defend'; 'the womb they pack with soldier armed'; 'he exhausted every asset,' for 'all the assets'; in Cicero, 'we imposed on the people and are   5 considered orators,' which means 'I imposed' as he is speaking only of himself; in Virgil we have 'a plain we have traversed in spaces limitless,' also 'features' or 'looks' of a man for 'face' or 'countenance,' as in 'Is it granted your features to behold?' We also have 'spirits' for 'spirit.'

It is particularly common to use the plural instead of the singular in the   10 first person, sometimes to make the statement sound more modest. It is not done in the second person, except to indicate a class, for example, 'such is your [plural] desire,' meaning 'men in general.' In the third person Terence substituted plural for singular to make a statement more disparaging: 'When it comes to wives, then they feel old men,' referring to Chremes   15 alone. Martial says 'obscure Platos,' meaning just Plato. When we use words indicating a class, the shift in number is both frequent and unremarkable; these are so-called collective nouns, such as populace, nation, flock, class, part. For example: 'Part cut them up into portions' [where 'part' is followed by a plural verb]. Similarly with words indicating not an   20 individual but a class or species. It makes no difference whether you say 'The elephant does not reproduce until the tenth year' or 'Elephants reproduce in the tenth year.'

PERSON   25

There are also several ways of varying the person. We can use a definite personal form with only a vague reference, for example, what are you to do? you must take people as you find them; you would see even the rivers dried up (this means 'it was possible to see ...'). Both the first and second persons

* * * * *

2 victorious in battle] Livy 31.36.3, quoted in Quintilian 8.6.20
4 country to defend] Virgil *Georgics* 3.346
4 soldier armed] Virgil *Aeneid* 2.20
5 Cicero] See Quintilian 8.6.20, quoting a lost letter of Cicero to Brutus.
7 Virgil] *Georgics* 2.541, quoted by Quintilian 9.3.20
9 features to behold] Virgil *Aeneid* 6.688
13 Terence] *Phormio* 1010
16 Martial] 9.47.1
16 When we use ... tenth year] Added in *1534* (LB I 15A)
19 Part cut them up] Virgil *Aeneid* 1.212
22 Elephants] Pliny *Naturalis historia* 8.28
28 as you find them] Terence *Adelphi* 431
28 even the rivers dried up] Virgil *Eclogues* 7.56

LB I 14E

are used in this way: 'Never at that season may the fancy take me / Beneath
the open sky sweet sleep to snatch / Nor on woody hill-top in the grass to
lie.' Or again: 'Plant not your vineyards on a westward slope.'

It is quite common to use the third person instead of the first or even
the second, as in 'Clodius says ... Cicero denies,' that is, 'you say ... I deny,'
or as in Virgil: 'Nor shall I sorry be to recall Elyssa,' that is, to recall you; 'Let
him in battle now make trial of Turnus,' that is, trial of me; 'Proclaim among
your fathers' shades / It was Camilla's hand that slew you,' that is, my hand.

Here belongs the figure of speech known as apostrophe, when we
address either a person, or a thing as if it were a person, as in these two
examples from Virgil: 'Scipio's race, war-hardened, and thee, / Caesar,
greatest of all'; [and] 'Polydorus he murdered, the gold he won by force. / O
devilish love of gold, what power thou hast / For evil over human hearts!'
Virgil combines apostrophe with parenthesis in the following well-known
passage: 'Close by that scene, / A team of horses, whipped to pull this way
and that / Had dragged the sundered limbs of Mettus in their wake. / – Ah,
man of Alba, thy word shouldst thou have kept! – / And Tullus there the
liar's broken corpse was whirling ...'

This figure also includes the interchange of personal and impersonal
forms, for example, do these things not shame you? or, is there no shame for
this?; there is continuous fighting among barbarian nations, or, the barbarians fight without ceasing; there is a general rumour that the pope is
coming, or, most people say that the pope is coming; it is impossible to say
how much I love you, or, no one could easily say how much I love you.

VOICE, GENDER
Considerable variety can be obtained by changing the voice of a verb;
[some verbs for example can be active or deponent]: *lachrimat* or *lachrimatur*
'weeps'; *luxuriat* or *luxuriatur* 'runs riot'; *fluctuatur* or *fluctuat* 'fluctuates.'

* * * * *

1 Never at that season] Virgil *Georgics* 3.435–6
3 Plant not your vineyards] Virgil *Georgics* 2.298
6 Virgil] *Aeneid* 4.335
6 recall Elyssa] After this *1512* and *1514* have: 'Never could Erasmus forget
   William,' i.e., never shall I be able to forget you.
6 'Let him ... my hand] Added in *1534* (LB I 15B)
7 make trial of Turnus] *Aeneid* 7.434
8 hand that slew you] *Aeneid* 11.689
11 Virgil] *Georgics* 2.170; *Aeneid* 3.55–7
14 well-known passage] *Aeneid* 8.642–4. All main editions read Metius (modern
    texts Mettus).
20 not shame you] Terence *Adelphi* 754

LB I 15B

Other verbs with this possibility are *praeverto* 'anticipate'; *praecipito* 'rush headlong'; *averto* 'turn aside'; *reverto* 'return'; *impertio* 'impart'; *assentio* 'agree'; *soleo* 'be accustomed' (*solebat fieri* [imperfect, active], *solitum est fieri* [perfect, deponent], both meaning 'it used to happen'); *queo* 'be able' (either *non quivit compesci* [active] or *non quita est compesci* [passive], both meaning 'she could not be restrained'); *desinere* 'cease' (either *desiit haberi in pretio* or *desita est haberi in pretio* 'the thing ceased to be valued'); *coepi* 'begin' (either *causa coepit agi* or *causa coepta est agi* 'the case began to be dealt with'); *assentio* 'agree'; *conspicio* 'catch sight of' (in this case the deponent form *conspicor* belongs to a different conjugation).

Diomedes lists some other active forms of verbs usually deponent: *frustro* 'trick,' *patio* 'suffer,' *moro* 'delay,' *demolio* 'destroy,' *auxilio* 'help,' *populo* 'lay waste,' *digno* 'deem worthy'; but in my opinion these and others like them should be left where they are in the old writers, unless they come into verse, where they can be employed with more excuse.

Likewise nouns can belong to different genders; *pilleum* n. or *pilleus* m. 'cap,' *ficus* m. or f. 'fig,' *barbitus* m. or f. *barbiton* n. 'lyre,' *elleborus* m. or *elleborum* n. 'hellebore.' Plautus used *nasum* n. for *nasus* m. 'nose.'

CASE

Different case usages are also possible: *eius rei* [gen.], *ea res* [nom.] *mihi venit in mentem* 'this thing came to mind'; *non sum id* [acc.], *eius rei* [gen.] *nescius* 'I am not unaware of this matter.' A number of words have two constructions even in their literal, non-metaphorical meaning: *utor* [with accusative or ablative]: *utor hanc rem, hac re* 'I use this'; *egeo* [with genitive or ablative]: *egeo tui, egeo te* 'I have need of you'; *dives* [with ablative or genitive]: *dives pecore, dives pecoris* 'rich in flocks;' *dono: dono te libro* 'I present you with a book,' *dono tibi librum* 'I present a book to you'; *impertior: impertior heram hoc malo* 'I acquaint my mistress with this misfortune,' *impertior herae hoc malum* 'I communicate this misfortune to my mistress.'

WORD TYPE

The word type is varied if we use a derivative instead of the primary form, for example, *magnis negotiis prohibitus* 'prevented by important business,' or *magnitudine negotiorum prohibitus* 'prevented by the importance of his business'; or a diminutive instead of the basic form, for example, *loquaculus* 'a wee bit talkative' for *loquax* 'talkative,' *nasutulus* 'rather large-nosed' for

* * * * *

11 Diomedes] *Ars grammatica* I in Keil I 400
27 *dives pecore*] Horace *Epodes* 15.19; *dives pecoris*: Virgil *Eclogues* 2.20
29 *heram hoc malo*] Terence *Adelphi* 320

LB I 15D

nasutus 'large-nosed,' *paucula* 'rather few' for *pauca* 'a few,' *pauxillum* 'tiny little bit' for *paulum* 'a little'; or if we use a frequentative verb form instead of the simple form: *dictito* for *dico* 'keep saying' for 'say,' *volito* for *volo* 'flutter' for 'fly,' *iactito* for *iacto* 'keep throwing about' for 'throw about'; or nouns instead of adjectives, like calling someone 'a pest' instead of 'pestilent,' or 'a wickedness' instead of 'wicked.' Similar to this is the use of the form *Italus*, really 'a person from Italy,' instead of the adjective *Italicus* 'Italian,' for example, *Italae artes* 'Italian arts'; likewise *Batavus* for *Batavicus*, for example, *Batavae aures* 'Dutch ears'; *Hispani mores* 'Spanish customs' for *Hispanici*; or the comparative or superlative instead of the positive: 'Downcast, her eyes bright with unshed tears' [where 'downcast' is the comparative *tristior*, literally 'rather sad, sadder than usual']; or *facundissimus* 'most eloquent' for 'exceedingly eloquent.' These points we shall discuss in the proper place.

Or a patronymic can be used instead of the primary name, for example, 'sons of Scipio' for 'Scipios.' This may be allowable in poetry, but no one would accept it in prose.

WORD FORM

Richness of expression can also be assisted by change in the figure or word form, for example, by the substitution of the simple form for the compound or vice versa, whether this involves a metaphorical use or not; for example, simple *temnere* for *contemnere* 'scorn,' simple *ruere* for *eruere* 'destroy, hurl down,' *ponere* for *deponere* 'lay aside,' *mittere* for *omittere* 'leave out'; or, the other way round, *conscribere* for *scribere* 'compose,' *comedere* for *edere* 'consume,' *demirari* for *mirari* 'wonder,' *inaudire* for *audire* 'hear of,' *incognoscere* for *cognoscere* 'find out,' *consipere* for *sapere* 'be sensible,' *complacare* for *placare* 'pacify,' *dependere* for *pendere* 'be suspended,' *deridiculus* for *ridiculus* 'laughable,' *quandoquidem* for *quando* 'since.'

[It is also a change of word form when we substitute a form containing *fieri* 'be made' for an intransitive form, for example,] *non potest pudescere* or *pudefieri* 'he cannot feel shame' or 'be made ashamed,' *tempus est ut expergiscaris* or *expergefias* 'it is time for you to rouse yourself' or 'be roused,' *calescere* or *calefieri* 'grow hot' or 'be made hot.'

* * * * *

6 wickedness] As in Terence *Andria* 607: *ubi ille est scelus.*

9 Dutch ears] Martial 6.82.6; 'Dutch' or 'Batavian' ears were proverbial for insensitivity and boorishness: *Adagia* IV vi 35.

11 unshed tears] Virgil *Aeneid* 1.228

14 proper place] Chap 42

16 'sons of Scipio'] *Georgics* 2.170; see 325:11.

20 change in the figure] See Quintilian 9.1.4–5, 10ff.

LB I 16A

Under this heading we should possibly list the usage by which we
paraphrase a compound form by using its component elements separately,
for example, *magnanimus vir*, or *vir magno animo* 'noble-souled man' or 'man
of noble soul,' *relege* 'reread it' or *denuo lege* 'read it again,' *magnopere te
rogabat* or *magno te rogabat opere*' he asked you earnestly' or 'with great   5
earnestness,' *non animadvertit* 'he did not attend to it,' *non advertit animum*
'he did not pay attention,' *non satisfacit* 'he does not satisfy me' or *non facit
mihi satis* 'he does not give me satisfaction.'

Sometimes the variation depends on using compounds made up of
different elements, for example, *exprobrare* or *opprobrare* 'reproach,' *persol-*   10
vere, dissolvere, exsolvere, resolvere aes alienum 'pay off one's debts.'

TENSE

There can also be changes in tense: [the present and perfect infinitives can
be interchanged, as in] *memini legere* or *legisse* 'I remember reading' or   15
'having read'; [the imperfect subjunctive can be used in place of the pluper-
fect, for example,] *praediceres* or *praedixisses* 'you should have warned'
(which can also be expressed by *praedicere debuisses* 'you ought to have
warned'); [in the phrase] *laurus erat* for *laurus esset* 'it is a laurel' for 'it would
be a laurel' [the imperfect indicative has the force of a present indicative];   20
[or a past tense can be used instead of a future:] *vicimus* for *vincemus* 'we
have conquered' for 'we shall conquer'; [or a future imperative instead of a
present one:] *salutato* 'greet hereafter' for *saluta* 'greet'; [or a historic present
instead of a past indicative:] *imus, venimus, videmus* 'we go, we come, we
see,' equivalent to 'we went,' etc.   25

MODE

Similar to variety in tense is variety in mode [for example, the future
subjunctive or future indicative]: *vicero* or *vincam* 'I shall succeed in conquering' or 'I shall conquer'; [future indicative or future imperative:]   30
salutabis 'you shall greet' or *salutato* 'greet'; [present imperative or present
subjunctive:] *ne crede* or *ne credas* both meaning 'do not believe'; [or again,

* * * * *

19 *laurus erat*] Virgil *Georgics* 2.133
21 *vicimus*] Livy 21.43.2
24 *imus, venimus, videmus*] Terence *Phormio* 103
28 mode] The ancient grammarians disagreed as to the number of modes of the
verb. Probus *Institutio artium* in Keil IV 155 gives indicative, promissive
(future indicative), imperative, infinitive, optative, conjunctive (subjunctive), impersonal, gerund. On future subjunctive see below 439.

future indicative or future subjunctive:] *si voles, si volueris* 'if you (shall) want,' *ubi voles, ubi volueris* 'whenever you (shall) want, *cum vacabit, cum vacaverit* 'whenever there is (shall be) time'; [indicative for subjunctive:] *quia bene natus est* or *sit* 'since he is well born'; [historic infinitive or imperfect indicative:] *venari* or *venabatur* 'people went hunting.'

DECLENSION

Quite often it will be possible to vary the declension also: *hilarus, hilaris* 'cheerful,' *violens, violentus* 'violent,' *imbecillus, imbecillis* 'weak,' *contagium, contagio* 'contagion,' *iuger, iugerum* 'measure of land,' *capo, capus* 'capon,' *pavo, pavus* 'peacock,' *scorpio, scorpius* 'scorpion,' *senectus, senecta* 'old age,' *iuventus, iuventa* 'youth.'

CONJUGATION

Sometimes [one can vary] the conjugation: *lavere* [3rd] and *lavare* [1st] 'wash,' *férvere* [3rd] and *fervēre* [2nd] 'boil,' *accérsere* [3rd] and *accersire* [4th] 'summon.'

The following procedures also produce variety: prosthesis [initial addition] for example, *tetuli* for *tuli* 'I carried,' *gnatus* for *natus* 'offspring'; epenthesis [internal addition], for example, *Mavortis* for *Martis*; prosparalepsis [augmentation], for example [the longer infinitive forms], *admittier, accingier, dicier* for *admitti, accingi, dici* 'to be admitted, girded, said'; paragoge [addition of a letter or syllable at the end of a word], for example, *potestur* for *potest* 'it is possible'; aphaeresis [initial shortening], for example, *ruit omnia late* 'destroys all things far and wide' instead of *eruit*, or *linquere castra* for *relinquere* 'abandon camp'; syncope [internal shortening], for example, *extinxti dixti* for *extinxisti dixisti* 'you destroyed, said'; apocope [final shortening], for example, *mage* for *magis* 'more,' *vin* for *vis ne* 'do you wish?'

These are all types of metaplasm [transformation], for they all give a different form to the utterance. I am deliberately omitting other types of metaplasm because they do not seem to contribute much to richness of style, and it is my intention to deal only with those points which are strictly relevant to the matter in hand.

* * * * *

25 *ruit omnia late*] Virgil *Aeneid* 12.454
26 *linquere castra*] *Aeneid* 10.68
30 metaplasm] For the whole section on metaplasm see Diomedes *Ars grammatica* II in Keil I 441, where these examples are used.

D. Erasmi Roterodami de dupli
ci Copia rerū ac verborū commentarii duo.
De ratione studii & instituendi pueros commentarii totidé.
De puero Iesu Concio scholastica: & Quædam carmina ad eandem rem per
tinentia.

Venundantur in ædibus Ascensianis.

Title page of the first edition of *De copia*
Paris: Bade July 1512
This volume also included the first authorized edition of *De ratione studii*.
By permission of the Houghton Library, Harvard University

14 / Variety (3): Antonomasia

The next form of variation consists in *antonomasia*, that is, substituting
something else for a person's proper name, like calling Achilles 'the son of
Peleus' or 'the grandson of Aeacus,' the Romans 'the descendants of
Romulus,' the Trojans 'the sons of Priam' or 'the race of Dardanus,' Hercules 'the man from Tiryns,' Venus 'the Cytherean' or 'the Cyprian,' Diana
'the Cynthian goddess,' Jove 'the son of Saturn,' Mercury 'the god of
Cyllene.' An ordinary epithet can often be substituted for the proper name,
as in Virgil's: 'Which he, the faithless, left hanging in our chamber,' where
'the faithless' *impius* is Aeneas; or there is Livy's 'the Phoenician' for
Hannibal. In Terence 'the old man' is often used for 'the master.' We have
the same kind of thing where 'the poet' is used for Homer, and 'the
philosopher' for Aristotle, just as the Greeks called the king of the Persians
βασιλεύς [the king]. Similar to this is the practice of calling a robber a
Verres, an effeminate man a Sardanapalus, a rich man a Croesus, or a cruel
one a Phalaris (all of which I shall discuss in the appropriate place).

15 / Variety (4): Periphrasis

If we replace the name with a phrase consisting of several words, we are
using what is known as periphrasis, which some call *circuitio*, 'circuitous
expression,' like calling Scipio 'the destroyer of Carthage and Numantia,'
just as Horace called Homer 'the recorder of the Trojan war.' Or one could

* * * * *

3 *antonomasia*] See Quintilian 8.6.29–30; such usages occur frequently in poets
   of the classical period and were extravagantly developed by later poets and
   prose writers.
10 Virgil's] *Aeneid* 4.495–6
11 Livy's] As in 23.42.1, a frequent usage
12 Terence] As in *Phormio* 865
16 Verres] The notorious governor of Sicily, found guilty of flagrant oppression
   of the people of that province. Cicero spoke for the prosecution at his trial.
   Erasmus quotes from the *Verrine Orations* frequently in *De copia*.
16 Sardanapalus] A favourite example of Erasmus'; *Adagia* III vii 27
16 Croesus] A king of Lydia whose wealth was proverbial; *Adagia* I vi 74
17 Phalaris] Tyrant of Acragas in Sicily, notorious for cruelty, especially for
   roasting victims alive in a brazen bull; *Adagia* I x 86
17 appropriate place] Book I chap 46
23 periphrasis] See Quintilian 8.6.59.
24 Scipio] See Quintilian 8.6.30, section on antonomasia.
25 Horace] *Epistles* 1.2.1

LB I 16F

put 'the Mantuan bard' for Virgil, 'the poet of Venusia' for Horace, 'head of the Peripatetic school' for Aristotle, 'father of the Stoic family' for Zeno, 'pleasure's champion' for Epicurus.

There are several types of periphrasis: etymology, signification, and definition.

ETYMOLOGY

Etymology is an explanation of the meaning of a word, for example, *heredipeta* 'a legacy-hunter' is a man who 'lies in wait (*appetat*) and fishes for other people's inheritances (*hereditates*)'; a parasite 'a man who is a slave to food and his belly'; a philosopher 'a man pursuing wisdom'; a grammarian 'one who teaches grammar'; *assiduus* 'a taxpayer or householder' is one 'who pays (*det*) money (*aera*)'; *locuples* 'a wealthy man' is one 'who possesses many (*plurima*) places (*loca*)'; *pecuniosus* 'a moneyed man' is one 'who possesses an abundance of cattle (*pecus*).'

SIGNIFICATION

Signification is description of something by indicating the signs that accompany it; if, for example, someone, meaning 'anger,' were to speak of 'a seething of the mind or bile which brings pallor to the face, a glare to the eyes, and a trembling to the limbs'; or to say 'those who scratch their head with one finger' to mean effeminate and unmanly persons, or 'he wipes his nose on his arm', meaning 'a salt-fish dealer.'

DEFINITION

Definition is, for example, 'the art of good speaking' for 'rhetoric,' 'one who plundered the public funds' for 'peculator,' or 'one who forcibly crushed law and the liberty of citizens' for 'tyrant.'

* * * * *

1 Mantuan bard] Cf Apuleius *Apology* 10.
2 Zeno] Cf Apuleius *Apology* 9: *Zenonis Stoicae sectae conditoris.*
9 *heredipeta*] Word found in Petronius *Satyricon* 124.2
12 *assiduus ... locuples ... pecuniosus*] Aulus Gellius 16.10.15; Quintilian 5.10.55
19 anger] See Seneca *De ira* 1.1.4
22 with one finger] Juvenal 9.133
22 his nose on his arm] *Ad Herennium* 4.54.67
26 Definition] Quintilian 5.10.54; *Ad Herennium* 4.25.35

16 / Variety (5): Metaphor

Another kind of variation is provided by metaphor, for which the Latin
term is *translatio* 'transference,' so called because a word is transferred away
from its real and proper signification to one which lies outside its proper
sphere. There are various types of this.

DEFLECTION
First of all deflection; when a word is deflected to some closely related
concept, like 'see' for 'understand,' 'hear' for 'obey' or 'believe,' 'sense' for
'discern,' 'perceive' for 'comprehend,' 'scent, smell' for 'surmise, detect,'
'digest' for 'endure,' 'swallow' for 'destroy' or 'submit to,' 'embrace, kiss'
for 'love,' 'look up to' for 'admire,' 'look down on' for 'despise.' Similarly
'numbed' can be applied to mind, and eyes, as well as teeth. In all these a
word is transferred from the physical to the mental sphere. No type of
metaphor occurs with greater frequency. Possibly we may also include here
'sing' for 'say,' 'rehearse' for 'write,' 'publish' for 'praise,' 'trumpet' for
'celebrate.'

TRANSFERENCE FROM IRRATIONAL TO RATIONAL
The next type of transference is from irrational to rational creatures, and
vice versa, like saying that a man who keeps on talking in a repulsive and
tasteless manner 'brays' or 'bleats' or 'grunts' or 'snarls.' We can use 'yelp at'
for 'decry,' 'bark at' for 'revile.' On the other hand, we can call the swan a
singer, the nightingale a musician, the fox a traitor, the lion conceited, the
dog a flatterer, the ant thrifty, the bee a hard worker. Virgil attributes many
characteristics of this sort to the bee when he transfers to this creature all the
situations that arise in the human community.

* * * * *

3 metaphor] See Quintilian 8.6.3ff, where many of these examples are used;
  Diomedes *Ars grammatica* II in Keil I 457; and Erasmus Ep 312 (dedicatory
  letter to *Parabolae,* CWE 23 130:27ff).
14 numbed] *stupet.* Cf Jeremiah 31:29.
23 'bleats'] See Nonius Marcellus 44, quoting Plautus.
24 'bark at'] Quintilian 8.6.9
26 thrifty] See Virgil *Georgics* 1.186.
26 the bee] *Georgics* 4 passim

FROM ANIMATE TO INANIMATE AND VICE VERSA

The transference is made from slightly further afield if it is from animate to
inanimate, or vice versa. As in Virgil: 'If there grows such firmness in thy
heart,' where 'firmness' is transferred from wood to man. Or again: 'But
seeing them far off from the mountain's crown,' where the transference is
from animate to inanimate, 'crown' being used for 'summit.'

Likewise: 'Now every field, every tree, swells with progeny'; and,
'The land smiles.' Vice versa: 'Both in the flower of their youth,' a 'green'
age, 'youth in bloom'; or, 'the angry sea,' 'the Araxes chafing,' 'the greedy
sea,' 'Gargara marvels.' There are plenty of examples of this type of
metaphor, and they occur so obviously and so frequently that it is unnecessary for me to quote more here. Sometimes the transference is

FROM ONE ANIMAL TO ANOTHER,

for example, a crow using a pig for a horse, bees browsing. Or

FROM ONE INANIMATE THING TO ANOTHER
AND VICE VERSA,

for example, the wood gushes into leaf, a word properly used of springs; or,
hatred sprouts, properly used of bushes; or, hair shoots, or, the beard gets
overgrown, properly used of trees; or, speech flows, or, the waves or tides
of trouble; or if you call a hillock a wart, as Cato does.

* * * * *

3 Virgil] *Aeneid* 11.368
5 mountain's crown] *Aeneid* 5.35
7 swells with progeny] *Eclogues* 3.56
8 'The land smiles'] Cf *Eclogues* 7.55 *omnia rident;* flower of their youth: *Eclogues*
7.4 *ambo florentes aetatibus;* a green age: cf *Aeneid* 5.295 *viridis iuventa,* 6.304
viridis senectus; youth in bloom: cf *Culex* 410 *vernantia tempora.*
9 angry sea] Horace *Epodes* 2.6
9 Araxes chafing] Virgil *Aeneid* 8.728
9 greedy sea] Horace *Odes* 1.28.18
10 'Gargara marvels'] Virgil *Georgics* 1.103
15 bees browsing] Virgil *Georgics* 4.181; *Eclogues* 5.77
20 hair shoots] Juvenal 9.15
21 speech flows] A common metaphor, for example Cicero *De oratore* 3.172
21 waves or tides of trouble] Two more common Ciceronian metaphors; see
below 337:10–13.
22 as Cato does] Quoted in Aulus Gellius 3.7.6

17 / Reciprocal metaphor

Some metaphors are reciprocal or common, and these the Greeks call
ἀκόλουθαι [consequent]. As you can call a steersman a charioteer, so you
can call a charioteer a steersman. Some are one-sided only, and these they
call ἀνακόλουθαι [inconsequent]. The word 'crown' can be transferred
from a man to a hill, but 'summit' cannot be transferred to a man.

Metaphor contributes to richness of style by ensuring, as Quintilian
remarks, that we never find ourselves with a concept for which there is no
word available. It also provides embellishment, dignity, clarity, sublimity,
charm. Sometimes metaphor is unavoidable, as when countrymen speak of
'gems' for the buds on vine-stems, of the vines putting forth 'gems,' of the
fields being 'thirsty,' the crops 'suffering,' the corn 'running riot.' We speak
of a man as 'hard,' as 'rough,' for there is no other word.

It is not relevant to my present purpose to discuss in detail the
different ways of applying metaphor or how it differs from related figures of
speech, but I shall offer this useful piece of advice. The man who wishes to
practise the rich style should provide himself with extensive lists of striking
metaphors culled from the best authors, and should add as many similes as
he can find. Cicero has some excellent ones and there are a good many in
Quintilian, but Plutarch is possibly more prolific than anyone. Quite a
number can be collected from proverbs, as most proverbs contain either
allegory or some form of metaphor. These I myself have laboured to collect,
and whether I was successful or not, I certainly worked long hours at it. But
there is nothing to prevent us inventing metaphors of all kinds for ourselves, based either on our reading or on our observation of the world
around us, provided the transference is not harsh, coarse, overdone, unlikely, or used too frequently, especially within the same sphere of meaning. It is also worth reminding you that metaphor can sometimes lie simply
in the use of a noun, for example, if someones calls a man who is a slave to
his belly, a beast; or in an epithet: a man with a stony heart, an iron writer,

* * * * *

4 steersman] As in *gubernator magna contorsit equum vi*, quoted in Quintilian
8.6.9

8 Metaphor] See Quintilian 8.6.6.

23 have laboured to collect] In his *Adagia*. See Phillips '*Adages*.' Many phrases in
De copia are treated at greater length in the *Adagia*.

27 not harsh] Cf *Ad Herennium* 4.34.45.

31 beast] See Sallust *Catilina* 1.1: *veluti pecora ... ventri oboedientia*.

31 stony heart] As in Pliny *Epistles* 2.3.7: *saxeus es*

31 iron writer] A phrase used by Porcius Licinus, quoted in Cicero *De finibus* 1.5

glassy waves, blooming years; or in a verb: time flies away, the years slip
past. Sometimes something is added to explain the metaphor: he inflamed
the man with the desire for glory; he fired him with wrath.

18 / Variety (6): Allegory

Allegory has the same effect as metaphor. In fact, allegory is nothing more
than a metaphor carried on beyond the bounds of a single word: for
example, 'fight hand to hand,' equivalent to 'get down to arguing'; 'strike at
the throat,' equivalent to 'attack the central issue'; and 'shoot a dart,'
equivalent to 'try to catch out.' Likewise, 'so as to scuttle the ship he is
sailing in,' that is, 'to overthrow the state whose destruction must necessarily involve his own ruin.' This usage is quite frequent in proverbs and
proverbial sayings; for example, 'smoke is not far from flame,' meaning
'one should start taking precautions against danger in good time'; 'good
wine needs no bush,' that is, 'a good thing does not need any other
recommendation'; 'treat a Cretan like a Cretan,' that is, 'a treacherous and
shifty person must be countered with lies and cunning.' In proverbs of this
sort allegory often results in enigma. This is no bad thing if you are
speaking or writing for an educated audience, and not even if you are
writing for the general public, for one should not write so that everyone can
understand everything, but so that people should be compelled to investigate and learn some things themselves.

19 / Variety (7): Catachresis

Similar in force is catachresis, for which the Latin word is *abusio* 'abuse' or

* * * * *

1 glassy waves] Virgil *Aeneid* 7.759
1 blooming years] Catullus 68.16
1 years slip past] Horace *Odes* 2.14.2
8 Allegory] See Quintilian 8.6.47.
10 fight hand to hand ... strike at the throat] Quoted in Quintilian 8.6.51 as
hackneyed law-court phraseology
11 'shoot a dart'] Plautus *Epidicus* 690
12 scuttle the ship] See line 8n, quoted from an unknown speech of Cicero;
Adagia II i 10.
15 not far from flame] Plautus *Curculio* 53; *Adagia* I v 20
17 needs no bush] *Adagia* II vi 20
18 like a Cretan] *Adagia* I ii 29
29 catachresis] For this section see Quintilian 8.2.6; 8.6.34.

'misapplication,' and it differs from metaphor in that we resort to misapplication where a proper word does not exist, to metaphor where we substitute something for the proper word; for example, we use the word 'parricide,' that is, 'father-killer,' for one who kills his brother, because 'fratricide' is not used; and *piscina* 'fish-pond' for a bathing-pool, although   5
there are no fish (*pisces*) in it. Other examples are: *short* powers of man, the
long wisdom of the man, *diminished* courage (for 'little').

Quintilian particularly recommends a style of speech which offers the
attractiveness of all three figures in combination – simile, allegory, and
metaphor. He quotes as an example this passage from Cicero: 'Do you think   10
that any sea-strait, any channel, displays motions, agitations, alterations,
fluxes and refluxes that can match the surging and turbulence manifested in
our electoral procedures? One day allowed to pass, one night interposed,
can unsettle the entire situation, and the faintest breath of rumour can
change the whole popular attitude.'   15

A simile is a metaphor that is made explicit and specifically related to
the subject. Cicero's word for this is *collatio* 'comparison.' 'He was white-
hot with anger' is a metaphor; 'his whole face was suffused with rage just as
iron glows in the fire' is a simile. It is a simile when Cicero compares the
tides of a narrow sea-strait with the uncertainty of elections. 'Turbulence   20
manifested' is an allegory, 'the breath of rumour' a metaphor.

These figures of speech are also involved in richness of subject-matter,
which I shall deal with in book II.

25

20 / Variety (8): Onomatopoeia

Variety is also provided by onomatopoeia or word-making, for example,
taratantara for the sound of a trumpet, or *sibilus, murmur, mugitus* 'whistle,

* * * * *

4 'fratricide'] *Fratricida* does occur in Cicero, *De domo sua* 26, where it appears to
be invented for the occasion: *patricida fratricida sororicida.*
5 *piscina*] Festus 318 (Lindsay): *ad quam et natatum et exercitationis alioqui causa
veniebat populus.*
6 Other examples]*Ad Herennium* 4.33.45
10 Cicero] *Pro Murena* 35, quoted in Quintilian 8.6.49
16 A simile ... book II] Added in *1534* (LB I 19C)
17 *collatio*] Cicero *De inventione* 1.49: *collatio est oratio rem cum re ex similitudine
conferens.* See below 623:19.
17 white-hot with anger] Cicero *Tusculan Disputations* 4.43
28 onomatopoeia] For all this section see Quintilian 8.6.31ff.
29 *taratantara*] Ennius *Annals* 140 (Vahlen): *at tuba terribili sonitu taratantara dixit.*

murmur, moo.' Paragoge also belongs here, that is, the derivation and extrapolation of new words by analogy with existing forms.

I really do not see why we should be afraid to resort to this procedure if ever our sentence requires it. The verb *sullaturire* [was invented to mean] 'to want to behave like Sulla.' Other verbs in *-turire* that we use are *cacaturire*, *micturire, esurire* 'to want to evacuate the bowels, to make water, to eat.' Why should we not use other similar forms created by analogy: *dormiturire, scripturire, proscripturire, dicturire, bellaturire, nupturire* 'want to sleep, write, have a proscription, speak, fight, get married'? As we have the verb *graecari* meaning 'play the Greek,' why should we not also use *iuvenari, poetari, cornicari, rhetoricari, philosophari, theologari* meaning 'play the youth, poet, crow, rhetorician, philosopher, theologian'? Plautus was not afraid of using *vulpinari,* 'play the fox,' translating the Greek ἀλωπεκίζειν. [We have derivatives in *-atus* meaning 'provided with, wearing,' for example,] *laureati* 'laurel-decked,' *nummati* 'moneyed,' *scutati* 'shield-bearing.' Why not the similar words *pilleati, larvati, personati* meaning 'capped, demon-possessed, masked,' and so on? Why not a verb *siccescere* [derived from *siccus* 'dry'] meaning 'to dry up,' as well as *arescere* [from *aridus*]?

It is true that the Greeks are far more successful than speakers of Latin in creations of this kind; they invented *cretissare, platonissare* 'to act the Cretan, to try to be a Plato' and many more. All the same I think we should sometimes be venturesome, especially in verse and in translating from the Greek. We can certainly make bold use of forms already in authors of the right sort, nor should we consider harsh or obsolete any word that occurs in a reputable writer. Here I totally disagree with those who wince at any word they have not actually found in Cicero, as if it were a barbarism.

You should also observe that there can be various forms of derivative from one basic word, as I mentioned earlier: *voluptuosus* and *voluptuarius* 'voluptuary,' *edax* and *edo* 'glutton,' *homunculus, homulus, homuncio* 'manikin,' *pauxillum* and *paucula* 'rather few.'

* * * * *

4 *sullaturire*] Invented by Cicero *Ad Atticum* 9.10.6: *ita sullaturit animus eius et proscripturit* (line 8). Many of the words mentioned by Erasmus are noncewords occurring somewhere in Latin literature, though some are not classical at all (see line 24): *cacaturire,* Martial; *micturire,* Juvenal; *graecari,* Horace. Some are words used by Cicero and therefore acceptable (see next paragraph): *esurire, laureatus, nummatus, personatus, philosophari, arescere; scutatus, pilleatus* are classical words which happen not to occur in Cicero; *larvatus* occurs only in ante- and post-classical Latin.

12 Plautus] According to Nonius Marcellus 46, not Plautus but Varro; ἀλωπεκίζειν in Aristophanes *Wasps* 1241; *Adagia* I ii 28

26 barbarism] See 313:25n.

28 earlier] Chap 13

The observation of all these points will contribute a great deal to your linguistic resources, because much of the wealth of the Latin language lies in created forms of this sort.

21 / Variety (9): Metalepsis

Very similar to catachresis is metalepsis, in Latin *transumptio* 'transition.' In this we move by stages towards our meaning, for example: 'hid in lustreless caverns'; lustreless implies black, black implies dark, dark finally implies dropping away into vast depths. Similarly the Greeks call something 'sharp-pointed' when they mean 'swift.' This figure of speech is more likely to occur in poetry than in prose. It could be considered a form of synecdoche, like the following.

22 / Variety (10): Metonomy

This next figure, known as metonomy, 'shift of name,' is also very helpful in expanding our resources. There are various forms of it. We can, for example, put the discoverer for the thing discovered: 'Ceres by sea-water spoiled' (Virgil); 'Without Ceres and Bacchus Venus stays cold' (Terence); 'Neptune with the land conjoined / Walls off the fleets from northern blasts' (Horace); 'to consecrate to Vulcan'; 'to fight with Mars' favour fluctuating'; 'Venus adds to eye and voice.' In all these the discoverer or the presiding deity is put for the thing itself. If the process is reversed the effect is rather harsh: 'Let us Wine adore.' The god is truly present here in the wine, and so Wine is put for Bacchus.

* * * * *

10 lustreless caverns] Virgil *Aeneid* 1.60
12 'sharp-pointed'] See Quintilian 8.6.37, where, according to modern texts, he says the opposite: that the Greeks use 'swift' for 'sharp-pointed' (as in Homer *Odyssey* 15.299); Erasmus' text of Quintilian may well have had the former reading (found for example in the Paris 1543 text of Quintilian).
19 metonomy] For this whole section see Quintilian 8.6.23ff.
22 Virgil] *Aeneid* 1.178; Ceres for corn
22 Terence] *Eunuchus* 732; Bacchus for wine, Venus for love
24 Horace] *Ars poetica* 64; Neptune for sea
24 consecrate to Vulcan] That is, burn; Marcus Aurelius writing to Fronto (*Correspondence of Fronto* 4.5, Loeb Classical Library 1 178)
24 Mars'] For battle; also Vulcan for fire: see Quintilian 8.6.24.
27 'Let us Wine adore'] Diomedes *Ars grammatica* II in Keil 1 458; line from Plautus quoted by Servius in commentary on Virgil *Aeneid* 1.724

LB I 19F

Second, we can use the container for the thing contained: wine-jars 'drunk to the lees'; river 'beloved of heaven' (that is, of the dwellers in heaven); 'a prosperous age.' Again we can reverse the process, though the result is harsher and more violent: 'Next burns Ucalegon,' as Virgil wrote, putting the man for his house. Terence says 'Let's go to us' for 'to our house'; or we can say 'the man is being devoured,' meaning his property is being squandered: 'I hand this man on to you to be devoured'; or, as in Horace, 'had a taste of one old chap' (that is, of his money). Here the possessor is put for the possession.

Thirdly, we can indicate the effect by expressing the cause: 'he was better at the oars.' [Virgil] is here talking of his speed, which was achieved by oars. Vice versa: 'sluggish cold,' 'away with sad fears,' 'pallid Death,' 'bold youth,' 'pale sicknesses dwell there and sad old age,' 'headlong wrath,' 'gay youth,' 'unthinking love,' 'immodest night,' 'bold wine.'

The leader can be used for those he leads: sixty thousand troops were slain by Hannibal at Cannae; or the author for his works: the Virgil is for sale; one should constantly be consulting Pliny.

It is a similar usage to say 'a sacrilege has been detected' instead of 'a sacrilegious man,' or 'to have knowledge of arms' not 'of the art of arms.'

I think we should include in this class those words that can be applied both to persons and to things: an eloquent man or an eloquent speech, a bold man or a bold deed, you have confuted the man or you have confuted his arguments.

As examples of this sort are ready to hand on all sides, I desist from pursuing the matter any further.

* * * * *

2 'drunk to the lees,' 'a prosperous age'] Quintilian 8.6.24
2 'beloved of heaven'] Virgil *Aeneid* 8.64
4 Virgil] *Aeneid* 2.311
5 to us] *ad nos,* passim in Plautus and Terence for *ad aedes nostras*
7 to be devoured] Terence *Eunuchus* 1087, quoted Nonius Marcellus 33
8 Horace] *Satires* 2.5.22
11 Virgil] *Aeneid* 5.153
12 'sluggish cold'] *Ad Herennium* 4.32.43
12 sad fears] *Aeneid* 1.202
12 'pallid Death'] Horace *Odes* 1.4.13
13 'bold youth'] Virgil *Georgics* 4.565: *audaxque iuventā*
13 pale sicknesses ... old age] Virgil *Aeneid* 6.275
13 'headlong wrath,' 'gay youth'] Quintilian 8.6.27
15 The leader ... arms] See Quintilian 8.6.26, who quotes this type of figure as oratorical and poetic.
20 I think ... any further] Added in *1534* (LB I 20D)

23 / Variety (11): Synecdoche

Synecdoche is also extremely useful. Some people call it intellection, because we understand one thing from another, like understanding *many* from *one*, as in the example I gave earlier: 'the Roman, victorious in battle'; or, 'the Carthaginian routed' for 'Carthaginians.' We can also understand the whole from the part, for example, blade for sword, roof for house. Or the other way round: 'A mighty sea crashing down from the heights'; or 'Others brought fountain and fire': *sea* is for (storming) wave, *fountain* for a portion of spring-water. (Both examples are from Virgil.)

Or we can understand a class from one example: 'More stormy than the Adriatic' (Horace) for sea in general; 'draughts of Achelous' (Virgil) for any river. This type is not so satisfactory if reversed.

Or the thing made from the material employed: steel for sword, fir or pine for ship.

Or subsequent actions from previous ones: broke her virgin-knot, that is, deflowered; spurred on his horse, that is, galloped; washed and oiled, that is, clean and shining.

In short, whenever one thing is understood from another in any way whatsoever: they have lived, that is, they are dead; 'we too once knew our glory'; 'we Trojans are no more'; 'yonder, smoke is rising from the farm-house roofs.' In this last example we understand that night is falling, though something very different is said. We deduce the thing signified from the sign.

* * * * *

3 Synecdoche] See Quintilian 8.6.19ff; *Ad Herennuim* 4.33.44; Diomedes *Ars grammatica* II in Keil I 459.
5 earlier] Chap 13
10 Virgil] *Aeneid* 1.114; 12.119
12 Horace] *Odes* 3.9.23
12 Virgil] *Georgics* 1.9
16 virgin-knot] See Catullus 67.28.
17 spurred on his horse] Livy 2.20.2
17 washed and oiled] Terence *Phormio* 339
20 they have lived] *vixerunt*, used euphemistically to avoid the word 'dead'; see Plutarch *Cicero* 22.2, where it is used by Cicero to announce the execution of the Catilinarian conspirators.
20 knew our glory] Ovid *Tristia* 5.8.19
21 are no more] Virgil *Aeneid* 2.325; for these last three examples see *Adagia* I ix 50.
21 farm-house roofs] Virgil *Eclogues* 1.83

24 / Variety (12): Equivalence

Very effective is *ἰσοδυναμία* or equivalence. This is produced by adding, removing, or doubling a negative, combined with the use of opposites: he holds the first place, he is not among the last; a remarkably learned man, a man by no means ignorant; he did everything, there was nothing he did not do; one must not employ no deception against the man, that is, one must employ some deception. By using a word meaning the opposite and adding or removing a negative you can immediately give your speech a new look: it pleases, it does not displease; I accept the terms, I do not reject the terms. I shall deal in more detail with these and other equivalents in the appropriate place.

There are various ways in which pairs of words can contrast. Some are opposites: love, hate; angry, gracious; handsome, ugly. In some pairs one term marks an absence of some feature: blind, seeing; dead, alive; deaf, hearing; dumb, speaking. Such privative terms can only be applied where the nature of the thing is capable of either state. A stone cannot be described as dead or blind. In some pairs one contradicts the other: I refuse, I want; learned, unlearned; he approves, he disapproves; she is a plain girl, she is not at all pretty; she is by no means plain, she is extremely pretty; the man is by no means deaf, he has a good set of ears; he has not got very good ears, he is rather deaf: I cannot fail to approve [, I cannot approve].

I shall speak about correlated expressions shortly.

Pairs of expressions signifying activity and passivity belong here: he received a serious injury at his hands, he inflicted a serious injury on him; certain qualities are found lacking in Cicero by scholars, scholars find certain qualities lacking in Cicero.

These I have already discussed elsewhere.

25 / Variety (13): Paired expressions

In quite a number of paired expressions the transformation is operated without the use of negatives, simply by the interchange of the appropriate elements: he values reputation above money, he rates money lower than

* * * * *

11 appropriate place] Chap 47
13 various ways] See Aristotle *Categories* 10. Lines 13–28 'There are … elsewhere,' added in 1534 (LB I 21 A–B)
23 shortly] Chap 26
28 elsewhere] Chap 13

LB I 20F

reputation; he thinks less of reputation than money, he thinks more of money than reputation; he puts profit before honour, he puts honour second to profit. This form of linguistic resource depends on opposites, such as: look up to, look down on; care for, neglect; seek, reject; and countless others of the same sort.

26 / Variety (14): Interchange of correlated expressions

It is likewise easy to get variety by the use of correlated expressions, which themselves belong to this same class of opposites: she does not want to be his wife, she does not want him for a husband; he refuses to be his father-in-law, he rejects him as a son-in-law; I am ashamed to have her as my daughter-in-law, I am ashamed to be known as her mother-in-law; I would not wish for any other father, I would not prefer to be the son of any other man; how fortunate I am in my teacher, how fortunate I am to be your pupil; beware of hiring out your land to him, do not arrange to let him rent your land; she has been waiting a long time to get married to somebody, she is waiting for some man to marry her; I would not wish to be in your debt, I would not wish to have you as my creditor; you taught me this, I learnt this from you; Paul told me this, I heard this from Paul; a rock gave you birth, you were born of a rock; you will get considerable advantage from it, it will bring you considerable advantage; your literary pursuits will win you no little distinction, no little distinction will accrue as a result of your literary pursuits; the father was reconciled with his son, the son returned to good relations with his father.

27 / Variety (15): Heightening

We can also use auxesis, that is, increase, when we use a more violent word in place of the normal one in order to heighten what we are saying; for example, to say 'slain' for 'killed,' or 'highway robber' for 'dishonest'; to say that somebody 'is done for' when something unpleasant happens to him, or that someone is 'out of his mind' when he is struck by grief, 'murdered' when he is in pain, 'dumb' if he makes no reply, 'to have come to life again' if hope revives, to 'forget' an injury if he forgives it. We should include here

* * * * *

21 a rock gave you birth] Virgil *Aeneid* 4.366
31 auxesis] Quintilian 8.4.1ff
35 'out of his mind'] As in Terence *Phormio* 564: *exanimatam metu*

those exaggerated expressions I mentioned earlier, such as calling a cruel
man 'a hangman,' a wicked man 'a profaner of the sacred,' a bad woman 'a
poisoner'; also the use of the expressions 'a wickedness,' 'a portent,' 'a
pest,' 'a disaster' to refer to people; and finally using 'Atreus' for a cruel
man, 'Sardanapalus' for an effeminate one. These I shall deal with at greater
length in the appropriate place.

28 / Variety (16): Hyperbole

Next comes hyperbole, for which someone invented the Latin term *super-
latio* 'exaggeration.' In this, as Seneca says, we reach the truth by saying
something which is obviously false. Hyperbole says more than the situation warrants, yet the truth can be inferred from the falsehood: for example,
he could split rocks with his never-ending chatter; to touch heaven with
one's finger; swifter than the east wind; swifter than the wings of the
thunder; I shall strike the stars with my exalted head.

29 / Variety (17): Meiosis

The opposite of auxesis is μείωσις [meiosis], that is, diminution, saying
less than we mean, for example, 'touch' for 'hit,' 'hurt' for 'wound.'
     Diminution too can sometimes involve hyperbole: 'they scarce cling
to their bones'; 'shorter than a pygmy'; he has less than nothing. But again
I shall have something to say about this type when I reach the proper place.

* * * * *

 1 earlier] See Chap 14; this material will be treated in more detail in chap 46.
11 hyperbole] See Quintilian 8.6.67–74.
12 Seneca] See *De beneficiis* 7.22.1, especially: *quaedam praecipimus ultra modum ut
     ad verum et suum redeant.*
15 never-ending chatter] In *Adagia* prolegomena xiii (LB II 12A) Erasmus gives
     saxa clamore rumpit as an example of hyperbole.
15 touch heaven] *Adagia* IV iii 67: 'Caelum digito attingere,' also containing
     sublimi feriam sidera vertice
16 east wind] Virgil *Aeneid* 8.223; 12.733
16 wings of the thunder] *Aeneid* 5.319; 10.248
17 my exalted head] Horace *Odes* 1.1.36
22 The opposite] See Quintilian 8.4.1.
24 cling to their bones] Virgil *Eclogues* 3.102, of a sick flock
25 'shorter than a pygmy'] Juvenal 6.506
26 proper place] Chap 46

30 / Variety (18): Arrangement

We can also vary our expression by changing the way our phrases are linked
together. Various figures are involved here; asyndeton [that is, absence of
link]: 'I came, I saw, I conquered'; polysyndeton [that is, plurality of link]:
'and roof and home / And arms and Spartan hound and Cretan quiver'
(Virgil); zeugma, that is, when several concepts are related to one verb. This
can be done in three ways – by putting the verb first, last, or in the middle:
beauty fades through sickness or old age; through sickness or old age
beauty fades; through old age beauty fades, or through sickness. Here is an
example from Cicero: 'A victory was won over modesty by lust, over fear by
audacity, over reason by madness.' And an example of the other arrangement: 'You are not the sort of person, Catiline, that shame from crime, or
fear from danger, or reason from mad folly has ever recalled.'

Sometimes instead of repeating the link word we repeat a noun or
verb in the figure known as epanalepsis [that is, taking up again]: 'Are you
totally unmoved by our need of a night watch on the Palatine, unmoved by
the guards about the city, unmoved by the fears of the people, unmoved by
the assembling of all loyal citizens, unmoved by this impressive building
where the Senate has met, unmoved by the faces and the looks of all those
here?' A similar example would be: A victory was won over modesty by
lust, a victory over fear by audacity, a victory over reason by madness. Or
one could use not the same word but συνωνυμία [synonym]: A victory was
won over fear by audacity, madness conquered reason, lust carried modesty by storm.

Here is an example showing what variations on the same sentiment
can be achieved by the use of these figures: he scorns the gods, he scorns
men too; the gods he scorns, men he scorns; he scorns both gods and men;
both gods and men he scorns; the gods he scorns, and also men.

The following arrangements also belong under this head: [he could
endure lack of food more easily than cold]; lack of food could he endure
more easily than cold; profit rather than fame did he desire; he desired

* * * * *

5 I conquered] Suetonius *Julius* 37.2

7 Virgil] *Georgics* 3.344–5

9 beauty fades] See *Ad Herennium* 4.27.38.

11 Cicero] *Pro Cluentio* 15; see Quintilian 9.3.62, 77.

12 other arrangement] Cicero *Catilinarians* 1.22

16 Are you ...] *Catalinarians* 1.1 .

19 impressive] LB, like 1526, 1534, reads *magnificentissimus* but with a footnote,
lege munitissimus 'fortified'; this agrees with modern texts. The 1512 and 1514
editions read, in error, *munificentissimus*.

LB I 22A

profit rather than fame; profit he desired rather than fame; dearer do I hold
no one; no one do I hold more dear.

These uses do not contribute a great deal, but they play their part, as
does [the use of the 'connecting relative' as in] 'for which reasons'; or the
variations 'on that account,' 'on account of that,' 'for a reason so slight,' 'for
so slight a reason,' 'I will come to you since your father so wishes,' 'since
your father so wishes I will come.'

It is the same principle when we turn simple sentences into compound
ones, or vice versa; for example, 'you owe everything to me' is a simple
sentence, 'everything that you have, you owe to me' a compound one.

31 / Variety (19): Syntax or construction

Another thing which can contribute to variety is organization or construction, as I mentioned earlier. There are quite a number of expressions which
allow more than one construction: [*multus* 'much' can either be an adjective
in agreement,] *multum pudorem* 'much shame,' [or be used in the partitive
genitive construction,] *multum pudoris* 'a great deal of shame'; [*scribere* 'to
write' can be followed either by the dative case or by the preposition *ad* 'to'
governing an accusative case:] *scripsit mihi* or *ad me* 'he wrote to me';
[*diversus* and *alienus* 'different' can take either dative or *ab* 'from' governing
an ablative case:] *diversum, alienum huic,* or *ab hoc* 'different from this';
[likewise *idem* 'the same,' with either dative or *cum* 'with' governing an
ablative case:] *idem huic* or *idem cum hoc* 'the same as this'; [*iactare* 'to boast'
either with an accusative object or with *de* 'about' governing an ablative:]
iactat maiores suos or *iactat se de suis maioribus* 'he boasts of his forebears';
[*somniare* 'to dream of' with accusative or *de* with ablative:] *te* or *de te
somniavi* 'I dreamed of you'; [similarly *ridere* 'to laugh at':] *te* or *de te ridet* 'he
laughs at you'; [duration of time can be expressed by accusative case or
ablative:] *tota nocte* or *totam noctem potavit* 'he drank the whole night
through;' [*summus* 'the greatest' either with a genitive,] *Romanorum summus*
'the greatest of the Romans,' [or with a prepositional phrase,] *summus inter
Romanos* 'the greatest among the Romans'; [comparative expressions can be
followed either by the ablative case or by a phrase introduced by *quam*:]
servitus morte durior or *durior quam mors* 'servitude harsher than death';
[*damnare* 'to find guilty' is combined either with *de* governing an ablative or
with a genitive to express the charge:] *damnatus est de repetundis* or *repetundarum* 'he was found guilty of extortion'; [*natus* with dative or with *ad*

* * * * *

16 earlier] Chap 13

LB I 22D

governing an accusative:] *natus gloriae* or *ad gloriam* 'born for glory'; *tuae partes sunt* [nominative] or *tuarum est partium* [genitive] 'it is your role' or 'it belongs to your role.'

32 / Variety (20): Change in sentence form (various types)

The expression is also varied when it is given a different cast, a different outer garb so to speak, which we may for the moment call a change of form; that is, the form of a statement, such as 'Death is not bitter' can be transformed into a question (*interrogatio*), 'Is it then such a bitter thing to die?' or, 'There is nothing more contemptible than you' can become 'Could there be anything more contemptible than you?' Or we can use irony (*ironia*): 'You did not win much praise' can be rephrased as 'That was indeed splendid praise you won'; 'The people are not interested in all that' becomes 'That of course is of prime concern to the people.' Or we can change the tone by an expression of surprise (*admiratio*): 'He is passionately fond of money' becomes 'Ye gods, how he loves money!' or by an expression of uncertainty (*dubitatio*): 'He scorns both gods and men' becomes 'I do not know whether he is more contemptuous of gods or of men.' Or by an oath (*adiuratio*): 'Nothing do I hold more dear or more to be preferred than glory' becomes 'I'll be damned if I honour anything more than glory'; or by a vehement rejection (*abominatio*): 'Such a thought never entered my head' becomes 'Heaven forbid that I should think such a thing'; or by an exclamation (*exclamatio*): 'He is a man of remarkable vanity' becomes 'Oh the incredible vanity of the man!' Or by the figure called anticipation (*occupatio*): 'Not only did he assault several girls, he even violated a Vestal virgin' becomes 'He assaulted several girls, to say nothing at this point of his violation of a Vestal.'

Or by making suggestions and then rejecting them (*subiectio*), as in this passage: 'You are of obscure birth, and without a penny; you have no education, no looks, no ability; so why are you so proud of yourself?' This becomes: 'What makes you so arrogant? Distinguished parentage? But your family was totally obscure. Wealth? You are poorer than Irus. Education? You have never read a decent book in your life. Looks? You are uglier than

* * * * *

11 bitter thing to die] Virgil *Aeneid* 12.646, quoted by Quintilian 8.5.6
16 concern to the people] Terence *Andria* 185
34 Irus] A beggar in the house of Ulysses, proverbial for a poor man; Martial 5.39.9; *Adagia* I iii 57

Thersites. Ability? You are favoured with the thickest of brains. How can this bragging of yours be anything but sheer madness?'

Not only can the outer form of the whole utterance be varied, but also each separate topic. This however seems to belong rather with wealth of subject-matter, so I will discuss it in detail in book II.

Thus far I have briefly indicated most of the forms that can be employed to change the expression while the underlying meaning remains the same.

33 / Methods 1–20: Practical demonstration

To make it easier to understand what I have been saying, let us have a practical demonstration. We will take one or two sentences and see how far we can go in transforming the basic expression into a Protean variety of shapes – not that every method of variation can be applied to any one sentence, but we shall apply the ones that lend themselves to the example in question. Let us, for example, take this sentence: 'Your letter pleased me mightily' *tuae litterae me magnopere delectarunt.*

your: There is no synonym for 'your,' but a periphrasis is possible: Your excellency's, your highness's, your majesty's. If we insert a proper name such as 'Faustus' and say 'Faustus' letter', we employ two forms of heterosis, the substitution of a noun for a pronoun and of a third person for a second. If we say 'Faustine letters,' using a derivative adjective instead of the genitive of the noun, that is yet another form of heterosis.

letter: epistle, letter, note (synonym); epistolet, letterette, notelet (heterosis, [using a diminutive form]); pages, lines (synecdoche); what you wrote to me (periphrasis).

pleased: delighted, refreshed, exhilarated (synonyms, though 'exhilarated' is better considered a metaphor); brought pleasure, were a pleasure, were delightful (these and similar expressions illustrate periphrasis); bathed in delight, were honey-sweet, and so on (transferred or metaphorical expressions); were not unwelcome, not unpleasing (these result from the interchange of opposites).

* * * * *

1 Thersites] The ugliest man among the Greeks at Troy; *Adagia* IV iii 80
22 'Faustus'] Erasmus is presumably thinking of his friend of early days in Paris, the poet Fausto Andrelini. See Ep 84 introduction.
29 *pleased*] The arrangement of LB I 23E–F, where the sections follow the Latin word order of the specimen sentence, has been adjusted to accord with the English word order.

LB I 23B

me: my spirits, my heart, my eyes (periphrasis or synecdoche); us (enallage of the number); Erasmus (heterosis of the person).

mightily: greatly, intensely, extremely, wonderfully, marvellously, extraordinarily (synonym); mightily, hugely, superlatively, exceedingly, singularly (αὔξησις heightening); in no scant measure, on no small scale, in no common manner (opposites and negatives); it is impossible to say how much, it is beyond belief, I could not find words to express (these and similar expressions are on the way to hyperbole).

Other points can be conveniently illustrated only in the context of a complete sentence, so let us move on to our demonstration:

Your letter mightily pleased me; to a wonderful degree did your letter please me; me exceedingly did your letter please. (So far hardly anything has been changed but the word order.)

By your letter was I mightily pleased; I was exceedingly pleased by your letter. (Here only the voice of the verb is altered.)

Your epistle exhilarated me intensely; I was intensely exhilarated by your epistle; your brief note refreshed my spirits in no small measure; I was in no small measure refreshed in spirit by your grace's hand; from your affectionate letter I received unbelievable pleasure; your affectionate letter brought me unbelievable pleasure. (Here we have both hyperbole and reciprocal expression.)

Your pages engendered in me an unfamiliar delight; I conceived a wonderful delight from your pages; your lines conveyed to me the greatest joy; the greatest joy was brought me by your lines; we derived great delight from your excellency's letter. (Again we have examples of reciprocal expression.)

In the other examples the reader will easily identify the figure for himself:

From my dear Faustus' letter I derived much delight.

At your words a delight of no ordinary kind came over me.

I was singularly delighted by your epistle.

In these Faustine letters I found a wonderful kind of delectation.

To be sure, how your letter delighted my spirits!

Your brief missive flooded me with inexpressible joy. (Here we have a metaphor.)

As a result of your letter, I was suffused by an unfamiliar gladness.

Your communication poured vials of joy on my head. (Again a metaphor.)

Your epistle afforded me no small delight.

* * * * *

11 letter mightily pleased me] The variations on this (LB I 23F–6A) are numbered i–cxlvi in 1512.

36 vials of joy] Cf Terence *Phormio* 856: *delibutum gaudio*.

How delighted I was to read your letter!
The perusal of your letter charmed my mind with singular delight.
Your epistle was delightful to a degree.
Your letter affected me with extraordinary gladness.
As a result of your letter I was affected with singular gladness.   5
Your epistle was the greatest joy to me.
Your missive was to me a very great delight.
Your epistle was an incredible joy to me.
How exceedingly agreeable did we find your epistle!
You could scarce credit what relief I find in your missive. (Cicero frequently   10
uses 'find relief' in the sense 'take pleasure.')
Your epistle was to us one of great delightfulness.
Your letter was very sweet to me.
Your letter was the source of singular gladness.
Your letter made me positively jump for joy.   15
Your letter having arrived, I was transported with joy.
When your letter was delivered, I was filled with delight.
Once I had read your affectionate letter, I was carried away with a strange
happiness.
On receipt of your letter, an incredible delight seized my spirits.   20
Your epistle poured the balm of happiness over me.
Your writing to me was the most delightful thing possible.
The fact that you had written to me was extremely pleasurable to me.
Your honouring me with a letter was the most agreeable of occurrences.
Your brief note made me burst with joy.   25
How overjoyed I was by your letter!
I was both pleased and delighted that you communicated with me by letter.
When your letter arrived, you could have seen me jumping for all the joy I
felt.
That you paid your respects by letter was assuredly a satisfaction to me.   30
Nothing more wished for than your letter could have been brought me.
Your letter has reached us, and eagerly looked for it was.
Nothing more desired than your letter could have been brought us. (These
last three illustrate metalepsis, or at any rate synecdoche, for things that we
greatly desire are pleasurable when they arrive.)   35
Faustine letters cannot but be most delightful to Erasmus.

* * * * *

10 Cicero] For example, *Ad Atticum* 11.10.2: *quid est ubi acquiescam nisi quamdiu
tuas litteras lego.*
31 wished for] See Cicero *Ad familiares* 16.21.1, where the arrival of a letter is
exoptatissimus.
36 Faustine letters] See 348:22n.

Not unpleasing was your epistle to me.
Your by no means displeasing letter has arrived.
Your missive by no means failed of a welcome.
Your epistle was to me the sweetest of the sweet.
I read and reread your letter with great pleasure.   5
It was not without the greatest pleasure that I received your letter.
The man who delivered your letter conveyed a wealth of joy.
Wonderful to relate how your letter entranced me.
The pages I received from you sent a new light of joy stealing over my heart.
Your letter promptly expelled all sorrow from my mind.   10
I sensed a wonderful happiness in my spirits when your letter was handed me.
From your letter an unaccustomed happiness swept over my spirits.
Your letter caused me to rejoice to the full.
Because of your letter my whole self exulted with joy.   15
It is difficult to say how much happiness was occasioned in me by your letter.
I can hardly find words to express the extent of the joy to which your letter gave rise.
It is wonderful to tell what a ray of delight beamed forth from your letter.   20
Good God, what a mighty joy proceeded from your epistle!
Heavens, what causes for joy did your letter provide!
Ye gods, what a power of joy did your missive supply!
The happiness occasioned by your communication is greater than I can describe.   25
Your messenger brought me a deal of pleasure.
You could scarce credit the load of happiness your letters conveyed to my mind.
I cannot find words to tell the joys that your letter loaded on me. (Why hesitate to use such an expression, when Terence spoke of the day being   30 'loaded' with blessings?)
Your letter heaped joy upon me.
I rejoiced greatly at your letter.
I found singular pleasure in your letter.
Your missive showered a wealth of gladness upon me.   35
Your epistle was most delightful to me.
Your letter caused me quite to smooth my brow.

* * * * *

30 Terence] *Phormio* 842
37 smooth my brow] See Terence *Adelphi* 839: *exporge frontem.*

At the sight of your letter the frown fled from my mind's brow.
As I read the words you wrote me, a marvellous happiness stole over my mind.
As soon as I looked into your letter, a strange force of joy occupied my mind.
As my eye fell on your letter, an incredible tide of joy swelled in my breast.
When I received your most gracious letter, boundless happiness occupied every recess of my soul.
May I die the death if anything more delightful than your letter ever came my way.
May I perish if I ever met with anything in my whole life more agreeable than your letter.
As I aspire to the love of the Muses, nothing more gladsome than your letter has ever ere this befallen me.
Never believe that fortune could cast anything more delightful in my path than your letter.
As you are dear to my soul, even so does your letter delight me.
Ye heavens, what joy your letter roused in me!
What gaiety, what applause, what exultation your letter occasioned!
Reading your tasteful letter, I experienced an uncommon joy.
Your pen sated me with delight.
Your epistle provided me with much pleasure.
Your graceful epistle filled me wholly with delight.
Your charming epistle filled every corner of my heart with delight.
Your letter cast a dew of rare joy upon me.
Your epistle bedewed my spirit with an unfamiliar delight.
Nothing more delightsome than your letter ever came my way.
I never set eyes on anything more gladly than your letter.
There is not a thing that I would receive with more pleasure than the latest letter from my dear Faustus.
Can you imagine the tide of joy on which I rode as I perceived in your letter your affection for me?
When the messenger handed me your letter, my spirit immediately felt the motions of an inexpressible delight.
What need have I to tell you of the pleasure that stirred the soul of your Erasmus on the receipt of your letter?
My soul overflowed with joy when your letter was delivered.
How glad I was to receive your epistle!
After your note was handed me, my spirit quite bubbled over with joy.

* * * * *

1 my mind's brow] See Horace *Satires* 2.2.125: *explicuit vino contractae seria frontis.*

LB I 25[A]

I was beside myself with joy when I received your letter.

The charm of your letter put shackles of delight on my soul.

I cannot but rejoice mightily whenever a missive of yours comes flying to me.

Your letter was pure honey to me.

Whatever kind of a letter leaves your hand seems to me flowing with sweetness and honey.

I was most luxuriously refreshed at the sumptuous banquet of your letter.

What you wrote is sweeter to me than any ambrosia.

The pages of my dear Faustus were more splendid to me than Sicilian feasts.

There is no pleasure, no delight, that I would willingly compare with your letter.

All else is utterly repellent compared with your letter.

In the perusal of your affectionate letter the heart of Erasmus leapt for joy.

The pages scratched by your pen filled every part of me with joy.

Anything that arrives written by you is pure delight to my heart.

Your epistle exudes nothing but joy.

The man who brought your letter brought a feast day.

A triumph came with the man who delivered your letter.

Nectar I would not prefer to a message from you.

Could I possibly compare Attic honey with your dear letter?

Sugar is not sugar when set beside your letter.

The lotus tastes not as sweet to any mortal man as your letters do to me.

Your letters are to me like wine to a thirsty man.

Like clover to the bee, willow leaves to goats, honey to the bear, even so are your letters to me.

Your highness's letter was to me more honeyed than any honey.

Once I had received your longed-for letter, you might have said Erasmus was drunk with joy.

When your letter was delivered, you might have seen us tipsy with excess of delight.

* * * * *

7 sweetness] *saccaro*. In *1526* this word replaced *synere*, which Erasmus decided, after a correspondent inquired about it, was probably corrupt and of uncertain meaning. See Allen Epp 1803:99–105; 1824:27–46.

10 Faustus] Substituted for 'More' in *1534* (LB I 25D)

10 Sicilian feasts] A proverbial expression; see Horace *Odes* 3.1.18: *Siculae dapes*; *Adagia* II ii 68; ultimately derived, like the expressions on 354:6, 8, 10, 12, from *Paroemiographi graeci*, a collection of proverbs originating in antiquity but given definite form in the early Middle Ages.

25 clover to the bee] See Virgil *Eclogues* 10.30: *nec cytiso saturantur apes, nec fronde capellae*

I love you as no one else, and I delight in your letters as in nothing else.

Your lines seem to me pure enchantment.

Sweetmeats do not so delight the palate as your letter charms my soul.

No delicacies give such pleasure to the palate as your communication to the
mind.

The man who delivered your letter brought ἀμάξας ἡδονῶν [cart-loads of
pleasure].

Your messenger brought Δάθον [an Eldorado] of joy when he delivered
your letter.

He who handed over your pages brought with him θάλασσαν [a sea] of
joys.

Your letter was to me a positive Διὸς ἐγκέφαλος [choice morsel] for a
Persian, as the Greeks say.

If anyone thinks that some of these suggestions would hardly be
tolerable in prose, he should remember that this exercise is designed for the
composition of verse as well.

Let us now test out our skill in variation in the same way on some other
sentence, and let us choose one that is not of itself particularly fertile or
suggestive, so that it may be all the more apparent how effective this
technique of substitution can be, when it is confirmed by practice and
constant use.

So let us take this sentence: 'Always, as long as I live, I shall remember
you' *semper dum vivam tui meminero.* In the first place, to take the adverb
semper 'always,' there is no other word corresponding to it that has the same
force, and *semper* itself cannot generate other forms by inflection. Then
vivam 'live' is likewise without anything closely corresponding, and, as it is
an intransitive verb, it has only forms belonging to one voice, and the only
noun derived from it is *vita* 'life.' *memini* 'remember' is not only an intransitive verb, but is also defective and incomplete, and almost entirely unproductive, as it has no offspring but *memor* 'preserving the memory of' and
memoria 'memory.' Besides, the two verbs paired with these, *mori* 'die' and
oblivisci 'forget,' are themselves both defective and unproductive. All the

* * * * *

6 cart-loads of pleasure] *Adagia* I iii 32

8 Eldorado] Dathus was a colony of the Thasians, proverbial for its wealth;
Adagia I iii 33.

10 sea of joys] *Adagia* I iii 29

12 choice morsel] See 353:10n; also *Adagia* IV vii 53.

16 composition of verse] Erasmus was himself an accomplished writer of Latin
verse, which is collected in Reedijk. Most humanists wrote Latin (and sometimes Greek) verse, with greater or less skill, and schoolboys were expected to
compose verses.

same let us make a start. The reader will recognize the different types of
variation from the examples given earlier.

Always, as long as I live, I shall remember you.

Never, as long as I live, shall I fail to remember you.

Never during the time I yet shall live shall forgetfulness of you overcome
me.

At no time while I have life shall you disappear from my thoughts.

Never while I live will you find oblivion in me.

Never, as long as I remain among the living, shall oblivion of you find us.

I will not cease to remember you before I cease to live.

The memory of you will not leave me before life itself departs.

As long as I have breath, I shall be found mindful of you.

While I enjoy the light of life, you shall be fixed in my thoughts.

I would leave the fellowship of the living sooner than have the memory of
you removed from my breast.

I shall myself depart from the living before More departs from my memory.

The light of day shall fail me, before I begin to be forgetful of you.

Life shall desert me not a moment later than the remembrance of one so dear
to me.

The same day shall snatch from me the memory of you that shall snatch life
from me.

That same dawn is destined to bring oblivion of you that shall bring our
death.

There shall be the same end for our memory of you and for our life.

As long as I shall be mindful of myself, I shall never be sorry to remember
you.

There shall be no other extinction of our memory of you than the extinction
of the light of day.

That day alone shall quench my memory of you that quenches my life.

I shall begin to forget myself before I begin to forget you.

The memory of More will not steal from our breast before this soul steals
from us.

Save only death, no mischance shall cast you forth from my heart.

    * * * * *

  3 Always, as long as I live] The variations are numbered i–cxcv in *1512*, i–cc in
      1534 (LB I 26B–9E), where there have been some changes. For the sentiments
      behind many of the variations which follow, cf Paulinus of Nola *Carmina*
      11.61–2: *neque finis idem qui meo me corpore / et amore laxabit tuo*.

 16 More] Sir Thomas More, Erasmus' dearest friend; see Ep 114.

 25 sorry to remember] Virgil *Aeneid* 4.335

 33 cast you forth from my heart] *expectorare*; see section on archaic words, above
      312:2n.

LB I 26B

Could I ever while alive forget so delightful a companion?

Only then will Erasmus prove able to forget his beloved More, when he ceases to be mindful of himself.

As long as any consciousness is left to me, you shall always be present to my thoughts.

You are too dear to my heart ever to pass into forgetfulness, at least while I have life.

More is hidden deep within my heart, and nothing can cast him out from thence, save only Death.

I shall myself be delivered to Death before I consign you to oblivion.

While my spirit rules these eyes, these hands, you shall be fixed within my breast.

While the spirit directs these limbs, I shall remember you.

As long as breath remains in us, I shall be incapable of forgetting you.

While I am active in life, so long shall the memory of you live in me.

That day will end my life that begins oblivion of you.

The same fate shall tear this soul away and tear you from my love.

While the gods above grant me existence, I shall continually bear you in my thoughts.

While any spark of vital heat shall pulse within this breast my remembrance of you shall never fade away.

Life shall not be more lasting than the recollection of your services to me.

My memory of you will prove no shorter than life itself.

The remembrance of your dear head will be no less lasting than this life I live.

The day that takes away the memory of you will separate me from myself.

I shall be stolen away from myself before I cease to hold you in my thoughts.

My enjoyment of the light of day will last no longer than my remembrance of your benevolence.

Life will not go on longer than my recollection of you.

I shall be outside this self before More ceases to be within this breast.

This life and my remembrance of you shall keep pace together to the goal.

Erasmus will no longer exist when he is heedless of More.

This person will not be in existence, when I prove capable of forgetting so unique a friend.

As long as I shall be active in this world, I shall not allow my remembrance of your kindness to fade away.

As long as I breathe this common air, you shall many a time be present in my thoughts.

* * * * *

13 these limbs] Virgil *Aeneid* 4.336

LB I 26D

It shall never be that Erasmus retain life longer than his memory of you.

I shall not make an end of thinking of you till Atropos severs the fatal thread.

If any day shall ever bring forgetfulness of you, it shall certainly never precede the one that deprives me of the very light.

This sun that beholds everything shall never behold me unmindful of you.

Death alone shall dislodge from this heart the recollection of you.

As long as any portion of life shall remain in these limbs, More will never be absent from the thoughts of Erasmus.

While any drop of blood retains its warmth in this feeble frame, the memory of More will never grow cold in my heart.

As long as life shall remain mine, you shall never be absent from my thoughts.

How long soever shall remain unbroken this union of soul and mortal clay, never for one moment shall you be severed from my thoughts.

Sooner shall there no longer be soul within this body than you no longer in my thoughts.

Rather shall the spirit remove from this poor body's lodging than your image be erased that I bear engraved upon my heart.

My recollection of you shall equal my course through life.

The same finishing-post shall be set for my life and my thoughts of you.

My remembrance of you shall know no narrower bounds than life itself.

As long as any vein shall pulse with vital heat, to remember you shall ever prove delightful.

However long Lachesis shall draw out my thread of life, so long shall be drawn out my memory of you.

Life and thoughts of you shall have equal measure.

So long as the vital state shall maintain this body's mass, I shall retain a mind that above all remembers you.

While heaven's kindness grants me to enjoy the light of day, I shall always bear you in my thoughts.

While the gods above grant us life, we shall not allow carelessness of our loyal confrère ever to take us unawares.

While consciousness remains to me, I will never lay aside these remembering grateful thoughts.

* * * * *

1 memory of you] *1512, 1514* add: 'Life shall not endure beyond my memory of you.'

2 Atropos] One of the three Fates presiding over the lives of individuals. Clotho held the distaff, Lachesis spun the thread of life, Atropos inexorably cut it off.

24 Lachesis] See preceding n.

LB I 27A

As long as heaven wills that I enjoy the circling sun, so long shall you have in me a man who is mindful of you.
He who finds Erasmus heedless of you will not find him alive.
For all the time that life shall last for me, this mind of mine shall continue full of thoughts of you.
As long as it shall be my lot to enjoy this sky above our heads, it will not be my lot to forget you.
As long as life continues, you will always be present to the eyes of my heart.
I will forget my own name before I forget so rare a friend.
I shall lose myself before I lose the image of your face.
More will never pass from Erasmus' thoughts, while Erasmus lives.
No passage of time shall ever obliterate my memory of you.
The memory of you will only be extinguished when I am.
You will never be cast out of the doors of memory before the day that brings my destined end.
I will not stop remembering you until my death.
I will not cease to recall you until my latest hour.
Not until the last threads in my web of life are spun could I be forgetful of you.
While Erasmus lives, More's memory will never fade away.
My recollection of you no passage of time shall ever take off the statute book.
Before my final day the memory of you that I bear shall never be rescinded.
No injury inflicted by place or time shall cause me in this life not to recall you vividly.
I will remember you throughout all my life.
However long I shall have this mortal life, it will always be joined with memory of you.
My recollection of you shall follow me as far as the very grave.
I shall lose consciousness of myself before I shall lose the memory of a man most dear to me.
I shall be torn from these very limbs before you are rent from my mind.
Death shall find me sooner than forgetfulness of a head so dear.
I shall assuredly meet my end rather than cease to preserve your memory.
Your memory shall never be buried in me till I am buried myself.
My recollection of you shall perish with me or not at all.
The memory of my beloved More shall breathe within me until I breathe my last.
So long as we shall sojourn in this world, never shall oblivion of your grace assail me.

Until I meet my end, never shall forgetfulness of you occur to my mind.
(Seneca uses an expression like this.)
This mortal life can produce no fate so harsh that it can hammer your
memory from this heart of mine.
Nothing so cruel can happen to me in this mortal life as to cause me
heedlessness of you.
While I live, nothing can arise that would occasion forgetfulness of your
kindness towards me.
The memory of you is so deeply rooted in me that it will give way before
none of those mischances that befall us in this life.
You are consecrated in my heart in a monument that no passage of years can
demolish, save only death to which every mortal thing must yield.
Were I not mortal myself, I would not hesitate to declare this memory of you
that I hold to be immortal.
If Erasmus were immortal, the memory of you that he bears would likewise
be immortal.
Your kindnesses have set up a statue in the inmost recesses of my heart such
that no mischance can cast it down, as long as the earth shall support me.
More is inscribed in my heart in letters that no injurious time can ever
erode.
My recollection of you will only grow old as the years grow old.
I shall be cast out of myself before the name of More is driven from my
heart's shrine.
This one thing I declare and shall make good, that as long as I shall be
numbered among mortal men, you shall never be removed from the records
of my memory.
Though Time has power over all, this one thing surely shall never be
granted him, to cause me to forget you while I live.
Always this spirit of mine shall remember you above all else, and no
passage of time, however long, shall teach me to forget.
As long as the earth shall nourish me, the one thing I shall never be able to
unlearn is the remembrance of my dear companion.
As long as I shall be ἐπιχθόνιος [earth-propped], to use a Homeric word, I
shall continually preserve the memory of More.
As long as it shall be my lot to be numbered among σῖτον ἔδοντας [the

* * * * *

2 Seneca] See *De beneficiis* 1.12.1: *ingrato quoque memoria cum ipso munere incurrit*, where Erasmus' edition has a marginal note *incurrit animo*.
33 Homeric word] *Iliad* 1.266

Thomas More

'More's memory will never perish within me, unless I perish myself' was one of the
two hundred variations on this theme in *De copia*. When *De copia* was published in
1512 More was one of the four governors of Lincoln's Inn, an office to which he had
been elected in the previous year. His father, Sir John More, was also a member of
that society of lawyers. The Lincoln's Inn miniature, which may be the work of
Holbein, shows More in his later years, but the date is uncertain.
By permission of The Honourable Society of Lincoln's Inn

eaters of bread], to speak in Homeric fashion, never shall the face of More fade from this breast.

ὄφρ' ἂν ἔγωγε / ζωοῖσιν μετέω καί μοι φίλα γούνατ' ὀρώρῃ [As long as I shall associate with the living and my limbs shall bear me about], as Homer says, you can never be forgotten.

ἐμεῦ ζῶντος καὶ ἐπὶ χθονὶ δερκομένοιο [As long as I am alive and capable of perception], as we find written in Homer, forgetfulness shall never bear you from me.

I shall prolong the memory of you to match the course of my life.

While Erasmus survives, no day shall ever expunge the recollection of your highness.

I may be separated from you in body, but I shall always behold you in my mind, so long as the gods grant me the gift of life.

So long as the breath of life shall govern these limbs, you shall never for one moment be absent from my thoughts.

The memory of you is so deeply impressed on my heart that it cannot by any means be erased from there.

All things fade and fail with time, but your memory will flourish to the close of my days.

My beloved More is so closely embraced in my soul that he cannot escape while I live.

The day that sees me mindless of you will also see me lifeless.

You have engraved such a living image of yourself on my heart that hardly death itself will wipe it away.

Erasmus will not be more long-lived than his recollection of you.

Your memory will be so enduring that I myself will not endure any longer.

More's memory will never perish within me, unless I perish myself.

You will always find this man mindful of you, as long as he has any share in life.

I shall be separated from life before I am alienated from my memory of you.

My recollection of you is so tenacious of life that I shall not survive it.

You are too deeply embedded in my memory for anything to be able to dislodge you from there.

You cling too tightly to my heart for anything but the mischance of death to be able to cast you out.

You are too deeply hidden in this breast of mine to be driven out by any means, as long as the fates shall not grudge me life.

* * * * *

1 Homeric fashion] *Odyssey* 8.222
4 as Homer says] *Iliad* 22.387–8
7 written in Homer] *Iliad* 1.88

LB I 28B

You are too deeply implanted in my thoughts for me to survive if you are
rooted out from there.

Your image is too firmly impressed on my heart for me to outlive it, should
it be torn from thence.

The picture of you is so deeply embedded in my thoughts that no passage of   5
time will ever efface it.

While life is mine, nothing that happens will ever be strong enough to cast
down the statue of More set up in my thoughts.

It will never be that I live and am heedless of you.

As long as I dwell among men, not even all the waters of Lethe will be able to   10
dissolve my recollection of you.

As long as I feed on the breezes of heaven, I shall constantly recall you.

Provided God grants me life, I promise you a mind always thoughtful of
you.

Far from forgetting you while I live, if there is any consciousness when life   15
is past, I shall recall my beloved friend.

The last thing that shall befall me in this life is forgetfulness of you.

The rivers will run backwards to their source, as the Greek proverb has it,
when Erasmus shall prove capable of forgetting his dear More.

Only that man will see me heedless of you who sees the rivers, as Horace   20
says, 'From the plains glide backwards up the mountain steep / And Tiber
reverse his stream.'

Sooner shall fleet-footed deer feed among the clouds than forgetfulness of
More take Erasmus while he lives.

Your portrait is painted on the tablet of my heart in colours so vivid that no   25
long line of years can ever make it fade.

The last day of my life will discover me still mindful of you.

My life being safe, your memory will not flee from me.

This life being preserved, my memory of you will not die.

As long as this life bears me company, so shall the remembrance of you.   30

This life will depart from one still mindful of you.

Except life fly away, my memory of you will never do so.

Our recollection of you will endure to the furthest confines of existence.

In preserving your memory I shall never be untrue to my nature, unless I
cease to live.   35

* * * * *

18 rivers will run backwards] A poetic commonplace; for example, Ovid *Amores*
2.1.26: *inque suos fontes versa recurrit aqua*; *Adagia* I iii 15
20 Horace] *Odes* 1.29.10–12
23 among the clouds] Virgil *Eclogues* 1.60
26 line of years] Horace *Odes* 3.30.5

LB I 28E

As long as the kindness of heaven shall preserve to me this gift of life, the
memory of your kindness will never die away within me.
I shall sooner have done with life than cease remembering you.
I will meet my end sooner than consign you to breezes and winds.
More is fastened in my memory with adamantine nails which death alone   5
can break.
I shall go on remembering you till I am nothing but ashes.
The memory of you shall keep pace with me to the furthest limits of old age.
Erasmus will remember More throughout his whole life.
The recollection of your kindnesses to me will be prolonged until I rest upon   10
the pyre.
Even that final fatal day shall find me mindful of you.
I shall see to it that the recollection of your kindness is preserved until my
encounter with Death.
No experience in life, whether glad or sad, will ever be able to expel from   15
my heart's recesses the memory of your name.
As long as this soul is tethered to this poor frame, More shall be no stranger
to my thoughts.
I am more likely to carry your memory with me to the other world than
abandon it in this.   20
I shall cast out my own soul before I cease to keep you in my thoughts.
If the body can escape from its own shadow, then this mind will be capable
of forgetting you.
Not until I conclude the very last day of my life shall I cease to carry in my
thoughts your generosity to me.   25
However long a life is granted me, my recollection of you will equal it.
Life and memory will be granted us in equal measure.
I shall recall you as long as I breathe in the vital air.
Heaven grant my recollection of you be not briefer than my life.
However long Erasmus shall survive, he will never find your memory   30
unwelcome.
I shall be deprived of life before your memory abandon me.
I shall be bereft of this upper light, as they said in olden time, sooner than
More be expunged from my mind.

* * * * *

  4 consign you to breezes and winds] Another commonplace; *Adagia* iii iv 46
  5 adamantine nails] Horace *Odes* 3.24.5–7
 14 Death] Libitina, the Roman goddess of death and burial; used for Death in
       Horace *Odes* 3.30.7
 33 upper light] See Ennius *Annals* 102 (Vahlen): *quom superum lumen nox intem-*
       pesta teneret.

LB I 29A

This feeble frame shall chill in death before your memory grow cold within me.

I shall always maintain your memory unquenched.

For all the time that I shall have the pleasure of my soul (for thus speaks Sallust), so long shall I remember you.

Without surcease shall I prove heedful of you.

Without end shall I recall you.

No event shall bring me oblivion of you, save one that takes me from the light.

I will change the world more easily than this mind that remembers you.

That event shall withdraw me from life, that introduces forgetfulness of you.

I shall find my rest among the cruel shades, as the poets say, ere I cease to recollect you.

I shall myself be borne to the grave before your memory is borne from my heart.

The recollection of you shall follow my corpse to the grave.

Not even when I have gone hence could I forget you, let alone while I live.

The recollection of a man so deservedly loved will never grow dim for me while living.

When shall it be that the memory of More fades from Erasmus' mind? Only when life shall be failing him.

I shall be mindful of you the whole time I am in this world.

As long as I breathe, I shall bear you in my heart.

As long as I shall be allowed to have the pleasure of my soul, to speak after Sallust's fashion, I will not cease to take pleasure in recollecting you.

But let us make an end, as it is not our purpose to demonstrate how far we ourselves can go in inventing alternatives, but to show students by actual example the value of this exercise for the development of wealth of expression, for we have put one basic sentence, and that not particularly fertile or productive of variation, into about two hundred different forms, I should think, and even so we have not pursued with finicking exactitude every minute possibility.

The next thing to do, it seems, is to set out examples illustrating various points of Latin usage. We do not intend to pursue every possible one, though this would be extremely useful, as it would involve endless

* * * * *

5 Sallust] See *Catilina* 1.3: *vita ipsa qua fruimur brevis est.*
13 as the poets say] See Virgil *Aeneid* 1.547: *crudelibus occubat umbris.*
26 Sallust's fashion] See line 5n.

work; but we shall provide a few by way of illustrative example, and either
our readers can invent similar phrases for themselves, or someone else who
has more leisure than we have can look for phrases illustrating the various
points in all the different authors, and so provide more copious and detailed information for our candidate for *copia*.

34 / How to combine predications of equal weight

est vir tum eruditus, tum probus: he is a man both learned and good.
est iuvenis et formosus et bene ingeniatus: he is a young man both handsome and of a fine disposition.
atque deos atque astra vocat crudelia mater: 'Both gods and stars she
heartless calls / Who once his mother was' (*atque* repeated like this is a
poetic usage, here illustrated from Virgil).
vir doctus pariter ac probus: he is learned even as good.
est vir doctus simul et integer: learned and at the same time upright
est vir tam doctus quam bonus: he is as learned as good.
vir est doctus iuxta ac bonus: learned and together with it good
vir est non minus probus quam litteratus: no less good than cultured
vir est non inferior litteris quam moribus: not inferior in learning to what
he is in character
est ex aequo probus atque doctus: in equal measure good as learned
vir est aeque litteratus ac incorruptus: equally cultured as honest
vir doctus aeque ac probus: learned equally as good
vir perinde doctus ac probus: in like manner learned and good
exquisite doctus est, itidem et facundus: a fine scholar, and likewise
eloquent
vir est non minore morum probitate quam doctrina praeditus: endowed
with integrity of character to match his knowledge
vir est quemadmodum doctus, ita et integer: as learned, in like manner
upright

* * * * *

    5 candidate for *copia*] See 304:6n. At the end of chap 33 (numbered 32), *1512* has
       plus et plusquam, ad summum, ut minimum; this material was transferred in *1514*
       to chap 96 (LB I 54D–F).
  10 est vir tum eruditus] This and succeeding examples were numbered i–xxxv in
       1512, the text going as far as 367:12 'it was insolent,' which is unnumbered.
       After this *1512* and *1514* have 'which is the opposite of what we had above.'
       The next two examples (367:13–16) were added in *1526*, the rest of the chapter
       (367:17–368:26) in *1534*.
  15 Virgil] *Eclogues* 5.23

vir est doctusque bonusque: and learned and good (repeated *-que*, a poetic usage.)

vir simul eruditus, simul integer: at one and the same time erudite and honest

vir est doctusque et integer: both learned and honest (*-que* followed by *et* is a poetic usage.)

vir est haud secius eruditus ac probus: not otherwise erudite than honourable

vir est ut doctus ita et probus: as learned, even so honourable

vir est doctus et idem probus; vir est optimus idemque doctissimus: he is learned, and he is honest too; he is excellent, and he is a scholar too [literally, and the same man is ...].

vir est pari vel doctrina vel probitate praeditus: a man endowed with an equal gift be it of learning or of moral honesty

vir est non tantum eruditus, sed et integer; vir est non modo doctus, verumetiam probus: he is a man not only learned, but also upright.

vir optimus quoque est, non modo doctissimus: he is the best of men as well, not only a great scholar.

non tantum ferunt sed impellunt: they not only allow but encourage it. (It is one of Seneca's mannerisms to omit *etiam*, as in this example.)

vir est praeter summam eruditionem etiam optimus: apart from his great erudition, an excellent man as well

vir praeterquam quod doctus est, etiam optimus: excellent, quite apart from being learned

vir est de quo dubites doctiorne sit an melior: a man of whom you might question whether he were more learned or good

vir est in quo cum litteris probitas morum ex aequo certet: a man in whom morality competes with culture on equal terms

vir est qui litteras aequarit cum vitae sanctimonia: a man who has combined learning equally with purity of life

vir est cuius eruditioni respondet morum integritas: a man whose integrity corresponds to his erudition

vir est qui parem vitae castimoniam cum eruditione copularit: a man who has linked with his erudition equal purity of life

vir summa quidem doctrina, verum morum integritate neutiquam inferior sese: a man of great learning, who by no means falls short of himself in moral stature

vel ... vel 'either ... or' can on occasion have the force of 'both ... and': litteris tuis maiorem in modum sum delectatus, vel quod essent elegantissimae, vel quod humanitatis plenae: I was excessively delighted by your letter, either for its elegance or for its kindness.

vir est in litteris egregius, neque sui dissimilis in moribus: he is outstanding in learning, and his own equal in character.

vir est clarus imaginibus, neque non illustris egregiis in rempublicam
meritis: he is a man of splendid family, and not undistinguished for his
outstanding services to the state.

officium beneficio cumulasti: you have enhanced duty with generosity.

corporis formam animi dotibus aequiparas: you balance beauty of body
with gifts of mind.

cum diis ex pari vivit: he lives on equal terms with the gods.

oratione tua graviter offensus est, partim quod esset incondita partim quod
arrogans: he was gravely offended by your speech, partly because it was
uncouth, partly because it was insolent.

in hoc probitas aequat eruditionem: in this man integrity equals learning.

in hoc fortuna cum probitate facit paria: in this man fortune makes a pair
with honesty. (*paria facere* 'make a pair, balance, equalize' is an expression
used by Seneca.)

vir est egregie doctus, atque item probus: he is outstandingly learned, and
likewise honest.

vir est similiter doctus ac facundus: he is learned and eloquent alike.

vir est haud dissimiliter eloquens ac doctus: he is not otherwise eloquent
than learned.

vir pari doctrina ac probitate: a man of equal learning and probity

vir est perinde facundus ut doctus: he is a man just as eloquent as learned.

Sallust uses *iuxta* 'in conjunction, combined' as the equivalent of
aeque ac 'equally, alike' in:

cives, hostes iuxta metuit: citizens and enemy he jointly feared.

fortunae corporis animique bonis iuxta dives: rich in the gifts of mind,
physique and fortune combined

plebi patribusque iuxta carus (Sallust again): popular jointly with people
and with Senate

hiemem atque aestatem iuxta pati (Sallust): in joint measure endure winter
cold and summer heat

Pliny also uses *iuxta* in this way:

iuxta diebus noctibusque tacitus labitur mundus: the heavens silently glide

* * * * *

9 with the gods] Seneca *Epistles* 59.14

16 Seneca] For example, *De beneficiis* 3.9.3: *cum aliter beneficium detur aliter
reddatur paria facere difficile est*, where Erasmus' edition has a marginal note,
paria facere.

26 he jointly feared] *Jugurtha* 72.2

29 people and with Senate] *Jugurtha* 85.33

32 summer heat] *Jugurtha* 88.1

LB I 30C

on, day conjoined with night.
in Italiae partibus quibusdam iuxta hieme et aestate fulgurat: in some parts
of Italy lightning is observed in winter and summer both.

The following also illustrate this usage:
iuxta mecum rem tenes (Plautus): you know the facts, conjointly with
myself (i.e., equally with me).
iuxta tecum, si tu nescis, nescio (Plautus again, in *Persa*): combined with
you, if you know not, I do not know.
quo in loco res sitae sunt, iuxta mecum omnes intelligitis (Sallust again, in
Catilina): in conjunction with myself, you all understand the situation we
are in.

We may include here some expressions which are less common, but
found in respectable authors nevertheless:
quo iure, quaque iniuria me in pistrinum dabit (Terence): by some justice,
by some injustice, he will send me to the mill, (i.e., whether rightly or
wrongly).
at quam honesta, quam expedita tua consilia, quam evigilata tuis cogi-
tationibus qua itineris, qua navigationis, qua congressus sermonisque
cum Caesare: how honourable, how efficient were your plans, how carefully thought out, where the journey was concerned, where the sea-
crossing, where the meeting and conference with Caesar (Cicero writing to
Atticus).
cum video te distentissimum esse, qua de Buthrotiis, qua de Bruto: seeing
you so distracted, what with the Buthrotii and with Brutus (again Cicero to
Atticus, again using *qua ... qua* 'where ... where' for the usual *tum ... tum*
'then ... then' in the sense of 'both ... and')

35 / Ways of linking adversative statements

vir est doctrina quidem egregia, verum moribus illaudatis: he is a man of
remarkable learning to be sure, but of reprehensible character.

* * * * *

1 conjoined with night] Pliny *Naturalis historia* 2.6
3 winter and summer both] *Naturalis historia* 2.136
5 Plautus] *Aulularia* 682
7 *Persa*] 249
10 *Catilina*] 58.5
14 Terence] Cf *Andria* 214.
21 to Atticus] 9.12.1
24 to Atticus] 15.18.2

est ille quidem vir bonus, verum parum eruditus: he is a good man to be sure, but inadequately educated.

vir est ut lingua blandissima, ita ingenii amarulenti: while he has a winning tongue, all the same he is of a sour disposition.

vir est ut optimis prognatus maioribus, ita pessimis praeditus moribus: while he is the scion of a noble family, all the same he is endowed with the most ignoble character.

vir est tam deformis animo quam corpore formosus: he is as foul in mind as fair in body.

Petrus quemadmodum est tacitus conviva, ita est loquacissimus susurro: while Peter has little to say in company, even so he is a gossiping tale-bearer [literally, 'even as ... just so'].

hic salutator quidem est comis, sed virulentus obtrectator: this man is certainly affable in his address, but he is a virulent traducer.

blandus est vultu ceterum animo truculento: for all his bland expression, his mind is savage.

ferox est in timidos at in feroces timidus: he is fierce towards the timid, but in contrast timid towards the fierce.

aestate friget, contra hieme calet: in summer it is cold, on the other hand in winter it is hot.

Plautus uses *item* 'likewise' with the force of *contra* to mean 'on the other hand,' as in the following example: venit hoc mihi in mentem, Megadore, te esse hominem divitem factiosum, me item esse hominem pauperum pauperrimum: it occurs to me, Megadorus, that you are rich and influential, likewise I am the poorest of the poor.

inimicis supplex, in amicos contumeliosus: grovelling to enemies, insolent to friends. (Here no adverb is used at all.)

voluptas parit dolorem, contra dolor voluptatem: pleasure brings forth pain, on the other hand pain brings forth pleasure.

36 / How to combine negative statements having equal weight

vir est neque doctus neque probus: he is neither learned nor good.

nec litteris nec moribus probatus: approved neither in learning nor in character

* * * * *

8 vir est ... brings forth pleasure] These lines (8–29) were added in *1534* (LB I 30E–F)

22 following example] *Aulularia* 226–7

26 contumeliosus] Sallust *In Ciceronem declamatio* 3.5

vir est non indoctus modo verumetiam improbus: he is not merely uneducated but shameless in addition.
vir est ut indoctus ita et improbus: as he is uneducated so he is also
shameless.
non minus improbus quam illiteratus: no less shameless than illiterate   5
vir est tum indoctus tum improbus: he is both uneducated and shameless.
aeque indoctus atque improbus: just as uneducated as shameless
nescias praestare velint minus an possint (Quintilian): you cannot tell
whether they are less willing than able to perform this task (i.e., they are
just as incapable as unwilling).   10
pariter et indoctus et improbus: in equal measure ignorant and shameless
vir pessimus est et nihilo doctior: he is the worst of men in character, and
not a whit better in learning.
flamma deprimi non potest non magis quam quiescere (Seneca): the flame
cannot be suppressed any more than lie dormant.   15
vir cui nihil sit omnino bonarum litterarum, bonorum quoque morum
tantundem: a man with absolutely nothing of good learning, and an equally
small amount of good character
       In short we use more or less the same means to make negative state-
ments as positive ones.   20

37 / How to combine predications of unequal weight

vir est cum doctus tum probus: he is a learned man, but also a good one.   25
iuvenis cum eleganti forma, tum vero moribus optimis: a young man of
handsome appearance, but furthermore of excellent character
non pecuniam modo, verumetiam vitam tibi paratus sum impendere: I am
ready to spend not only my wealth but even my life in your cause.
vitam etiam tibi impenderim non modo pecuniam: I would even spend my   30
life for you, not merely my wealth.
(It will be seen that *non solum* and similar expressions can be used where the
statements are of equal weight, as well as where one is more emphatic.)
non sat erat impulisse nisi et proderet: it was not enough to incite them
without betraying them as well.   35

       * * * * *

   8 Quintilian] 4.2.37
  11 pariter ... improbus] After this 1512 has: *quam bene pingis quam male fingis* 'You
     are as good a painter as you are a bad liar.'
  14 Seneca] See *Epistles* 57.8: *quem ad modum flamma non potest opprimi, nam circa id
     diffugit quo urgetur.*

non sufficiebat spoliasse nisi et iugularet: it was not sufficient to rob them without slaughtering them besides.

parum erat deformem esse nisi mores forma dignos addidisset: not content with being ugly, he added a character to match his body.

nihil erat deformi esse vultu, nisi moribus etiam esset taeterrimis: being hideous in face was nothing, he had to be repulsive in character as well.

In this type of expression the second and more emphatic part is sometimes, by an elegant stylistic variation, left to be understood: Chrysostom, not only golden-tongued (i.e., but also golden-hearted); some letters of Cornelia, the mother of the Gracchi, have been preserved, not merely to honour her sex (i.e., but also out of admiration for her eloquence); you have seen a man twisted not only in body (i.e., but also in mind).

38 / How to combine negative statements of unequal weight

non modo non intelligit, verum ne legit quidem: not only does he not comprehend, he does not even read.

non solum parum intelligit, sed nec legit: not merely is his understanding inadequate, but he does not read either.

non tantum nihil intelligit, immo nec legit: not only does he understand nothing; furthermore he does not read.

ne legere quidem novit, nedum intelligat: he does not even know how to read, let alone understand.

non novit vel legere, tantum abest ut intelligat: reading is beyond him, so far is he from understanding.

tantum abest ab intelligendo ut ne legere quidem norit: so far is he from comprehension that he does not even know how to read.

adeo non intelligit ut nec legat: so far does he not understand that he does not even read.

usque adeo non intelligit ut nesciat vel legere: to such an extent does he not comprehend that he does not even know how to read.

hic in Graecis litteris nihil quid dicam intelligere, immo nec legere potest:

* * * * *

7 In this type ... in mind] Added in 1534 (LB I 31B–C)

8 Chrysostom] Dio Cocceianus, c AD 40–112, Greek orator and philosopher, nicknamed Chrysostomos, 'the golden-mouthed'

11 her eloquence] Erasmus has compressed two examples from Quintilian 1.1.6: Cornelia the mother of the Gracchi, whose elegant language is preserved for posterity in her letters, and Hortensia, Quintus' daughter, 'whose speech is read not merely to honour her sex.'

in Greek literature he is quite incapable, why say of grasping anything, he is incapable of reading it at all.

hic nihil in bonis litteris non dicam intelligit immo ne legit quidem: of good literature I will not say he grasps nothing, he does not even read it.

ingenium quoque senectus deterit, nedum corporis vigor perpetuo duret: old age also weakens the mental faculties, still less is bodily vigour likely to endure.

nedum sermonis stet honos et gratia vivax (Horace): still less should words keep honour and favour / By passing time undimmed. (Horace innovated here in using *nedum* as the equivalent of *tantum abest ut* 'so far is it from being the case that.')

ne pecuniam quidem impenderet amico, nedum vitam: he would not spend even his money for his friend, still less his life.

Quintilian introduced a variation on this figure: nec enim de omnibus causis dicere quisquam potest, saltem de praeteritis, ut taceam de futuris: there is no one who can discuss all cases, previous ones at least, to say nothing of future ones (i.e., not even previous ones, so far is he from discussing future ones).

39 / Positive or negative statements of proportion

[First, using the superlative]
ut quisque est gloria dignissimus, ita gloriae est negligentissimus: those most worthy of glory care about it least.

ut quisque gloria est maxime dignus, ita gloriae minime est avidus: in proportion as a man is especially worthy of glory, so he covets it least.

optima quaeque vitae pars quam ocissime praetervolat: the best part of life flies past the quickest.

tanto pessimus omnium poeta, / quanto tu optimus omnium patronus (Catullus): so much the worst of poets all, as you the best of patrons

quam vos facillime agitis, tam vos maxime aequum est aequa facere: as you have the greatest freedom of action, so it is most reasonable that you act with fairness [i.e., your obligation to act fairly is proportionate to your freedom of action].

* * * * *

8 Horace] *Ars poetica* 69
14 Quintilian] 5.1.3
28 optima quaeque] Cf Virgil *Georgics* 3.66: *optima quaeque dies ... aevi / Prima fugit*.
31 Catullus] 49.6–7
32 aequum est aequa facere] Cf Terence *Adelphi* 501–4.

40 / The same idea expressed by means of comparatives

quo quisque dignior est qui laudetur, hoc minus laudari gaudet: as a man is more worthy of praise, so he delights less in being praised.

quanto quisque fama dignior, tanto minus affectat famam: according as a man is more worthy of praise, so he aspires less to win it.

quo quisque magis promeretur honorem, eo minus honorem appetit: in proportion as a man is more deserving of honour so he desires it less.

We can also put it the other way round:

hoc minus ducitur laudis cupidine, quo quisque laude sit dignior: a man is less influenced by the desire for praise, according as he is more worthy to receive it.

tanto quisque minus optat pecuniam quanto minus possidet pecuniae: a man desires money so much the less, according as he has less of it.

41 / Ways of intensifying the positive

The force of the basic word can be enhanced by combination with *per, perquam*, and *prae*, as in *perdifficile, perquam difficile* 'extremely difficult,' *praelongus* 'very long,' *praevalidus* 'very strong,' *praepotens* 'very powerful.' This applies to verbs also: *pervelim, perquam velim*, 'I should very much like,' *percupio* 'I am very eager.' The same effect can be produced in verbs by means of *de*: *deamo* 'I love passionately,' *demiror* 'I am extremely surprised.' *ad* also has this force: *adprobe* 'quite thoroughly,' *adfabre* 'most ingeniously,' *adprime* 'right at the beginning,' *adamo* 'love dearly.'

Lawyers also employ compounds formed with *in* as having the same effect, but in my opinion they are mistaken; where they read *indifficile est* 'it is very difficult,' the correct reading is *in difficili est* 'it lies in the sphere of difficulty'; like *in proclivi est* 'it lies in the realm of ease,' equivalent to *proclive est* 'it is easy' and *in promptu est* 'it is at the ready' for *promptum est* 'it is ready'; similar phrases are *in tuto est, in causa est, in vitio est* 'it lies in the area of safety ... cause ... fault.'

The positive can also be enhanced not by composition but by the addition of *quam*. This involves the figure of exclamation: *quam tenere amat filium* 'how tenderly he loves his son!'; *quam nihil pudet* 'how nothing

* * * * *

13 tanto ... pecuniae] Material included at the end of this chapter in 1512 appears in subsequent editions as chaps 61–3 (LB I 42D–4E).
28 but in my opinion ... fault'] Added in 1534 (LB I 32A)

LB I 31E

shames him!' *ut* has the same force: *ut gaudet* 'how he rejoices,' *ut est severus* 'how stern he is.'

We can also include here expressions such as *immane quantum distat* 'vast is the extent of the difference,' *papae quam is sibi placet* 'heavens, how pleased he is with himself!'

The meaning can also be intensified by the adverbial phrases *oppido quam, sane quam, nimis quam, antigerio* (this one is archaic), all meaning 'very,' and, as I have said, these may be freely combined with verbs: *perquam velim* 'I would very much like,' *percupio* 'I am most eager,' *sane quam cupit* 'to be sure how he longs.' The particle *ne* appears to have an effect not very different: *ne ego infelix homo sum* 'I am an unlucky fellow to be sure,' *faciunt ne intelligendo ut nihil intelligant* 'in truth, by being so clever, they show their ignorance.'

Likewise by all those adverbial phrases indicating intensification of some kind: *admodum* 'to a degree,' *valde* 'greatly,' *egregie* 'eminently,' *insigniter* 'markedly,' *insignite* 'remarkably,' *magnopere* 'mightily,' *maximopere* 'vastly,' *summopere* 'supremely,' *in primis* 'principally,' *adprime* 'chiefly,' *cum primis* 'in the front rank,' *in paucis* 'among the few' (which Quintus Curtius uses in the sense of 'uncommonly'), *tantopere* 'to such an extent,' *quantopere* 'to what an extent' (these last two employ the figure of exclamation), *adeo* 'so' equal to *valde* 'very' as in *fratrem adeo nobilem* 'so noble a brother,' *maiorem in modum* 'to a considerable extent,' *mirum in modum* 'to a marvellous extent,' *supra modum* 'beyond measure,' *praeter modum* 'exceedingly,' *singulariter* 'singularly,' *unice* 'uniquely,' *eximie* 'outstandingly,' *impendio* 'lavishly,' *impense* 'exuberantly,' *effuse* 'profusely,' *abunde* 'abundantly,' *affatim* 'amply,' and many more.

vel not only means 'either,' but can also emphasize:

ut vel perire maluerit (Cicero): so that he would even prefer death

vel umbra satis est (Seneca): even a shadow is enough.

amico non vel teruncium impertiat: he would not spend even a halfpenny on his friend.

quibus rebus supra bonum et honestum perculsus (Sallust): cast down by these events beyond, that is, more than was proper for, a good and honorable man

* * * * *

3 *immane quantum distat*] Cf Horace *Odes* 1.27.6: *immane quantum discrepat*.
12 *ut nihil intelligant*] Terence *Andria* prologue 17; Erasmus is here following the interpretation preferred by Donatus' commentary.
19 Quintus Curtius] 4.8.7, 6.8.2, and passim
28 Cicero] Cf *Pro Roscio Amerino* 26: *ut mori mallet quam de his rebus Sullam doceri.*
32 Sallust] *Jugurtha* 82.2

Like *magis quam, plusquam* has intensifying force:
homo plus quam insanus: a man more than mad
senex plus quam delirus: an old fellow more than crazed
plus aequo saevit: his rage is more than can be justified.

Related to this is *non tantum* 'not only,' which is not the equivalent of
Greek μόνον οὐχί 'all but' [literally 'only not'], but has the same effect as
plusquam:
homo non tantum vino temulentus: a fellow drunk not just with wine
vir non tantum imaginibus nobilis: a man noble not merely in ancestry
(See my earlier discussion of *non tantum*.)

A usage such as *terque quaterque beati* 'three and four times blest' is
originally a Greek usage, but it is employed by Latin writers, especially in
poetry.

Here are some other more out-of-the-way usages:
incredibile dictu quam elegans: beyond belief to tell how elegant
immane dictu (Sallust): beyond bounds to tell
dici non potest: it cannot be told
sermone consequi nequeam: I cannot find words to express
rara quadam modestia: of a strange rare modesty
praecipuum honorem: a principal honour
primariam laudem: praise of the first rank
incredibili sapientia, haud vulgari doctrina: of incredible wisdom, of uncommon learning
Deum immortalem, qua doctrina virum: Good God, a man of what learning
(i.e., of outstanding learning)
plus satis animosus: more spirited than enough
plus nimio tristis: too sad by far (i.e., more than is meet)

Many other similar examples might well be added to this list. An
especially common form of amplification is to use the superlative instead of
the positive, for example, *plurima* 'most' for a very large number, *maxima*
'greatest' for very large.
dicere tibi promptissimum est, mihi facere facillimum: speaking comes
very readily to you: I find doing easy.

* * * * *

10 earlier] End of chap 37
11 four times blest] Virgil *Aeneid* 1.94
16 Sallust] *Epistula ad Caesarem* 1 (*Oratio*) 2.7
33 find doing easy] Cf Ovid *Metamorphoses* 13.10: *nec mihi dicere promptum / nec
facere est isti.*

We often use the comparative instead of the positive, as Quintilian himself
states, as, for example, if someone says *infirmior* 'rather feeble,' that is,
'fearful.'

42 / Making the positive less emphatic

The positive force of an expression can be diminished by the addition of the
preposition *sub* [literally 'under'], for example to adjectives: *subtristis*
'rather sad,' *subrusticus* 'a bit countrified,' *subobscurus* 'rather obscure,'
subasper 'somewhat harsh,' *subinvidus* 'slightly envious,' *subinanis* 'rather
vain,' *subfuscus* 'dusky'; or to verbs: *subpudet* 'feel somewhat ashamed,'
subirascitur 'be fairly angry,' *subolet* 'get a whiff of,' *subridet* 'show the
beginnings of a smile,' *subodoratur* 'get an inkling of,' *subtimet* 'feel slightly
afraid.'
    The same effect is produced by the addition of various adverbs:
non nimis molestum est: not over-troublesome
utcunque iucundum fuit: pleasing in one way or other
aliquantulum mordax: somewhat biting
These adverbs can also be combined with verbs:
utcunque sapit: he has some sort of sense.
paululum delirat: he is slightly mad.
    Or we can employ one of the various forms of diminutive: *argutulus*
'somewhat talkative,' *acutulus* 'sharpish,' *minutulus* 'smallish, paltry,' *ran-
cidulus* 'rather loathsome,' *putidulus* 'somewhat disgusting,' *diutule* 'a lon-
gish time,' *saepicule* 'fairly often,' *ebriolus* 'slightly drunk,' *sciolus* 'with a
smattering of knowledge,' *tenellus* 'somewhat delicate,' *nigellus* 'blackish,'
integellus 'pretty safe,' *philosophaster Tullius* 'Cicero who had pretensions to
philosophy.'
    A comparative used in place of a positive has the effect of a diminu-
tive, for example, *tristior* 'rather sad'; but the usual effect is to express
censure, with the addition of the adverb *paulo* 'to some extent,' and an
ellipse, for example, *vir integer quidem, sed severior* 'an honest man, but
rather harsh,' that is, *paulo severior quam convenit* 'somewhat harsher than
he need be'; or *facundus homo, sed paulo loquacior* 'a man of ready speech,

* * * * *

2 Quintilian] 9.3.19
29 *philosophaster Tullius*] Augustine *De civitate Dei* 2.27
32 *tristior*] As in Virgil *Aeneid* 1.228, an example used at 327:12

but somewhat over-talkative.' This has the effect of toning down the criticism.

The meaning of a verb can also be modified by the use of a derivative: *vellico* 'pluck at,' *cantillo* 'sing under one's breath, hum,' *cantito* 'warble,' *volito* 'flutter,' *dormito* 'snooze, take a nap,' *victito* 'subsist, eke out a living.'

The same effect is produced by *parum* 'insufficient' and *non admodum* 'not so much': *ne parum multa scire viderentur* 'lest they should seem insufficiently knowledgeable'; *vir non admodum senex* 'not such an old man'; *non admodum adolescens* 'not so very young'; *non perinde sapiens ut dives* 'not just as wise as rich'; *non satis mihi liquet* 'it is not sufficiently clear to me'; *parum mihi liquet* 'it is insufficiently plain'; *minus compertum habeo* 'I am not adequately informed.'

vix and *semis* have the same force: *vix vivus* 'hardly alive'; *semi-vivus* 'half alive'; *vix bene Graeca* 'Greek hardly well'; *parum bene Graeca* 'Greek insufficiently well'; *cum semiviro comitatu* 'with half-male retinue' (i.e., unmanly, effeminate).

Similarly *saltem* and *at*: *si non eodem die, at postridie* (Cato) 'if not the same day, at least the next'; *si non propinquitatis at aetatis suae, si non hominis, at humanitatis rationem haberet* (Cicero) 'to take account if not of his relationship, at least of his age, if not of a man, at least of humanity'; *si non primus, certe non postremus* 'if not first, certainly not last.'

43 / Making the comparative more emphatic

There are a number of adverbs particularly associated with the comparative which intensify its meaning: *longe* 'by far,' *multo* 'considerably, much,' *nimio* 'excessively'; also these phrases: *multis partibus* 'in many respects,' *in immensum* 'vastly,' *in infinitum* 'infinitely,' *infinitis partibus* 'in countless respects':
longe venustior: far lovelier
multo gravior: much more serious
nimio severior: far too severe
ne doleas plus nimio, memor / inmitis Glycerae (Horace): Do thou grieve not o'ermuch / Thinking on Glycera's disdain.

* * * * *

7 *scire viderentur*] *Ad Herennium* 1.1
13 *vix* and *semis* ... not last] Added in *1534* (LB I 33A)
15 *cum semiviro comitatu*] Virgil *Aeneid* 4.215
17 Cato] *De re rustica* 2.1
19 Cicero] *Pro Quinctio* 97
34 Horace] *Odes* 1.33.2

LB I 32F

multis partibus praestantior: in many respects superior
in infinitum utilior: infinitely more useful
infinitis partibus divina humanis sunt potiora: the divine is in countless respects superior to the human.

tanto and *quanto* which introduce a figure [of exclamation] produce the same effect: *tanto corpore praestantior est animus* 'so superior is mind to body' (i.e., much superior).

The addition of *eo* or *quo* has the same effect: *est praedives, quo magis admiror hominis sordes* 'he is extremely rich, so that I am all the more amazed at his meanness'; *eo magis admiror* 'I wonder all the more'; *papae, quanto satius est amicis quam pecuniis abundare* 'Really, how much better it is to be rich in friends than in money.'

MAKING THE COMPARATIVE LESS EMPHATIC

Modifying adverbs can also make the meaning less emphatic: *paulo venustior est Gellius quam Macrobius* 'Gellius is a little more genial than Macrobius'; *aliquanto brevior est hic quam ille* 'this man is slightly shorter than that one'; *nihilo ditior* 'not a penny the richer'; *ne tantillo quidem melior eris si dives fueris* 'you will not be one scrap better if you become rich'; *minimo fuerit honoratior si titulus accesserit* 'he would not be in the slightest degree more respected if he got a title.'

quantulo 'by how small an amount' is like *quam paulo* 'by how little,' equivalent to *paene nihilo* 'by practically nothing.' *quantulo* is actually an exclamatory form: *papae, quantulo hic homo sapientior est* 'Gracious, how little wiser this fellow is!'

A similar diminution of meaning results from the use of derivatives such as *grandiusculus* 'somewhat bigger,' *meliusculus* 'slightly better,' *celeriuscule* 'rather more quickly.'

44 / Making the superlative more emphatic

The superlative can be intensified by the adverbs *longe* and *multo* which were used with the comparative, and also by *facile* 'easily':
Cicero longe facundissimus: Cicero by far the most eloquent
et idem vir multo omnium optimus: and also much the best of all men

* * * * *

8 The addition ... the more] This 1534 insertion breaks the continuity of examples for *tanto, quanto*.
16 Gellius] The same sentiment is expressed in Ep 61:148–9.

eius civitatis longe princeps, facile princeps, primus: by far the most
significant figure in that state, easily the most significant, easily the first

The same effect is produced by *tanto* and *quanto*, again used figuratively:

deum immortalem, quanto Socrates philosophorum omnium optimus:
Good Lord, how much the best is Socrates of all philosophers.

The superlative can also be intensified by composition with *quam*:
quam plurimos vidi 'I saw the greatest possible number'; *ut quam optime res
cadat, tibi nihil commodi fuerit* 'even if things turned out as well as possible, it
would be no advantage to you.'

Exaggerated intensification (hyperbole) can be expressed in the following ways: *mulier plusquam pessima, pessima peior* 'a woman more than
worst, worse than the worst'; *homo non loquacissimus sed ipsa loquacitas* 'not
just a talker but talkativeness itself'; *et ipsa loquacitate loquacior* 'a greater
talker than Talk personified'; *ipsa Venere venustior* 'more lovely than Loveliness.'

Sallust's well-known phrase: *quam quisque pessime fecit, tam maxime
tutus est* 'according as each man has acted the worst, so he is most secure,'
expresses equivalence, not intensification.

The superlative cannot have its meaning made *less* emphatic except by
the addition of *quidem* or a similar word: *est ille quidem doctissimus, verum
moribus non perinde probatus* 'he is very learned to be sure, but his character
is not just so admirable.'

45 / Periphrastic substitutes for the comparative

Comparison can also be expressed by a periphrasis containing the comparative adverbs *magis* and *minus* 'more' and 'less': *avidior voluptatum* or
magis avidus voluptatum quam pecuniae 'greedier, more greedy for pleasures
than for money.'
potius 'rather' functions in the same way: *voluptatum avidus potius quam
pecuniae* 'greedy for pleasures rather than for money.'
Other expressions with the same effect are:
non tam voluptatum appetens quam pecuniae: not so desirous of pleasures
as of money
minus avidus pecuniae quam voluptatum: less greedy for money than for
pleasures

* * * * *

17 Sallust's] *Jugurtha* 31.14

LB I 33C

non perinde litterarum admirans quam pecuniae: not just as impressed by learning as by money

In short, we can here employ all those expressions which we said earlier could be used to combine concepts, one of which carries greater emphasis.

Some verbs have an inherent comparative meaning:
praestat lucrum pudori: profit stands in front of (i.e., is preferable to) self-respect.

Cicero Platone facundior, Plato Cicerone doctior: Cicero more eloquent than Plato, Plato more learned than Cicero; Cicero Platonem *superat* eloquentia, Plato Ciceronem *antecellit* eruditione: Cicero surpasses Plato in eloquence, Plato excels Cicero in learning.

Hieronymus Augustinum *vincit* rerum scientia, Augustinus Hieronymum *anteit* ingenii subtilitate: Jerome beats Augustine in factual knowledge, Augustine outstrips Jerome in subtlety of intellect.

Pol maerores mihi *anteverterunt* gaudiis (Plautus): Truly in my case sorrows have taken precedence over joys.

quanto herum *anteeo* sapientia (Terence): How far I outstrip my master in commonsense!

praeverti hoc certum est aliis rebus omnibus (Plautus): I am determined to let this take precedence over all else (i.e., prefer).

conati novi consules omnibus eam rem *praeverti* (Livy): the new consuls endeavoured to give this matter precedence over all else.

si vacas animo neque habes aliquid quod huic sermoni *praevertendum* putes (Cicero): if you can spare me your attention and do not feel you have something that ought to take precedence over a conversation of this sort (Plautus used *antevenire* 'get the start of' for 'excel.')

homines qui per virtutem soliti erant nobilitatem *antevenire* (Sallust): men who by virtue had become accustomed to excel the nobility

Other verbs of the same sort are *anteponere* 'put first,' *praeferre* 'prefer,' *posthabere* 'put second,' *praecellere* 'rise above.'

* * * * *

4 earlier] Chap 37
16 Pol maerores ... nobility] This passage (lines 16–29) was added in 1534 (LB I 33F).
16 Plautus] *Captivi* 840: *antevortunt*
18 Terence] *Phormio* 247
20 Plautus] *Cistellaria* 781
22 Livy] 8.13.1; modern texts read *coacti*, not *conati*.
25 Cicero] *De divinatione* 1.10
28 Sallust] *Jugurtha* 4.7

Sallust introduced a new use when he wrote: *invidia atque superbia postfuere*
'jealousy and arrogance came after' (i.e., took second place). Another usage
from the same writer: *facundia Graecos, gloria belli Gallos ante Romanos fuisse*
'the Greeks came before the Romans in eloquence, the Gauls in military
glory' (i.e., were more eminent).

Other phrases are *cedere* 'yield,' *secundum esse* 'come second,' *praeripere
laudem*' carry off the glory,' and so on, for these all provide variations in the
expression of the comparative:

magis amat pecuniam quam famam: he loves money more than reputation.

pecuniae Socrates amans est magis quam famae: Socrates is in love with
money rather than fame.

pecuniarum amantior est quam famae: he is more loving of wealth than
reputation.

famam pecuniae posthabet: he puts reputation second to money.

famae pecuniam anteponit: he puts money before reputation.

minus famae cupiditate ducitur quam pecuniae: he is influenced less by a
desire for fame than by a desire for money.

impensius amat pecuniam quam famam: he loves money more passionately than reputation.

huic potior est pecunia quam fama: in his eyes money is preferable to
reputation.

huic prius est lucrum quam honesta fama: in his eyes money takes precedence over a good name.

huic antiquius est laudari quam admoneri: he finds praise preferable [liter-
ally 'previous'] to advice.

huic vilior est vita quam pecunia: to him life is of less value than money.

prae [preposition with ablative] 'in comparison with' has the same force:
omnium minas atque omnia pericula prae salute sua levia duxerunt 'they considered the threat to the whole company and all the danger trivial compared
with their own safety'; *non tu quidem vacuus molestiis, sed prae nobis beatus*
'you have your own troubles to be sure, but you are happy compared with
us' (i.e., happier than us). (These last two examples are both from Cicero.)
[*prae* can also be combined with *ut* to introduce a clause:] *ludum iocumque*

* * * * *

1 Sallust introduced ... eminent] Added in *1534* (LB I 33F–4A)
1 Sallust] *Catilina* 23.6
3 same writer] *Catilina* 53.3
6 *praeripere laudem*] For example, Cicero *Pro Roscio Amerino* 2: *eam [laudem]
praereptam velim*
22 huic prius est ... *praeut*] The passage to 382:5 added in *1534* (LB I 34A–B)
32 Cicero] *Verrines* 2.156; *Ad familiares* 4.4.2

alterum dices illum, prae ut huius rabies quae dabit (Terence) 'you will call that
other just a game and joke, compared with what this one's fury will produce'; *nihil hercule hoc quidem, prae ut alia dicam* (Plautus) ' 'Pon my word,
this is just nothing compared with what else I could mention.' Plautus also
used *praequam* instead of *praeut*.   5

46 / Varying the expression of the superlative

The expression of the superlative may be varied by using a verb or positive   10
adjective modified by an adverb: *amat te maxime* [verb plus adverb], *aman-*
tissimus est tui [superlative adjective], *effusissime te diligit* [verb plus adverb]
all meaning 'he is extremely fond of you.' *vir indoctissimus* [superlative
adjective] 'a most ignorant man,' *vir minime doctus* [positive adjective plus
adverb] 'a man by no means educated'; *minime multos* [positive adjective   15
plus adverb] 'by no means many,' equivalent to *quam paucissimos* [superla-
tive] 'the very smallest possible number.'
 Another variation is the use of the comparative: *Cicero reliquis omnibus*
eloquentior 'Cicero, more eloquent than all the rest.' However, it is not usual
to employ the comparative in a positive expression like this; a clause   20
containing some kind of negative is commoner:
Cicero quo non alius eloquentior: Cicero than whom no one was more
eloquent
quo non praestantior alter: than whom no other was more distinguished
(i.e., the most distinguished of all)   25
nihil minus amat quam assentationem: there is nothing he likes less than
flattery.
nulla re minus capitur quam gloria: there is nothing with less attraction for
him than glory.
nihil hunc aeque delectat atque musica: nothing delights him as much as   30
music.
nihil prius habet quam adesse conviviis: there is nothing he likes better
than going to parties.
nihil pulchrius ducit quam divitem vocari: he thinks nothing finer than
being called a wealthy man.   35
nihil minus faciam, nihil minus sentiebam quam quod tu suspicabare:
there is nothing I am less likely to do, nothing was further from my
thoughts, than what you suspected.

 * * * * *

1 Terence] *Eunuchus* 300–1: *dicet fuisse illum alterum*
3 Plautus] *Miles* 20

[Or we can use *potius quam*:]
homo quidvis potius quam doctus: a man anything rather than (i.e., anything but) educated
efficiam ut intelligas omnia mihi defuisse potius quam fidem ac diligen-
tiam: I will make you understand that I was deficient in anything but loyalty
and industry.
omnia potius quam illud agnoscet: he will acknowledge anything but that.
quidvis potius quam vanitatem fatebitur: he will admit to anything you like
but vanity.
    [Here is another idiom:]
nullo inferior: lower than none (i.e., the highest)
nullo non inferior: than none not lower (i.e., the lowest of all)
nemine non deformior: than none not more ugly (i.e., the ugliest of all)
    The same superlative effect can be produced by verbs:
Cicero superat omnes dicendi copia: Cicero surpasses all in eloquence.
vincit omnes candore: he excels all in clarity.
nemini cedit candore: he yields to none in clarity.
in dicendo principatum obtinet: in eloquence he occupies the first rank.
primas tenet: he holds the primacy.
arcem tenet: he stands at the peak.
    Here are some other variations:
vir praeter ceteros spectatae fidei: a man of proven loyalty above all others
praeter omnes te diligit: he loves you above all.
supra cunctos tuae gloriae favet: beyond all he supports your advancement.
ante omnia rei studendum: before all else we must put our minds to the
business.
    Words such as *unicus* 'unique, unparalleled,' *solus* 'only,' *primus*
'first,' *singularis* 'singular,' have an inherent superlative signification:
unice te amat: he loves you with unparalleled affection.
solus est homo homini amicus: he alone is a real friend in need.
singulari benevolentia te prosequitur: he cherishes you with singular benevolence.
primam laudem obtinet: the chief praise is his.
Tullius eloquentiae princeps: Cicero the prince of eloquence
paenulatorum alpha (Martial): Grade One in poncho-wearers
    Here is another type:
tam facundus ut cum hoc nemo sit conferendus: so eloquent that none can
be compared with him

    * * * * *

30 homo homini amicus] Cf Terence *Phormio* 562.
35 Martial] 2.57.4; *Adagia* II iv 18

tam eruditus ut ei nemo sit aequandus: so learned that none can be classed
with him
tam prudens ut parem non invenias: so wise you could not find his equal
sic ut mihi numquam in vita fuerit melius (Horace): so that things were
never better in my life   5
adeo placet ut magis non possit: so pleasing that it could not be more so
     Yet another type:
quis hoc uno facundior? who is more eloquent than this one man?
quid invenias pecunia vilius? what can you find more vile than money?
an quicquam est patria dulcius? can anything be dearer than fatherland?   10
erras si credis mihi quicquam esse uno te carius: you are mistaken if you
think any single thing dearer to me than you are.
     Here is an idiom worth noting:
officium tuum tam mihi gratum fuit quam quae gratissima: your service to
me was as gratifying as anything could be.   15
tam te amo quam qui maxime: I love you as much as anyone could.
amabat ut cum maxime tum Pamphilus (Terence): Pamphilus was then as
much in love as he could be.
domus celebratur ita ut cum maxime (Cicero): the house is as crowded as it
can possibly be.   20
     Here are some other types:
hoc crede mihi si quid unquam es crediturus: believe me in this, if you ever
are going to believe anything.
homo doctus si quisquam est omnino doctus: a man of learning, if anyone
ever was learned   25
homo vorax ut si quis alius: a guzzler if ever there was one
homo quantum alius nemo doctus: a man learned as no other ever was
nullus aeque pernovit hominis ingenium atque ego: no one knows the
fellow's nature as well as I.
haud alium reperies perinde tui studiosum: you will not find another who   30
supports you quite so wholeheartedly.
neminem adaeque timet atque te: he fears no one quite as much as you.
si alias umquam nunc summa vigilantia utendum est: we must employ the
greatest vigilance now if ever (i.e., now especially).
si quando alias amicum praestitisti, nunc ostende quanti me facis: if you   35

* * * * *

4 Horace] *Satires* 2.8.3–4
17 Terence] *Hecyra* 115
19 Cicero] *Ad Quintum fratrem* 2.4.6

LB I 34D

have ever played the friend at any time, demonstrate now how much you value me.

Phrases like *quantum potest* 'as much as possible,' *quoad fieri potest* 'as far as possible,' clearly have superlative force:
tu quantum potes abi: do you go away to the best of your ability (i.e., as fast   5
as possible).
enitar quoad potero: I will strive to what extent I can (i.e., as hard as possible).

It will be appropriate to include here examples of metonymy that depend on hyperbole, like calling a very cruel man an Atreus, a very   10
eloquent one a second Cicero, a very harsh one a third Cato; also comparisons that involve hyperbole: whiter than snow, more barbaric than a Scythian, more talkative than a jackdaw or turtle-dove.

It will prove instructive if I give a number of examples of this last type, which can be derived in various ways. The comparison can be drawn from   15
some substance remarkable for the quality in question, such as: whiter than snow, blacker than pitch; or from an abstract noun: blinder than blindness itself; or from some creature known for that quality: blinder than a mole, sharper-eyed than a roe-deer; or from a notable person: more cruel than Phalaris; or one can employ plain metonymy, like calling something that is   20
very sweet, honey or nectar, something very bitter, gall; a very old man, eld itself, a very wicked one, wickedness personified; an offensive person, a nastiness; a glutton, a sink; a squanderer, a pit; a dissolute man, a running sore; a despicable one, trash; a vile one, dirt; a pernicious one, a pest; a trickster, a murky spot; a filthy person, a gutter; a notorious one, a scandal;   25
a monstrous one, a monster; a discreditable one, a disgrace; a troublemaker, an ulcer; a vicious one, dregs; a hateful one, an offence of a fellow; a stupid one, a brute; a poisonous one, a viper; an utterly unseeing one, a mole; a thoroughly rapacious one, a wolf; an utterly ugly one, a Thersites.

* * * * *

  5 tu quantum potes abi] Terence *Adelphi* 350; *quantum potest* is frequent in both
      Plautus and Terence.
 10 Atreus] See 389:7n.
 11 Cato] See 391:5n.
 13 Scythian] See 392:7n.
 13 turtle-dove] *Adagia* i v 30
 18 mole] *Adagia* i iii 55
 19 roe-deer] Jerome Ep 70.6: *ne ... oculos caprearum talpa contemnat*
 20 Phalaris] See 391:1n.
 29 Thersites] See 389:9n.

EXAMPLES OF DIFFERENT TYPES OF VARIATION
The following nouns can be associated with a comparative to express a
superlative concept: sweeter than honey, blacker than pitch, whiter than
snow, softer than a feather, calmer than oil, softer than the ear-lobe, purer
than gold, duller than lead, slower than a stump, more stupid than a block, 5
harder than a rock, lighter than bark, more unresponsive than the seashore
or the sea, more stormy than the Adriatic, more bibulous than a sponge,
thirstier than the sands, more incessant than the bronze of Dodona, more
fragile than glass, more unstable than a ball, more accommodating than an
actor's sock, taller than an alder, harder than a whetstone, brighter than the 10

* * * * *

2 The following nouns] The order of examples in the series that fills the rest of
this section follows that given in Erasmus' authorized editions of *De copia*.
The order in LB I 35B–6D is clearly inferior and unsatisfactory; it arose from the
typesetter's reading the short lines in the double columns of *1534* downwards
instead of across.
3 honey] Ovid *Tristia* 5.4.29–30: *o dulcior illo melle*; also a stock phrase in writers
on rhetoric, as in *Ad Herennium* 4.33.44
3 pitch] Ovid *Metamorphoses* 12.402: *totus pice nigrior atra*
4 snow] Ovid *Amores* 3.7.8: *bracchia ... candidiora nive*
4 feather] Plautus *Poenulus* 812: *levior pluma est gratia*
4 oil] *Poenulus* 1236: *hanc canem faciam tibi oleo tranquilliorem*
4 ear-lobe] Cicero *Ad Quintum fratrem* 2.15a.4: *oricula infima scito molliorem*;
Adagia I vii 36
4 purer than gold] See 1 Pet 1:7; *Adagia* IV i 58.
5 lead, stump, block] Cf Terence *Heautontimorumenos* 877: *in me quidvis harum
rerum convenit / quae sunt dicta in stulto, caudex, stipes, asinus, plumbeus*
6 rock] Ovid *Metamorphoses* 9.303–4: *moturaque duros verba ... silices*
6 bark] Horace *Odes* 3.9.22: *tu levior cortice*
7 sea] A poetic commonplace, for example, Ovid *Metamorphoses* 13.804: *surdior
aequoribus*; *Adagia* I iv 84
7 Adriatic] Horace *Odes* 3.9.23; *Adagia* IV vi 89
8 sands] Cf Ovid *Heroides* 19.201: *bibulis inlisit fluctus harenis*
8 bronze of Dodona] *Adagia* I i 7; talkative people are set off by an appropriate
word, just as the bronzes of Dodona rang when struck.
9 ball] Apuleius *Metamorphoses* 2.4: *pilae volubilis instabile vestigium*
10 actor's sock] *Adagia* I i 94: 'Cothurno versatilior'; the actor's sock fitted right or
left foot equally well, and so suggested those who could not be trusted to
remain on the same side.
10 alder] Ovid *Metamorphoses* 13.790: *longa procerior alno*; the alder is not strikingly tall, but cf Virgil *Eclogues* 6.63, where the sisters of Phaethon become 'tall
alders.'
10 whetstone] *Adagia* I i 20

LB I 35B

sun, paler than box-wood, bitterer than the Sardonic herb, more despised
than sea-weed, rougher than butcher's broom, colder than ice, more seething than Etna, more tasteless than a beet, more just than the scale, more
crooked than a thorn, emptier than a bucket, lighter than a feather, lighter
than a shaving, more changeable than the wind, more hateful than death,   5
more capacious than the abyss, more inflexible than a dry bramble, more
voracious than Charybdis, darker than periwinkle leaves, cheaper than
chick-peas, more revolting than warmed-up cabbage, lighter than cork,
cleaner than a rudder, more licentious than the Floralia, an intellect blunter
than a pestle, more attractive than a magnet, more parched than pumice,   10

* * * * *

1 sun] Plautus *Miles* 2: *clarior quam solis radii esse ... solent*

1 box-wood] Ovid *Metamorphoses* 4.134: *oraque buxo pallidiora gerens*

1 Sardonic herb] Sea-weed, butcher's broom; Virgil *Eclogues* 7.41–2: *immo ego
Sardoniis videar tibi amarior herbis / horridior rusco, proiecta vilior alga*. The
'Sardonic' herb grew in Sardinia and was poisonous, causing the eater to die
in agony with the lips drawn back in a 'Sardonic' grin; *Adagia* III v 1.

2 ice] Ovid *Heroides* 1.22: *frigidius glacie pectus amantis erat*

3 Etna] *Appendix Virgiliana Aetna* 93: *aestuet Aetna*

3 beet] *beta*; the word is used later by Erasmus as a nickname for Beda (Noel
Bédier), one of his Parisian critics. See Thompson *Colloquies* 395.

3 scale] *Adagia* II v 82

4 bucket] *Appendix Virgiliana Catalepton* 5.1: *inanes ... ampullae*

4 feather] Plautus *Menaechmi* 488: *homo levior quam pluma*

5 shaving] Plautus *Bacchides* 512–13: *quam illa ... ramenta fiat plumea propensior*

5 wind] Ovid *Heroides* 7.51: *tu quoque cum ventis utinam mutabilis esses*

6 abyss] *Adagia* III vii 41

6 bramble] *Adagia* II i 100

7 Charybdis] A fabulous monster situated on one side of the straits between
Italy and Sicily, where it sucked in ships passing through the narrows; Cicero
Philippics 2.67: *quae Charybdis tam vorax?*; see line 6n, abyss.

7 periwinkle leaves] Literally the Egyptian clematis, a low creeping plant, used
as a figure for those who were long, thin, and dark-skinned; *Adagia* I i 22

8 chick-peas] *Corchoros*, a cheap bitter-tasting plant used as a vegetable by poor
Egyptians; *Adagia* I vii 21

8 cabbage] Cf Juvenal 7. 154: *Crambe repetita*, of re-hashed themes served up in
schoolboys' exercises; *Adagia* I v 38

8 cork] *Adagia* II iv 7

9 rudder] Because washed by the sea; *Adagia* II iv 95

9 Floralia] The Roman Flower Festival, 28 April–3 May, traditionally a time of
great licence, especially among women; see Juvenal 6.250.

10 pestle] *Adagia* III vi 21

10 magnet] *Adagia* I vii 56

10 pumice] Plautus *Aulularia* 297: *pumex non aeque est aridus atque hic est senex;
Adagia* I iv 75

drier than horn, drier than currants, more incontinent than a holed cask, less reliable than a sieve, more transparent than a lantern, purer than spring water, more unquiet, more inconstant than the Channel, dearer than one's eyes, more beloved than the light.

Examples of hyperbole, repeating the same stem: blinder than blindness, wickeder than wickedness, hungrier than famine, thirstier than thirst itself, more voracious than voracity, more pestilent than any plague, more captious than captiousness personified, more garrulous than garrulity, uglier than ugliness, more monstrous than any monster, more confident than confidence itself, older than old age, stupider than stupidity incarnate, more calamitous than calamity.

The following usage is similar: lovelier than Venus, more pugnacious or warlike than Mars, more eloquent than Mercury, sounder than Health, luckier than Luck, unluckier than an accident, more inconstant than Vertumnus, more mutable than Proteus, more changeable than Empusa, more elegant than the Graces, more mordant than Momus, more lewd than Priapus, more learned than Minerva, more melodious than Euterpe,

*****

1 horn] Catullus 23.12: *corpora sicciora cornu*
1 currants] *Adagia* II viii 67
1 holed cask] Cf Plautus *Pseudolus* 369: *in pertussum ingerimus dicta dolium*; *Adagia* I x 33
2 sieve] Used of the forgetful; *Adagia* I iv 60
2 lantern[Plautus *Aulularia* 566: *perlucet quasi laterna Punica*
3 Channel] The one between Attica and Euboea which was notorious for its shifting currents; *Adagia* I ix 62
4 eyes] Terence *Adelphi* 702: *magis te quam oculos nunc ego amo meos*
4 light] Virgil *Aeneid* 4.31: *luce magis dilecta*
12 Venus] Virgil *Eclogues* 7.62: *gratissima ... formosae myrtus Veneri*
13 Mercury] *Adagia* II x 10; see also book II 642:24ff.
14 Vertumnus] An Italian divinity whose name was thought to be connected with *vertere*, 'turn'; see Ovid *Metamorphoses* 14.642ff.
15 Proteus] The Old Man of the Sea, who would evade capture by changing his shape; see Ovid *Metamorphoses* 8.731ff; Virgil *Georgics* 4.440 ff.
15 Empusa] A horrible apparition in the underworld, made up of parts of all kinds of creatures, which kept constantly changing its shape; see Aristophanes *Frogs* 293; for all these see below 643:5 and *Adagia* II ii 74.
16 Momus] *Adagia* I v 74
17 Priapus] The guardian spirit of gardens, usually represented by a coarse wooden statue; see Ovid *Metamorphoses* 14.640; Horace *Satires* 1.8; and below 589:3.
17 Minerva] Roman goddess equated with Athena, the goddess of wisdom, invention, and skilled trades
17 Euterpe] One of the nine Muses, presiding over lyric poetry; the Muses were

wealthier than Plutus, poorer than Poverty, fiercer than a Fury, more rapacious than a Harpy.

Similar is the use of names of persons taken from tragedy, comedy, or other tales: more fawning than Gnatho, more boastful than Thraso, more confident than Phormio, more versatile than Geta, more grasping than Euclio, more winsome than Thais, harsher than Demea, milder than Micio, more voracious than a sponger, thirstier than Tantalus, crueler than Atreus, madder than Orestes, madder than Ajax, craftier than Ulysses, uglier than Thersites, more eloquent than Nestor, longer-lived than Nestor, more

5

* * * * *

named as early as Hesiod, but were not assigned specific functions until late antiquity.
1 Plutus] The spirit of wealth; see Aristophanes *Plutus*.
1 Fury] One of a number of avenging spirits which hounded evil-doers at the command of the gods; see line 8n, Orestes.
2 Harpy] A fabulous monster, half woman, half bird, which snatched the food from men's lips; see Virgil *Aeneid* 3.212ff.
4 Gnatho] A parasite in Terence's *Eunuchus*, used as a typical example of his kind; see Cicero *Philippics* 2.15: *putate tum Phormioni alicui, tum Gnathoni*.
4 Thraso] A bragging soldier in Terence's *Eunuchus*
5 Phormio] A self-confident scheming parasite in Terence's play of that name
5 Geta] Name of a scheming slave in *Phormio* and *Adelphi*
6 Euclio] A miser in Plautus' *Aulularia*
6 Thais] A courtesan in Terence's *Eunuchus*
6 Demea ... Micio] Two brothers of contrasting character in Terence's *Adelphi*; see below 584:10–14.
7 sponger] A frequent type in ancient comedy, for example, Phormio
7 Tantalus] A notorious sinner, punished in hell by submersion in a pool whose waters receded whenever he tried to quench his terrible thirst; Horace *Satires* 1.1.68: *Tantalus sitiens*; *Adagia* II vi 14
7 Atreus] Perpetrator of many crimes, the most notorious being his murder of his brother's children, whom he served up cooked as a meal for their father; *Adagia* II vii 92
8 Orestes] Son of Agamemnon and Clytemnestra; he killed his mother at the bidding of the gods to avenge her murder of his father, and was then hounded into madness by pursuing furies; Horace *Satires* 2.3.133: *demens Orestes*.
8 Ajax] One of the Greek heroes at Troy, who became temporarily deranged in consequence of a humiliation over the armour of Achilles, which he had hoped to acquire; *Adagia* I vii 46
8 Ulysses] Craftiest of all the Greeks at Troy; *Adagia* II viii 79
9 Thersites] An ugly trouble-maker among the common soldiers at Troy; *Adagia* IV iii 80
9 Nestor] Lord of Pylos in Peloponnesian Greece, who outlived three generations of men; he was present before Troy, where he proffered advice at great length; *Adagia* I ii 56; the order of the examples here is as in *1512, 1514*.

LB I 35D

tuneful than Orpheus, more foolish than Glaucus, more savage than a
Cyclops, more destitute than Irus, chaster than Penelope, fairer than
Nireus, longer-lived than Tithonus, chaster than Diana, bolder than Achilles, hungrier than Erysichthon, more prolific than Niobe, louder than
Stentor, blinder than Tiresias, more ill-famed than Busiris, more enigmatic   5
than the Sphinx, more intricate than the Labyrinth, more inventive than
Daedalus, more daring than Icarus, more overweening than the Giants,
stupider than Grunter, more unremitting than the Hydra.

* * * * *

1 Orpheus] Mythical singer who sang so sweetly that he charmed animals,
  trees, winds, and rivers; Horace *Odes* 1.12.7: *vocalem ... Orphea*
1 Glaucus] Trojan warrior who exchanged his own golden armour for
  Diomedes' bronze armour; Homer *Iliad* 6.234 says Zeus took away his wits;
  Adagia I ii 1.
2 Cyclops] The savage one-eyed giants encountered by Odysseus in his ten-
  year journey home from Troy; *Odyssey* 9.152ff
2 Irus] Beggar at the court of Odysseus in Ithaca; *Adagia* I vi 76
2 Penelope] Odysseus' faithful wife who repulsed all offers of marriage during
  her long wait for her husband's return
3 Nireus] The handsomest Greek at Troy; Horace *Odes* 3.20.15: *qualis aut Nireus
  fuit*
3 Tithonus] Husband of Aurora, the Dawn; he was given immortality, but not
  immortal youth; *Adagia* I vi 65.
3 Diana] The virgin huntress goddess, sister of Apollo
3 Achilles] The bravest warrior on the Greek side at Troy
4 Erysichthon] Punished with raging hunger for a sin against Ceres, the goddess of crops
4 Niobe] Mother of six sons and six daughters, who were killed by Apollo and
  Diana to punish their mother for boasting of her large family; Juvenal 6.177:
  scrofa Niobe fecundior alba; *Adagia* III iii 33
5 Stentor] The Greek with the loudest voice at Troy; *Adagia* II iii 37
5 Tiresias] The blind prophet of Thebes; *Adagia* I iii 57
5 Busiris] A king of Egypt who sacrificed all foreigners who entered the land;
  Virgil *Georgics* 3.5: *quis ... illaudati nescit Busiridis aras?*
6 Sphinx] A fabulous monster dwelling near Thebes, which put riddles to
  travellers and tore them in pieces when they could not answer; *Adagia* II iii 9
7 Daedalus] The craftsman who among other achievements built the Labyrinth
  at Cnossos in Crete to house the Minotaur; he and his son Icarus escaped the
  wrath of the ruler of Cnossos by flying away on wings made of feathers and
  wax; Icarus was too adventurous and flew so high that the sun melted his
  wings, so that he fell into the sea and was drowned.
7 Giants] Attempted to overthrow the rule of Zeus and the Olympians by
  scaling heaven by means of mountains piled one on top of the other; *Adagia* III
  x 93
8 Grunter] Gryllus, an ex-man turned into a pig by Circe and appearing in
  conversation with Ulysses in a dialogue by Plutarch, *Bruta animalia ratione uti*
8 Hydra] One of the monsters overcome by Hercules; it was a snake which

The following are taken from history: crueler than Phalaris, happier than Timotheus, luckier than Polycrates, more churlish than Timon, more despicable than Sardanapalus, more religious than Numa, juster than Phocion, more incorruptible than Aristides, richer than Croesus, more intransigent than Cato, wealthier than Crassus, poorer than Codrus, more debauched than Aesopus, more ambitious than Herostratus, more cautious

* * * * *

sprouted three fresh heads whenever one was cut off, and its defeat was accounted the most dangerous and praiseworthy of Hercules' labours; Horace *Odes* 4.4.61–2: *non hydra secto corpore firmior ... crevit in Herculem*

1 Phalaris] Notorious tyrant of Acragas in Sicily who, among other enormities, roasted victims alive in a brazen bull; taken as a typical example of cruelty in Seneca *De beneficiis* 7.19.5; *Adagia* I x 86

2 Timotheus] Athenian general who achieved his ends more by good luck than management, and became a proverbial example of those who get what they want without trying; *Adagia* I v 82

2 Polycrates] Ruler of Samos, famous for his good fortune in every aspect of life, until he eventually met a cruel death

2 Timon] Celebrated misanthrope of Athens; Lucian *Timon*

3 Sardanapalus] Famous king of Assyria who acquired an apparently undeserved reputation for effeminacy; Juvenal 10.362: *venere et cenis et pluma Sardanapali*; *Adagia* III vii 27

3 Numa] Second king of Rome in succession to Romulus; he was devoted to religious observance rather than war, and put religion in the city on an organized basis; Livy 1.18.1: *inclita iustitia religioque ... Numae Pompili erat*; Plutarch *Numa Pompilius*

3 Phocion] Athenian general of the fourth century BC, renowned for fearlessness and fair dealing, whom the Athenians mistakenly executed for treason; Plutarch *Phocion*

4 Aristides] Athenian of the fifth century BC, renowned for integrity; he was exiled because his fellow-citizens could not stand his virtue; Cicero *Pro Sestio* 141: *Aristides ... unus omnium iustissimus*; Plutarch *Aristides* 6.

4 Croesus] Last king of Lydia in Asia Minor, famous for his wealth; Ovid *Tristia* 3.7.42: *Irus et est subito qui modo Croesus erat*; *Adagia* I vi 74

5 Cato] *Catone praefractior*: Cicero *De officiis* 3.88: *nimis mihi praefracte videbatur aerarium vectigaliaque defendere* [*Cato*]; both the Elder Cato, second century BC, and his grandson, the Younger Cato, first century BC, were famous for high principles, obstinacy, and outspokenness.

5 Crassus] Marcus Licinius Crassus Dives (Crassus the millionaire), an unscrupulous Roman financier and politician contemporary with Cicero

5 Codrus] A poor man who lost all when his garret was burnt out; Juvenal 3.203

6 Aesopus] Son of Cicero's friend, the tragic actor Aesopus; he squandered his father's immense fortune by extravagances such as dissolving jewels in wine; see Horace *Satires* 2.3.239.

6 Herostratus] He set fire to the temple of Diana at Ephesus in 356 BC in order to win himself immortal fame; in consequence it was generally agreed never to mention his name; see Valerius Maximus 8.14 ext 5.

LB I 35F

than Fabius, more saintly than Socrates, stronger than Milo, more acute
than Chrysippus, sharper-eyed than Lynceus, more melodious than
Trachalus, more eloquent than Demosthenes, more forgetful than Curio,
more astute than Hannibal, obscurer than Heraclitus, more learned than
Aristarchus.

Some national names can be used in this way: more treacherous than
the Carthaginian, rougher than the Scythian, more inhospitable than the
Taurians, more mendacious than a Cretan, more fugitive than the Parth-

* * * * *

1 Fabius] Quintus Fabius, the Roman general who outmanoeuvred Hannibal,
  the brilliant and astute Carthaginian commander (see line 7n) in the Second
  Punic War; he avoided confrontation with the enemy and thus acquired the
  title *Cunctator*, 'the Delayer'; Virgil *Aeneid* 6.846: *unus qui nobis cunctando
  restituis rem.*

1 Socrates] The Athenian sage, teacher of Plato, treated as a kind of saint by the
  humanists; see book II 639:16ff; Thompson *Colloquies* 67–8.

1 Milo] See 303:14n.

2 Chrysippus] Distinguished Stoic philosopher; Cicero *De oratore* 1.50: *acutis-
  simum ... Chrysippum*

2 Lynceus] One of the Argonauts; he had such sharp sight that he could see into
  the ground, and was the first to discover veins of precious metal; *Adagia* II i 54;
  Horace *Epistles* 1.1.28: *non possis oculo quantum contendere Lynceus.*

3 Trachalus] An orator of the first century AD, especially noted for his fine
  delivery; Quintilian 10.1.119

3 Demosthenes] The most famous of Greek orators; see Cicero *Orator* passim.

3 Curio] The elder Gaius Scribonius Curio, an orator among whose defects was
  a poor memory; Cicero *Brutus* 216–8

4 Heraclitus] Sixth century BC Greek scientist and philosopher, famous for the
  obscurity of his pronouncements, for which he acquired the nickname 'the
  Obscure'; Cicero *De finibus* 2.15: *Heraclitus cognomento qui σκοτεινός
  perhibetur*

5 Aristarchus] Literary critic of Alexandria in the third century BC, especially
  famous for his criticisms of the accepted text of Homer; Ovid *Ex Ponto* 3.9.24:
  magnus Aristarcho maior Homerus erat

7 Carthaginian] The Carthaginians, especially their wily general Hannibal,
  were considered the personification of treachery by the Romans; *Adagia* I viii
  28.

7 Scythian] Typical examples of crudity and barbarity; those who lived in the
  Tauric Chersonese (Taurians 7) sacrificed to their gods all strangers who set
  foot in their land; see Euripides *Iphigenia in Tauris.*

8 Cretan] The Cretans were renowned as a nation of liars and cheats; *Adagia* I ii
  29.

8 Parthians] Their mounted cavalry would fire a volley of arrows and immediately gallop out of range of spears and similar weapons; Ovid *Remedia
  amoris* 155: *fugax Parthus; Adagia* I i 5.

ians, more vain, more lightweight than the Greeks, more drunken than the
Thracians, more untrustworthy than a Thessalian, more contemptible than
a Carian, more luxurious than the men of Leontini, haughtier than a
Sybarite, more effeminate than the Milesians, wealthier than the Arabs,
shorter than a pygmy, more stupid than an Arcadian, less trustworthy than
a Cretan, more debauched than an Asotus.

The following examples use the names of living creatures: more talkative than a woman, lustier than a sparrow, more lecherous than a billy-goat,
longer-lived than a stag, raven, or crow, more talkative than a jackdaw,
more melodious than a nightingale, more deadly than a viper, more deceit-

* * * * *

1 Greeks] Romans of the classical period looked on contemporary Greeks as
worthless and despicable descendants of the noble Greeks of the past; for
example, Cicero *ad Quintum fratrem* 1.1.16: *praeter hominum perpaucorum, si
qui sunt vetere Graecia digni ... fallaces sunt permulti et leves et diuturna servitute
ad nimiam assentationem eruditi.*

2 Thracians] *Adagia* II iii 17: 'Episcythizare,' meaning 'to drink heavily'

2 Thessalian] For Thessalian fraudulence, *Adagia* I iii 10

3 Carian] A by-word for worthlessness; *Adagia* I vi 14

3 Leontini] Wealthy Greek town in East Sicily, reduced to idleness after Phalaris
took away its weapons; *Adagia* I iii 22

4 Sybarite] Inhabitant of Sybaris, a prosperous Greek town in South Italy,
notorious for luxury and immorality; *Adagia* II ii 65

4 Milesians] Inhabitants of Miletus on the coast of Asia Minor, another wealthy
town, known as the home of 'Milesian Tales,' a collection of erotic and
fantastic stories, and the source of fine-woven transparent clothes; *Adagia* I iv
8

4 Arabs] Proverbial for wealth, which they derived from trade in perfumes and
incense; Horace *Odes* 3.24.1: *opulentior thesauris Arabum*

5 pygmy] Known to the ancients since Homer; see *Iliad* 3.3–6 for a battle
between cranes and pygmies; Juvenal 6.505–6: *brevior ... virgine Pygmaea*

5 Arcadian] Notoriously stupid; *Adagia* III iii 27

6 Cretan] See 392:8n.

6 Asotus] A Greek word meaning 'debauched'; for the habits of *asoti* see Cicero
De finibus 2.23.

8 woman] *Adagia* IV i 97

9 stag, raven, crow] Proverbial examples of long life, mentioned together by
Hesiod in a fragment quoted by Plutarch in *De defectu oraculorum* 2.415c: 'a
crow lives nine times as long as a man, a stag four times as long as a crow, a
raven three times as long as a stag.'

9 jackdaw] Cf Isidore *Etymologiae* 12.7.45: *graculus a garrulitate nuncupatus ... est
enim loquacissimum genus*

10 nightingale] Pliny *Naturalis historia* 10.81ff

10 viper] *dipsas*, a snake whose bite caused the victim to die of thirst; Lucan
9.737ff. The *hydra* (water-snake 394:7) lurked beside rivers and lakes; Virgil
Georgics 3.425ff. The *iaculus* (tree-snake 394:5) was so called because it lurked

ful than a fox, more prickly than a sea-urchin, more slippery than an eel, more timid than a hare, sounder than a fish, more playful than a dolphin, rarer than a phoenix, more prolific than a white sow, rarer than a black swan, rarer than a white raven, greedier than a vulture, grimmer than a scorpion, more unexpected, more deadly than a tree-snake, slower than a   5 tortoise, tucked up tighter than a snail, sleepier than a dormouse, more ignorant than a pig, slower than an ass, crueler than a water-snake, more fearful than a hind, thirstier than a blood-sucker, more quarrelsome than a dog, stronger than an ox, wilder than an unbroken horse, shaggier than a bear, lighter than a water-spider, more mischievous than a monkey, more   10 fawning than a spaniel, more thieving than a cat, deafer than a deer with

* * * * *

in trees and hurled itself (*iacere*) at its victim with such force as to be able to penetrate it; Lucan 9.822ff. For all these see Nicander *Theriaca*.
1 fox] *Adagia* I ii 28
1 sea-urchin] *Adagia* II iv 81
1 eel] *Adagia* I iv 95
2 hare] *Adagia* II i 80
2 fish] Refers to the ancient belief that fish did not suffer from disease; *Adagia* IV iv 93
2 dolphin] See Pliny *Epistles* 9.33 for the famous dolphin of Hippo.
3 phoenix] Ovid *Amores* 2.6.54: *phoenix unica semper avis*
3 white sow] Referring to the white sow with thirty young sent as a sign from heaven to Aeneas on his arrival in Italy; Virgil *Aeneid* 8.81ff; Juvenal 6.177: *scrofa Niobe fecundior alba*
3 black swan] Juvenal 6.165: *rara avis in terris nigroque simillima cycno*; *Adagia* II i 21
4 white raven] Juvenal 7.202: *corvo … rarior albo*
4 vulture] *Adagia* I vii 14: *Si vultur es, cadaver exspecta*, of grasping characters like legacy-hunters
5 tree-snake] See 393:10n, viper.
6 tortoise] *Adagia* I viii 84
6 dormouse] Martial 3.58.36: *somniculosos … glires*
7 pig] For the pig's stupidity see *Adagia* I i 40: *Sus Minervam docet*, 'the pig tells Minerva her business.' See 388:17n.
7 ass] Ovid *Metamorphoses* 11.179: *lente gradientis aselli*
7 water-snake] See 393:10n, viper; Ovid *Metamorphoses* 13.804: *calcato immitior hydro*.
8 hind] Virgil *Eclogues* 8.28: *dama timidior*
9 ox] Misplaced in 1534, before 'blood-sucker'
10 bear] Ovid *Metamorphoses* 13.836: *villosae catulos … ursae*
10 water-spider] Plautus *Persa* 244: *neque tippulae levius pondus quam fides lenonia*
11 deer] See Pliny *Naturalis historia* 8.114, where it is stated that deer are deaf unless their ears are pricked up.

unpricked ears, stupider than a gull, more demanding than a cuckoo, cheekier than a beetle.

Some are derived from occupations: more brutal than a hangman, more perjured than a parasite, more effeminate than a pansy, more boastful than a soldier, more muscular than an athlete, more magnificent than a king, more severe than an Areopagite, more inexperienced than a monk, more flattering than a legacy-hunter, more violent than a tyrant, more hardened than a labourer.

The same effect is produced by using adjectives derived from these nouns: honeyed for extremely pleasing; snow-white morals for very pure; a golden age for very prosperous and desirable; leaden, stony for hard; an iron writer, grass-green, or turnip-headed for fatuous; fig-like for soft; adamantine for hard and able to bear toil; glassy for fragile; a vulturine stomach, a foxy mind, leonine ferocity, Thrasonian boasting, Demean harshness, Stentorian voice, Ciceronian eloquence. This type is too numerous for me to endeavour to give a more comprehensive list. Some expressions are more far-fetched, but they belong here nonetheless: as a wolf cares for numbers, or rivers in flood their banks; I am no more bothered by his insults than an Indian elephant by a gnat; I don't care a pin, I don't give a fig, I don't care a straw. But these phrases will be dealt with elsewhere.

47 / An alternative expression for all three degrees of the adjective

An adjective, whether in the positive, comparative, or superlative degree, can be replaced by a periphrasis:

[positive:] *vir magnopere doctus* 'a man greatly learned' or *vir magna doctrina praeditus* 'a man endowed with great learning'

[comparative:] *magis doctus* 'a man more learned' or *maiore doctrina praeditus* 'a man endowed with greater learning'

* * * * *

1 gull] *Adagia* II ii 33

2 beetle] Refers to its unremitting feud with the eagle; *Adagia* III vii i

6 Areopagite] Member of the Areopagus, the upper council at Athens, composed of men of dignity and mature years, known as severe judges; *Adagia* I ix 41

7 legacy-hunter] See 394:4n, vulture.

12 grass-green] *Adagia* II iv 72 (on *bliteus*)

18 rivers in flood their banks] Virgil *Eclogues* 7.52

20 elsewhere] Many of these comparisons are treated at greater length in the *Adagia*; the whole section on 385–95 is repeated to a large extent verbatim in *Adagia* prolegomena xiii (LB II 12C–13D). For *pin, fig, straw* see chap 71.

[superlative:] *doctissimus* 'most learned' or *maxima doctrina praeditus* 'endowed with the greatest learning.'
res cum magna, cum maiore, cum summa turpitudine coniuncta est: 'the affair involves great, greater, the greatest infamy.'

[EQUIVALENT EXPRESSIONS]
So called ἰσοδυναμίαι or equivalences contribute in no small degree to richness of expression. My next task will therefore be briefly to indicate how various equivalent words are differentiated.

[Words for 'all' first]

totus refers to the complete thing, while suggesting possible divisions:
si mors totum hominem absumeret, merito tantopere formidaretur: if Death carried off the whole man, it would deserve to be so greatly feared.
totum hunc mensem, totam hanc noctem sine fruge transegi: I have spent this whole month, this whole night, without profit.

cunctus refers collectively to all the separate individuals included in the main concept, as if it were derived from *coniuncti* 'conjoined':
cunctos Romanos, cunctos mortales: all the Romans, all mortal men

universi means 'all gathered together':
aut nullam aut universam pecuniam vult: he wants no money, or all of it (i.e., all at once).
id illa nunc abripiet universum (Terence): that she will now grab, all of it.

singuli differs from this in that it means 'all, but each individual separately':
in singulas naves singuli milites accensebantur: the soldiers were all being assigned, one to each separate ship.

omnis is a general word that does for all contexts. We can say *omne corpus, omnis populus* 'the whole body, the whole people' using it instead of *totus*; and *omnem diem* 'each day' using it instead of *singulus*, as in *omnem crede diem tibi diluxisse supremum* (Horace) 'believe each day that dawns to be thy last.'

It can also be used for *cuncti* and *universus*: *at ut omne reddat* (Terence) 'But if only he will pay back the lot' – though in this example it may be replacing *totus*.

* * * * *

18 *coniuncti*] Festus 156 (Lindsay)
23 Terence] *Phormio* 45
31 Horace] *Epistles* 1.4.13
33 Terence] *Adelphi* 280

[Words for 'each']

quisque implies the distribution of something into individual units:
sua cuique sententia: to each individual his own opinion
natura animantium sua cuique dedit arma: nature has given to each creature its own means of defence.
suas cuique dotes largitus est Deus: God has endowed each individual with his own gifts.

unusquisque does not appear to differ from *quisque*, except that it can also be used instead of *singulus*:
unumquemque sua cupiditas ducit: his own desire leads on each individual.
nunc unumquodque crimen cuiusmodi sit excutiamus: now let us scrutinise each individual charge separately to see of what kind it is.

There is nothing to prevent *singuli* also being used in a distributive sense in the same way:
singulis navibus singulos duces praefecit: he put separate officers in command of each individual ship.

[Words for 'whoever']

An utterance introduced by *quisquis* is not complete and independent, whereas one introduced by *quicumque* is sometimes complete, sometimes incomplete:
quisquis gravabitur sementem facere, is non metet: whosoever shirks the sowing will reap no harvest.
quicumque recusabit laborem, non feret fructum: whoever rejects the toil will gain no reward.
quisquis can however introduce a clause that is more or less independent when it expresses ignorance:
quisquis fuit ille deorum: whosoever it was among gods.
quisquis es armatus, qui nostra ad limina tendis: whosoever thou art, that bearing arms, / Advancest on our doors.

Both words are sometimes used in cases other than the nominative in phrases dependent on another verb: rem facias quocumque modo: you must manage it somehow.
hominem quoquo modo absolvas: you must get the man's acquittal in some way (i.e., in whatever way you like, *quovis modo*).

* * * * *

5 means of defence] Cf Cicero *De officiis* 1.11.
10 individual] Cf Virgil *Eclogues* 2.65: *trahit sua quemque voluptas.*
28 quisquis fuit ille deorum] Ovid *Metamorphoses* 1.32
29 ad limina tendis] Virgil *Aeneid* 6.388. The manuscript tradition offers both *flumina* and *limina; flumina* is preferred in modern texts.

LB I 36F

quilibet and *quivis* are used with no distinction between them to mean 'whoever you like,' as in: *quaelibet in quemvis opprobria dicere saevus* (Horace) 'A hard-mouthed hurler of any chance insult / At any you care to name.' But the implication of these two words is 'this *or* that,' whereas *omnis* 'all' and most of the rest imply 'this *and* that,' for example, *quemvis arbitrum cedo* 'produce whom you will as arbiter between us' (i.e., this man *or* that, it makes no difference to me); *qualibet hirsutas fronde tegente comas* 'with any bough that chanced / Shading their shaggy locks.' The Greek word for this idea is τυχόν [accidental], not chosen, but fortuitous and haphazard.

unusquilibet is very similar. It means 'one individual out of many, whoever he might be': *deligas tibi auctorem unumquemlibet* 'choose yourself any one author you fancy.' *unusquivis* is exactly the same.

All these four, *quilibet, quivis, unusquilibet, unusquivis,* already contain a verb form and admit no other verb in the same clause, since they make an utterance complete.

The indefinites *quantuscumque, quantusquantus* 'however big,' *qualiscumque, qualisqualis* 'of whatever sort' behave like *quicumque* and *quisquis.* Likewise the adverbs *utut, utcumque* 'howsoever,' *ubiubi, ubicumque* 'wheresoever,' *quoquo, quocumque* 'whithersoever.' To put the matter briefly, compounds always follow the nature of the second included element: *undevis, undelibet* 'from wheresoever you wish' contain a verb form and make complete utterances, whereas *undecumque* 'from wheresoever' is undetermined, like *quocumque, quoquo* 'to wheresoever, to whatever place.' But *quolibet, quovis* 'to wherever you want' contain verbs and so are not undetermined. *quoquoversum, quaquaversum* 'in whatever direction' are undetermined; *ubivis, ubilibet* 'wherever you want' contain verbs and make complete utterances. *ubicumque* 'wherever' is undetermined; and likewise *ubiubi* 'wheresoever' and *utut* 'howsoever,' for these do not make an utterance finite either.

['whichever,' 'each']

uter means 'whichever of two,' and its usage varies according to the way it is compounded: *utercumque* is indeterminate, whereas *utervis, uterlibet* make finite utterances. Similarly with *utrocumque* 'in whichever of two directions,' which is different from *utrovis, utrolibet* 'in whichever of two directions you choose.'

uterque implies 'each in conjunction' [i.e. both], like *utroque* 'in both

* * * * *

3 Horace] *Epistles* 1.15.30
5 *quemvis arbitrum cedo*] Terence *Adelphi* 123
7 *fronde tegente comas*] Ovid *Ars amatoria* 1.108

LB I 37A

directions,' *utrinque* 'from both directions,' *utroqueversum* 'turned both ways.'

['some,' 'any']

aliquis means 'any one individual' in an indefinite sense, as in *quid si hoc aliquis voluit deus?* 'suppose some (individual) god willed this?' *quis* means the same, but is nearly always preceded by *si, ne, num, ec, ubi*:
si quid extiterit novi: if anything fresh happens
ne quid temere faxis: don't do anything rash.
num quem tuorum offendi? have I offended anyone of yours?
ecquid tui tetigi? have I ever touched anything of yours?
ubi quis te laeserit: whenever anyone injures you ...

ubi 'where' is used for *alicubi* 'somewhere, anywhere,' and *unde* 'whence' for *alicunde* 'somewhence,' at any rate in compounds: *sicubi* 'if anywhere,' *necubi* 'lest anywhere,' *nuncubi?* 'is there anywhere?' *sicunde* 'if from anywhere,' *necunde* 'lest from anywhere.'

quidam means 'some definite individual': *quendam volo visere*: 'I want to call on a certain person' – unless it is used in a contemptuous sense, or in association with a metaphorical expression: *Isidorum quendam mihi citabat* 'he kept citing to me some Isidore or other' (where it has the same derogatory sense as *nescio quis* 'some unheard-of'); *lacrimas emisit quendam animi sanguinem* 'the tears he wept were (so to speak) the life-blood of his spirit'; *seditio morbus est quidam civitatis* 'sedition is (as it were) a disease of the state.'

quispiam covers the functions of both *quidam* and *aliquis*. Although Valla contests this, one can quote a good many authorities for opposing his view.
mittito ad me tuorum quempiam: send me one or other of your people.
est domi tuae quispiam cum quo iure debeam expostulare: there is in your household a certain person with whom I have every right to take issue.

quisquam [pronoun] and *ullus* [adjective] 'any' agree in meaning. They

* * * * *

5 *aliquis voluit deus*] Terence *Eunuchus* 875: *quispiam voluit deus*

8 ne quid temere faxis] Cf Terence *Andria* 205: *ne temere facias*.

10 ecquid tui tetigi] Cf Terence *Adelphi* 178: *tetigin tui quicquam?* After *ecquid tui tetigi* 1512 and 1514 have *ecquam habes uxorem?* 'what sort of a wife have you got?'

16 *quendam volo visere*] Horace *Satires* 1.9.17

22 civitatis] Cf Cicero *Catilinarians* 1.31: *hic morbus qui est in republica*.

25 Valla] Lorenzo Valla, Italian humanist for whom Erasmus had a high regard. See Ep 23:108n. This chapter of *De copia* is clearly indebted to the corresponding part of Valla's *Elegantiae*. On the pronouns mentioned in line 24 see *Elegantiae* 3.63 and Erasmus' *Paraphrasis in Elegantias Vallae* (LB I 1073E, 1113D, or ASD I-4 221, 308).

LB I 37C

are somewhat more emphatic than the terms given above, and also have the
special feature of preferring a context containing a negative, or *si*, or *ne*
introducing a negative final clause, or an interrogative:
haud ullus mortalium ista possit praestare: not any mortal could perform
what you ask.
haud possit mortalium quisquam ista praestare: not anyone among
mortals ...
si quisquam est qui sapientiam cum eloquentia coniunxit, certe Tullius is
est: if anyone there is who has combined wisdom and eloquence, that one is
certainly Cicero.
vide ne quisquam hinc aufugiat: prevent anyone escaping from here.
cave ne quoquam oculos tuos a meis dimoveas: see that you do not shift
your eyes away from mine in any direction.
an est quisquam qui suam amicam se praesente ...? can there be anyone
who would let his girl before his eyes ...?
num quisquam est mortalium tam patiens? surely there is not any mortal
man so long-suffering?
    The adverbs *usquam* and *uspiam* 'anywhere' occur in the same sort of
context.

48 / Generalizing statements

Having said all this by way of basic introduction, I shall now proceed with
ἰσοδυναμίαι or equivalent expressions.
    To take first of all generalizing or universal statements. These can be
made in various ways: first by using those words with a definite meaning
that fit this kind of sentence, such as *omnis* 'all': *omnes amicos alienavit* 'he
alienated all his friends.' Next by means of negatives: *neminem non alienavit*
'there was no one he did not alienate.' Third by means of a question: *quem
non amicum alienavit?* 'which of his friends did he not alienate?' *quas gentes
Italum, aut quas non oraveris urbes?* (Virgil) 'What tribes of Italy, what cities, /
Shalt thou not as suppliant entreat?'

* * * * *

12 a meis dimoveas] Terence *Adelphi* 170: *cave nunciam oculos a meis oculis
    quoquam demoveas tuos*
14 amicam se praesente] Cf Terence *Heautontimorumenos* 913: *quemquamne ...
    putas qui se praesente amicam patitur suam ... ?*
32 Virgil] *Aeneid* 6.92

The type employing negatives, for example, *nulli non maledicis* 'there is none you do not slander,' cannot however be used as an alternative for one containing two generalizing words, such as *cum omnibus omnia minabatur* (Cicero) 'when he was threatening everyone with everything,' or *omnibus omnia invidet* 'he grudges everyone everything.' It would not be correct to substitute here *nihil non invidet alicui* 'there is nothing he does not grudge someone.'

omnibus maledicis: you slander everybody.

quis est cui non maledicis? who is there that you do not slander?

omnia dixit: he said everything.

quid non dixit? what did he not say?

We have just seen that a question containing a negative is the equivalent of a generalizing positive statement; a question without a negative makes a generalized negative statement: *quid possit dici stultius?* 'what more stupid thing could be said?' (i.e., nothing could be said that was more stupid).

Generalizing statements can also be made by using indefinite adjectives and pronouns: *haud pepercit cuiquam* 'he did not spare anyone'; *non est ullum veritus, haud ullum veritus* 'he did not fear any'; *haud ullum est facinus reliquum quod non peregerit* 'there is not any crime left that he has not committed'; *non excepit aliquem* 'he did not except any person,' that is, 'he excepted no one.'

Another possibility is to use *quantum, quidquid* 'however much, whatever there is,' and *si quod aliud* 'if any beside': *quantum est hominum venustiorum* 'the whole supply of charming fellows,' that is, 'all the charming fellows'; *quidquid erat copiarum, eo traduxit* 'he took across whatever he had by way of forces,' that is, all his forces; *si quid erat copiarum amisit* 'if there were any forces, those he lost,' that is, he lost them all; *siquid alias sibi bonae famae compararat, id nunc perdidit* 'if he had acquired any decent reputation anywhere else, that he now threw away.'

A proverbial turn of phrase can also express generality: you will confound the holy and the profane, that is, everything; young men and old, that is, all; something neither large nor small, that is, nothing. There are

* * * * *

4 Cicero] *Pro Milone* 33
14 *stultius*] Cicero *Pro Caecina* 40
24 *hominum venustiorum*] Catullus 3.2
32 holy and the profane] Horace *Epistles* 1.16.54; *Adagia* I iii 82
32 young men and old] *Adagia* IV vi 45

also indefinite expressions of this sort, such as 'by fair means or foul,' 'by
right or by wrong,' that is, 'in some way or other.'

Finally we have *ad unum* 'to a man,' equivalent to 'all': *si non exosus ad
unum Troianos* (Virgil) 'If thou hatest not the Trojans to a man.'

5

49 / Specific statements

[First, using *nonnihil* and *non nemo*:]
nonnihil est vel aspicere: it is not nothing to get even a look (i.e., it is   10
something).
nonnulli pluris faciunt pecuniam quam fidem: there are not none (i.e.,
there are some persons) who value money more than good faith.
non nemo etiam in illo sacrario reipublicae, in ipsa inquam curia non nemo
hostis est (Cicero): right in the inmost shrine of the state, in this very House   15
I say, there are some persons who are traitors to our nation.
quum esset non nemo in senatu qui diceret non oportere (Cicero): though
there were not lacking individuals in the Senate to say it was not right.
inest et infantibus nonnihil ingenii: even in infants there is a certain
amount of intelligence.   20
[Next, using *non omne*:]
non omnem pecuniam absumpsit: he did not use up all the money (i.e.,
there was some he did not use up).
qui legat argentum factum, non omne legat argentum: he who bequeathes
silver in the form of money does not bequeath all his silver.   25
nonnulli and similar words can be omitted in this type of sentence
without altering the sense:
sunt qui pecuniam anteponant famae: there are (people) who put money
before reputation.
est ubi peccet (Horace): there are (certain points) wherein [the crowd] errs.   30
est qui plures agros occupet: there is (one) who seizes on many a field.

* * * * *

1 'by fair means or foul'] *per fas nefasque*; see Donatus on *Andria* 214; *Adagia* I iii
   82.
1 'by right or by wrong'] *quo iure quaque iniuria*; Terence *Andria* 214; see previous n.
3 *ad unum Troianos*] Virgil *Aeneid* 5.687
15 Cicero] *Pro Murena* 84
17 Cicero] *Pro lege Manilia* 62
24 legat argentum] Cf Quintilian 5.14.26.
30 Horace] *Epistles* 2.1.63

LB I 38B

quiddam is often understood, as in this example: *est in quo mihi possis magnopere gratificari* 'there is (a certain matter) in which you could do me a great service.'

A double negative sometimes indicates not just a positive concept but necessity:
non possum non ridere: I cannot not laugh [i.e., I can't help laughing]. non possum non mirari: I can't help wondering.
non potest non volvi caelum, non potest non stare terra: the heaven must of necessity revolve, and the earth stand firm.
non potest non verum dicere veritas: truth cannot fail to speak the truth. This happens only with the verb *possum* 'to be able.'

50 / Precision in the use of words

In introducing variations one must take care not to confuse the different implications of words, as most professors of dialectic do. *non erit tibi res cum quoquam* 'you will not have to deal with anyone' means 'you will have to deal with no one,' whereas *non erit tibi res cum quolibet homine* 'you will not have to deal with *any*one' means 'you will have to deal with a remarkable and outstanding man.' One is negative in effect, the other is positive, and has a very different force. *non cuivis homini contingit adire Corinthum* 'Not *any* body can reach the city of Corinth' means 'only the outstanding.' You can see how different this is from *non ulli* 'not anybody.' *non amat quempiam e ministris* 'he does not care for someone among his servants,' but *non amat aliquem* 'he does not care for anyone' (i.e., he cares for no one). *non satis amat quendam* 'he does not care much for a certain person' indicates a definite individual whom he dislikes.

non satis tibi favet quidam 'there is a certain person who is not very well inclined towards you.' (Some people use *certus* in this last sense: *per certos homines hoc foedus diremptum est* 'certain individuals were responsible for breaking this treaty'; *iussus est ad certum diem adesse* 'he was ordered to appear on a certain day.') *non tibi favet quisquam* 'not a single person supports you' is entirely different in implication.

non recuso quemquam 'I do not refuse anyone' is correct, whereas *non recuso quemlibet* 'I do not refuse everyone' is incorrect, unless you mean something different. Similarly, *non exclusit omnes* 'he did not exclude all'

* * * * *

22 *adire Corinthum*] Horace *Epistles* 1.17.36; see 295:10n.
33 *non tibi favet quisquam*] The continuity of the text has been broken by the note on *certus*, inserted in 1534.

means 'some people he did not exclude,' but *non exclusit quoslibet* 'he did
not exclude all and sundry' means that a choice was exercised and some
were excluded, some admitted.

omnia folia huic arbori decident 'all the leaves will fall off this tree' is a
true statement; *universa decident* 'the whole mass of leaves will fall off' is
not. *singulos salutavit* 'he greeted single individuals,' but he did not greet
quemlibet 'all and sundry,' whereas *lupae unumquemlibet admittunt* 'prosti-
tutes do receive all and sundry' (i.e., any whatsoever without distinction).

*vide ne cui dicas, vide ne dicas cuiquam, vide ne cuipiam dixeris, vide ne
dixeris alicui, vide ne mortalium ulli dixeris* all have the same force and mean
'mind you do not tell any person at all' (i.e., tell no one), whereas *vide ne
cuivis* or *ne cuilibet dixeris* 'mind you do not tell anyone you fancy' implies
'take care whom you tell, mind you do not blab it out without thinking to
any chance person.'

omnes sibi malunt esse recte quam aliis 'all men prefer things to be right
for themselves rather than for other people' has the same force as *quisque
vult* 'each man prefers,' and also *nemo non malit ...* 'there is no one who
would not prefer ...' and *singuli sibi malunt ...'* 'every single individual
prefers.' But *universi sibi malunt ...* 'the whole lot together prefer ...' is a silly
expression because of the special implications of *universi*.

To the universal term *totus* 'the whole' corresponds *aliquantum* 'a
considerable portion'; to *semper* 'always' corresponds *aliquamdiu* 'a certain
length of time'. As we said earlier, *omnia* 'all' can be replaced by *quantum*
'how much, whatever the amount,' likewise *totus* 'the whole' by *quantum*
and *quam longus* 'whatever the length': *homo quantus erat humi prostratus est*
'the man's whole length was sprawled along the ground'; *nunc hiemem inter
se luxu quam longa fovere* (Virgil) 'Now they were keeping warm all the
winter's length / In mutual comfort and indulgence.'

EACH, NEITHER
uterque utrique est cordi 'each to either is dear,' *uterque alteri est odio* 'each to
the other is hateful' are both positive reciprocal expressions, equivalent to
mutuo sese amant, mutuo sese oderunt 'they love each other, hate each other.'
The negative form is *neuter alteri fidit* 'neither trusts the other'; one would
not however say *neuter neutri* [like *uterque utrique*].

There are a number of ways of varying this type of expression:

* * * * *

15 *omnes sibi malunt*] *Adagia* I iii 91
23 earlier] See 401:23ff.
27 Virgil] *Aeneid* 4.193
31 *uterque utrique est cordi*] Terence *Phormio* 800

uterque alterum odit: each one hates the other.
uterque utrumque odit: each hates each.
alter alterum odit: one hates the other.
oderunt alter alterum: they feel hatred each towards the other.
mutuum oderunt: they feel a mutual hate.
oderunt se mutuo: they hate mutually.
oderunt in vicem: they feel a reciprocal hate.
oderunt inter sese: they hate each other.
mutuum inter ipsos est odium: there is a mutual hatred between them.
neuter alterum amat: neither loves the other.
alter alterum vicissim odit: one hates the other in retaliation.

ALWAYS

semper 'always' indicates time in general; its opposite is *numquam* 'never';
aliquando 'at some time or other' is a subsection of *semper*:
semper litigas: you are always wrangling in the courts.
numquam non litigas: there is never a time when you are not wrangling ...
quando non litigas? when are you not wrangling ...?
num quando non litigas? there is never a time, is there, when you are
not ... ?
an est quando non litigas? is there ever a time when you are not ... ?

OFTEN

alioquoties 'sometimes' is the indefinite term corresponding to *saepe* 'often,'
aliquot 'quite a number' to *multi* 'many,' and *aliquantus* 'a considerable
amount' to *magnus* 'great.' The opposite of *saepe* is *raro* 'rarely.'
neque raro admonui: nor did I warn him but rarely (i.e., I frequently
warned him).
haud saepe me visit: he does not often visit me.
   plerumque 'for the most part,' *ferme fere* 'usually, on the whole,' *nonnumquam* 'not never' [(i.e., on occasion),] all have a certain generalizing
force:
ita ferme ingenium est hominum: such is the nature of men on the whole.
eo ingenio plerique sumus: we are like that for the most part.
fere fit ut divites habeantur in pretio: it is usually the case that the rich are
valued.
   In a negative sentence *temere* 'casually' acquires this sort of meaning:
haud temere pervenit ad frugem: not casually (i.e., not readily, practically
never, hardly ever) does it reach fruition.
   * * * * *

38 pervenit ad frugem] Cf Quintilian 1.3.3.

51 / Varieties of negative

Observe that sometimes a single negative has the same effect as two:
neminem audit: he listens to no one.
ne parentem quidem audit; non audit vel parentem: he does not listen even
to his father.
nemo parem referre gratiam parenti potest, ne malo quidem: no one can
return adequate thanks to a parent, not even a bad one.
nec malo parenti quisquam parem referre gratiam potest: not even to a bad
parent can anyone return adequate thanks.
non potest par gratia rependi patri, vel malo: it is not possible for adequate
gratitude to be shown to a parent, even a bad one.
non reliquit ille nec ruinam: he did not leave anything, not even remains.
ne ruinam quidem reliquit: he did not leave even remains.

TRIPLE NEGATIVES
Sometimes a triple negative has no more effect than one or two: *non veretur
neque deos neque homines* [three negatives], *neque deos neque homines veretur*
[two], *non veretur aut deos aut homines* [one]: 'he respects not either gods or
men.' In poetry one can say *non metuit hominesve deosve* for this.
   The practice of doubling a negative for emphasis is found among Latin
speakers as well, provided the repeated negative has some other words to
accompany it, for example, *non faciam, non inquam* 'I will not do it, not, I
say.' The Greeks however use the bare negatives side by side, sometimes
without any particular emphasis: οὐ μὴ πίνω ἔτι 'I will not drink any more'
[where οὐ and μή are both negatives]. It is a common habit among writers
of Attic Greek to heap up several negatives in place of one.
   One can use the same vocabulary and still vary the expression of a
statement, or one can change the vocabulary and keep the basic statement
the same, by altering the verb, as in the following examples:
omnes admittit: he receives everyone.
omnes reicit: he rejects everyone.
neminem non reicit: there is no one he does not reject.
neminem admittit: he receives no one.
omnibus displicet: he displeases everyone.
nemini placet: he pleases no one.
nulli non displicet: there is no one he does not displease.
nulli placet: he pleases none.
Here we must observe which words are incompatible with which.

SYNONYMOUS NEGATIVE EXPRESSIONS

There are various ways of expressing the negative: *non, haud* 'not,' *nec, neque* 'and not, neither,' *haudquaquam, neutiquam* 'not at all, not by any means,' *minime* 'by no means,' *minus* 'less,' *parum* 'not enough,' *absit* 'heaven preserve us,' *dii prohibeant* 'God forbid,' *bona verba* 'don't say it,' *quidvis potius* 'anything but,' *omnia citius* 'anything sooner,' and so on.

Of these *haud* and *haudquaquam* are rather more emphatic than *non*. *neutiquam* has its own particular emphasis. *minime* indicates rather more than plain negation: *homo minime malus* 'a man by no means bad' (i.e., anything but bad). *parum* makes a more tentative negation: *parum eruditus* 'not quite educated enough'; *ne parum multa scire viderentur* 'lest they should appear inadequately informed' (i.e., to know little or not enough).

minus has diverse functions, in that sometimes it merely compares:
utrumque diligit, famam et pecuniam, sed illam minus quam hanc: he loves
both things, fame and money, but fame less than money;
sometimes it merely negates:
homo minus mihi notus: a man less (i.e., insufficiently) known to me
nam cum ea voce minus convenit: it is not really consistent with that
statement;
sometimes it does both at once:
cum interim, quod tamquam facile contemnunt, nescias praestare velint
minus an possint (Quintilian, in his chapter on how to state the facts of a
case): all the time you cannot tell whether they are less willing than able to
perform a task which they despise as something easy.
non tibi illud factum minus placet quam mihi, Laches (Terence, in *Hecyra*):
That deed is unpleasing to you, Laches, not any less than to me.
placet 'pleases' is not put here for *displicet* 'displeases,' as the grammarians
choose to explain the line [i.e., 'it is not less *displeasing* to you than to me'],
for what man in his right mind would write such a thing? *minus* here has the
same force as in:

* * * * *

9 *minime malus*] Cicero *Tusculan Disputations* 2.44: *homo minime malus vel potius vir optimus*, an example used in Charisius *Ars grammatica* II in Keil I 206
11 *ne parum multa*] *Ad Herennium* 1.1
22 Quintilian] 4.2.37
25 Terence] *Hecyra* 647
27 grammarians] See Donatus *Commentary* on this passage; he suggests either that *non minus* equals *magis*, or, the view which Erasmus rejects, that *placet* is used ironically instead of *displicet*.

non amat me Dionysius et minus te: Dionysius mislikes me and mislikes
me rather than you (i.e., he hates me more than you).
So in the Terence example we have to understand that the situation pleases
neither of them, and *minus* is at the same time expressing both a negative
and a comparison.

52 / Linking sentences together

To go into all this in more detail is really the task of the logicians, but I think
that my treatment of it, albeit brief, is adequate for the scope of this work.

    Now let us tackle some of the other formulae, first of all those function-
ing as connectives, since we observe that even those of a fairly high
standard of education are deficient in the art of coupling together in a neat
and elegant manner, as with tendons, the limbs and joints of their speech.
To explain what links can be employed to join up the smaller subsections of
an utterance would be an almost endless task, but the major segments can
be connected with the following expressions: *praeterea* 'moreover'; *deinde*
'thereafter,' frequently employed by Cicero; instead of *deinde* Seneca
employs *subinde* 'thereupon,' but with a connotation of speed, equivalent
to *mox* 'directly, soon'; Suetonius does the same.
praecipuum est stercus columbarum, proximum caprarum, ab hoc ovium,
deinde boum: the best fertiliser is pigeon-droppings, next goat-dung, after
that sheep-dung, thereafter ox-dung.
in nostro orbe proxime laudatur Syriacum, mox Gallicum: in our part of the
world the next most highly esteemed is the Syrian, immediately thereafter
the Gallic. (Pliny uses *mox* in a number of places for *deinde* 'thereafter.')
in quo principatum tenuit Boeotia, deinde Sicilia, mox Africa: in this
Boeotia took first place, next Sicily, thereafter Africa.

* * * * *

19 instead of ... the same] Added in *1526* (LB I 40B)
19 Seneca] See *De beneficiis* 6.27.6: *si accusatorem submitteres quem deinde remo-
veres, si aliqua illum lite implicares, quam subinde discuteres,* where the 1529
edition of Seneca has a marginal note, *subinde pro mox.*
21 Suetonius] For example, *Augustus* 95, *Galba* 1 (Suetonius also uses *subinde* to
mean 'often'); there is a comment on the usage in Erasmus' 1518 edition of
Suetonius where most of the phrases quoted in *De copia* are listed in the index.
22 praecipuum est ... third place'] Added in *1514* (LB I 40B)
23 deinde boum] Pliny *Naturalis historia* 17.52
25 Gallicum] *Naturalis historia* 12.45, on nard
29 Africa] *Naturalis historia* 18.63, on wheat

Next we have *primo, secundo, tertio loco* 'in first, second, third place,' *proximum ab hoc* 'next after this'; *porro, porro autem* 'furthermore,' which is appropriate to the start of a fresh and more important utterance, as Donatus remarks; *ceterum* 'for the rest' should be employed whenever the speech moves on to a different section; *tum* 'then,' can be used instead of *praeterea,* and we also have *ad hoc, ad haec* 'in addition to this,' equivalent to Greek πρὸς τούτοις; *cum hoc* 'along with this' is similarly employed. Suetonius in several places employs *super haec* 'over and above this' for *praeter haec* 'besides this': *super ingenuorum paedagogia* 'over and above the seducing of free-born boys,' *super innumeram turbam* 'over and above the vast crowds.' *adde his* 'add to this,' *accedit his, accedit ad haec, huc accedit* 'there is the added fact,' *huc pertinet* 'connected with this,' *eodem pertinet* 'connected with this same point,' *huic confine est illud* 'related is this,' *his finitimum est* 'very closely associated with these points,' *ad hanc formam pertinet* 'under this same head belongs,' *ad hunc ordinem referendum est* 'we must include in this class,' *huic proximum est* 'the point that follows on from this,' *illud haudquaquam praetereundum silentio* 'we should by no means pass over in silence,' *sed operae pretium est illud audire* 'it is worth while hearing about this.' *iam* 'already, by now' sometimes has this connective function; it is a favourite word of Quintilian's.

When the speech begins to take fire under its own impetus, we find *iam vero* 'now indeed,' *age vero* 'come now,' *quid quod?* 'what of?' and so on:
iam vero quid referam? and now indeed what shall I tell you of?
age vero, ad bellum in Africa gestum veniamus: come now, let us look at the war in Africa.
quid quod suos etiam incessit? what of the fact that he assailed even his own supporters?
quin, quinetiam, insuper 'over and above all that' also belong to this type.

Sometimes the figure known as *occupatio* (anticipation) functions as a connective:
ut ne dicam interim: to say nothing meantime
ut omittam domesticas huius sordes: to pass over the disgusting quality of his private life
nam illud quid attinet commemorare? what is the point of mentioning?
nam haec alias: but this belongs elsewhere.

* * * * *

3 Donatus] Commentary on Terence *Adelphi* 419: *porro autem, at, vero, et huius-modi principia sunt narrationum quibus superiora sequentibus conectuntur*
9 *paedagogia*] Suetonius *Nero* 28

sed illud suo loco dicetur: but I shall discuss that in the appropriate place.

Sometimes the expression of doubt so functions: *eloquar an sileam?*
'shall I speak or keep silent?' *nunc* 'now' has the same effect: *nunc ad id quod*
secundo loco dicturos nos sumus polliciti 'now to the subject which I undertook
to discuss in second place.'

53 / Phrases to operate transitions

Sometimes the connection is made by the figure known as transition, in
which what has just been said and what is going to be said are brought
together in various ways. The two subjects can be treated as on a par: 'all
that was extremely delightful; neither did what followed provide pleasure
in any less degree'; or the second can be given more weight: 'but even if all
that were forgivable, who could endure this?' 'you have heard serious
charges laid against this man, but you will hear yet more serious ones'; the
subjects can be treated as similar: 'all this was devised by treachery, as were
also the deeds he is said to have performed but recently in Rome'; or they
can be contrasted: 'that was his private conduct; now to his public life'; 'so
far we have considered his achievements on the home front; now let us look
at his military career'; 'these were the misdemeanours of a young man; now
you shall hear of the virtues of his later years'; or we can move on to a
different topic: 'there you have his character – it remains for me to speak of
his teaching.'

We can use a kind of *occupatio* or anticipation: 'we shall quickly move
on to our remaining points, but before doing so add this one remark.' Or we
can employ self-reproof: 'but that is more than enough on that subject'; 'but
how far off course have I been driven by the blast of my indignation!' 'but
we must return to the subject'; 'why dwell on this topic?' 'my speech must
move quickly on to that subject which is the nub of this whole case.' Finally
we can proceed to consequential or relative concepts: 'there you have an
account of the benefits I bestowed upon him – now hear what thanks he
returned'; 'we have set forth what he undertook to do – now hear briefly
what he actually performed.'

* * * * *

2 *eloquar an sileam*] Virgil *Aeneid* 3.39
10 transition] See *Ad Herennium* 4.26.35.

LB I 40D

54 / Interchange between 'person' and 'thing'

One general method of variation is the interchange of nouns for persons
and things: you have no need of my advice, you have no need of me as an
adviser; with you as persuader, on your persuasion; with you as prompter,
at your prompting; instigator, instigation; encourager, encouragement;
guiding hand, guidance; leader, leadership; consul, consulship; with you
as my teacher I have made progress, I have progressed under your teaching;
he never stops boasting of his consul-father, ... of his father's consulship;
he exults in his beautiful wife, ... in his wife's beauty; I offer heaven thanks
that you are safe, I thank heaven for your safety; his shameless wife, his
wife's shamelessness, is a torture to him.

55 / Various phrases to express 'customary'

ex more (Suetonius), de more (Virgil), pro more: according to custom
patrio more (with no preposition): by ancestral custom
more hominum facit: he is acting after the manner of men.
non insolens istud facis: what you are doing is nothing unusual for you.
pro vetere consuetudine: in accord with long-standing habit
solens meo more fecero: I shall but do as I always do [i.e., keeping to my
ways, after my fashion].
nihil praeter solitum: nothing out of the ordinary, [i.e., beyond what is
usually done]
hoc apud Scythas solenne est: this is established usage among the Scythians. (Suetonius uses *solenne* in this way.)
mos est, moris est: it is customary.
usu publico receptum est: it is received practice, [i.e., accepted in general
usage].

* * * * *

1 Interchange] In 1512 chaps 54–7 occur at the end of book I (numbered 150–3).
17 Suetonius] For example, *Julius* 80.2
17 Virgil] For example, *Aeneid* 4.57
22 meo more fecero] Plautus *Amphitryo* 198
27 Suetonius] *Augustus* 44.2

LB I 40F

56 / 'Suborning'

subornavit accusatorem: he suborned an accuser.
submisit e consularibus viris qui regio genere ortam peierarent: he put up
men of consular rank to swear falsely that she was born of a royal line.   5
supponi puerum: to have a child substituted
subdere ova in nidum alienum: introduce eggs into another's nest
submissicii, suppositicii, subditicii partus: suppositicious offspring
ne credas a me allegatum hunc senem (Terence): do not think that I have
inveigled this old man (equivalent to *subornatum*)   10
allegarem ad te illos a quibus intelligo me praecipue diligi (Cicero): I would
send as a deputation to you those whom I know to have my interests
especially at heart.
et ad eos allegandum est (Quintilian): representations must be made to
them (i.e., persons must be induced to persuade them).   15
servi allegant precatorem: slaves procure an intercessor.

Thus the noun *allegatio* 'representation' comes to mean *instigation*,
and the verb *allegare* 'to adduce' is used of those who cite the authority of
writers, who are thus *procured* or *deputed* when our own authority is
insufficient.   20

57 / 'Reviving'

vetus Atheniensium exemplum renovemus: let us revive the old example of   25
the Athenians.
pristinum morem revocemus: let us recall the custom of olden times.
gratias egit quod pristinum morem retulisset: he thanked him for restoring
the ancient custom.
redeamus ad intermissa studia: let us return to our interrupted studies.   30
studium intermissum repetamus: let us resume our interrupted pursuits.
bellum redintegrarunt: they started up the war afresh.

* * * * *

4 submisit ... peierarent] Suetonius *Nero* 28
6 supponi puerum] Terence *Eunuchus* prologue 39
9 ne credas a me ... insufficient] The passage to line 20 added in *1534* (LB I 41B–C)
9 Terence] *Andria* 899
11 Cicero] *Ad familares* 15.10.2: *allegarem ... illos a quibus intelligis*
14 Quintilian] Not Quintilian, but Quintus Cicero *Commentariolum petitionis* 5
16 allegant precatorem] See Terence *Heautontimorumenos* 976: *nec precatorem
pararis*

LB I 41B

divum instauramus honores: we celebrate anew the honours of the gods.
templum instar prioris quod conflagrarat excitavit: he raised the temple
again exactly in the form of the earlier one which had burned down.
libertatem amissam restituit: he restored lost liberty.
odium vetus eo dicterio recruduit: this remark caused the old hatred to
break out afresh.
recanduit ira: his anger blazed up again.
refricuit illi veteris iniuriae memoriam: he stirred up the memory of the old
injustice.
cras ingens iterabimus aequor (Horace): Tomorrow a second time we embark / Upon the mighty sea [*iterare*, literally 'do a second time'].
iteranti noxam non est ignoscendum: there should be no forgiveness for
one who commits the same offence twice.

58 / The expression of purpose

tu vigilas uti ditescas, ego laboro quo doctus evadam: you reject sleep in
order to grow rich; I toil so that thereby I may become learned.
obiurgo te quo reddam meliorem: I reprimand you so that thereby I may
make you a better man.
ut melior evadas, ob id obiurgo te: for this cause I reprimand you, that you
may be improved.
in hoc reperta musica, ut animos delectet: for this purpose was music
discovered, that it might beguile the spirit.
ad id adhibendae litterae, ut nos reddant melius moratos: for this cause
should letters be applied, that they may make us better mannered.
cui rei paras opes? for what are you laying up riches?
demulcendis animis excogitatus est usus vini: the use of wine was devised
for the soothing of the spirit.
huc repertae sunt disciplinae: to this end was education discovered.
hunc litteris genui, hunc negotiationi destinavi filium: this son I begat for
learning, this one I intended for business.
quo mihi divitias? to what end wealth?
quorsum opus est nummis? to what purpose need we money?

* * * * *

7 recanduit ira] Ovid *Metamorphoses* 3.707
10 Horace] *Odes* 1.7.32
34 divitias] Cf Horace *Epistles* 1.5.12: *quo mihi fortunam*? The idiom is also much
employed by Seneca.
35 nummis] Cf Horace *Satires* 2.7.116: *quorsum est opus*?

quo spectas? quo tendis? quem scopum tibi proponis?: what end have you
in view? whither are your footsteps pressing? what goal have you set before
you?

Under this head belong all those expressions which I listed in connection with the first supine: *spectatum veniunt*, etc. 'they come to look.'

59 / The expression of reason or cause

non dico quo quemquam habeam cariorem: I do not say this in that I hold
anyone more dear.

non dico quod parum tua mihi placeant: I do not say this because your
proposals are not sufficiently attractive.

ob id te saepius reprehendo quod impensius amo: I often find fault with
you for the very reason that I am extremely fond of you.

quoniam impensius te diligo, ob id te saepius admoneo: because I am
extremely fond of you, that is why I so often take you to task.

ideo nulli places, quia tibi nimium places: the reason why you please no
one is that you are too pleased with yourself.

quando tu me neglegis, tui quoque curam abiciam: since you neglect me, I
too shall abandon my care for you.

age, revocentur copiae, quandoquidem ita tibi videtur: very well, let the
forces be recalled, since that seems the best course to you.

iubeas miserum esse libenter, quatenus id facit (Horace): Tell him to be
miserable, seeing / That he wants to be just that. (Pliny uses *quatenus* in the
same way in his letters.)

maneat puella, postea quam sponso iucunda est: let the girl remain, now
that she pleases her betrothed.

postea quam mihi non credis, alios in consilium adhibe: now that you do
not believe me, bring others into your counsel.

quando haec te cura remordet (Virgil): since this care eats deep into thy
heart

neminem ex animo amat, in causa est pecuniae studium: he loves no one
from the heart; the reason is his passion for money.

* * * * *

4 listed] At 322:32ff; see also 426:6ff.
5 *spectatum veniunt*] Ovid *Ars amatoria* 1.99
10 cariorem] Cf Terence *Eunuchus* 96: *non pol quo quemquam plus amem … eo feci.*
24 Horace] *Satires* 1.1.64
25 Pliny] For example, *Epistles* 3.7.14
31 Virgil] *Aeneid* 1.261

The following are also *causal* phrases, for which the Greek word is
αἰτιολογικὴ.
amo Socratem utpote virum integerrimum: I love Socrates as a man of the
highest integrity.
odi Dionysium, quippe tyrannum: I hate Dionysius inasmuch as he is a
tyrant.
amplector Petrum, ut optime de me meritum: I have the warmest regard for
Peter, as one who has done me great service.
demiror te qui fidem habeas Afro: I am surprised at you for trusting an
African.
erras qui credas alios tua diligentius curaturos quam teipsum: you are
wrong to imagine that others will guard your interests better than you
yourself.
stultus es qui id speres, impudens qui id postules: you are a fool to hope
that, impudent to demand it.
delector Augustino, viro nimirum festivissimo: I am delighted with Augustine, really a most agreeable person.
delector Augustino, ut qui vir sit moribus festivissimis: I am delighted with
Augustine inasmuch as he is a man of the most agreeable nature.
amo Nicolaum tanquam hominem mei amantissimum: I am very fond of
Nicholas, as one who is most attached to me.
contemne pecuniam, quid enim ad bonam mentem confert? despise
money, for what does it contribute to the good of the mind?
amandus est tibi Cicero, siquidem te diligit effusissime: you ought to like
Cicero, inasmuch as he is extremely partial to you.
semper in manibus habendus Tullius, nam hoc uno auctore Latine disces:
your Cicero should be always in your hands, for from this writer alone will
you learn Latin.
unus Cicero vere Latinum potest reddere, proinde pueris hic semper in
sinu gestandus: only Cicero can truly make a Latinist; accordingly schoolboys should always carry him in their breast-pockets.

* * * * *

5 Dionysius] Probably a reference to Dionysius I of Syracuse, a notorious tyrant;
Erasmus often attacks and satirizes tyranny.
8 Peter] Erasmus had several friends called Peter; Pieter Meghen and Pieter
Gillis belong to the years before the first publication of *De copia*. See Bierlaire.
9 trusting an African] In 1512 'trusting a Norman'
16 Augustine] Possibly a reference to Augustin Vincent (Caminade), a literary
acquaintance of Erasmus' who helped him on several occasions, but a person
he never really liked. See Ep 131 introduction.
29 in sinu gestandus] This also denotes affection; Terence *Adelphi* 709: *hicine non
gestandus in sinust?*

optimus dicendi magister Terentius, quare semper est evolvendus: Terence
is the best model of diction; consequently you should be always turning his
pages.

quo mihi rectius esse videtur, eo magis, hoc lubentius, id negotii sus-
cepimus: for the reason that I consider it more correct, for that reason the
more, for that reason the more gladly, have we undertaken this business.

non habes quam ob rem mihi succenseas: you have nothing to justify your
anger against me.

non est cur mihi succenseas: you have no reason to be angry with me.

non est quod multa loquamur (Horace): there is no reason to say very much.

in viam quod te des hoc tempore nihil est (Cicero): there is no reason why
you should travel at the moment.

succenset, eaque gratia nos non visit: he is rather annoyed, and on that
account does not visit us.

luget atque ob id vocatus ad cenam excusavit: he is in mourning, and for
that reason refused an invitation to dinner.

On occasion one can leave out the word meaning 'because': *parentem
amo, parricidam non amo* 'I love a father, a parricide I love not' (i.e., because
he is my father, on this count I love him; because he is a parricide, for this
cause I do not); *pontifici debeo honorem, Alexandro non debeo* 'to a pontiff I
owe respect, to Alexander I owe none.'

60 / *Quod εἰδικῶς* [specifying *quod*]

quod 'that, the fact that, as for the fact that' is taken εἰδικῶς [in a specifying
manner] when it subjoins a species to a genus: *gaudeo* 'I rejoice' is a wide
concept (a genus or class); *quod me amas* 'that you love me' narrows it down
and indicates a species of joy – a person can rejoice, hope, grieve, for many
different reasons. (Incidentally I use the terms genus and species here as a
grammarian, not a logician.)

quod meae nugae non omnino displicent doctis, gaudeo: the fact that my

* * * * *

1 evolvendus] See Quintilian 12.2.8: *evolvendi penitus auctores.*
10 Horace] *Epistles* 2.1.30
11 Cicero] *Ad familiares* 14.12
21 Alexander] Presumably Alexander VI, pope 1492–1503
26 *quod* 'that ... logician] Added in 1534 (LB I 42B)

scribblings do not altogether displease the learned world gives me satisfaction.

[The accusative with infinitive construction can also be used here:] gaudeo meas nugas non omnino displicere doctis: I am glad my scribblings do not altogether displease the learned world.

quod res tibi feliciter evenerit, laetor: as for things turning out well for you, I am pleased about that; laetor rem feliciter evenisse: I am pleased things have turned out well for you.

quod uxorem duxeras nondum audieram; uxorem duxisse te nondum audieram: as for your taking a wife, I had not yet heard of it; I had not yet heard that you had taken a wife.

quod puellam repudiaris, demiror; demiror te repudiasse puellam: I am very surprised at your jilting the girl.

quod litteras reliqueris, doleo; doleo te reliquisse litteras: it grieves me that you have abandoned literature.

quod εἰδικῶς is here functioning like ὅτι [that] in Greek, though the ὅτι construction in Greek is commoner; Latin prefers the accusative with infinitive construction, unless the more specific idea is put first: quod pater revaluit gaudeo: the fact that your father is in good health again gives me great happiness.

61 / *Ut* used εἰδικῶς [in specification]

ut 'that, so that' frequently has the same specifying force: spero fore ut facto gaudeas: I trust that the situation will be that you approve what has been done.

confido futurum ut te minime facti paeniteat: I am confident that you will find that you feel not the slightest regret for this.

non committam ut usquam videar officio meo defuisse: I will not act so that I appear to have failed my duty in any respect.

efficiam ut intelligas mihi quidvis potius quam fidem defuisse: I will see that you realize that I was lacking in anything rather than good faith.

da operam ut revalescas: take care that you get strong again.

cura ut valeas: mind you keep well.

fac uti nos ames: continue your affection for me.

fac uti sciam: see that I am informed.

* * * * *

35 cura ut valeas ... fac uti nos ames] Formulae for ending a letter

WORTHY AND UNWORTHY

dignus 'worthy' [can be followed by a consecutive clause introduced by *qui*:] *dignus qui quam diutissime vivat*, [or by *ut*:] *dignus ut quam diutissime vivat*, [or can be combined with an ablative:] *longissima vita dignus*, all of which mean 'worthy of a very long life.' [It can also be followed by an infinitive:] *dignus quam diutissime vivere* 'worthy to live for many years,' but this construction is poetic: *dispeream si tu Pyladi praestare matellam / dignus es* (Martial) 'I'll be damned if you are fit / A chamber pot to hold for Pylades'; *digna sequi potius quam tortum ducere funem* (Horace) 'Fit to follow the rope, not pull it.' [Similarly *mereri* 'to deserve' can be followed by a *qui* clause:] *meritus est cui laurea imponatur* 'he deserves to be crowned with laurel,' [or by *ut*:] *promeritus es ut tibi decernatur triumphus* 'you have thoroughly deserved to have a triumph decreed you.'

indignus 'unworthy' [can be followed by an ablative]: *indignus tuo amore* 'unworthy of your love,' [or by a *qui* clause:] *indignus quem ames*, [or by an *ut* clause:] *indignus ut abs te diligatur* 'not fit that you should love him.' Again, in poetry [it can be followed by an infinitive:] *indigni fraternum rumpere foedus* (Horace) 'not fit to sever the bond of brotherly love.'

idoneus 'fit': *idoneus est qui bellum gerat* [*qui* clause], *idoneus ut bellum gerat* [*ut* clause] 'fit to conduct the war'; *idoneus bello gerendo* [dative of the gerundive] 'fit for waging war.' [Again the infinitive is poetic:] *idoneus bello gerere; fons etiam rivo dare nomen idoneus* (Horace) 'a fountain fit to lend its name / To a mighty stream.' *idoneus ad gerundum bellum* [*ad* with accusative of the gerundive] 'fit for waging war.'

dignari 'deign, consider worthy': *non me dignatur alloquio* [ablative] 'he does not consider me worthy of address'; *non me dignatur alloqui* [infinitive] 'he does not deign to address me.'

dignus 'worthy': *dignum patella operculum* [ablative of noun] 'cover worthy of the dish'; *res digna cognitu* [ablative of supine] 'thing worth the knowing'; *res digna quae cognoscatur* [*qui* clause] 'thing worthy of being known.'

indignus 'unworthy': *res indigna tua cura* [ablative] 'thing unworthy of

* * * * *

1 WORTHY AND UNWORTHY] Material from this point to the end of chap 63 was transferred from the end of chap 40 in *1514*.

7 Martial] 10.11.3

9 Horace] *Epistles* 1.10.48

18 Horace] *Epistles* 1.3.35

22 Horace] *Epistles* 1.16.12

28 *dignum patella operculum*] *Adagia* I x 72

your attention'; *indigna quam tu cures* [*qui* clause] 'thing not worthy that you should trouble about it.'

Finally, *res est infra tuam dignitatem* 'the matter is beneath your dignity.'

APPROPRIATENESS
haud decet simiam purpura, dedecet simiam purpura: royal robes do not become an ape.

indecora est simiae purpura: royal robes are unseemly on an ape.

parum decorum est loquacem esse virginem: it is hardly befitting for a young girl to be always chattering.

ornat mulierem silentium, dedecorat garrulitas: silence adorneth a woman, but chatter bringeth her shame.

haudquaquam decora est simiae purpura: purple is by no means seemly for an ape.

haud decet imperatorem una cum amica ire in via: it is not right for a commander-in-chief to walk down the road with his mistress.

haud decet ut te loquente ego sileam: it is not right that you should speak and I keep silence.

quod solus ambulas id parum te decet: your walking alone is not very proper.

demitte pallium, nam sic indecore sedes: pull your cloak down, you are not sitting decently like that.

hic gestus virgini indecorus est: this gesture is unseemly for a girl.

ista petulantia iuveni dedecorosa est: that impudence does no credit to a young man.

quod huic pulchrum est, tibi est inhonestum: it may be fine for him, for you it is infamous.

quod huic pulchrum est, tibi foedum est: what is all right for him is shameful for you.

non congruit, non convenit, non quadrat: it does not agree, it does not fit, it does not square.

* * * * *

8 ape] *Adagia* I vii 10
10 parum decorum ... shame] Added in *1526* (LB I 42E)
12 ornat mulierem silentium] *Adagia* IV i 97
16 ire in via] Cf Terence *Eunuchus* 494–5
22 demitte ... shameful for you] Added in *1534* (LB I 42F)
31 non congruit ... square] Added in *1526* (LB I 42F)

NECESSITY

exorandus est pater: you must prevail on your father [literally, your father is
to be entreated].

vigilandum ei qui velit ditescere: he who wishes to grow rich must keep his
wits about him.

vigilet oportet qui cupit ditescere: he who desires to grow rich must needs
exercise vigilance.

vigilare necessum est eum, qui rem cupit facere: it is essential for the man
who wants to make money to keep on the alert.

vigilet necesse est, necessum est, qui velit dives evadere: of necessity the
man who desires to finish up rich must keep his eyes open.

qui litteras assequi cupiat, uti sudet necessitas est: it is essential for the man
who desires to achieve learning to put his back into the task. (*necessitas* is a
favourite word of Quintilian's).

non potest non dolere qui laesus est: one who is injured cannot help feeling
indignation.

fieri non potest quin doleat is cui fit iniuria: it is impossible for one who
suffers an injury not to feel indignation.

abibis volens nolens, velis nolis hinc abibis: you shall go away, willy-nilly.

non mihi possum temperare quin lachrimem: I cannot keep myself from
weeping.

non me contineo quin clamem: I cannot refrain from crying out loud.

cogor, compellor: I am forced, compelled.

huc me adegit inopia: poverty has driven me to this.

huc redegit fortuna: fortune has reduced me to this.

ad haec traxit necessitas: necessity has drawn me to this course.

huc fatis pertrahor: it is fate that brings me to this pass.

huc obtorto collo trahor: I am dragged here by the scruff of the neck.

invitus dicam, coactus dicam: I shall speak against my will, under compulsion.

FREEDOM

utcumque voles facito: do just as you wish.

ut lubet rideto: laugh how you like.

quidlibet et dicas et facias licebit: you will be free to say and do whatever
you choose.

tuo arbitratu facito: act as you please.

* * * * *

2 exorandus est pater] See Terence *Andria* 167: *restat Chremes / qui mi exorandus
est.*

28 obtorto collo] See *Adagia* II i 19; Plautus *Poenulus* 790.

tuo arbitrio rem gere: deal with it the way you want.

utcumque visum erit agito: act as seems best to you.

animo tuo gerito morem: you should please yourself.

obsequere animo tuo: follow your fancy.

ex animi tui libidine facito: act according to your own inclinations.

pro animi tui sententia rem tractabis: you will treat this matter as you see fit.

ut animo lubitum erit tuo, ita facies: you shall do whatever you feel inclined to do.

utcumque feret animus, ita facito: act according as your inclination leads you.

liberum est seu velis a pacto discedere, seu manere conventis: it is up to you whether you choose to withdraw from the agreement or abide by what was decided.

nunc integrum non est tibi hac de re quod velis statuere: you no longer have carte blanche to come to whatever decision you choose.

mihi ius est creditum abs te reposcere: I have been given authority to require you to repay the loan.

ius tibi facio pro tuo arbitrio transigendi negotium: I grant you authority to conduct this negotiation in accordance with your own judgment.

tibi permitto quomodocumque velis vivere: I permit you to live your life in any way you wish.

age tuo more: act in your own way.

sine me nunc meo more vivere: allow me now to live in my own fashion.

tibi in manu est utrum malis efficere: which course of action you prefer lies in your own hands.

penes illum est ius vitae ac mortis: he holds the power of life and death.

summa rerum penes te est: you have supreme power.

ut ad te familiariter et quasi pro meo iure scriberem (Cicero): to write to you as a friend, and exercise my rights so to speak.

quem iure suo adire aut appellare posset (Cicero, in one of his speeches *In Verrem*): whom he could approach or appeal to as of right.

DECIDING

decretum est: it was decreed.

deliberatum est: it was resolved after deliberation.

certum est: it has been decided.

* * * * *

23 sine me nunc] Terence *Andria* 153: *meo … modo*
28 Cicero] *Ad familiares* 13.50.1
30 Cicero] 2.36

stat sententia: the view is

visum erat: it seemed best.

in animo habebam: I had in mind.

erat in animo: it was in my mind.

non est animus: I do not have the inclination.   5

non est sententiae, non est sententia: it is not within my view, ... not my
view.

non est consilium, consilii: it is not our purpose, ... not within our purpose.

non erat ratio (in Cicero): it did not seem reasonable.

placebat: it was found acceptable.   10

placitum est senatui: the senate was agreed.

decrevit senatus: the senate decreed.

in eam senteniam pedibus ibant omnes: everyone began to vote in support
of this motion.

statueram in animo: I had decided in my own mind.   15

mecum statueram: I had inwardly decided.

utrum utro melius nondum statui: I have not yet made up my mind which
of the two courses is better.

constitui hoc anno navigare: I have decided to make the voyage this year.

est mihi in animo hoc vere navigare: I have in mind to sail this spring.   20

si mihi non animo fixum immotumque sederet (Virgil): Did not the fixed
resolve abide / Within my heart immutable.

mihi nihil aeque propositum in vita, quam tibi per omnia gratificari: my
greatest aim in life is to please you in everything.

si ita animum induxisti tuum: if you have so set your thoughts   25

destinaram in animo: I had designed in my heart

hic murus aeneus esto: This shall be your wall of brass.

AGREEING

assentior tibi: I agree in opinion with you.   30

tecum sentio: I think with you.

consentiebant universi: everyone was in accord.

in tuam sententiam pedibus eo: I vote for your proposal.

in eam sententiam reliqui omnes discedebant: everyone else began to move
out in support of that motion.   35

* * * * *

9 Cicero] *Verrines* 1.24

21 Virgil] *Aeneid* 4.15

25 animum induxisti tuum] Terence *Andria* 883

27 aeneus esto] Horace *Epistles* 1.1.59, that is, an unshakable decision

frequentes ierunt in alia omnia (Cicero): large numbers voted for the counter-proposals.

accedo tuae sententiae: I accede to your view.

non his accedo qui Pythagorae sequuntur opinionem: I do not accede to those who follow the opinion of Pythagoras.

tuo iudicio subscribo: I subscribe to your judgment.

sententiae tuae meum addo calculum: I add my vote to your expressed opinion.

ea sententia plerisque probatur: this proposal finds favour with the majority.

idem sentio quod tu: I think the same as you.

sententiae tuae nemo non suffragabitur: there is no one who will not vote in support of your proposal.

haec mihi tecum conveniunt: this is common ground between us.

hactenus omnia mihi tecum constant: so far my views and yours coincide completely.

hac de re summus est inter philosophos consensus: on this point there is complete agreement among philosophers.

huic sententiae frequenter acclamatum est: this proposal met with loud acclaim (ὁμόψηφοι is the word the Greeks use for those sharing the same opinion and voting the same way, ὁμόδοξοι for those of the same beliefs and of the same group).

idem uno omnes ore confirmabant: all confirmed this with one voice.

omnibus eruditorum calculis sive punctis, eloquentiae princeps M. Tullius: Cicero voted the prince of eloquence by the whole learned world

DISAGREEING

longe lateque abest: it differs in length and breadth.

dissentio: I disagree.

ego longe diversa sentio: my view is quite opposed.

multo aliter atque tu sentio: my view is very different from yours.

ei sententiae refragabuntur omnes: everyone will contest this view.

isti sententiae nemo non reclamabit: there is no one who will not cry out against this view of yours.

mihi tua sententia neutiquam probatur: I cannot possibly approve your sentiments.

* * * * *

1 Cicero] *Ad familiares* 1.2.1

7 calculum] See next n.

24 calculis, punctis] Refers to the ancient custom of recording votes by means of pebbles or marks made on a wax tablet; *Adagia* i v 60; cf 501:24.

LB I 43D

magnopere nostra cum tua pugnat opinio: my opinion is totally at variance
with yours.
variatum est sententiis: various opinions were expressed.
id unum nobis est controversum: this was the one point of disagreement
among us.
id solum est in controversia, in controverso: this is the one point in dispute.
equidem ab opinione tua minimum absum: I at any rate stand only a slight
distance away from your position.
multum a tua mea discrepat sententia: my view is very discrepant.
longe secus atque tu sentio: I think quite differently from you on this.
haud mediocriter a tua mea dissidet opinio: there is no slight quarrel
between your view and mine.
nimium inter tuam atque meam interest opinionem: there is an excessive
difference between your view and mine.
plurimum a tua mea distat opinio: my view is poles apart from yours.
mihi secus videtur: I think otherwise.
diis aliter visum est: heaven willed otherwise.
huic sententiae milites adversabantur: the soldiers offered resistance to this
suggestion.

WISHES AND PRAYERS
quod agis bene fortunent superi: may the gods above prosper your activities.
quod agis bene vertat: may what you are doing turn out well.
feliciter cadat quod instituisti: may there be a successful conclusion to what
you have instituted.
dii coepta secundent: may heaven favour our undertaking.
optime cecidit: things turned out excellently.
bene vertat rei publicae: may the outcome be beneficial to the country.
sit felix faustum bonumque rei publicae: may it bring good fortune, felicity,
and well-being to our nation.
feliciter cedat nobis omnibus: may the result be happy for us all.
hanc affinitatem precor ut Deus nobis omnibus laetam esse velit: I pray God
to grant that this alliance bring joy to us all.
feliciter exeat quod coepisti: may what you have begun see a happy end.
prospere succedat quod agis: may your activities see prosperity and success.

      * * * * *

17 diis aliter visum est] Seneca *Epistles* 98.4
27 dii coepta secundent] Virgil *Aeneid* 7.259: *incepta*

ex animi sententia procedat quod aggressus es: may what you have embarked upon go according to plan.

Deum optimum maximumque precor ut istud consilium quam est honestum tam sit etiam auspicatum: I pray almighty God that your honourable course of action be attended by the success it deserves.

precor ut bonis avibus Italiam adeas, melioribus redeas: I pray that you may go to Italy with good omens and return with better ones.

precor ut hic annus tibi laetis auspiciis ineat, laetioribus procedat, laetissimis exeat ac saepius recurrat semper auspicatior feliciorque: I pray that this year may commence with happy auspices for you, proceed with happier ones, conclude with the happiest, and ever return more prosperous and more fortunate.

precor ut hic dies tibi candidus illuxerit: I pray that this day has dawned serene and bright for you.

incolumem reditum opto liberis tuis: I hope your children return safely.

precor ut apud tuos omnia laeta reversus offendas: I hope you find all well when you return home.

utinam prospere naviges similique successu renaviges: may you sail out with prosperity and no less prosperously return to port.

bonis auspiciis ancoram solvas: may you weigh anchor with happy auspices.

precor ut tuis optatis omnia respondeant: I pray that everything may correspond to your desires.

faxint superi ut alba tibi contingant omnia: may heaven grant all things bright to you.

velim ut ex voto res omnis succedat: I would like everything to go according to your prayers.

o si res ita ut volumus nobis eveniat: if only things turn out as we wish.

precor ut tibi secunda occurrant omnia: I pray that you meet with nothing but success.

precor ut diis secundis faventibusque negotium hoc conficias: I pray that you conclude this business with the favour and blessing of heaven.

quaeso ut hanc rem stultissime coeptam superi nobis bene vertant: I only hope that heaven turns to our good this business we have commenced so foolishly.

nihil malim quam ut his pulcherrimis coeptis dextra aspirent numina: above all else I hope that the powers above look favourably upon this splendid undertaking.

quaeso ut quod instituisti superis bene fortunantibus absolvas: it is my wish that what you have begun you may with the aid of heaven complete.

precor ut hic contractus commodo sit utrisque: I trust that this contract may
be beneficial to both parties.
precor ut hoc matrimonium voluptati sit omnibus nobis: I pray that this
marriage may bring pleasure to us all.

VARIATIONS ON THE FIRST SUPINE
[The supine is used to express purpose:] *venit repetitum depositum* 'he has
come to ask back his deposit.' [The following sentences with the same
meaning illustrate alternative constructions:] *venit ad repetendum depositum, venit ad repetendam pecuniam* [*ad* governing a noun in the accusative case with the gerundive in agreement]; *venit repetendi depositi causa*
[*causa* 'for the sake' governing a noun in the genitive case with the gerundive in agreement]; *venit ut depositum repetat* [final clause introduced by *ut*];
venit repetiturus depositum [future participle]; *venit repetere depositum*
[infinitive]. This last is more of a Greek usage than a Latin one, but the Latin
poets are quite ready to employ it, especially Horace.

62 / Subdividing

omnis eloquentia rebus constat et verbis: the whole of eloquence consists in
subject-matter and expression.
rerum universitas decem generibus continetur: everything there is falls
under one of ten genera.
officium oratoris in quinque partes distribuitur: the function of the orator
can be distributed over five areas.
oratio sex partes complectitur: the speech comprises six sections.
oratio sex partibus absolvitur: the speech is made up of six sections.
primum genus sex continet species, quidam in septem species secant: the
first genus contains six species, though some divide into seven.
reipublicae tres sunt formae: there are three forms of constitution.
respublica in tres dividitur formas: government can be divided into three
forms.
enthymema non simpliciter accipitur: enthymeme is not to be understood
in one way only.

* * * * *

21 rebus constat et verbis] See Cicero *De optimo genere* 4: *eloquentia constat ex
    verbis et ex sententiis.*
31 three forms] See Cicero *De republica* 1.26.
34 enthymema] See Quintilian 5.10.1

syllogismus trifariam dividitur: every syllogism requires three components.

omnis argumentatio in formas octo diducitur: all processes of argument can be separated into eight forms.

id genus in partes septem derivatur: this type is channelled off into seven subsections.

huic generi species subiectae sunt decem: there are ten species subordinate to this genus.

summa divisione in duo genera digeritur, quorum utrumque in species complures distrahitur: at the first subdivision it is distributed among two genera, and each of these is in turn divided up into a considerable number of species.

praeiudiciorum vis omnis tribus in generibus versatur: all previous decisions come within three types.

63 / Distributing

bis me tuae delectarunt litterae, partim quod essent mirum in modum elegantes, partim quod eximiam quandam in me benevolentiam prae se ferrent: your letter pleased me doubly, partly because of its marvellous elegance, partly because it expressed such remarkable good will towards me.

pars ingenium alii corpus exercebant: a section trained their minds, others their bodies. (In alternating *pars* and *alii* in this way Sallust employed a somewhat strained but nevertheless stylish expression.)

utrumque fratrem alienavit a sese, unum morum asperitate, alterum sordibus: he alienated both brothers, one by his uncouth behaviour, the other by his meanness.

corpore atque animo constat homo, alterum cum pecudibus habet commune, alterum cum diis: man consists of body and intelligence; the one he shares with the beasts, the other with the gods.

neminem non lacessit, hunc scriptis, illum conviciis, alium minis: not one does he fail to provoke – this person by writings, that one by insults, another by threats.

hunc neglegit, hunc odit: this one he neglects, this one he hates (though the repetition of *hic* like this fits poetry better).

* * * * *

13 tribus in generibus versatur] Quintilian 5.2.1
25 Sallust] *Catilina* 2.1
30 corpore atque animo] See Sallust *Catilina* 1.2

geminatio verborum interdum habet vim, leporem alias (Cicero): the repetition of words provides force on occasion, in other contexts charm.

alios assentatione delinit, alios muneribus corrumpit, alios promissis illectat: some he butters with flattery, others he bribes with presents, yet others he inveigles with promises.

modo ait, modo negat: sometimes he says yes, sometimes no.

interim obiurgat, interim inepte blanditur: at times he is vituperative, at others absurdly toadying. (The repetition of *interim* is a mannerism of Quintilian's.)

nunc neminem admittit, nunc omnibus occurrit: now he will admit no one, now he greets all with open arms.

64 / Words for hindering and preventing

nemo prohibet ire quemquam publica via: no one prevents anyone from walking on the public highway.

tu me prohibes ne publica ingrediar via: you are preventing me from going on the public road.

quo minus assecutus sis, fortuna in culpa fuit, non ego: fortune was to blame, not I, that you failed to achieve it.

impedimento fuit quo setius lex ferretur: he acted so as to block the passage of the law.

hactenus rescribere non licuit per valetudinem, etiamsi per occupationes licuisset: until now my health has kept me from replying to your letter, even if my affairs had allowed me to do so.

ego id agam qui ne detur (Terence): I'll so behave as to make sure she's not given to me.

metuo ut ferre possis: I am fearful as to your ability to bear it, i.e., *ne non possis*: I am afraid lest you may not be able (though *ut* here might be taken as equivalent to *quomodo* 'how').

id utile, ut ne quid nimis: a useful precept is 'nothing in excess' (an example showing how *ut ne*, like *uti ne*, 'with the intention that not' can be used instead of *ne* 'lest' by itself, just as ἵνα μή [to the end that not] is used in Greek).

* * * * *

1 Cicero] *De oratore* 3.206
6 modo ait, modo negat] Terence *Eunuchus* 714
16 nemo prohibet ire quemquam publica via] Plautus *Curculio* 35; *Adagia* III v 27
22 lex ferretur] Cf *Ad Herennium* 1.12.21: *impedimento est quo setius feratur.*
27 Terence] *Andria* 335
32 ut ne quid nimis] Terence *Andria* 61: *in vita esse utile ut ne quid nimis*

non veto quin quae velis facias: I raise no objection to your doing what you want.

intercessit quo minus in acta sua iuraretur (Suetonius in his *Life of Tiberius*): he interposed his veto so that people should not swear to observe his legislation (i.e., *obstitit, inhibuit, impedimento fuit*: he set himself against, he restrained, he blocked).

per me non stetit quo minus viceris: it was not through me that you failed to win.

exclusus tempore non venit: excluded by time he did not come (i.e., the shortage of time hindered him from coming).

DOUBT

non dubito quin cupias redire: I have no doubt but that you desire to return.

non dubito te cupere reditum: I have no doubt that you long for your return.

res in ambiguo est: the matter is undecided.

nondum satis constitui: I have not yet sufficiently made up my mind.

adhuc anceps animi sum: I am still divided in my own mind.

adhuc haereo: I am still at a loss.

etiam dum ἐπέχω: I am as yet suspending judgment. (ἐπέχω is a term used by the Academic philosophers.)

nondum huc aut illuc inclinat sententia: my view does not as yet incline one way or the other.

adhuc in aequilibrio vacillat animus, utroque nutans: so far my mind balances in equilibrium, dipping in both directions.

hactenus suspendo decretum animi: thus far I refrain from a decision.

nondum liquet: more evidence is required [literally, it is not yet clear].

ampliatum est iudicium: the case is deferred.

WITHOUT

citra praeceptoris operam doctus evasit, sine praeceptore doctus evasit, nullo praeceptore doctus evasit: without help of a teacher, without a teacher, with no one to teach him, he acquired an education.

* * * * *

3 Suetonius] *Tiberius* 26

9 exclusus tempore non venit] Caesar *Bellum Gallicum* 6.31.1

21 Academic philosophers] Adherents of the later Academic school held that absolute knowledge was not within man's reach, and that he should therefore refrain from committing himself to dogmatic assertion while continuing to act on a basis of reasonable probability. The Academics adopted part of this teaching from Pyrrho, the founder of Scepticism (see 438:21).

LB I 44F

absque pecuniis nihil efficias: you can achieve nothing apart from money.
extra iocum (Cicero): joking apart (equivalent to *sine ioco*)

VAUNTING
ostentat ingenium: he flaunts his abilities.
iactitat natales suos: he is always boasting about his aristocratic connections.
iactat se de natalium splendore: he puts on airs over his aristocratic lineage.
vendicat sibi eloquentiam: he claims eloquence for his own.
mire sibi placet de specie corporis: he is remarkably satisfied with his own appearance.
ubique maiorum imagines depraedicat: everywhere he brags of his distinguished forbears.
sunt qui se vulgo sanctimoniae specie venditant: there are some people who seek to ingratiate themselves with the crowd by a show of sanctity.
ipse sui praeco est: he sells his own wares.
ipse sui ipsius tibicen est: he blows his own trumpet.
ipse suarum virtutum apud omnes canit encomium: he sings his own praises everywhere he goes.
mirum quam ipse sibi pulcher est: it is marvellous how handsome he is in his own eyes.
de maiorum nobilitate gloriatur: he vaunts his aristocratic ancestors.
plurimum sibi tribuit: he has the highest opinion of himself.
suis ipsius suffragiis tantum non deus est: on his own vote he is all·but God.
sibi Suffenus est: he thinks he is the world's greatest poet.
de generis nobilitate dictu mirum quas tollat cristas, quae erigat cornua: on the subject of his family's nobility it is marvellous to tell how he ruffles his crest and rears his horns.

REMEDYING AND HEALING
huic incommodo paulo mederi possis: you can deal with this inconvenience at little cost.
huic malo illud erit remedio: that will remedy this ill.
quod iactu cecidit, arte corrigas: you must by skill amend the way the dice did fall.
mendum litura tollitur: an error is removed by erasure.

* * * * *

2 Cicero] *Ad familiares* 7.16.2
10 mire sibi placet ... his horns] The passage to line 28 added in 1534 (LB I 45B)
25 sibi Suffenus est] See Catullus 22 for Suffenus' efforts at poetry.
34 dice did fall] Cf Terence *Adelphi* 740: *illud quod cecidit forte, id arte ut corrigas.*

animi morbos sanat philosophia: philosophy heals the diseases of the mind.

corporis vitia ingenii dotibus pensantur: faults of the body are compensated by the rich endowment of the intellect.

febre levatus est: he was relieved of the fever.

malis omnibus mors semel liberat: death delivers from evils once for all.

oculorum vitia ruta emendat: rue improves defects in the eye.

orationis vitia grammatica castigat: grammar corrects defects of speech.

philosophia morbos animi pellit medicaturque: philosophy heals and drives out the sicknesses of the mind.

dentium cruciatum vinum lenit: wine soothes a toothache.

uteri tormina levat malva: mallow relieves cramps in the womb.

capitis dolores mitigat somnus, sedat tormina, fugat pruritum, sopit dolorem, levat dolorem: sleep reduces a headache, eases colic, sends away an itch, lulls pain, relieves pain.

stomachum labascentem fulcit vinum vetus: old wine firms a fluid stomach.

stomacho conducit pervigilium: staying awake aids the digestion.

uxoris vitium aut mutandum est, aut ferendum: a wife's faults must be either altered or endured.

morbis omnibus arte succurritur, soli senectuti subveniri non potest: skill brings succour for all diseases; only for old age is there no remedy available.

adversus podagram efficax est apium: parsley is effective against gout.

contra carcinomata valet mel: honey is efficacious in the treatment of carcinomata.

obstitit ebrietati cicuta: hemlock is a preventative against drunkenness.

adversus alvi tormina remedio est crepitus: breaking wind is a help for griping pains in the bowels.

WHEEDLING, URGING

dic age: come, tell.

dic sodes: tell me if you will.

dic obsecro: tell me, I beg you.

dic quaeso te: pray tell me.

dic amabo: tell me, please. (*amabo* is often used by Cicero.)

blanditur: wheedles; assentatur: flatters; palpatur (Horace): strokes.

* * * * *

19 altered or endured] See Aulus Gellius 1.17, quoting Varro.
35 (*amabo* ... they flatter] The passage to 432:8 added in *1534* (LB I 45D)
36 Horace] *Satires* 2.1.20

palpum obtrudere (Plautus): cajole [literally, hold out the hand to]
demulcere caput: pat on the head
ad gratiam loqui: curry favour
dare auribus: speak to the ear of, for example (Trebonius writing to Cicero),
noli putare, mi Cicero, me hoc auribus tuis dare: do not think, my dear 5
Cicero, that I speak this merely to your ears.
auribus Vari serviunt (Caesar): they serve the ears of Varus (i.e., they
flatter).
fac virum te praebeas: see that you show yourself a man.
quid habes quod ad haec respondeas? what have you to say in reply? 10
cedo: come now, out with it.
agedum: come then.
eia age: well then, up and on with it.
vide sis: see to it, if you please.
quin uno tu verbo rem expedis? why not say one word and settle the affair? 15

FOR YOUR SAKE
nolim id esse verum vel tua causa: I would not like that to be true, even for
your sake.
tibi metuo: I fear for you. 20
mihi gaudeo: for my own part, I am quite delighted.
omnium nomine doleo: I grieve on everyone's account.
nam ego eo nomine sum Dyrrachii hoc tempore, ut quam celerrime quid
agas audiam (Cicero): I am at Dyrrachium at this moment on that very
account, that is to hear what you are up to as early as possible. 25
eone nomine imperator unice / fuisti in ultima occidentis insula? (Catullus): was it on that account that you went, / a general of incomparable
abilities, / to the furthest island of the west?
tua gratia munus hoc suscepi: I have undertaken this task for your sake.
vicem tuam doleo: I grieve on your account. 30
commoda illi respectu mei: be obliging to him out of regard for me. (Quinti-

* * * * *

1 Plautus] *Pseudolus* 945
2 demulcere caput] Terence *Heautontimorumenos* 762; *Adagia* III i 37
4 to Cicero] *Ad familiares* 12.16.1
7 Caesar] *Bellum civile* 2.27
21 mihi gaudeo] A rather unusual expression used by Cicero in *Ad familiares*
6.15, a letter famous as one possibly written by Cicero to congratulate one of
the conspirators for his part in Caesar's murder
24 Cicero] *Ad familiares* 14.3.4: *quid agatur audiam*
26 Catullus] 29.11–12
31 Quintilian] For example, 12.9.11: *respectu communium officiorum*

lian employs this form *respectu*. We also find *contemplatione tui* 'out of consideration for you.')
tui causa: for your sake.
in tuam gratiam haec feci: I did this to please you.

DOUBLE QUESTIONS
vise utrum redierit annon: see whether he has come back or not.
vise num iam redierit an nondum: see whether he has already come back, or not yet.
vise redieritne domum: see whether he has come home.
vise an redierit an non: see whether he has come back or not.
vise redieritne domum necne: see whether he has come home or not.
vise redierit an non: see whether he has come back or not.
cogita utrum famae malis consulere an pecuniae, cogita famaene malis consulere an pecuniae, cogita famae malis consulere an pecuniae, cogita an famae malis consulere an pecuniae: consider whether you prefer to take thought for reputation or money.
cogita num famae malis consulere quam pecuniae: consider whether you prefer to take thought for reputation rather than for money.
vide si potes esse possessor: watch out if you can gain possession (Cicero in the second book of his *De oratore*, using *si* instead of the usual *an* in imitation of Greek, where εἰ [if] introduces both questions and conditional clauses).

CONCEDING
finge hominem vivere: imagine that the fellow is alive.
fac ita esse: suppose that it is so.
fac potuisse: suppose that he could have.
facite hoc meum consilium legiones novas non improbare (Cicero): suppose that the fresh legions have not disapproved of this plan of mine.
ut donemus ita esse: to grant that it were so
ut hoc interim tibi concedamus: to concede you this point in the meantime
ut hoc interim tibi largiar: to yield this point meantime
ut non referat pedem, insistat tamen (Cicero): even if it does not retreat, it would at any rate stand still.
non est in nostra potestate sed in natura, ut tamen multum sit in nobis

* * * * *

20 Cicero] *De oratore* 2.283
29 Cicero] *Philippics* 12.29
34 Cicero] *Philippics* 12.8

LB I 45E

(Cato): it lies not in our power, but with nature, though even so much depends on ourselves.

pone sic esse in tabulis: assume that this is what the will said.

esto sane, sit ita sane: very well, let it be so.

ut maxime iusserim, non erat tuum id facere: I may have given any amount of orders, but it was not your business to do it.

etiam si quid asperius dixisset, tuum erat obticescere: even if he did say something sharp, your place was to keep quiet.

sed imaginare me donasse, non potes tibi rem vindicare: but suppose I have donated it, you cannot claim it for yourself.

et si maxime donassem, non tibi ius est rei vindicandae: I may have given it as much as you like, that does not give you the right to claim the thing.

donarim sane, non statim tibi ius est iniciendi manum: granted I have given it, you do not immediately acquire the right to lay hands on it.

NEARLY

paene scopum attigeras, prope scopum attigeras, propemodum attigeras scopum: you almost hit the mark.

parum aberas a scopo: you were not far off the mark.

parum abfuit ut scopum attigeris, parum abest quin scopum attigeris: it was, it is, only by a small amount that you failed to hit the mark.

res parum aberat a pugna: the situation was not far from a fight.

parum aberat quin pugnarent: they were not far from fighting.

minimum aberat ut homini manus iniceret: it wanted but little before he laid hands on him.

minimo minus scopum attigeras: you missed the mark by a hair's breadth.

nihil fuit propius quam ut perirem (Plautus): nothing was more in the offing than my ruin.

vix hominem cohibui quo minus manum iniceret: I hardly restrained the fellow from laying hands on him.

tantum non conserebant manus: they were all but coming to blows; tantum non adorabant: they all but adored. The corresponding idiom in Greek μόνον οὐχί [only not] has a wider extension.

* * * * *

1 Cato] Not Cato, but Varro *Res rusticae* 1.4.4
27 Plautus] *Miles* 476: *quid propius fuit*
31 tantum non] See Seneca *De beneficiis* 5.16.3: *impunitatem, pecuniam, tantum non civicam acciperet*, where Erasmus' edition marks this as a Senecan usage.

Suetonius, in his *Life of Tiberius*, puts: *civilem admodum inter initia, ac paulo minus quam privatum egit* 'at the start he acted very much the citizen and practically the private citizen,' where he uses *paulo minus* 'missing by little' as the equivalent of *propemodum* 'almost.' A little later he writes' *quod paulo minus utrumque evenit* 'both things very nearly happened,' the equivalent of: *parum abfuit quin utrumque evenerit* 'it wanted but little for both to occur.' In the same work he writes: *sed tantum non statim a funere ad negotiorum consuetudinem rediit* 'he returned all but immediately from the funeral to his normal activities.' Terence used *modo non* for *tantum non*: *is senem pellexit per epistolam, modo non montes auri pollicens* 'he inveigled the old man by means of a letter, promising all but mountains of gold.'
nihil longius abfuit quam ut hosti me dederem: nothing was further off than my surrendering to the enemy.
nec mihi longius quicquam est quam videre hominum vultus (Cicero): and there is nothing further from me than observing the faces of men.

UNCERTAINTY
annos natus est ferme viginti: he is about twenty years old.
annos natus circiter octoginta: round about eighty years old
circa lustra decem (Horace): in years almost ten times five
annos natus est plus minus quadraginta: he is more or less forty years old.
ad dies viginti: up to twenty days
quum annos ad quinquaginta natus esset (Cicero): though he was about fifty
hora quasi decima (Suetonius): about four o'clock
annos habet haud scio an duodeviginti: he is, I should imagine, about eighteen.
puerum annos natum fortasse decem: a boy maybe ten years old
diu in incerto habuere (Sallust): for a long time they were in uncertainty.

* * * * *

1 Suetonius] *Tiberius* 26
4 A little later] *Tiberius* 39
7 same work] *Tiberius* 52
9 Terence] *Phormio* 67
14 Cicero] *Pro Rabirio Postumo* 35
20 Horace] *Odes* 4.1.6
23 Cicero] *Pro Cluentio* 110
25 Suetonius] *Caligula* 58.1: *hora quasi septima*
29 Sallust] *Catilina* 41.1

65 / Correcting a statement or anticipating an objection

in pietate praecipua felicitatis pars, vel tota potius felicitas hominis sita est:
man's chief happiness, or rather entire happiness, lies in love of God.
vulgi more magis quam iudicio (Sallust): in the manner of the crowd rather
than advisedly
doctrina nihil ad virtutem conducit, immo nonnihil officit: learning is in no
way conducive to virtue, in fact it is something of a hindrance.
tibi praecipue atque adeo tibi uni calamitatem hanc acceptam ferre pos-
sumus: we can set this calamity down chiefly to your account, indeed to
yours alone.
ducem hostium intra moenia atque adeo in senatu videmus: we see the
leader of the hostile forces within our walls, indeed within the very Senate.
tuum opus vidi magis quam legi: I glanced at your work rather than read it.
Graecas litteras degustavit verius quam didicit: he acquired a smattering of
Greek literature rather than studied it.
bonas litteras sedulitate sua depravavit vel (ut verius dicam) evertit: he
applied himself to the corruption of good learning, or, more correctly, to its
destruction.
bonas litteras non dico depravavit, sed funditus evertit: good learning I will
not say he corrupted, but totally destroyed.
suos omnes laesit; quid dixi laesit, immo subvertit: he injured everyone
connected with him. Injured, did I say? He ruined them rather.
sed in hoc ferendus meus error, ferendus autem? immo etiam adiuvandus
(Cicero): but in this matter you must bear with my error. Bear with? Yes
indeed, but also help it.
quem historicum citius dixeris quam poetam: you could call him a historian
sooner than a poet.
Lucanum relegi, non tam poetam quam historicum: I re-read Lucan, not so
much a poet as a historical writer.
ni pater esses, dicerem te desipere: if you were not my father I would say
you were a fool.
hic exercitus ductor, paene dixeram seductor: this leader of the army, I
almost said misleader.

* * * * *

1 Correcting] For this section see *Ad Herennium* 4.26.36.
5 Sallust] *Epistula ad Caesarem* 2.4
12 in senatu videmus] Cicero *Catilinarians* 1.5: *videtis*
25 Cicero] *Ad Atticum* 12.43.2

vertit Homerum, paene dixeram pervertit: he translated Homer, I almost said transmogrified.

respondebo non orationi tuae sed convicio: I will reply not to a speech on your part, but to a slanderous assault.

To sum up, correcting can be done by amplification, diminution, or alteration.

Amplification: qui de huius urbis atque adeo orbis terrarum exitio cogitant (Cicero in his speech *In Catilinam*): who are contemplating the destruction of these walls, indeed of the whole world; insector, posco, atque adeo flagito (Cicero again, in his speech *Pro Plancio*): I press, I urge, in fact I demand. Cicero often employs this form of speech.

Diminution: sic hic vivimus, aut victitamus verius: thus we live here, or more truly eke out an existence.

Alteration involves transfer to a word that is opposite, or more appropriate and more striking:

pro hospite hostem fovi domi meae: for friend I cherished a foe within my home.

his legationibus non immoratur sed immoritur: when this man is on a mission, he does not pass time, he passes out.

hic patrimonium omne absumpsit, aut ut melius dicam, abligurrivit: his whole inheritance he swallowed up, or to use a truer word, he swallowed down.

The same effect can be produced by *at* [which has a strong adversative force]:

fucum factum mulieri. at quem deum? (Terence): thus by the god did the woman have dust thrown in her eyes. But what a god!

una mater oppugnat, at quae mater? (Cicero): his mother alone stands in the way, but what a mother! A person who ... etc.

* * * * *

3 convicio] Cf Cicero *De domo sua* 3: *respondebo hominis furiosi non orationi ... sed convicio.*

5 To sum up] The passage to line 28 'person who ... etc' was added in *1534*, with minor insertions earlier (LB I 46D–E).

8 *In Catilinam*] 1.9

10 *Pro Plancio*] 48. Erasmus' text here and at 475:20 has *Planco*.

18 immoritur] For a similar incident see Quintilian 9.3.73.

20 abligurrivit] See Terence *Eunuchus* 235: *patria qui abligurrierat bona.*

25 Terence] *Eunuchus* 589–90

27 Cicero] *Pro Cluentio* 199

66 / Citing authorities

ut Ciceroni placet: as Cicero has it
auctore Platone: on Plato's authority. *auctor* is used in three senses: the
person cited may express an opinion, urge a course of action, or give an   5
account of something.
teste Varrone: as Varro bears witness
si Terentio credimus: if we accept what Terence says
uti refertur apud Plinium: as we find reported in Pliny
ut ait Protagoras Platonicus: as Protagoras says in Plato's dialogue   10
ut apud Xenophontem Simonides dixit: as Simonides said in Xenophon
Epicuro teste, felicitas in voluptate sita est: according to Epicurus, happiness lies in pleasure.
Aristoteles bonorum tres ordines fecit: Aristotle set up three ranks of
desirable things.   15
non spirare animal cui non sit sanguis calidus auctor est Theophrastus:
Theophrastus propounds the view that only warm-blooded animals
breathe.
apud Plinium scriptum est elephantos decimo demum anno parere: it is
stated in Pliny that elephants do not reproduce until their tenth year.   20
Pyrrho negat quicquam sciri posse: Pyrrho denies the possibility of knowledge.
id verum esse testis est Livius: Livy witnesses to the truth of this.
extat in annalibus: the annalistic records contain the statement.
veterum litteris proditum est: it is recorded in early documents.   25
eius sententiae complures citat auctores: he cites a number of authorities
holding this opinion.
ad eam sententiam quam plurimos allegat testes: he adduces a great
number of witnesses to this view.
eam sententiam multorum auctoritate tuetur: he defends this view by citing 30
the authority of many writers.
huic opinioni Plinius astipulatur: Pliny concurs in this opinion.
huic sententiae suffragatur Plato: Plato lends his support to this view.
idem sentit Pythagoras: Pythagoras is of the same opinion.
Aristoteli animal est etiam spongia: for Aristotle the sponge also is an   35
animal.
Plinio sentiunt et arbores: for Pliny trees too have sensation.

* * * * *

20 Pliny] *Naturalis historia* 8.28
21 Pyrrho] See 429:21n.

67 / Variations on the imperative

The imperative, for example, *vale* 'farewell,' can be varied by [using a present subjunctive] *valeas* 'you are to fare well' or [*fac* with a dependent present subjunctive] *fac valeas* 'see to it that you fare well,' or [a future imperative] *valeto* 'henceforth fare well,' or [a future indicative] *valebis* 'you shall fare well.'

In some verbs we can use the future subjunctive: *memineris* 'you are to remember' [the subjunctive of *memini* 'remember'] has the same force as *memento* [the future imperative] 'remember henceforth'; and *oderis* 'you are to hate' [the subjunctive of *odi* 'hate'] has the same force as [the future imperative phrase] *odio habeto* 'henceforth hold as an object of hatred.'

In other verbs, this form can only be used in negative clauses: *ne dixeris* 'you are not to remark at some point', [a variant for] *ne dicas* [present subjunctive] or *ne dic* [present imperative] 'do not say.'

68 / Various ways of expressing futurity

paenitebit olim te: one day you will be sorry.
futurum est ut olim te paeniteat: the time will come when you will be sorry.
spero te gavisurum facto: I hope you will be pleased with what has been done.
brevi opinor taedebit te huius vitae: before long, I believe, you will tire of this life.
opinor fore ut brevi te huius taedeat vitae: I think that the situation will soon be that you are tired of this life.
spero futurum ut facto gaudeas: I hope the case will be that you are pleased with what has been done.
dixeris egregie (Horace): you will have spoken splendidly.
alligaris filium (Terence): you will find you've got your son tied down.
abibit hinc propediem: he will leave here forthwith.

* * * * *

8 future subjunctive] This term, not used today, is derived from ancient grammatical terminology; see for example Donatus *Ars grammatica* in Keil IV 360–1: 'coniunctivo modo ... tempore futuro *cum legero legeris legerit*,' etc. *memini odi novi* form a group of defective verbs often mentioned specifically by ancient grammarians: as they have no present stem they do not have present subjunctive, imperative, or future indicative, which are derived from the present stem. For this whole section see Charisius *Ars grammatica* III in Keil I 258–9.

30 Horace] *Ars poetica* 47

31 Terence] *Adelphi* 844

abiturus est hinc propediem: he is about to depart forthwith.

futurum est ut repeat creditum: what is about to happen is that he will ask for his loan back. In this periphrasis, *futurum est ut*, Latin speakers seem to be giving an equivalent of the Greek construction with μέλλει [to be on the point of], for example, μέλλει λέγειν [he is on the point of speaking], which could be expressed by *dicturus est*. Cicero makes great use of this periphrasis. It is in any case unavoidable whenever we meet a verb which has no future participle; for example, we must say *spero fore ut artem brevi perdiscas* 'I trust that the case will be that you are soon thoroughly versed in the art,' since the future participle *perdisciturus* does not exist.

There is one form that combines both future and preterite signification [i.e., the future perfect]:

prius quam tu domum redeas, ego epistolam perscripsero: before you can return home, I shall have the letter written.

antequam in portum pervenies, navis solverit: before you reach the harbour, the ship will have sailed.

si tales animos in pugna praestabitis, vicerimus, *or* vicimus [using the perfect as an alternative]: if you display such a spirit on the field, the victory shall already be ours (or, then have we already won).

This seems very like μετ' ὀλίγον μέλλειν [to be right on the point of], though the usual Latin way of expressing this idea is by a periphrasis employing the adverbs *iam, iamiam, mox*:

iam aderit: he will be here any minute.

similis iamiam morituro: like to one at the very door of death.

mox audies: you will hear straightway.

In some verbs we are obliged to use the future subjunctive, that is, *meminero, odero, novero* 'I shall find I recall, hate, know.'

The following usages also belong with the future:

confido commentarium hoc studiosis probatum iri: I trust that the outcome will be the approval of this commentary by scholars [i.e., that this commentary will be approved].

et perspicio te perditum ire filium: and I perceive that you are proceeding to ruin our son.

69 / A periphrastic alternative for verbs in general

A periphrasis containing *fieri* 'happen, come about' or some similar verb can be used for practically any verb form:

* * * * *

26 obliged] See 439:8n.

ita carus eris omnibus: so you will win everyone's affection; ita fiet ut carus
sis omnibus: so it will come about that you win ...
hoc modo effugit invidiam: in this way he escaped odium; hoc modo
factum est ut effugerit invidiam: in this way it was managed that he escaped
odium.

utinam ex aequo me amares: if only you loved me as much as I do you;
utinam fieret ut ex aequo me amares: if only it were the case that you loved
me ...
in uxorem pessimam incidi: I have fallen in with a terrible wife; mihi usu
venit ut in pessimam uxorem inciderim: it has been my lot to fall in with ...

70 / The potential

The potential includes nearly all expressions which imply possibility, obligation, or some similar concept:
quid agas cum eo qui nihil intelligit? what are you to do with someone who
understands nothing?
est quod rideas: you may well laugh.
non est quod invideas: you have no reason for jealousy.
videas et flumina sicca: you would see even the rivers run dry.
cerneres alios trepidare, alios circumspectare fugam: you would have observed some in confusion, others looking round for a way of escape.
vidisses omnes obmutescere: you would have seen everyone fall speech-
less.
equidem istud non affirmarim: I at any rate would not assert that.
dixerit hic aliquis: someone at this point might make the remark.
maturius venisses: you should have come earlier.
Terence uses *praediceres* for *praedicere debuisses* 'you should have warned
me.'
   In this sort of sentence the Greeks add the particle ἄν, as in λέγοις ἄν
[you would say, you might say].

71 / Words for 'valuing'

plurimi me facit: he values me highly.
parvi habet: he holds it cheap.

* * * * *
21 flumina sicca] Virgil *Eclogues* 7.56
26 assert that] Cf Quintilian 11.3.5: *equidem ... affirmarim.*
29 Terence] *Andria* 793; see 328:17n.

pro nihilo ducit: he thinks it worthless.

nihili pendit: he considers it of no account.

pro minimo ducit: he thinks it of very slight importance.

ne huius quidem facio: I do not think it worth this (δεικτικῶς [with a gesture], showing a hair or a thread).

maximo in pretio est apud omnes: he is held in high esteem by all.

plurimi fit apud omnes: he is greatly valued by all.

magni habetur apud suos: his own people think a great deal of him.

pili, nauci, flocci non facio: I don't give a fig, a rap, a straw for it.

boni consulere: take in good part

tranquillissimus autem animus meus qui totum istud aequi bonique facit (Cicero): my mind is absolutely at rest as it is quite indifferent to all that.

istud aequi bonique facio (Terence): I don't mind that at all.

supra ea veluti ficta pro falsis ducit (Sallust): anything beyond this he takes as an invention of the author and consequently false.

fidem suam interposuit, quam non minoris quam publicam ducebat (Sallust): he gave him his personal pledge, which he considered of no less value than that of the state.

quae prima mortales ducunt (Sallust): which mortals put first (i.e., which men value most highly)

in gratiam habere (Sallust): take as a favour; denique regi patefecit quod pollicebatur senatum et populum Romanum quoniam armis plus valuissent non in gratiam habituros: finally he indicated to the king that the Roman senate and people would not take kindly to his offer, seeing that they had had the better of the fighting.

nihil habere pensi (Sallust): care not a whit; neque id quibus modis assequeretur dum sibi regnum pararet quicquam pensi habebat: nor did he care a whit what methods he employed, provided he acquired dominion for himself.

* * * * *

5 a thread] Cf Terence *Adelphi* 163: *huius non faciam; Adagia* I viii 7.

10 boni consulere ... he did] Material to 443:8 was added in *1534* (LB I 47F–8A) except for *unius aestimemus assis, cassa nuce non emam.*

10 boni consulere] Quintilian 1.6.33: *boni consulas*

12 Cicero] *Ad Atticum* 7.7

13 Terence] *Heautontimorumenos* 788

14 Sallust] *Catilina* 3.2

16 Sallust] *Jugurtha* 32.5

19 Sallust] *Catilina* 36.4

21 Sallust] *Jugurtha* 111.1: *in gratia habituros*

26 Sallust] *Catilina* 5.6

nihil pensi, nihil moderati habere (Sallust): reck nothing, show no restraint
vilia habere (Sallust): hold cheap, despise; fidem fortunas pericula vilia
habere: hold honour, possessions, dangers, cheap
unius aestimemus assis (Catullus): let us value at a copper. (This in spite of
the grammarians' rules.)
cassa nuce non emam: I wouldn't give an empty nutshell for it.
filius est eodem apud me pondere quo fuit ille (Cicero): his son carries the
same weight with me as he did.

72 / Buying, etc

nimio emisti, non revendes tantidem: you paid too much for it; you will not
be able to re-sell it for as much.
nimio liceris: you are bidding too high.
minoris addicturus erat: he was going to knock it down for less.
quanticumque indicaris, tanti mercabor: I will purchase it for whatever
price you suggest.
vide ut quam maximo aestimes: mind you assess it as high as possible.
non refert quanti res ipsa sit sed quantopere tibi sit opus ea: it does not
matter how much the thing is worth but how much you need it.
tu tuum agrum pluris conducis quam ego meum emerim: you are paying
more to rent your land than I bought mine for.
paulo locas aedes tuas: you are charging a low rent for your house.
cupiam maximo si queam: I would like a high rent if I could get it.
eme quam potes minimo, revende quam potes plurimo: buy as cheap as
you can, sell as dear as you can.
asse non emerim totam Ciceronis famam: I would not give a brass farthing
for Cicero's entire reputation.
labore di bona sua vendunt: the price of the gods' blessings is hard work.

* * * * *

1 nihil ... moderati habere] *Catilina* 12.2
2 vilia habere] *Catilina* 16.2
4 Catullus] 5.3
5 rules] That specific value and price should be expressed by a nominal form in
the ablative case, not genitive; see next chapter.
6 nutshell] Cf Plautus *Rudens* 1324: *cassam glandem*.
7 Cicero] *Ad Atticum* 10.1.1
11 Buying] With this chap cf Thompson *Colloquies* 608–11.
21 how much you need it] See Cato: *quod non opus est, asse carum est*, quoted in
Seneca *Epistles* 94.27.
28 brass farthing] Cf Catullus 33.8: *non potes asse venditare*.
30 hard work] *Adagia* II ii 53

LB I 48A

vili vendunt, minoris non possunt: they are selling them cheap; they could not ask less.

non emit qui nihilo emit, care emit qui rogat: he buys not who buys for nought; he pays dear who has to beg.

extrude merces quanticumque potes, vel gratis alicui obtrudito, si secus non potes: sell off this merchandise for whatever price you can get; give it away free to someone if you cannot push it off any other way.

redimas te captum quanti potes, quam potes pro minimo, si nequeas paulo at quanti potes: you are to buy your freedom for whatever sum you can, the lowest price you can manage, but if not for a small amount, then for whatever price you can.

cui addictus est ager? Lodovico. quanti? to whom was the land knocked down? to Louis. How much for?

frumentum addictum est, sed nondum admensum: the grain has been allocated, but not yet assessed.

quanti proscripsit aedes? ducatorum myriade: for how much did he advertise his house? For ten thousand ducats.

quanti cenastis? percare: what did your dinner cost you? Extremely dear.

magno hic vivitur: the cost of living is high here.

amatur vilissime: loving comes cheap.

Bassus carius cacat quam bibit: it costs Bassus more to go to the lavatory than to have a drink.

magna mercede canit: he asks a large fee for singing.

maxima tacuit Demosthenes: Demosthenes took a very large fee to keep silent.

quanto / metiris pretio? (Juvenal): at what price do you assess?

quanti stipulatus es? what price did you agree on?

Thais decem milibus drachmarum noctem venditabat: Thais used to charge ten thousand drachmas per night.

nimio constat elegantia: it costs a great deal to be fashionable.

* * * * *

4 has to beg] See Seneca *De beneficiis* 2.1.4: *quoniam quidem ut maioribus nostris ... visum est, nulla res carius constat quam quae precibus empta est; Adagia* I iii 20.

5 extrude merces ... ducats] This passage (lines 5–17) was added in 1534 (LB I 48B).

6 merchandise] Cf Horace *Epistles* 2.2.11: *extrudere merces.*

8 redimas te] See Terence *Eunuchus* 74–5: *ut te redimas captum quam queas / minumo; si nequeas paululo at quanti queas.*

21 Bassus] See Martial 1.37.

24 Demosthenes] See Aulus Gellius 11.9 where Demosthenes withdraws his opposition in return for a bribe.

26 Juvenal] 9.70–1

28 Thais] The name of several celebrated courtesans in Athens and Rome

quorum uni mellita quadragies sestertium constiterunt (Suetonius): the cakes cost one of them four million sesterces. Here the ablative *centum milibus* is understood after *quadragies*, that is, forty times (one hundred thousand).

73 / Making a difference

nihil interest facias an dicas: it makes no difference whether you do or say.
nihil refert per te facias an per alium: it does not matter whether you do it yourself or through an agent.
parvi mea refert quid nolis aut velis: it matters little to me what you want or do not want.
at mea plurimum refert: but it matters a great deal to me.
quid interest utrum facias an instiges? what difference does it make whether you actually do it or incite another?
plurimum interest, maxime refert, quo tempore virum adeas: it makes a great deal of difference, it is very important, at what moment you approach the man.
equidem haud magno in discrimine pono (Livy): I at any rate do not make a great issue of
respondit se vita malle excedere quam metu violentae mortis amicos inimicosque iuxta ponere (Valerius Maximus): he replied that he preferred to depart this life rather than put friend and foe on a par through fear of a violent death.
adero, me vosque omnibus in rebus iuxta geram (Sallust): I shall be there, and shall treat myself and you alike in all things.
Tros Tyriusque mihi nullo discrimine agetur (Virgil): Trojan and Tyrian will find no distinction with me.
utrum probes an improbes manum non verterim: I would not lift a finger whether you approve or disapprove.
ad ista sum indifferens: I am indifferent to that. (Suetonius has this use of *indifferens*.)

* * * * *

1 Suetonius] *Nero* 27.3
20 Livy] Preface 8: *haud in magno equidem ponam discrimine*
23 Valerius Maximus] 3.8 ext 5
26 Sallust] *Jugurtha* 85.47
28 Virgil] *Aeneid* 1.574
30 manum non verterim] Cicero *De finibus* 5.93
32 Suetonius] *Julius* 53: *Caesarem … circa victum Gaius Oppius adeo indifferentem docet …*

quaedam perquam tenui limite dividuntur (Quintilian): there is an extremely fine dividing line between some of the divisions advocated.

verane haec sint an ficta nihil laboro: I am not bothered whether this is true or false.

utrum scripseris an dixeris feceris necne manum non verterim: I would not give a hand's turn whether you wrote or said or did it or not.

susque deque fero, susque deque habeo: rain or shine, it is all one to me [literally, I take it up or down].

instigasti, perinde est ac si feceris: you encouraged him, so it is just the same as if you actually did it.

ex aequo in noxia es: you are equally to blame.

tantundem peccasti: you have done wrong just as much.

citra discrimen amat ac laudat omnes: he showers approval and praise on everyone without discrimination.

citra delectum omnes in familiaritatem receptat: he accepts everyone as an intimate acquaintance without any distinction.

omnes promiscue mordet: he backbites everyone indiscriminately.

passim haec praedicat: he is proclaiming this everywhere.

apud quoslibet haec dicit: he is saying this before all and sundry.

amussis alba in albo lapide: a white line on a white stone [i.e., something undistinctive].

74 / Affirming

promisit se venturum? promisit, maxime, etiam: did he say he would come? he did, certainly, yes. (The Greek word for 'yes' is ναί.)

si non, quomodo tabulas conficis? si etiam, quamobrem ... (Cicero): if no, how do you keep your accounts? if yes, why ... ?

quasi aut etiam aut non, non modo verum esset sed necessarium (Cicero): as if yea or nay were not only true but inevitable. (I have quoted this example because there are some who do not consider *etiam* an affirmative particle.)

scilicet: evidently

admodum: to a degree

* * * * *

1 Quintilian] 9.1.3
7 susque deque fero] See Aulus Gellius 16.9.1; *Adagia* I iii 83.
20 amussis alba] *Adagia* I v 88
28 Cicero] *Pro Roscio comoedo* 9
30 Cicero] *Academica priora* 2.97 (4.97)

quam lubentissime: most willingly
benigne: thank you very much.
sic habet: that is the case.
sic erit: that is how it will be.
ita est: quite so   5
factum est: that's what happened.
plane: obviously
mirum ni: naturally
haud dubie: without a doubt
dubio procul: indubitably   10
liquet: that's evident
constat: it is quite clear.
confessum est: it is acknowledged fact.
in confesso est: it goes without saying.
extra controversiam est: it is beyond dispute.   15
certum est: it is established.
pro certo: for certain
compertum: ascertained
liquido: evidently
indubie: doubtless   20
indubitato: undoubtedly
certo certius, vero verius est: assurance doubly sure
veriora his quae apud Sagram gesta sunt: truer than what happened on the
Sagra
                                                                                         25

75 / Accusing

accusatus est sacrilegii: he was accused of sacrilege.
hic se furti alligat: he shows himself guilty of theft.   30
postulatus est repetundarum: he was called to account for extortion.
delatus proditionis: indicted for treason

* * * * *

24 Sagra] Refers to a battle in southern Italy in which 15,000 Locrians, with divine
    aid, defeated a many times larger army from Croton; the report of the victory
    miraculously reached Greece the same day and was not believed. The incident
    became a proverbial example of something rejected and then found to be
    completely true: see *Paroemiographi graeci*: ἀληθεστερα τῶν ἐπὶ Σάγρα.
27 Accusing] This chap (75) was gradually expanded in successive editions.
30 alligat] Terence *Eunuchus* 809
31 repetundarum] Cf Suetonius *Julius* 4.1: *Dolabellam repetundarum postulavit.*

principes civitatis insimulati proditionis ab Romanis (Caesar in his seventh
book of Commentaries): the tribal chiefs were charged with treachery by
the Romans.

reum egit, peregit: he brought to trial.

in ius voca: take him to court.

lege agito: take legal proceedings.

in ius ambula: come along to court.

in ius duxit hominem: he haled the fellow off to court.

in ius trahis: you drag him to court.

litem intendit: he threatens a law suit.

dicam scripsit: he brought an action.

filius cum patre litem agitat: the son is conducting a law suit against his
father.

cum opulentissimo viro illi lis est: he is engaged in a legal dispute with a
very wealthy man.

cum Mida iudicio decertat: he is arguing it out in court with a Midas.

accersitus est capitis: he was summoned on a capital charge.

delatus est sacrilegii: he was indicted for sacrilege.

peculatus reum peregit: he brought him to trial for peculation.

ad tres viros deferam tuum nomen (Plautus): I will lay your name before the
triumvirs.

nomen hominis amicissimi detuli (Cicero): I brought a charge against one
who was a close friend.

delationem nominis postulavit (Cicero): he demanded the indictment.

Roscii nomen deferendum curavit (Cicero): he organized the indictment of
Roscius.

diem illi dixit: he laid an accusation against him.

Caesoni capitis diem dicit (Livy): he brought Caeso to trial for his life.

rei capitalis diem Postumio dixerunt (Livy): they charged Postumius with a
capital offence.

eum talionis agentem exceptione reppulit: he eluded him by means of an
exception clause when he claimed damages.

* * * * *

1 Caesar] *Bellum Gallicum* 7.20.1: *Vercingetorix ... proditionis insimulatus*

7 in ius ambula] For example, Plautus *Rudens* 860

18 delatus est ... capital offence] Material to line 30 was added in 1534 (LB I 49A).

20 Plautus] *Aulularia* 416

22 Cicero] Cf *Pro Caelio* 76: *nomen amici mei de ambitu detuli.*

24 Cicero] *In Quintum Caecilium* 64

25 Cicero] *Pro Roscio Amerino* 132

28 Livy] 3.11.9

29 Livy] 25.4.8

agit cum eo malae tractationis: he challenges him with malpractice.

damnatus est repetundarum (or, de repetundis): he was found guilty of extortion.

absolutus iniuriarum: acquitted of a charge of injury

an quisquis gratiam cum possit non refert ingrati teneatur?: is anyone who does not show gratitude, in spite of the fact that he can, liable to prosecution for ingratitude?

an teneatur reipublicae laesae qui quod sibi licuit fecit? would anyone be liable to a charge of acting against the public interest for doing what he was entitled to do?

laesae religionis sit actio: let the point at issue be contempt for religion.

nec audacem timoris absolvimus (Seneca): nor do we acquit the bold man of fear.

All the expressions listed in the chapter on praising and blaming belong here.

qui iam de maiestate postulavit (Cicero): who had already brought to trial for treason

cras subscribam homini dicam (Plautus): tomorrow I will bring an action against the fellow.

cum istam causam subscriberent (Plautus again): since they subscribed to that case. From this comes the use of the word *subscriptor* for those who second the accuser and assist the principal: accusabat M'. Aquilium, subscriptore C. Rutilio Rufo (Cicero): he was accusing Manius Aquilius, seconded by Gaius Rutilius Rufus. Hence also *subscriptio* 'subscription, signature.'

incusat senis parsimoniam: he finds fault with the old man's meanness.

insimulat herum malitiae: he accuses his master falsely of spite.

causatur tutorum perfidiam: she pleads the dishonesty of her guardians.

* * * * *

4 iniuriarum] See *Ad Herennium* 2.13.19: *iudex absolvit iniuriarum.*

5 an quisquis ... religion] *1514* (LB I 49A–B)

5 ingrati teneatur] See Seneca *De beneficiis* 3.6.

12 nec audacem ... fear] *1526* (LB I 49B)

12 Seneca] *De beneficiis* 4.27.2

14 All the expressions ... guardians] This passage to line 28 *1534* (LB I 49B)

14 chapter] 130

16 Cicero] *Ad Quintum fratrem* 3.1.15

18 Plautus] *Poenulus* 800

20 Plautus] Not Plautus, but Cicero *Pro Cluentio* 119

23 Cicero] *In Caecilium* 69

LB I 49A

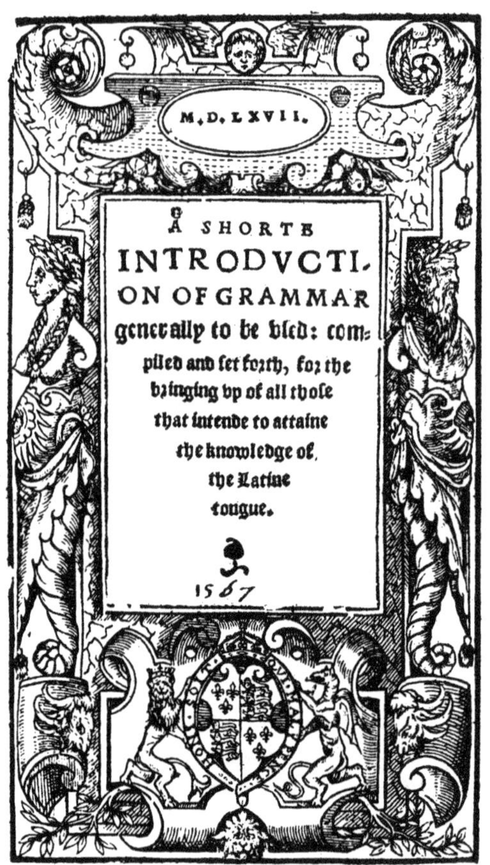

Title page of *A Shorte Introduction of Grammar*
London: R. Wolfe 1567
A booklet in English consisting of an accidence by Colet and a syntax by William
Lily, the first high master of St Paul's School, was succeeded by a Latin syntax
prepared by Lily and later revised by Erasmus. This revised work was published as
De octo orationis partium constructione (London: Pynson 1513).
These writings, with supplementary material from other grammarians, grew into
this grammar (actually two, one in English and the other in Latin, in the same
volume) which in its 1542 edition included a royal proclamation forbidding the use
of any other grammar in schools.
Folger Shakespeare Library

76 / Usefulness

nihil aeque conducit ad beate vivendum: nothing is so conducive to the good life.

nihil ad parandas opes conducibilius: nothing is more instrumental in the acquisition of wealth.

nihil ad eam rem confert: it contributes nothing to this end.

plurimum adferet adiumenti: it will offer considerable assistance.

utilis ad parandos amicos assentatio: flattery is useful for winning friends.

plus adfert voluptatis quam utilitatis: it provides more pleasure than profit.

plurimas ad res hic libellus usui futurus est: this little book will prove useful for many purposes.

ad id patruus in primis adiutare poterit: your uncle will be able to help particularly in this matter.

quid faciunt ad virtutem nummi? what does money do towards virtue?

libet quidem verum non expedit: it is attractive, but not beneficial.

visum est mihi hoc ad multa quadrare (Cicero): I felt it fitted in with many things.

utinam haec res tam frugifera tibi sit quam futura est honesta: I hope this course will prove as profitable to you as it is honourable.

utinam tantundem frugis adferat quantum adfert gloriae: if only it brings as much profit as it now brings glory.

ad id sola doctrina fuerit adiumento: only an informed mind could be of assistance to that end.

ad hoc pecunia magno adminiculo futura est: money will provide strong support to this end.

ad id haud mediocriter adminiculantur vires corporis: bodily strength is no slight support in this.

in id quoque prodest ornatus: ornament also has the advantage that ... (an idiom employed by Quintilian).

non parum ad id efficiendum momenti habet fama integra: an unblemished reputation is of no little moment in bringing this about.

neque vero illud mediocriter profuerit: nor indeed would that prove but a slight advantage.

adiuvat hoc quoque: this too helps.

hac ratione nihil profecimus, reliquum est ut diversam ingrediamur viam: by this method we have made no progress; it remains for us to enter upon a different course.

* * * * *

17 Cicero] *Ad Atticum* 4.19.2
30 Quintilian] Cf 8.3.9: *protinus in id quoque prodest ut ...*

LB I 49B

nihilo plus explicet ac si insanire paret (Horace): he would get no further
than if he planned to lose his wits.
eruditio ad pietatem plus adfert dispendii quam compendii, et non tam
promovet quam moratur: learning brings more loss than gain where piety
is concerned, and does not so much advance as retard.
calida sunt amica stomacho, dulcia conducunt hepati: hot things are helpful
to the stomach; sweet things are good for the liver.
quod stomacho confert, idem prodest cerebro: what does the stomach good
also benefits the head.
quod ad stomachum facit, idem capiti salutare est: what helps the stomach
is also healthy for the head.
quod stomacho bonum est, idem cerebro commodum est: what is good for
the stomach is also beneficial to the head.
lactucae alvo deiciendae efficaces, et ad somnum conciliandum idoneae:
lettuces are effective in loosening the bowels, and good for inducing sleep.
ad ciendos menses valet malva: mallow is potent in inducing menstruation.
alvo sistendae sunt utiles fabae assae: dried beans are a useful remedy to
make the bowel costive.
stomachum acuunt, excitant, irritant appetentiam edendi: these substances
sharpen, excite the appetite, stimulate a desire for food.
hac in re solus hic tibi poterit commodare: in this matter only he can be of
assistance to you.
plurimum commoditatis adferet pecunia studioso: money will prove a
considerable convenience to a scholar.
utinam tam tibi commodo sit quam mihi fuit grave: I only hope it will be as
much benefit to you as it has been a burden to me.
magno meo malo tentavi: I tried it to my own great detriment. (The possessive adjective may be omitted.)
loquendo quae in rem non essent die consumpto (Livy): having wasted the
day in speeches which were not to the purpose
si e republica censeret, veniret (Livy): ... if he thought it was to the public
interest, he should come ...
facis ex tua dignitate et e republica (Cicero): you are acting in a manner
consonant with your own position and with the public interest.
scio quae studio dixerit e republica dixisse (Cicero): I know that what he
said under the pressure of emotion he said in the public interest.

* * * * *

1 Horace] *Satires* 2.3.270–1; *Adagia* II ii 80
29 Livy] 26.17.9
31 Livy] 23.24.1
33 Cicero] *Ad Brutum* 1.2.2

fecisti tuo commodo, nostro incommodo: you acted so as to convenience
yourself, and inconvenience us.
si iudicabis in rem tuam esse: if you judge it to your advantage
si putabis ex usu tuo fore: if you think it will be to your gain
si putabis e re tua fore: if you think it will serve your ends
pro te facit quod dico: what I say is for your good.
ad philosophiam dialectica viam aperit, viam sternit, viam praestruit:
dialectic opens up the way, paves the way, prepares the way to philosophy.
ad eam rem iam iacta sunt fundamenta: for that purpose the foundations
have already been laid.
aetites partus adiuvat: the eagle-stone prevents miscarriage.
inflationem stomachi discutit: disperses flatulence in the stomach
pectoris dolores levat: relieves pains in the chest
bilem extrahit: draws off bile
pituitam detrahit: loosens phlegm
mensium abundantiae auxiliatur: helps heavy menstruation
adversus serpentes in vino datur: is given in wine as a remedy for snakebite
deploratis auxilio est chironia: black bryony helps in hopeless cases.
morbis omnibus medicatur panace: panacea heals all ills.
elleboro phthiriasis emendatur: the condition of phthiriasis is ameliorated
by hellebore.
datur ad serpentum ictus chelidonia: celandine is given to counteract
snakebite.
rhododaphnes folia homini praesidio sunt adversus serpentes: rhododendron leaves are a protection for man in cases of snakebite.
aviditatem cibi facit acetum, valet ad ciborum appetentiam irritandam:
wine-vinegar creates a desire for food; it is effective in stimulating the
appetite.
absinthium fulcit stomachum labentem: absinth firms a fluid stomach.
The Greeks call substances which aid the digestion εὐστόμαχα.
nullum operae pretium fuerit: it would not be worthwhile.

* * * * *

11 partus adiuvat ... appetite] Text to line 28 added in *1514* (LB I 49E–F); *aetites*
   added in *1534*
11 eagle-stone] See Pliny *Naturalis historia* 36.149–51, a stone supposedly found
   in the nest of an eagle.
19 panacea] See Pliny *Naturalis historia* 25.30: *panaces ipso nomine omnium mor-*
   borum remedia promittit.
21 hellebore] *Naturalis historia* 25.61
29 absinthium ... εὐστόμαχα] Added in *1526* (LB I 49F)
31 nullum ... while] Added in *1534* (LB I 49F)

77 / Predicting and foretelling

sol purus oriens neque fervens serenum diem nuntiat: if the sun rises clear
and does not burn, it announces a day of fine weather.

concavus oriens pluvias praedicit: if it rises with a hollow look, it predicts 5
wet weather.

si circa occidentem rubescunt nubes, serenitatem futurae diei spondent: if
the clouds gather round the setting sun and glow red, they promise a fine
day to follow.

sin spargentur pluviam ventosque significabunt: but if they are dispersed 10
over the sky, they will signify rain and wind.

cum oriente radii non illustres eminebunt, pluviam portendent: if the sun's
rays at his rising do not burst out clear into the sky, they will portend rain.

si in exortu rubescent nubes, maxima ostendetur tempestas: if the clouds
are red at sunrise, a violent storm will be indicated. 15

si oriens cingitur orbe, ex qua parte is se aperit, exspectetur ventus: if the
rising sun has a ring round it, wherever it opens up, you may expect wind
from that quarter.

si totus defluxerit, serenitatem dabit: if the whole ring fades away, it will
give fine weather. 20

lunae cornu septentrionale acuminatum, inde praesagit ventum: if the
moon's northern horn tapers, it presages wind from that quarter. (Pliny
often uses the word *praesagire* to mean not 'to foreknow' but 'to foretell.')

si quartam orbis rutilus cinget ventos et imbres praemonebit: if there is a
reddish ring round the moon on the fourth day, it will give warning of a 25
period of wind and rain.

nascens obatro cornu pluvias decrescens dabit: if the new moon has one
horn obscured, it will bring rain when it wanes.

rubicundam venti protinus sequuntur: windy weather follows a red moon.

autumni serenitas ventosam hiemem facit: a calm autumn brings a stormy 30
winter.

volitantes stellae ventos nuntiant: shooting stars announce wind.

eaedem in plures disiectae partes inconstantes ventos effundent: if they
shoot in all directions, they will cause inconstant winds.

cum ab aquilone nocte serena fulguraverit, ventum et imbrem demon- 35

* * * * *

1 Predicting] This chapter (77) was introduced in *1514*, and expanded in *1526*; it
intrudes between *Usefulness* and *Harming*.

3 sol purus ... that quarter] *1514* (LB I 49F–50A)

22 (Pliny ... foretell.')] *1526* (LB I 50A)

24 si quartam orbis ... from Pliny] Text to 455:18 *1514* (LB I 50A–B). The rest of the
chapter *1526*

strabit: when lightning is observed to the north in a clear night sky, it will indicate wind and rain.

nubes vehementius atrae ab oriente in noctem aquam minantur: clouds ominously black to the east threaten wet weather towards night.

nube gravida candicante grando imminebit: when the cloud is heavy and whitish, a hailstorm will be imminent.

nebulae caelo cadentes serenitatem promittunt: mists trailing from the sky promise fine weather.

pallidi ignes tempestatum nuntii sunt: fires burning palely are harbingers of stormy weather.

mare in tranquillo portu intra se murmurans ventum praedicit: when the sea within the harbour wall emits a subdued murmur it predicts wind.

camporum fragor et caeli murmur non dubiam habet tempestatis significationem: a roaring in the fields and a murmuring in the sky offers an infallible indication of rough weather.

echini affigentes sese tempestatis signa sunt: sea-urchins attaching themselves to rocks are a sign of a coming storm.

(All these examples are taken from Pliny.)

ipsa caeli facies futuram tempestatem loquitur: the very face of the sky tells what the weather will be.

exoriens nothus venturam pluviam praemonet: a rising south wind gives warning of rain to come.

Iris imbrium est nuntia; the rainbow is harbinger of rain.

halcyones nidulantes futurae tranquillitatis fidem non dubiam faciunt: halcyons building their nests make us absolutely confident of calm weather to come.

praecox pueritia vaticinium est vitae brevis: a precocious childhood is a prophecy of a short life.

immodica felicitas signum est venturae calamitatis: excessive good fortune is a sign of calamity to come.

crispantes undae nautis coorituros ventos demonstrant: dancing waves indicate to sailors that the wind will rise.

qui bene coniciet hunc vatem puta optimum: judge that man the best prophet whose conjectures prove right.

stridor dentium in aegrotis mortis indicium est: a grinding of the teeth in the sick is an indication of the nearness of death.

dentium series brevis et continua longaevitatem arguit: an unbroken row of small teeth is a prognostication of longevity.

* * * * *

18 Pliny] *Naturalis historia* 18.340–64
33 qui bene coniciet] Cf Cicero *De divinatione* 2.12.

occursus puellae nuper nuptae felix auspicium est: it is lucky to meet a bride.
occursus virginis parum laeti ominis est: it is a bad sign to meet an unmarried girl.
nec dubias significationes saepe iecit ne reliquis quidem se parsurum: and he often gave quite unmistakable indications that he would not spare the rest either.
evidens specimen dedit qualis sit futurus princeps (Suetonius): he gave clear tokens what sort of an emperor he would be.
ex pueritia divina qualis sit futurus senex: divine from his childhood what kind of an old man he will be.
hinc collige, hinc augurare, hinc ratiocinare: deduce, predict, infer from this.

78 / Harming

pirorum esus stomacho gravis: pears are indigestible.
dulcia stomachum laedunt: sweet things harm the stomach.
acida concoctioni officiunt: sharp things are detrimental to the digestion.
salsa noxia sunt hepati: salt things are harmful to the liver.
lac virilem stomachum offendit: milk is offensive to the male stomach.
adusta inimica biliosis: dried foods are injurious to the bilious.
non obsistam: I will not oppose.
non fuero impedimento: I will not prove a hindrance.
non obturbabo: I will not cause any disturbance.
non reluctabor: I will not resist.
non obstrepam tuis conatibus: I will not cry out against your endeavour.
non renitar: I will not withstand.
non reclamo: I do not raise objection.
non remorabor institutum tuum: I will not obstruct your intention.
aures minus feriunt (Quintilian): they beat on (i.e., offend) the ears less.

* * * * *

5 se parsurum] Cf Suetonius *Tiberius* 62.3: *ne reliquis quidem ... parsurus creditur.*
8 Suetonius] Cf *Nero* 6.2: *signum evidens; Domitian* 1.3: *ut iam tum qualis futurus esset ostenderet.*
18 pears] Cf Pliny *Naturalis historia* 23.115.
19 stomachum laedunt] Cf Ovid *Amores* 2.19.26: *stomacho dulcis ut esca nocet.*
32 Quintilian] 9.3.4

79 / Fulfilling a function

gessit consulatum: he held the consulship.
ubi tum proconsulem agebat: where he was at that time functioning as proconsul
praetoris officio fungebatur: he was carrying out the duties of praetor.
dictator erat: he was dictator.
bellum administrabat: he had the management of the war.
Siciliam obtinebat: he was governor of the province of Sicily. (Cicero frequently uses *obtinere* in the sense 'govern, administer.' Otherwise *obtinet* means 'obtain.')
provinciae praesidebat: he was in charge of the province.
annonae praefectus erat: he was superintendent of the corn supply.
regia negotia procurabat: he was managing the king's affairs.
munia tribunicia obibat: he was discharging the duties of the office of tribune.
obire bella (Livy): prosecute wars
obire legationes (Cicero): undertake embassies
censui praeerat: he was superintending the census.
cum imperio esse: hold a magistracy [literally, be empowered with the right to command]
gerere potestatem (Cicero in his fourth speech against Verres): wield power
piraticam facere (Cicero again): practise piracy
hoc negotii tibi mandamus: we entrust this piece of business to you.
tibi provinciam hanc delegamus: we delegate this sphere of operations to you.
duram suscepisti provinciam: you have undertaken a difficult office.
duram sustines provinciam: you are sustaining a difficult charge.
fac ut imperatorem te praebeas: see that you act the emperor.
vide ut praestes amicum: be sure to show yourself a friend.
scurrae non amici functus es officio: you played the part of a man of the world, not a friend.
ego te absente tuis fungar vicibus: I will carry out all your duties in your absence.

* * * * *

9 Cicero] For example, *Pro Plancio* 95
17 Livy] 4.7.2
18 Cicero] *Academica priora* 2.5 (4.5)
22 Cicero] *Verrines* 2.138
23 Cicero] *Oratio post reditum in senatu* 11
27 provinciam] Terence *Phormio* 72–3: *cepisti*

tuas agam partes: I will play your part.

tuarum partium est, tuae partes sunt, retundere petulantiam hominis: it is part of your job, it is your part, to check the fellow's insolence.

defunctus consulatu: having discharged the consulship

defunctus vita: having laid aside this life

defunctus malo: having emerged from misfortune

defuncte periculis (Virgil): o thou from perils escaped

defendere vicem: sustain a role

defendente vicem modo rhetoris atque poetae (Horace): taking the part now of orator and poet

pontificis personam gerit: he sustains the character of pontiff.

paulatim exercuit principem (Suetonius): gradually he practised the prince (i.e., he performed the functions of a prince).

tractare, gubernare rem publicam: conduct public affairs, govern the state

ducere, gerere, exercere bellum: conduct, wage, prosecute war

navare operam: carry out a task with vigour

satagit rerum suarum: he has his hands full.

ductare exercitum: conduct an army

patrare bellum: wage war

(Quintilian notes that Sallust innovated in using *ductare* and *patrare* in a decent sense, whereas they had been indecent before.)

in familia bene instituta omnes in officio sunt: in a well-organized household everyone performs his proper function.

non deero officio meo: I shall not fail my duty.

numquam cessabo in officio meo: I shall never be remiss where my duty is concerned.

Sallust used *curare* absolutely, as in:

nam is in ea parte curabat: for he was in charge in that sector.

80 / Attribution of qualities

summo ingenio puer, summi ingenii puer, summus ingenio puer: a boy with great ability, of great ability, a boy outstanding in ability [descriptive

* * * * *

7 Virgil] *Aeneid* 6.83
9 Horace] *Satires* 1.10.12
12 Suetonius] *Tiberius* 33.1
17 suarum] Cf Terence *Heautontimorumenos* 225: *suarum rerum sat agitat.*
20 Quintilian] See 316:18–22.
24 deero] Cf Cicero *Ad familiares* 7.3.1: *ne officio deessem.*
27 Sallust] *Jugurtha* 60.5

ablative, descriptive genitive, ablative of respect]. *summus ingenium* 'outstanding with reference to ability' [with a so-called accusative of respect] would be a poetic expression.

vir admiranda sapientia, vir admirandae sapientiae, vir admirandus sapientia: a man of remarkable wisdom, remarkable for his wisdom. Again, *vir admirandus sapientiam* would be poetic.

vir incredibili praeditus sapientia: a man endowed with incredible wisdom

vir omniiugis corporis atque animi dotibus exornatus: a man adorned with every possible gift of body and mind

vir omnibus instructus dolis: a man equipped with every kind of cunning

vir ex meris mendaciis conflatus atque compositus: a man composed and compounded of nothing but deceit

id omnibus natura insitum est: that is innate in all men.

id natura nobis indidit: that nature has imparted to us.

ita natura comparatum: so things have been arranged by nature.

id cunctis attribuit natura: nature has attributed that to all.

multa vitia nobis recepta consuetudo conciliat, nonnulla natura ingenerat: many vices become acceptable through established habit; quite a number are engendered in us by nature.

omnibus innatum est ut vitam suam incolumem esse velint: the urge to self-preservation is innate in all creatures.

id vitii non tibi natura adiunctum est, sed accersitum ac receptum prava consuetudine: that particular fault was not contributed to your character by nature, but introduced and fostered by bad habits.

inest in homine incredibilis quaedam astutia, inest homini: an incredible astuteness is native to man.

81 / Titles

eius rei meminit Plato in dialogo qui inscribitur Συμπόσιον: Plato mentions this in the dialogue entitled *The Symposium*.

testis Cicero in eo libro quem inscripsit oratorem perfectum: Cicero bears witness to this in the book which he entitled *The Complete Orator*.

Plinius in opere cui titulus historia mundi: Pliny in the work which bears the title *Natural History of the World*

Varro in satyra cui titulum fecit 'nescis quid serus vesper vehat': Varro in the satire to which he gave the title 'You know not what the closing day will bring'

* * * * *

37 Varro] See Aulus Gellius 13.11.1.

LB I 51A

Vergilius in Alexide: Vergil in the *Alexis*
Terentius in Adelphis: Terence in the *Adelphi*
Hesiodus in opere cui titulum nuncupavit opera et dies: Hesiod in the work
to which he gave *Works and Days* as a title
in libello cui titulum indidit de verborum copia: in the little book on which 5
he bestowed the title '*Copia*: Abundance of Expression'
in commentariis quibus titulum praetulit de nugis aulicorum: in the essays
to which he prefixed the title *On the Follies of Courtiers*
in odarum libro quem Silvas nuncupavit: in the book of odes which he
called *Silvae* 10
in Phormione Terentiana: in the Terentian *Phormio*

82 / Congratulating

15

gaudeo te nobis optantibus incolumem esse redditum: I am glad that you
have been restored to us unharmed in answer to our prayers.
gratulamur tibi victoriam: we congratulate you on your victory. Suetonius
and Seneca use this construction with *gratulor*; also Cicero: appellat
hominem et ei voce maxima victoriam gratulatur: he called out to the fellow 20
and congratulated him on the victory in a loud voice.
isto nomine tibi gratulor: I congratulate you on that account.
gratulamur de victoria: we offer congratulations on account of your victory.
gratulor vicisse te: I congratulate you on winning.
quod victor redieris vehementer gaudeo: I am extremely pleased that you 25
have returned victorious.
te nova prole auctum esse gaudeo: I am delighted that you have been
blessed with another child.
salvum te advenire volupe est: your safe arrival is a great satisfaction.
laetor tuo nomine quod uxor feliciter peperit: I am happy on your account 30
that your wife has been safely delivered.

* * * * *

1 *Alexis*] *Eclogue* 2
7 de nugis aulicorum] Perhaps a reference to Lucian's *De iis qui mercede conducti
degunt*, which Erasmus translated. See also 582:6–7; 603:17n.
9 in odarum libro] Erasmus in 1497 edited a book of poems *Sylva odarum* for his
friend Willem Hermans; see Ep 49.
18 Suetonius] *Claudius* 6.1; *Vitellius* 2.5
19 Seneca] For example, *De beneficiis* 3.23.3
19 Cicero] *Verrines* 1.19
29 volupe est] An archaic form found in Plautus and Terence. See Terence
Phormio 610.

quod gener tibi tantopere probatur magnopere tua causa gaudeo: I am extremely pleased for your sake that you find your son-in-law so satisfactory.

voluptati mihi est quod tibi res ex sententia cesserit: it is a pleasure to me that things have turned out as you wanted.

tua gratia gaudeo quod res praeter spem bene verterit: on your account I am glad that things have unexpectedly taken a turn for the better.

tuam vicem laetor quod prospere pugnaris: I am pleased for your sake that you have been successful in the fight.

macte: bravo!

macte istius animi: congratulations on your attitude!

abi, virum te iudico (Terence in the *Adelphi*, spoken by Syrus): on you go, you're a real man.

83 / Expressing thanks

quod tam officiose me commendaris principi tuo gratiam et habeo et habiturus sum immortalem: I am and shall be eternally grateful to you for commending me so obligingly to your prince.

quod tanta fide mea negotia procuraris pares gratias agere vix possum, referre nequaquam: I can hardly thank you enough and can never repay you for looking after my affairs so scrupulously.

quod me passim amantissime praedicas video quantum debeam tuo in me studio: I can see how much I owe to your partiality towards me, in that you commend me with the greatest affection wherever you go.

quod meis commodis tantopere studes et habetur a me gratia et semper habebitur: I do indeed feel gratitude towards you for supporting my interests so enthusiastically, and I shall always do so.

quod argentum ad diem promissum reddidisti amo te et habeo gratiam: thank you, I am grateful to you for returning the money by the day you promised.

ecquid nos amat de virgine? (Terence): is she at all pleased with us about that girl?

quod mihi polliceris valde te amo (Cicero): I am very grateful to you for promising ...

* * * * *

12 Terence] *Adelphi* 564, spoken by Demea not Syrus
33 Terence] *Eunuchus* 456: *ecquid nos amat de fidicina istac?*
35 Cicero] *Ad Quintum fratrem* 3.9.4

multum te amo quod spopondisti M. Octavio (Cicero): I am much obliged to you for telling Marcus Octavius ...

factum bene quod epistolam obsignatam remiseris: you did right to send the letter back unopened.

quod nos pro tua virili tueris gratum est: it is gratifying that you are exerting all your powers to protect us.

grates persolvere dignas non opis est nostrae (Virgil): it lies not in our power to render worthy thanks.

fateor me tibi magnopere devinctum esse: I am indeed under a great obligation to you.

hoc nomine plus tibi debeo quam ut umquam solvendo esse possim: on this score I owe you more than I can ever be in a position to pay.

hoc officio artius me tibi astrinxisti: by this service you have bound me even closer to you.

obligatiorem me tibi fecisti: you have made me even more beholden to you.

devinctiorem reddidisti: you have put me under a greater obligation.

magis obnoxium effecisti quam ut vel verbis agere gratias possim: you have made me too indebted to find even the words to thank you.

maior est nostra necessitudo quam ut vel tu mihi vel ego tibi pro ullo officio debeam gratias agere: we are too closely connected for either of us to feel any obligation to thank the other for any service.

maius est hoc beneficium quam ut orationem postulet: this benefit is too great to call forth a speech.

84 / Repaying a service

gratiam referre: make requital
reponere merita: return services
rependere officia: recompense good offices
pensare beneficium: repay a kindness
remunerare beneficium: reward a kindness
remetiri beneficium: do an equal kindness in return
reddere beneficium: render back a kindness
persolvere beneficium: refund a kindness
respondere meritis: answer one good turn with another
par esse beneficiis acceptis: be quits for benefits received

* * * * *

1 Cicero] *Ad Atticum* 5.21.5: *quod respondisti*
7 Virgil] *Aeneid* 1.600–1

LB I 51E

efficiam ut tuum in me officium ad te non sine faenore redeat: I will make sure that your good offices to me do not return to you without interest.

faeneratum hoc beneficium tibi pulchre dices: you will say that this good deed has brought a splendid rate of interest.

dispeream nisi beneficium istud tibi conduplicaverit: I'll be damned if he does not double up the value of this good deed.

statim regerere beneficium est nolentis debere: to reciprocate a kindness at once is the act of a man who does not wish to be in anyone's debt.

hoc non est referre beneficium sed refutare: this is not returning a kindness, but rejecting it.

certemus mutuis inter nos officiis: let us compete in doing each other service.

beneficium ultro citroque commeare debet: a kindness should keep travelling back and forth.

cum faenore reponendum quod acceperis: benefits received should be repaid with interest.

quisquis grate munus accepit iam gratiam retulit: he who receives a gift with grateful heart has already offered thanks.

retaliare 'to retaliate' is only used in a bad sense, for example, *retaliare iniuriam* 'make retaliation for injury.' Practically all the verbs mentioned above can be used in a bad sense as well as a good one: *respondere malefactis* 'answer one bad turn with another'; *reponere, pensare, remetiri, referre iniuriam* 'return an injury,' etc. *retaliare* is found in a good sense in Gellius, and there is nothing against this in the nature of the word itself, but such a usage is rather uncommon.

85 / Origin

haud dubito quin haec ab amore quodam in me singulari proficiscantur: I have no doubt but that all this proceeds from a singular affection towards myself.

universum hoc malorum agmen e bello nobis natum est: this entire string of misfortunes was produced for us by the war.

* * * * *

3 pulchre dices] Terence *Phormio* 493: *faeneratum istuc beneficium pulchre tibi dices*

5 conduplicaverit] Cf Terence *Phormio* 516: *idem hic tibi, quod boni promeritus fueris, conduplicaverit.*

17 gratiam retulit] See Seneca *De beneficiis* 2.30.2: *qui libenter beneficium accepit reddidit.*

23 Gellius] 20.1.16

hinc omnis illa simultas inter eos orta est: hence arose the whole of that famous quarrel between them.

tu malorum omnium auctor: you are the author of all these ills.

cupiditas pecuniae vitiorum omnium parens: the love of money is the mother of all vices.

invidia totius huius odii seminarium fuit: envy was the soil in which all this hatred took root.

natura nobis parvulos igniculos dedit: nature has bestowed on us little tiny sparks ...

hinc omnis illa turba venit: hence comes all that confusion.

hinc fluxit: hence has flowed

hinc manat omne quo beati reddimur: hence emanates everything by which we are made truly happy.

Graeco fonte cadunt (Horace): drop from a Greek fountain-head

hinc scatet omnis illa vitiorum colluvies: it is from here that this filthy flood of vice gushes forth.

his fontibus totus ille tumultus rerum extitit: from this source all this civil commotion has come into being.

hinc surgunt odia: it is from this that hatreds arise.

hinc lites proveniunt: from this disputes develop.

hinc veniunt iurgia: hence come hard words.

ab his exordiis Romana nobilitas ducitur: from these origins is Rome's nobility derived.

omnium magnarum rerum a diis immortalibus principia ducuntur (Cicero, in his speech *In Vatinium*): the inception of all great achievements is derived ultimately from the immortal gods.

regibus ortus: of royal lineage

Roma oriundus: a man of Roman origin

atavis edite regibus: scion of an ancient line of kings

maximis prognatus ducibus: descendant of mighty leaders

sate sanguine divum: o thou begotten of the race of gods

ex his pullulant odia: from this burgeons hatred.

gliscunt invidiae: ill will spreads.

subnascitur simultas: enmity springs up in succession.

fruticantur dissidia: the weed of discord puts forth its shoots.

silvescunt factiones: the thicket of faction springs up.

* * * * *

8 igniculos dedit] Cicero *Tusculan Disputations* 3.2
14 Horace] *Ars poetica* 53: *cadent*
24 Cicero] *In Vatinium* 14
29 edite regibus] Horace *Odes* 1.1.1
31 sanguine divum] Virgil *Aeneid* 6.125

illa e philosophorum fontibus haurienda: this draught must be drawn from philosophers' springs.

reliqua e poetis petenda: the rest you must look for in the poets.

86 / Compensating

quod corporis viribus deest, id ingenii dolis exaequa: make up with cunning of mind the deficiencies of your physical strength.

quod corporis formae detractum est, id animi dotibus natura pensavit: nature has compensated with endowment of mind the absence of physical beauty.

tu opulentior, nos eruditiores atque ita tecum paria fecimus: you have more money, we have more education, and so we balance each other.

absentiam nostram crebris litteris sarciamus: let us write often to repair the breach of our absence.

quod hactenus cessatum est, id oportet diligentia recuperare: you must recover by application the loss incurred by your earlier slackness.

quod illius stultitia peccatum est id tua sapientia restituas oportet: you must correct by your good sense the errors of his stupidity.

quod illius inscitia admissum id oportet ut tua prudentia redimas: it is appropriate that you offset by your common sense the consequences of his foolishness.

supplendum diligentia quod ingenio deest: one must make up for lack of ability by hard work.

quod corpori detractum id ingenii dotibus accessit: the gifts which nature did not give his body were added to his mind.

studio reponendum quod negligentia praeteritum est: one must recover by application opportunities lost through negligence.

quod ademptum est fortunae, id ingenii dotibus additum est: what he lost in worldly wealth was added to the endowment of his mind.

quantum corporis viribus deest, tantum animi virtutibus superest: the powers of the intellect are so much the stronger as bodily strength is weak.

natura quod alibi detrahit alibi reddit: what nature takes away in one place she restores in another.

quod suis eripit hoc hospitibus accumulat: what he snatches from his family's hands he heaps upon his guests.

ingenio formae damna rependo meae (Ovid): beauty of mind makes good the plainness of my face.

* * * * *

38 Ovid] *Heroides* 15.32

famae dispendium pecuniae compendio resarcit: he mends a lost reputation by the acquisition of wealth.
famae iacturam pecuniario lucro solatur: he consoles a damaged reputation with financial success.

87 / Suitability

quaere uxorem aptam tuis moribus, aptam ad tuos mores: look for a wife who suits your ways.
amicum delige tuis moribus appositum, accomodatum, ad tuos mores: choose a friend appropriate to, according to, after your own character.
amicum delige qui tuis moribus, ad tuos mores, conveniat: choose a friend who fits in with your ways.
non est natura compositus ad artem poeticam: he is not qualified by nature for the poetic art.
ostentationi compositum (a phrase of Quintilian's): organized for display
iuri magis an aequo sit appositus (Quintilian): whether he has more regard for the letter of the law or for justice (*magis appositus* 'more adapted' here being equivalent to *propensior* 'more inclined')
constatque rebus ad faciendam fidem appositis (Quintilian): it consists of material particularly adapted to the purpose of generating confidence.
ad mathematica videtur esse propensior: he seems to have more of a propensity towards mathematics.
vir maximis rebus natus, ad maximas res natus: a man born for great things
vir factus ad huius nequitiam: a man made for this fellow's nefarious schemes
ad huius mores factus fictus sculptus esse videtur: he seems made, moulded, and modelled to match this fellow's ways.
adeo ad huius mores quadrat: he so squares with his ways.
oratio non est naturae consentanea: the speech is not consistent with the person's character.
facta non respondent orationi: the facts do not correspond to the statements.
haec non competunt in senem: this does not befit an old man.
haec non competunt viro gravi: this is not appropriate to a man of standing.

* * * * *

9 uxorem aptam] *Adagia* I viii 1
17 Quintilian's] 8.3.11
18 Quintilian] 4.3.11
21 Quintilian] 5.8.1

non haeret in Catonem huiuscemodi crimen: an accusation of this sort does not stick on Cato.

non consentiunt tui mores cum huius moribus: your ways and his do not agree.

non concinunt tua atque huius studia: your interests and his do not harmonize.

non concordat huius institutum cum tuo: his way of life and yours do not accord.

concinnus transitus: a neat transition

concinna digressio: an elegant digression

ista non cohaerent, non consistunt: that is not coherent, not consistent.

non cadit in sapientem animi perturbatio: it is inappropriate to the sage to experience any disturbance of the emotions.

non recipit tua simplicitas adulationis suspicionem: the simplicity of your nature does not admit the suspicion of flattery.

non congruunt litterae cum studio pecuniae: literature and the pursuit of wealth are incompatible.

non bene conveniunt, nec in una sede morantur / maiestas et amor: Royal dignity cannot combine, nor share its throne / With love.

88 / Getting rid of

hic mihi est ablegandus aliquo: I must send him off somewhere.

puerum hunc prius amanda quopiam: get this boy out of the way to some place or other first.

hunc Argum aliquo si potes amolire: get rid of this Argus somewhere if you can.

non possum hunc amovere quopiam: I cannot remove him to some place or other.

ego hunc neque uti amittam a me neque ut retineam scio: I do not know how to let him go or hold him tight.

non possum memet ex hoc grege nebulonum excutere: I cannot shake myself free of this gang of ne'er-do-wells.

* * * * *

12 cadit in sapientem] See Cicero *Tusculan Disputations* 3.7.

18 maiestas et amor] Ovid *Metamorphoses* 2.846–7

24 ablegandus] Cf Terence *Hecyra* 413: *aliquo mihist / hinc ablegandus.*

27 Argus] The hundred-eyed watchman, used for an astute person

31 retineam scio] Cf Terence *Phormio* 507: *nam neque quo pacto a me amittam neque ut retineam scio,* where the speaker has 'caught a Tartar.'

hinc utcumque est extrudendus aliquo: somehow or other he must be pushed off somewhere.

89 / Departing

rus hinc abeo: I am going away from here to the country.
rus hinc concedo: I am leaving here for the country.
discedo, abscedo, decedo: I remove, withdraw, depart.
Galliam repeto, inde Britanniam aditurus: I am returning to France; and intend to go on from there to Britain.
in Italiam iter instituit: he set off for Italy.
tum Neapolim cogitabam: I was intending for Naples.
apparas iter: you are getting ready for the road.
adornas profectionem: you are making preparations for your departure.
componis sarcinas: you are collecting your baggage.
ingressus est viam: he set foot on the road.
quo paras proficisci? where are you getting ready to go?
quo paras profectionem? to what place are you making ready your departure?
quo tendis? where are you making for?
quo te, Moeri, pedes? whither, Moeris, so hot-foot?
quo tenetis iter? whither do you hold your course?
quonam iter est? whither lies your road?
rus me confero: I am taking myself off to the country.
domum me recipio: I am going back home.
domum revertor: I am returning home.
certum est in patriam revolare: I have made up my mind to hurry back to my own country.
certum est veteres amicos revisere: I have made up my mind to visit my friends of long ago again.
redde te patriae: restore yourself to the fatherland.
fac recurras in patriam: be sure to hurry back to your own land.
restitue te tuis: take yourself back to your own kin.

* * * * *

13 cogitabam] An elliptical construction used by Cicero in letters; in *Ciceronianus* (LB I 986F), Erasmus mocks those who imitate it to excess.
16 sarcinas] Cf Varro *Res rusticae* 1.1.1: *ut sarcinas conligam*, said of an old man tidying up in readiness for death.
19 profectionem] Cf Caesar *Bellum civile* 1.27.2: *profectionem parare incipit*.
22 pedes] Virgil *Eclogues* 9.1

fac te quam primum reducem videamus: mind we see you back as soon as possible.

ad rem inutile est subinde movere castra: it does not help the situation to be continually moving camp.

haud temere ditescunt qui crebro vertunt solum: not easily do they grow rich who constantly change their abode.

90 / Effort

da operam ut convalescas: put your mind to getting better.

cura ut revalescas: take care to recover.

enitere ut cum parentibus in gratiam redeas: endeavour to be reconciled with your parents.

adnitere totis nervis ut in virum tuo genere dignum evadas: strain every nerve to become a man worthy of your family.

illud totis viribus agito, ut parentum expectationi facias satis: pursue with all your powers the goal of fulfilling your parents' hopes.

pro virili conatus sum, pro mea virili, pro viribus: I tried to the best of my ability.

hoc unum stude, ut te in regis benevolentiam insinues: make it your one aim to insinuate yourself into the king's favour.

litteris incumbas: you are to apply yourself to literature.

in haec studia incumbite: apply yourselves to these studies.

ad id eluctare: struggle to that end.

ad hoc invigila: be vigilant to this end.

efficies si modo advigilaris: you will manage it provided you keep your wits about you.

vigilandum est qui sua negotia velit tempori conficere: That man must surely early wake / Who will his business in good time complete.

manibus pedibusque connitere: strive with might and main [literally, with hands and feet]

id unum elaborat: that is the one thing for which he is working.

eo velis equisque contendit: he makes for the place with ship and horse.

huc velis remisque festinat: he is hurrying here with sail and oar [i.e., with all possible speed].

* * * * *

29 tempori conficere] Cf Plautus *Rudens* 921: *vigilare decet hominem qui volt sua temperi conficere officia.*

31 connitere] Cf Terence *Andria* 161: *manibus pedibusque obnixe omnia / facturum.*

34 velis equisque] *Adagia* I iv 17

35 velis remisque] *Adagia* I iv 18

hoc studium parvi properemus et ampli (Horace): small folk or considerable, we should / Press on with this endeavour.

ut doctus evadas, dies noctibus continua: join day to night to become a scholar.

in ea re vehementer est sudatum: much sweat was expended over that.

in id plurimum laboris exhaustum, exanclatum: a vast amount of toil was endured, expended in this cause.

rem perdifficilem conamur: we are attempting an extremely difficult feat.

rem arduam molimur: we are toiling at a hard task.

summo nixu: with supreme effort

summa ope: with all our ability

summa vi: with all our strength

quantum potes adlabora: work at this as hard as you can.

pecuniae causa nihil non tum facit, tum patitur: there is nothing he will not do or endure for the sake of money.

91 / Extricating and involving

ubi his malis emersero: when I emerge from these misfortunes

ubi his turbis memet extricavero: when I extricate myself from all this trouble

ubi ex his negotiis me expedivero: when I disentangle myself from these problems

cum ex his negotiorum exiero labyrinthis: when I find the way out of this maze of problems

simulatque his me tumultibus exolvero: as soon as I get myself free of all this confusion

ubi his e nugis memet excussero: when I get myself shaken free of these foolish pursuits

siquando licebit memet ex his negotiorum fluctibus emoliri: if ever I manage to heave myself out of this sea of troubles

si licebit ab his curis discedere: if I manage to leave these cares behind

si continget liberari, levari: if I am lucky enough to be freed, relieved

si quando ab iis negotiis meipsum vindicavero, asseruero, absolvero: if

* * * * *

1 Horace] *Epistles* 1.3.28
3 dies noctibus] See Seneca *Controversiae* 1 preface 14: *iungebantur noctibus dies.*
6 exanclatum] Literally 'drain to the dregs,' then 'endure'; a word found mainly in early Latin writers; also Cicero *Tusculan Disputations* 1.118: *cum exanclavisset omnes labores*

ever I assert my freedom, set myself free, liberate myself from these cares
ubi ex iis malis eluctatus fuero: when I struggle clear of these misfortunes
ubi ex his calamitatibus enataro: when I swim clear of these calamities
implicatus malis: ensnared by misfortune
involutus negotiis: involved in affairs   5
districtus curis: distraught with worries
occupatus negotiis: occupied with business
distentus: distracted
distendi, distineri negotiis: be distraught, distracted, by conflicting concerns   10
distorqueri curis: be tortured with worry
immersus, obrutus, opertus negotiis: immersed, overwhelmed, swamped
with problems
intricatus, impeditus, illigatus, obvinctus, dispunctus, obsaeptus, onera-
tus, negotiis: entangled, ensnared, encumbered, tied up, marked down to,   15
hedged in, weighed down with responsibilities
oppressus, oppletus: oppressed, stuffed with
tot me res circumvallant: so many things fence me round.
tot me pericula circumstant, circumsistunt, obsaepiunt, cingunt, obsident,
premunt, urgent: so many dangers surround, invest, fence in, encircle,   20
besiege, press on, bear hard upon me.

92 / End or goal
                                                                           25
Stoici in una virtute summum bonum constituunt: the Stoics locate the
supreme good in virtue alone.
Epicurus felicitatem voluptate metitur: Epicurus measures happiness by
pleasure.
Peripatetici usu virtutis beatitudinem definiunt: the Peripatetics define the 30
good life as the practice of virtue.
Herillus in scientia summum bonum collocat: Herillus establishes the supreme good in knowledge.
quidam in indolentia boni finem posuerunt: some have placed the limits of
the good in absence of pain.   35
est qui in pecunia felicitatem sitam esse existimet: there are persons who

* * * * *

14 dispunctus] *dispungere*, a book-keeping term, 'mark off, check'; for example,
   Seneca *De beneficiis* 4.32.4: *apud me istae expensorum acceptorumque rationes
   dispunguntur*
18 circumvallant] Cf Terence *Adelphi* 302: *tot res repente circumvallant se*.

consider that happiness lies in money.

maxima pars hominum spectat utilitatem, pauci sibi proponunt honestum: the majority of mankind has its eye on the advantageous; only a few have the honourable as their goal.

huc omnes conatus tui spectant ut ditescas: your every effort is directed to the sole end of getting rich.

huc respicis, huc tendis: it is this that you have in view, to this goal that you are making.

omnes spes meas in te uno fixi: all my hopes I have founded on you alone.

quidam famae serviunt, alii lucri rationem habent: some are slaves of reputation, others think only of gain.

hic voluptatem ubique sequitur, ille captat gloriam: this man pursues pleasure in every circumstance; that one is out to win glory.

hic ad privatam utilitatem omnia refert: this man refers everything to his personal advantage.

huc reliqua omnia sunt conferenda: everything else must be assessed by this standard.

huc omnia illa pertinent, spectant: all those other things relate, have regard to this.

quorsum haec tam putida tendunt? (Horace): what is the aim of these disagreeable remarks?

in hoc etiam popularem laudem petit: even in this he is seeking popular acclaim.

admirationem Aristoteles maxime petendam putat: Aristotle considers admiration very worthy of pursuit.

illud genus ostentationi compositum solam petit audientium voluptatem: this style, being organized for display, has no aim but the pleasure of the audience.

negotiatorum unicus scopus est pecunia: the one goal of businessmen is money.

93 / Such is his impudence

si crimen illi palam obicias, sat scio, qua est impudentia, *or* cuius est impudentiae, *or* ea est hominis impudentia, infitias ibit: if you were to charge him openly with it, I know quite well, such is the fellow's impudence, he will deny it.

* * * * *

20 Horace] *Satires* 2.7.21
26 audientium voluptatem] Quintilian 8.3.11

sat scio, ut est impudens, infitias ibit: I know quite well, impudent as he is, he will deny it.

sat scio, pro solita sua impudentia, infitiabitur: I know quite well, in view of his usual impudence, he will reject the charge (though this last expression is not so vehement as the others).

adeo est impudens ut mox sit infitiaturus: he is so impudent that he is going to refute it immediately.

ut nunc sunt mores: as customs are now (i.e., in view of the ways of the present generation)

ut est barbarorum ingenium: as the abilities of savages go (i.e., in view of the nature of savage minds)

94 / Too ... to

vir melior est quam qui velit mentiri, simplicior quam qui possit: he is too fine a man to want to lie, too straightforward to be able to.

superbior est quam ut velit doceri, stupidior quam ut possit discere: he is too proud to be prepared to be taught, too stupid to be able to learn.

adeo pauper est ut nec obolum habeat, adeo ignavus ut malit inedia perire quam artem discere: he is so poor that he has not got a brass farthing, and is so lazy he would prefer to die of hunger rather than learn a trade.

sic de me meritus es ut tibi succensere non debeam, sic mihi carus ut irasci ne si velim quidem possim: you have conferred such benefits on me that I ought not to feel the slightest anger towards you, and you are so dear to me that I could not be angry with you even if I wanted to.

melius de me meritus es quam ut tibi possim succensere: you have done me too great a service for me to be able to be angry with you.

95 / All's well

bene res habet, bene se res habet, bene habet, bene est: all's well, things are fine.

optime est: things are excellent.

bene tibi habent principia: things are starting off well for you.

optimo in loco res est: things are in an excellent position.

peiore in loco res esse non potest: things could not be in a worse position.

quonam in statu res sunt tuae? how are things with you?

* * * * *

38 peiore in loco] Terence *Adelphi* 344: *peiore res loco non potis est esse*

96 / In my opinion

mea quidem sententia, pro mea quidem sententia: in my opinion, at any rate

ut ego quidem sentio: as I see it, at any rate

ut mea fert opinio: as far as my opinion goes

meo quidem animo (a Plautine phrase): to my mind

meo iudicio: in my judgment

ut mihi quidem videtur: as it seems to me, at any rate

ni fallor: unless I am mistaken

si quid iudico: if I have any powers of judgment

meo quidem suffragio M. Tullius vicit Demosthenem: on my vote Cicero beats Demosthenes.

tuo calculo victus est: on your verdict he lost.

MORE THAN

audivi plus milies, audivi plus quam milies: I have heard it more than a thousand times.

calesces plus satis, *or* plusquam satis: you will get more than hot enough.

Before a numeral or an adverb *quam* can be inserted or omitted; before a verb there is no choice; it must be inserted:

sapit plus quam expedit: he knows more than is convenient.

mulier plus quam decet erudita, plus quam necesse facunda: a woman more educated than is suitable, more eloquent than is necessary

vixit annos plures quam decem, *or* plures decem: he lived more years than ten.

plus quingentos colaphos infregit mihi: he rained more than five hundred blows about my ears. [This could also be expressed by] *plus quam quingentos,* or *plures quingentis.*

amplius quadraginta (Suetonius): more than forty

So there are four ways of expressing 'more than' with numerals. *amplius* and also *non amplius* can be put first, last, or in the middle:

* * * * *

7 Plautine] For example, *Aulularia* 539, *Bacchides* 102; etc

16 MORE THAN ... with numerals] The passage to line 31 transferred from the end of chap 32 (= 33) in *1514*

17 audivi plus milies] Terence *Eunuchus* 422: *plus milies audivi*

19 calesces plus satis] Terence *Eunuchus* 85

27 infregit mihi] Terence *Adelphi* 199

30 Suetonius] *Augustus* 72.1

32 *amplius* and also ... *plures ducentis*] The passage to 475:30 added in *1534* (LB I 54E–F)

LB I 54C

cum enim Syracusis amplius centum cives Romani cognoscerent (Cicero):
though more than one hundred Roman citizens at Syracuse knew him.
amplius horas quattuor fortissime pugnaverunt (Caesar): they fought with
great courage for more than four hours.
non amplius quattuordecim cohortes Luceriam coegi (Pompey writing to
Lucius Domitius): I have concentrated not more than fourteen cohorts at
Luceria.
(In these three examples it precedes.)
sexaginta annos natus es, ut conicio, et eo amplius (Terence): you are sixty, I
should guess, or more.
Laodiceae viginti pondo, paulo amplius (Cicero): at Laodicea, twenty
pounds or a little more
(Here it is put after.)
tres pateat caeli spatium non amplius ulnas (Virgil): three ells extends the
space of heaven, no more.
(Here it is inserted.)
     plus is used in much the same way: it precedes in these two examples:
ac tecum plus anno vixit in Gallia (Cicero, in his *Pro Quinctio*): and he lived
with you for more than a year in Gaul.
sed non plus duobus aut tribus mensibus (Cicero again, in his *Pro Plancio*):
but not more than two or three months
It is inserted here:
dies triginta aut plus eo in navi fui (Terence): thirty days or more than that
was I in the boat.
It is put last in:
centum desiderati sunt, aut plus eo: a hundred were required or more.
     Accordingly, 'more than two hundred were required' can be variously
expressed as follows: *amplius ducenti desiderati sunt; ducenti et eo amplius
desiderati sunt; ducenti desiderati sunt et eo amplius; desiderati sunt plus quam
ducenti; desiderati sunt plures ducentis.*

* * * * *

1 Cicero] *Verrines* 1.14
3 Caesar] *Bellum Gallicum* 4.37.3: *horis*
5 Pompey] Cicero *Ad Atticum* 8.12c.2
9 Terence] *Heautontimorumenos* 63
11 Cicero] *Pro Flacco* 68
14 Virgil] *Eclogues* 3.105
18 Cicero] *Pro Quinctio* 41
23 Terence] *Hecyra* 421

LB I 54E

AT THE MOST, AT THE LEAST

semel hominem salutavi, aut ad summum bis: I said 'Good day' to the man
once, or at the most twice.
ut multum, ut plurimum: at most
non minus: no less
saltem: at least
ut minimum: at the least
ut minimum dicam: to say the least
non amplius cum plurimum quam septem horas dormiebat (Suetonius): he
never slept more than seven hours at the most.

97 / Humouring

mos gerendus est patri, morigerandum est patri: you must fall in with your
father's wishes.
obsequendum est patri: you must humour your father.
patri obsecundandum: you must comply with your father.
patri concedendum, inserviendum: you must give way to, submit to your
father.
observiendum paternis moribus: you must fit in with your father's ways.
accommoda te paternis moribus: adapt yourself to your father's ways.
praebe te illis ad tempus: fall in with them for the time being.
attempera te moribus omnium: conform to the general pattern of behaviour.

98 / Asking

maiorem in modum te rogo: in all seriousness do I ask you.
etiam atque etiam oro: again and again I entreat you.
obsecro te atque obtestor: I beg and beseech you.
illud unum abs te magnopere peto contendoque: this one thing do I earnestly desire and urge of you.
illud a me vehementer contendebat: that he besought from me most passionately.

* * * * *

1 AT THE MOST ... say the least] Transferred from the end of chap 32 (=33) in 1514
9 Suetonius] *Augustus* 78.1
15 mos gerendus] Cf Terence *Eunuchus* 188: *mos gerundust Thaidi; Adelphi* 218: *si
... adulescenti esses morigeratus.*

efflagitasti cottidianis conviciis: you have demanded it with daily clamour-
ings.
imploravit opes hominis: he implored the man's assistance.
eblanditus est favorem: he coaxed the favour out of him.

One finds *exambiit* 'solicited' in some writers.

extorsit potius quam exoravit: he forced it out of him rather than prevailed
upon him.
at istud poscere est non rogare: that is claiming, not asking.
flagitabant verius quam orabant: they demanded rather than requested.

99 / Forgiving

remisere multam: they remitted the fine.
hanc unam ignosce culpam: pardon this one fault.
remisit offensam: he excused the offence.
condonamus admissum: we forgive the wrong you have done.
condonamus argentum quod habes (Terence): we make you a present of the
money you have.
condonare creditum (Sallust): abolish debt
da veniam iuvenilibus erratis: be lenient to the mistakes of youth.
iurisiurandi gratiam facere pupillus non potest: a ward cannot grant dis-
pensation from taking an oath. This example comes from the *Pandects*.
The same usage is found in Sallust:
ceterum Boccho quoniam paenitet delicti gratiam facit: yet, since Bocchus
expresses repentance, they pardon him for his offence.
And in Suetonius:
coniurandi gratiam fecit: he granted them pardon for conspiring.
ad quaedam vitia convenit connivere: it is best to turn a blind eye to some
faults.

* * * * *

 5 some writers] Late writers such as Cyprian, Symmachus, Ammianus
18 Terence] *Phormio* 947
20 Sallust] *Epistula ad Caesarem* 1 (*Oratio*) 2.6
23 *Pandects*] Part of the *Digest*, a codification of Roman law prepared for the
   emperor Justinian, which formed the basis of later studies in civil law. It
   consisted of extracts from earlier authorities such as Scaevola; this extract
   12.2.32.
24 Sallust] *Jugurtha* 104.5
27 Suetonius] *Augustus* 17.2

100 / Annulling

rescindere conventa: rescind an agreement
abrogare legem: repeal a law
abdicare legem: reject a bill
antiquare, abolere legem: vote against, abolish a law
obsolescere 'go out of use' is intransitive.
sustollere legem: remove a law
irritare pacta: irritate, invalidate a settlement
in integrum restituere: restore the original legal situation
mutare pacta: alter an agreement
oblitterare legem: erase a law
haec lex abiit in desuetudinem: this law has fallen into disuse.
Pliny used the phrase *exolescere metum dominorum* 'fear of overlords becomes obsolete' in his *Letters; exolescere* here is the equivalent of *extingui,*
intercidere 'be done away with, disappear.'
nusquam tui beneficii memoria apud me intermorietur: at no time shall the
memory of your services to me die away.
deposuit imperium: he laid down his command.
abdicavit magistratum: he resigned his magistracy.
abdicatus a magistratu (Sallust): relieved of his magistracy by resignation

101 / Adorning

comere: dress up
expolire: polish
perpolire: put a gloss on
exornare: adorn
venustare: beautify
picturare: embroider
honestare: embellish
pigmenta: colouring
flosculi: ornaments

* * * * *

14 Pliny] *Epistles* 1.4.4: *nam mitium dominorum apud servos ipsa consuetudine metus exolescit*
21 Sallust] *Catilina* 47.3; modern editors prefer *abdicato magistratu*, which some old texts also read.
24 Chapter 101] These are all metaphorical terms used in the criticism and discussion of varieties of style by Cicero and Quintilian.

LB I 55C

lecythi: paint box
veneres: charms
venustas: loveliness
lepos: attractiveness
nitor: elegance   5
gratia: grace
decus: comeliness
lenocinia: allurements
emblemata: inlay
compositio: arrangement   10
colores: highlights
myrothecia: scent-bottles
fuci: false colours
phalerae: decorations
dignitas: dignity   15
cultus: style
polities: refinement

102 / During dinner   20

inter cenam (which Suetonius and Seneca use), *inter cenandum, super cenam, cenantibus nobis, in cena* all mean 'during dinner.' *inter iocum* (Suetonius again), *inter iocandum*, 'during the fun, jokingly.' Suetonius also uses *inter conventum* 'in a company,' *inter poenam* 'while the punishment was being 25 inflicted,' *per iocum* 'by way of a joke.'
inter pocula: while they were in their cups
inter potandum: during the drinking

                                                                   30
103 / After dinner

post cenam, a cena, sub cenam all mean 'after dinner.' *sub* [literally, under, close up to] means either 'shortly before' or 'immediately after':

    * * * * *

    22 Suetonius] For example, *Augustus* 71.2
    22 Seneca] For example, *De beneficiis* 3.27.1
    23 Suetonius] *Julius* 4.2
    24 Suetonius] *Galba* 5.1: *inter conventum*
    26 *per iocum*] Suetonius *Nero* 6.2

    LB I 55D

sub haec lectae sunt tuae litterae (Cicero): immediately after, your letter was read.

a tuo reditu, post tuum reditum: after your return

104 / Similitude

est et diversarum rerum quaedam inter se similitudo, affinitas, cognatio, vicinia: even diverse things have a certain similitude, affinity, connection, closeness.

his finitima, confinia sunt illa: that has a proximity to this.

simiae figura multum ad hominis formam accedit: the shape of a monkey approaches very close to the human form.

puro tamen fonti quam flumini propior: yet nearer to a pure spring than to a river

non multum a tuis moribus haec abludit imago: this picture's range does not fall so far short of your own ways.

huc alludit illa Terentiana sententia: it is to this that the well-known Terentian saying makes playful allusion.

Virgilianam dictionem aemulatur, exprimit, refert: he is imitating, copying, echoing Virgilian diction.

haud multum abest, dissidet, discrepat a tuis moribus: it is not very far, not very different, not very discrepant from your own behaviour.

ab hac ratione non multum abhorret (Quintilian): it is not very different from this procedure.

eiusdem generis est et illud: this too is of the same sort.

eiusdem farinae (a proverbial expression): of the same kidney [literally, of the same flour]

eiusdem notae: of the same brand

eiusdem classis: of the same squad

mei loci atque ordinis hominem: a man of my own rank and class

ex aliquo circulo (a Ciceronian phrase): from some social circle

* * * * *

1 Cicero] Cf *Ad familiares* 10.16.1: *sub eas statim recitatae sunt tuae.*

6 Similitude] Cf Quintilian 8.4.12.

16 abludit imago] Horace *Satires* 2.3.320: *Haec a te non multum abludit imago*

24 Quintilian] See 9.2.78.

27 proverbial] Occurs in Persius 5.115; *Adagia* III v 44

31 mei loci atque ordinis hominem] Terence *Eunuchus* 234

32 Ciceronian] *De oratore* 1.159

e sinu suo (Cicero and Plutarch): one of his bosom friends
ex eo numero est: he is of that number.
ex illo conventu quadruplatorum (Cicero in his fourth speech *In Verrem*):
one of that corporation of tricksters
e suis gregalibus (Cicero again): one of his comrades   5
sub hac facie latet adulatio: flattery lurks behind this facade.
plerumque vitia virtutis personam induunt ac virtutis simulacrum re-
praesentant: usually vices don the mask of virtue and present the semblance of virtue.
sub virtutis specie, virtutis titulo, virtutis praetextu: under the appearance 10
of virtue, under the title of virtue, under the pretext of virtue
sub imagine pietatis: under the guise of piety
sub umbra pietatis: under the sham of piety
patrem ore refert: he is his father over again in looks.
parentem moribus exprimit: his ways are just like his father's.   15
patruum nomine reddit: he is named after his uncle.
avum voce repraesentat: his voice recalls his grandfather's.
patronum imitatur oculis: he has the same kind of eyes as his patron.
amitam nulla re prorsus exhibet: she is not at all like her aunt.
alter Cicero, alter Hercules: a second Cicero, a second Hercules   20
faciem mentita Lyciscae: donning the mask of Lycisca
formata in admirationem (Suetonius): pretending astonishment [literally,
arranging her features into astonishment]
vultu ad hilaritatem composito: contriving an expression of cheerfulness
praetexere, prae se ferre: make a pretence of   25
ante se gerit: makes a show of
effigie pietatis: under the semblance of piety
dissimilis huic, dissimilis huius [with dative or genitive case]: different
from this
non absimilis facie Tiberio: not unlike Tiberius in features   30
The same writer also uses *adsimilis* for *similis* 'resembling.'
　　　* * * * *
　　1 Cicero] *Catilinarians* 2.22
　　1 Plutarch] *Pompey* 25, where Erasmus' text may have read ἐκ τῶν κόλπων;
　　　most texts read εἰς τοῦ Πομπηίου συνήθων (as do the Venice text of 1519 and
　　　the Florentine of 1517).
　　3 Cicero] *Verrines* 2.22
　　5 Cicero] *De haruspicum responso* 53; see *Adagia* III vi 86, which deals with
　　　conventus also.
　21 Lyciscae] Juvenal 6.122: *titulum mentita Lyciscae*
　22 Suetonius] *Claudius* 37.2
　30 Tiberio] Suetonius *Otho* 1.2
　31 same writer] Suetonius *Galba* 18.1

105 / Lending and borrowing

mutuum dare: make a loan
mutuo dare: provide on loan
mutuare: borrow   5
commodato dare: oblige with a loan
commodare: lend, put at someone's disposal
utendum dare, accipere: lend, borrow something
accipit usurariam (Plautus): takes on loan
opera commodaticia praestat operas mutuas: one good turn deserves   10
another.
mutuum muli scabunt: mules scratch each other, [i.e., you scratch my back,
I'll scratch yours].

                                                                            15

106 / Deceiving

imposuimus reipublicae: we have imposed on the nation.
fefellit nos: he has deceived us.
decepit, circumvenit adolescentem: he tricked, cheated the young man.   20
circumscripsit, circumduxit (legal terms): circumvented, misled
verba dare mihi difficile est: it is difficult to get me to swallow a story.
si senseris eos fucum velle facere: if you get the impression that they are
trying to throw dust in your eyes
imposturam fecit, imposturam passus est: carried out, was the victim of, an   25
imposture
delusit, elusit: played false, made game of
frustratus est nos sperato lucro: he has cheated us out of the profit we
expected.
non te fraudabo debita gloria: I will not rob you of the glory you have   30
earned.
technae, doli, fuci, praestigiae, vafrities, versutia, astus, astutia, fraus:
trick, guile, deception, jugglery, slyness, artfulness, cunning, astuteness,
fraud

        * * * * *

    9 Plautus] Cf *Amphitryo* 498: *uxore usuraria*.
   12 mutuum muli scabunt] *Adagia* I vii 96
   18 reipublicae] See 324:5.
   23 fucum velle facere] Cf Quintus Cicero *Commentariolum petitionis* 9.35: *si eum ...*
      audieris fucum ut dicitur facere aut senseris.

os mihi sublitum est: I was bamboozled [literally, I got my face smeared].

in fraudem illexit, pellexit: he enticed me, inveigled me into this trap.

arte me tractavit: she played me skilfully.

dolo mecum egit: he dealt cunningly with me.

in specie: to all appearances – a Ciceronian usage: praeclara classis in specie, sed inops et infirma: a splendid fleet to all appearances, but badly equipped and weak

quod si mea fiat captione: if this were to happen to my loss

absit omnis captio: away with all sophistry

cur igitur vos inducitis in eas captiones quas numquam explicetis? (Cicero): why are you tying yourselves up in mental knots you can never undo?

107 / Be friends

utor patre familiariter: I am on friendly terms with his father.

est mihi cum illo artissima necessitudo: I am very closely associated with him.

sum illi summa familiaritate coniunctus: I am on terms of great familiarity with him.

sum illi amicus: I am a friend of his.

summa mihi cum illo familiaritas intercedit: there exists a considerable intimacy between myself and him.

multus mihi cum homine quondam usus fuit: at one time I saw a great deal of the man.

mutua quaedam benevolentia iam pridem inter nos est: there has long been a feeling of mutual good will between us.

imperator Iugurtham in amicis habebat (Sallust): the general numbered Jugurtha among his friends.

108 / Hoping

spero fore: I hope that

nonnulla spes est fore: there is some hope that

* * * * *

1 sublitum est] See Plautus *Captivi* 783.

2 illexit] See Plautus *Miles gloriosus* 1435.

3 tractavit] Cf Terence *Heautontimorumenos* 366.

5 Ciceronian] *Verrines* 5.86

10 Cicero] *De divinatione* 2.41

28 Sallust] *Jugurtha* 7.6

LB I 56C

venio in spem: I am coming to hope.
vocor in spem: I am encouraged to hope.
erectus in spem: roused to hope
concipio spem de te optimam: I have the highest hopes of you.
nonnulla me spes habet: a considerable feeling of hope pervades me.   5
maxima teneor spe: I am filled with the great hope.
magna me spes tenet: a great feeling of hope pervades me.
adducor in spem: I am led to hope.
nonnulla me spes cepit: a certain hope has come over me.
spei nonnihil affulsit, arridet, blanditur: a ray of hope has shone out, smiles   10
on us, encourages us.
omnia summa mihi de te promitto: I am making the highest promises to
myself concerning you.
is est de quo tibi possis omnia polliceri boni viri officia: he is the sort of
person from whom you can promise yourself all the kind offices a good man   15
will perform.
nihil mediocre de te tui cives exspectant: your fellow citizens expect nothing ordinary from you.
inicere spem: inspire hope
sollicitare spe: tempt with hope   20
ostendere spem: hold out the hope
ostendit futurum: holds out future prospects
ducimur spe: we are led by the hope.
lactamur spe: we are beguiled by hope.
ad comoediae gratiam Latini ne aspirarunt quidem: the Latin writers did   25
not even aspire to the charms of comedy.
ad eam laudem quam volumus aspirare non possunt (Cicero): they cannot
approach that praise we desire.
ut omnia bona in spe haberet (Sallust): so as to have all that was good in
prospect (i.e., there was nothing he could not hope for).   30

109 / Word for word

ad verbum edidicit: he learned it word for word.   35
quem locum ad litteram subieci (Quintilian): which passage I have quoted
verbatim

* * * * *

27 Cicero] *Orator* 140
29 Sallust] *Catilina* 31.7
36 Quintilian] 9.1.25

eius verba subieci: I append his actual words.
The common expression for this is *in forma*.
ipsa hominis verba tibi reddam: I shall give you the man's actual words.

110 / εἰρωνεία [Irony]

heus bone vir: hey there, my fine fellow
scilicet is superis labor est: so that is what concerns the powers above!
is nunc si diis placet nos docebit qui nihil umquam didicit ipse: so now, if
heaven please, we shall take instruction from a man who has never learnt a
single thing himself.
o mirum amicum: oh what a marvellous friend!
mira vero militi quae placeant: marvellous indeed what pleases the soldier.
sane vero: of course
quasi vero: as if, indeed

111 / Drag out the time

sic ille dies extractus est: so that day was dragged out.
hoc agebant ut dies eximeretur: their purpose in so acting was to get
proceedings suspended [literally, to have the day declared invalid].
ducere tempus: prolong the time
terere tempus: waste time
ducere bellum: prolong the war
iam dies excesserat: the time allowed had already run out.

112 / Ready, easy

paratum: prepared
promptum: set out, available
in promptu: at the ready
in procinctu: stripped for action, in readiness
proclive, in proclivi: on the slipway, down hill, ready to go, easy

* * * * *

9 labor est] Virgil *Aeneid* 4.379
14 militi quae placeant] Terence *Eunuchus* 288
36 in proclivi] Sallust *Epistula ad Caesarem* 2.8.6

LB I 56F

obvium: not out of the way
expositum: accessible
expromptum: laid out ready
in numerato habere: have in ready money
in statione: at one's post   5
ad manum: to hand
extempore, extemporarium, extemporaneum: extemporaneous

113 / Averting   10

deprecari invidiam: beg the laying aside of ill will
deprecari culpam: beg release from blame [i.e., forgiveness]
depellere crimen: rebut an accusation
aversari: turn from, refuse   15
abominari: say words to avert ill omen
reicere: reject
refellere: refute
negare: disclaim
infitiari: deny   20
infitias ire: make denial
propulsare: repulse
profligare: strike down
amoliri: put out of the way
di meliora piis (Virgil): God grant a better end to the just!   25
quod deus avertat: from which God preserve us!
divi prohibeant: heaven forbid!

114 / Acknowledging   30

agnovit hereditatem: he accepted the inheritance.
agnoscit crimen: he acknowledges the validity of the accusation.
accipio condicionem: I accept the stipulation.
admitto testamentum: I allow the will.   35
            * * * * *
    4 in numerato habere] Quintilian 6.3.111: *ingenium eum in numerato habere,*
      according to Seneca *Controversiae* 2.5.20, a *mot* of Augustus' concerning
      Lucius Vinicius
   12 deprecari invidiam] Cicero *Pro Cluentio* 81
   13 deprecari culpam] Aulus Gellius 11.8.4, quoting Cato
   25 Virgil] *Georgics* 3.513

adiit testamentum: he consulted the will.
ut admirationem etiam plausu confiteretur: so as to show his admiration by applauding
amorem re testatus est: he bore witness to his love in deeds.
odium et vultu prae se fert: he lets his hatred show even in his face.
morbum incessu vultuque fatetur: by his gait and looks his sickness he confesses.

115 / From youth

iam inde a puero: right from boyhood
ab adulescentia: from youth
a teneris unguiculis: from our baby nails
sic a pueris assueti sunt: such had been their custom since they were boys.
usque a pueris curavi ambos (Terence): I have cared for them both ever since they were boys.
mihi magna cum eo iam inde usque a pueritia semper fuit familiaritas (Terence): he has always been a great friend of mine ever since we were boys together.
iam inde a cunabulis (Varro): right from the cradle
inde ab incunabulis imbutus odio tribunorum (Livy): imbued with a hatred for tribunes right from his cradle
a rudibus annis: from our unformed years
a prima pueritia: from earliest boyhood
ab ipso vitae exordio: from the opening of life
ab ipso vitae limine: from life's very threshold
ab incunabulis: from the cradle
cum ipso nutricis lacte sugimus errorem: we drink in error with our nurse's milk.
ab ipsis crepundiis: since we played with a rattle

* * * * *

6 sickness he confesses] Juvenal 2.17
14 unguiculis] Cicero *Ad familiares* 1.6.2: *a teneris, ut Graeci dicunt, unguiculis; Adagia* I vii 52
16 Terence] *Adelphi* 962
19 Terence] *Heautontimorumenos* 184
21 Varro] Erasmus has possibly misremembered. On *cunabula* see *Adagia* I vii 53.
22 Livy] 4.36.5
28 ab incunabulis] For example, Cicero *De oratore* 1.23
29 sugimus errorem] See Cicero *Tusculan Disputations* 3.2: *ut ... suxisse videamur ...; Adagia* I vii 54.

LB I 57B

P. MOSELLANI

TABVLÆ DE

SCHEMATIBVS

ET TROPIS IN

Rhetorica.

ITEM

IN ERASMI ROTERO-
dami libellum de duplici copia.

¶EXCVDEBAT

Iohannes kyngſtonus.
Anno 1573.

Peter Schade (Mosellanus) *Tabulae de schematibus et tropis* (London 1573)
Title page and c4ᵛ of this popular text on rhetoric
This edition, like many others, includes Georgius Major's compression of *De copia*,
which fills only fifteen pages of the book.
Folger Shakespeare Library

TABVLÆ

Pathopœia, affectuum { *Sexu,*
varietas, quæ petitur { *Temporibus,*
à circunstantijs, *à* { *Locis,*
{ *Personis,*
{ *AEtatibus, &c.*

In Erasmi librum de Co-
pia Tabulæ.

TRIPLEX EST COPIA

Videlicet, { *Dictionum,*
{ *Orationum,*
{ *Sententiarum.*

DICTIONVM COPIA,

Dictionum copia, quæ fit singulis vocabulis, consi-
stit in Synonymia, quæ est, quum diuersa verba ean-
dem omnino rem declarant.

vt, { *Ensis, gladius.*
{ *Domus, ædes.*

Huc pertinent quoque, Sordida, Inusitata, Poë-
tica, Prisca, Obsoleta, Dura, Peregrina, Nouata.

ORATIONVM COPIA.

Ora-

116 / Carefully

accurate: carefully, elaborately
exacte: exactly
elaborate: painstakingly   5
ad unguem: to a nicety [literally, tested with a fingernail]
ad amussim, examussim, amussatim, examussatim: with precision [liter-
ally, using a ruler]
ad perpendiculum: by plumbline
summa cura: with the greatest care   10
exquisite, conquisite: with an eye to detail
circumspecte: with circumspection
attente: with attention
    Cicero used *consideratus* 'deliberate' in the sense of *attentus* 'atten-
tive,' also the phrases *ad perpendiculum exigere* 'test by plumbline,' *sagaciter*   15
pervestigavit 'tracked down by scent,' *divinitus dicta* 'divinely spoken' in the
sense 'exceedingly well,' *pressius agamus* 'let us pin down' (in his fourth
book *De finibus*), and *nunc comminus agamus* 'let us now come to grips.'

                                                                          20

117 / Completing

absolvit: settled, finished
perfecit: carried through
exegi monumentum: I have completed a memorial.   25
finem imposui: I put an end to
finem dicendi faciam: I shall make an end of speaking.
finiit: ended
summam manum imposuit: put the finishing touches to
ad umbilicum duxit: reached the last page   30

    * * * * *

  6 ad unguem] See Horace *Ars poetica* 294: *praesectum decies non castigavit ad*
    unguem.
  7 examussim] Plautus *Mostellaria* 102; *Adagia* I v 90
 14 Cicero] *consideratus*: for example, *Pro Quinctio* 11, *una in re paulo minus*
    consideratus; *ad perpendiculum exigere*: *Verrines* 1.133; *sagaciter pervestigavit*:
    see *De oratore* 1.223; *divinitus dicta*: *De oratore* 1.28; *pressius agamus*: *De finibus*
    4.24; *nunc comminus agamus*: *De divinatione* 2.26
 25 monumentum] Horace *Odes* 3.30.1
 27 finem dicendi faciam] Cicero *Pro Sestio* 136
 30 ad umbilicum duxit] See Horace *Epodes* 14.8; *Adagia* I ii 32–5 for this and
    491:1, 3, 4.

    LB I 57D

fastigium imponere: set the capstone
colophonem addere: add the crowning glory
supremam addidit manum: added the final touch
extremum actum addere: add the last act
fabulam vitae peregit: he completed his play of life. 5
exacta aetate: having spent a long life
ad metam usque perduxit: he brought to the finishing-post.
peregit fabulam: he performed the play to the last scene.
depuduit: shame has fled.
desultavit canticum (Suetonius): he danced the solo to the end. 10
depugnatum est: they fought to a standstill.
perdoluit: she has hurt you at last.
deferbuit: went off the boil, cooled down
vita defunctus est: he departed this life.
desiit artem: he left off the art. 15

118 / Setting against

leges inter se colliduntur eventu: laws are brought into conflict by events. 20
ut non compositi melius cum Bitho Bacchius: so that Bacchius matched
with Bithus would not be a better pair
quis te cum isto commisit homine? who set you to fight that man?
concertasti cum ero: you had a bit of a set-to with my master.
conferre pedem: engage at close quarters 25
conserere manum: fight hand to hand
congredi cum viro: come to grips with the man
confligere: be in conflict
colluctari: wrestle with
conflictari: contend 30

* * * * *

1 fastigium imponere] Cicero *De officiis* 3.33
2 colophonem] *Adagia* ii iii 45
3 supremam addidit manum] Cf Cicero *Brutus* 126; Petronius 118.
6 exacta aetate] Cicero *Tusculan Disputations* 1.93
9 depuduit] Ovid *Heroides* 4.155
10 Suetonius] *Caligula* 54.2
12 perdoluit] Terence *Eunuchus* 154
15 desiit artem] Suetonius *Tiberius* 36
20 colliduntur eventu] See Quintilian 7.7.2.
21 Bitho Bacchius] Horace *Satires* 1.7.20
24 cum ero] Cf Terence *Adelphi* 211: *te audio … concertasse cum ero.*

119 / Loving

unice te diligit: he has a singular regard for you.
amat effusissime: he loves extravagantly.
carissimum habet: he holds most dear.
admiranda quadam caritate prosequitur: he shows him a wonderful affection.
fama nihil habet antiquius: he gives nothing priority over fame.
non amat modo verum etiam observat: he not only loves but also respects.
singulari benevolentia prosequitur: he treats him with singular benevolence.
animo toto te complectitur: he embraces you with his whole heart.
oculis atque animo fert hominem: he carries him in his mind's eye.
Corydon ardebat Alexim: Corydon was on fire for Alexis.
deperibat virginem, deperibat in virginem: he was desperately in love with
the girl.
perdite amat: he loves to distraction.
deperdita amore (Suetonius): madly in love
flagrat amore tui: he burns with passion for you.
amantissimus est tui: he is most affectionate towards you.
tui tuorumque est observantissimus: he is most attentive to you and all
your family.
studiosissimus est tui: he is most attached to you.
tui cupientissimus: longing eagerly for you
ex animo tibi bene vult: he wishes you well from the heart.
bene cupit tibi: he desires your good.
hunc unum habet in deliciis, habet in oblectamentis: he is his one darling,
his sole heart's delight
non perinde illi adfectus erat: he was not all that well disposed towards
him. Suetonius uses this in the sense of *non perinde diligebat* 'he was not all

* * * * *

8 antiquius] See Cicero *De divinatione* 2.78: *antiquiorem sibi fuisse laudem et
gloriam.*
14 ardebat Alexim] Virgil *Eclogues* 2.1
15 deperibat virginem] Cf Terence *Heautontimorumenos* 525: *Clinia hanc ... de-
perit.*
18 Suetonius] *Domitian* 3.1
20 amantissimus est tui] Cicero *Ad Atticum* 7.7.1
30 Suetonius] Cf *Tiberius* 52.1.

that fond of him.' He also uses *pronior Dolabellae* 'more prone to Dolabella'
in the sense 'more inclined towards.'
sic omnia tua exosculatur: he so kisses all that is yours (i.e., he so loves).

120 / Desiring

laudis avidus: avid for praise
laudis avarus: greedy for praise
avens gloriae: gasping for glory
cupiens famae: desirous of fame
tui sitientissimus: thirsting for you
famelicus gloriae: hungering after glory
sitit famam: he thirsts for fame.
sitit aurum: he thirsts for gold.
esurientissimus laudis: ravenous for praise
mira gloriae fames habet hominem: an incredible hunger for glory has the
fellow in its grip.
ambit honores: he solicits office.
nullius rei quam laudis ambitiosior: ambitious for nothing more than
praise
privati commodi studiosus: intent on personal advantage
alieni appetens: covetous of others' possessions
appetens laudis: covetous of praise
eloquentiae candidatus: an aspirant to eloquence
inhiat lucris: he is agape for gain.
imminet exitio vir coniugis, illa mariti: the husband plots his wife's destruction, and she in turn her husband's.
gestio videre hominem: I am all agog to see the man.
prurit illi tergum: his back has an itch [i.e., he is asking for trouble].

* * * * *

1 He also] *Galba* 12.2
3 exosculatur] See 316:8n.
23 alieni appetens] Sallust *Catilina* 5.4
25 eloquentiae candidatus] Quintilian 6 preface 13; see 304:6n.
27 illa mariti] Ovid *Metamorphoses* 1.146
30 tergum] Cf Plautus *Miles gloriosus* 397: *dorsus totus prurit.*

LB I 58A

121 / Cursing

quoties caput tuum diris devovit: how often has he wished you in hell
[literally, devoted your life to the dreadful powers].
execratus est tum sese tum suos omnes: he called down curses on himself
and all his family.
ut te di perdant: may heaven bring you to destruction.
abi in malam rem, in maximum malum, in crucem: go to the devil; to hell
with you; go and be hanged.
di te eradicent: heaven destroy you root and branch.
di tibi factis dignum tuis supplicium dent: may heaven punish you as you
deserve.
di mentem tibi dent tuam: heaven do to you what you intend for others.
βάλλ᾽ ἐς κόρακας [away to the crows with you]: go and be hanged (the
commonest Greek expression).
quae res illi vertat male: and bad luck may it bring him.
in morbo consumat (a proverbial expression): may he spend it on an illness.
capiti vestro istud quidem (Plautus): I hope *that* happens to *you*.
di capiti ipsius generique reservent (Virgil): heaven lay it up in store for
him and all his kin!
quod illorum capiti sit (Cicero): on their own heads be it!
di sint irati huiusmodi Graeco (Cicero again): may heaven turn against this
sort of Greek.

122 / Promising

nescio quid magni promittunt sidera: the stars presage something great.
magnifice pollicentur amantes: lovers make splendid professions.
promissis ductat hominem: he inveigles the man with promises.
pollicitis dives quilibet esse potest: in promises can anyone be rich.
cave fidas huiusmodi pollicitationibus: mind you do not trust professions
of this sort.

* * * * *

13 tibi dent tuam] Martial 7.67.16; *Adagia* IV i 91
16 vertat male] Cf Plautus *Curculio* 273: *quae res male vortat tibi.*
17 proverbial] Seneca *De beneficiis* 4.39.2
18 Plautus] *Poenulus* 645
19 Virgil] *Aeneid* 8.484
21 Cicero] *Ad familiares* 8.1.5 (a letter from Caelius)
31 pollicitis] Ovid *Ars amatoria* 1.444

LB I 58B

spondeo futurum: I give my word that it will be so.

despondeo: I pledge.

sponde, noxa praesto est: become surety for another and misfortune awaits you.

ego tibi huius nomine fideiubeo: I go bail on his account.

recipio tibi facturum hunc: I undertake to see that he will perform it.

recipio ad me: I take it upon myself; in se recipiunt (Sallust): they take it upon themselves.

hoc tibi meo periculo promitto: I promise you this on my own responsibility.

ita mihi stipulanti pactus est: when I proposed these conditions, he made a firm bargain with me.

litoribus nostris ancora pacta tua est: your anchor held fast to our shore.

do fidem futurum, confirmo futurum: I give you my assurance, I confirm, that it will be so.

fidem suam interposuit: he gave him his personal promise.

Clodio Tiberius ea lege cenam condixit (Suetonius): Tiberius engaged himself to come to dinner with Clodius on condition that ...

nam cum mihi condixisset cenavit apud me (Cicero): he dined with me, since he had engaged to do so.

The ancients used the phrase *lingua nuncupatum* 'named by tongue' for a verbal undertaking in specific terms, for example, Cicero in his work *De officiis*: *nam cum ex duodecim tabulis satis esset ea praestare quae essent lingua nuncupata*: 'since the Twelve Tables required only the fulfillment of what had been named by tongue.'

vovere 'to vow' is used of pledging to God.

at non haec quondam blanda promissa dedisti (Catullus): these are not the promises with honeyed tongue once made.

quem ille casu oblatum promissis onerat (Sallust): this man, whom chance offered him, he loaded with promises.

dare promissa: make promises; for example, cum hic esses longe alia promissa dedisti: when you were here you made quite different promises.

* * * * *

13 pacta tua est] Ovid *Heroides* 2.4

16 fidem suam interposuit] Sallust *Jugurtha* 32.5

17 Suetonius] *Tiberius* 42.2; Cestius Gallus, not Clodius

19 nam cum mihi ... 'one-day givers'] The passage to 496:5 added in *1534* (LB I 58D–E)

19 Cicero] *Ad familiares* 1.9.20

22 Cicero] *De officiis* 3.65

27 Catullus] 64.139

29 Sallust] *Jugurtha* 12.3

sollicitat ingentibus promissis: he tempts him with huge promises.

spes amplissimas ostendit: he holds out splendid hopes.

In the sayings of the ancients the sort of people who made great promises were called χρηστολόγοι 'speak-fairs' and *dosones* 'one-day givers.'

123 / Leadership

est copiosum dicendi genus in quo Cicero principatum obtinet: there is a copious style of oratory in which Cicero has the primacy.

breve in quo Sallustius regnat: a succinct style in which Sallust holds sway

subtile in quo dominatur Hortensius: a plain style which Hortensius dominates

floridum in quo primas tenet Plinius: a florid one in which Pliny occupies first rank

varium in quo praecipuus est Hieronymus: a varied style in which Jerome stands out

grave in quo princeps est Seneca: a serious one in which Seneca is leader

festivum in quo singularis est Martialis: a witty style in which Martial has none to equal him

simplex in quo primus est Terentius: a simple one in which Terence is the chief

acutum in quo praecellit Quintilianus: an incisive one in which Quintilian excels

suave in quo vicit Statius: an agreeable one in which Statius defeats all comers

antiquum in quo nulli secundus est Cato: an archaic one in which Cato comes second to none

inaffectatum in quo nulli cedit, nullo inferior est, nemine posterior est Caesar: a natural style in which Caesar yields to none, is inferior to none, is preceded by none

huius negotii velut antesignanus, dux, vexillifer, signifer exstitisti: you have come forward as a sort of commander, leader, standard-bearer, ensign in this business. (In Greek, κορυφαῖος [headman], leader of the chorus)

Homerus omnes procul a se reliquit: Homer has left everyone far behind.

omnes a tergo reliquit: he left everyone behind him.

* * * * *

4 χρηστολόγοι ... *dosones*] *Adagia* I x 54, IV v 92

10 dicendi genus] A reminiscence of Macrobius 5.1.7

15 Pliny] The Younger Pliny

longo intervallo praecellit, praecedit, praecurrit, praeit, anteit, antecellit:
he is in advance, precedes, outruns, goes ahead, outstrips, excels by far.
in litteris Graecanicis palmam tenet: he holds the palm in literature after the
Greek manner.
eloquentiae M. Tullius arcem tenet: Cicero occupies the summit of eloqu-   5
ence.
primam laudem obtinet: he obtains the chief praise.
primum locum obtinet: he holds the chief place.
praemia prima feres: you shall win the first prize.

                                                                              10

124 / Shows

munera gladiatoria populo exhibuit: he exhibited shows of gladiators before the people.   15
edidit circenses: he organized games in the circus.
fecit ludos scaenicos (Suetonius in his *Life of Caligula*): he laid on stage
shows.
commisit et subitos (Suetonius in the same work): he arranged extra contests on the spur of the moment.   20
praeter consuetudinem musicum agona commisit (Suetonius again, in his
Life of Nero): he arranged a musical contest, which was hitherto unprede-
cented.
dedit populo centum gladiatorum paria: he gave the people a hundred pairs
of gladiators.   25
centum camelos produxit: he brought on a hundred camels.

125 / Recruit

                                                                              30
habuit delectum: he levied troops.
agere delectum: to conduct a levy
delectibus undique acerbissime actis: having conscripted men unmerci-
fully in all areas
          * * * * *
    12 Shows] All these phrases are based on Suetonius.
    14 munera gladiatoria] Cf Suetonius *Caligua* 18, *Claudius* 21.
    16 circenses] *Caligula* 18
    17 scaenicos] *Caligula* 18
    19 subitos] *Caligula* 18
    21 musicum agona] *Nero* 23.1
    33 acerbissime actis] Suetonius *Caligula* 43

    LB I 58F

cogere exercitum: raise an army
contrahere copias: muster forces
conscribere exercitum: enlist an army
parare manum: assemble an armed force
comparare vim militum: raise a military force
collectis copiis: amassing his forces

126 / Relieving of an office

deposuit dictaturam: he laid down the dictatorship.
amotus est consulatu: he was removed from the consulship.
abrogatum est illi imperium, ademptum imperium: his command was
rescinded, revoked.
abdicavit se magistratu (Suetonius): he abdicated his magistracy.
privavit honore (Suetonius again): he deprived of office.
redactus est in ordinem: he was reduced to the ranks; multos coegit in
ordinem: he reduced many to the ranks, i.e., [in this context] reduced to the
level of private citizens.
missionem petiit: he asked for his discharge.
rude donatus est: he was honourably discharged [literally, presented with
the *rudis*].
dimisit cum ignominia: he dismissed him with ignominy.
exauctoravit totam legionem: he dispensed with the services of the whole
legion.

127 / Persuading

fecit mihi lacrimis paenitentiae fidem: he has convinced me of his peni-
tence by his tears.
lacrimis mihi persuasit sese facti paenitere: he persuaded me by his tears
that he was sorry for what he had done.
lacrimae mihi persuaserunt illum paenitere facti: his tears have persuaded
me that he is sorry for what he has done.

* * * * *

15 Suetonius] Cf *Claudius* 29.2: *abdicare se praetura coactus.*
16 Suetonius] *Nero* 43.2
17 redactus est in ordinem] Suetonius *Vespasian* 15.1
22 *rudis*] Originally a wooden fencing-stick presented to gladiators on their
retirement; *Adagia* I ix 24
24 totam legionem] Cf Suetonius *Augustus* 24.2.

lacrimis effecit ut crediderim illum paenitere: his tears have caused me to believe that he repents.

adduxit, pertraxit, pellexit, perpulit me in suam sententiam: he has brought, drawn, enticed, forced me over to his point of view.

coactus est verius quam persuasus: he was compelled rather than persuaded.

128 / Inferring or reasoning

quod animal est idem corpus sit necesse est, quod autem corpus est non statim et animal: that which is animal must of necessity be material, but that which is material is not inevitably animal.

is pauper est qui plurimum cupit; porro quo quisque magis abundat opibus hoc est opum appetentior; igitur ditissimus quisque pauperrimus sit necesse est: the poor man is the one who desires the most; but the man with the greatest wealth is the one most desirous of wealth; therefore the richest man must be the poorest.

si deus est animus, animi puritate non victimis corporeis eum convenit colere: if God is a spirit, it is fitting to worship him not with offerings of material substance but with purity of spirit.

cum animus sit corpore praestantior, virtutes autem animi sint possessiones, pecuniae corporis, consentaneum est virtutes pecuniis anteponendas esse: since the soul is superior to the body, and virtues are the possessions of the soul, while wealth is the possession of the body, it is only reasonable that virtues should be set above wealth.

in quem cadit misereri, in eundem cadit invidere; non cadit autem invidere in sapientem; ergo ne misereri quidem: the man who finds it possible to feel pity can also feel envy; but the sage is not capable of feeling envy; therefore he cannot feel pity either.

ipse sibi utilis esse nequit, et vobis erit usui? he cannot do himself any good, so will he prove of any use to you?

felix non est cui multa desunt; atqui divitibus desunt plurima; qui possunt igitur divites esse felices? a man who lacks much cannot be happy; but the rich lack many things; how then can the rich be happy?

solum bonum virtus, nam id demum bonum est quo nemo male potest uti; virtute nemo male uti potest, bonum est ergo virtus: virtue is the sole good,

* * * * *

15 pauperrimus sit necesse est] See Cicero *Paradoxa Stoicorum* 6.
27 in quem cadit misereri] Cicero *Tusculan Disputations* 3.21

LB I 59C

for only that is good which no one can put to a bad use; no one can put virtue
to a bad use, therefore virtue is good.
bonum est virtus ut qua nemo male uti potest; an bonum pecunia qua
quisque potest male uti? virtue is a good inasmuch as no one can put it to a
bad use; can money be a good when any of us can put it to a bad use?
i nunc 'go then' has an inferential force, but carries with it an overtone of
censure, as in: i nunc, argentum, marmor vetus etc.: go then, fancy your
silver and marbles antique …
quae cum ita sint, quis audeat infitias ire? seeing that these are the facts,
who would dare to deny?
hoc cum sic habeat annon dedisti damnum? utrum damnum dedisti an
non? et dubitamus adhuc? since this is the situation, can it be that you did
not cause him loss? did you cause him loss or not? are we still in doubt?

129 / Nothing but

nil nisi poeta es: you are nothing but a poet.
nil aliud es nisi poeta: you are nothing else but a poet.
nil aliud quam poeta es: you are nothing other than a poet.
tantum poeta es: you are merely a poet.
poeta es, praeterea nihil: you are a poet, and besides that nothing.
nihil es praeterquam poeta: you are nothing more than a poet.
nisi poeta esses nihil esses: if you were not a poet you would be nothing.
nil aliud quam flebat: he did nothing but weep (the equivalent of *tantum
flebat* 'he merely wept'), an example from Quintilian; the construction is
commoner in Suetonius, for example: nihil aliud quam vectabatur: he did
nothing but ride about; nihil amplius quam monuit: he did nothing more
than warn him.
non tantum expresses the opposite idea: non tantum osculatus est: he did
not merely kiss.

* * * * *

7 i nunc, argentum] Horace *Epistles* 1.6.17
26 Quintilian] Cf *Declamationes minores* 252: *tamquam ego nihil aliud quam de
amissa virginitate filiae queror;* two sets of declamations, *maiores* and *minores,*
are extant under Quintilian's name, both today considered spurious.
27 vectabatur] *Augustus* 83.1
28 monuit] *Claudius* 16.1

130 / Praising and blaming

non omnes probabunt istud consilium, culpabunt plurimi: not everyone
will approve this plan of yours; most people will find fault with it.
animum insimulabunt nonnulli: a good many people will cast doubt on
your intentions.
nemo mihi vitio verterit: no one is to blame me.
nunc quam rem vitio dent quaeso animadvertite (Terence): now please
observe the fault they tax him with.
dare crimini (Cicero in *Brutus*): make an accusation out of
istud vituperio dabunt omnes: everyone will make that something to blame
you with.
tu tibi laudi ducis: you consider it to your credit.
gloriae tibi tribuis, honori putas fore: you think it glorifies you; you think it
will bring you credit.
at omnes dedecori dabunt, probro dabunt, criminabuntur, damnabunt,
reprehendent, improbabunt, suggillabunt, taxabunt, notabunt: but
everyone will consider it a disgrace, will make it a reproach, will accuse,
condemn, blame, censure, jeer, tax, brand it with infamy.
atro calculo notabunt: they will put a black mark against you.
quoniam adeo Sullam non paenitet ut et facta in gloria numeret (Sallust):
since Sulla is so far from repenting that he even numbers these deeds
among his glories
album addere calculum: throw in a white pebble (i.e., give a favourable
verdict)
subscribere sententiae: subscribe to a view
suffragari, refragari: support, oppose
laudibus ferre: extol
ad caelum ferre (Horace), in caelum ferre (Cicero): exalt to the skies
laudibus vexit (Pliny in his letters): carried aloft with praise

* * * * *

8 Terence] *Andria* 8
10 *Brutus*] 277
21 Sallust] *Histories* 1.55.19
24 white pebble] Cf Pliny *Epistles* 1.2.5: *si ... album calculum adieceris;* Ovid
   Metamorphoses 15.42–3: *mos erat antiquis niveis atrisque lapillis / his damnare
   reos illis absolvere culpa; Adagia* I v 53.
29 Horace] *Epistles* 1.10.9
29 Cicero] *Pro Flacco* 103
30 Pliny] *Epistles* 4.27.2

scis vitio nigrum praefigere theta: you know how to set death's black sign
on vice.

avaritiae singulos increpans (Suetonius): rebuking different ones for their
avarice

tibi malum imputabitur: the misfortune will be imputed to you.

tibi feretur acceptum: it will be set down to your account.

tu fueris in crimine: you would be the one blamed.

tam est in vitio qui deserit amicum in periculo quam qui prodit (Cicero):
the man who deserts a friend in danger is as much at fault as one who
betrays him.

in te residet facti suspicio: the suspicion of the deed rests on you.

in te redundabit: it will redound on you.

in te cudetur haec faba (a proverbial expression): you will smart for this
[literally, this bean will be pounded on you].

male audies apud omnes qui hactenus audisti bene: hitherto you have been
well spoken of, and now you will be ill spoken of by all.

quiquis de meliore nota (Catullus): anyone of the better quality

vir pessimae notae: a man of the worst mark

homo nullo numero, nihil illo contemptius (Cicero): a fellow of no account,
nothing more contemptible than he

vir primae notae: a man of first mark

vir extremae notae: a man of the lowest mark

homo quintae classis, homo ultimae sortis: a fifth-class fellow, a fellow of
the meanest condition

homo bonae frugis, bonae frugi, homo frugi (this last without the adjective): a worthy fellow

* * * * *

1 praefigere theta] Persius 4.13: *potis es vitio*; *Adagia* I v 56; *theta* was supposed
   to stand for Greek *thanatos* 'death.'
3 avaritiae singulos ... by all] Text to line 16 added in *1526* (LB I 60A–B)
3 Suetonius] *Caligula* 39.2
8 Cicero] *De officiis* 1.23: *qui autem non defendit ... tam est in vitio, quam si parentes
   aut amicos ... deserat.*
13 proverbial] Occurs in Terence *Eunuchus* 381; the general meaning is explained
   in Donatus' commentary on the passage; see *Adagia* I i 84.
17 quisquis ... fellow] Added in *1534* (LB I 60B)
17 Catullus] 68.28; 107.6
19 Cicero] *Philippics* 3.16
22 extremae notae] *Adagia* III vii 80

131 / In short

ad summam (Horace), in summa: in short
ut summatim dicam: to put it briefly
denique, demum, postremo: finally, in short   5
breviter: in brief
ut semel dicam: to say once for all [i.e., in a word]
ut semel finiam: to define it in a word
dicam in genere: I shall speak in the broadest terms.
rem omnem verbo complectar: I shall sum up the whole business in a word.   10
quid quaeris? 'what would you?' has the force of *denique* 'in fine,' and is often
used by Cicero.
quid multa? why more?
quid multis moror? why keep you with much talk?
dicam universim: I shall treat of it as a whole.   15
in universum habeo quod respondeam: I have something to say by way of a
general reply.
dicam verbo: I shall say it in a word.
ad ultimum 'at the last' was used in the sense of *denique* by Quintus Curtius;
Suetonius used *ultimo* in this sense, Cicero *ad extremum*.   20

132 / Wasting effort

lusit operam: he wasted his efforts.   25
luditur opera: the effort is all in vain.
opera et impensa periit: toil and expense have gone for nothing.
frustra ego hanc operam sumo: I am taking all this trouble to no good
purpose.
nihil agis: you are getting nowhere.   30
laterem lavas: you are labouring in vain [literally, trying to wash the colour
out of a brick].

    * * * * *

  3 Horace] *Epistles* 1.1.106
  7 ut semel dicam ... ut semel finiam] Quintilian 10.1.17, 11.3.59
19 Quintus Curtius] For example 3.1.7: *ad ultimum pro fide morituros*
20 Suetonius] For example, *Nero* 32.4
20 Cicero] For example, *Pro Cluentio* 50
25 lusit operam] Cf Plautus *Pseudolus* 369: *operam ludimus.*
31 laterem lavas] Terence *Phormio* 186: *lateram lavem.* See 621:12.

actum ago, actam rem agis: I am, you are, redoing the done.
in silvam fers ligna: coals to Newcastle [literally, you are carrying logs into the wood].
And all the other proverbial expressions which indicate wasted effort.

5

133 / Profit

magnum ex ea re fructum retulit: he received a considerable income from it.
cepit emolumentum: he made a profit.
lucrum reportavit: he obtained a return.
sensit commodum: he experienced the benefit.
commoditatem demessuit: he reaped the advantage.
collegit utilitatem: he gathered the profits.
frugem accepit: he took the proceeds.
lucrum fecit: he did well out of it.
compendium paravit: he provided himself with winnings.
ea res illi frugifera fuit, fuit emolumento, fuit commodo, fuit usui: this was profitable to him, gainful, advantageous, useful.
ex ea legatione messem opimam messuit: he reaped a rich harvest from that posting.

10

15

20

134 / Impudence

25

nihil pudet: nothing shames him.
depuduit, depuditum est: he is past shame, shame is gone.
dedidicit pudorem: he has forgotten the lesson of shame.
oblitus est pudoris: he has forgotten shame.
dedidicit pudescere: he no longer knows how to feel shame.
nescit pudescere: he does not know how to feel shame.
exuit pudorem: he has cast away shame.
perfricuit faciem, perfricuit frontem: he wears a bold face, bold brow [literally, has wiped the blushes off].
nihil habet oris, nihil frontis: he is quite without a blush, without the look of modesty.
quo ore? qua fronte? will you have the cheek to …? [literally, with what face, what brow?]

30

35

* * * * *

1 actum ago] Cf *Phormio* 419: *actum, ut aiunt, ne agas*; *Adagia* I iv 70: 'Actum agere,' meaning 'to bring up again a matter already decided in the courts.'

135 / Straining after

affectata verba: artificial expressions
affectatus ornatus: overdone ornamentation
ascitus ornatus: imported ornamentation
asciticius decor: contrived embellishment
et gratiam rei nimia captatione consumpsimus (Quintilian): we exhausted
the attractiveness of the subject by excessive straining after effect (*captatio*
is here equivalent to *affectatio* 'affectation').
captat laudem: he chases praise.
venatur gloriam: he is on the scent of glory [literally, hunts].
aucupatur famam: he is out to snare fame [literally, catch like a bird].
accersit sibi malum: he is riding for a fall [literally, summoning misfortune
to himself].

136 / Not knowing and its opposite

scio: I know.
non ignoro: I am not ignorant.
non me fugit: it does not escape me.
non me latet: it is not hidden from me.
non me praeterit: it does not pass me by.
non sum nescius: I am not unaware.
non me clam est: it is not unbeknownst to me.
quis nescit? who does not know?
nemini dubium: no one can doubt.
intelligo, video, sentio: I understand, I see, I perceive.
compertum habeo, exploratum, perspectum, cognitum habeo: I have it as
ascertained fact, established, evident, acknowledged fact.
non est obscurum mihi: it is by no means obscure to me.
non me fallit: it does not elude my notice.
nec ea res me falsum habuit (Sallust): nor did events find me mistaken.

* * * * *

7 Quintilian] 8.6.51. All major editions of *De copia* read *cooptatione*; LB I 60E has
  a note: *meliores editiones habent captatione.*
23 non me praeterit] Quintilian 10.1.12
24 non sum nescius] For example, Cicero *De oratore* 1.45: *non sum nescius ... ista
  inter Graecos dici*
25 clam est] Terence *Hecyra* 261
33 Sallust] *Jugurtha* 10.1

LB I 60E

indoctus disci: with no skill at quoits
rudis horum malorum: with no experience of these misfortunes
imperitus fallendi: unpractised in deception
ignarus loci (an expression of Sallust's): unfamiliar with the place

5

137 / Disgraceful, etc

turpe est: it is disgraceful.
cum turpitudine coniunctum est: it cannot be separated from disgrace.   10
laudabile est: it is laudable.
cum laude coniunctum est: it brings approbation with it.
cum vitio coniunctum est: it is tied up with error.
vitio confine est: it borders on offence.
non vacat vitio: it is not free from fault.   15
non caret vitio: it is not devoid of defect.
non abest a vitio: it is not clear of offence.
periculosum: perilous
cum periculo coniunctum: involving peril
in vitio est: is at fault.   20
in probro est: is in disgrace.

138 / Without doing

25

ruere illa non possunt ut haec non eodem labefacta motu concidant (Cicero,
in his speech *Pro Pompeio*): that cannot come crashing down without all this
collapsing too, overthrown by the same tremor. [One could also say:] quin
haec eodem labefacta motu concidant.
non potes studere opibus ut animi tranquillitatem non perdas: you cannot   30
pursue wealth without losing your peace of mind; *or* non potes quin perdas
... ; *or* non potes, nisi perdas ... : you cannot, unless you were to lose ...

* * * * *

1 indoctus disci] Horace *Ars poetica* 380
4 Sallust's]*Jugurtha* 12.5. All major editions of *De copia* read *ignarus ioci* in error.
20 in vitio] Cicero *De officiis* 1.62
21 in probro] Terence *Phormio* 825
26 Cicero] *De imperio Cnaei Pompei (Pro lege Manilia)* 19

139 / That which, just as

Cicero often uses *id quod* for *quod*, and *ita ut* for *ut*:
ita ut facis: just as you are doing
id quod facis: which thing you are doing
quod quidem facis: which indeed you are doing

140 / Amplifying a statement

cedendum erat hospiti praesertim seni, maxime seni: you should have
deferred to a guest, especially when he was an old man, most of all to an old
man.
pulsavit hospitem eumque senem, idque senem, atque hunc senem, atque
adeo senem: he struck his guest, and he an old man at that.

141 / Some verbs with two constructions

erit humanitatis vestrae magnum civium numerum calamitate prohibere
(Cicero): you will demonstrate your feeling for your fellow men by keeping
from disaster a great number of citizens.
prohibe infandos a navibus ignes (Virgil): keep from the ships the abominable fires.
defendit capellas ab aestu: he protects the goats from the heat.
defendit aestum capellis: he wards off the heat from the goats.
spargere humum foliis: sprinkle the ground with leaves
spargere folia humi: sprinkle leaves on the ground
sternere pallio lectum: cover the bed with a coverlet
insternere lecto pallium: lay a cover on the bed
inscripsit poculum litteris: he inscribed the cup with letters.
inscripsit poculo litteras: he inscribed letters on the cup.

* * * * *

21 Cicero] *De imperio Cnaei Pompei (Pro lege Manilia)* 18
23 Virgil] *Aeneid* 1.525
26 aestum capellis] Horace *Odes* 1.17.3: *aestatem capellis*
27 humum foliis] Virgil *Eclogues* 5.40: *spargite humum foliis*

142 / Not content

non contentus victoria: not content with victory
non contentus vicisse: not content to have won
non sat habebat vicisse: he did not consider it enough to have won.
non sat erat vicisse: it was not enough to have won.
parum erat vicisse ni in victos etiam saeviret: victory was not enough unless
he wreaked his fury also on the vanquished.
non sufficiebat vicisse: it was not sufficient to have won.
paenitebat rapinae nisi parentem quoque spoliasset: he was not happy
with his plundering unless he had also stripped his father bare.

143 / Satisfying

interdum non satisfacit Ciceroni Demosthenes: at times even Demosthenes
does not satisfy Cicero.
non implet aures Ciceronis Demosthenes: Demosthenes does not content
Cicero's ears [literally, fill].
non respondet optatis meis: it does not answer my desires.
non facit satis hominum de se exspectationi: he does not come up to men's
expectation of him.
Tullius in Demosthene nonnumquam desiderat aliquid: Cicero quite often
finds deficiencies in Demosthenes.
non is es quem exspectaram: you are not the person I had expected.
non talis est qualem vellem: he is not as I would wish him to be.
nonnihil in te requiro adhuc: I still find something missing in you.
non facit ad huius cupiditatem: it does not do for his greed.

144 / Impunity and its opposite

omnes plura habere cupimus et tamen id nobis impune est: we all desire to
have more, and yet it brings no penalty on us.
haud impune feres: you will not get away with it.
haud impune feceris: you will not find you can do it with impunity.

* * * * *

16 Demosthenes] Cicero *Orator* 104: *ut nobis non satis faciat ipse Demosthenes ... non semper implet auris meas*
21 come up to ... of him] After this *1512* and *1514* have *non respondet hominum de se exspectationi* 'he does not answer to men's expectation of him.'
33 impune est] Cato, quoted in Aulus Gellius 6.3.37

LB I 61C

non fuit illi fraudi magistratum prohibuisse vi: it proved no detriment to him that he had used force to prevent the magistrate ...

sine fraude esto: let it be without detriment. (The early Romans said *se fraude*.)

non sic auferes: you will not carry it off like this.

tulit ne cui fraudi secessio esset (Livy): he passed a law to the effect that no one should be penalized because of the secession (i.e., granting impunity to all).

mirabar hoc si sic abiret: I was surprised if it was going to turn out so easily.

militem impunitate donavit: he granted the soldiers impunity.

nullum facinus impunitum esse oportet: no crime ought to go unpunished.

quo impunius dicax esset (Cicero, in his speech *Pro Quinctio*): so as to employ his sharp tongue with the greater impunity

nullas poenas dedit eius facti: he paid no penalty for that deed.

poenas pendit: he paid the penalty.

tum pendere poenas / Cecropidae iussi: the sons of Cecrops next, the penalty paying perforce

irrogare multam (Cicero): impose a fine

exemplum in illos editum: an example was made of them.

persolvit, exsolvit, luit, dependit: paid, rendered, expiated, discharged

nullum de eo sumptum supplicium: no punishment was exacted from him.

ei facto nulla irrogata poena: no penalty was imposed on the deed.

de tanto flagitio non est animadversum: no punitive measures were taken in consequence of this scandalous deed.

in omnes graviter animadversum: severe measures were taken against them all.

exacta poena: the penalty was exacted.

opinor capite plectendum: I consider it deserves the death penalty.

noxae deditus est: he was delivered up to punishment.

Suetonius speaks of offences being 'seen to, dealt with' (*animadversa*) with the force of *punitus* 'punished.'

nec in deditos gravius consultum (Quintus Curtius): nor were any particularly harsh counsels adopted with reference to those who surrendered.

* * * * *

5 sic auferes] Cf Terence *Adelphi* 454: *haud sic auferent.*
6 Livy] 7.41.3
9 si sic abiret] Terence *Andria* 175
12 Cicero] *Pro Quinctio* 11
16 Cecropidae iussi] Virgil *Aeneid* 6.21
18 Cicero] For example, *Pro Milone* 36
30 Suetonius] *Nero* 16.2
32 Quintus Curtius] 5.6.16

in te cudetur haec faba: you will smart for this.

unus dependes pro omnibus: you alone shall pay the penalty for all.

tergo lues: you will atone for it with your back.

145 / Persuading or advising

idne estis auctores mihi? so you come as backers for *that* course?

te auctore suscepi negotium: I undertook the business on your advice.

tuo impulsu feci: I did it at your prompting.

te impulsore feci: you were the one who impelled me to this deed.

tuo suasu, tuo inductu (Cicero): on your urging, your inducement

te suasore, te consultore: with you as encourager, adviser

tuo consilio: by your counsel

abs te persuasus id feci: I did it because I was persuaded by you.

tuo instinctu: on your instigation

amorem in consilium adhibuisse videris: you appear to have applied to affection for advice.

tuo persuasu (Cicero): through your persuasion

te flagitatore suscepi negotium: I undertook it because you asked me to do so incessantly.

Quintus Curtius uses *tuo verberatu* 'by your dunning, flogging' in this sense.

146 / Knowingly

prudens fecit, sciens fecit: he did it knowingly.

de industria fecit: he did it on purpose.

studiose fecit: he did it voluntarily.

data opera, dedita opera fecit: he did it of set purpose.

Seneca uses the phrase *destinato fecit* 'he did it deliberately.'

* * * * *

1 haec faba] See 502:13n.

8 auctores mihi] Terence *Adelphi* 939

11 te impulsore] Cf Terence *Adelphi* 560: *me impulsore.*

12 Cicero] utrum casu ... an huius persuasu et inductu, quoted in Quintilian 5.10.69 from the lost *Pro Oppio* of Cicero

19 tuo persuasu] See previous n.

32 Seneca] *De beneficiis* 6.23.4: *adice quod destinato iuvant* (Erasmus' reading; modern texts read *ex destinato*).

studio, consulto, consilio fecit: he did it intentionally, designedly, advisedly.
The opposite idea is expressed as follows:
imprudens, nesciens fecit: he did it unawares.
per errorem, errore factum est: it was done by mistake.
per imprudentiam: by inadvertence
peccavi inconsulte: I went wrong through indiscretion.
Quintilian on several occasions uses *ex industria* instead of *de industria* 'on purpose.'
composito factum, ex composito factum: done by arrangement
Suetonius in his *Life of Caligula* uses *ex destinato* 'by design' in the sense of *consulto.*

147 / Reason

plurimis de causis mihi tuae litterae iucundae fuerunt: for very many reasons your letter was a delight to me.
duas ob res hominem odi: I hate the fellow for two things.
multis modis tua mihi iucunda fuit epistola: your epistle was in many a way delightful to me.
duobus nominibus es mihi carissimus: on two counts you are most dear to me. (An alternative expression is *duplici nomine* 'on a double count.')
duplici de causa tuis scriptis delector: for a double reason do I find delight in your lines.
bis mihi iucunda fuit epistola tua: your epistle was doubly delightful to me.
multifariam me tuae litterae delectaverunt: in many a way did your letter charm me.

148 / Dates

calendis Ianuariis: on the January Calends [i.e., on the first of January]
ad calendas Ianuarii: round about the Calends of January
sub idem tempus: about the same time (a phrase used by Suetonius on several occasions)
* * * * *
8 Quintilian] For example, 5.7.32; 10.1.20
10 ex composito] Suetonius *Claudius* 37.2
11 Suetonius] *Caligula* 43.1
34 round about ... appointed time] Added in *1526* (LB I 62C); the insertion breaks the continuity of the text.

statis temporibus: at fixed intervals

Quintus Curtius uses *stata vice* with the same meaning as *certis vicibus* 'at the appointed time.'

calendarum die: on the day of the Calends

nonis Ianuarii: on the Nones of January [i.e., on the fifth]

ad nonas: round about the Nones

die nonarum: on the day of the Nones

idibus Maiis: on the May Ides [i.e., on the fifteenth of May]

ad idus Maii: about the Ides of May

iduum Novembrium die: on the day of the November Ides [i.e., on the thirteenth of November]

pridie calendas, pridie calendarum [using accusative or genitive]: on the day previous to the Calends

pridie nonas Maias, pridie nonarum: on the day previous to the May Nones

pridie Idus, pridie Iduum Novembrium: on the day previous to the November Ides.

postridie calendas Ianuarias: on the day after the January Calends; *alternatively*, quarto nonas Ianuarias: on the fourth day before the January Nones [two ways of saying 2 January]

postridie nonas Ianuarii: on the day after the Nones of January; *or* octavo idus Ianuarii: on the eighth day before the Ides of January

postridie idus Ianuarii: on the day after the Ides of January; *or* decimo nono calendas Februarii: on the nineteenth day before the Calends of February

decimo calendas Februarias: on the tenth day before the February Calends

ad decimum calendas Februarii: about the tenth day before the Calends of February

The other months and days are to be expressed in the same manner.

149 / Numerals

A general variation to be found in numerals is that the link-word *et* can be added or omitted: *annos natus quattuor et viginti,* or *annos natus viginti quattuor* 'four and twenty,' or 'twenty-four years old'; *annos natus centum et viginti,* or *centum viginti,* or *viginti supra centum*: 'one hundred and twenty years old,' or, 'one hundred twenty years,' or, 'twenty over the hundred.'

Another variation is that the two numerals preceding a multiple of ten may be expressed by a compounded or an uncompounded form: 'eighteen' can be *octodecim* or *duodeviginti* 'two off twenty,' 'nineteen' can be *noven-*

*****

2 Quintus Curtius] For example, 9.9.9: *stata vice oceanus exaestuans*

decim or *undeviginti* 'one off twenty,' 'twenty-eight' can be *duodetriginta* 'two off thirty,' 'twenty-nine' *undetriginta* 'one off thirty,' and so on up to a hundred.

Plural hundreds are expressed either by a compounded form functioning as an adjective in agreement with a noun, or by a non-compounded form functioning as an adverb: 'two hundred' is either *ducentos* [compounded adjective, here in the accusative case, *exempli gratia*] or *bis centum* 'twice a hundred'; 'three hundred' is either *trecentos* or *ter centum*, and so on right up to a thousand.

Thousands are expressed either by the noun *mille* 'a thousand' [governing another noun in the genitive case], or by *mille* functioning as an adjective [in agreement with the other noun] plus a numeral adverb:
mille nummum [genitive plural]: one thousand of sesterces [noun]
mille nummos: one thousand sesterces [adjective]
bis mille nummos: twice one thousand sesterces [adjective]
duo milia nummorum: two thousands of sesterces [noun], and so on with the other thousands up to a thousand thousands, which can be expressed by *mille milia* 'a thousand thousands,' or *milies mille* 'a thousand times a thousand.'

The so-called cardinals and ordinals can often be used indifferently to express the same notion: *annos natus viginti* [cardinal] 'twenty years old'; or *annum egressus vigesimum* [ordinal] 'emerging from his twentieth year'; or *annum excessit vigesimum* 'he has passed his twentieth year'; or *annum agit primum et vigesimum* 'he is spending his twenty first year';
biennium est quod patriam non reviserim 'it has been a two-year stretch that I have not revisited my country'; or *tertius hic annus agitur quod patriam non revisi*, or *cum non revisi* 'this is the third year now going by that I have not revisited ...'

dic quotus esse velis? 'say what number you want to be,' that is, how many guests you want. There is no idea of succession or order implied here, but simply number.

In poetry distributives may be used in place of simple numerals; but even in prose, wherever some word is included which implies distribution, one is free to use either distributives or cardinals: *quotannis duo talenta capit*, or *quotannis bina talenta capit* 'every year he takes two talents,' or 'two talents a time'; *in singula capita mille nummum distribuit*, or *millenos nummos* 'to *each* individual he distributed a thousand sesterces *per head*', or 'a thousand a time per head.'

* * * * *

29 *quotus esse velis*] Horace *Epistles* 1.5.30

LB I 62D

The phrase *in diem vivunt* 'they live one day at a time' is used of those who spend their lives without any concern for the future. *qui in horam viverent* (Cicero) 'persons who lived for the moment,' that is, without forethought, extempore. *in dies* means 'as each day comes, day by day': *senescit in dies et mutatur in horas* (Livy) 'declines day by day, and alters every hour.' Horace used the phrase *in diem* to mean 'daily': *ille potens sui / laetusque deget, cui licet in diem / dixisse vixi* 'in happiness that man shall dwell / And his own master be / Who can say at each day's close / "Life have I lived this day".'

Observe that when forming compounds from a larger and a smaller number one can use the word *alter* [literally, 'another'] instead of *unus* 'one' or *primus* 'first': *litteras accepi tuas, quas mihi Cornificius altero et vigesimo die reddidit* (Cicero) 'I have received your letter, which Cornificius delivered to me on the twenty-first day'; *centesima lux est haec ab interitu P. Clodii et opinor altera* (Cicero again, in his *Pro Milone*) 'it is the hundredth day since the demise of Publius Clodius, no, the hundred and first, I think.' Livy has the same usage: *anno trigesimo altero quam condita Roma erat* 'in the thirty-first year from the foundation of Rome.' Apart from this type of combination, *alter* is often used in place of *secundus* 'second': *unum alterum tertium annum Saxa quiescebat* (Cicero) 'Saxa lay low for a year, for another year, for a third year.' Similarly *unus et alter* 'one and again one,' *unus vel alter* 'one or a second one,' that is, one or two.

In adverbs the phrase *semel atque iterum* 'once and a second time' is equivalent to *bis* 'twice.'

Whenever the genitive plural *sestertium* is added to a numeral adverb, one understands *centies mille* 'a hundred times a thousand': for example, *decies sestertium* means *decies centum milia sestertiorum* 'ten times a hundred thousands of sesterces.'

150 / Adverbs of time

The immediate past is expressed by the adverb *modo* 'just,' a more distant

* * * * *

1 The phrase ... sesterces] The passage to line 28 added in *1534* (LB I 62F–3A)

3 Cicero] *Philippics* 5.25

5 Livy] 22.39.15: *eum qui senescat in dies*

6 Horace] *Odes* 3.29.42

13 Cicero] *Ad familiares* 12.25.1

15 *Pro Milone*] 98

17 Livy] 3.33.1: *anno trecentesimo*

20 Cicero] *Pro Cluentio* 178

past by *dudum, iamdudum* 'a little while ago,' a time even further back by
nuper 'recently' and *pridem* 'some time ago,' and the most distant past by
olim and *quondam* 'in time past, once upon a time.'

The gradations of future time are as follows: *mox aderit* 'he will be here
any moment now'; *iam veniet* 'he will come directly.' The adverbs *protinus*
'forthwith,' *continuo* 'immediately,' *ilico* 'on the spot,' *extemplo* 'straightaway,' *e vestigio* 'instantly' can indicate the immediate future, but they are
usually associated with a past context: *litteris tuis lectis extemplo domum me
contuli* 'after reading your letter, I straightaway took myself home'; *accepto
hoc nuntio e vestigio me domum conieci* 'on receiving this message I instantly
rushed off homewards.'

olim can be used for both past and future time: *olim floruerunt Graeci* 'at
one time the Greeks were a distinguished people'; *forsan et haec olim
meminisse iuvabit* 'one day perhaps even this / You will be happy to recall.'

proximus 'the next' can likewise refer to either time: *proximo anno
strenue se gessit* 'the next year he acted with vigour'; *in proximum annum
summas copias parat* 'he is assembling huge forces for next year'; *proximis his
diebus* 'in these next, or last few days'; *proximo mense* 'next or last month';
proximo partu 'at her last or next lying-in'; *proximo bello* 'in the last or next
war.' *novissimus* 'the newest, most recent' refers only to the past.

superiore anno 'the previous year'; *superiore mense* 'the previous
month'; *superiore bello* 'in the previous war'; *superioribus diebus* 'during the
days just past,' a phrase used of something done recently or shortly before;
likewise *paucis his diebus* 'in the last few days.' Horace uses *quinque diebus*
'in five days' to mean 'inside, or after, five days,' and Sallust has a similar
usage: *paucis diebus in Africam proficiscitur* 'in a few days he set off for
Africa'; *ante pauculos dies* 'before a very few days'; *paucis post diebus* 'a few
days later'; *post paucos dies* 'after a few days'; *aliquanto ante* 'some time
before'; *aliquanto post* 'some time after'; *paulo, multo ante, paulo, multo post*
'a little, much earlier, a little, much later.'

dein, deinde, deinceps, exinde 'next, thereafter, thereupon, after that.'
sub haec can mean 'shortly before' or 'shortly after this.'
secundum orationem praetoris murmur ortum (Livy): following on the
praetor's speech a murmuring arose.
secundum haec silentium fuit (Livy again): after this there was a silence.

* * * * *

14 *meminisse iuvabit*] Virgil *Aeneid* 1.203
24 Horace] *Satires* 1.3.16: 'Horace ... for Africa' added in 1534 (LB I 63C)
25 Sallust] *Jugurtha* 39.4
33 secundum orationem ... silence] Added in 1534 (LB I 63D)
33 Livy] 32.22.1
35 Livy] 32.33.1

The following words indicate a specific time: *hodie* 'today,' *heri* 'yesterday,' *nudiustertius* 'the day before yesterday' [literally, now is the third day], *nudiusquartus* 'three days ago' [literally, now is the fourth day], *quinto, sexto, septimo, octavo abhinc die* 'the fifth, sixth, seventh, eighth day from now' [i.e., four, five, six, seven days ago]. *hodie* 'today,' *cras* 'tomorrow,' *perendie, perendino die* 'the day after tomorrow,' *quarto abhinc die, quinto, sexto, etc* 'the fourth, fifth, sixth, day from now' [in the future]. The addition of a verb makes clear the time reference of phrases with *abhinc*: *septimo abhinc die mecum cenabat* 'he was having dinner with me six days ago'; *septimo abhinc die istic me videbis* 'you will see me there six days from now'; *me abhinc annis amplius xxv spopondisse dicit* (Cicero, writing to Atticus) 'he says that I made the promise more than twenty-five years ago'; *quo tempore? abhinc annis quindecim* (Cicero again) 'when? fifteen years from this time.' [*abhinc* 'from now' can be used with an accusative case or an ablative, but] the use of the accusative is somewhat harsh, especially when the phrase does not express a period of time during which an extended action is performed, for example, in this Terentian sentence: *abhinc triennium ex Andro commigravit huic viciniae* 'three years ago she moved from Andros to this neighbouhood' – the woman did not take three years over her move, but three years had intervened between her leaving Andros and coming to Athens; *quaestor C. Papirio consule fuisti abhinc annos quattuordecim* (Cicero) 'you were quaestor in the consulship of Gaius Papirius, fourteen years ago'; *scriptor abhinc annos qui centum decidit* (Horace) 'a writer who came to an end a hundred years ago.' The usage is somewhat less harsh in this example from one of Cicero's speeches against Verres: *horum pater abhinc duos et viginti annos mortuus est* 'their father deceased twenty-two years ago' (for to be deceased is a lasting state).

Here is another way of expressing an interval of time that has elapsed: *septimus hic dies est quod mecum cenavit* 'as for dining with me, this is the seventh day since he did so' [i.e., he dined with me six days ago]; *annus est quod nullas a te litteras accepi* 'it is a whole year that I have not had a letter

* * * * *

1 *heri*] See Plautus *Mostellaria* 956–7: *nam heri et nudius tertius / quartus, quintus, sextus usque*

10 *me abhinc annis* ... lasting state] The passage to line 27 added in 1534 (LB I 63D–E)

11 Cicero] *Ad Atticum* 12.17.1

13 Cicero] *Pro Roscio comoedo* 37

17 Terentian] *Andria* 70

21 Cicero] *Verrines* 1.34

23 Horace] *Epistles* 2.1.36

25 Verres] *Verrines* 2.25

from you' [i.e., I have not had a letter from you for a year]; *multum temporis est, diu est, quod nos non visis* 'you have not been to see us for a long time'; *saeculum exisse mihi videtur ex quo nullas abs te litteras accipio* 'it seems an age since I had a letter from you.' Terence used the obviously exaggerated expression *iamdudum aetatem* 'a whole lifetime ago' for 'some time ago.'

Some writers use *cum* instead of *quod*: *iam biennium est cum ille mecum esse coepit* (Plautus) 'it's two years now since he started meeting me'; *multi anni sunt cum ille in aere meo est* (Cicero) 'it's many years now that he has been at my disposal'; *vigesimus annus est cum omnes scelerati me petunt* (Cicero again) 'every criminal in the country has been after me for twenty years.'

In Cicero and others of the old writers one finds various usages with *quam*: *postridie aut post diem tertium quam lecta erit* (Cato) 'the next day or two days after it has been gathered'; *post annum tertium quam severis incendito* (Cato) 'the second year after sowing burn it off'; *postero die quam illa erant acta* (Cicero) 'the day after all this was done'; *aliquando venerunt post diem quadragesimum et sextum quam a nobis discesserant* (the younger Cicero) 'at long last they arrived, on the forty-sixth day after they had left us'; *post annum quam pro Cornelio dixerat* (Asconius Pedianus) 'a year after he had spoken in defence of Cornelius'; *post annos complures quam fecit testamentum* (Scaevola in the *Pandects*) 'a good many years after he made the will.' *ante*, whether preposition or adverb, functions in the same way: *ante sedecim annos quam haec dicta sunt* (Asconius Pedianus) 'sixteen years before this statement was made.' This type of expression is made easier by the fact

* * * * *

4 Terence … their fashion] The passage to 518:17 added in 1534 (LB I 63F–4A)
4 Terence] *Eunuchus* 734
7 Plautus] *Mercator* 533
8 Cicero] *Ad familiares* 15.14.1
10 Cicero] *Philippics* 12.24
13 Cato] *De re rustica* 65.1
15 Cato] *De re rustica* 161.2
16 Cicero] *De oratore* 2.12
17 younger Cicero] Cicero's son, writing to his father's freedman Tiro, *Ad familiares* 16.21.1. Modern editions have *vobis* for *nobis*.
19 Asconius] He wrote a commentary, only partially preserved, on some of Cicero's speeches; this example is from his commentary on *Oratio in senatu in toga candida* 73. The manuscript of Asconius was found by Poggio at Saint-Gall in 1416; the editio princeps appeared in Venice in 1477.
21 *Pandects*] *Digest* 32.41.4; cf 477:23n.
23 Asconius] See line 19n; this example is possibly a conflation of *Commentarium in Cornel.* 68: *post xvi annos quam reges exacti sunt* with 57: *ante xxiii annos quam haec dicta sunt.*

that *post* and *ante* have inherent comparative force, like *secus* 'otherwise,'
contra 'contrariwise,' *aliter* 'differently.' The expression is somewhat more
strained if none of these words is present, a form of speech frequently
employed by Livy; for example, *Lilybaeum tertio die quam profectus inde erat*
rediit 'he returned to Lilybaeum on the third day after he had set out from
there'; *die vigesimo quam creatus erat dictatura se abdicavit* 'he resigned the
dictatorship on the twentieth day after he had been appointed.'
id aetatis erat ut turpe sibi duceret discere: he was of such an age that he
considered it shameful to be learning.
non pudet te istuc aetatis lascivire? are you not ashamed to be fooling about
at your time of life?
hoc aetatis cum sim, non admodum timeo mortem: seeing that I am the age I
am, I am not particularly afraid of death.
pleramque noctem studet: he studies for most of the night.
crebris ignibus factis plerumque noctis barbari suo more laetari (Sallust):
the barbarians lit many fires and passed the best part of the night in
merriment after their fashion.

151 / Numbering with

in deos relatus; in numerum deorum relatus est: he was enrolled in the list
of gods.
inter quos referendus erit? (Horace): with whom shall he be numbered?
ascribe me in numerum tuorum: count me among your supporters.
ascribe me tuis amicis: add my name to the roll of your friends.
ascribito me inter amicos tuos: write me down among your friends.
veteribus annumerandus: to be counted in with the veterans
inter summos annumerandus: to be counted among the greatest
inter primos censendus, ponendus, collocandus: to be rated, placed, set
among the first
recipe me in tuum gregem: receive me into your company.
multos obscuros legit in senatum: he appointed many men of no distinction
to the senate.
cur hunc hominem ascivistis in vestrum contubernium? why have you
admitted this fellow into your society?

* * * * *

4 Livy] 25.31.14; 6.29.10
15 Sallust] *Jugurtha* 98.6
22 in numerum deorum relatus est] Suetonius *Julius* 88.1
24 Horace] *Epistles* 2.1.41
32 in tuum gregem] Cf Terence *Eunuchus* 1084: *ut me in vostrum gregem recipiatis.*

cooptatus in collegium augurum: co-opted into the college of augurs
ascitus, additus ordini senatorio: brought in, admitted to the senatorial
order
accersitus, ascitus in militum numerum: summoned to, included in his
forces
ut civitate donatum in decurias adlegeret (Suetonius): to admit to the panel
of jurors a man who had been given the citizenship
adde hunc amicorum tuorum catalogo: add this man to the catalogue of
your friends.

152 / Beginning and ending

in ipsis vitae primordiis: at the first beginnings of life
in ipsis vitae rudimentis: in the very first stages of life
in primis litterarum elementis: when one first starts learning to read
in capite tuarum litterarum: at the head of your letter
in prima statim fronte: at very first view
in ipso vitae limine: on the very threshold of life
in ipso quasi vestibulo vitae: at the very entrance to life
ab ipsa statim linea: from the starting-block
ab ipso carcere: from the gates
in exortu: at the rising
in exordio vitae: at the commencement of life
ab ineunte aetate: since entering on man's estate
lubricum tempus ineuntis adulescentiae: the hazardous period of first
youth
ineunte vere mox cum hirundinibus advolabo: when spring starts I shall
come flying in with the swallows.
exacta aetate nupturit: he is itching to marry when his life is done.
provecta aetate, vergente aetate, affecta aetate, effeta, decrepita aetate,
ingravescente aetate, inclinata et praecipitata, inclinata et praecipiti aetate:
    * * * * *

  6 Suetonius] *Tiberius* 51.1
 12 Beginning] This chapter (152) was expanded in both *1526* and *1534*.
 16 primis litterarum elementis] Quintilian 1.1.23
 21 ab ipsa statim ... gates] *1526* (LB I 64C)
 25 ab ineunte aetate ... its end] The passage to 520:3 *1526* (LB I 64C); for *ab ineunte
    aetate*: Cicero *Pro lege Manilia* 1.1
 26 lubricum tempus] Cf Seneca *Controversiae* 2.6.4: *adulescens ... lubricum tempus
    ... transiit.*
 31 affecta aetate] Cicero *De oratore* 1.200

LB I 64B

in advanced old age, in the decline of life, with life nearing its end, at the out-worn, decrepit stage of life, when the years become burdensome, when life sinks and hastens to its end

piget hoc aetatis depugnare: I cannot be bothered to fight it out at my time of life.

ad serum usque diem (Tacitus): until late day

praecipiti iam die (Livy): with the day by now declining

flexo in vesperam die (Tacitus): as the day wound towards evening

primis tenebris movit (Livy): he moved just as darkness fell.

prima vespera, primo diluculo, primo crepusculo (Livy again): in the early evening, at first light, at dusk

aestate iam adulta (Tacitus): when summer was at its peak

adulto autumno (Livy): when autumn was in mid-career

adulta nocte; in exitu iam annus erat (the same author): when night was full grown; the year was on the way out.

quinto anno exeunte (Cicero): as the fifth year drew to its end

decurso vitae spatio: having run his course in life

cygneam vocem 'swan song' was used by Cicero for 'last utterance' in book 3 of his work *De oratore*.

in principio: in the beginning

in initio operis: at the commencement of the work

in calce tuarum litterarum: at the foot of your letter

in extremis tuis litteris: at the end of your letter

in postrema parte tuarum litterarum: in the final part of your letter

nunc ad metam festinat oratio: now my speech is speeding towards the finishing-post.

in extremo vitae actu: in the last act of life

* * * * *

4 piget hoc ... *De oratore*] The passage to line 19 1534 (LB I 64D)
6 Tacitus] *Histories* 3.82.3
7 Livy] 25.34.14
8 Tacitus] *Annals* 1.16.3
9 Livy] 31.23.4
10 Livy] *prima vespera*: 36.29.5
12 Tacitus] *Annals* 2.23.1
13 Livy] Not Livy, but Tacitus *Annals* 11.31.2
14 same author] *adulta nocte*: Tacitus *Histories* 3.23.3; *in exitu ... erat*: Livy 38.35.1
16 Cicero] *De divinatione* 1.53
17 decurso ... spatio] Cicero *De senectute* 83
18 Cicero] *De oratore* 3.6
22 in calce tuarum litterarum] *Adagia* I ii 37

LB I 64C

in portu impingere: wreck the ship in the harbour

in porta cantherio: fall off the nag at the gate

ne in apiis quidem: they have not even started yet [literally, they are not even at the parsley]

in ipso operis ingressu: in the introductory paragraphs

in ipso statim operis frontispicio: on the very frontispiece

in ipsis vitae foribus: at the very portals of life

vitae ianua: the door of life

fauces inferorum: the jaws of hell

in philosophiam nondum intulit pedem, nondum fecit vestigium: he has not yet set foot in the realms of philosophy; he has not yet taken a step. *vestigium facere* is common in Cicero.

ordiri telam: lay the warp

pertexere: complete the warp

fundamenta iacere: lay the foundations

auspicari: make a (ceremonial) beginning

iniit consulatum: he entered upon the consulship.

ineunte vere: as spring came in

hoc ultimum utrimque initum finitumque est proelium (Livy): this was the last battle begun and concluded on either side.

vellem a principio te audisse (Cicero): I wish I had listened to you from the start.

tuas epistolas a primo lego (Cicero again): I am reading your letters from the beginning.

* * * * *

1 in portu impingere] Quintilian 4.1.61: *gubernator qui dum portu egreditur impegit; Adagia* I v 76

2 in porta cantherio] *Adagia* I v 78; this saying and the previous one refer to those who come a cropper before they have even started.

3 ne in apiis quidem] *Adagia* I x 89: either because parsley was the first thing one came to in a Greek garden, or because children who were intended to be athletes were laid in a bed of parsley soon after birth

5 ingressu] Quintilian 10.1.48

6 in ipso statim ... frontispiece] *1526* (LB I 64D)

10 in philosophiam ... finishing touches on] Text to 522:25 *1534* (LB I 64E–F)

13 ordiri telam] *Adagia* II vi 68

14 pertexere] Cicero *De oratore* 2.145

17 iniit consulatum] For example, Livy 24.9.7

18 ineunte vere] For example, Cicero *Pro lege Manilia* 35

19 Livy] 26.6.13; the usual reading is *utcumque*; Erasmus may be thinking of Sallust *Histories* 1.11: *discordiarum et certaminis utrimque finis fuit*, a fragment which he could have known from Augustine *De civitate Dei* 3.17.

21 Cicero] *Ad Atticum* 7.1.2

23 Cicero] *Ad Atticum* 9.6.5

LB I 64D

utinam a primo tibi esset visum (Cicero yet again): if only you had thought
so from the first.
hoc ab initio fuit: this was the case at the start.
utinam initio adfuisses: if only you had been here at the start.
principio quod amare velis reperire labora (Ovid): strive in the first place to
discover / The object of your passion.
ad extremum ridendus (Horace): a laughing stock at the last
consuli non animus ab initio, non fides ad extremum defuit (Cicero): the
consul did not lack courage at the start, nor credit at the end.
habes operis primam manum: you have the first draft of the work.
oratorem tibi delineavi: I have sketched the orator for you.
adumbratum accipies oratorem, non expressum: you will receive your
orator in outline, not in detail.
incohatum non absolutum: started only, not completed. Cicero employed
the term *informatum* 'roughed out' for *incohatum*. It means something of
which a rough outline has been made, and is a metaphor drawn from
sculpture and painting.
exitus acta probat: the proof of the pudding is in the eating [literally, the
result tests the actions].
ordimur hic ferratam fabulam, quae sit futura catastrophe nescio: we are
entering on a drama of violence; I do not know what the dénouement will
be.
coronidem addere: add the final flourish
colophonem imponere: add the crowning glory
supremam manum addere: put the finishing touches on

153 / More than is supposed

maiora fide: greater than anyone's capacity for belief
maiora quam ut vera credi queant: too much for anyone to be able to believe
minor opinione doctrina: his lectures are not up to expectation.
minor doctrina quam pro hominum opinione: his teaching is inferior to
men's expectation of him.

* * * * *

1 Cicero] *Ad Atticum* 16.7.4
5 Ovid] *Ars amatoria* 1.35
7 Horace] *Epistles* 1.1.9
14 Cicero] See *Orator* 33: *ad eum ... incohandum ... et formandum.*
20 catastrophe] *Adagia* I ii 36
24 colophonem] See 491:2n.
30 maiora fide] See Ovid *Metamorphoses* 4.394: *resque fide maior.*

citius spe aderat: he was there sooner than anyone hoped.
celerius exspectatione redibat: he was on the way back quicker than anyone
expected.
citius ac sperabatur: sooner than was hoped
ante exspectatum redibat: he was on the way back before expectation.
par famae doctrina: his lectures come up to his reputation.
non minor doctrina quam fama celebratur: his teaching is not inferior to
what rumour proclaims it to be.
supra fidem omnia: it is all beyond belief; that is, maiora fide: greater than
anyone's capacity for belief.
maiora veris renuntiabant: their report was exaggerated.
minora, inferiora veris praedicabant: they did not reveal the full state of
affairs [literally, they asserted what was less than the truth].
infra verum erant quae nuntiabat: what he reported was less than the truth.
minor consulari dignitate cognitio: the inquiry is beneath the dignity of a
consul.
minus est quam ut a consule cognoscatur: it is too small a matter to be
investigated by a consul.
maior consulis dignitas quam ut hanc causam cognoscat: the standing of a
consul is too high for him to investigate this case.
tua virtus maior est omni praeconio: your virtue is greater than any commendation.
vincit omnem laudem tua virtus: your goodness defeats all praise.

154 / Falling to the lot of

hoccine tantum malum mihi derepente obiectum esse! to think that such a
misfortune has all of a sudden cropped up.
ingens huic venit (*or* obvenit) hereditas: a huge inheritance came his way.
obtigit uxor qualem volebam: it has been my good fortune to find the sort of
wife I wanted.

* * * * *

5 ante exspectatum] There are several examples in poets and Silver Latin prose,
for example, Ovid *Metamorphoses* 4.790: *ante exspectatum tacuit*; and see
555:2n.
9 supra fidem] See Quintilian 2.10.5: *supra fidem et poetica themata*.
26 Falling to the lot of] This (chap 154) is the final chapter of book I in *1514*; *1512*
has four more (numbered 150–3), which in *1514* were transferred to new
positions as chaps 54–7 (LB I 40F–1D).
28 obiectum esse] Terence *Adelphi* 610

non cuivis homini contingit adire Corinthum: not every man has the luck to
reach the city of Corinth.
nactus es uxorem te dignam: you have acquired a wife worthy of you.
felicissimum ingenium sortitus es: you drew an enviable disposition in
life's lottery.
similes habent labra lactucas: the mouth matches the lettuce.
habet quod amet: he has found something to suit him.
is nunc reperit: he's learning it now.
merito nobis accidit ut mali videamur dum nimium studemus nos videri
bonos: it rightly happens that we give a bad impression when we strive too
hard to make a good one.
non omnibus datum ut impune quae lubeat dicant: not everyone is granted
the privilege of saying what he fancies with impunity.
non quibuslibet licet quae libeat facere: it is not permitted to all and sundry
to do just what they fancy.
mihi usu venit (*or* usus venit) ut cum intractabili monstro conflictarer: it
was my lot to wrestle with an intractable monster.

155 / Shrinking from

refugit consuetudinem feminarum: he shrinks from any association with
women.
alienus est a studiis: he is a total stranger to study.
abhorret a litteris: he turns from literature with loathing.
Suetonius uses *abhorret ostentum* 'recoils from the portent' in the sense of
exhorret 'is horrified at.'
execratur, detestatur, abominatur litteras: he loathes, detests, abominates
literature.
ad studiorum mentionem nauseat: the mention of study makes him sick.
horret mortem: he has a horror of death.
exhorret mare: he is terrified of the sea.
aversatur omnes: he shuns everyone.
avertitur miseros: he turns his back on the unfortunate.

* * * * *

1 adire Corinthum] Horace *Epistles* 1.17.36, a favourite example of Erasmus'; see
295:10n, 403:22n.
6 labra lactucas] An ass's tough mouth munches tough thistles; that is, it meets
its match; *Adagia* I x 71.
20 Shrinking from] Chaps 155–71 were added in *1526*.
26 Suetonius] *Galba* 4.2

LB I 65A

ad poetices mentionem nauseat, vomiturit: if poetry is mentioned, he feels
like throwing up.
deprecatur publica munia: he begs to be excused from public duties.
gravatur splendidos mensae apparatus: sumptuous banquets are a vexation
to him. *gravatur* 'be weighed down by' is the equivalent of *moleste fert*
'bears ill, takes offence at.' Suetonius and Horace both use *gravor* with an
accusative like this. Horace, for example, has:
equitem gravatus / Bellerophontem: resenting Bellerophon, set upon his
back.

156 / Positions

erat illi a pedibus: he was footman in his service.
aberat qui mihi est a manibus: my secretary was away.
nam tum aberat meus amanuensis: at the time my clerk was away.
qui regi sunt a corpore, a secretis, a sacris scriniis: the king's valets, his
clerks to the council, officials of the royal secretariat
rationales, qui sunt a rationibus: treasury officials
a libellis: ministers of petitions
ab actis, actuarii: financial clerks, quartermasters
laterones, anteambulones: bodyguards
a cyathis, a poculis, pocillator: cup-bearer
nomenclator: prompter, remembrancer
a consiliis, consiliarius (Suetonius): counsellor

157 / Interests

totus est in litteris: he is absorbed in his literary studies.
vacat congerendis opibus: all his time is taken up with accumulating
wealth.
dat operam rei nummariae: he is devoting his attention to financial matters.
attendit huic negotio: he is considering this business.
attendit iuri (Suetonius): he paid attention to, that is, studied, law.

* * * * *

6 Suetonius] For example, *Augustus* 72.3: *ampla et operosa praetoria gravabatur*
7 Horace] *Odes* 4.11.27
22 laterones] On this word Varro *De lingua latina* 7.52
25 Suetonius] *Tiberius* 33; Suetonius also uses *a manu, amanuensis, actuarii,
anteambulones.*
35 Suetonius] *Galba* 5.1

LB I 65B

intentus est lucris, intendit lucris: he is intent on gain.
inhiat gloriae: he is agape for glory.
appulit animum ad scribendum: he put his mind to writing.
adiecit animum ad virginem: he has set his heart on the girl.
accommoda te rebus praesentibus: adapt yourself to present circumstances.
applica animum tuum ad uxoris ingenium: accommodate your attitudes to
fit in with your wife's nature.
dedidit se mammonae: he surrendered himself to Mammon.
dedicavi me Christo: I have dedicated myself to Christ.
dica te totum optimis litteris: devote yourself entirely to what is best in
literature.
dedit se ad leges (Cicero): he gave himself up wholly to the law.
servos ad remum dedit (Suetonius): he sent slaves to man the oars. (The
same writer also uses the phrase *ad terram dedit* 'sent to the ground' with the
force of *deiecit* 'beat down.')
inservit honori: he dances attendance on honours.
incumbite honestis disciplinis, incumbite in honestas disciplinas: direct all
your energies to honest learning.
devotus harenae (Suetonius): a sports addict. Suetonius also uses *devotus
vobis* 'devoted and dedicated to you.'
adiunxit animum ad ea quae ratio temporum postulabat: he acquiesced in
the demands of circumstance.
ut animum ad aliquod studium adiungant: to give themselves up to some
craze

158 / Corrupting

corrumpunt bonos mores colloquia mala: evil communications corrupt
good manners.
inficiunt, vitiant, primam aetatem stultae nutrices: young children can be
sullied and tainted by stupid nurses.

* * * * *

3 ad scribendum] Terence *Andria* 1
4 ad virginem] Terence *Eunuchus* 143
13 Suetonius] *Augustus* 16.1
14 same writer] *Augustus* 96.1
16 inservit honori] Horace *Ars poetica* 167
19 Suetonius] *Caligula* 30.2; *Tiberius* 67.4
23 studium adiungant] Terence *Andria* 56
29 colloquia mala] 1 Cor 15:33

aurum plumbo adulterant: they adulterate the gold with lead.

gemmae adulterinae: false gems

depravant bonam causam mali rhetores: bad speakers ruin a good case.

deterunt laudem ducis indocti poetae: ignorant poets dim a leader's reputation.

malus vicinus scabiem suam adfricat vicino: a bad neighbour spreads his scab by contagion.

vas insincerum afficit infusum liquorem: a dirty vessel contaminates any liquid poured in.

obtrusit mihi subaeratos nummos pro aureis: he passed off gold-washed coins on me for gold ones.

vereor ne quid veneni tuis afflet: I fear his noxious breathings may taint your supporters.

ne quid pestis instillet in tenerum animum: ... he may drop some baleful poison into this young mind.

ne quod sincerum est trahat in vitium: ... he may draw to evil courses what is pure.

ne tibi morbum inhalet suum: ... he may pass on his sickness to you.

ne suum virus insibilet: ... his hissing tongue may inject you with his venom.

ne quid inspiret mali: ... his evil breath may contaminate.

puerilem animum impiis opinionibus imbuit: he imbued the boy's mind with irreverent views.

malitiam una cum lacte nutricis imbibit, suxit, hausit: he drank, sucked, drew in malice with his nurse's milk.

frequentes offensae reddunt suppuratam amicitiam: injury, if it repeated be, an ulcer gnaws in fair friendship's flesh.

gloriam tuam dedecore contaminasti, inquinasti, conspurcasti, foedasti, obscurasti, deturpasti, offuscasti, denigrasti: by this disgrace you have marred, stained, smirched, polluted, dimmed, disfigured, obscured, blackened your great name.

inussit tibi notam ignominiae: this has branded you with the mark of infamy.

* * * * *

6 malus vicinus] See Seneca *Epistles* 7.7.

8 vas insincerum] Cf Horace *Epistles* 1.2.54: *sincerum est nisi vas, quodcumque infundis acescit.*

10 gold-washed coins] See Persius 5.106: *subaerato ... auro.*

24 cum lacte nutricis] See 487:29n.

29 deturpasti] Suetonius *Caligula* 35.2

LB I 65E

venenare 'poison' is a verb used by the poets; *potionare* 'medicate' occurs in Suetonius.

159 / Solitude

secum vivit: he lives by himself.
secum loquitur: he talks to himself.
solus est: he is alone.
solitarius est: he is solitary.
incomitatus incedit: he proceeds unattended.
solus ambulat: he is walking alone.
in locis solis ambulare tutum non est: it is not safe to walk in lonely places.
agit in solitudine: he spends his days in solitude.
ne musca quidem adest: there is not even a fly with him.
secretum agere 'to exercise withdrawal' occurs in Suetonius in the sense 'be alone.'
foris se venditant, cum apud se sunt, nihil illis sordidius: in public they make a great show, at home you could not imagine anything more squalid.
vix asse emeris, si totum hominem per se aestimes: you would hardly pay a brass farthing if you put a price on the whole man just as he stands.

160 / Have a sense of

oratio tua sapit tyrannidem: your speech has the savour of tyranny.
resipit stultitiam: it smacks of folly.
olet hircum: he stinks of goat.
redolet vinum: he reeks of wine.
vox tua sonat asinum: your voice sounds like an ass's bray.
rusticus obolet allium: the rustic sends out a gust of garlic.
vineta crepat mera: he prates of nothing but vineyards.
scripta tua spirant Italum: your letter wafts the aroma of Italy.

* * * * *

1 poets] For example, Horace *Odes* 1.22.3: *venenatis sagittis*
2 Suetonius] *Caligula* 50.2: *potionatus*
15 ne musca quidem adest] See Suetonius *Domitian* 3.1, a witty remark made about Domitian, who used to shut himself away and torture flies to death.
16 Suetonius] *Tiberius* 60.1
29 redolet vinum] Cicero *Philippics* 2.63
31 obolet allium] Cf Plautus *Mostellaria* 38: *oboluisti allium*.
32 crepat mera] Horace *Epistles* 1.7.84

LB I 65F

tinnit aurum: it has a gold ring.

fragras unguentum: you breathe odours.

Phrases like *torvum tueri* 'direct a savage gaze,' *titanicum obtueri* 'turn a giant's glare' belong here. The figure is less harsh in Greek, for example, μανικὸν βλέπειν [roll a frenzied eye].

161 / Fulfilling

fac promissa appareant: make your promises come true.

exhibe quod toties polliceris: put into practice what you keep on promising.

talem et se et exercitum adprobavit ut nulli praemia maiora perceperint: he so demonstrated the excellence of himself and his army that they received greater rewards than any others. (These last two examples both from Suetonius.)

si fortuna obstabit quo minus praestem quod recepi, certe hunc animum tibi probabo: if fortune prevents me from actually doing what I have undertaken, I shall certainly convince you of the reality of my intentions.

promittis amplissima, das nihil: you promise the earth and give nothing.

si munificus videri vis, repraesenta beneficium: if you want to look generous, pay out your benefit on the spot. (Both Seneca and Suetonius use *repraesentare* 'pay out in cash' in this way, meaning 'put into practice without delay.')

162 / Repenting

nondum huius animi me paenitet: I do not so far repent of my attitude.

me quantum hic operis fiat paenitet: I am not happy about the amount of work going on here (here *paenitet* is equivalent to *non satisfacit* 'it is not satisfying').

* * * * *

3 *torvum tueri*] Virgil *Aeneid* 6.467

10 fac promissa appareant] Terence *Eunuchus* 310

16 Suetonius] Possibly a memory of *Tiberius* 24.1: *ceteros quod polliciti sint tarde praestare, sed ipsum quod praestet tarde polliceri; Galba* 6.3

22 Seneca] See *De beneficiis* 2.4.2: *repraesentanda sunt beneficia quae a quibusdam accipere difficilius est quam impetrare.*

22 Suetonius] For example, *Caligula* 58.1: *repraesentare spectaculum*

capit me pristinae benignitatis paenitudo: regret for my early generosity
now moves me.

paenitentia ductus, paenitentia tactus: moved by repentance, touched by
repentance

agere paenitentiam has the same sense as *paenitere*. The Younger Pliny uses
it: rursus eius paenitentiae paenitentiam ago: and now in turn I experience
regret for my earlier regret (i.e., I am sorry I was sorry).

paenitet can be used with reference to people or things: nec te paeniteat
istius patris: nor need you feel any regret at such a father as you have.

initi matrimonii me paenitet: I regret ever entering on the married state.

163 / Strife

male sarta / gratia nequicquam coit, et rescinditur: good will / If ill sewn up,
begins to heal in vain; / Ere long the wound opens up again.

interrupta familiaritas: acquaintance broken off

mala lingua dirimit multorum amicitias: evil speaking sunders the friendships of many.

orta est inter illos simultas: dissension arose between them.

refrixit benevolentia: his good will cooled.

amor versus in odium: love turned to hate.

discordant: they are at loggerheads.

intercessit offensae nescio quid: some offence or other came between them.

Sallust on several occasions uses *offensa* for *discordia*.

dissuenda est amicitia, non abrumpenda: friendship should be unstitched,
not torn away.

dissiluit gratia fratrum: the good will of the brothers burst asunder.

parum inter eos convenit: there is little agreement between them.

miror non bene convenire vobis: I am surprised that you do not get on
together.

utrique cum altero convenit: each is in agreement with the other.

concordant: their hearts are as one.

concordes sumus: we are of one mind.

* * * * *

5 Younger Pliny] *Epistles* 7.10.3: *agatque paenitentiam paenitentiae suae*
9 patris] See Horace *Satires* 1.6.89: *nil me paeniteat sanum patris huius.*
15 et rescinditur] Horace *Epistles* 1.3.31
25 Sallust] For example, *Jugurtha* 102.7
26 non abrumpenda] Cf Cicero *De amicitia* 76.
28 gratia fratrum] Horace *Epistles* 1.18. 41–2

oratio tua cum factis non consentit: your speech does not agree with your deeds.

summo omnium consensu: with the approval of the entire company

magna inter molles concordia: deep concord reigns in gentle hearts.

nulla inter nos discordia: there is no point of disagreement between us.

dissident inter sese: they are at variance.

obortum est inter illos subitum dissidium: a sudden discord sprang up between them.

digressa est a marito (Suetonius): she parted from her husband.

divertit ab illo: she separated from him.

divortium fecit cum illo: he and she went their separate ways.

repudiavit uxorem: he repudiated his wife.

dimisit matrimonio: he put her away from the state of matrimony.

dimisit matrimonium: he put away (i.e., rescinded) the marriage.

renuntiavit illi amicitiam: he renounced his friendship; which has the same meaning as: denuntiavit illi inimicitiam: he declared a state of enmity.

dissedit cum uxore: he was at odds with his wife; that is, discidium habuit: he was estranged from her.

missam fecit uxorem: he sent his wife packing, a phrase which Suetonius uses for *repudiavit*.

serere dissidia: sow dissension

est illi offensior: he is on rather bad terms with him. Suetonius again; *subiratus* 'rather angry' would be an equivalent.

est mihi cum illis ἄσπονδος πόλεμος: there is war to the death between us.

164 / Reconciling

sarcire, resarcire gratiam: repair, patch up good relations

reducere, reponere, restituere in gratiam: bring back, return, restore to good relations

redigam vos in gratiam: I shall put you on good terms again.

reconcinnare pristinam amicitiam: to set to rights the ancient friendship

recollige mihi illius animum: win back his feelings for me.

* * * * *

9 Suetonius] *Julius* 43.1
13 dimisit matrimonio] Suetonius *Tiberius* 49
16 denuntiavit ... inimicitiam] Cicero *Philippics* 5.19
17 dissedit cum uxore] Suetonius *Tiberius* 7.3
19 Suetonius] *Caligula* 25.2
22 Suetonius] *Tiberius* 13.2

fac ut mecum redeat in gratiam: get him to be reconciled with me.

instaura pristinam inter nos benevolentiam: restore the good will that once existed between us.

in gratiam iam cum voluptate redeamus (Cicero): so that we can now be on good terms with pleasure.

Pompeius a me valde contendit de reditu in gratiam, sed adhuc nihil profecit (Cicero): Pompey is making great efforts to get me to agree to a reconciliation, but so far he is getting nowhere.

sicuti regi libuerat, pax convenit (Sallust): peace was arranged on the terms the king had proposed.

165 / Sense and its opposite

pol homo tu non es sobrius? good heavens, man, can you be sober?

insanit, delirat, desipit: he is crazy; his wits are out of course; he is out of his senses.

vesanire (Catullus): rage insanely

non est integrae mentis: he is not of sound mind.

non est compos mentis: he is not compos mentis.

non constat animo: he is not stable mentally.

laborat errore mentis: he suffers from delusions.

motae, commotae mentis est: he is of disturbed mind.

mente lapsi (Suetonius): those who had lost their wits

defectus animo: mentally defective

mente excidit: he took leave of his senses.

valet animo: he is mentally sound.

laborat ab animo: he is weak in the head.

Sophocles reus actus est dementiae: Sophocles was taken to court on a charge of insanity.

destituit illum vis animi: his mental powers deserted him.

* * * * *

4 Cicero] *De senectute* 56

7 Cicero] *Ad Quintum fratrem* 3.1.15

9 Sallust] *Jugurtha* 38.10

15 es sobrius] Cf Terence *Andria* 778.

18 Catullus] 25.13

24 Suetonius] *Augustus* 48

29 Sophocles] By his sons who wished to depose him, at the age of 90, from the conduct of the family's affairs; he refuted the accusation by reading from his latest play, the *Oedipus Coloneus*; see Cicero *De senectute* 22.

166 / Excepting, excluding

nullus istuc auderet nisi tu solus: no one would dare that but you alone.
nemo praeter unum te: no one apart from just you
nemo praeterquam tu solus: no one beyond you alone
nullus aderat extra unam aniculam: no one was present beyond one old dame.
fortunatus sum ceteris in rebus absque una hac: I am fortunate in all other things barring this one.
extra ducem paucosque praeterea (Cicero): outside the general and a few others besides
extra praedam: outside, that is, apart from, the spoil
Cicero quite often uses this idiom with *extra* in imitation of the Greeks; but *extra iocum* 'outside a joke, in all seriousness,' *extra causam* 'apart from a reason, unmotivated' are not quite in the same class.
omnium facundissimus excepto Cicerone: the most eloquent of all, Cicero excepted
omnibus nisi uno Cicerone facundior: surpassing all in eloquence but Cicero alone
omnium doctissimus si unum aut alterum excipias: the most learned of all, if you exclude one or two others
nemini cedit uno te excepto: he yields to no one, except for you alone.
excepto can also be used without a nominal form: excepto quod non simul esses, cetera laetus (Horace): except that you were not with me, / Happy for the rest
In legal language we find *recipere* instead of *excipere*: recepit sarta tecta: he set aside buildings roofed and repaired.
uni tibi permitto, praeterea nemini: I allow you alone, and apart from that no one.
tibi quidvis apud me licet: as far as I am concerned, you may do what you like.
alioqui non ferrem, alias non ferrem, aliter non ferrem: otherwise, in other circumstances, I would not put up with it. This last phrase occurs in Cicero, in his *De officiis*.
We often find *super* 'above' for *praeter* 'apart from' in Suetonius, but the force of *super* is not so much to exclude as to set apart from the rest: super

* * * * *

6 unam aniculam] Cf Terence *Phormio* 98.
10 Cicero] *Ad familiares* 7.3.2
13 Cicero] For example, *De finibus* 5.77: *quicquam extra virtutem*
24 Horace] *Epistles* 1.10.50

LB I 67A

Angelo Poliziano
Portrait medal attributed to Niccolò Fiorentino, c 1494
Erasmus regarded the 'exquisite' Poliziano (1454–94) as one of the very few modern
writers 'whom I should not hesitate to include among the greatest' (Ep 126:150–1).
On the reverse of the medal is inscribed 'STUDIA,' and a winged figure hands a
branch plucked from a laurel tree to a seated female figure who may be a
personification of Florence.
Münzkabinett, Staatliche Museen zu Berlin

veteres amicos et familiares: over and above his old friends and acquaintances

Politianus secundum te primas tenet: after you, Poliziano holds first rank (i.e., except for you).

167 / As you wish and its opposite

uxorem nactus sum ex animi mei sententia: I have acquired a wife after my own heart.

uxor mihi contigit qualem volebam: I have been fortunate enough to find the kind of wife I wanted.

hic venatus male respondet votis nostris: this hunting answers ill to our prayers.

non successit pro votis navigatio: the voyage did not succeed as he had prayed.

nihil accidit non praeter animi sententiam: nothing happens that is not contrary to my dearest wish.

omnia secus quam volebam, omnia contra quam volebam: everything quite different from, quite the opposite of what I wanted

fortuna non respondit optatis meis: fortune did not answer to my desires.

fac ut lubet: do as you please.

fac pro tuo arbitrio: act as seems best to you.

vive tuo arbitratu: choose your own way of life.

nihil faciam nisi de concilii sententia: I shall do nothing except in accordance with the will of the council.

faciam ut voles: I will act as you shall desire me.

faciam pro tua voluntate omnia: I shall do everything in accordance with your wishes.

168 / Known, proved

homo spectatae probitatis: a man of proved integrity

vir probatissimae fidei: a man of tried and tested loyalty

* * * * *

1 amicos et familiares] *Tiberius* 55.1

3 Poliziano] Angelo Poliziano, 1454–94, secretary to Lorenzo de' Medici, and a member of the Platonic Academy in Florence; he was a distinguished humanist for whom Erasmus had a high regard, quoting him in the *Adagia* as an authority and as representative of the best Italian scholarship; see Ep 126:151–7.

LB I 67B

animum in me tuum habeo multis iam argumentis exploratissimum: I am
quite convinced of your feelings towards me, which have been demonstrated by many a proof.

compertum, perspectum, exploratum habeo quanti me facias: I have it as
ascertained, evident, established fact [i.e., I am well aware] how much you
care for me.

delectus est ut industriae vir expertae (Suetonius): he was chosen as a man
of acknowledged energy.

periclitatos mores (Cicero); tried and tested character.

(In these two examples *expertus* and *periclitatus* are the equivalent of *spec-
tatus*.)

comperta mihi est hominis perfidia: I know the fellow's treachery through
and through.

deprehensa est astutia: the trick was detected.

re compertum est: it was definitely ascertained.

pro certo, pro comperto dicis: you say for sure, as ascertained fact.

certum non habeo: I am not sure about

cum certum sciero, scribam ad te: when I know definitely, I shall write to
you.

169 / Abundance

abundat opibus: he is rolling in money.

exuberat, redundat, exundat, superfluit; superfluens (Seneca): abounds,
overflows, outpours, superabounds; superabundant

est apud illos ingens aquarum et graminis copia: they have an enormous
supply of water and grain.

Cicero and Suetonius both use *copiae* 'resources' for 'riches.'

multum, plurimum, satis vini: much, a great deal of, enough wine

abunde potentiae gloriaeque (Suetonius): enough power and glory and to
spare

nimium licentiae: an excess of licence

* * * * *

7 Suetonius] *Vespasian* 4.5
9 Cicero] *De amicitia* 63
25 Seneca] For example, *De beneficiis* 1.11.5: *hic erit pecunia non superfluens*
29 Cicero] Frequently; for example, *Verrines* 1.127
29 Suetonius] *Vitellius* 7.1
31 Suetonius] *Julius* 86.2

nimis insidiarum: too much of a trick, a phrase used by Cicero in the sense
'definitely a trick.'
affatim vini: wine to satiety
ne cui maior quam quinquaginta iugerum agri modus esset (Livy): that no
one's measure of land should exceed fifty iugera
hoc erat in votis, modus agri non ita magnus (Horace): this did I pray for: a
parcel of ground / Of modest size.
frumenti in summa caritate maximum numerum miseram (Cicero): when
corn was in very short supply, I had sent an enormous quantity.
maximus vini numerus fuit, permagnum optimi pondus argenti (Cicero
again, in one of his *Philippic Orations*): there was a very large quantity of
wine, a huge weight of valuable silver.
magno invento numero hordei olei vini fici, pauco tritici (Hirtius): discovering a large quantity of barley, oil, wine, and figs, but not much wheat
immensa pecuniarum vis reperta est: a huge sum of money was discovered.
quibus mala abunde omnia erant (Sallust): who were well supplied with
misfortunes
abunde libertatem rati quia tergis abstinetur (Sallust again): thinking you
have liberty in full since your backs are spared
inopem et coopertum miseriis effecit (same writer): turned me into a man
impoverished and overwhelmed with misfortune.
haec talia facinora impune suscepisse parum habuere (again Sallust): they
were not content with having committed these atrocities with impunity.
satis habebatis animam retinere (Sallust): you were satisfied with merely
being alive.

170 / Without a hearing

indicta causa coniecit servos in vincula (Cicero): he flung the slaves into
prison without a hearing.

* * * * *

 1 Cicero] *Orator* 170
 4 ne cui maior ... alive] The passage to line 25 added in *1534* (LB I 67E–F)
 4 Livy] 26.34.10
 6 Horace] *Satires* 2.6.1
 8 Cicero] *Pro Plancio* 64
10 Cicero] *Philippics* 2.66
13 Hirtius] *Bellum Africum* 67
16 Sallust] *Catilina* 21.1; *Histories* 3.48.26; *Jugurtha* 14.11, 31.9, 31.20
30 Cicero] *Verrines* 5.18, misremembered

LB I 67E

quosdam inauditos condemnavit (Suetonius): some persons he condemned unheard.

inauditum capite puniebat: he would execute without a chance to speak.

citra causae cognitionem damnatus est: he was condemned without the case being investigated.

The term used by the lawyers is ἐρημοδίκιον [an undefended action, judgment by default].

171 / Prosperity and its opposite

prospera valetudine: in flourishing health

incolumi valetudine: in unimpaired health

incolumi fama: with undamaged reputation

secundiore fama fuit: won a more favourable repute, the equivalent of

minus laboravit infamia: suffered less from notoriety

secundo vento, secundo aestu: with a following wind, tide

secundo amne, flumine: downstream

secundo rumore (Tacitus): exciting favourable comment

adverso rumore: exciting adverse comment, a phrase of Tacitus', where *adversus* has the sense of *sinister* 'malicious.'

Tacitus also uses the following phrases:

secundis numinibus: by the favour of the powers above

secunda tempestate ac fama: blessed by fame and good weather

secundante vento: with a following wind

Tacitus and Livy both use the phrase *secunda proelia* 'favourable battles' for 'successfully fought.'

et Iunone secunda (Virgil): with Juno's blessing too

dextro Hercule: with Hercules' blessing [literally, with Hercules on the right (i.e., propitious) side]

* * * * *

1 Suetonius] *Galba* 14.3

3 capite puniebat] Suetonius *Vitellius* 14.4

10 Prosperity] This (171) is the final chap of book I in *1526*.

15 secundiore fama fuit] Suetonius *Julius* 2; that is, by comparison with the doubtful reputation acquired by Caesar's activities in the East

19 Tacitus] *secundo rumore: Annals* 3.29.4; *adverso rumore: Histories* 2.26.2; *sinister rumor: Histories* 2.93.2; *secundis numinibus: Annals* 15.34.1; *secunda tempestate ac fama: Agricola* 38.5; *secundante vento: Annals* 2.24.3

26 Tacitus] *Histories* 4.79.4; Livy, for example 40.35.4

28 Virgil] *Aeneid* 4.45

secundam existimationem collegit (Suetonius): collected good opinions.

si quem numina laeva sinunt: if this to any man the grudging spirits grant

hic tibi si alias umquam mens laeva fuit: on this occasion, if ever, your thoughts were ill-fated.

reflante fortuna nihil ages (Cicero): you will achieve nothing if fortune blows contrary.

rebus adversis, rebus afflictis, rebus tristibus erigendus est animus: in difficulty, affliction, misfortune, an effort must be made to rouse the spirits.

cedidit belle: it turned out nicely.

ita cecidit ut volebam: it turned out just as I wanted.

hoc cecidit opportune: this turned out very well.

valde optanti utrique nostrum cecidit: what happened is exactly what we were both longing for.

hoc adhuc percommode cadit: so far things are turning out very conveniently (these five all from Cicero).

male cecidit: it turned out badly.

hac non successit (Terence): this way has not proved successful.

172 / Past history

ab orbe condito non extitit homo sceleratior: since the foundation of the world there has not arisen a greater villain.

duo post homines natos taeterrima capita Dolabella et Antonius: the two most loathsome creatures that have ever appeared since mankind was born, Dolabella and Antony

consules post hominum memoriam taeterrimi atque turpissimi: the most abominable and infamous consuls in the whole history of our nation

post homines natos: since mankind was born

nostra aetate 'within our own life-time' is used for something that we ourselves have experienced, *nostra memoria* 'within our own recollection' for something seen by an older generation which we have been able to hear

* * * * *

1 Suetonius] *Claudius* 7.1
2 laeva sinunt] Virgil *Georgics* 4.7
5 Cicero] Cf *De officiis* 2.19: *cum (fortuna) reflaverit affligimur.*
15 Cicero] *Ad Atticum* 13.33a.1; *Ad Atticum* 3.7.1; *De oratore* 2.15; *De oratore* 1.96; *Verrines* 1.5
17 Terence] *Andria* 670
20 Past history] Chaps 172–206 were added in *1534.*
24 duo post homines natos] Cicero *Philippics* 11.1
27 consules ... turpissimi] Cicero *Pro Plancio* 86

of from them; *patrum memoria* 'in the recollection or experience of our forefathers' goes further back than either of these, and refers to something that happened in the time of our great-grandfathers and remote ancestors. Cicero used *ex omni memoria* 'from all time past' in his speech *Pro Publio Sestio,* and *superiore memoria* 'in earlier times' in his speech *Pro Lucio Cornelio Balbo.*

post orbem conditum: since the foundation of the world
post urbem conditam (Cicero): since the foundation of Rome

173 / Entirety

a capite usque ad calcem: from head to heels
a summo capillo usque ad imum pedis: from the top of his head to the soles of his feet
debes in solidum: you are liable for the whole amount.
reddes ad assem (the Younger Pliny): you shall pay to the last farthing.
quod iis ad denarium solveretur (Cicero in his speech *Pro Publio Quinctio*): the amount to be paid them down to the last penny
bona fide reddidit depositum vel cum pulvisculo: in good faith he handed back what had been entrusted to him, even including the dust it had accumulated.
cum tota erugine (Juvenal): rust and all
quantus quantus est nihil nisi somnium est: taken all together he's nothing but stuff and nonsense.
hiemem inter se quam longa est (Virgil): throughout all the winter's length

* * * * *

1 *patrum memoria*] For example, Cicero *De natura deorum* 2.165
4 *ex omni memoria*] Cicero *Pro Sestio* 27
5 *superiore memoria*] Cicero *Pro Balbo* 28
8 post urbem conditam] Cicero *Catilinarians* 4.14
13 a capite usque ad calcem] *Adagia* I ii 37
17 Younger Pliny] *Epistles* 1.15.1
18 Cicero] *Pro Quinctio* 17
23 Juvenal] 13.61
24 somnium est] Cf Terence *Adelphi* 394: *tu quantus quantu's nil nisi sapientia es, ille somnium.*
26 Virgil] *Aeneid* 4.193

174 / Clarity

dilucide expedivi quibus oportuit: I have clearly set it out before the proper persons.

vel caeco perspicuum est: even a blind man could see that.

explanatius dicam: I shall make it more explicit.

dicam crassiore Minerva: I shall express it with a more homespun wit.

enodatius explicare (Cicero, in his work *De finibus*): set out in a rather simple and straightforward manner

enucleate (Cicero again): stripped of unnecessary verbiage

dic exserte, velis an nolis: state plainly and openly whether you will or no.

candidus sermo: unclouded (i.e., clear, lucid) speech

The Greeks use the phrase λευκὸς λόγος [bright speech] meaning 'clear, lucid,' and λευκότερον λέγειν [to speak more brightly] meaning 'say with greater clarity.'

sole meridiano clarius: plainer than the sun at midday

significavit verius quam expressit: suggested rather than stated plainly

lex hoc expresse vetuit: the law expressly forbade.

declara mentem tuam: declare your intention.

planum facere: make plain; often used by Cicero with the force of *declarare* 'declare.'

oculis subicere, ob oculos ponere: set under, set before the eyes of

solidum est: it is solid reality (i.e., plain fact), used by Cicero in his first speech against Verres: at enim illud solidum est ut me Siculi maxime velint, alterum illud credo obscurum est: it is plain fact that the Sicilians wanted me more than anybody; the other question I believe is less clear ...

luce clarius, tuba clarius (two Greek expressions): clearer than day, louder than a trumpet

* * * * *

3 quibus oportuit] Terence *Phormio* 399

7 crassiore Minerva] Cf Quintilian 1.10.28: *quosdam imperitiores etiam crassiore ut vocant Musa*; Horace *Satires* 2.2.3: *crassaque Minerva*; *Adagia* II vi 75.

8 Cicero] *De finibus* 5.27

10 Cicero] For example, *Tusculan Disputations* 4.33

13 λευκὸς λόγος] *Adagia* IV vii 100

20 Cicero] For example, *Verrines* 2.81

23 first speech against Verres] *In Caecilium* 22; modern texts read *solum id est*; Erasmus also prefers to read *solidum* in Seneca *De beneficiis* at 7.17.1, where modern texts have *hoc absolutum et verum beneficium*.

175 / Nobility and its opposite

vir apprime nobilis: a man noble in the highest degree
minime obscuris natalibus: anything but obscurely connected
homo minime novus: by no means a parvenu   5
homo cum primis illustris: a particularly illustrious personage
vir clarissimus: the right honourable
vir antiquae nobilitatis: a man of ancient family
vir honesto apud suos loco natus: a member of a highly respected local
family   10
summo loco nata: a woman of exalted birth
domi splendidus: a man of high standing in local society
maiorum imaginibus clarus: a man eminent by reason of distinguished
ancestors
ex illustri stirpe progenitus: the descendant of an illustrious line   15
avitis stemmatibus clarus: a brilliant figure whose family tree reaches back
for centuries
homo domi nobilis: one of the local gentry, a phrase often used by Cicero
and Sallust of a man belonging to a family of some distinction
homo domi suae cum primis locuples atque honestus: a man with highly   20
respected and wealthy connections in his home town
hominem veteris prosapiae ac multarum imaginum (Sallust): a man of
ancient lineage, boasting many ancestral portraits
Philargus in amplissima civitate amplissimo loco natus (Cicero): Philargus,
a man born of a noble house in a noble city   25
adolescentes nec tenui loco orti (Livy): young men, and not ones of base
parentage at that
femina splendide nata (Pliny): a lady of exalted rank
obscurus: undistinguished; homo loco obscuro tenuique ortus fortuna
(Livy): a man of undistinguished origin and humble condition   30
humili loco, infimo loco natus: low-bred, base-born
homo novus: self-made man

* * * * *

18 domi nobilis] *Adagia* IV ix 49
18 Cicero] For example, *Verrines* 3.80; 2.35; Sallust *Catilina* 17.4
22 Sallust] *Jugurtha* 85.10
24 Cicero] *Verrines* 5.122. Modern texts have Phalacrus.
26 Livy] 2.3.2
28 Pliny] *Epistles* 6.33.2
30 Livy] 26.6.13

LB I 68E

Sallust calls Cicero *reperticius* 'up-start,' because he came of a family undistinguished in public life.
vir equestri loco: a man of knightly status
vir senatorii generis: of the senatorial class
Cicero used *vicanus* 'bumpkin' for a person of low birth. Horace called ignoble persons *ignotos* 'unknown.'

176 / Violence

vix a manibus temperatum est: they hardly refrained from coming to blows.
res ad vim et arma spectabat: things were moving towards violence and the use of weapons.
a verbis ventum est ad verbera: words led to blows.
rixa in pugnam versa est: the quarrel turned into a fight.
vi geritur res: violence rules the day.
ferro non rationibus decertabatur: the issue was being resolved with weapons rather than arguments.
in manibus ius erat: might was right.
ad saga properatum est (frequently used by Cicero): there was a rush to get out the greatcoats, [i.e., to prepare for war]; *sagum* 'cloak' is a military garment, as the toga is a civilian one.
collo obtorto reduxit hominem: he dragged the fellow back by the scruff of the neck.

177 / Rumour

vulgo fertur: it is commonly reported.
diu fuit populi fabula: for a long time there was talk among the people.

* * * * *

1 Sallust] *In Ciceronem declamatio* 1.1; Cicero, who made his own way in politics without the backing of a powerful and established family, was an outstanding example of the *novus homo* (see 542:32), the term regularly used in the first century BC for such a figure in Roman public life.
5 Cicero] *Pro Flacco* 8
5 Horace] *Satires* 1.6.6, 24
16 vi geritur res] Ennius *Annals* 268 (Vahlen); quoted by Aulus Gellius 20.10.3; Erasmus' next example echoes the sense of the rest of the passage.
20 Cicero] *Philippics* 14.3, hardly frequent; *Adagia* IV viii 10
23 collo obtorto] See 420:28n.

LB I 68F

rumore vulgatum est: rumour noised it abroad.

constans rumor est: there is a persistent rumour.

fama passim iactatum est: it was put about everywhere by common report.

in ore est omni populo: it's on everyone's lips.

erat in sermone res: the thing was the subject of talk, a phrase used by 5
Cicero with the same meaning as *rumor erat* 'the news spread.'

vox erat una totius provinciae: nothing else was being talked about in the
whole province.

in ore et sermone omnium (Cicero): on everyone's lips, the subject of
everyone's conversation   10

male audire, bene audire: to hear ill or good, a phrase used of those who are
ill or well spoken of

178 / Example   15

maiorum suorum vestigiis ingreditur: he is following in his family's
footsteps.

vetus institutum revocavit: he revived the ancient custom.

a prisca reipublicae consuetudine non recessit: he did not depart from 20
long-established political custom.

agere ad praescriptum (Caesar): act according to orders

vetus exemplum est, veteris exempli res est, fallere amicum: there is long
precedent for deceiving friends.

more hominum fecit, sibi quam amico maluit consulere: he did as men 25
always do; he preferred to consult his own interests rather than his friend's.

novo more: in novel fashion, that is, without precedent (frequently used by
Cicero).

To quote an example, we can use *ut* or *velut: simile gaudet simili ut sus sue,
velut puer puero* 'like is attracted to like as pig to pig, even as boy to boy'; or 30
we can use *quod genus* 'to exemplify which sort of thing' (the Greek expression is οἷον 'such as'), or *verbi causa, verbi gratia, exempli causa* (all three in
Cicero) 'to give an example.'

* * * * *

4 in ore est omni populo] Terence *Adelphi* 93
6 Cicero] *Verrines* 2.35
9 Cicero] *Verrines* 2.56
22 Caesar] *Bellum civile* 3.51.4
28 Cicero] For example, *Verrines* 2.67: *novo more, nullo exemplo*
33 Cicero] For example, *Tusculan Disputations* 1.12; *De finibus* 5.30; *De inventione*
1.66

179 / Extermination

funditus periit: has been utterly destroyed
radicitus exstinctus est: has been rooted out and annihilated
cupiditas radicitus extrahenda est: greed must be torn out by the roots.
a stirpe subversa est respublica: the state has been overturned from its
foundations.
a stirpe interiit (Sallust): has perished root and branch.
pristinae disciplinae ne vestigium quidem ullum superest: not the faintest
trace remains of that early system.
The Greek word for this concept is *panolethria* 'total destruction.'
extirpari et funditus tolli (Cicero in his book *De fato*): be extirpated and
fundamentally destroyed

180 / Shocking

atrox iniuria: grievous injury
indignum facinus: shocking deed
infandum (a poetic word): unutterable
nefarium scelus: deed that affronts heaven
gravis contumelia: grave affront
non ferenda superbia: intolerable arrogance
intolerandam ferociam (Cicero, in his speech against Rullus): insupport-
able savagery
factum non una cruce dignum: a deed for which crucifixion is too good a
punishment
facinus culleo dignum: deed worthy of the worst punishment we have
noxa capitalis: a capital offence
crimen inexpiabile: a crime past praying for
piaculare facinus: deed that calls down the wrath of heaven [i.e., requiring
atonement]

* * * * *

5 cupiditas radicitus extrahenda est] Cicero *De finibus* 2.27
8 Sallust] *Catilina* 10.1
12 Cicero] *De fato* 11
19 indignum facinus] Terence *Andria* 145
24 Cicero] *De lege agraria* 2.91
28 culleo] Literally, worthy of the sack; parricides were sewn up in a leather sack
and thrown into water. See Cicero *Pro Roscio Amerino* 71–2; *Adagia* IV ix 18.

LB I 69D

181 / Harshness

ad vivum exigere: demand one's pound of flesh
summo iure mecum agitur: I face the full severity of the law.
rigide, severe, praecise mecum agitis: you deal with me inflexibly, severe- 5
ly, abruptly (in Greek, ἀποτόμως 'brusquely, sharply').
inique, duris condicionibus, duris legibus mecum agitur: I am dealt with
harshly, under harsh conditions, under harsh terms.
etiam si mecum agas obsignatis tabulis: even if you were to deal with me
with everything signed and sealed [i.e., in the strictest possible form] 10
pergitisne vos tamquam ex syngrapha agere cum populo? (Cicero, in his
speech *Pro Lucio Murena*): do you insist on proposing to the people, as if
there were some kind of written document obliging them ... ?
In the same speech Cicero uses the phrase *austere et Stoice agere* 'act with
true Stoic austerity.' One can also use *Scythice agere* 'behave like a Scythian' 15
of someone who behaves in a rather boorish fashion.

182 / Ascribing, attributing

20

assignare, adscribere, attribuere 'assign, ascribe, attribute' are usually used
with reference to bad things, though occasionally they refer to good ones.
si perturbatior est, tibi assignato (Cicero, writing to Atticus): if it is rather
confused, blame yourself.
haec si minus apta videntur huic sermoni, Brute, Attico assigna (Cicero, in 25
his *Brutus*): if this seems not particularly relevant to our conversation,
Brutus, you may blame Atticus.
flens petiit ne unius amentiam civitati assignaret (Livy): he begged with
tears in his eyes that he would not ascribe to the whole state the madness of
one individual. 30
peto a te ut id non modo neglentiae meae sed ne occupationi quidem
tribuas (Cicero, in *Brutus* again): I ask you not only to refrain from attribut-

* * * * *

6 ἀποτόμως] Cicero *Ad Atticum* 10.11.5
9 obsignatis tabulis] Cicero *Tusculan Disputations* 5.33
11 Cicero] *Pro Murena* 35
14 same speech] *Pro Murena* 74
23 Cicero] *Ad Atticum* 6.1.11
25 Cicero] *Brutus* 74
28 Livy] 35.31.15
32 Cicero] Not *Brutus*, but *Ad Atticum* 4.2.1

ing this to indifference on my part, but not to attribute it to my preoccupation either.

omnes id Verri tunc attribuebant (Cicero again): everyone was laying it at Verres' door.

ut aliis causam calamitatis attribueret (Cicero): to shift the blame for the disaster onto others

si quid mali acciderit, tuae socordiae imputato: if anything goes wrong, charge it to your own slovenliness.

quod vivo, tuae clementiae acceptum fero, acceptum refero: the fact that I remain in life I put down to your clemency, that is, I acknowledge that I owe to ...

creditores suae negligentiae expensum ferre debent (Scaevola, in the *Pandects*): creditors must charge this to their own carelessness.

So far our examples have referred to bad things. Now for expressions for something good:

si quid feliciter evenit, non fortunae sed deo ascribendum est: if anything turns out well, it should be ascribed not to good luck but to God.

assignandum est, tribuendum est, attribuendum est, acceptum ferre oportet, imputandum est: it should be assigned, entered to, inscribed, put down to the account of, accredited to

The following expressions have the same suggestion of something good *vindico, assero, arrogo*:

totius negotii laudem sibi vindicat, sibi arrogat, sibi asserit, sibi usurpat: he claims, arrogates, assumes, appropriates the credit for the entire business to himself.

The expressions in the first group are derived from the language of accountancy, and are the terms expressing who owes what, or to whom what sum is due. The second group is drawn from the terminology of legal actions in which someone formally asserts his claim to a person or thing.

Some more expressions:

totum me tibi debeo: I owe myself entirely to you.

quod spiro et valeo tui muneris est: my life and health is of your giving.

si quid habeo id totum tuae munificentiae est: whatever I have is due entirely to your generosity.

* * * * *

3 Cicero] Cf *Verrines* 3.156: *omnes ei tum attribuebant.*

5 Cicero] *Verrines* 5.106

12 Scaevola] *Digest* 42.8.24, see 477:23n.

26 first group] Lines 18–20

32 quod spiro et valeo] See Horace *Odes* 4.3.21–4: *totum muneris hoc tui est ... quod spiro et placeo ... tuum est.*

si quid in me boni est, abs te venit, profectum est, fluxit: if there is any good
in me, it has come from you, it has its origin, its source in you.

183 / Addiction

gulae deditus, voluptati addictus: given over to gluttony, made over to
pleasure (a metaphor taken from auctions)
ventris mancipium: a slave to his belly
servit lucro: he is dominated by gain.
inservit honori (Horace): he dances attendance on honours.
in hoc totus incumbit: he directs all his energies to this end.
assidet litteris: to sit close to, be devoted to literature
affixus est poeticae: he is set on poetry.
et ad genus id quod quisque vestrum in dicendo probaret adhaerescerent
(Cicero): and be associated with that style which each of you would approve
of in public speaking
Juvenal used *devotus* in a good sense: quod ni tibi deditus essem / devotus-
que cliens, uxor tua virgo maneret: were I not your devoted / Faithful client,
your wife would yet be a maid.
animum ad scribendum appulit (Terence): he put his mind to writing.
ut animum ad aliquod studium adiungant (Terence): to give themselves up
to some craze
adiecit animum ad virginem (Terence): he has set his heart on the girl.
dedit se ad leges (Cicero): he gave himself up wholly to the law.
me totum meaque omnia tibi dico, dedico, consecroque: myself and all I
have I make over, surrender, and dedicate to you.

184 / Ability

tibi in manu est ne fiat (Terence): it's in your hands to prevent it.
verum id frustra an ob rem faciam in manu vestra est Quirites (Sallust): it

* * * * *

11 Horace] *Ars poetica* 167
13 assidet litteris] Pliny *Epistles* 3.5.19
16 Cicero] *De oratore* 3.37
18 Juvenal] 9.72
21 Terence] *Andria* 1, 56; *Eunuchus* 143; cf chap 157.
25 Cicero] Cf chap 157.
32 Terence] *Hecyra* 493
33 Sallust] *Jugurtha* 31.5

lies in your hands, citizens, whether I do so in vain or to some good purpose.

id in te situm est: it rests with you.

istuc non est meae facultatis: that is not within my means.

non opis est nostrae (Virgil): it is not within our power.

nos pro nostris opibus exstruimus moenia: we build walls in accord with our resources.

non est in potestate mea: it is not in my power. Sallust used both *in potestate* and *in potestatem habere*, 'to have in, to get into one's power.'

si in mea potestate esset: if it were in my power

filius nondum emancipatus in patris est potestate: a son who has not yet been emancipated is in his father's (legal) power.

penes te est ius vitae ac necis: with you lies the right of decision for life or death.

non est mearum virium: my strength is not equal to it.

meis auspiciis, meis copiis, meo Marte confectum est hoc negotium: I completed this business under my own command, with my own troops, by my own unaided efforts.

The following example from Sallust contains a novel use of *copia*:

quibus in otio vel molliter vel magnifice vivere copia erat: who when times were quiet had the means of living in ease or in splendour. He also used the plural phrase *in manibus* 'in one's hands.'

Cicero used various phrases, such as *pro mea parte adiuvi, pro mea parte virili, pro viribus, pro mea virili,* all meaning 'I helped to the best of my ability.' Sallust used *pro parte virili* without the possessive pronoun.

We can also include the following expressions in this group:

impetravit commeatum: he was granted leave of absence.

facta est illi dicendi potestas: he was given the opportunity to speak.

post ubi fide publica dicere iussus (Sallust): later, offered the chance of speaking under an official pledge of pardon

si fides publica data esset (Sallust): if he were given an official pledge of pardon

* * * * *

5 Virgil] *Aeneid* 1.601
8 Sallust] *Jugurtha* 83.1, 112.3
19 Sallust] *Catilina* 17.6
22 *in manibus*] *Catilina* 20.2; *Jugurtha* 73.6
25 Sallust] *Epistula ad Caesarem* 1 (*Oratio*) 8.10
29 Sallust] *Catilina* 47.1
31 Sallust] *Catilina* 48.4

eumque interposita publica fide Romam perduceret (Sallust again): and
bring him to Rome under an official safe-conduct
magnatibus quidquid libet licet: the mighty may do whatever they will.
utinam per fortunas liceret pro tuis in me beneficiis gratiam reponere: if
only I had the means to show my gratitude as your generosity deserves.
utinam tam adesset facultas quam adest prompta voluntas tibi gratificandi:
if only the means were as readily available as my desire to do you a favour.

185 / Oath-swearing

per caput hoc iuro: I swear on my life.
sancte deierat: swears by all that is holy that it is not so.
at sunt qui nihil vereantur conceptis verbis peierare: but some people are
not afraid to perjure themselves in the most solemn terms.
in verba iurabas mea: you promised, repeating the words I spoke.
non ego perfidum / dixi sacramentum (Horace): no false oath have I sworn.
sacramenta militaria: the soldier's oath of loyalty
non verear vel Iovem lapidem iurare: I would not hesitate to swear even by
Jove, the mighty stone.
sic me deus bene amet: as I hope for God's loving kindness
sic mihi propitius sit Christus, ut ego te salvum cupio: as I hope for Christ's
mercy, I desire your well-being.
sollicitat, ita vivam, me tua mi Tiro valetudo (Cicero): upon my life, I am
worried about your health, my dear Tiro.
ne sim salvus si aliter scribo ac sentio (Cicero): a curse on me if I write
differently from what I think.
ne vivam si scio (Cicero again): as I expect to die, I do not know.
moriar si quisquam me tenet praeter te (Cicero): let me die if anyone holds
me but you.
male mihi sit si umquam quicquam tam enitar (Cicero): woe betide me if I
ever make such an effort over anything again.

* * * * *

1 Sallust] *Jugurtha* 32.1
13 sancte deierat] Terence *Hecyra* 771
16 in verba iurabas mea] Horace *Epodes* 15.4
17 Horace] *Odes* 2.17.9–10
19 Iovem lapidem] See Cicero *Ad familiares* 7.12.2; the most ancient and binding
oath known to the Romans.
24 Cicero] *Ad familiares* 16.20.1; *Ad Atticum* 16.13a.1, 4.17.5; *Ad familiares* 9.15.2;
Ad Atticum 13.25.3

LB I 70D

dispeream ni optimum erat (Horace): I'll stake my life this would have been the best.

abiuratae rapinae (Virgil): the thefts he had disclaimed

fidem prodiderat, creditum abiuraverat (Sallust): had broken her word, repudiated her debts.

iusiurandum dabitur (Terence): an oath will be taken.

In legal language *deferre iusiurandum* 'tender an oath' is used of offering the other party an oath which he may swear if he wishes, *referre iusiurandum* 'reject an oath' of refusing to swear the oath offered and demanding that the proposer swear it himself.

huic citius credam iniurato quam tibi iurato: I would sooner believe him without an oath than you with one.

186 / Dictating

praetor dictat iusiurandum: the praetor dictates the oath.

facile ero facundus si tu dicenda dictaveris: I shall easily be eloquent if you dictate what I should say.

praei verbis quod vis (Plautus): lead off with what you want (i.e., dictate the formula you want me to use).

agedum pontifex praei verba quibus me pro legionibus devoveam (Livy): come, priest, repeat ahead of me the words in which I may offer myself up on behalf of the legions.

id votum in haec verba praeeunte P. Licinio pontifice maximo consul nuncupavit (Livy): the consul then spoke the vow using these words, saying them after Publius Licinius the high priest. Livy used *praefari* as well as *praeire*: sunt qui M. Fabio pontifice maximo praefante carmen devovisse sese eos pro patria Quiritibusque Romanis tradant: some authorities record that they offered themselves up for their country and the

* * * * *

1 Horace] Cf *Satires* 1.9.47: *dispeream ni / summosses omnes.*
3 Virgil] *Aeneid* 8.263
4 Sallust] *Catilina* 25.4
7 legal language] See Quintilian 5.6; *Digest* 12.2, 25.2.
11 quam tibi iurato] Cf Plautus *Amphitryo* 437: *nam iniurato scio plus credet mihi quam iurato tibi*; Juvenal 5.5; *Adagia* I viii 23.
20 Plautus] *Rudens* 1335
22 Livy] 8.9.4
26 Livy] 36.2.3
27 Livy] 5.41.3

LB I 70F

citizen body of Rome, saying the solemn formula of consecration after the
high priest Marcus Fabius.
ut vobis voce praeirent quid essetis pronuntiaturi (Cicero): to dictate to you
(i.e., prescribe) the verdict you were to pronounce
praescribere modum, praescribere finem: appoint a limit or end 5
non ad alienum praescriptum sed ad suum arbitrium imperare (Caesar):
exercise power not to somebody else's order but as they themselves willed

187 / In time, etc 10

opportune advenis: you come just at the right time.
fac adsis in tempore, tempori: mind you turn up in good time.
vigilet oportet qui tempori vult sua conficere negotia: a man must wake up
early if he wants to get his business completed in good time. 15
in ipso articulo supervenit: he arrived in the nick of time.
satis erat diei ut Puteolos excurrere possem et ad tempus redire (Cicero):
there would have been enough time for me to take a trip to Puteoli and get
back in time.
aderis autem ad tempus (Cicero again): but you will be there in time. 20
matura reditum: get back early.
fac curentur ista mature: see that this is dealt with quickly.
per tempus hic venit miles (Plautus): here comes the soldier just in time.
non potuisti per tempus magis advenire (Plautus again): you could not have
come at a better time. 25
fac adeas hominem in tempore: see that you approach him in time.
tempestivis conviviis delectantur et philosophi: even philosophers enjoy
parties on appropriate occasions.
tempestiva viro (Horace): of age to know a man
tempestivius ista dixeris a cena: after dinner would be a better time to talk 30
about that.
nihil suave quod est intempestivum: nothing is pleasant if it comes at an
inappropriate time.

* * * * *

3 Cicero] *Pro Milone* 3
6 Caesar] *Bellum Gallicum* 1.36.1
14 conficere negotia] Cf Plautus *Rudens* 921; see 469:29n.
17 Cicero] *Ad Atticum* 13.45.2
20 Cicero] *Ad Atticum* 5.9.2
23 Plautus] *Bacchides* 844
24 Plautus] *Menaechmi* 139
29 Horace] *Odes* 1.23.12

LB I 71A

The dead of night is called *nox intempesta* 'unseasonable' because it is not a
time (*tempus*) suitable for doing anything.
commodum supervenit Chremes: Chremes arrived most opportunely.
incommode me revocavit senex: the old man called me back most incon-
veniently.
suo quidque tempore agendum est: everything should be done at the
proper time.
pleraque differat et praesens in tempus omittat (Horace):much he post-
pones and for the present leaves (i.e., until an appropriate and convenient
time). This word *praesens* 'present' can refer to any time: Cato was praised
by Augustus 'because he did not wish the present constitution altered,' that
is, the one contemporary with Cato.

188 / Before time

sed cadat ante diem (Virgil): may he perish before his time.
praematura morte exstinctus est: he was carried off by a premature death.
ante tempus sapit: he is wise before time.
et rerum prudentia velox ante pilos venit (Persius): and wisdom in affairs
has speedily arrived, before your beard has grown.
praepropere duxit uxorem: he got married in too much of a hurry.
nondum matura nuptiis elocata est: she was married off before she was
ready.
abi hinc cum tuo praepropero amore (Livy): away with you and your
over-hasty love.
illud praecox ingeniorum genus non temere pervenit ad frugem: this precocious type of intelligence hardly ever comes to fruition.
praecocia, praecoqua mala pluris emuntur: people pay more for early fruit.
accelerata consilia raro sunt felicia: hurried decisions are rarely good ones.

* * * * *

1 *nox intempesta*] See Macrobius *Saturnalia* 1.3.15; and the example in Sallust
  Jugurtha 38.4.
3 commodum supervenit Chremes ... incommode me revocavit senex] These
  are not actual quotations from Plautus or Terence, but echo the language of
  those writers.
8 Horace] *Ars poetica* 44. Erasmus' text reads, in error, *in praesens tempus*.
17 Virgil] *Aeneid* 4.620
20 Persius] 4.4
25 Livy] 1.26.4: *cum immaturo amore*; Erasmus has misremembered this example,
  but Livy does often use *praeproperus*.
27 pervenit ad frugem] *Quintilian* 1.3.3.

festinata consilia raro prospere cadunt: hastily made plans rarely turn out successfully.

praecipitata consilia vix umquam felicem exitum sortiuntur: impetuous decisions hardly ever have a successful outcome.

et adhuc tua messis in herba est (Ovid): and your corn is still in green leaf. 5

189 / After time, late

sero sapiunt Phryges: Phrygians are wise after the event.

sera est nunc consultatio: it is too late to seek advice now. 10

serum est mortuo adhibere medicinam: it is too late for medicines once the patient has died.

nulla aetas ad discendum sera est: it is never too late to learn.

sera est in fundo parsimonia: it is too late to spare when all is spent.

advenit, sed post tempus: he came, but too late. 15

sera rosa: the late rose; so Horace, using *serus* instead of [the usual] *serotinus* as in *serotini fructus* 'late fruits,' that is, those which ripen after the usual time

post festum, ut aiunt, advenitis: you come a day after the feast, as the saying goes. 20

190 / Haste

mox te revisam, brevi te revisam: I shall see you again soon, shortly.

prope diem te revisam: I shall see you again at an early date. 25

primo quoque tempore conveniam hominem: I shall meet him at the earliest possible moment.

puncto temporis fortuna versa est: fortune changed in an instant.

momento temporis corruunt omnia: everything collapsed in a moment of time. 30

extemplo Aeneae solvuntur frigore membra (Virgil): straightaway cold fear unstrings Aeneas' limbs.

* * * * *

5 Ovid] *Heroides* 17.263

9 sero sapiunt Phryges] A line from a tragedy *Equos Troianus* by an unknown author; see Cicero *Ad familiares* 7.16; *Adagia* I v 61.

11 adhibere medicinam] English equivalents: 'after death the doctor,' or 'bolt the stable door when the horse has gone'; *Adagia* III vi 17

14 in fundo parsimonia] Seneca *Epistles* 1.5

16 Horace] *Odes* 1.38.3

31 Virgil] *Aeneid* 1.92

de improviso (Sallust); unexpectedly

ante exspectatum (Virgil): before expectation

dicto citius tumida aequora placat: he spoke and it was done: the heaving sea fell calm.

simul cum dicto manus adfert homini: with the words he laid hands on him.

actutum se domum contulerunt: forthwith they took themselves home.

haec locutus e vestigio se domum recepit: having said this he straightaway made off home.

protinus, ilico, continuo, statim: directly, on the spot, immediately, instantly

in ipso statim vitae limine exstinctus est: he was cut off right on the very threshhold of life.

confestim se in pedes coniecit: he took to his heels with all speed.

simul atque haec dixerat repente abiit: as soon as he had said this, he departed abruptly.

simul ut accepit nummos aufugit: the moment he received the money, he fled.

vix dum dictum erat, illa dedit (Martial): hardly were the words out when she gave.

Sallust used the phrases *quam maturissime* or *quam maturrime* 'as seasonably as possible' for *quam primum* 'as soon as possible'; also the phrase *quam ocissime* 'as speedily as possible.'

incisis venis mortem approperat (Tacitus): he speeds up death by opening his veins.

nec mora, manum inicit homini: without a moment's delay he seized him.

omnium opinione celerius redisti: you have returned sooner than anyone expected.

omnium exspectationem celeritate vicisti: you have surpassed everyone's expectations with your speed.

huc fac quam primum recurras: mind you hurry back at the first moment.

volasse dices: you will say I must have flown.

ubi me his negotiis extricaro nihil cunctatus ad vos advolabo: once I have freed myself of these problems, I will let nothing keep me from coming to you with all speed.

* * * * *

1 Sallust] For example, *Catilina* 28.1
2 Virgil] *Georgics* 3.348; see 523:5n.
3 aequora placat] Virgil *Aeneid* 1.142
21 Sallust] *quam maturrime: Histories* 1.77.16; *quam ocissime: Jugurtha* 25.5
24 Tacitus] *Annals* 16.14.3

LB I 71E

ANTICIPATING

We can include here verbs meaning 'anticipate,' some of which we have
reviewed elsewhere:
praevenire, antevertere, praevertere, praeverti: anticipate, forestall, take
priority, give priority   5
haec dies illi antecessit (Terence): this day has got ahead of that one.
occupare: do something first; cum assectaretur 'numquid vis' occupo
(Horace): he strolls beside me; 'Good morning then,' I interrupt / And try to
take my leave
fortiter occupa portum (Horace): stoutly make for the harbour in time   10
antevenire: get in ahead of
sed ea omnia luxu antecapere (Sallust): anticipate all these in self-
indulgence (i.e., minister to hunger and thirst before they felt them)
ac priusquam legiones scriberentur multa antecapere quae in bello usui
forent (Sallust): seize in advance much that would be of use in the war   15
before levying troops
consul optimum factu ratus noctem quae instabat antecapere (Sallust): the
consul, thinking the best thing to do was to act in advance of the coming
night
        maturare 'to bring to maturity, bring on' frequently implies speed: 20
maturate fugam (Virgil): haste your flight.
nisi maturasset pro curia signum sociis dare (Sallust): if he had not been in
too much of a hurry to give the signal to his associates before the senate-
house
at mature (Terence): but *soon*   25
But the noun *maturitas* 'maturity, readiness' and the adjective *maturus* 'ripe,
ready' do not carry this implication of speed.

* * * * *

    3 elsewhere] Chap 45
    6 Terence] *Phormio* 525
    8 Horace] *Satires* 1.9.6
    10 Horace] *Odes* 1.14.2
    12 Sallust] *Catilina* 13.3
    15 Sallust] *Catilina* 32.1
    17 Sallust] *Catilina* 55.1
    21 Virgil] *Aeneid* 1.137
    22 Sallust] *Catilina* 18.8
    25 Terence] *Eunuchus* 208

191 / Small extent in space

si ex isto loco digitum transversum aut unguem latum excesseris (Plautus):
if you shift off that spot a finger or a nail's breadth sideways
pedem ubi ponat non habet: he hasn't anywhere to put a foot down.
palmum non habet: he hasn't a hand's breadth.
pollicem latum agri non habet: he hasn't a thumb of land.
cave digitum latum ab hoc discesseris loco: take care not to stir a finger's
breadth from this spot.
pedem latum numquam a tuis praescriptis digrediar: I shall never depart so
much as a foot's breadth from your instructions.
culmum latum numquam recedit ab Epicuro: he never went a straw's width
away from Epicurus.
pilum latum non recedit a pristinis moribus: he did not retreat from the
ways of old by so much as a hair's breadth.

192 / Considerable extent in space or time

longe usque a campis ultimis (Plautus): right over there, the other side of
the fields
usque a mari supero Romam proficisci (Cicero): to set out for Rome right
from the Adriatic
ex Aethiopia est usque haec (Terence): she comes all the way from
Ethiopia.
usque a pedibus ad summum capillum: right from the soles of his feet to the
crown of his head
usque ex unguiculis (Plautus): right from our fingertips
quod augures omnes usque a Romulo decreverunt: which decision was
upheld by all augurs right down from Romulus

* * * * *

3 Plautus] *Aulularia* 57
5 pedem ubi ponat] Cicero *De finibus* 4.69: *sapientia pedem ubi ponat non habebat*
8 digitum latum] Cf Plautus *Bacchides* 423: *digitum longe a paedagogo.*
10 pedem latum] Cf Plautus *Mostellaria* 433: *me pedem latum imposisse.*
20 Plautus] *Rudens* 1034
22 Cicero] *Pro Cluentio* 192
24 Terence] *Eunuchus* 471
28 Plautus] *Stichus* 761
29 decreverunt] Cicero *In Vatinium* 20

omnia qua visus erat constrata telis armis cadaveribus (Sallust): everywhere as far as the eye could see was strewn with weapons, armour, bodies.

usque a proavis vetus ordinis aetas (Virgil): an ancient heritage of rank, right from father's father

193 / Fearing

metuo ne quod vis non liceat per patrem: I am afraid that what you want will not be possible because of your father.

timeo ne mihi succenseat: I fear he will be angry with me.

nullus metus est ne tibi quisquam det verba: there is no fear of anyone pulling the wool over your eyes.

nihil periculi est ne regno excutiaris: there is absolutely no danger of your being driven from the kingdom.

metuo ut substet hospes (Terence): I am afraid our friend won't stand up to this. (Note that *ut* is the equivalent of *ne non* [and introduces negative fearing clauses].)

firmae vereor ut hae sint nuptiae (Terence): I have my fears as to this marriage being permanent.

o puer ut sis vitalis metuo (Horace): dear lad, I fear you will not be long-lived.

omnes labores te excipere video, timeo ut sustineas (Cicero): I see you undertaking all the labours involved; I fear you will not be able to stand them.

accepi a te litteras quibus vereri videris ut epistolas illas acceperim (Cicero): I have received a letter from you in which you seem to be afraid that I didn't receive those other letters.

sollicitus sum ut tantum laborum possis sustinere: I am anxious about your being able to bear so much toil.

* * * * *

1 Sallust] *Jugurtha* 101.11
4 Virgil] Not Virgil but Ovid *Amores* 3.15.5: *ordinis heres*
17 Terence] *Andria* 914
20 Terence] *Hecyra* 101
22 Horace] *Satires* 2.1.61
24 Cicero] *Ad familiares* 14.2.3
27 Cicero] *Ad Atticum* 11.22.1

194 / Appropriateness and its opposite

eloquentiae caput est apte dicere, neque enim diserte dicitur quod inepte dicitur: the fundamental requirement for eloquence is to speak as the occasion demands, and no utterance is well spoken which is lacking in this quality of appropriateness.

nihil ad eam rem dici potuit accommodatius: nothing could have been said which was more to the point.

delige uxorem tuis accommodam moribus: choose a wife who fits in with your ways.

splendide dixit magis quam apposite: he spoke brilliantly rather than appositely.

nihil adferri poterat appositius: no more apposite point could have been made.

elegans iocus sed parum in loco dictus: it was a neat piece of wit, but that was hardly the occasion for it.

tua institutio non quadrat ad huius ingenium: the instruction you offer is not suited to his abilities.

mulieri mulier magis convenit, magis congruit: a woman is better for a woman; a woman suits a woman better.

hic militiae natus est: he is a born soldier.

hic ad huius mores factus scalptusque est: he is formed and fashioned to match this fellow's ways.

magnifica loqueris sed nihil ad Bacchum, ut aiunt: what you say is splendid, but nothing to do with Bacchus, as the proverb says; in Greek, ἀπροσ-διόνυσα or οὐδὲν πρὸς ἔπος [nothing to do with Dionysus, nothing to do with the subject].

ista sarcina non sedet humeris tuis: that burden does not sit well on your shoulders.

haec inter se non cohaerent: this does not hold together.

istuc ingeniose interseruisti verius quam concinne: your interposition was clever rather than relevant.

* * * * *

19 mulieri mulier magis convenit] Terence *Phormio* 726

24 nihil ad Bacchum] *Adagia* II iv 57; this saying, according to one ancient explanation, came into use when poets first began writing plays dealing with material other than the myth of Bacchus, which was their original and proper subject.

25 ἀπροσδιόνυσα] Title of one of Erasmus' colloquies; see Thompson *Colloquies* 422.

non sibi constat tua oratio: your speech is not consistent with itself.
non consonat vita doctrinae: his practice is not in accord with his preaching.
non concordant facta cum dictis: his words and deeds to not agree.
multa dixit extra causam, nihil ad rem pertinentia: he said a great deal that
lay outside the case, that had nothing to do with it.
quid cani cum balneo? a bath is no place for a dog.
istuc praeclare quidem dictum sed alieno loco: a splendid remark, but quite
out of place
alieno tempore sementem facis: you are sowing out of season.
alieniore aetate post faceret tamen (Terence): later on at years unseemly do
it all the same
ne bovi clitellas: as well does a saddle fit a cow
feli crocoton addidisti: a cat in a saffron gown
in lente unguentum: sweet oils on lentils
non facit ad luctum cithara: music sorts not well with grief.

195 / Dying

mortem obiit: he met his end.
vita defunctus est: he has done with life.
vixit: his life is over.
in vivis esse desiit: he has ceased to be numbered with the living.
excessit e vivis: he has departed from amongst the living. *excessit* can also
be used without any further addition, like *decessit* 'he has gone.'
satius est milies mortem oppetere quam turpitudinem admittere: it is
preferable to encounter death a thousand times rather than allow oneself a
disgraceful act.

* * * * *

7 quid cani cum balneo] *Adagia* I iv 39 – said of someone in an inappropriate
place
11 Terence] *Adelphi* 110
13 ne bovi clitellas] *Adagia* II ix 84: 'Non nostrum opus, bos clitellas?' – said of
someone undertaking an unsuitable office
14 feli crocoton addidisti] Literally 'you have given a beautiful dress to a cat';
Adagia I ii 72; the adage means an outer covering that is at variance with the
essential nature underneath; see the story of the cat that became a beautiful,
elegantly dressed woman but at her wedding feast forgot herself and chased a
mouse: *Paroemiographi Graeci* Zenobius 2.93.
15 in lente unguentum] See 308:2n.

mihi ipsi fuit mors aequo animo oppetenda (Cicero): as for myself, I should have had to face death calmly.

obiit supremum vitae diem: he came to his last day of life.

diem obiit: he met his fated day; or *obiit* alone, which Cicero uses.

vitam morte commutavit: he changed life for death.

concessit in fata: he passed to his fated end.

concessit vita (frequent in Tacitus): he passed from life.

mortalitatem explevit (again Tacitus): he fulfilled his allotted span. Tacitus also uses *supremum diem explevit* 'he fulfilled his final day.'

animam reddidit: he yielded up his spirit.

spiritum finiebat: he was drawing his last breath.

spirare desiit (Livy): he ceased to draw breath.

efflavit animam (Cicero): he sighed forth his soul.

cuius in complexu libenter extremum vitae spiritum ediderim (Cicero): in whose arms I would gladly yield up my dying breath

exspiravit: he expired.

antequam ex hac vita migro, emigro, demigro (all Ciceronian usages): before I remove, depart, transfer from this life

exire de vita (Cicero): exit from life

e medio excessit (Terence): she has departed from our midst.

emori malim: I would rather perish.

e vita discessit inedia: he starved himself to death.

mortem occubuit (Tacitus): he succumbed to death. Tacitus also uses *occubuit* without further qualification.

* * * * *

1 Cicero] Cf *Ad familiares* 4.7.4: *equidem etiam si oppetenda mors esset domi atque in patria mallem.*

4 Cicero] For example, *De legibus* 1.61

7 Tacitus] For example, *Annals* 3.30.1

8 Tacitus] *Annals* 6.50.4

8 Tacitus] *Annals* 3.76.1

12 Livy] Not, it seems, Livy or Tacitus

13 Cicero] *Pro Milone* 48; *Tusculan Disputations* 1.19: *et agere animam et efflare dicimus*

14 Cicero] *Philippics* 12.22

17 Ciceronian usages] *De republica* 6.9; *De legibus* 2.19.48; *Tusculan Disputations* 1.74

19 Cicero] *De amicitia* 15

20 Terence] *Phormio* 1019: *ea mortem obiit, e medio abiit*

22 discessit inedia] Cf Cicero *Tusculan Disputations* 1.84: *per inediam discedens*

23 Tacitus] Not, it seems, in Tacitus, but several times in Livy, for example, 2.7.8; used absolutely by both Livy, for example 23.24.11, and Tacitus, for example *Histories* 4.60.2

LB I 72F

voluntariam occubuit necem (a phrase which Suetonius used): he succumbed to a self-inflicted slaughter.

seu certae occumbere morti (Virgil): or yield to an inevitable death

vivis exemptus est: he was removed from the living.

inter vivos agere desiit: he ceased to move among men.

agere animam 'to breathe one's last' is used of someone actually in the death
agony.

deo naturaeque concessit: he paid his debt to God and nature.

ubi anima naturae cessit, demptis obtrectatoribus ipsa se virtus magis
magisque extollit (Sallust): once the soul has paid the debt to nature, with
the removal of the fault-finders, plain virtue of itself becomes ever more
glorious.

pater uti necesse erat naturae concessit (Sallust): my father, as was inevitable, has gone the way of all flesh.

vitae peregit fabulam: he has played his last scene in life.

leto datus est: he has received his quietus.

luce orbatus est, vita orbatus est: deprived of the light of life, deprived of
life

lumine cassus: reft of light (a poetic expression)

mortuus 'dead' is used without further qualification; *demortuus* is used of
someone who by his death has left his place or office empty, and the man
who replaces him is said *succedere in demortui locum* 'step into the dead
man's shoes.'

The noun *excessus* 'departure' is found in good authors for 'death,' and
Tacitus often uses *exitus* in the same way: *exitu demum Neronis positis odiis in
medium consuluere* 'with Nero's departure at long last they laid aside their
hatreds and took thought for the common good'; *laudatis antiquorum mor-
tibus pares exitus* 'departures comparable to the much-praised deaths of
ancient heroes.' However, the verb *exire*, as in *exire a vita* 'depart from life,'
is usually used of those who submit to a voluntary death, and *exitus* usually
refers to a voluntary departure from life.

* * * * *

1 Suetonius] *Augustus* 13.2
3 Virgil] *Aeneid* 2.62
10 Sallust] *Epistula ad Caesarem* 2.13.7
13 Sallust] *Jugurtha* 14.15
16 leto datus est] See Varro *De lingua latina* 7.42: *ollus leto datus est,* the official
formula for announcing a death.
19 poetic] Virgil *Aeneid* 2.85: *cassum lumine lugent*
22 *in demortui locum*] A technical term in Roman political life
25 Tacitus] *Histories* 2.5.2
28 *pares exitus*] *Histories* 1.3.1

oppetere mortem 'to encounter death' is used of an end that is striking or peculiar in some way.

Tacitus used *finis* 'end' for *excessus*: comperto fine Augusti: when Augustus' end was made known.

196 / Voluntary death

e vita tamquam a theatro exeamus (Cicero): let us depart from life as we would from the theatre.

impatiens malorum, mortem sibi conscivit, necem sibi conscivit: unable to endure his sufferings, he took his own life.

inedia vitam finiit: he ended his life by refusing to eat.

veneno sumpto mortem accersivit: he summoned death by taking poison.

incisis venis mortem approperat (Tacitus): he speeds up death by opening his veins.

desperatis rebus decrevit sibi adferre manus: in utter despair he determined to lay violent hands on himself.

vim suae vitae attulit (Tacitus): he brought violence to bear on his own life.

Tacitus often uses the phrase *mortem sumere* 'lay hold of death' to mean 'take one's own life': haud creditus sufficere ad constantiam sumendae mortis: not believed capable of the firmness of character necessary to lay hold on death.

morte spontanea vitam abrupit: he cut short his life by a voluntary death.

intercluso spiritu mortem invenit: he found his death by cutting off his breath.

suspendio quaesita mors est: he hanged himself and so found death.

197 / Unnatural death

occidit, interfecit, peremit, necavit, exstinxit: slew, murdered, cut off, put to death, destroyed

iure caesus est: he was rightly killed.

* * * * *

3 Tacitus] *Annals* 2.39.1
9 Cicero] *De finibus* 1.49
15 Tacitus] *Annals* 16.14.3
19 Tacitus] *Annals* 12.59.2
20 Tacitus] *Annals* 13.30.2

LB I 73B

neci dedit: dispatched to a violent death; dede neci: dispatch to death (both
from Virgil)
vitam et cantharides eripere possunt: cantharides too can extinguish life.
animam seni extinguerem (Terence): I would squeeze the breath out of the
old chap.
vita privavit: deprived of life
vita orbavit, luce orbavit: robbed of life, of light
Nero Senecae denuntiavit ultimam necessitatem: Nero sent Seneca a message saying that the ultimate exigency had come.
ad necem adegit: drove to death

198 / Intention

si te propositi nondum pudet (Juvenal): if you are still unashamed of your
design
erat animus, erat in animo: I was minded, it was in my mind.
proposueram, statueram, decreveram, constitueram urbem relinquere: I
had planned, decided, determined, resolved to leave the city.
si stat sententia litteris te addicere: if your intention of devoting yourself to
literature holds firm
non est sententia frustra niti: it is not my intention to make great efforts to
no purpose.
non fuit consilium socordia atque desidia bonum otium conterere: I had no
intention of wasting my good leisure in idleness and sloth.
non sum huius animi ut inanem operam velim sumere: I am not of a mind to
take on pointless toil with any eagerness.
non est consilii: it is not within my purpose.
non est ratio: it is not reasonable, there is no thought of ...
visum erat ad vos remigrare: the best thing seemed to be to return to you.
habebam in animo: I had in mind.

* * * * *

2 Virgil] *Aeneid* 12.341; *Georgics* 4.90
3 cantharides] A substance derived from the Spanish blister-fly, used as both a
medicine and a poison; see Pliny *Naturalis historia* 29.93ff.
4 Terence] *Adelphi* 314
8 ultimam necessitatem] Tacitus *Annals* 15.61.4
15 Juvenal] 5.1
24 bonum otium conterere] Sallust *Catilina* 4.1
29 non est ratio] Cicero *Verrines* I.24

sic apud animum meum statuo (Sallust): so I have determined in my own mind.

199 / Imminent danger

non sentis quid tibi malorum impendeat, quanta immineat calamitas, quanta instet tempestas: you do not realise what misfortunes threaten you, what a calamity hangs over your head, what a storm is bearing down on you.
non ea procul abest: it is not far from you.
iam urget ac premit: already it is besetting you and pressing you hard.
in foribus adest ultio: vengeance is at the doors.
dux hostium cum exercitu supra caput est (Sallust): the enemy leader with his army is on our heads. Livy also uses *supra caput* in a number of places.
nihil malorum non intentabatur: every kind of misfortune threatened.
praesentemque intentant omnia mortem (Virgil): all things threaten instant death.
haec prooemia nobis dira minitantur: this preamble bodes ill.
in propinquo est discrimen: the crucial moment is at hand.
non sentis quae te circumstent pericula, quae malorum procella te circumvallet: you do not realize what dangers beset you, what a tumult of disaster presses in on all sides.
quis te maneat exitus: ... what an end awaits you
quam tenui discrimine absis ab exitio: ... what a fine dividing line separates you from disaster
vicinius est malum quam credis: the evil is nearer at hand than you believe.
propior es periculo quam suspicaris: you are closer to danger than you suspect.
quousque cunctando rempublicam intutam patiemini? (Sallust): how long will you delay and leave the state defenceless? (by 'defenceless' he meant 'in the path of danger').
eo respublica in extremo sita est (Sallust): this is why the state is in this ultimate situation.

* * * * *

 1 Sallust] *Epistula ad Caesarem* 2.6.2
14 Sallust] *Catilina* 52.24
15 Livy] 3.17.2, 4.22.6
17 Virgil] *Aeneid* 1.91
30 Sallust] *Histories* 1.77.17
33 Sallust] *Catilina* 52.11

LB I 73D

ubi intelligit omnes fortunas suas in extremo sitas (Sallust again): when he
realized that his whole life and lot was now at the ultimate point
et gnati vita in dubium veniet: your son's life too will be called in question.
in dubiis rebus consilium adhibendum est: in precarious situations one
should get advice. 5
omnia sunt hominum tenui pendentia filo (Ovid): the affairs of men hang
all by a slender thread.
et incedis per ignes / suppositos cineri doloso (Horace): and you tread on
glowing embers / Concealed under deceptive ash.
periculosae plenum opus aleae: a task with hazard and danger fraught 10

200 / Easy, difficult

dictu quam factu facilius: easier said than done 15
nihil facilius: nothing easier
facile est, perfacile est, proclive est, in proclivi est: it is easy, very easy,
ready to go, at the ready.
nihil negotii est: it is no bother.
nullo negotio rem conficies: you will manage it without any trouble. 20
denique omnes Romani usque ad nostram memoriam sic habuere, alia
omnia virtuti suae prona esse (Sallust): finally, every Roman right down to
our own times has always considered that everything else would go down
easily before their valour.
et profecto diis iuvantibus omnia matura sunt (Sallust): and assuredly, by 25
the grace of God, everything is now ripe.
id cuivis promptum est: that is available to anyone.
hoc mihi in promptu non est: this is not something I can readily do.
si hoc itinere uti decreveritis, cetera in promptu erunt (Sallust): if you
decide to employ this way, everything else will come easily. 30
in procinctu habere: have in readiness
ad manum esse: be to hand
difficile est, perdifficile est: it is difficult, very difficult.
rem arduam moliris: you are toiling at a hard task.

* * * * *

1 Sallust] *Jugurtha* 23.2
3 in dubium veniet] Terence *Adelphi* 340
6 Ovid] *Ex Ponto* 4.3.35
8 Horace] *Odes* 2.1.8, 6
22 Sallust] *Jugurtha* 114.2
25 Sallust] *Jugurtha* 85.48
29 Sallust] *Epistula ad Caesarem* 2.12.2: *decreveris*

201 / Pretext

hoc praetexit nomine culpam (Virgil): with this name she cloaked her sin.
hoc colore tegit culpam: thus he glozes over his guilt.
obtentu pietatis rem impiam moliebatur: he was working out his foul
purpose under a cover of piety.
specioso titulo molitur facinus omnium turpissimum: under a specious
pretence he is plotting the foulest crime of all.
plausibili titulo: under a plausible name
religionis fuco sese venditant: they ingratiate themselves with a false
semblance of religion.
amici specie gessit inimicum: under the appearance of friendship he played
the part of an enemy.
quicumque rempublicam agitavere honestis nominibus (Sallust): whoever
stirred up political unrest ostensibly for respectable causes
sed haec res mire sunt vitiis obtentui (Sallust): but this provides a marvellous screen for vice.
magni nominis umbra sese tuentur: they protect themselves by skulking in
the shadow of a mighty name.

202 / Rashness

nihil habet pensi: he recks nought.
inconsultis consiliis agit omnia: he does everything on ill-considered conclusions.
pro sua libidine rem gerit: he is dealing with it as his fancy takes him.
audacia illi pro sapientia in consilio est: boldness counsels him, not wisdom.
aequi atque iniqui nulla ratio est: there is no consideration of justice or
injustice.
quid deceat quid non susque deque habet: what is proper and what is not is
all one to him.

* * * * *

3   Virgil] *Aeneid* 4.172
14 Sallust] *Catilina* 38.3
16 Sallust] *Histories* 1.55.24: *quia secundae res*
18 sese tuentur] Cf Quintilian 12.10.15: *umbra magni nominis delitescunt.*
24 nihil habet pensi] Cf Sallust *Catilina* 5.6: *nec quicquam pensi habebat.*
32 susque deque habet] See 446:7n.

quae etiam mediocres viros spe praedae transversos agit (Sallust): which
drives even quite ordinary men off course through hope of gain
quos privata amicitia Iugurthae parum cognita transversos agit (Sallust):
who are carried away through a private involvement with Jugurtha, the
implications of which they have not sufficiently realized
impetu fertur magis quam iudicio ducitur: he is swept away by impulse,
not guided by judgment.
nihil habet pensi quid in quem dicat: he cares not a whit what he says or
against whom.

203 / Burial

exequias ire: follow to the grave
curare funus: see to the funeral
parentare: offer rites in honour of deceased relations
parentalia peregimus: we celebrated the Parentalia.
postquam illi more regio iusta magnifice fecerunt (Sallust): after they had
performed the last offices for him in magnificent style as befitted a king

204 / Habit and its opposite

insuevit fallere: he has got into the habit of deceiving.
assuevit mentiri: he has grown used to lying.
consueta relinquere durum est: it is hard to leave what we are used to.
optimis assuescendum: one ought to grow into the way of what is best.
armis belloque desueti: had lost the habit of arms and war
ad ista iampridem occalluit animus: their mind has long since become
hardened to such things.
longo usu callum duxi: I have grown a thick skin by long usage.
quid tu Athenas insolens? (Terence): what brings you to Athens? you don't
often come.
insolens iniuriarum: unaccustomed to wrong-doing
interdum timidos insolentia itineris levare manu: at times he gave a help-

* * * * *

1 Sallust] *Jugurtha* 6.3
3 Sallust] *Jugurtha* 14.20
17 Parentalia] Roman rites in honour of the dead
18 Sallust] *Jugurtha* 11.2
32 Terence] *Andria* 907

ing hand to those alarmed by the strangeness of the route (these last two examples both from Sallust).
nihil novi facit: he is not doing anything novel.
istuc insolens facis: that is unusual for you to do.
istuc tuo more facis: it is just like you to do that.
istuc tibi solenne est: that is your usual practice.
moris est: it is customary.
in usu est: it is usual.
in usu esse desiit: it ceased to be usual.
ne vetustissima Italiae disciplina per desidiam exolesceret (Tacitus): so that a traditional Italian discipline should not disappear through being allowed to lapse
Graeci amictus iam exoleverant (Tacitus): Greek dress had by then gone out of fashion.
res aut nova aut vetustate exemplorum memoriae iam exoletae (Livy): a situation which was either a novelty or something the memory of which had been forgotten because the last example had occurred so long before
ista iam in desuetudinem abiere: that has by now all passed into desuetude.

205 / Slowness

tardat: delays, lingers, the equivalent of Greek χρονίζει [take one's time]
tardus corpore sed ingenio tardior: slow of body but slower of mind
lentus abes: stay away and take your time.
festina lente: more haste, less speed
age pedetemptim: go a step at a time, cautiously.
paulatim, sensim infunde: pour it in bit by bit, gradually.
cunctari: hold back, drag the war on, as in Sallust: quem ubi cunctari accepit et dubium belli atque pacis rationes trahere: when he learned that he was holding back and weighing up the prospects of war and peace, unable to make up his mind

* * * * *

2 Sallust] *Catilina* 3.4: *insolens malarum artium; Jugurtha* 94.2
10 Tacitus] *Annals* 11.15.1
13 Tacitus] *Annals* 14.21.4
15 Livy] 37.1.9
25 lentus abes] Ovid *Remedia amoris* 243: *lentus abesto*
26 festina lente] *Adagia* II i 1
29 Sallust] *Jugurtha* 97.2

LB I 74D

Ptolemaeus pretio ad dies bellum prolatans (Sallust again): Ptolemy daily
extending the war by bribes
diem ex die prolatabant (Tacitus): they put it off from day to day.
cum is diem de die differet (Livy): since he was deferring it from one day to
another 5
diem ex die ducere (Caesar): drag out day after day
procrastinare, comperendinare (Cicero): put off till tomorrow, adjourn

206 / No further 10

intra convicia rixa constitit: the quarrel went no further than hard words.
citra sanguinem pugnatum est: the fight remained this side of bloodshed.
perbenignus est sed non ultra promissa: he is very kind, but not beyond
what he promised. 15
The same effect is produced by the word *tenus* 'to the limit,' to which
the ancients, more readily than we do, added a noun, either in the ablative
or genitive case:
crurum tenus (Virgil): to the level of the shins
non patruum saltem porta tenus obvium (Tacitus): no uncle coming at least 20
as far as the gate to meet him.
modo pectore modo ore tenus extantes (Tacitus): rising out sometimes to
chest level, sometimes to face level only
usurpatas nomine tenus urbium expugnatas dictitant (Tacitus): they continually assert that his sackings of cities had been performed in name only. 25
ianua ac limine tenus domum claudit (Tacitus): he closed up the house at
the limit of door and threshold.
unum addiderim, nusquam latius dominari mare, multum fluminum hinc
atque illuc ferre, nec litore [tenus aut] accrescere aut resorberi (Tacitus, in
his life of Agricola): I would add this last statement, that nowhere does the 30

* * * * *

1 Sallust] *Histories* 4.69.12: *in dies prolatans*
3 Tacitus] *Annals* 6.42.4
4 Livy] 25.25.4
6 Caesar] *Bellum Gallicum* 1.16.4
7 Cicero] procrastinare: *Pro Roscio Amerino* 26; comperendinare: *Verrines* 4.33
19 Virgil] *Georgics* 3.53
20 Tacitus] *Annals* 3.5.2
22 Tacitus] *Annals* 1.70.3
24 Tacitus] *Annals* 15.6.4; *expugnatas* is an error for *expugnationes*.
26 Tacitus] *Histories* 1.33.1
29 Tacitus] *Agricola* 10.7

sea hold wider sway, that it carries many currents to and fro, nor is its rise
and fall confined to the limit of the shore ... (He means that the sea
penetrates beyond the shore).
in quos iecit magis hoc consul verbo tenus quam ut re insimularet (Livy): at
whom the consul threw this accusation more as a manner of speaking than
as a real charge.
Livy also used the phrase *vulneribus tenus* 'as far as the inflicting of
wounds'; Quintilian used *aurium tenus* 'only as far as the ears.'
pauci hostium tenus exacti penetravere usque ad Porum (Quintus Curtius):
a few of them were driven as far as the enemy line and reached Porus.
pallio tenus philosophos imitatur (Apuleius): he copies philosophers as far
as the philosopher's cloak.

* * * * *

4 Livy] 34.5.5
7 Livy] 41.20.12
8 Quintilian] 12.2.17
9 Quintus Curtius] 8.14.9; *1534* and LB read *ad portum* in error.
11 Apuleius] *Florida* 7

BOOK II
ABUNDANCE OF SUBJECT-MATTER

Enrichment of material: Method 1

We have now presented as briefly as possible such thoughts as occurred to
us on the subject of abundance of expression, so our next task is to review
with equal conciseness abundance of subject-matter. To start off this part of
the work with material as similar as possible to that used in the corresponding section in book I, the first method of enriching what one has to say on
any subject is to take something that can be expressed in brief and general
terms, and expand it and separate it into its constituent parts. This is just
like displaying some object for sale first of all through a grill or inside a
wrapping, and then unwrapping it and opening it out and displaying it
fully to the gaze.

Here is an example of the method. Let us take the sentence: *He wasted
all his substance in riotous living*. This is expressed in summary fashion, and
is, so to speak, wrapped up. We can open it out by enumerating all the
different types of possessions and setting out the various ways of wasting
them: All he had inherited from mother or father or acquired by the death of
other relatives, all that was added by his wife's dowry (and that was
nothing in the ordinary run of things), all the increase that accrued from
various legacies (and that increase was very considerable), all he received
by the prince's generosity, all that he raked in during his military service,
all his money, plate, clothes, estates and land, together with farm buildings
and stock, in short everything, chattels and real estate, even his very
household, he threw away on degrading affairs with low women, revelry
every day, extravagant parties, nights spent wining and dining, luxurious
foods, perfumes, dicing and gambling, and all in a few days so squandered,
gobbled up, and sucked it out that he did not leave himself two half-
pennies to rub together.

In this way the two phrases 'all his substance' and 'wasted in riotous
living' are explicated via their constituent parts.

Here is another example: *He completed a thoroughly comprehensive
education*. This general statement can be expanded by listing all the separate
disciplines and every aspect of learning: There is absolutely no area of
learning in which he is not meticulously versed; there is no branch of
learning which he has not grasped down to the last detail, and so grasped

* * * * *

14 through a grill] Cicero *De oratore* 1.162; *Adagia* III i 49

5

10

15

20

25

30

35

that he would appear to have laboured at it to the exclusion of the rest; he
has such a wonderful knowledge of all the tales of all the poets; he is so
richly supplied with the finest turns of expression employed by the orators;
he has so sifted the laborious rules of the grammarians; he is skilled in the
subtleties of dialectic; he has probed the secrets of physical science; he has
scaled the heights of ultramundane knowledge; he has penetrated the
inmost recesses of the theologians; he has a thorough understanding of the
demonstrations of mathematics; such is his knowledge of the movements of
the stars, the principles of number, the dimensions of the various lands, the
position and name of cities, mountains, rivers, springs, the harmony and
intervals of musical sounds; such is his memory of ancient and modern
history; every good writer, whether of ancient or of modern times, he has
them all; add to all this an equal skill in Greek and Latin language and
literature; in short, whatever learning has been discovered and handed on
by distinguished authors, this one man has completely assimilated and
understood and holds fast in his memory.

Again, to expand the phrase *Endowed with every blessing of nature and
fortune,* one can mention every separate good point of the body and then
every separate gift of intelligence and spirit, and finally birth, wealth,
nationality, success, and whatever comes to us from fortune. A third example is provided by *Hippias the omniscient.* To elaborate this, one may
introduce all the things listed by Apuleius in his description of this person
in the *Florida,* a passage that is incidentally not devoid of diversity and
richness of expression.

There is a very good example of this procedure in Lucian's *Harmonides,* where he could have said baldly τὴν αὐλητικὴν ὅλην ἐκμεμάθηκα
[I have thoroughly learned the art of flute-playing], but he preferred to
make a display of *copia* by setting out the parts inherent in the total idea.
The passage does not go very easily into Latin, but I will make some attempt
to translate it for the sake of those who do not know Greek: 'You have by
now taught me to tune the flute accurately and breathe into the mouthpiece

* * * * *

21 *Hippias*] Of Elis, a sophist (297:14n and 583:5) contemporary with Socrates;
equipped with a wide if superficial knowledge of many branches of learning
and of art, combined with practical skills; he professed to be able to speak on
any topic, and declared that everything he wore was made with his own
hands. He was a celebrated figure, though criticized for arrogance and boast-
fulness.
23 *Florida*] 9; see 583:6n.
25 Lucian's] *Harmonides* 1. Erasmus quotes the Greek text; the Latin translation
and the following sentence (LB I 76A–B) were added in 1534. He neglected to
translate the final sentence.

gently and tunefully, to put the fingers down flexibly and in time with the constant rise and fall of the melody, to move with the beat and play in unison with the chorus, and to observe the characteristics of the different modes, the sublime frenzy of the Phrygian, the Dionysiac storming of the Lydian, the solemnity and dignity of the Dorian, the elegance of the Ionian. [All this I have learned from you.]'

If we had decided to do with all the separate disciplines in our example above what Lucian has done here with the single discipline of music, you can see what riches of material would have been thus provided.

Here I would make what I think is a helpful suggestion: have the general statement set out right at the beginning, and then take it up again in a different form of words, returning to the basic idea as if you have wearied of enumerating details, even if in fact nothing has been omitted.

Furthermore, we should take care not to throw the proper order of the various parts into confusion by mixing everything up in an indiscriminate chaos of utterances, and piling up a boring mass of words totally devoid of attraction; but instead we should rather prevent tedium in reader or hearer by skilful arrangement, appropriate allocation and elegant disposition.

DIVISION OF A WHOLE INTO PARTS

We may include here the kind of example where some whole made up of subordinate parts rather than of a group of disparate items is separated out into its parts. Take the sentence: *He is a total monster*. This will be filled out by first dividing the man into body and mind, and then touching on the separate parts of the body followed by the separate parts of the mind: He is a monster both in mind and in body; whatever part of mind or body you consider, you will find a monster – quivering head, rabid eyes, a dragon's gape, the visage of a Fury, distended belly, hands like talons ready to tear, feet distorted, in short, view his entire physical shape and what else does it all present but a monster? Observe that tongue, observe that wild beast's roar, and you will name it a monstrosity; probe his mind, you will find a horror; weigh his character, scrutinize his life, you will find all monstrous; and, not to pursue every point in detail, through and through he is nothing but a monster.

It is clear what fulness the speech would acquire if anyone chose to dwell on the depiction of any of these separate items.

Here is another example: *He was quite drenched*; he was drenched with rain from the top of his head to the soles of his shoes; head, shoulders, chest, belly, legs, his entire body in fact, dripped with rainwater.

A small point, but one quite worth mentioning as possibly applicable to this type, is the introduction of the genus if we are speaking of a species.

This is usually done just for the sake of amplification: Learning of every kind both adorns and assists the race of men, but philosophy does so pre-eminently; Lust is disgusting at any age, but is most disgusting of all in old age; Prudence is of great importance in all human affairs, but especially in war. Here the simple statement would have been: Prudence is of great importance in war. Cicero has an example of this type in his speech *De domo sua*, delivered before the college of priests: 'Our ancestors, your reverences, invented and established many practices in their extraordinary wisdom, but nothing was more striking than their decision that you, the priests, should direct both the worship of the immortal gods and the highest affairs of state.'

But there is little point in quoting this one specimen when examples of the type lie ready for the finding on every side.

Variation: Method 2

The second method of variation is very like the first. It arises when we are not satisfied with stating the final outcome and leaving preceding events to be deduced, but rehearse in detail everything which led up to the final result. Here is an example of what I mean: *Cicero crushed Catiline's designs*. This may be elaborated as follows: The wicked designs of Catiline, put into effect through young men of desperate character plotting the ruin and destruction of the whole Roman state, the consul Marcus Tullius Cicero immediately sniffed out with his customary sagacity, hunted down with remarkable vigilance, caught by exercising great prudence, revealed with wonderful devotion to the country, convicted with incredible eloquence, broke by the weight of his authority, extinguished by the use of force, and with the aid of fortune removed for ever.

Here is another: *He acknowledged a son born to him from the girl*. You may expand this as follows: He fell passionately in love with the girl, who was extremely pretty. Unable to control his affection, he assailed her simple mind with promises, bribed her with gifts, cajoled her with flattery, induced her by kindnesses to return his affection, and overcame her by his insistence. Finally he became intimate with her and deflowered her. After some time the girl's belly began to swell as, of course, a child had been conceived. At the end of nine months she went into labour and produced a boy.

Here is yet another example: *He took the city*, which may be amplified

* * * * *

6 Cicero] *De domo sua* 1.1

LB I 76D

as follows: First of all the heralds were sent to demand reparations and also
to offer terms of peace. When the inhabitants refused to accept these, he
gathered forces from all quarters, brought in a great supply of engines of
war, and moved his army and the machines up to the city ramparts. The
inhabitants replied by fiercely repelling the enemy from the walls, but the
general eventually got the upper hand in the fighting, and, scaling the
walls, invaded the city and seized control of it.

Method 3

The third method again is not so very different from the second. In the third
we do not set out the fact unadorned, but look for causes of it, even some
distance back, and try to explain what gave rise to it; for example, if one
were not content with saying that a state of war developed between the
French and the Neapolitans, but added the reasons for the enmity, said who
instigated it, what was the pretext for commencing hostilities, what hopes
they had of victory, and on what each party based its confidence. This
precept is too obvious to need detailed instruction, and it would be difficult
to set out an example except at very great length. Consequently we shall
dispense with any attempt to do so and shall refer the reader to Sallust and
Livy.

Method 4

The fourth method is not all that different again. Here we do not simply
state some situation, but enumerate all the circumstances that accompany it
or result from it. For example: *We shall blame you for the war*, which may be
enlarged by saying: The emptying of the treasury on barbarous troops, the
breaking of the youth of the country by hardship, the trampling underfoot
of the harvests, the abduction of cattle, the burning of farm and village on
every side, the deserted fields, tumbled walls, looted homes, plundered
shrines, old men left childless, children fatherless, mothers widowed, girls
shamefully raped, the morals of the young ruined by licence, so many
deaths, so many sorrows, so many tears, the extinction of the arts, the
suppression of law, the obliteration of religion, the total confusion of every

* * * * *

16 the French and the Neapolitans] Such as existed following the outbreak of the
Italian wars, mainly between France and Spain, after 1494, Naples being
under the control of an Aragonese dynasty

LB I 77B

divine and human value, the undermining of all civil discipline, all this train of evils, I say, which is born of war, we shall write down to your account alone, if, on your advice, war is declared.

Method 5

The fifth method of enrichment primarily involves ἐνάργεια, which is translated as *evidentia* 'vividness.' We employ this whenever, for the sake of amplifying or decorating our passage, or giving pleasure to our readers, instead of setting out the subject in bare simplicity, we fill in the colours and set it up like a picture to look at, so that we seem to have painted the scene rather than described it, and the reader seems to have seen rather than read. We shall be able to do this satisfactorily if we first mentally review the whole nature of the subject and everything connected with it, its very appearance in fact. Then we should give it substance with appropriate words and figures of speech, to make it as vivid and clear to the reader as possible. All the poets excel in this skill, but Homer above all, as I shall indicate when I reach the appropriate place. It consists mainly in the description of things, times, places, persons.

I   DESCRIPTION OF THINGS
First, the description of 'things' as a method of enrichment. We can take an action which is either in process or completed, and instead of presenting it in bare and insubstantial outline, bring it before the eyes with all the colours filled in, so that our hearer or reader is carried away and seems to be in the audience at a theatre. (The Greeks call this *hypotyposis*, because it gives the subject visual form, though this word is used for any kind of presentation to the eyes.) If one were to say that a city had been taken by storm, he would of course imply by such an overall statement all the subsidiary events that such a calamity admits. But, to go on in the exact words of Quintilian: 'If you make explicit everything included in this one phrase, we shall witness the flames spreading through homes and temples, and the crash of falling buildings, and all the cries blending into one overriding sound; some people fleeing, not knowing where they are going, others locked in a last embrace of their loved ones, the wails of babies and women, and old men cruelly preserved by fate to see this day; then we shall see the inevitable plundering of secular and sacred, the running to and fro

* * * * *

19 appropriate place] At 579, 580, 654–5
32 Quintilian] 8.3.67ff

of men carrying off loot or looking for more, prisoners in chains, each in the charge of his personal robber, mothers resisting the abduction of their children, and, wherever anything of greater value has come to light, the victors fighting among themselves. Though the one word "destruction" includes all this, this is a case where to state the whole is less effective than   5
to state all the parts.'

Quintilian also cites as an example of vividness this passage from Caelius directed against Antonius: 'They discover our hero flat on his back in a drunken stupor, snoring as loud as his lungs would let him and belching constantly, with his special "companions-in-arms" lying   10
sprawled sideways off the various couches, and the other ladies lying about all round the room. These were terrified out of their wits when they took in the arrival of the enemy, and tried to get Antonius awake. They shouted his name, and lifted him up by the neck, without any effect; one of them called lovingly into his ear; several of them slapped him quite hard. When he   15
began to take in their voices and hands, he tried to put his arms round the necks of the nearest girls, and could neither sleep being woken, nor keep awake being drunk, but was pulled about in a half-asleep daze between the centurions and the girl-friends.'

'No more credibly imagined scene,' says Quintilian, 'no more power-   20
ful denunciation, no more unambiguous exposure would be possible.'

Quintilian also quotes the description of a wild party: 'I seemed, he says, to see different people going in and out, some of them reeling about from the wine, others yawning as a result of the previous day's indulgence. The floor was filthy, awash with wine, and littered with wilted garlands and   25
fish-bones.'

But on all sides you will find a plentiful supply of examples of this sort, especially in the works of the poets, as I said earlier, and in the historians, whose style approximates most closely to poetry. In particular, this characteristic of vividness is especially remarkable in messengers' speeches in   30
tragedy, for these take the place of a real scene and report something which either cannot be represented on the stage for practical reasons or which is not the sort of thing one wants to represent; for example, when Talthybius in Euripides' *Hecuba* tells how Polyxena was slain, and the messenger in

* * * * *

7 Quintilian] 4.2.123–4; not the famous Mark Antony but his uncle Antonius
   Hybrida, a notorious spendthrift
22 Quintilian] 8.3.66, quoting from the lost *Pro Gallio* of Cicero
31 and report something ... chariot race] Text to 579:7 added in 1534 (LB I 78C–D)
34 *Hecuba*] 518ff

LB I 78A

Iphigenia in Aulis describes the sacrifice of Iphigenia. In Seneca's *Troades* the messenger tells Andromache how her son Astyanax met his end. This is sufficient indication by way of example, since all the tragedies present us with narrations of this sort at every turn. Nor does it matter for this convention whether the narrative is true or false, as in Sophocles' *Electra*, where the old man gives Clytemnestra a false account of how Orestes lost his life in the chariot race. Marcus Tullius too is a wonderful craftsman in this line.

I think I should remind you that descriptions of this sort consist mainly in the exposition of circumstantial details, especially those which make the incident particularly vivid, and give the narrative distinctiveness. Not a little is contributed to such descriptions by the adducing of parallels, the introduction of similes and contrasts, by comparison, metaphor, allegory, and by any other figures of speech that will light up a topic.

Epithets are also very effective here: for example, airy cliffs, turret-crowned cities, sky-blue or glassy sea, stooped ploughman, supercilious philosopher, spreading beech, black cave; or, to take some examples from Homer, δυσηχὴς πόλεμος [dread-resounding war], κορυθαίολος Ἕκτωρ [Hector of the flashing helm], βροτολοιγὸς Ἄρης καὶ τειχεσιπλήκτης [man-destroying, wall-breaching Ares] – this particular poet teems with phrases of this sort.

In a description not only do we take in things that happened before, during, and after the incident in question, but we also point out that something that did not happen could have happened if such and such had come to pass, or could still happen. One could for example say: See what a narrow escape we all had when you engaged the enemy with so little thought for the consequences: if by some mischance the enemy had been victorious, this and that would have happened. Or someone speaking against the introduction of monarchy could by his description set before the eyes of his hearers the whole drama of tyranny, and urge them to imagine that they see before them what they will soon be actually experiencing if they change from democracy to kingship.

* * * * *

1 *Iphigenia in Aulis*] 1540ff; both these plays were translated into Latin by Erasmus and published in 1506; text in ASD I-1 195–359.
1 *Seneca's Troades*] 1068ff
5 *Electra*] 673ff
15 Epithets] These phrases are all quotations from or reminiscences of Virgil.
18 Homer] *Iliad* 2.686, 2.816, 5.31
22 things that happened] See Quintilian 9.2.41.

LB I 78D

If we are speaking on some serious issue, ὑποτυπώσεις [vivid descriptions] are to be introduced only insofar as they contribute to the matter in hand; but when the whole business has no purpose but pleasure, as is usually the case with poetry, and with ἀποδείξεις [display pieces] which are handled precisely for the purpose of exercising and demonstrating one's ingenuity, one may indulge rather more freely in graphic descriptions of this sort. We may include under this head such Homeric descriptions as the arming of his gods and heroes, banquets, battles, retreats, and councils. Is there anything he does not display vividly before our eyes by putting in the appropriate circumstantial detail, which, even if it sometimes seems insignificant, yet somehow or other presents the thing marvellously to our eyes? He also gets his effect by the use of epithets and similes. Then there are descriptions of whirlwinds, storms, and shipwrecks, such as we find in a good many places in Homer, in Virgil in *Aeneid* 1, and in Ovid in *Metamorphoses* 11. There is a battle between two barbarian races in Juvenal, and a plague in Virgil *Georgics* 3, also in Ovid *Metamorphoses* 7 and in Seneca's *Oedipus*, and another one in Thucydides. There is a splendid description of a famine in one of Quintilian's display speeches. Then there are descriptions of prodigies, eclipses of the sun, snowstorms, torrential rain, lightning flashes, thunder, earthquakes, fire and flood, such as Ovid's description of Deucalion's flood; likewise seditions, armies, battles, slaughter, destruction, sackings, single combat, naval battles (as in Lucan book 3); banquets, parties, weddings, funerals, triumphs, games, processions, like Plutarch's description of Cleopatra's barge in his life of Mark Antony; sacred rites, ceremonies, incantations, witchcraft (as in Lucan book 6, and in Horace's *Satires*, where Priapus describes a scene at which he

* * * * *

 1 If we are speaking] See Quintilian 9.2.40.
14 Virgil] *Aeneid* 1.81ff
14 Ovid] *Metamorphoses* 11.478–572
15 Juvenal] 15.33ff
16 Virgil] *Georgics* 3.478ff
16 Ovid] *Metamorphoses* 7.523–81
17 Seneca's] *Oedipus* 37ff, 110–20
17 Thucydides] 2.47–54
18 Quintilian's] *Declamationes maiores* 12: *Pasti cadaveris*; see 500:26n.
21 Ovid's] *Metamorphoses* 1.262–312
22 Lucan] 3.521ff
24 Plutarch's] *Antony* 26
25 Lucan] 6.430ff.
26 Horace's] *Satires* 1.8

had been an onlooker); hunts (as for example in a poem by Cardinal Hadrian, though scholars do in fact deny that he wrote it); also descriptions of living creatures, like the electric ray and the porcupine in Claudian; the phoenix both in Claudian and Lactantius; the parrot in Ovid's *Amores* and in Statius; serpents in Lucan 9; all kinds of fish in Oppian; in Pliny the physical appearance, nature, and habits of vast numbers of living creatures, together with their natural enemies and allies, and in particular his description of the gnat; in Virgil the depiction of the horse and the ox and the wonderful portrayal of the bee; statues, like the statue of an old man in Pliny's *Letters*; paintings and other representations, like the Gallic Hercules in Lucian; and several expositions of works of art in Philostratus; and the similar expositions of tapestries, carvings, and suchlike, of which there are innumerable examples in the poets and historical writers, such as Arachne's web in Ovid *Metamorphoses* 6, and Homer's representation of the shield of Achilles, and Virgil's of the shield of Aeneas; or a ship, or a dress, or πανοπλία [full armour], or an engine of war, a chariot, a Colossus, a pyramid, or anything else the description of which will afford delight.

We may include here, I think, accounts of a people's physical appearance and social customs – Scythians, cannibals, Indians, troglodytes, and so on; or some delineation of the life of a soldier, philosopher, courtier, countryman, private citizen, or royal personage.

* * * * *

2 Hadrian] Adrian de Castello, c 1460–1521; his poem *Venatio* was published by Aldus in 1505; see *Dictionary of National Biography* I.

2 though scholars ... deny] This reservation added in 1534 (LB I 79C)

4 Claudian] *Carmina minora* IX (XLV), XLIX (XLVI) in J. Koch's Teubner edition (Leipzig 1893)

4 Lactantius] *De ave phoenice*

4 Ovid's] *Amores* 2.6

5 Statius] *Silvae* 2.4

5 Lucan] 9.700ff

5 Oppian] *Halieutica*, a poem on fishing

8 gnat] Pliny *Naturalis historia* 11.2

8 Virgil] *Georgics* 3.72ff; 51ff; bee: *Georgics* 4 passim

10 Pliny's] *Epistles* 3.6

11 Lucian] *Hercules Gallicus*, an essay translated by Erasmus; see 603:17n.

11 Philostratus] One of four Philostrati living in the period second to third centuries AD; this one wrote Εἰκόνες, descriptions of pictures in a Neapolitan collection, which are exercises in the art of rhetorical description.

14 Ovid] *Metamorphoses* 6.1ff

14 Homer's] *Iliad* 18.483ff

15 Virgil's] *Aeneid* 8.626ff

To give a satisfactory account of all these things not only requires skill
and imagination, but it is very helpful to have seen with your own eyes
what you wish to depict. There are indeed descriptions of imaginary
things, but even these have some similarity to real ones, descriptions for
example of the Ages of Gold, Silver, and Iron; or the picture of human life in
Cebes; or of the Court, or Slander, or Learning, or several other things in
Lucian. Homer has descriptions of Rumour, Folly, Prayers, Ovid of Famine
and Envy, and both he and Virgil describe Rumour.

If anyone prefers to include these under description of persons, which
I am just about to deal with, I have no very great objection.

II DESCRIPTION OF PERSONS

Descriptions of persons are indeed very like this last type. The technical
term for the realistic presentation of persons is προσωποποιία [dramatiza-
tion]. Somewhat different from this is προσωπογραφία [delineation of
persons], mainly in that it has a wider application. You could with reason
speak of the προσωπογραφία of Famine, Envy, and Sleep, which I have
just been discussing, as these are presented as if they were persons. To this
type belongs the personification of Virtue and Pleasure, which, as
Xenophon tells us, the sophist Prodicus imagined disputing before Hercules; likewise the personification of Death and Life, which, according to
Quintilian, Ennius introduced arguing together in one of his satires;
likewise Slander in Lucian, and Learning and Sculpture; Opportunity in
Ausonius; Fortune in Horace's odes and in Quintus Curtius; Love in
Moschus; Poverty and Wealth in Aristophanes; Justice in Chrysippus, as

* * * * *

5 Ages of Gold] Hesiod *Works and Days* 110ff
6 Cebes] A sophist, one of the disciples of Socrates; the description of human
   life occurs in the Πίναξ, probably wrongly attributed to him.
7 Lucian] *De iis qui mercede conducti degunt* on court life; *De calumnia (Non temere
   credendum esse delationi)* on Slander; *Imagines* 16 on Learning; see 603:17n.
7 Homer] *Odyssey* 24.413; *Iliad* 9.502ff
7 Ovid] *Metamorphoses* 8.799; *Ex Ponto* 3.3.101–2; *Metamorphoses* 12.53ff
8 Virgil] *Aeneid* 4.173ff
20 Xenophon] *Memorabilia* 2.1.21–34, quoted in Quintilian 9.2.36
22 Ennius] See Quintilian 9.2.36.
23 Lucian] Slander: see line 7n; Learning and Sculpture contend for the young
   man's allegiance in *De somnio sive vita Luciani.*
24 Ausonius] *Epigrams* 33.3
24 Horace's] *Odes* 3.29.49
24 Quintus Curtius] 7.8.24–5
25 Moschus] Eros Drapetes, Love as a runaway slave *Idyll* 1
25 Aristophanes] *Plutus*, in which Wealth and Poverty are characters
25 Chrysippus] See Aulus Gellius 14.4.

LB I 79E

Gellius records; Philosophy in Severinus Boethius; the Lamia in Poliziano; also the Muses, Graces, Furies, War, Sphinx, Scylla, Charybdis, and so on, in the poets.

Some descriptions have more relation to reality, yet give considerable scope for display, like the description of Hippias in Lucian, and again in Apuleius' *Florida*. Such 'characterizations' however are more suitable for the orator. Characterization is the name given to the depiction of a lover, rake, miser, glutton, drunkard, sluggard, chatterer, boaster, vaunter, envier, sycophant, hanger-on, or pimp. There is an example in book 4 of the *Rhetorica ad Herennium*, where all the marks of the pseudo-rich man are set out, that is the man who is not rich but puts on a parade to give the impression that he is. You may draw any number of examples from comedy, for that is what comedy is all about. We have extant the *Characters*, supposedly by Theophrastus, which provide material for the sort of characterization we find in comedy. In my opinion they are the work of some grammarian rather than the philosopher. Such a delineation of character is built up of all the accompanying attributes; this could be nationality or country; and we could describe the physical appearance, dress, voice, language, gestures, gait, religious practices, cast of mind, and moral behaviour, of a Carthaginian, Greek, Gaul, Scythian, Hibernian, Spaniard, Scot, or Briton; we shall have to depict the Carthaginian as an inveterate breaker of agreements, cunning, insolent, and showily dressed; and so with all the rest. Cities have their individual characteristics too: the Athenian is soft, and better at talking than doing, Romans are hard, Florentines tight-fisted. Or we may take sex as a basis, and depict man on the one hand as firm, woman on the other as talkative, fickle, and superstitious; or make a characterization on grounds of age as Horace does in the *Ars poetica*; or of fortune, showing the wealthy man as haughty, the poor man as humble and diffident; or of employment, the soldier being arrogant and a great bragger about his own brave deeds, the pimp never keeping his word, the countryman inclined to pessimism, the courtier to flattery, the city man mild, the medical man concerned to make money, the poet eager for fame, delighting in springs and groves and lonely places, despising wealth and political office, the sophist more talkative than wise.

* * * * *

1 Boethius] *Consolatio philosophiae* 1.1
1 Poliziano] See 535:3n; an essay *Lamia, Praelectio in priora Aristotelis Analytica*
5 Lucian] *Hippias* 3
6 Apuleius'] *Florida* 9; see 573:22n.
10 *ad Herennium*] 4.50.63
27 Horace] *Ars poetica* 158ff, the 'Ages of Man'

Nor should we neglect the universal emotions, the feelings of father for children, husband for wife, citizen for country, prince for people, people for nobles, and all the others discussed in detail by Aristotle in his *Rhetoric*.

There are however individual characteristics even within these general types. It is not enough to grasp what is consistent with the character of an old man, a young man, a slave, the head of a house, or a pimp. Otherwise representatives of the various types would all be indistinguishable from each other. The comic poets especially seem to have aimed at variety in characters belonging to the same general type. What could be more dissimilar than Demea and Micio in Terence? Micio is mild even when he is trying to reprimand his son severely, Demea is cross-patched even when he is doing his best to be pleasant. Yet they are both old men, and brothers at that. What could be a greater contrast than Chremes who is always easygoing and pleasant-spoken, and Simo who is vehement and suspicious? or Pamphilus, who is a young man of spirit, and Charinus who is lacking in courage and initiative? What more dissimilar than Phaedria struggling to overcome his passion, and Chaerea who cares nothing for the consequences? There is a great difference between Davus who is determined to look on the bright side, and Byrria who has nothing to offer but despair, between the two parasites Gnatho and Phormio, and between these and the sort of parasites depicted by Plautus. Likewise Plautus' courtesans are very different from Terence's, who for the most part depicts good courtesans, like Philotis and Bacchis in the *Hecyra*. Plautus makes his old men lecherous and cheerful, and old hands at deceiving their wives, though he does in one play invent a different sort of character in Euclio, who is unbelievably miserly and suspicious.

If we handle a character whom another writer has treated before us, we must take the salient characteristics from those who invented or described him earlier; for example, you must make Achilles fierce, unrelenting, direct, hostile to kings, hostile to any form of deceit, and swift of foot, for that is how Homer first depicted him; Ulysses must be cunning, lying,

* * * * *

3 Aristotle] *Rhetoric* 2.12–17
11 Terence] *Adelphi*
14 Chremes ... Simo] Characters in Terence's *Andria*
16 Pamphilus ... Charinus] In *Andria*
17 Phaedria ... Chaerea] In *Eunuchus*
19 Davus ... Byrria] In *Andria*
21 Gnatho and Phormio] In *Eunuchus, Phormio*
26 Euclio] In *Aulularia*
30 must make Achilles fierce] See Horace *Ars poetica* 120–2.

LB I 80D

deceitful, able to endure anything; Agamemnon rather lacking in force but
eager for power, fearful of the people, keener on pleasure than war; Hector
noble-souled, careless of death and omens, putting everything second to
his love for his country; Ajax better able to prove himself by deed than
word, resentful of humiliation and rejection. In short, as the character was   5
first created by Homer, so it has to be preserved by the tragic poets.
Similarly, anyone who wishes to depict Aristides, Themistocles, Phocion,
Alcibiades, Pisistratus, Julius Caesar, Fabius, Camillus, Timon, Socrates,
Plato, or Epicurus must look for the appropriate characteristics in the
historical writers.   10

This form of exercise obviously appealed to those who forged letters
and speeches going under the names of Menelaus, Phoenix, Achilles,
Phalaris, Brutus, Seneca, and Paul. Likewise anyone writing dialogues
must consider what words he puts in the mouth of which character. In the
case of non-real characterizations, the appropriate features – Philosophy   15
with firm and authoritative face, the Muses wholesome and winning, the
Graces holding hands with robes flowing free, Justice with straight and
unflinching gaze, and so on – must be derived from the nature of the thing
alluded to.

There are also appropriate characteristics to be observed in fables, and   20
this no one will be able to manage unless he has observed and studied the
natures of living creatures, and knows that the elephant is quick to learn
and reverent, the dolphin an enemy of the crocodile and a friend of man,
that the eagle builds its nest on heights, that the beetle has a habit of
pushing along balls of the dung in which it mates and reproduces, and   25
disappears during the season when eagles are incubating, that the lark lays
its eggs in harvest-fields, that the hedgehog likes ranging about and is an
enemy to snakes. All this, and less well-known facts too, may be easily
discovered in Aristotle, Pliny, and Aelian. Orators also make use of fables.
A type of fable that is less natural is one that attributes speech to inanimate   30
objects such as trees or stones.

More common in oratory are those προσωπογραφίαι [delineations

* * * * *

22 elephant] Pliny *Naturalis historia* 8.1
23 dolphin] *Naturalis historia* 8.91, 9.24–8; Younger Pliny *Epistles* 9.33, the fam-
    ous dolphin of Hippo
24 eagle ... beetle] See *Adagia* III vii 1: 'Scarabaeus aquilam quaerit'; Aesop *Fables*
    4 (Chambry)
26 lark] Aulus Gellius 2.29.3
29 Aristotle] *Historia animalium*
29 Pliny] *Naturalis historia* passim
29 Aelian] *De natura animalium*

of persons] in which a definite person is painted in all his colours, in so far as this is relevant to the matter in hand, for example, Catiline in Sallust, Hannibal in Livy, Trajan in Pliny.

Rarer are descriptions of physical appearance, but they do occur; for example the depiction of a beautiful woman feature by feature, or of a hideous hag, or Homer's description of Thersites, or Helen's pointing out of many of the Greek leaders from the walls of Troy, in response to Priam's queries. Virgil imitates Homer when he describes many of the great Romans in book 6.

Particularly appropriate to character delineation is διαλογισμός or dialogue, in which we supply each person with utterances appropriate to his age, type, country, way of life, cast of mind, and character. Utterances of this kind may be introduced into historical writing, hence all the speeches in Thucydides, Sallust, and Livy. Letters and striking sayings may also be composed, and even thoughts expressed, as of a man talking to himself, though this is commoner in the poets.

The term προσωποποιία [dramatization] may be most properly applied when we introduce a person far away or long dead and make him speak in a manner appropriate to his character, as for example in a passage like this: Suppose that those leaders of our city in times long past were to come to life again and observe the manner in which we now conduct ourselves. Would they not burst out in words such as these? Then a speech will follow. Or this: What if that famous forbear of yours were now with us, would he not have good reason to reprimand you in words like these? or: Suppose Camillus were now to return to the light of day, would he not with reason take us to task in words such as these? Already I seem to hear him speaking to me and saying ... or: Imagine Plato himself expostulating with you after this fashion.

Representation of persons like this does not offer any challenge to credulity, as we make them say things that they probably would say if they were really here. A less easily acceptable form of representation, but one that can be used in real speeches, not just practice ones, if the seriousness of

* * * * *

2 Sallust] *Catilina* especially chap 5
3 Livy] 21.4
3 Pliny] *Panegyricus* especially chaps 2, 4
6 Homer's] *Iliad* 2.212ff
6 Helen's] *Iliad* 3.161ff
8 Virgil] *Aeneid* 6.756ff
23 famous forbear] See Cicero *Pro Caelio* 33.
27 Imagine Plato] See Cicero *De finibus* 4.61: *quid si reviviscant Platonis illi ... et loquantur?*

the occasion requires it, is to put words into the mouth of Nature, or the State, or a province, or our native land. Cicero did this in his speeches against Catiline: 'She [i.e., the country] speaks to you, Catiline, and silently addresses you.' Or again: 'For if my country, which I love more than life itself, if the whole of Italy, if the entire state were to address me and say: "Marcus Tullius, what are you at?" ...' In Plato's *Crito* Socrates introduces the laws arguing with himself. This type occurs whenever we lend speech to the gods, or to places, or to all sorts of other things. Examples to which the term προσωπογραφία [delineation of persons] may be properly applied are given brilliance by metaphors, similes, and parallels, and such examples occur in great numbers in the poets.

III DESCRIPTION OF PLACES
Another method of enrichment is by inserting descriptions of places, which the Greeks call τοπογραφίαι. This is a very common method of introducing a narrative, used by poets and historians, and by orators too on occasion. In this the whole appearance of a place is described so that we can see it, a city for example, a hill, a region, a river, a harbour, a country estate, gardens, a sports arena, a spring, a cave, a temple, a grove. If the descriptions are of real places, the accepted term is τοπογραφίαι [descriptions of place], but if imaginary τοποθεσίαι [depictions of place]. Real ones include Virgil's description of Carthage and its harbour, Pliny's accounts in his *Letters* of his Laurentine villa, and Statius' account of Pollio's villa at Sorrento and Manilius' villa at Tivoli; imaginary ones include Ovid's evocation of the Abode of Sleep, the House of Fame, the Palace of the Sun, Virgil's of the Underworld and the lair of Cacus, the description of Taenarum in Statius, a hall in Lucian, and Psyche's fairy palace in Apuleius. We must include among real descriptions the account of the eruption of Vesuvius in the Younger Pliny, and the fires of Etna in Claudian, and any account of the

* * * * *

2 Cicero] *Catilinarians* 1.18
4 Or again] *Catilinarians* 1.27, both examples used in Quintilian 9.2.32
6 Plato's] *Crito* 50B ff
21 Virgil's] *Aeneid* 1.418ff
22 Pliny's] *Epistles* 2.17
23 Statius'] *Silvae* 2.2, 1.3
24 Ovid's] *Metamorphoses* 11.592ff, 12.39ff, 2.1ff
25 Virgil's] *Aeneid* 6.268ff, 8.225ff
26 Statius] *Thebaid* 2.32ff
27 Lucian] *De domo*
27 Apuleius] *Metamorphoses* 5.1–2
29 Pliny] *Epistles* 6.16 and 20
29 Claudian] *De raptu Proserpinae* 1.153ff

Nile, the cave of the Sybil, the rainbow, and so on. The more unfamiliar the things are, the more pleasure the description will give and the longer one may dwell on it, provided it is not totally irrelevant.

IV DESCRIPTION OF TIMES

Next we come to description of times, which the Greeks call χρονογραφία. This is often used to begin an account of events, but on occasion is employed merely for the sake of giving pleasure, as when poets describe day, night, dawn, or dusk, but even in this case such descriptions should not be introduced if they have absolutely no connection with the rest of the material. Take for example the famous passage in Virgil:

> It was night, and over all the earth
> Weary bodies lay in quiet sleep;
> The woods, the cruel sea had sunk to rest,
> Stars in mid-course were wheeling on,
> And every field lay hushed;
> The beasts, the speckled birds, the creatures of the pools
> Liquid and wide beneath the sky, and thickets
> Standing rough across the land, wrapped in sleep
> Beneath the silent night, hushed their cares,
> And let their hearts forget their grief.

Now this description of the stillness of the night is intended to throw into relief Dido's grief which would not abate when all else was still. For the poet goes on: 'But not the heartsick Tyrian queen / Never does she yield and sink to sleep.'

Under this head belong descriptions of spring, winter, autumn, summer, vintage, mourning, festivals, which often have an additional value in helping to demonstrate a point. Descriptions are complex if we set out the characteristics of the times and seasons we are depicting, for example, peace, war, sedition, party strife, monarchy, democracy, and as well as describing them, indicate what good or bad features are particularly associated with them.

All these topics should be dealt with separately on occasion as an exercise for our ingenuity, but a complete description contains them all. In

*****

1 Nile] For example, Virgil *Georgics* 4.287ff
1 cave of the Sibyl] For example, Virgil *Aeneid* 6.237–40
1 rainbow] See 297:22n.
11 Virgil] *Aeneid* 4.522ff

LB I 82B

the satire I mentioned a short while ago, Horace first describes the place on
the Esquiline where the scene took place, then the time, then the person of
Priapus and the witches, and finally he gives a graphic account of the
sacrifice and the flight of the hags when alarmed by the noise of the fart.

Method 6 (Digression)

Very like the methods of enrichment which I have just been discussing is
the sixth method, which the Greeks call παρέκβασις, variously translated
as diversion, digression, or excursus, or, as Quintilian defines it, the
handling of a topic which does have a contribution to make to the successful
outcome of the case, in a manner which digresses from the strict arrangement of the material. Such a digression may be introduced to praise someone, like Cicero's popular recital in his speech *Pro Lucio Cornelio* of the
virtues of Gnaeus Pompey, into which topic the divine orator (to use
Quintilian's own words) diverges, breaking off the argument he was pursuing, as if the current of his speech had met a barrier in the shape of the
general's name. Digressions can also be used to attack someone, or for
adornment, delight, or preparation. They find their subject-matter for the
most part in the topics I have just discussed, the exposition of actions, the
descriptions of places and regions, the presentation of persons, and also in
the handling of stories and fables. Further material is supplied by topics of
universal relevance or commonplaces, when we decide to expand what we
have to say by inveighing against glory, luxury, lust, avarice, base affection, tyranny, wrath, and other vices, and (as if forgetting our case for a
time) dwell on these subjects. Alternatively, we can eulogize careful use of
money, generosity, self-control, application to study, piety, and control of
the tongue. Such topics are so valuable in promoting wealth of expression
that a good many distinguished authors have handled them specifically as
an exercise, in which form they are known as χρεῖαι [useful maxims].

* * * * *

1 Horace] *Satires* 1.8; see 580:26.

11 Quintilian] 4.3.14

15 Cicero's] This speech is lost; the whole passage is quoted from Quintilian
4.3.13.

31 χρεῖαι] One of several forms of exercise used to instruct schoolboys in the
elementary techniques of the art of speaking; it consisted of a maxim illustrated by an anecdote. The various exercises were illustrated in *Progymnasmata* (preliminary exercises) by rhetoricians such as Theon, Hermogenes (see
607:14n), Libanius, and Aphthonius (whose work was still being used in the
seventeenth century). Collections of such maxims were also made by writers
such as Diogenes Laertius and Plutarch.

LB I 82D

Another set of commonplaces not very different from these depicts things like the advantages of freedom compared with the disadvantages of slavery, the fickleness of fortune, the equal inevitability of death for us all, the power of money in the affairs of men, the brevity of human life, and innumerable other similar topics.

One may dwell rather longer on digressions at the beginning of one's speech, as with Lucian's description of the Gallic Hercules and Poliziano's of the Lamiae, or at the end, so as to refresh the listener who by now may well be weary, which is more or less what Virgil does in the *Georgics*. If one wishes to make a digression in the middle, one should return quickly to the point from which the digression was made, unless the completion of a section in the speech provides a suitable handle on which to hang a digression: one could be inserted after the exposition of the facts, to stimulate the hearer ready for the argumentation which will come next, or after the section where the arguments are enumerated, or after any of the less attractive sections, in order to dispel the mental fatigue induced by detailed exposition. If our subject-matter of itself provides opportunities for digressions, we may of course dwell on them when thus invited to do so.

Method 7

The seventh method consists in the addition of epithets or descriptive words. Diomedes considers the epithet a variety of antonomasia and defines it as follows: the epithet is a differentiating adjunct to a proper noun, which may enhance, detract, or particularize; enhance, as in 'divine Camilla'; detract, as in 'Ulysses, originator of foul deceits'; particularize, as in 'Thessalian Achilles.'

Such descriptive phrases may be derived from mental characteristics: Plato, wisest of the philosophers; or from physical ones: Thersites, ugliest of all Greeks; from externals (this type is manifold, as it covers the whole range of fortune's gifts): birth: high-born Maecenas; wealth: Croesus,

* * * * *

9 Virgil] *Georgics* 1.464ff: digression on the death of Julius Caesar and prayer for the safety of Octavian; 2.475ff: the blessedness of farmers and the joys of poetry; 3.478ff: the plague; 4.315–558: the story of Aristaeus, itself containing the story of Orpheus and Eurydice

24 Diomedes] *Ars grammatica* II in Keil I 459

24 antonomasia] See book I chap 14.

27 Camilla] Virgil *Aeneid* 11.657

27 Ulysses] *Aeneid* 2.164

28 Achilles] *Aeneid* 2.197

LB I 83A

richest of kings; beauty: most handsome Nireus; strength: Milo, the strongest athlete; country: Ulysses, the Ithacan; deeds: Hercules, reducer of monsters; occurrences: twice-captured Phrygians; in short, every good or evil gift of fortune.

It does not matter whether the descriptive word consists of a noun in apposition or not, provided that some differentiating characteristic is contributed to persons, or indeed to things; for example: precipitate youth; love, a headstrong and unwise councillor; pleasure, the food of evil; peevish and difficult old age; philosophy, the banisher of vice; comedy, the mirror to human life; history, the teacher of life.

In poetry one may use natural descriptive phrases, such as: white snow, liquid founts, chilly night, rolling river, golden sun; but these should not be employed in prose unless they carry some particular emphasis and are relevant to what we are trying to achieve; for example: You will not win a case so unjust before Aristides, the most just of men; or: Do you dare to keep carnival in the presence of Cato, the severest critic of moral conduct? This will apply particularly to stock examples and well-known sayings, such as: Aristarchus, the most learned of men and the most meticulous; Cicero, the prince of eloquence; Plato, the most reliable authority.

Method 8

The eighth type of expansion uses the circumstances peculiar to the case, for which the Greek term is *peristases*. These consist partly of non-personal and external details: contributory events, place, opportunity, instrument, time, method, and so on; partly of personal details: race, country, sex, age, education and training, physical state, material circumstances, place in society, type of personality, occupation, previous conduct, motivation, intention, reputation. The apt and timely employment of 'circumstances' serves several ends: amplification or building up, and extenuation or toning down, about both of which I shall have something to say shortly;

* * * * *

2 Hercules, reducer of monsters] Apuleius *Apology* 22: *purgator ferarum, gentium domitor*

3 twice-captured Phrygians] Virgil *Aeneid* 9.599

9 philosophy, the banisher of vice] Cicero *Tusculan Disputations* 5.5

9 comedy, the mirror to human life] Attributed to Cicero by Donatus; see *Comicorum graecorum fragmenta* ed. G. Kaibel (Berlin 1899) i i 67.

10 history, the teacher of life] Cicero *De oratore* 2.36

24 eighth type] For the whole of this section see Quintilian 5.10.104.

vividness, which I have just spoken of above; also confirmation and credibility. It fills out the whole case and reinforces it with close-packed convincing details, and even if you do not deploy them and lead them out to battle,
so to speak, they fight on their own and contribute not a little to the winning
of the case. Accordingly, just as one can recognize the trained athlete or   5
musician even when he is not concentrating particularly, so one can perceive the true orator anywhere in the speech by the way details of this sort
are aptly added to the mixture in the appropriate place.

Since this feature pervades the whole speech, it cannot be illustrated
by a short example.   10

Method 9

The ninth method consists of amplification or building up, of which Quinti- 15
lian lists a considerable number of types. We shall briefly deal with those
that are relevant to our present purposes.

The first type uses augmentation, in which one advances by regular
steps not only to the maximum, but even in a way beyond the maximum.
An example of this may be found in Cicero's fifth speech against Verres: 'It 20
is an offence to tie up a Roman citizen, a crime to flog him, equal to the
murder of a kinsman to put him to death. What shall I call crucifying him? It
is not possible to find a word to fit such a heinous act.'

There is also a variety of this figure in which we heap up 'circumstances' while observing some kind of order, and let one run on from   25
another so arranged that the next thing is always greater than the one that
went before, as in Cicero's passage in the *Second Philippic* about Antony's
vomiting: 'What a disgusting thing, not only to see but even to hear! If this
had happened at dinner when you were quaffing those monstrous tankards
of yours, who would not think it disgraceful? But it was in a formal   30
assembly of the people of Rome, engaged in conducting the business of the
state, holding the office of Master of the Horse, for whom it would be a
disgrace even to belch, that this fellow spewed up morsels of food stinking
of wine all over himself and all over the speakers' platform.' Here each
individual word has more effect than the one before. In the first place the 35
action was disgusting in itself even if it had not been in an assembly, or if in
an assembly not one of the people, or not of the Roman people, or if he had

* * * * *

15 Quintilian] 8.4, from which chapter Erasmus takes his examples
20 Cicero's] *Verrines* 5.170; quoted in Quintilian 8.4.4
27 Cicero's] *Philippics* 2.63; Quintilian 8.4.8

not been conducting formal business, or not formal public business, or if he were not Master of the Horse.

If anyone took these items separately and dwelt on the individual stages, he would indeed extend his material, but an amplification of this type would be less effective than the one we have.

The opposite method to this is comparison. In augmentation, the movement is constantly towards something more impressive; a comparison gets its effect by starting from something less striking. The comparison may be based on a supposition or may employ a real event. We had a supposition, for which the Greek term is ὑπόθεσις, in the first part of the example we quoted from Cicero, for he puts forward the supposition that it happened at a dinner party to a person holding no public office. There is another one in the well-known passage from one of the Catilinarian speeches: 'Upon my word, if my slaves feared me the way all your [fellow citizens] fear you, I should feel that I had better get out of my house.'

When a real situation is used, we put forward a genuine circumstance that has some similarity with the thing we are boosting, and proceed to show how this is very close to it, or equal to it, or even greater. This is what Cicero does in the *Pro Cluentio*. He describes how a certain woman of Miletus received money from the reversionary heirs in return for having an abortion. He goes on: 'While Oppianicus shares the crime committed, he deserves much greater punishment. She ill-treated her own body, and brought suffering on herself, but he achieved the same result through another person's suffering.'

In this type we not only compare one whole situation with another, but we can compare one detail with another, as is done in this passage from the *Pro Milone*: 'Scipio, that distinguished figure, when holding no public office, killed Tiberius Gracchus when he was causing a moderately serious political upheaval in Rome; shall we, when clothed with the dignity of consul, stand by while Catiline seeks to lay the whole world waste with fire and slaughter?' Here Catiline is compared with Gracchus, the situation in Rome with the world, a moderate upheaval with slaughter and burning and desolation, a man holding no office with those who are entrusted with the highest. Again if anyone wished to expand these sections, he would have topics full of possibility at every point.

The second method of amplification uses the rhetorical figure known as inference; in this we actually build up one thing, and this suggests the

* * * * *

13 Catilinarian] 1.17; Quintilian 8.4.10
19 Cicero] *Pro Cluentio* 32; Quintilian 8.4.11
27 *Pro Milone*] Actually *Catilinarians* 1.3; Quintilian 8.4.13; see 609:15.

build-up of another, as in this passage: 'You, with a gullet of that capacity, with a chest of that girth, with a physique which would do credit to a gladiator, swilled so much wine at Hippias' wedding that the next day you couldn't help being sick in full view of the Roman people.' Here one can infer how much wine Antony drank because, in spite of his gladiator's physique, he was not able to carry so much and digest it.

Associated with this is the procedure by which we take the most dreadful deeds and rouse the strongest resentment against them, and then deliberately tone them down so that what follows may seem even more serious, as in this passage from Cicero: 'In a prisoner like this these crimes are trivial. The commander-in-chief of the fleet of a noble city had to pay money to save himself from the fear of being flogged. But that's a human enough crime.' We must needs expect something absolutely appalling, if deeds which are shocking seem human and normal beside it.

Another method of build-up is the piling up of words and phrases meaning the same thing. This is very like συναθροισμός [accumulation of synonyms] which I discussed earlier. Cicero uses this in his speech *Pro Ligario*: 'What was that sword of yours doing, Tubero, that you drew on the field of Pharsalus? Whose ribs was that weapon-point seeking? what was the purpose of your weapons? what was your own mind? what sort of eyes, what sort of hands did you have, what passion drove you on? what did you seek? what desire?' Here the speech grows like a heap by addition. Sometimes the emotional tone of the additions rises ever higher with each one, as in this: 'Present was the keeper of the prison gate, the praetor's thug, the destruction and terror of allied and Roman citizens alike, the lictor Sextius.'

We can also build up by using a form of 'self-correction,' as Cicero does in this passage from the Verrines: 'We have brought to your court not a mere thief but a brigand, not an adulterer but a stormer of chastity, not a temple-robber but a sworn enemy of religion and all that is sacred, not a cut-throat but a savage murderer of citizens and allies alike.'

There are just as many ways of toning down what we have to say as there are of building it up.

Our utterances may be expanded by everyday and unremarkable methods such as adding adverbs, nouns, and other parts of speech, either

* * * * *

1 this passage] See 592:27n.
10 Cicero] *Verrines* 5.117; Quintilian 8.4.19
16 συναθροισμός] See 320:6.
17 Cicero] *Pro Ligario* 9; Quintilian 8.4.27; see above 320:28ff.
24 in this] Cicero *Verrines* 5.118; Quintilian 8.4.27
26 'self-correction'] See book I chap 65.
26 Cicero] *Verrines* 1.9; Quintilian 8.4.2

to express approval or censure: Cicero delights me to an inordinate extent: it is beyond words how well disposed your father-in-law is towards you; I cannot find words to express what pleasure I take in Cicero – but I have dealt with these methods of extension in book I.

A well-known and common method of expansion is to attach a species to its genus: All the disciplines of a liberal education bestow on a man either grace or advantage; eloquence does so beyond all others – though I have dealt with this method before too.

Method 10

The tenth method of expansion depends on inventing as many propositions as possible. I am speaking of rhetorical propositions or themes, which are demonstrated to be true by the exposition of arguments. As for inventing propositions, Quintilian says that this skill cannot be learned as a technique, but comes from imagination and practice. Hence we find that a group of people may have received the same instruction, and may use similar types of argument, and yet one will discover more material than another.

Propositions or themes are derived partly from generalities, partly from the circumstances of the case. We can demonstrate the method with an example chosen by Quintilian: 'When Alexander overthrew Thebes, he discovered documents recording that the Thebans had lent the Thessalians a hundred talents. These documents he handed over to the Thessalians as a reward for supporting him with troops in the campaign. The Thebans later had their fortunes restored by Cassander, and demanded repayment of the debt from the Thessalians. The case was taken before the Amphictyonic Council. It was not disputed that the Thebans had lent a hundred talents, and that this sum had not been repaid – the point at issue was the claim that Alexander had given the Thessalians the documents. Nor was it disputed that Alexander had not actually presented them with the money they owed the Thebans.'

In arguing this out we need to invent themes and sections of the

* * * * *

4 book I] Chap 46
8 before] At 574:41ff
13 propositions] See Quintilian 4.4.
16 Quintilian] 5.10.119–21
23 Quintilian] 5.10.111–18; Erasmus changes Quintilian's statement of the case slightly.

following sort to provide the framework for our case: (1) Alexander's gift
was of no effect; (2) he had no power to give; (3) he did not actually give.

In the first section the first proposition on behalf of the Thebans will be
that one has the right to demand back through the law what has been taken
away by force. On behalf of the Thessalians it will be propounded that the
documents were not simply removed by force but by war, and the rights of
war are the most powerful ones known in human affairs; by them are
determined kingdoms and peoples and the territories of nations and cities.
In answer to this the Thebans declare that not everything falls into the
victor's power by the rights of war; the rights of war have no validity in
matters which belong to the sphere of civil justice; that things seized by
force of arms can only be retained by exercising that same force of arms;
where arms hold sway, there is no place for a judge, but where there is a
judge, arms have no authority. Here we argue from the circumstances
special to the case, which enables us to show why this particular case differs
from others. To support this last proposition, we can put forward as a
parallel a statement of general validity: Captives become free again if they
regain their native land, because ownership of things acquired in war can
only be asserted by exercising the same physical force by which they were
first acquired. The third proposition on behalf of the Thebans will also
depend on the special circumstances of this case: In any case in which the
Amphictyonic Council is the judge, the main consideration must be equity.
(The same lawsuit requires different handling according to where it is
heard, for example, before the Centumviral Court or before an arbitrator.)
The effect of these arguments is again to show that this case is on a different
footing from those where the rights of war should determine the issue.

In the second section we can state on behalf of the Thebans that the
victor had no power to make a gift of a right, because only what can be
seized belongs to the victor: a right is an incorporeal thing, and cannot be
physically held. To support this proposition we can bring in an argument
from the dissimilar: An heir and a conqueror are not in the same case; the
right passes to the heir, the material object to the conqueror. The circumstances of the case provide the next proposition, which reinforces the
previous one: Even if we concede that in other cases a right passes to the
conqueror, certainly the right attached to a state loan could not in any way

* * * * *

22 Amphictyonic Council] Because it was associated with the shrine of Apollo at
   Delphi, which in theory meant that the council had dignity and authority and
   that its decisions carried religious sanction
24 Centumviral Court] A court in ancient Rome dealing with property suits;
   Pliny began his legal career there, and speaks of it in his *Letters*.

LB I 85C

pass to the conqueror, because if a loan is made by the whole people, the sum is owed to the whole people, and as long as one individual survives, he is the creditor to whom the sum is due; but not all the Thebans fell into Alexander's power. This argument needs no further support.

In the third section we can have a general proposition (that is, one not specifically tied to any case): When he gave the documents, Alexander did not really give anything, for rights do not reside in documents. This proposition can be supported by arguments of all kinds; such as arguments from a similar case: The man who possesses documents proving inheritance does not necessarily have the right of inheritance; or: If a creditor happens to lose his documentary proof, the debtor is not forthwith released from his debt. The second proposition in this section depends on conjecture: Alexander did not present the Thessalians with the documents to reward them, but to deceive them. This will have to be demonstrated by various suggestions and hypotheses. The third one is not simply a contribution to this stage of the argument, but is more or less the introduction of a new issue. It depends on material proper to the case, and takes this form: Even if we grant the Thessalians all this – that the law of war has authority in civil disputes in general, and before these judges in particular, and in the case of a state loan, and all the other points – all the same, whatever the Thebans lost when conquered by Alexander, they should have recovered when restored by Cassander, especially when this was Cassander's express wish.

[EXAMPLE TAKEN FROM SPEECH DISCUSSING
COURSE OF ACTION]
To give a second example: anyone urging Cicero not to accept Mark Antony's proposal that he should keep his life in return for burning the *Philippics* could use the following propositions: No man of eminence ought to buy his life at the cost of his immortal fame. This general proposition could be reinforced by one dependent on the specific circumstances of this case: Especially Cicero, who by his labours won for himself a name and a glory that will live for ever and eloquently demonstrated in so many wonderful books that death is of no account, particularly as, being already an old man, he probably has not many years still to live. A second major

* * * * *

26 To give a second example ... poor health] The passage to 598:19 added in *1514*
   (LB I 86A–C)
26 Mark Antony's proposal] A stock theme debated in the ancient schools of
   rhetoric; see Seneca *Suasoriae* 6.
32 wonderful books] For example, *Tusculan Disputations* 1
33 already an old man] See *Philippics* 2.119.

LB I 85E

proposition can be derived from the circumstances of the case: Nothing
could be more distressing than to have a fine man like Cicero indebted for
his life to a villain like Antony. The third proposition will be conjectural:
Antony is acting treacherously; when the *Philippics*, which he knows
enshrine his own eternal infamy and Cicero's deathless glory, have been
burned, he will then take Cicero's life and so blot out the man entirely.

[SECOND EXAMPLE OF THE SAME KIND]
Again, if you are dissuading someone from matrimony, propositions like
this may be used: (1) if you consider your duty to God, matrimony is an
impediment to those who strive towards Christ; (2) if you consider your
comfort in this life, even a happy marriage brings innumerable cares in its
train (and here a wide field opens up of comparison of the advantages of
celibacy with the disadvantages of matrimony); (3) if you consider freedom,
which many people rate higher than life itself, this above all else the bond of
matrimony takes away. Then you may turn to specific propositions, and
these can be very numerous: You should not marry this particular woman;
you should not marry at this time; you should not marry, because you are
poor, old, a student, in poor health.

The number of available propositions increases when we start from a
hypothetical situation, as Cicero does in his defence of Milo: 'Suppose that
Clodius had been killed in the ambush by Milo, Milo should nevertheless
be considered worthy of the highest honours for removing such a pernicious member of society, and for risking his own life for the well-being of
the state.' But then he returns to reality: 'But he did not kill him.'

The number increases also if, to prepare the way for our case, we set
up in advance and outside our main line of argument a proposition that is
somewhat startling, so that the one we are really trying to carry seems easy
to accept by comparison. Suppose that someone in a consultation were
trying to persuade the pope not to make war on the Venetians. Remembering the saying, 'Demand the outrageous in order to achieve the reasonable,'

* * * * *

9 matrimony] Erasmus discusses marriage in many writings (see Thompson
Colloquies 99–100), including an early *Encomium matrimonii* (c 1498; printed
1518; from 1521 on it formed part of *De conscribendis epistolis*) and a treatise,
Institutio christiani matrimonii, published in 1526. See *De conscribendis epistolis*
chaps 47–8, where arguments for and against matrimony are set out at length
(LB I 414E–26A, ASD I–2 400–32).

21 Cicero] A summary of what Cicero says in *Pro Milone* 77ff

30 not to make war on the Venetians] For this example Erasmus is drawing on his
experiences in Italy, 1506–9, where he saw for himself the belligerence and
secular ambition of Pope Julius II, whose goal was to reassert the temporal

he would first seek to undermine the proposal as follows: There are authorities of no little weight who consider that empire and earthly sway are inconsistent with the dignity of the supreme pontiff, and with the peace of the church, and with the Christian charity which he should foster, disregarding all else. This proposition may be demonstrated with a wealth of argument almost without trying, there is so much to choose from.

The speaker may then move on to his second proposition as follows: Such arguments and others like them might well be put forward by another; but even if we grant that temporal power does not involve inconsistency, yet to seek to win or regain earthly dominion by force of arms, tumult, slaughter and bloodshed is totally opposed to the mercy that should be seen in the representative of the Christ who said, 'Learn of me, for I am meek and lowly of heart.'

Then he will move on to his third proposition: Even if it were entirely right, all the same it would be unsafe, because the outcome of war is never to be relied upon; consequently, in trying to restore the status of the church through the temporal and the changeable, he is in danger of utterly overthrowing it. This too can be supported by a considerable number of examples, including those drawn from similar situations.

Then he will proceed to his third [sic] proposition: Even if it were fitting, even if it were permissible, even if you were successful, yet such a foul swill of evils follows in the train of even the justest of wars, that even a temporal prince, if he were a Christian, should not consider paying such a

* * * * *

power of the papacy and recover lands nominally under the church's jurisdiction by playing off the various temporal powers against each other and even resorting to war. In 1506 Erasmus was in Bologna, from which he fled to Florence in October, fearing a siege by approaching French forces; the siege came to nothing, and with the departure of the tyrant Bentivoglio the city agreed to acknowledge papal suzerainty; Erasmus was back in Bologna in November at the time of Julius' triumphal entry into the city.

The arguments against war in these pages of *De copia* reappear in the important essays 'Dulce bellum inexpertis' (*Adagia* IV i 1), 'Sileni Alcibiadis' (*Adagia* III iii 1), 'Scarabaeus aquilam quaerit' (*Adagia* III vii 1), and *Querela pacis* (all of 1515; printed separately 1517); and see *Institutio principis christiani* (1516). Erasmus' hatred of war is expressed in many of his writings, including *The Praise of Folly* and the *Colloquies* (for example *Charon*). His detestation of Julius II is found most memorably in his brilliant satire, *Julius exclusus*. He did not publish this, but few scholars question his authorship. The text is available in *Opuscula* 65–124; a translation in *The Julius exclusus of Erasmus* trans and ed Paul Pascal and J.K. Sowards (Bloomington, Indiana 1968). On its connection with *De copia* see E.V. Telle 'Le "De copia verborum" d'Erasme et le "Julius exclusus e coelis"' *Revue de littérature comparée* 22 (1948) 439–47.

LB I 86D

price to regain by the sword a few lands or cities, let alone that prince who
bears the title of Most Holy. One could add a proposition dependent on the
particular person involved: Though it might be fitting for another pontiff, it
is not fitting for Julius, if we mean that Julius whose mild nature and
unequalled holiness of life seem totally incompatible with war.

After our speaker has demonstrated all these propositions by argument, he will then turn to the point at issue: Even if none of the arguments
we have advanced deters you from this course, it does seem somewhat
unwise at the present time to undertake a war with the Venetians. (This
proposition also depends on the details of the actual situation.) This theme
will then be subdivided: first, such a conflict cannot be entered upon
without grave danger to the whole church; second, the Roman see, which
has always honoured and rewarded deeds done for the benefit of the
church, will seem to have forgotten the services performed time and again
by that nation with grave peril to their own lives for the Christian religion;
third, there is not even a satisfactory reason to justify taking up arms
against those who have done nothing to deserve it.

These might well be considered reasons rather than propositions, but
there is nothing to prevent the same statement being a proposition and a
reason.

To take yet another example: if someone were trying to persuade some
king not to undertake a war against the most Christian king of France, he
could construct his line of argument with propositions of this sort: first, to
engage in war is not natural to man who was born to feel good will, but to
brute beasts whom nature has supplied with weapons of a sort (a general
proposition). The next proposition will reinforce this one: it is not natural to

* * * * *

1 let alone that prince ... war] Added in *1514* (LB I 86F)
3 another pontiff] Julius Caesar, who as Pontifex Maximus was the supreme
religious head of the ancient Roman republic. Erasmus on several occasions
compares Pope Julius with Julius Caesar (for example below 625:1), a comparison not meant to be flattering; see Ep 205:42–3 (from Bologna, concerning the
pope's triumphal entry).
18 These might ... propositions] Added in *1514* (LB I 87A)
18 but ... and a reason] Added in *1534* (LB I 87A)
21 To take yet another ... with these forces] Text to 601:29 added in *1514*, with
some further minor modifications in *1526* and *1534* (LB I 87B–D)
21 some king] Among his other moves against the French subsequent to 1510,
Julius II induced the young Henry VIII of England to send expeditions against
France in 1512–13 (see below 601:20–9). This was a disappointment to Erasmus, who had formed high hopes of Henry as an enlightened Christian
prince. In *Julius exclusus* the pope boasts of fostering war against the Venetians and of inciting Henry to attack France.

LB I 86F

all beasts, but only to wild ones; and the next again supports this one: and
not even wild beasts fight among themselves in the way that mortal men do:
tiger does not war with tiger, nor lion with lion; but man does not show to
any other animal the savagery that he shows to his fellow men; wild beasts
only fight to defend their young, or when driven mad by hunger; man is   5
incited to bloody wars by vain ambition and foolish and pretentious titles.
The next proposition will be more specific, and will function as a new stage:
Granted that men do make war, it is the mark of uncivilized ones to do so,
men not all that different from wild beasts, not of those that live under the
rule of law. A fifth point could be that, even if civilized men make war, it is   10
not the mark of Christian men to do so, seeing that the Christian faith is
peace pure and simple. As a sixth we could say: Even if it were proper to
undertake the war, it would not be to your advantage because, when all is
weighed up, the evils that are endured for the sake of war are far greater in
number than the advantages that even the victor secures. (This will have to   15
be argued out.) Seven: Even if it were advantageous, it would not be safe, as
the outcome of war is always uncertain, nor do those always win whose
cause is the better, or whose equipment is superior, and quite often the
troops turn their arms against their own leader.

     All these propositions are for the most part general ones; one may next   20
proceed to the particular ones derived from the issues more specifically
related to the case in question: Leaving aside everything else, no war
should be undertaken by you, especially with such an adversary. This one
admits of many subdivisions: because you are a boy with no experience of
war, or have only recently come to the throne (and so on – I am only showing   25
how one sets about it); again, you should not fight this king who is so
powerful, or who did your father such great service, or who is bound to you
by so many ties, or who has shown such regard for you; or, not on this
pretext, not at this time, not with these forces.

                                                                            30

[ANOTHER EXAMPLE]
Similarly, someone who was intending to convince a person that he should
not study Greek literature could start off by stating that literature of any sort

               * * * * *

  33 not study Greek literature] This illustrates the ability of the trained man to
     argue on either side of a case, according to the precepts of the ancient schools
     of rhetoric. Erasmus was convinced of the humane value of Greek studies, and
     himself persevered in the acquisition of Greek in the late 1490s and early 1500s
     in spite of having no suitable teacher and no money to buy books (see Ep 138);
     but in the company of More and other English scholars his Greek studies
     flourished. In 1516 and 1518 he published a translation of books I and II of
     Theodorus Gaza's Greek grammar to encourage the study of Greek.

LB I 87B

Luciani viri q̃ difertiſſimi cõpluria opuſcula longe feſtiuiſſima ab Eraſmo Ro
terodamo & Thoma moro interpretibus optimis in latinorum linguam tra
ducta:hac fequentur ferie.

Ex Eraſmi interpretatione

Toxaris ſiue de amicicia Luciani dialogus.
Alexander qui & Pſeudomantis eiuſdem.
Gallus ſiue Somnium eiuſdem quoq; luciani
Timon ſeu Miſanthropus.
Tyrannicida ſeu pro tyrannicida eiuſdem declamatio.
Cum declamatione Eraſmica eidem reſpondente.
De iis qui mercede conducti degunt dialogus eiuſdem.
Et quædam eiuſdem alia

Ex Mori traductione.

Tyrannicida Luciani Moro interprete.
Declamatio Mori de eodem.
Cynicus Luciani a Moro verſus
Menippus ſeu Necromantia Luciani eodem interprete.
Philopſeudes ſeu incredulus Luciani ab eodé Moro in latiná linguá traductus:

Ex ædibus Aſcenſianis.

Title page of Erasmus' and More's Lucian

Paris: Bade 1506

Many of Erasmus' versions of Lucian were made during his second visit to England
in 1505–6 and were published, with More's, near the end of 1506. Lucian was a
popular author in the sixteenth century, and these translations were often reprinted.
University of Michigan Library, Department of Rare Books
and Special Collections

is no great help towards Christian happiness, and can even be an obstacle. Having demonstrated the validity of this by argument, he can then come to the point at issue: Granted that there is reason why we should study other literatures, we should certainly refrain from studying Greek literature, because it is so difficult that the life of man, fleeting, brief, and feeble as it is, is not equal to the task of learning it; and even if one had years enough, it does not bring sufficient reward to make it worth acquiring at the cost of even moderate toil; finally, those who have devoted themselves to the literature of Greece have themselves been overtaken, through some fate or other, by the misfortune suffered by that ruined and oppressed land. Or we could say that, even if other people should study it, this particular person should not. We have now moved on to specific propositions, and there will be plenty of these one can use.

With these propositions it is important, I think, to arrange them as far as possible so that one moves comfortably from one to another as down a flight of steps. Lucian does this splendidly in *Tyrannicida* (a work which we have translated into Latin): If I had only attempted such a deed of derring-do at such risk to my own life, I should deserve a reward for that; but (he goes on) I did not only attempt it – I actually beat off the bodyguard and killed the son. Shall I not receive a reward? But (moving on to the next point) I also removed the father, by providing the occasion of his death.

* * * * *

10 Or we could say ... can use] Added in 1514 (LB I 87F)
17 translated into Latin] Lucian was a favourite author with Erasmus, as with Thomas More, Rabelais, and many other Renaissance writers. Lucian's literary influence endures in Erasmus' and More's most popular writings, *The Praise of Folly* and *Utopia*. In 1505–6, when Erasmus was in England, he and More made Latin versions of thirty-two works by Lucian: twenty-eight (some very brief) were by Erasmus, four by More. These, and a declamation by each replying to Lucian's *Tyrannicida*, which each had translated, were published in Paris by Bade late in 1506. A later edition (Paris: Bade 1514) contained seven additional translations of Lucian by Erasmus. His authorship of another work (*Longaevi*) formerly attributed to Lucian is disputed. The text of Erasmus' translations, ed Christopher Robinson, is available in ASD I-1 361–627; of More's in the Yale Edition of the Complete Works of St Thomas More III 1 (1974): *Translations of Lucian* ed Craig R. Thompson.
21 the occasion of his death] *Tyrannicida* is a display speech on a fictitious subject: the speaker intended to kill the tyrant, but finding only his son killed him instead; the tyrant, discovering his son's body, committed suicide; the speaker now claims reward as a tyrannicide. On this declamation and the replies to it by Erasmus and More see *Translations of Lucian* ed Thompson xxx–xxxix, 79–127, 147–56.

LB I 87E

He does it again in *Abdicatus*, which we have also translated into Latin: It is not allowed to disinherit someone whom you have already disinherited once and received back into the family. Even if it were allowed, there is this good reason for not being allowed to do so now. Finally, even if there were very good cause for doing so now, his earlier services are so great that out of regard for them a father should overlook his faults.

If we are not happy with a whole troop of propositions, we can embrace the essentials of the case in three or four, and then, as we handle each of these, move off into other propositions if we feel like it. These main propositions are quite often advanced in the division, by which I mean the section of the speech immediately before we step off into the argument, where we set out in general terms what we are going to say, and in what order. Quite often as we handle the case, we find we can move from one proposition to another by natural steps, but if they do not cohere naturally, we shall ourselves invent suitable transitions which will connect them neatly together.

Anyone aiming at the abundant style must observe three things: he must discover those propositions which embrace in entirety everything pertaining to the case; he must properly subdivide them; and finally arrange them in the order most appropriate to the case. By this means the speech is not confused by the wealth of material, as the listener always has something definite either to concentrate on now, or to remember, or to look forward to. Besides, the speaker will not flounder in his argument while the next point is ready to hand to help him back onto his course.

As I said, Quintilian does not consider that the invention of propositions can be taught, though it is both an essential preliminary and something difficult. There are, however, things that help: primarily those which are especially effective in any sphere, that is, natural ability and imagination; next, a knowledge of the law, particularly valuable in law-court speeches, and of moral philosophy, history, and a wide range of authors, in speeches intended to urge a course of action or do someone honour; finally, experience, practice, and imitation. Similar situations will readily provide propositions based on similarities, and also on dissimilarities, though general propositions will be suggested by the overall nature of the case, specific ones by a careful scrutiny of the special circumstances involved on

* * * * *

1 *Abdicatus*] Another display speech: a disinherited son studies medicine and so is able to cure his father's madness; he is received back into the family, but on refusing to heal his stepmother is disinherited again; he claims this is unjust.

25 As I said] See 595:16.

each occasion. Finally a lively imagination will be stimulated by the precepts of the rhetoricians concerning the main types of issue, which Quintilian calls *status*, the Greeks στάσεις [categories]. The 'persuasive' type of speech has its natural topics which may act as a source of propositions – the right, the praiseworthy, the expedient, the safe, the easy, the unavoidable, the pleasant. The laudatory or vituperative type likewise has its own topics, I mean the main types of 'good thing' with all their subsidiary concepts.

Method 11

The eleventh method of enriching our style depends on the accumulation of proofs and arguments. The Greek word for these is πίστεις [reasons for belief]. Different reasons can be brought forward to confirm one and the same proposition, and the reasons themselves can be supported by further arguments.

Proofs fall into two classes: ἔντεχνοι [of the art], invented or artificial proofs, and ἄτεχνοι [not of the art], given proofs. This second type is drawn mainly from previous legal judgments, hearsay, evidence extracted under torture, written evidence, oaths, and witnesses. The former type is derived first from 'indications,' which are very like the ἄτεχνοι. (Of these 'indications,' some are 'compelling', for which the Greek term is τεκμήρια [evidence], some are 'non-compelling,' σημεῖα [signs].) Second, they are derived from 'arguments' – Quintilian at any rate makes a distinction between these and 'indications.' Arguments can be likely, possible, and not impossible. Most of these are derived from the circumstances of the case, which cover persons or things. 'Persons' takes in family, nation, country, sex, age, education, physical condition, material circumstances, state, disposition, occupation, ambition, previous actions, previous statements, motives, purpose, name; 'things' includes cause, place, time, opportunity, previous contemporary and subsequent events, means, instrument, method.

COMMONPLACES
There are also certain topics appropriate to all types of speech or even to all sections of a speech, whereas the ones I have just been discussing, though they can on occasion be handled in other contexts, are more suited to

* * * * *

2 Quintilian] 3.6.3
12 eleventh method] This section summarizes material in Quintilian 5.9 and 10. The material is so compressed as to be difficult to follow; Quintilian's more extended version with examples is much clearer.
17 ἔντεχνοι, ἄτεχνοι] Quintilian 5.1

LB I 88C

controversial issues dealt with in a court of law, and within this class, to cases which turn on a question of fact.

Generally speaking, arguments are derived from definition or defining formulae, from description, from exposition of the meaning of a word, which is a form of definition, or from things which definition by its very nature includes: genus, species, properties, differentiating characteristics, subdivision, classification (this last takes various forms, for example, a consideration of aspects such as commencement, completion, development); or from deductions based on similar or dissimilar situations; from contraries, contradictions, consequences, related propositions, causes, results, comparisons (of which there are three forms: comparison with something greater, smaller, or equivalent), and from self-evident statements; and from all the others that have been suggested, since writers agree neither on the order of presentation, nor on the number, nor on the names to be used. The subject has been dealt with at length by Aristotle and Boethius, in fair detail but not very clearly by Cicero, briefly by Quintilian. Anyone training with a view to acquiring eloquence will have to look at all the possible topics in turn, go knocking from door to door so to speak, to see if anything can be induced to emerge; but with practice the right ones will come to suggest themselves naturally, without this process being necessary.

Again, arguments can be derived from a 'supposition,' which is itself appropriate to many contexts, and finally from the circumstances peculiar to the case in question.

[ILLUSTRATIVE EXAMPLES]
A most effective means of making what we are saying convincing and of generating *copia* at the same time is to be found in illustrative examples, for which the Greek word is παραδείγματα. The content of the examples can

* * * * *

6 genus, etc] See Quintilian 6.3.66, a section on sources of jests.
12 self-evident statements] For example, those who perform a just act, act justly; Quintilian 5.10.58
13 and from all ... being necessary] Added in 1534 (LB I 88F–9A); the insertion breaks the continuity of the section on arguments.
15 Aristotle] *Topica*
15 Boethius] He translated Aristotle's *Topica* and wrote a commentary in six books on Cicero's *Topica*.
16 Cicero] In *Topica*, professedly based on Aristotle's work
16 Quintilian] 5.10, a long chapter dealing with all kinds of argument
18 knocking from door to door] Quintilian 5.10.122
29 παραδείγματα] Quintilian 5.11.1

be something like, unlike, or in contrast to what we are illustrating, or
something greater, smaller, or equivalent. Contrast and dissimilarity reside
in features such as type, means, time, place, and most of the other 'circumstances' I enumerated above. We include under 'examples' stories,
fables, proverbs, opinions, parallels or comparisons, similitudes, anal-   5
ogies, and anything else of the same sort. Most of these are introduced
not only to make our case look convincing, but also to dress it up and
brighten, expand, and enrich it. Anyone therefore who chooses to furnish
himself with a mass of material from the possibilities here listed can make
what he has to say as copious as he likes, without thereby producing a   10
meaningless accumulation of words; furthermore the variety of the material
will prevent boredom. This is not the place to discuss how to discover such
material or how to apply it, but anyone who wants this information may
find it in Aristotle, Hermogenes, and Quintilian, who have written in great
detail on these very topics. I shall deal with anything relevant to *copia*, but   15
only briefly, so as not to appear to have written a whole book rather than a
set of notes.

In the development of *copia*, then, illustrations play a leading role,
whether the speech is the sort that debates what action should be taken, or
urges to a particular course of action, or is intended to console someone in   20
grief, or is laudatory or vituperative; in short, whether one is trying to
convince one's audience, move them, or give them pleasure.

It is not enough to provide oneself with an enormous and very varied
supply of illustrations, and to have them ready for use at a moment's notice;
one must also be able to handle them with variety. Variety can be provided   25
by the very nature of the illustrative examples themselves. They can be
things done or said in the past, or be derived from the customs of various
nations. There will be differences according to whether they are drawn
from historians, or from poets (and poets include writers of comedy,
tragedy, epigrams, epic, and pastoral poetry), or from philosophers (and   30
again there are various schools of philosophers), or from the theologians, or
the books of the Bible. Some variety will be provided by the differences
between nations: the institutions and illustrative examples of the Romans
are different from those of the Greeks, and among the Greeks those of the
Spartans are not those of the Cretans and Athenians; nor again do we find   35

* * * * *

12 not the place] He deals with it later, at 635ff: Assembling illustrative material
14 Aristotle] *Rhetoric* 2.20ff
14 Hermogenes] Rhetorician of the second century AD, who wrote a series of
   textbooks on rhetorical technique much read in succeeding centuries, including four books, περὶ εὑρεσέων, on invention; see 589:31n.
14 Quintilian] See 606:16n, 29n.

the same habits among the Africans, Jews, Spaniards, French, English, or
Germans. Or it may be a question of period: early times, then the subsequent periods of antiquity, recent history, and things in our own lives; or
some inherent quality in the incident recorded: military or civil actions,
examples of clemency or bravery or wisdom (and so on ad infinitum, for   5
there is no end to this list); or the status of the person concerned: one finds
different behaviour in a prince, judge, parent, slave, rich man, poor man,
woman, girl, or boy.

One should therefore apply as many different illustrations as possible
at each point, derived not only from the whole range of Greek and Latin   10
literature, but also from the history of other nations. We can also derive
material from popular sayings. People are most impressed however by
examples that are ancient, splendid, national, and domestic. In fact each
nation, each class of person prefers what is his own, or else something that
makes him feel superior, such as anecdotes about women, children, slaves, 15
and barbarians.

But examples not only acquire variety in our handling of them; they are also
enlarged and expanded. I shall indicate some of the ways of doing this: first 20
by 'commendation,' when we introduce a section in which we praise the
incident, or the author, or the nation from which the illustration is drawn. If
one quoted something done or said by a Spartan, for example, one could
preface the anecdote by remarking that this people was always superior to
the rest in wisdom and in military and civil organization, and abounded in   25
splendid moral object-lessons. Or an example from Plutarch could be introduced by saying that this writer was of all authors particularly worthy of
respect in that he combined a thorough knowledge of philosophy with the
eloquent style of a historian, so that one would rightly expect to find in him
not only a trustworthy account of events, but also the authority and judg-   30
ment of a revered and learned philosopher. If one wished to use as an
illustration the story of how Marcus Atilius Regulus returned to the enemy,
one could begin with something like this: Among all the honourable exam-

* * * * *

23 a Spartan] For Spartan discipline see Plutarch *Apophthegmata Laconica, Instituta Laconica, Lycurgus.*
32 Regulus] Consul during the First Punic War between Rome and Carthage; he
was captured in Africa by the Carthaginians and sent to Rome to arrange an
exchange of prisoners, under strict oath to return if he were unsuccessful. He
dissuaded the Roman Senate from accepting the terms offered and returned to
the enemy, who tortured him to death; see Cicero *De officiis* 3.99.

LB I 89D

ples of Roman courage, there was never any act finer or more celebrated than that of Marcus Atilius.

One may invent little passages of commendation like this, making them long or short according to the requirements of the context; but one should take care to invent one that is appropriate; for example, if one is quoting something to illustrate faithfulness, one will commend one's source for seriousness and good faith, or if one wishes the audience to see something as an example of proper feeling, one will make proper feeling the subject of one's remarks. And so with other qualities.

SECOND METHOD OF EXPANDING [EXAMPLES]
Next illustrative anecdotes can be presented in a richer form if we expand them and broaden the treatment by incorporating amplifications and extensions. Anyone who is concerned to be brief will find it enough merely to refer to the incident as being well known, as Cicero does in the *Pro Milone* when he says: 'If it were a crime to put villains to death, we would have to view as criminals famous men like Servilius Ahala, Publius Scipio Nasica, Lucius Opimius, and the whole senate headed by myself as consul.' But the speaker whose purpose is the rich treatment will narrate the incident in a more substantial manner, as we find Cicero doing in another passage from the same speech. An officer in the army of Gaius Marius, who was a relative of the commander, made a sexual assault on one of the soldiers, and was killed by the man he was trying to force. Cicero then added one of those remarks which effectively round off a story (*epiphonema*): 'The fine young man preferred to act and incur peril rather than submit and incur disgrace.' The great Marius acquitted him of guilt and let him go free.

In passages introduced for display purposes one may spend even longer on elaborating such illustrative anecdotes, especially if the subject is such that sheer pleasure will induce the audience to pay attention. For example, if someone were trying to urge the idea that foreign travel and the enlargement of personal experience do much to make a man wiser, he could

* * * * *

15 Cicero] *Pro Milone* 8; Servilius Ahala as Master of Horse in 439 BC killed Spurius Maelius on suspicion of aspiring to tyranny; Scipio Nasica, an exconsul, led the mob of senators that killed the reformer Tiberius Gracchus in 133 BC (see 593:27ff); Lucius Opimius as consul hounded down Gaius Gracchus in 121 BC.

18 myself as consul] A reference to Cicero's execution of the Catilinarian conspirators when he was consul in 63 BC

21 same speech] *Pro Milone* 9, quoted in Quintilian 8.5.11; a speech in defence of the young man is found in Quintilian *Declamationes maiores* 3, *Miles Marianus*; see 500:26n.

dwell for a time on the praise of Solon, and then launch into an extended account of the city that Solon left, his reasons for going, the seas he crossed, the foreign peoples he visited, the dangers he encountered among them, the persons he met, the wonders he saw, how long he was away, and how much more famous and more wise he was when he returned to his native land.

Of the same sort are Jerome's anecdotes about the wanderings of Pythagoras and Apollonius in the preface to his complete edition of the Holy Scriptures. But the most convenient example of the whole procedure is to be found right at the beginning of the second book of Cicero's *De inventione*, where he tells the story about Zeuxis, who, when he was going to paint a picture of Helen, asked for a number of girls of outstanding beauty so that he could take the best feature from each and so produce a flawless portrait of beauty.

FICTIONAL EXAMPLES

The same applies to fictional examples, for these too can be treated extensively or concisely as the subject-matter and context demand. When we use an anecdote which cannot possibly be believed, it will be best, unless we are being humorous, to preface it by saying that those wise old men of long ago did not invent stories like this for no good reason, nor was it for nothing that they have been current by general consent for so many centuries. Then we can interpret the meaning. For example, if a speaker is saying that one should not pursue that for which one is not naturally suited, he can point out that those wise old writers were well aware of this truth, and demonstrated it by inventing the very apt tale of the Giants whose rash attempts came to no good end. Or if he is depicting a miser, he can first say that the miser is deprived of what he actually possesses as well as of what he does not possess, and then go on to the story of Tantalus. Or if he is arguing that the function of the wise man is to control his emotions by reason and judgment, he can bring in Homer's story in book 1 of the *Iliad* where Achilles is already laying his hand on the hilt of his sword and Pallas Athene calls him back from behind. Again, if one is putting forward the idea that a genuine reputation for courage can only be won by the man who

* * * * *

1 Solon] See Plutarch *Solon*.
8 preface] Ep 53.1, Ad Paulinum
10 Cicero's] *De inventione* 2.1–3
26 Giants] See 390:7n.
29 Tantalus] See 389:7n.
31 *Iliad*] 1.188ff

has been tossed by misfortune and tested by all sorts of danger, after the
sort of introduction I have indicated, he can bring in Ulysses as Homer
depicts him.

Although the principle of the allegory or hidden meaning is not
equally obvious in every case, experts in antiquity are agreed that under all
the inventions of the ancient poets there does lie a hidden meaning,
whether historical, as in the story of Hercules fighting the twin-horned
Achelous; or theological, as in that of Proteus turning into all kinds of
shapes or of Pallas springing from the head of Jove; or physical, as in the
story of Phaëthon; or moral, as in the case of the men whom Circe turned
into brute beasts with her cup and wand. Quite often there is a mixture of
more than one type of allegory. In some instances it is not particularly
difficult to grasp the sense of the allegory: it is quite obvious (I prefer to take
examples of moral allegories) that the tale of Icarus falling into the sea warns
that no one should rise higher than his lot in life allows, and the story of
Phaëthon that no one should undertake to perform a task that is beyond his
powers. Salmoneus cast headlong into hell teaches us not to emulate what
lies far beyond our fortunes, and Marsyas flayed alive teaches us not to try
conclusions with those more powerful than ourselves. The story of Danaë
tricked with gold can only mean (and this is how Horace interprets it too)
that there is nothing so walled in that money cannot storm the defences,
nothing of such integrity that it cannot be corrupted by bribery; the labours
of Hercules tell us that immortal renown is won by effort and by helping
others; the wish of Midas that the greedy and insatiable are suffocated by

* * * * *

6 ancient poets] In *Enchiridion* (LB V 7F) Erasmus says that all of Homer's and
  Virgil's poetry may be read allegorically.
7 Hercules] Ovid *Metamorphoses* 9.1–97
8 Proteus] Virgil *Georgics* 4.405–10, 440–2
9 Pallas] Ovid *Fasti* 3.841–2
10 Phaëthon] Ovid *Metamorphoses* 2.1ff
10 Circe] Homer *Odyssey* 10.233ff; see *Adagia* III iii 1.
14 Icarus] Ovid *Metamorphoses* 8.183ff; see 390:7n.
17 Salmoneus] Who made himself equal with Zeus (Virgil *Aeneid* 6.585–6)
18 Marsyas] Ovid *Metamorphoses* 6.382ff; Marsyas presumed to challenge Apollo
  to a musical context which the god won.
19 Danaë] Horace *Odes* 3.16
23 Hercules] For his exploits see Ovid *Metamorphoses* passim; for the allegorical
  interpretation *Adagia* III i 1.
24 wish of Midas] When offered a wish by Apollo, he chose that all he touched
  might turn to gold; even his food turned to gold in his mouth and choked him.

their own wealth, the judgment he gave that intellectual power is incompatible with the desire for money; Bacchus set on fire by the thunderbolt and plunged into the waters of the nymphs that the fire of wine must be quenched by the sober element (an interpretation which we find in one of the Greek epigrams). The story of Circe turning men into beasts by her spells can only indicate that those who will not be guided by reason, which is man's prerogative, but abandon themselves to base desires no longer have any human characteristic except the name of man, and have sunk to the nature of beasts, lust turning them into bears, somnolence and sloth into pigs, savagery into lions, and so on. Ulysses, who was the only one not changed after drinking the cup and being touched with the magic wand, demonstrates that firm and constant purpose characteristic of the wise man, which cannot be weakened by fear or deflected from what is honourable by any blandishments of the emotions. The lotus, which prevented his companions from leaving after they had once tasted it, teaches that the sweet, insidious poison of base pleasures, from which it is not all that difficult to abstain, is very difficult to give up once one has tasted it. The songs of the Sirens teach that flattery is the most seductive thing there is, and the most pernicious. Scylla and Charybdis, separated by such a narrow space, teach that the path of virtue is a narrow one, with related vices threatening on either side, for example, the path of frugality between extravagance and meanness; and one must steer one's course in life between them in such a way that, since it is extremely difficult to pursue an exactly middle course in all things, one inclines to the side where there is less danger, as Ulysses did. And the moly, with its black root and milk-white flower, 'a plant very difficult for mortals to find,' can only indicate wisdom, towards which the first steps are difficult and full of effort, but the fruits are very sweet. Similarly the golden bough in Virgil typifies wisdom set apart in a hidden place and found by only a few.

But not to go on at too great length, any number of interpretations of

* * * * *

1 the judgment he gave] He was freed from the curse of the golden touch, but continued to choose the worse rather than the better; he judged Pan's playing superior to Apollo's, and to punish him for his crassness his ears were changed into those of an ass; see Ovid *Metamorphoses* 11.85–179; *Adagia* I iii 67.

5 Greek epigrams] *Anthologia palatina* 9.331; cf *Adagia* II ii 96.

5 Circe] See 611:10n.

14 lotus] Homer *Odyssey* 9.94–9

18 Sirens] *Odyssey* 12.165ff

19 Scylla and Charybdis] *Odyssey* 12.73ff

25 moly] *Odyssey* 10.302–6

28 golden bough] Virgil *Aeneid* 6.136ff

this sort can be found in Eustathius, the commentator on Homer. I myself, in my young days, wrote quite a lot on this subject in the books I called *The Antibarbarians*.

Somewhat easier are the things invented by the poets for this very purpose, like their inventions about the gods which imitate human life, such as Homer's tale about Mars caught in the net by Vulcan, or where he makes Jupiter ἀγκυλομήτης [crooked in counsel] send out a dream which makes the Greeks think that they will capture Troy, though what he was purposing was very different: it is the policy of kings deliberately to spread certain rumours among the people when they have decided on something very different in their own minds.

Even easier are stories which are so handled by the poets that we think of them as true stories rather than invented ones, like the story of Orestes who murdered his mother, and the friendship between him and Pylades. Some people think that these stories really do record an actual event, like Alcestis saving her husband's life by sacrificing her own, which Valerius Maximus mentions as well as the poets. Likewise the deaths of Codrus and Menoeceus can be classed together with the deeds of Q. Curtius and the two Decii, and among pairs of friends we count Theseus and Peirithous, and Castor and Pollux. There is also the story of Arion carried to his homeland on the dolphin's back, which St Augustine considers to be true.

Certainly there is no doubt that a good many incidents in Virgil and particularly in Lucan are real historical events – though much that Herodotus puts into his history is quite unbelievable, and Xenophon wrote

* * * * *

1 Eustathius] Twelfth-century scholar and ecclesiastic who wrote, among other things, a vast commentary on the Homeric poems
3 *Antibarbarians*] Translated in CWE 23
6 Homer's] *Odyssey* 8.266ff
7 Jupiter] *Iliad* 2.1ff
13 Orestes] A theme treated by all three Greek tragedians, Aeschylus, Sophocles, and Euripides
16 Alcestis] See the play by Euripides of that name.
16 Valerius Maximus] He wrote a whole series of *exempla (factorum dictorumque memorabilium liber)* dedicated to the emperor Tiberius. Codrus, Curtius, and the two Publii Decii occur in 5.6 on patriotism ('De pietate erga patriam'), Alcestis in 4.6 on married love ('De amore coniugali').
18 Curtius] The text says Q. Curtius but probably Marcus Curtius is intended; see Livy 7.5.6.
21 Augustine] *De civitate Dei* 1.14
24 Herodotus] Erasmus had no high opinion of the integrity of ancient historians. Herodotus and Xenophon are quoted as untruthful in his life of Jerome (*Opuscula* 135:40ff).

his *Cyropaedia* more as a manifesto on the training of the young than as a genuine historical record. If the audience take these as true, they will be effective because people believe them; if they take them as inventions, since they are the productions of wise and revered authors, they will be effective for the very reason that they were put out by men whose authority gave what they wrote the force of precept.

On the other hand, poetry provides a lot of material which is to be taken as genuine historical fact, dealing for example with Scipio, Hannibal, Augustus, Pompey, or Julius Caesar; again poetry also offers passages which no one would deny are fictional, but since it is generally accepted that they were invented precisely for the purpose of functioning as examples, and what is more were invented by great writers, they have all the weight of examples; I mean things like the goddess Envy, Rumour, Discord, and Prayers which I mentioned earlier, and also characters in dramatic or mixed poetry, especially comedy, with which dialogues have much in common.

For example, if anyone were speaking to the theme that parents should take care, if they do anything wrong, not to do it so that their children know, an effective illustrative example would be provided by the son Clitipho in the play about the old man tormenting himself with remorse, when the son says:

> Blow me, when he's had a drop too much to drink
> What tales he tells me of the things he used to do!
> And now he says 'From another's fate take note and learn
> What will be of use' – the cunning rogue!
> Little does he know my ears are deaf
> To all his prosing.

Or if one were trying to convince an audience that, as the wise man replied to a questioner, a man should take a wife of the same social class as himself (since otherwise, that is if you, being poor, join to yourself a rich woman, you get not a wife but a ruler), an illustration could be provided by Chremes in the *Phormio* who fears his wife Nausistrata as if she were his owner. Again if one were saying that a friendship between a poor man and a rich one is neither secure nor reliable, one could use as an illustration Euclio in

* * * * *

14 earlier] See 582:7–8.
20 play] Terence *Heautontimorumenos* 220–2
30 wise man] Pittacus, one of the Seven Sages of Greece; in Diogenes Laertius
   1.79–80; *Adagia* I viii 1

LB I 92A

Plautus' *Aulularia*, who is trying to avoid acquiring a connection with the
rich Megadorus and says: 'It occurs to me ...' (I quote no more – the passage
is very well known); or if you were enlarging on the sentiment that it is
unjust of fathers to be furious with their sons when they do wrong, when
they themselves do worse things in their old age, you could quote the same
Nausistrata I mentioned above when she says:

> Does it seem such a shocking thing to you
> That your son, who begins to feel himself a man,
> Should have one mistress while you have two wives?
> Are you not ashamed? Have you the face
> To censure him for this? Just tell me that.

But it is foolish to give one or two examples when the whole of comedy
is nothing but a picture of human life. I could have produced similar
specimens from tragedy, pastoral poetry, and dialogues, but for a work on
this scale I think I have sufficiently indicated to students of lively intelligence the way they should proceed.

In my opinion examples may be properly derived not only from the
sources I have discussed but also from dumb beasts and even inanimate
objects, though these possibly belong rather with ὁμοίωσις [simile or
parallel case]. I mean things like holding up the industry of the ant as an
encouragement to people to work hard to get what they want, or describing
the social organization of the bees in order to promote respect for law and
civil discipline. To discourage lack of respect for parents, one could cite the
young of the stork who are said to feed and carry the old birds about in their
turn when age has made them weak; or when exhorting an audience to
show proper care for their children, one could bring in the she-ass which
will go through a raging fire to rescue its foal; or if one wanted to hold up
ingratitude to obloquy, one could use the story of the lion which Gellius
quotes from Apion, or of the snake which, according to Pliny, saved its
rescuer when he was beset by robbers; or to censure a man entirely without
affection, neither loving anyone nor being the object of anyone's love, one

* * * * *

1 *Aulularia*] 226ff; see 369:21–5.
6 Nausistrata] Terence *Phormio* 1040–2
15 picture of human life] See 591:9.
19 examples] Quintilian 5.11.22
26 stork] Aristotle *Historia animalium* 9.13; Aristophanes *Birds* 1353–7
30 lion] See Aulus Gellius 5.14, the story of Androclus and the lion.
31 Pliny] *Naturalis historia* 8.61

LB I 92C

could introduce the dolphin that loved a boy, or the eagle seized by a
burning passion for a girl, or the magnet that draws metal to itself. I shall
probably say more about such topics when I get to the section on fables.
Meanwhile, to return to my subject.

THIRD METHOD OF EXPANDING EXAMPLES
Illustrative examples of both kinds, that is both invented and real ones, can
be expanded by yet other procedures: first, by the 'parable,' also known as
ὁμοίωσις [simile], which Cicero translates by *collatio*; second, by introducing a comparison or antithesis. In the 'parable' an appropriate simile
reveals the fresh image as like, unlike, or in contrast to the original; first, an
example of the like: Just as Camillus by his bravery repelled the barbarian
foe and rescued Rome when it was hard pressed by the Gauls and brought
to the edge of disaster, so Lorenzo Valla summoned from the grave and
restored to their former splendour Latin letters, corrupted, crushed, and
extinguished by barbarian ignorance; second, the unlike: We should not
feel the same way towards Lorenzo and Camillus, because Camillus was
moved by patriotism to risk his own life in saving his country from the
barbarians, but Lorenzo was led by the desire for fame, or rather by a
passion for attacking as many people as possible, not to restore the oppressed Latin language, but to reduce it to rigid rules, when it could be
learnt more satisfactorily from the reading of eloquent authors; third, a
contrasting example: Marcellus restored their works of art to the Syracusans
though they were our enemies; Verres took them away from them when
they were our allies. ('Restore' is the opposite of 'take away,' 'enemy' the

* * * * *

1 dolphin] Pliny *Naturalis historia* 9.25
1 eagle] Pliny *Naturalis historia* 10.18
2 magnet] *Adagia* I vii 56; a number of the examples quoted in the above
  paragraph are assembled in *Adagia* III vii i: 'Scarabaeus aquilam quaerit,'
  including two more grateful-snake stories.
3 fables] See 631.
9 *collatio*] See 337:17n.
12 Camillus] A successful Roman general who was recalled from exile to save
  Rome after it had been captured by the Gauls in 390 BC
14 Valla] See 399:25n.
23 Marcellus ... son's bravery] To 618:2: these two examples are given in reverse
  order in all editions previous to 1534 (LB I 193A).
23 Marcellus] Marcus Marcellus, the conqueror of Syracuse in 212 BC
24 Verres] See 331:16n; the two are contrasted at length in Cicero *Verrines* 4.115ff.

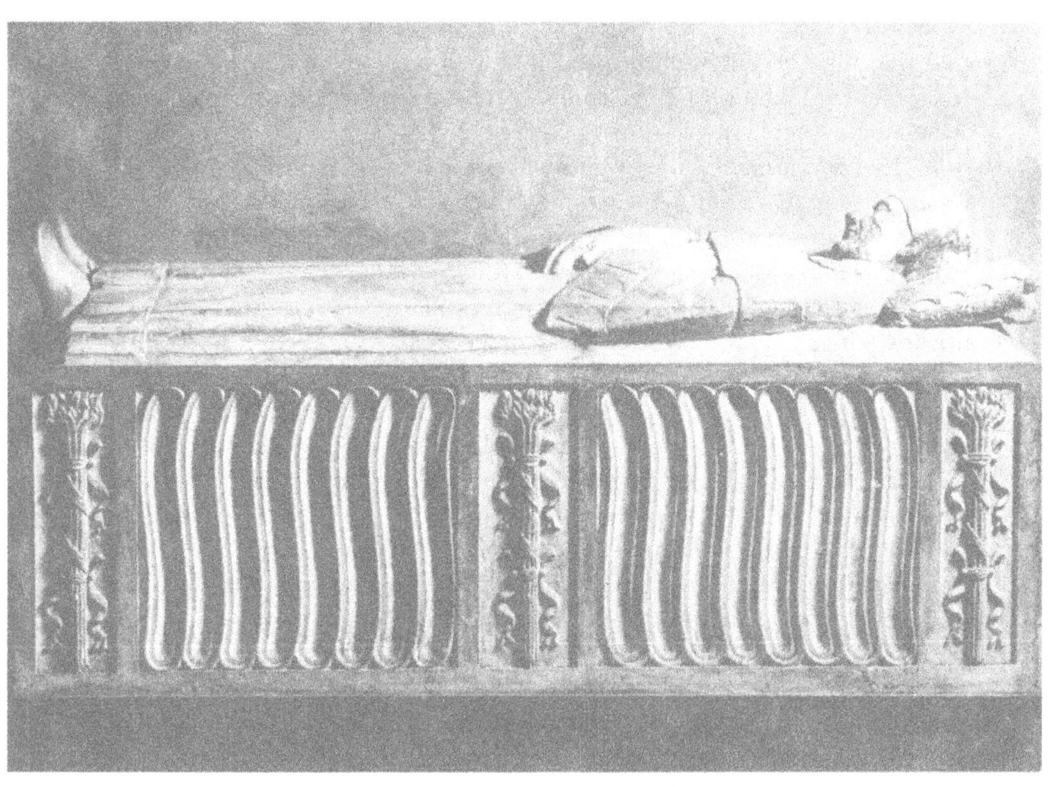

Tomb of Lorenzo Valla
Church of St John Lateran, Rome
To Erasmus, Valla (1406–57) was the greatest of 'modern' restorers
of correct and elegant Latinity. Erasmus was particularly appreciative of Valla's
Elegantiarum linguae latinae libri vi (printed 1471) and wrote (c 1489)
an 'epitome' of it which was published in 1529, issued in revised form in 1531,
and often reprinted. In 1505 he had published an edition of Valla's notes
on the Vulgate New Testament, a work which evidently had considerable
influence on his own decision to investigate the text of the New Testament.
Alinari/Scala

opposite of 'ally.') Here is another example: Brutus slew his sons when they were plotting treason; Manlius punished with death his son's bravery; and one from Virgil: 'But the great Achilles, / Whose son thou falsely proclaim'st thyself to be / Acted not thus towards the foe.'

The comparison shows the fresh example as something smaller or greater or equal; smaller: If cities have been overthrown for the sake of broken marriages, what is the appropriate treatment of the adulterer? or another example: 'Our ancestors often fought wars because their traders and merchant-men had been insultingly treated; what should be your attitude when so many thousand Roman citizens have been murdered by one edict at the one time? Your fathers were prepared to extinguish the light of Greece, the city of Corinth, because their ambassadors had been insolently addressed; will you leave that king untouched who bound and flogged the consular legate of the Roman people, and most cruelly tortured him to death?'

Cicero is again the source for our example of something equal: 'It so happened that I stood for election along with two men of noble family, one a scoundrel, the other a decent, good man; yet I surpassed Catiline in standing, Galba in popularity.' Something greater is exemplified in the *Pro Milone*: 'They deny that it can be the will of heaven that that man should look upon the light of day who confesses that he has slain a fellow-man. Now in what city are fools putting forward an argument like this? Why, in that very city where the first trial ever on a capital charge was the trial of Marcus Horatius, who, although the city itself was not as yet free, was freed from the charge in the assembly of the Roman people, and that though he admitted killing his sister with his own hand.'

To sum up, in the illustrative example properly so called, which is a reference to a genuine or apparently genuine occurrence designed to induce people to accept what we are saying, we can either indicate our chosen incident in a few words, as in that example from St Jerome: 'Remember

* * * * *

1 Brutus] Not Caesar's murderer, but his ancestor, considered as the founder of Roman liberty in the fifth century BC for his part in the expulsion of the kings; he slew his sons for attempting to restore them.

2 Manlius] Manlius Torquatus, as consul in 340 BC, executed his son for disobeying orders and engaging (victoriously) in single combat; see Livy 8.7ff.

3 Virgil] *Aeneid* 2.540–1

8 another example] Cicero *Pro lege Manilia* 11

16 Cicero] *Pro Murena* 8.17

19 *Pro Milone*] 7

Dares and Entellus'; or we can employ a broader treatment and bring it in as an analogous example involving something similar, dissimilar, in contrast, greater, less, or equal. The point of departure may be any special circumstance attaching to things or persons. The example can be further improved by the artifices of language, when we deliberately tone down or exaggerate different points by the use of suitable vocabulary or figures of speech.

Anyone who wishes to give his example the fullest treatment possible will set out all the separate points of similarity and dissimilarity and will compare one with another. This is what Cicero does in the example I quoted above about the murdered legate. He deliberately sets one feature beside another: 'They did not put up with any diminution in the liberty of Roman citizens; are you going to ignore their loss of life? They avenged a verbal affront to the rights of ambassadors; will you leave unavenged an ambassador tortured to death? Their splendid achievement was to bequeath to you a great glory of empire; take care that it is not your disgrace to be unable to guard and preserve what you have received.'

This kind of thing can be treated very extensively if the speaker compares as many of the attendant circumstances as possible. One could, for example, if urging someone to bear the death of a son with controlled grief, confront him with the woman in pagan tradition who bravely bore the death of several sons. After telling the story, the speaker will proceed to compare the two: Can you, a grown man, not bear what a feeble woman could? She overcame both her sex and her feelings as a parent; will you be defeated by one of these alone? She bore with uncrushed spirit the loss of several sons; do you mourn inconsolably the extinction of one? Furthermore, all her sons perished together in a shipwreck, an inglorious end; yours fell fighting bravely on the field of battle. She had no one to whom she could with honour impute the loss of her sons; you sacrificed yours for your country. They perished wholly and utterly; your son will live for ever in his immortal fame. She gave thanks to nature that once she had been the mother of so many sons; you recall only that you have lost an excellent son. She had no hope of repairing her loss, being of an age past child-bearing; you have a fertile wife, and are still healthy and virile yourself. Can you, a Roman and a man, not evince the qualities that a weak barbarian woman

* * * * *

1 Dares and Entellus] Combatants in a boxing match in which the old but experienced man defeats the young and cocksure; Virgil *Aeneid* 5.387ff; Jerome Ep 102.2; *Adagia* III i 69. On Erasmus' edition of the letters of Jerome (1516) see Ep 396 introduction.
10 quoted above] At 618:8ff

could? She was ignorant of learning and yet she could scorn something that shatters you in spite of your education and your great profession of philosophy. Finally, will a Christian man not manifest the firmness of spirit shown by a pagan woman? She believed that nothing survives the pyre, and still held grief unseemly; you have been taught that those who depart this life with glory have at last truly begun to live, and yet you cry endlessly that your son is lost for ever. Can you not give back to God when he asks it what she calmly resigned to nature? She bravely submitted to necessity; do you rebel against God?

This specimen makes it clear enough what methods one should use in comparing one's examples; but in genuine lawsuits, since there is a greater supply of circumstantial detail, it is even easier to discover different sorts of antitheses.

One should mention, by the way, that in antitheses of this sort sententious sayings and clinching summaries can be very appropriately worked in. To take the same example again, after the first contrast – 'Can you, a grown man, not bear what a feeble woman could?' – one could introduce striking sayings such as 'Nature made a distinction in sex; do you make no distinction in mind?'; 'A woman is not expected by anyone to win praise for courage, but if a man is not courageous he is not even classed as a man'; 'The name man indicates both the stronger sex and strength of mind; it is shameful to sport a beard and be surpassed by a woman in firmness of heart.' After the antithesis 'She had no one to whom she could with honour impute the loss of her sons; you sacrificed yours for your country,' one could invent sayings like this: 'It is a great comfort in sorrow to have something or someone to whom one can with honour attribute what has happened'; 'One cannot sacrifice one's son for anyone more reasonably or more gloriously than for one's country.' After the antithesis, 'They perished wholly and utterly; your son will live for ever in his immortal fame,' one could go on 'It is far better to live by fair fame than by the common breath of man. The life of the body is ill-starred, and (even without accidents) brief, and held in common with the beasts; that other life is glorious and everlasting, and carries a man into the company of heaven.'

Such striking sayings or maxims could be appended to each section of the compared passages, but these indications will be enough for the time being, as I shall be discussing maxims in the proper place.

* * * * *

36 proper place] At 627

PARALLELS

The more pedantic may wish to distinguish the illustrative example from
the parallel, taking the example as something definitely done by someone,
the parallel as an analogous situation to be found in events in general, or
natural or chance accompaniments of events. Atilius' return to the enemy
would be an *example* of adhering to principle and keeping faith; but a ship
raising or lowering sail to suit the force of the wind, and tacking from one
side to the other, would be a *parallel*, showing that the sensible man should
yield to circumstances and accommodate himself to his situation. Even so,
the methods of expanding the parallel are exactly the same as those I have
illustrated for the example. Sometimes a single phrase is enough: Do you
not realize you must turn your sail into the wind? or: Stop washing a brick
white. In this form it will be an allegory or metaphor. Sometimes it is
expanded and the application made more specific. We have an example of
such an expansion in Cicero's *Pro Murena*: 'Those just sailing into harbour
after a long sea-voyage eagerly give information to those setting out about
the likelihood of storms and the pirate situation and what the different
places are like, because it is natural to feel kindly towards those who are
about to face the dangers which we have just escaped. What then should be
my feelings, who am just coming into sight of land after a terrible tossing,
towards this man who, as I can see, must go out to face dreadful storms?'

Here is another example from the same speech: 'It is commonly said
that among Greek musicians those take up the flute who cannot play the
lyre; in the same way we observe that quite a number of people who have
not managed to become orators have fallen back on the study of the
technicalities of the legal system.'

St Jerome imitated the first of these parallels used by Cicero in one of
his letters to Heliodorus: 'In giving you this advice I am not like a man
whose ship and cargo are unharmed, an inexperienced sailor who knows
nothing about currents. I am more like a man just cast up on the shore from a
shipwreck, in a frightened voice warning those about to set sail. In that
tide-race the Charybdis of self-indulgence engulfs a man's health of soul;
on the other side lust smiling like Scylla with fair face entices the ship of
modesty onto the rocks. Here is the shore beset with barbarian foes; here is

*   *   *   *   *

    5 Atilius'] Regulus; see 608:32n.
   12 washing a brick] Terence *Phormio* 186
   15 Cicero's] *Pro Murena* 4
   22 same speech] *Pro Murena* 29
   27 Jerome] Ep 14.6

that pirate, the devil, with all his crew, ready with chains for those he hopes
to seize. Do not trust it, do not feel at ease. The sea may smile, smooth as a
mill-pond, the surface of the motionless element may hardly be ruffled by a
breath of wind, yet this flat plain contains great mountains. Under the
surface is danger; under the surface is the enemy. Ready the ropes, take in
the sails. Let the yard-arm be the sign of the Cross before you. That calm is a
storm.'

This could be greatly extended if the speaker took all the separate
dangers which threaten virtue because of sin or wicked men or any other
cause and collated them with the various things that endanger the lives of
sailors, and then brought in comparisons using situations that were greater, or less, or different, or contrasting, and finally ornamented the passage
where appropriate with neat sayings and striking remarks in conclusion.

This is done in the following example: The more precious an object is,
the more carefully it is guarded, the more cautiously it is spent. So one
should take the greatest care of time which is the most precious thing there
is, and make sure that none of it slips by without profit. If guardians are
appointed for those who thoughtlessly squander jewels and gold, what
madness will it be to throw away time, the fairest gift of immortal God, on
disgraceful idleness and dishonourable pursuits? When you waste time,
you are wasting your life, and what can be more valuable than life? If one
small jewel goes, you call that a loss; but when the whole day has gone, that
is, a good portion of your life, do you not call that a loss? especially when
lost things like jewels can be replaced by some means or another, but the
loss of time is irreparable. Losses that you suffer are usually other people's
gain, but the waste of time is no profit to anyone. There is no loss from
which someone does not gain some advantage except the loss of time.
Further, the loss of material possessions is often to our spiritual good, for
riches usually furnish the material for sin, so that it is often better to have
thrown them away than to have preserved them carefully. The better the
use to which a thing can be put, the more shameful is its waste. But there is
nothing finer, nothing more splendid than the good application of good
time. However carefully you preserve material possessions, you often have
them snatched from you by chance or by man, so that the loss makes you
wretched, but nothing more; it does not shame you as well. But the waste of
time, which happens through no fault but our own, not only brings misery
in its train, but discredit in addition. The worst kind of ill fame is that for
which no one can be blamed but the sufferer. With material possessions

* * * * *

13 striking remarks in conclusion] See 629:6ff.
14 more precious] See Seneca *Epistles* 1.

LB I 94E

you could have bought estates and houses, you could not have bought a worthwhile mind; with time you could have acquired other graces of the spirit, and immortality as well. There is no portion of life so brief that it could not have been used to make a great stride towards happiness. Finally, possibly you would have had to account to your father for your bad use of wealth; for your badly spent hours you must account to God.

This is only an indication of how one can expand a parallel example by comparing and elaborating the separate details, but I feel this is sufficient.

One could deal in the same way with parallels based on dissimilarity: A new ship is better than an old one, but it is not so with friendship: A woman who makes free with her wealth deserves praise, but not one who makes free with her beauty; In a relay race the man who takes the torch is better than the one who hands it over, but in a war the general who hands over an army is better than the one who receives it from him.

My earlier remarks have shown how every imaginable thing can be used as a source for the derivation of such analogous cases.

LIKENESSES

The εἰκών, in Latin *imago* 'likeness,' is very like the parallel or simile. In fact, if it is expanded, it becomes a simile. For example, the following is a simile: As an ass will not be driven by blows from the pasture until it has had its fill, even so a warrior will not cease from slaughter until he has sated his soul. If however you were to say that someone leapt on the foe like a snake or a lion, that would be an εἰκών. To say that Achilles advanced to battle glowing like fire or the sun in his armour is a likeness rather than a simile. Homer uses both figures very frequently and with great effect.

In a speech the εἰκών is more useful in the cause of vividness or impressiveness or stylistic attractiveness than for proving any point. Examples and parallels also serve these ends, but they often help considerably in generating an attitude of consent in our hearers, especially when they are combined with induction, for which the Greek is ἐπαγωγή. Plato's Socrates makes great use of this.

Here is an illustration of induction combined with example: Tell me,

* * * * *

10 A new ship ... A woman] Examples taken from Quintilian 5.11.26
12 In a relay race] Example taken from *Ad Herennium* 4.46.59, where the explanation is given: because the exhausted runner hands over to a fresh one, whereas the experienced general hands over to an untried one
19 In fact ... effect] Added in 1534 (LB I 95C)
20 simile] See Erasmus' *Parabolae sive similia* in CWE 23.
24 Achilles] Homer *Iliad* 19.375ff

LB I 95B

what good did Demosthenes ever get out of his remarkable eloquence?
Apart from other misfortunes, an unhappy and pitiable end. What reward
did eloquence bring to Tiberius and Gaius Gracchus? A violent death, and
that a wretched and shameful one. What to the highly praised Antonius? He
too was mercilessly stabbed to death by thugs. Take Cicero, the father of all   5
eloquence, what reward did he get? Death, and a bitter and pitiable one at
that. Very well, then, burn the midnight oil and strive to achieve the
highest glories of eloquence, when it has always brought destruction on
anyone who excelled in it.

Here is induction combined with a parallel: Do you not expect a sailor   10
to talk more knowledgeably about sailing than a doctor? and a doctor more
authoritatively about medicine than a painter? and a painter better about
the techniques of colour and light and shade and perspective than a cobbler? Will not a charioteer be better at discussing the art of driving a chariot
than a sailor? (A number of comparisons like this will make everyone   15
prepared to accept the idea that each person will speak best about the thing
he knows best. Then one brings in one's parallel case.) But what will the
orator discuss best, when he professes to be able to talk on any topic?

There is a very well-known anecdote about Aspasia, illustrating induction from parallel cases, taken from Aeschines.   20

COMPARISONS IN EPIDEICTIC ORATORY
There is also a general type of comparison, used especially in panegyric or
vituperative speeches, when we confront one person with another for

* * * * *

1 Demosthenes] The most famous of Greek orators; he eventually took poison to
  avoid capture by his enemies.

3 Tiberius and Gaius Gracchus] Two brothers, democratic reformers of the
  popular party, both murdered in the political upheavals of the second century
  BC; see 609:15n.

4 Antonius] Grandfather of the famous Mark Antony; he was killed in the civil
  wars in the time of Marius, and his head was hung in the Forum.

5 Cicero] Eventually killed by Antony's thugs in 43 BC; his head was hung in the
  Forum with a needle through the tongue, in revenge for the *Philippic Orations*
  in which Antony had been mercilessly attacked. See Juvenal 10.114ff, Cicero
  and Demosthenes destroyed by their eloquence.

20 Aeschines] Not the orator but a pupil of Socrates, whose writings include
  Socratic dialogues; passage translated by Cicero in *De inventione* 1.51–2:
  Aspasia gets Xenophon's wife incautiously to agree that she would prefer her
  neighbour's gold ornaments if they were better than her own, likewise her
  dress and other adornments; would she then prefer the other woman's husband? Xenophon likewise is led from neighbour's horse and estate to
  neighbour's wife. See further Quintilian 5.11.27–9.

purposes of praise or blame. If one wished to praise Pope Julius, one could set him beside Julius Caesar and compare the benefits conferred by the two men; if one wished to attack him, one could compare their crimes. Likewise, one could praise Maximilian by comparing him with the Emperor Marcus Aurelius Antoninus.

Things can also be compared. A writer praising history could compare its uses with the benefits of those who have advanced the state by deeds of war; or if he wished to praise poetry, he could compare and balance its advantages with those of philosophy.

One thing can be compared with many: anyone wishing to glorify history could compare it with all the other most highly valued disciplines. There are two ways of using this sort of comparison. For you may tone down the virtues on one side and build up those on the other; or you may praise the other side extravagantly while showing the thing you are really praising to be better or certainly not inferior. In attacking, you magnify the faults, while showing the person you are assailing to be more villainous, or at least equally villainous.

In doing this you must take care that the examples used for comparison are well known and beyond question. A good ruler should be compared with Trajan or Marcus Aurelius the philosopher-emperor, a bad one with Nero or Caligula. A vicious critic should be compared with Zoilus or Hyperbolus, a tale-bearer with a viper or Regulus, an effeminate voluptuary with Sardanapalus.

You will increase the material available for your comparison if, as I just suggested, you bring in several persons or things when praising or attack-

* * * * *

1 Pope Julius] See 600:3n.
4 Maximilian] A reference to the reigning German emperor, Maximilian I
5 Marcus Aurelius] The Roman philosopher-emperor, 161–80 AD, author of the famous *Meditations*
7 deeds of war] See Sallust *Catilina* 3.
18 In doing this ... sudden death] Text to 626:12 added in *1534* (LB I 96B–C)
20 Trajan] Second of the five so-called 'Good Emperors,' 98–117 AD; Marcus Aurelius (see line 5n) was the fifth.
21 Nero, Caligula] The two maddest and most vicious of the Julio-Claudian line of Roman Emperors
21 Zoilus] Famous for the asperity of his criticisms of Homer; *Adagia* II ii 55
22 Hyperbolus] Athenian demagogue of the fifth century BC, who violently attacked rival political figures; see Plutarch *Alcibiades* 196.
22 viper] See 393:10n.
22 Regulus] Not the hero, Marcus Atilius Regulus, but a notorious informer contemporary with the Younger Pliny, who describes him in his *Letters*
23 Sardanapalus] See 391:3n.

ing just one person or thing. In praising a ruler, for instance, one could
extract the best feature from each of a number of people: success and
presence of mind from Julius Caesar, generosity of spirit from Alexander,
affability from Augustus, courtesy from the elder Titus, purity of life and
clemency from Trajan, contempt for glory from Marcus Aurelius, and so on.   5
The same principle is to be used in making an attack.

If you were expressing abhorrence for anger, you could compare it
with uncontrollable drunkenness, delirium, epilepsy, demonic possession;
or if vituperating a poisonous tongue, you could liken it to the noxious
breath of a man suffering from the plague, to the exhalations of snakes   10
which breathe the deadliest poison, and the miasma from certain lakes and
caves which causes sudden death.

JUDGMENTS

As I said, with examples we can include judgments, which the Greeks call   15
κρίσεις. These are *sententiae* or striking sayings of famous writers, of nations, of wise men, of distinguished citizens. A great supply can be discovered in the celebrated poets of old, also in the historiographers, the
philosophers, and mystic writings. Judgments accordingly show the same
variety as examples. Collections of such things have been made by some of   20
the Greeks, notably by one Stobaeus. There are also apophthegms of wise
men, like 'The sayings of famous men,' and the things recorded by

* * * * *

1 praising a ruler] As in Allen Ep 964, where Erasmus writes to Henry VIII of
England
3 Alexander] The Great; see Plutarch *Life*.
4 Augustus] See Suetonius *Life*.
4 elder Titus] The Emperor Titus Vespasianus (71–9 AD), known usually as
Vespasian; his elder son, also Titus Vespasianus, was known as Titus; see
Suetonius *Vespasianus* 12.1: *ab initio principatus usque ad exitum civilis et
clemens.*
5 Trajan] See 625:20n.
5 Marcus Aurelius] See 625:5n.
11 lakes and caves] Such as Avernus, which provided one of the entrances to hell,
Virgil *Aeneid* 6.237ff; see Pliny *Naturalis historia* 2.207 for places whose fumes
kill birds, men, and other animals.
19 mystic writings] Erasmus means books of the Bible, especially those that lend
themselves to an allegorical interpretation; he mentions these as a source in
Adagia prolegomena V (LB II 5C).
21 Stobaeus] author of an anthology of excerpts from earlier literature; see *Adagia*
prolegomena iii (LB II 4A) where he is cited as a source.
21 apophthegms] Erasmus published a collection of such sayings, *Apophthegmata*, in 1531 (LB IV 93A–380D).

LB I 96B

Plutarch. Here too the material is varied: as regards subject-matter, we have
military and philosophical sayings; as regards speakers, we have kings,
wise men, ordinary citizens; as regards tone, we have serious, humorous,
and witty sayings. We can include here proverbs, whether extracted from
authors or from popular speech. National customs are in my opinion no
different from examples; oracles and replies from higher powers can certainly be included with judgments, for example, if one were to approve
Socrates as a wise man, because this was the judgment pronounced by the
oracle of Apollo.

MAXIMS

Next we come to *sententiae* or maxims, which are not extracted from authors
but invented by ourselves to suit the matter in hand. These can be introduced into any part of the speech. One passage often generates quite a
number of maxims. They can occur in the narration and in passages intended to stir the emotions of the audience, as well as in the proof section.
Quite often the transition from one section to another is made by means of
one of these terse sayings. By introducing them in appropriate contexts you
will provide yourself with a not inconsiderable source of *copia*, which at the
same time will lend your speech weight or attractiveness.

There are various forms of maxim. Some of them are καθολικαί [of
universal application], such as: Envy brings its own punishment. Others
will only do in certain contexts, such as: Nothing is so popular as generosity. Some need a specific person: A prince who will know everything has
many things to learn.

Some *sententiae* are simple: Love conquers all. Some have some kind
of reason incorporated: In every dispute the richer party, even if he is the
victim, nevertheless seems the aggressor because he has more power. Some
are double, composed of two contrasting statements, without any reason
being expressed: Complaisance wins friends; truth begets ill will. Some
consist of two distinct statements: Death is not unpleasant; the approach to

* * * * *

1 Plutarch] Collected sayings of kings and commanders, *De scite dictis regum ac
  imperatorum* (*Apophthegmata*)
9 oracle of Apollo] See Plato *Apology* 21A.
21 various forms] For this whole section see Quintilian 8.5.3ff.
23 generosity] Cicero *Pro Ligario* 37
25 many things to learn] This translates the readings of *1512, 1514, 1526, 1534,*
  and LB: *necesse habet multa cognoscere.* Modern texts of Quintilian read *ignos-*
  cere 'must pretend not to know many things.'
27 In every dispute] Sallust *Jugurtha* 10.7
30 Complaisance wins friends] Terence *Andria* 68; see 319:26n.
31 Death] Cf Thompson *Colloquies* 359 (*Funus*).

LB I 96D

death is unpleasant. If the argument is spelled out in each section, the
sententia becomes fourfold: Those who think the faults of youth should be
condoned are wrong (this is the first section; now the reason is appended),
because that age is [not] a hindrance to sound study; (now the third section)
those think wisely who punish the young most severely (now the reason) in   5
order that they may wish to acquire at the age most suitable those virtues
which will assist them throughout their lives. Although this example occurs
in the *Rhetorica ad Herennium*, I do not think much of it. However, it is not
difficult to invent another one of the same sort: Hard work is a good thing in
the young, because (reason) it is disgraceful to squander on idleness and   10
base pleasures those gifts which nature supplies in those years so that we
may acquire worthwhile skills; but, on the other hand, affluence is a good
thing in old age, so that (reason) that period of life which is somewhat
lacking in the resources of nature may at least be supported by the props of
material benefits. Or another: Old age, if destitute, is piteous; if ignorant, 15
disgraceful; for it is misery to be in need just when the weakness of nature
especially needs the support of money, and shameful to be ignorant of all
that is best just at the time when not to be learning is right and proper, to be
instructing others particularly becoming.

A maxim can be plain: The miser is without what he has as much as   20
what he has not; or it can incorporate a figure of speech: I had the power to
preserve – and dost thou ask / Whether I have power to destroy? The
straightforward way of expressing this would be: It is easier to destroy than
to preserve. It may have a general reference: It is easy to harm, harder to
help; or be adapted to specific persons, in which case it is less clearly a   25
maxim, as in this example from Cicero: 'Caesar, your exalted position has
bestowed on you no greater gift than your ability to save, nature no better
gift than your willingness to do so.'

There is also the kind of unspoken and concealed maxim that we find

* * * * *

2 Those who think] Example taken from *Ad Herennium* 4.17.25, the section on
   sententiae; see below line 8. The sentiment is expanded by Erasmus in *De
   pueris instituendis* introduction (1529); see ASD I-2 23:4. '[not]' is inserted in
   line 4 on the authority of these texts.
20 A maxim] For this section see Quintilian 8.5.6ff.
20 The miser is without] Publilius Syrus *Sententiae* ed W. Meyer (Leipzig 1880)
   628; part of a collection of moral sayings drawn from the *Mimes* of Publilius
   and from other writers, going under the name of Seneca throughout the
   Middle Ages. Erasmus extracted those belonging to Publilius and ascribed
   them to their true author in an edition of 1514 which included the *Disticha
   Catonis* and other texts (see Ep 298:11–16).
22 power to destroy] From Ovid's lost tragedy *Medea*, quoted in Quintilian 8.5.6
26 Cicero] *Pro Ligario* 38

in Virgil's line: 'She is consumed with hidden fire.' Ovid makes it explicit:
'More fiercely burns the fire that is concealed.' Another form is the type that
narrates a past event: The larger party has defeated the better. If this were
made explicit, it would be: It usually happens that the larger party defeats
the better.

Another form of maxim is the type the Greeks call ἐπιφώνημα, Quintilian 'acclamation,' that is a final triumphant remark appended either to a
narrative, as in Virgil's: 'Such toil it was to found the Roman race'; or to the
conclusion of an argument, as in this example from Cicero's *Pro Ligario*:
'The pardon of these people, Caesar, is the glory of your clemency. Shall
their language goad you into cruelty like their own?' Not every *epiphonema*
is automatically a maxim, though it usually is, but anything in the closing
section of an utterance which strikes on the ear as shrewd and pungent can
be called an ἐπιφώνημα.

This is a particular feature of epigrams, as in the one about the sheep
feeding with her milk the cubs of the wolf: Never once is nature changed by
kindness. Martial's poems very often end with such a clinching remark:
'Either don't sleep, Nasidienus, or dream about yourself'; or this one: 'Shall
I tell you what you are? You're a jack-of-all-trades.'

Valerius Maximus makes great use of this sort of thing, and Seneca
also usually closes his *Epistles* with a summing-up remark. There have been
people so fond of using the *epiphonema* that they thought they must work in
such an exclamatory appendage all over the place after anything they said.
One should however show discretion in using all maxims, including these
triumphant conclusions, and only employ them where the context demands
it, or at least allows it.

The *noema* is a form of terse remark which is not expressed but
understood, as in the story of the man who sued his sister for damages after
she had cut off his thumb while he slept, because she was tired of buying
him out of the gladiatorial school. She said 'you were fit to have your hand
complete,' implying 'so that you could go back and fight as a gladiator all
your days.'

Hortensius' famous remark is much the same, I think. He said he had

* * * * *

1 Virgil's] *Aeneid* 4.2
1 Ovid] *Metamorphoses* 4.64
6 Quintilian] 8.5.11
8 Virgil's] *Aeneid* 1.33
9 *Pro Ligario*] 10, quoted in Quintilian 8.5.10
16 changed by kindness] *Adagia* II i 86; *Anthologia palatina* 9.47
17 Martial's] 7.54; 2.7
28 man who sued his sister] See Quintilian 8.5.12

never been reconciled with his mother or sister, which gives one to understand that he had never quarrelled with them.

There are novel types of maxim based on the unexpected, on allusion, on metaphorical uses, on using two words instead of one, on contraries. Examples of these may be found in Quintilian by anyone who wants them.

ELABORATION
There is a certain affinity between the type of maxim which, as I showed above, consists of four subsections and the procedure known as 'elaboration.' In this we dwell for some time on the same point, vary the same maxim in all kinds of different ways, and thus enrich it. We may employ variation in language, expressing the same sentiment in different words and different figures of speech; or variation in delivery, using different facial expressions, gestures, and tone of voice; or variation in treatment, first saying something in our own person, then putting it into the mouth of someone who expresses it rather differently; or we can put forward an argument coolly, and then produce it in a fierce and heated manner.

A complete 'elaboration' contains seven parts: statement, reason, rephrasing of statement (to which one can add the reason restated), statement from the contrary, comparison, illustrative example, conclusion. Here is a specimen: The wise man will shirk no danger required by his country, because it often happens that a man who refuses to perish for his country of necessity perishes with it; and, since all blessings are received as the gift of our native land, no burden should be considered irksome when borne for our native land. (This is the first part, where the basic statement is simply set out and supported by its reasons. Next comes the rephrased statement, expanded by an equal or greater number of reasons.) For men are fools to run away from a danger that must needs be faced for the country's sake (statement – reason) because such a danger cannot be escaped, and because to do so reveals them as ungrateful to the state. (Next comes the section using the contrary statement.) The really wise men are those who at peril to themselves ward off the perils of their native land – (reasons) as they both render the state the respect they owe it, and prefer to perish for the multitude rather than with it. (Now we get opposites.) It is quite indefensible to surrender to nature, when you are forced, that life which you indeed received from nature but preserved by means of the state, and to refuse to

* * * * *

3 novel types] A very compressed recollection of Quintilian 8.5.15–18
9 'elaboration'] See *Ad Herennium* 4.42.54–8.
21 specimen] The whole example is taken from *Ad Herennium* 4.44.57. Erasmus merely interposes his own comments.

LB I 97E

give that life freely to the state when you are asked; to prefer, when you could perish for your country with courage and honour, to live in shame and cowardice; to be prepared to face danger for friends and parents and relations, to be unprepared to enter into peril for the state, which holds within itself every name revered by men, including the revered name of Fatherland. (Next we have a comparison.) Just as we rightly despise a voyager who prefers his own safety to that of the ship, so we execrate a man who, when the state is in peril, consults his own safety rather than the safety of all. (Now we put in the kind of parallel in which we move towards something bigger.) When a ship has been wrecked, many have often escaped unharmed; no one can swim away with his life from the wreck of the ship of state. (Now an illustrative example.) This was well understood by Decius, who, according to the story, vowed his own life, and to preserve the legions hurled himself into the midst of the enemy. (Next some maxims.) He parted with his life; he did not lose it. In return for something of little worth, he bought something of great value. He gave his life; he received his country. He gave his soul, and received a glory which, transmitted with renown from times long past, each day shines forth ever more splendidly. (Finally we have the conclusion as a kind of epilogue.) If we have proved by reasoning and demonstrated by example that one should embrace danger for the sake of the state, we must consider those men wise who shirk no danger that involves the safety of their native land.

Boys being trained in *copia* may be usefully exercised with themes of this sort – although I do not myself care much for this particular example either, which I have again taken from the *Rhetorica ad Herennium*, except that it does at least illustrate the method. It could be expanded even further if you piled in several rephrasings and reasons to go with them, several similes, and several examples.

FABLES

Fables are very similar to legendary tales, except that fables are more immediately attractive and make the point more effectively. Their attraction is due to their witty imitation of the way people behave, and the hearers give their assent because the truth is set out vividly before their very eyes. Fables are particularly effective with uneducated and unsophisticated people, and anyone else whose ways still have a whiff of the days of yore.

The most famous fables are those that go under the name of Aesop, who was numbered among the sages on their account. Quintilian thinks

* * * * *

39 Quintilian] 5.11.19

they were written by Hesiod, but certainly recognizes in them the work of
some outstanding intellect. If fables are thought of so highly, it is not
surprising that Menenius Agrippa persuaded the Roman populace to
abandon a most dangerous sedition by inventing for the occasion the fable
of the parts of the body conspiring against the belly, as recorded in Livy, or   5
that Themistocles persuaded the Athenians not to replace all their magistrates with his story of the fox covered with flies.

Each person is perfectly at liberty to invent material of this sort,
according to his subject, but if you are going to invent something appropriate, you need to be a person of lively imagination, and you must have   10
observed closely the nature of living creatures, and these are of infinite
variety. As for using fables, they can be indicated by a single word, just as
illustrative examples can, especially if the fable is well known. You could for
example say: If the ignorant criticize your work and tear it to shreds, don't
be upset. Those who know anything about the subject think highly of it.   15
After all, the cock in Aesop's fable did not appreciate the jewel. Or this: One
should not despise or disregard any enemy, however weak and humble,
seeing that the eagle in Aesop's tale had to pay for scorning the beetle. Or
this: Rely on your own achievements, not on the glory of your ancestors, or
you may suffer the same fate as Aesop's crow.   20

Fables are expanded by an introductory paragraph of commendation.
We can commend the author of the fable, or fables as a class. This is what
Aulus Gellius does in expounding the fable of the lark. He begins: 'Aesop,
the famous story teller from Phrygia ...' (the passage may easily be referred
to). Or you may dwell a little on the description of the appearance and   25
nature of the living creatures and things you introduce, since this is just the
kind of thing that people enjoy, and is itself part of a liberal education; you
can, for example, introduce a description of the dung-beetle and tell how it
is born from dung, and raises itself on its hind legs, and pushes along balls
of dung, and other things of this sort; or say that the eagle holds sway over   30
the race of birds, is Jove's armour bearer, is never struck by lightning, stares
unblinkingly at the burning rays of the sun, and soars beyond the clouds on
swiftest wing – anything whatsoever in fact that contributes to magnifying

* * * * *

5 Livy] 2.32.8ff
16 Aesop's fable] Phaedrus 3.12
18 Aesop's tale] *Fables* 4 (Chambry)
20 Aesop's crow] *Fables* 162 (Chambry); Phaedrus 1.3, the jackdaw in borrowed
    peacock's plumes; Erasmus' crow is from Horace *Epistles* 1.3.19.
23 Gellius] 2.29.3
31 stares ... the sun] Pliny *Naturalis historia* 10.10

LB I 98E

the lowliness of beetles or glorifying the nobility of the eagle. All this material I have dealt with in a light-hearted way in my *Adagia*.

We should be sure to include anything told us about the various creatures in the stories of the poets: that the first wolf originated from Lycaon, the first partridge from a young man; that the swan is sacred to Apollo and sings most sweetly at the hour of its death; that the crow is Apollo's messenger and was turned from white to black for dawdling on the way; or any remarkable deed of an animal recorded in historical writings, like the eagle that fell in love with a girl in Pliny, or Bucephalus, Alexander the Great's horse, and so on, for again I am only showing how one goes about it.

Next, when we come to the fable itself, we may tell it fairly easily and expansively. This will not prove boring if we wittily transfer the characteristics of human society to the situation in the fable, especially if we invent conversations, aphorisms, and maxims to match. There is a very good example in Horace's *Satires*:

> A country mouse once, as the story goes,
> Received a town mouse to his humble hole,
> A friend of old repaying a stay of long ago;
> A rough soul he was, and close, and yet prepared
> To open up and do him proud ...

(You can refer to the passage.)

There is an example of an expansively told tale in Apuleius about the crow and the fox, and in Aulus Gellius about the lark.

As for the so-called ἐπιμύθιον [moral], that is, the interpretation of the fable, it does not matter much whether you put it at the beginning or the end. You can in fact both begin with it and end on it, provided you incorporate variety of language.

* * * * *

2 *Adagia*] III vii 1
4 wolf] Ovid *Metamorphoses* 1.209ff
5 partridge] *Metamorphoses* 8.236ff
5 swan] Cicero *Tusculan Disputations* 1.73
6 crow] Ovid *Metamorphoses* 2.541ff
9 eagle] Pliny *Naturalis historia* 10.18
9 Bucephalus] *Naturalis historia* 8.154
16 Horace's] *Satires* 2.6.80ff
25 Apuleius] *Florida* 23 (*De deo Socratis* prologue)
26 Aulus Gellius] 2.29.3

LB I 99B

DREAMS

Some people invent dreams as well, though possibly these should not be
introduced except in display speeches, like Lucian's dream, or when we
narrate them as genuine visions in order to encourage or deter our hearers.
This is the case with Prodicus' invention about Hercules debating whether
he should enter on the steep uphill path of virtue, or the downhill path of
pleasure; or the story of Momus finding fault with man because his creator
had given him a heart full of hidden corners but no window to look into it,
and with the ox because he had not put the eyes at the end of the horns so
that it could see what it was butting. Of the same sort seems to be St
Jerome's dream about being flogged for being a Ciceronian. In my young
days I too toyed with something on these lines.

FICTIONAL NARRATIVES

If entirely fictional narratives are introduced as if they were true because
they will help us to get our point across, we must make them as much like
the real thing as possible. There are well-known features, listed in the
handbooks of rhetoric, which make a story credible. As an example of this
type we may mention the story about Memmius in Cicero, and possibly the
one about Volteius in Horace. I observe that some people have been excessively fond of this sort of thing and, relying on the gullibility of the crowd,
have imported into Christian literature the most stupid miraculous events
as if they were absolutely true.

Stories which are invented to raise a laugh are the more entertaining
the further they are from the truth, provided they do not approach the
nonsense of old wives' tales, and can also win the ears of the educated by
learned allusions. To this type belong Lucian's *True History* and Apuleius'
Golden Ass which he copied from Lucian's example, further the *Icaromenippus* and lots of other things by Lucian; also nearly all the plots of Old
Comedy, which delight us not by presenting a picture of real life, but by
allusion and hidden meaning. The type of fiction which is deliberately
constructed so as to be a representation of reality is definitely to be classed

* * * * *

3 Lucian's] *De somnio sive vita Luciani*
5 This is the case ... these lines] Added in *1534* (LB I 99E)
5 Prodicus' invention] See 582:20.
7 Momus] See Aesop *Fables* 124 (Chambry); *Adagia* I v 74.
11 Jerome's dream] Ep 22.30
19 Memmius] See Cicero *De oratore* 2.240.
20 Volteius] Horace *Epistles* 1.7.55ff

LB I 99D

as an allegory, for example, the description of the cave in Plato, where men
are chained and look with pleasure on shadows, taking them for reality.

SCRIPTURAL ALLEGORIES
Whenever we are endeavouring to turn men towards piety or from wickedness, we shall find very useful anecdotes drawn from the Old or the New
Testament, that is from the Gospels. The hidden meaning of these can be
variously handled; it can be explained in terms of human life, or of the body
of the church joined and connected to Christ the head, or of the fellowship
of heaven, or of those early days when the faith was new-born, or of our
own times. However, I shall deal at greater length and in more detail with
this subject in a short work I have in hand on scriptural allegories.

All these types I have mentioned are to be classed as 'examples.' I have
spent rather a long time on this subject because it is from this depository in
particular that the equipment for *copia* is drawn. There are however still a
few points I should deal with briefly before leaving the topic altogether.

Assembling illustrative material

First of all, my earlier remarks have shown how any illustrative example
you choose may be variously incorporated by means of a simile, contrary,
comparison, hyperbole, epithet, likeness, metaphor, or allegory. I shall
now show by what means we may acquire an ample supply of examples,
have them ready in our pocket so to speak. What I shall advise is not so
much impressive as useful, and I only wish I had carried it out long ago in
my own youth (for it occurred to me even then), as I see how much my first
efforts at writing would have gained in weight had I done so. However, a
generous spirit does not grudge to young people of promise either what
was denied oneself by fortune or what one failed to acquire by application.

Having made up your mind to cover the whole field of literature in
your reading (and anyone who wishes to be thought educated must do this
at least once in his life), first provide yourself with a full list of subjects.

* * * * *

  1 Plato] *Republic* 7.514
12 scriptural allegories] Perhaps a reference to *Ratio verae theologiae* (1518),
    which uses the 'tropological' method of scriptural exposition, as does also
    Commentarius in Psalmum I (1515); LB V 75ff, 171ff. With certain reservations
    Erasmus accepted the conventional distinctions between literal and spiritual
    interpretation of Scripture. In *Enchiridion* (1503) he emphasized the danger of
    excessive literalism (LB V 8D–E, 29B–F). See also *Ecclesiastes*, his treatise on
    preaching (and last major publication, 1535), LB V 1026C–56E.

LB I 100A

These will consist partly of the main types and subdivisions of vice and virtue, partly of the things of most prominence in human affairs which frequently occur when we have a case to put forward, and they should be arranged according to similars and opposites. Related topics naturally suggest what comes next in the list, and one remembers opposites in the same way.

Suppose for the sake of example that the first heading is 'Reverence and Irreverence.' To these will be subjoined the related subordinate types. Under 'Reverence' we shall have different sorts of proper feeling: reverence towards God, patriotism towards one's country, love for children, respect for parents or for those whom one should honour as parents, such as teachers and those whose generosity has preserved us. The opposite of this is 'Irreverence,' and related to both is 'Superstition,' so that should be added here. A wide field now opens up covering outlandish forms of worship, and the different rites of various peoples, also the foolish indulgence of parents towards children, which is a misdirected love for the child.

The next heading could be 'Faith,' which you might subdivide into faith in God, human faith, faithfulness to friends, of servants to masters, good faith towards enemies; and 'Faithlessness' could be likewise subdivided. Then could come 'Beneficence,' and, after you have listed its subdivisions, 'Gratitude,' which is not a subsection of beneficence, nor its opposite, but its consequence and so naturally associated with it.

These topics can be developed through all the standard treatments: what reverence is, how it differs from other virtues, what is its particular characteristic, by what activities it is demonstrated or violated, what nourishes or destroys it, what advantages it brings to man. Here a whole field of illustrative examples and judgments opens up.

But each person should draw up a list of virtues and vices to suit himself, whether he looks for his examples in Cicero or Valerius Maximus or Aristotle or St Thomas. If he prefers, he can make his list alphabetical – it does not matter much; although I would not have him putting into his lists every smallest hair-splitting subdivision of a topic, but only those that look as if they will often be of use in speaking. This can be discovered by looking at the topics that occur in various types of speech, epideictic, deliberative, and judicial. The headings in Valerius Maximus are mostly of this sort, and quite a lot of those in Pliny.

Topics that do not come under the head of vices and virtues belong partly to 'examples,' partly to 'commonplaces.' The first group covers things

* * * * *

24 These topics ... opens up] Added in 1534 (LB I 100E)

LB I 100C

like: remarkable longevity, vigorous old age, old head on young shoulders, remarkable happiness, remarkable memory, sudden change of fortune, sudden death, self-inflicted death, horrible death, monstrous births, remarkable eloquence, remarkable wealth, famous men of humble birth, cunning, remarkable physical strength, remarkable beauty, outstanding mind in ugly body, and so on. To each of these heads should be attached their opposites and things associated with them: remarkable eloquence has as its opposite remarkable inarticulateness, and associated with it sweetness of voice, grace of movement, histrionic ability, and so on.

'Commonplaces' covers things like: It is very important what interests you develop as a boy; It matters what company you keep; His own is fair in each man's eyes; Offence is easy, reconciliation hard; The safest course is to believe no one; Love as one soon to hate, hate as one soon to love; He gives twice who gives readily; Each man manufactures his own fortune; The wrath of kings moves slowly; The friendship of princes is perilous: War is pleasant to those who have not experienced it; A shared kingdom is insecure; The best provision for old age is learning. But what is the point of going on quoting these when there are thousands of them? One must choose from them the ones that seem most suited to speeches.

'Commonplaces' also includes stock comparisons like: Is the married or unmarried state happier? private or public life? Is monarchy preferable to democracy? Is the life of the student better than that of the uneducated?

Any of the commonplaces I quoted above which seem to have some affinity with virtue or vice can be listed under the appropriate heading. For example, under 'Liberality' one could include things like these: He gives twice who gives readily; Nothing costs more than the thing for which you must beg; A service given to the worthy does a service to the giver; No gift is wasted as much as one bestowed on the ungrateful; The value of a kindness is destroyed if it is made a ground for reproach.

In order to avoid confusion caused by a disorganized mass of material, it will be a good thing to subdivide sections that cover a wide range. 'Liberality,' for example, could be subdivided as follows: benefits performed promptly and quickly, suitable benefits, benefits bestowed on the worthy and the unworthy, kindness made a ground for reproach, mutual

* * * * *

11 His own is fair] *Adagia* i ii 15
13 Love as one soon to hate] *Adagia* ii i 72
13 He gives twice] *Adagia* i viii 91
14 Each man manufactures] *Adagia* ii iv 30
15 wrath of kings] *Adagia* i ii 3
15 War is pleasant] 'Dulce bellum inexpertis,' the title of one of Erasmus' most important writings against war, *Adagia* iv i 1; see 598:30n.

LB I 100F

benefit; and anything else which you may consider more suitable, for I am just giving a few examples to illustrate what I mean.

So prepare for yourself a sufficient number of headings, and arrange them as you please, subdivide them into the appropriate sections, and under each section add your commonplaces and maxims; and then whatever you come across in any author, particularly if it is rather striking, you will be able to note down immediately in the proper place, be it an anecdote or a fable or an illustrative example or a strange incident or a maxim or a witty remark or a remark notable for some other quality or a proverb or a metaphor or a simile.

This has the double advantage of fixing what you have read more firmly in your mind, and getting you into the habit of using the riches supplied by your reading. Some people have much material stored up so to speak in their vaults, but when it comes to speaking or writing they are remarkably ill-supplied and impoverished. A third result is that whatever the occasion demands, you will have the materials for a speech ready to hand, as you have all the pigeonholes duly arranged so that you can extract just what you want from them.

No discipline is so remote from rhetoric that you cannot use it to enrich your collection. Mathematics seems utterly remote, yet it will provide you with comparisons: the sphere totally consistent with itself, the square standing firm with its four right angles whichever way it falls, with which one can compare the wise man, entirely self-reliant, independent, firm, and unshaken in his virtue whatever the onslaughts of fortune. To say nothing at the moment of the fact that the theologians frequently look to mathematics when expounding mysteries because of the hidden analogy between things and numbers.

Natural science provides not only similes but examples. A simile of this type would be: As the lightning most often strikes the tops of hills, so the position of highest authority is exposed to the worst misfortunes; or, As lightning liquifies bronze but leaves wax untouched, even so a prince should show the utmost severity to the rebellious and disobedient, but display clemency to all others. If one wished to inculcate modesty and reticence in pleasure even in the properly married, one could use as an example the elephant, which out of self-respect mates in concealment. Or to urge the care with which parents should guard and train those first vulnerable years of childhood, one could cite dolphins, which accompany their offspring until they are quite grown up, and do not allow their young to go anywhere unless an older dolphin is with them as tutor and chaperon.

* * * * *

35 mates in concealment] Pliny *Naturalis historia* 8.13

So our student will flit like a busy bee through the entire garden of literature, will light on every blossom, collect a little nectar from each, and carry it to his hive. Since there is such an abundance of material that one cannot gather everything, he will at least take the most striking and fit this into his scheme of work.

Some material can serve not only diverse but contrary uses, and for that reason must be recorded in different places. For example, if you are describing the incurable greed of a miser, you may properly bring in the tale of Charybdis; but if you are talking of insatiable gluttony or woman's inexhaustible lust Charybdis will fit again. Likewise, Aesop's fable about the goat and the fox getting into the water-hole together will do either to illustrate forethought, which means that you do not embark on an enterprise without first considering how you may get out of it, or to exemplify false friends who appear to be consulting a friend's interest but are really doing the best they can for themselves.

The death of Socrates can be used to show that death holds no fear for a good man, since he drank the hemlock so cheerfully; but also to show that virtue is prey to ill will and far from safe amidst a swarm of evils; or again that the study of philosophy is useless or even harmful unless you conform to general patterns of behaviour.

This same incident can be turned to Socrates' praise or blame. He deserves praise for showing such a courageous contempt for death when condemned for no fault of his own but purely out of animosity; he is to be blamed, inasmuch as by his useless pursuit of philosophy and disregard of accepted standards he caused bitter grief to his friends, disaster to his wife and children, and destruction to himself, while others are useful to their country, and are an ornament as well as a support to their families; and for that reason the duty of the true philosopher is at some point to abandon the crabbed precepts of philosophy and accommodate himself to the interests and opinions of the majority, to serve the times, as the saying goes.

If you look at this example of Socrates and determine its successive scenes, how many subject headings you will thus elicit! First of all, we find Socrates accused out of ill will by Anytus and Meletus, two most undesirable individuals. This suggests the subject: Truth begets hatred; or Outstanding virtue earns ill will; or Juries often take more account of noble birth than honest character; or There is nothing more shameless than

* * * * *

9 Charybdis] *Adagia* I v 4
10 Aesop's fable] 40 (Chambry)
16 death of Socrates] For all this material on Socrates see Plato *Crito* and *Phaedo*; also *Adagia* III iii 1.

LB I 102A

wealth allied to bad character. (For what could be more preposterous than to have Socrates brought to court by men discredited by every crime imaginable?) Another subject could be: Not every act befits all equally. It was for this reason that Socrates did not throw himself on the jury's mercy, for it was not fitting that a man who throughout his life had taught that death should not be viewed with horror unless it was shameful, should now sink to abject entreaties, apparently through fear of death. This too was the reason why he did not do anything to avoid being brought to court in the first place, did not half-way through the trial opt for exile, and finally would not agree to escape from the prison though the chance was offered him, lest he should appear to be deserting his own principles. This is just the first section.

Then when we find him engaging in philosophical discussion so calmly and unhurriedly as his execution rapidly drew near, and drinking the hemlock as cheerfully as he would wine, and, just before he died, joking with Phaedo and reminding him to sacrifice a cock to Aesculapius, this suggests the topic: Death is even desirable to those who are conscious of a well-spent life; or this one: The nature of a man's life is revealed most clearly at his death. This is a good illustrative example of a steadfast and entirely consistent life, since Socrates when faced with imminent death looked and spoke just as he had done throughout his whole life.

The third section tells us that, while Socrates was in prison, there was no sign of Alcibiades, Agathon, and Phaedrus, but only of Crito, Phaedo, and Simmias. This leads to the thought that danger reveals who one's real friends are, for those everyday friends whose presence we have when nothing out of the ordinary is required look to themselves at such times.

In the fourth section he spends a long time discussing the immortality of the soul with his friends, but sends away his wife and family after giving them a few instructions. This gives us the heading: The philosopher should not be deeply involved in human relationships. (This tallies splendidly with the teaching of Christ.)

The fifth section shows the crowd immediately after Socrates' death turning its fury on his accusers, and setting up a golden statue to the Socrates whose loss they now regret. From this we may extract the heading: Fickle is the love or hate of the crowd; or this: Virtue's present form we hate / But when 'tis gone, in discontent / We seek it then – too late; or this:

* * * * *

3 Not every act] *Adagia* II iv 16
3 for this reason] See Cicero *Tusculan Disputations* 1.71.
35 Virtue's present form] Horace *Odes* 3.24.31–2

Counterfeit glory vanishes with the life, but the splendour of true virtue grows ever brighter after death.

All this makes it quite plain, I think, how many purposes the same illustrative example can serve.

The same is true of the simile. What a wealth of parallels can be derived from ships and sailing! Just as storms demonstrate the good helmsman, so reverses reveal the good general. No one entrusts the rudder to his closest friend but to the expert in navigation; even so no one will hand over the direction of the ship of state to his favourite, but to the man he considers most competent. Even as the crew take in the sails when a following wind blows too strongly, and spread them when the wind is less favourable, likewise when all is prosperity, the spirit must be curbed to keep it from arrogance; yet when fortune is hostile, it must be expanded and strengthened by courage and hope of better things to come. Again: When we cannot hold a straight course ahead through the storm, we must take a roundabout route and make for our goal just the same. When the uncontrolled violence of a storm is too much for the sailors' skill, they furl the sails and drop anchor; in like manner, one must sometimes cease to resist the raging mob until such time as it becomes ready to listen and manageable. As the sailor does not hold his sail always in the same position but raises it or lowers it, or swings it to this side or that to match the way the wind blows, even so the wise man should not at all times and in all places and in all situations keep the tenor of his life unchanged, but should accommodate to present circumstances his expression, his words, his behaviour. As in great storms the most experienced sailors take suggestions even from the inexperienced because in a crisis like this different ideas occur to different people, even so a good king in great national dangers will be willing to listen to anyone's advice. When the danger is slight, the steering is still done by a man who has been tossed in grave dangers; even so, the state is safest when headed by a leader who has been tested in serious situations. Just as the helmsman does not consider he is properly performing his function unless he looks about him and tells each man what he should do, so no one properly acts the prince unless he directs and assumes responsibility for the functions of all his subordinate ministers. Any sailor would be crazy who allowed the vessel to be lost because of his hatred of some of the passengers, seeing that he could not survive himself if the ship foundered; likewise, any man is insane if he does not guard the safety of his country because of some party feeling, since he himself cannot

* * * * *

10 take in the sails] See Horace *Odes* 2.10.22ff.

remain in safety if the country is destroyed. As sailors drop the sheet anchor only in the most violent tempests, so one should not resort to the final remedy unless in the gravest peril when all hope is practically gone.

But it is foolish to go on like this, as you can see by now that this one topic can be the source of thousands of similes.

Quite often one aspect of a simile can be applied to various purposes. For example, the frequent changes of the moon can be used for the vicissitudes of fortune, or the mutability of human life, or the irresolution of the foolish. One basic idea can be adapted to various uses: A merry companion is a wagon in the way; Life is pleasanter if one does not pass it alone, but joins with pleasant and cheerful friends; One should always carry a good book, so that one can dispel boredom by reading; If a happy spirit and a clear conscience go with you, no part of life will ever be wearisome; The best companion on a journey is one who speaks of happy things; if he constantly reminds you of unpleasantnesses, he wearies you to death.

The same is true of proverbs and sayings, and the use of these I demonstrated at the beginning of my own collection of proverbs.

Some extracts must therefore be written out in more than one place, or at least jotted down, for sometimes it will be sufficient to indicate the contents by a word or two accompanied by a reference to the source, especially if it is something that cannot be set out properly in a few words.

To make the whole thing clearer by means of an example, I shall take the heading 'Changeableness' or 'Irresolution,' and see how much material I can collect under it. I shall start with the poets and take from them the god Mercury, a cunning divinity, whom we find assuming various shapes, and operating now among the gods, now in the underworld, now among men, and performing various functions, sometimes playing the part of Ganymede as Jove's cup-bearer or carrying messages, conducting the souls of the dead to Charon, giving help to businessmen and advocates, and playing his lyre or employing his wand. He has a parti-coloured hat, and rejoices in names of all kinds. These occur in Aristophanes' *Plutus*, where he is called στροφαῖος [versatile], ἐμπολαῖος [trafficking], δόλιος [wily], ἡγεμόνιος [guiding], ἐναγώνιος [games-presiding]. In Homer and Hesiod

* * * * *

1 sheet anchor] *Adagia* i i 24.
10 wagon in the way] Publilius Syrus *Sententiae* 104 Meyer (see 628:20n)
16 proverbs] *Adagia* prolegomena xii (LB II 9E): *varius proverbiorum usus*
25 Mercury] See 388:13n.
31 Aristophanes' *Plutus*] 1155–61
33 Homer] For example, *Odyssey* 1.84
33 Hesiod] *Works and Days* 77

he is διάκτορος [Guide] and Ἀργειφόντης [Slayer of Argos]. He is also
called God of Cyllene and ἐριούνιος [Bringer of Luck]. I shall also take the
god Vertumnus, who gets his name from the fact that he is continually
changing (*vertere*) his form, and also Proteus who transforms himself into
all kinds of incredible things. I shall take Empusa from Aristophanes' *Frogs*,   5
a kind of demon continually presenting itself under different shapes, also
Morpheus, assuming any appearance he chooses, and Circe transforming
men into various animal shapes with her spells and magic wand (for bad
men do not act consistently but are prey to shifting emotions); I shall take
Καιρός [Opportunity], the mobile god who never stays the same, and one   10
like him, if you will, the Rhamnusian goddess. I shall take Jove, transformed into an eagle, swan, bull, or shower of gold, and Chimaera with the
head of a lion, torso of a woman, tail of a dragon, and that variegated
monster which Horace invents right at the beginning of the *Ars poetica*. I
shall bring in two-faced Janus, and three-bodied Geryon, and Bacchus, to   15
whom the poets attribute εὐήθεια, that is a volatile and complaisant nature
(and that is how Aristophanes depicts him in the *Frogs*), and any other
figures in the poets which exemplify prodigious variety. I shall bring in
Ulysses, adopting different characters according to the circumstances,
which is why Homer, right at the beginning of his poem, calls him   20
πολύτροπος [versatile].

* * * * *

  3 Vertumnus] See 388:14n.
  4 Proteus] See 388:15n.
  5 Empusa] See 388:15n.
  7 Morpheus] Ovid *Metamorphoses* 11.633ff
  7 Circe] See 611:10n.
 10 Καιρός] The fleeting decisive moment which must be seized by the forelock as
    it passes; the divinity was variously represented in Renaissance art with
    wings, a precariously balanced pair of scales, a lock of hair, and, by fusion
    with the figure of Fortune, as standing on a wheel or a ball; see *Adagia* I vii
    70:'Nosce tempus,' where Erasmus quotes both Posidippus' epigram (*An-
    thologia palatina* 16.275) on Lysippus' statue of Καιρός, and Ausonius' (epi-
    gram 33) on Occasio where the wheel is already present.
 11 Rhamnusian goddess] Nemesis, so called from her celebrated shrine at
    Rhamnus in Attica; her function was to punish presumption and over-
    confidence by turning prosperity to misfortune, in which her activities re-
    sembled those of the fickle goddess Fortune; *Adagia* II vi 38.
 12 Chimaera] Homer *Iliad* 6.181; Ovid *Metamorphoses* 9.647–8
 14 Horace] *Ars poetica* 1–5
 15 Janus] Ovid *Fasti* 1.65–6
 15 Geryon] Virgil *Aeneid* 8.202
 20 Homer] *Odyssey* 1.1

LB I 103F

Next I shall turn to science, and use the image of the moon which never returns the same in appearance as before, but is half-full, or full, old, new, pale, reddish, whitish, now precedes the sun, now follows him from behind. I shall use the image of the sky different in spring or autumn, now cloudy, now clear, now calm, now boisterous with winds. I shall extract the simile of the sea continually ebbing and flowing with the alternating tides, especially the Euripus which surges back and forth seven times each day and night. I shall add the polyp, whose changeableness has become proverbial, and the chameleon constantly changing its colour, the panther and the pard with their parti-coloured spots, and any other animals of the same sort, also the slippery snake, and childhood whose moods change from hour to hour, the peculiar inconstancy of women, the crowd veering at the slightest impulse, the wonderful mobility of quicksilver, the reed bowing to every breeze, the lightness of dry leaves, feathers, shavings, the soft pliable nature of wax, the shifting images of dreams, the mobility of wheels, the weather-vane set atop towers and church spires to record as it swings around the direction of the wind, the pans of the scale lightly dipping to this side and to that, and mosaic work with the wonderful variety of all its little different coloured stones.

Some similes can be invented, like comparing the mind of the inconstant man, thinking first of one thing then another, to a reflecting globe hung up in a busy market place, and mirroring a constant succession of different figures as the crowd moves to and fro, or to a glass which appears to take on any colour you put beneath it, or to an iron pendulum oscillating to and fro without stopping under the influence of a positive and a negative magnet, or to a ball rolling about on a flat surface.

From the non-fictional writers I shall borrow the inborn light-mindedness of the Greeks, which Juvenal describes; the slippery loyalty of the Allobroges, the Carthaginians of like inconstancy of character, the Scythians changing their pastures daily and having no fixed abode, the rod of Moses changing into one thing after another; Aristippus, playing any part you like, who 'was suited by every shade of life,' as Horace says,

* * * * *

8 polyp] *Adagia* II iii 91
9 chameleon] *Adagia* III iv 1
11 childhood] Horace *Ars poetica* 160
28 Greeks] Juvenal 3.74ff
29 Allobroges] Caesar *Bellum civile* 3.59ff
29 Carthaginians] See 392:7n.
30 Scythians] Horace *Odes* 3.24.9–10
30 rod of Moses] Exod 7:8ff
31 Aristippus] Horace *Epistles* 1.17.23; *Adagia* I iii 86

wearing the Cynic's cloak or royal purple as the case may be; also the ἡμίλευκος [half-white man] mentioned by Lucian, Catiline with his incompatible characteristics out of Sallust, Hannibal from Livy and Valerius Maximus (both Catiline and Hannibal displayed a quite different tenor of life in youth and old age), Tigellius out of Horace's third satire: 5

No consistency that fellow had;
Often he passed as if fleeing for his life,
More often still with solemn gait he paced
Like one bearing Juno's holy symbols. 10

Comedy will provide us with an example of female inconsistency when Sostrata in the *Adelphi* says 'Why man, you must be mad. / Do you consider this a thing to tell abroad?' and then a few lines later says 'Not for all the world will I do that. / I'll tell it out.' The inconstancy of lovers is 15 demonstrated by Phaedria, who goes to the country and suddenly comes back, the inconstancy of youth by Antipho in the *Phormio*. It would however take too long to pursue this topic properly.

From tragedy I shall borrow Phaedra arguing with herself and changing her mind, now willing, now unwilling; and Medea too, before she 20 murders her children, swayed by different emotions; Byblis and Narcissus from Ovid; and Dido from Virgil at the point where Aeneas is preparing his departure. The poets provide us with countless characters of this type all over their writings.

From fables I shall bring in the countryman who could blow hot and 25 cold from the one mouth to the amazement of the satyr. I could go on, but for the moment I am only illustrating the method. From proverbs I shall borrow

* * * * *

2 Lucian] *Prometheus es* 4

3 Sallust] *Catilina* 5

3 Livy and Valerius Maximus] Both authors relate incidents illustrating, for example, Hannibal's skill as a general and his magnanimity, also his superhuman cruelty.

5 Horace's] *Satires* 1.3.9–11

13 *Adelphi*] 336–7, 342–3

16 Phaedria] In Terence's *Eunuchus*

17 Antipho] In Terence's *Phormio*

19 Phaedra] See Seneca's play of that name, especially 604–5: *vos testor omnes, caelites, hoc quod volo me nolle.*

20 Medea] See Seneca *Medea* 893ff.

22 Ovid] *Metamorphoses* 9.450ff; 3.344ff

22 Virgil] *Aeneid* 4.296ff

26 satyr] *Adagia* I viii 30

τὴν παναγαῖαν Ἄρτεμιν [ever-wandering Artemis], ἀνέμου πεδίον [a field
for the wind], εὐμεταβολώτερος κοθόρνου [more adaptable than an actor's sock], ὕδρου ποικιλότερος [more pied than a water-snake], Λιβυκὸν
θηρίον [a Libyan beast] and so on. (I have given the sources for all these in
my *Adagia*.) A rolling stone gathers no moss. A tree that is always being   5
moved does not flourish. From apophthegms I shall quote the remark made
against Cicero: 'to sit in two seats at once,' and Sallust's comment on him
(written, not spoken), 'He says one thing standing up and another sitting
down.' From Homer we have ἀλλοπρόσαλλος [on different sides at different times] – this is the word he uses of the War God when he is favouring   10
neither side definitely, but supporting first one party, then the other. From
Ovid, I think, 'Constant only in fickleness'; from Horace, 'Lighter than
bark,' and 'Turn round to square and square again to round,' and 'At Rome,
as fickle as the wind, / It's Tivoli I love, at Tivoli it's Rome'; from Plautus;
'lighter than a water-spider'; from Terence's *Phormio*, 'I will, I won't – I   15
won't, I will – what's said is unsaid again,' and so on; from Euripides, 'Your
mind does not run straight – this you think now, / But something else you
thought before, and soon / Will think something else again.'
     By now it is clear, I should think, what a wealth of equipment in this
line also we can discover out of all the writers at our disposal.   20
     The same considerations apply to maxims, which one may not only
extract from authors but invent according to one's requirements. If you
contrast each of these with its opposite, and subjoin related ideas to both
headings, you can see what a vast store of speech will be laid up. As all this
has so many applications (as I shall explain in detail in my work *De*   25
conscribendis epistolis), there is nothing which you will not be able to apply
somehow to the enrichment of your speech. Even opposite ideas can be

* * * * *

5   *Adagia*] Ἄρτεμιν: II ix 47; πεδίον: II v 70; κοθόρνου: I i 94, and see 386:10n;
     ὕδρου: I i 95; θηρίον III vii 8; rolling stone III iv 74
6   does not flourish] Seneca *Epistles* 2.3
7   two seats] *Adagia* I vii 2
7   Sallust's] *In Ciceronem declamatio* 4.7; *Adagia* III iii 56
9   Homer] *Iliad* 5.831
12 Ovid] *Tristia* 5.8.18
12 Horace] *Odes* 3.9.22; *Epistles* 1.1.100; *Epistles* 1.8.12; *Adagia* II v 70; see line
     5n.
14 Plautus] *Persa* 244
15 Terence's] *Phormio* 950
16 Euripides] *Iphigenia in Aulis* 332
25 *De conscribendis epistolis*] First authorized edition published in 1522; see
     chapter on *exempla quomodo tractanda* (ASD I–1 330ff).

LB I 105A

brought in through irony, or by the adducing of a contrast, or by a comparison. It would be irony if one called Socrates a man who never agreed with himself, when throughout his whole life he was always seen with the same expression. It would be contrast if one said that Julius Caesar never regretted anything he did, whereas this man never decreed anything that he did not before long rescind; a comparison if one said that it was just as difficult to make the famous Cato, whom Cicero calls inflexible, abandon his opinion as to make this man keep to his.

It is easy to modify related ideas and adapt them to neighbouring concepts. To take Persius' phrase, 'Live in your own house.' This properly applies to one aiming higher than his lot in life allows, but since being discontented with one's lot has affinities with inconstancy of mind, it can be wrested in this direction, especially when Seneca writes: 'It seems to me a strong indication of a well-ordered mind to be able to stay at home and keep oneself company.'

One can even twist material to serve the opposite purpose. If you were praising a man for all seasons, endowed with a versatile and dexterous mind, you could dip into your 'inconstancy' cupboard and bring out the polyp which changes colour according to the surface beneath it, and then the Euripus, saying that this sea is not so versatile as this man's mind. You could bring out the flame which cannot stand still, the sky which constantly presents a different face, the reed bending according as the breezes blow, and say that it is the mark of a wise man to change his views and his way of life according to events, circumstances, places. Only senseless rocks and the brute earth do not move. Of living creatures, those that are most impressive are the most mobile. In the universe things are nobler the further they are from immobility: earth which does not move is the lowest, then comes water which does move, then air which moves more, then fire which moves even more than air, and finally the heaven which moves most of all. This is why the ancients called the mind of man wind and fire, but the stupid, slow, and foolish they called stones and lead, things to which the word 'immovability' is particularly applicable.

By means of passages of this sort you will be able to divert much of

* * * * *

3 seen with the same expression] See Cicero *Tusculan Disputations* 3.31.
4 Julius Caesar] Erasmus specifically says Julius Caesar; according to Suetonius, Titus on his death-bed said: *neque enim exstare ullum suum factum paenitendum excepto dumtaxat uno* (*Titus* 10).
7 Cicero] *De officiis* 3.88; see 391:5n.
10 Persius' phrase] 4.52; *Adagia* I vi 87: 'Tecum habita'
13 Seneca] *Epistles* 2.1
17 man for all seasons] *Adagia* I iii 86: 'Omnium horarum homo'

LB I 105C

your equipment of 'constancy' to purposes of blame, and that for 'inconstancy' to praise. But as I said a short while ago, this will be dealt with more
opportunely elsewhere.

Now I shall deal with the remaining methods of expansion.

Expanding the formal divisions of a speech

The length of a speech will depend on how many of the recognized subdivisions of a speech are employed. Whereas the speaker who is aiming at
brevity will use as few of these as possible, the speaker who wishes to
spread himself will not only employ these legitimate subdivisions prescribed by the art of rhetoric, but will endeavour to supplement them
besides.

Fundamentally the orator has three functions – to inform, to give
pleasure, to influence. The speaker who wants to be brief will content
himself with one of these and will simply inform, which he will do by
stating the facts and arguing from them; the man who wishes to speak at
length will employ all three, in every section of the speech, not just in the
peroration or introduction. The brief speaker again can content himself
with the exposition of the facts, or, if the type of case allows it, omit this and
simply use the proof section. Even this section, while it cannot be entirely
omitted, can be narrowed down and kept brief. The expansive speaker will
use all six subdivisions: introduction, exposition of facts, division into
heads, proof, refutation, conclusion; but he will also expatiate on the
various topics provided by the introductory passages as they occur, and
throughout the speech, whenever the case gives him opportunity, he will
introduce little prefatory sections, by means of which he will retain or
regain the good will, attention, and receptivity of his hearers, or dispel
boredom, or prepare the way for what he is going to say. Such occasions
frequently arise.

The main method of restoring receptivity is by suitable transitions, for
which I supplied a number of formulae in book 1, such as: You have heard

* * * * *

9 subdivisions] The theory of the parts or divisions of a speech goes back in
some form to the Greek theorists of the fifth century BC and was variously
elaborated by later writers on rhetoric. The scheme given in lines 24–5 is
taken from *Ad Herennium* 1.3.4. This theory was combined in various ways
with the doctrine of the functions of the orator. Erasmus quotes the three-fold
function put forward by Cicero (probably based on Aristotle) *Brutus* 276: *tria
... esse quae orator efficere deberet, ut doceret, ut delectaret, ut moveret.*
33 book 1] Chap 53

that he acquired office by bribery, corruption, bloodshed, fornication, and every foul art; I shall now show you that what was shamefully acquired was more shamefully administered. Attention is restored by something like this: All this is important, but trival compared with what I am now going to say; Now I come to the heart of the whole matter, accordingly I beg you to hear this with all the attention you can muster; But I have dwelt on this possibly at too great length, so I shall deal with what remains briefly and clearly, if you are prepared to lend me your ears and minds as you have hitherto done; I shall go back rather a long way, but I shall so choose my words that you will derive both pleasure and profit from what you hear. And so on, for thousands of such remarks can be invented according to the nature of the case.

Boredom can be dispelled or avoided like this: Listen carefully, I beg you. The thing I am dealing with possibly seems trivial at first sight, but if you will attend for a little, you will assuredly realize that under this cover lurk the gravest perils to our national security; Bear with me for a while, I beg you, I will soon reveal what all this has in view; And now you will hear something never heard before; You will learn a thing more ridiculous than anything else.

Good will is resuscitated by the same means as were used to generate it.

In the introduction we can also employ argument if we must get something out of the way which otherwise would be an obstacle when we are dealing with other matters; but this must only be done very deliberately when the circumstances so require it.

The exposition of facts can be greatly enhanced by the figure which some call *sermocinatio* 'dialogue' in which we assign suitable utterances to one or more persons, as when Homer, in *Iliad* 22, makes old Priam try to dissuade Hector from taking part in the duel, and after him Hecuba, and in *Iliad* 6 makes Hector's wife Andromache try to deter him from battle, and shows Hector replying to them, in all of which he demonstrates a wonderful mastery of what is appropriate to each character. In this the historical writers are particularly worthy of admiration, for everyone accepts that they are allowed to put speeches into the mouths of their characters. I refer to pagan historians. It is doubtful whether Christian ones may do the same, except that something similar seems to be done in the story of the seven

* * * * *

26 The exposition ... *Life of St Agnes*] Text to 650:2 added in *1534* [LB I 106C–D)
28 Homer] *Iliad* 22.33ff
30 *Iliad* 6] 390ff

Maccabees, and, apart from others who have written lives of the martyrs, St Ambrose seems to have allowed himself to do so in his *Life of St Agnes*.

The exposition, apart from the fact that it can be developed expansively and filled out with demonstrations and descriptions of mental states, is also extended by ἐπιδιήγησις [additional exposition], which is, as Quintilian explains, a repeated narration in which an incident which has been set out briefly and simply is repeated at greater length and with more elaboration. This is done to rouse indignation or sympathy. The exposition can also be amplified by the appendage of a digression, which Quintilian only allows if such an excursus attaches itself as a natural conclusion to the narrative. For example, if our narrative has become vehement towards the end, we can prolong it as if the words are still tumbling out in indignation. This happens in real cases where something is at stake. But in a display piece, once the facts have been set out, there is no reason why you should not expatiate on some pleasing and attractive topic, which will both wipe away the weariness occasioned by the narration of facts, and by the sheer pleasure of listening make your audience more alert for the proof section which comes next. I discussed the nature of such topics earlier.

A proposition will be expanded if we double or multiply it instead of keeping it single, even if one would be enough, because different people are affected by different things. I mean a single one, like: If he had done it, he would have deserved reward rather than punishment; or a double one like: This proposal is not honourable or expedient, nor can it be carried out without great danger; but if it were honourable and expedient in the highest degree, and attended by no danger at all, it is none the less impossible for us to achieve.

Then we can put forward our proposition or thesis not in bare simplicity but with arguments incorporated and the warmth of emotion added, as we find in this passage from Cicero's *Pro Milone*: 'Everything happened just as I have described, gentlemen of the jury. The waylayer was defeated, violence was overcome by violence, or better, boldness was crushed by courage.' (Then he incorporates emotion.) 'I say nothing of the benefit reaped from this by the country, by you, by all loyal citizens, for this would do no good to Milo, who was fated not to be able to preserve even himself without at the same time preserving the country and yourselves.' (Then he

* * * * *

1 Maccabees] 2 Macc 7, the story of seven brothers tortured to death by Antiochus IV of Syria, all of whom die with defiant speeches on their lips

5 Quintilian] 4.2.128

9 Quintilian] 4.3.4

18 earlier] 589–90

29 *Pro Milone*] 30–1

adds to the effect by argument.) 'If he had no justification in so doing, then I have nothing which I can defend. But if reason enjoins upon the educated, necessity on barbarians, custom on civilized nations, the law of nature on wild beasts, that they should ward off every form of violence by whatever means they can from body, head, and life, you cannot judge this deed a crime without at the same time decreeing that all who fall into the hands of thugs must perish either by their weapons or your verdict.' (Then he returns to emotion.) 'If he had thought so, Milo would certainly have found it preferable to bare to Clodius the throat which he had attacked not once, nor for the first time on this occasion, rather than to have it cut by you for not surrendering himself to Clodius and allowing him to slash it.'

(Again, in the following section where he is establishing the point at issue – the passage is well known – Cicero repeats the gist of arguments which he had used in the introductory section. He was justified in doing this because he had touched on a number of issues in the opening paragraphs; but one can do the same satisfactorily under other circumstances, provided one has suitable intervening remarks, especially in the enumeration of heads and in the exposition, which is the second part of the division, which I dealt with above, when I was discussing propositions.)

A further example of this would be, if you were urging Cicero not to accept the gift of his life from Antony in return for burning the *Philippics*, to set out your propositions like this: First consider, my dear Cicero, whether it would be worthy of you suddenly to destroy the immortal fame of your genius, won by so much effort, and which has shed so much lustre on your whole house, for the sake of a span of life which cannot be long for one who is so old, by burning the finest of all your productions. Second, whether a brave man, who has always put liberty above all, should find it tolerable to owe his life, the best thing of all, in which all else is contained, to a monster to whom no free man would wish to be beholden on any count whatsoever. Finally, he should consider lest it be somewhat naive in such a vital matter to trust an enemy of the greatest perfidy who never kept faith even with his friends, and not to observe what even a blind man could see, that that most accomplished butcher Antony intends nothing else but the total extinction of Cicero.

All this could have been expressed in the simple propositions: one, life is not worth such a price; two, it is wretched to owe one's life to an enemy; last, Antony wants to deceive, not save.

* * * * *

19 dealt with above] 604:7ff
20 A further example] This example was discussed earlier; see 597:26ff.
32 blind man] *Adagia* I viii 93

LB I 107A

If any proposition seems rather difficult to swallow, one will have to prepare the way for it with a little introductory section. If you intend, for example, to praise Plato's doctrine that wives should be held in common, you will say that you are well aware that you appear to be proposing something absolutely ridiculous, but you will beg your audience to suspend judgment for a time until they have heard the main points of the argument, as you are quite sure that, once the case has been fully set out, they will be ready to endorse a very different opinion. They should consider that this theory, whatever its nature, was not advanced without due consideration by a philosopher of such eminence who earned the title 'divine' for his brilliance in other matters. The same thing happens in forming judgments as in looking at people. If you look at the outward appearance of some people from a distance and without much attention, you think nothing could be lovelier, as their outer varnish imposes on your eyes; but if you go closer and look more carefully, the very thing that delighted your eyes so much before you find increasingly displeasing. What could be more ridiculous than the Sileni, unless you explain their inner meaning? But once you explain them, what could be more worthy of reverence? Truth lurks in hidden places, and in judging one should not follow the lead of the crowd, which always takes the worst for the best. Accordingly, your hearers should lay aside for a time their received and built-in opinion and weigh the question on its own merits, and not decide one way or the other until they have heard the full complement of arguments. There will be some things which by themselves seem stupid, but looked at in combination produce the concord and harmony of the truth.

If you invent a little preface of this sort according to the nature of the case, you will often succeed in preparing the mind of your listener for the line of argument to follow.

The proof section will be expanded, apart from the methods of amplification which I demonstrated above, by refutation or preparation, and assertion. We refute or prepare the way by two means: first by propositions. What I mean by propositions on this occasion are not those that embrace the main points at issue in the case, but the summaries or recapitulations which it is the custom of orators to list at the beginning of their arguments and then repeat at the end with a heightened emotional tone, or as an epilogue. I spoke of this type in earlier sections.

* * * * *

3 Plato's doctrine] *Republic* 5.449–61
18 worthy of reverence] *Adagia* III iii 1: 'Sileni Alcibiadis'
36 earlier sections] At 650–1

In setting out such propositions we choose a form of expression which in itself inclines our audience to believe or disbelieve. For an example we may again take a passage from Cicero's *Pro Milone*: 'Before I come to speak about the business with which this court is directly concerned, I ought first to refute the insinuations often made in the Senate by the evil men who are his enemies, and in the assembly even earlier by his accusers.' By using the words 'evil' and 'enemies' he does much to discredit the other side's statement. He then undermines the statement itself by the use of irony: 'They deny that it can be the will of heaven that that man should look upon the light of day who confesses that he has slain a fellow-man.' These emotive words, which simply mean 'That man should be punished' must needs be pronounced with a certain sarcasm.

Preparatory passages of this sort are prefixed to the separate sections of the recapitulation.

In the same section of the *Pro Milone* Cicero is about to use illustrative examples to refute a statement of the prosecution, and prepares the way for this by saying: 'Now in what city are fools putting forward an argument like this?' Then he produces the example of Marcus Horatius being acquitted after murdering his sister.

Similar to these are asseverations. These are not arguments, but they often have a confirmatory force if they are combined with real proofs. I mean things like: Who is so blind as not to see this, so shameless as to deny it? This is too stupid to need rebuttal; Who does not realize ...? and so on; also Put a bold face on it, and dare to deny ...; In view of all this, what impudence to ...; and so on.

Each summarizing section can be enriched by its own epilogue. In this the main points are briefly summed up and recalled to the mind's eye of the audience, so that they will listen to the conclusion with greater receptivity. Cicero does this very often, because he tends to deploy his line of argument over a considerable area. We can take an example from his speech *Pro Pompeio*: 'Consider therefore whether you should have any hesitation in plunging whole-heartedly into a war which will defend the glorious name of the Roman people, the security of your allies, vast revenues, the investments of many of your fellow citizens, and the state itself.'

Recapitulations are also extended by excursus where we expand the

* * * * *

3 *Pro Milone*] 7, somewhat misremembered by Erasmus
9 They deny] Example used earlier, at 618:20
15 same section] See above 618:22.
30 *Pro Pompeio*] *Pro lege Manilia* 19, which recapitulates the preceding four sections

material by expressing the appropriate emotional tone to go with the
separate proofs. The conclusion is particularly suited to this. If we wish to
demonstrate *copia* at this point, we shall duplicate the section: we shall run
over the main arguments immediately and again as an epilogue, and also
handle the various emotions at all the appropriate points. (You may discover what these are from Aristotle and Quintilian.)

The poets are splendid at this. The more violent emotions, which the
Greeks call πάθη [passions] are to be discovered in Homer's *Iliad* and in
tragedy; the calmer ones, which are pleasant rather than disturbing, are
supplied by Homer's *Odyssey* and by comedy. Yet ἤθη [disposition, feel-
ings], which is what the Greeks call the emotions of comedy, are often
interspersed in the *Iliad* and Greek tragedy. Latin tragedy makes rather
sparing use of them.

Among the emotions we must include pleasure, though this should be
incorporated throughout the speech wherever appropriate, not just in the
peroration. What different people find pleasing is dealt with in detail by
Aristotle in his sections on the emotions, and Cicero has written on jokes
and Quintilian on laughter, discussing the theory of humour. The pleasure
derived from the milder emotions is particularly appropriate to the section
where the facts of the case are expounded, because they help to make the
description vivid and everyone is familiar with them. Is there anyone who
does not get pleasure from reading the passage in Homer where Andromache runs to meet Hector at the gate of the city by which he was
departing fully armed for battle? She is not alone (for that would not be
proper for a modest married woman) but has her maids with her, and she
carries in her arms young Astyanax, Hector's son, his father's dearly beloved, and (as Homer adds) 'fair as a lovely star,' hoping to sway her
husband's resolve through him. Hector smiles without saying anything
when he sees the child. Andromache stands close to him, puts out her right
hand, and calls him by name. Then after they have both said something in
keeping, Hector goes to take the child to kiss him, but the child is terrified
by the splendid armour and the plume nodding on top of the helmet, and
flings himself back screaming into his nurse's arms. The father and mother

* * * * *

6 Aristotle] *Rhetoric* 2.1–17
6 Quintilian] 6.2.8ff
7 The more violent ... use of them] Added in 1534 (LB I 108D)
17 Aristotle] See *Rhetoric* 1.11; 2.1–17.
17 Cicero] *De oratore* 2.217–90
18 Quintilian] 6.3.1ff, 37ff
18 The pleasure ... appropriate place] Text to 657:18 added in 1534 (LB I 108E–9C)
22 Homer] *Iliad* 6.369ff

both laugh; Hector removes his helmet, puts it on the ground, and then takes the boy in his arms and kisses him. After praying for a blessing on him, he hands him back to his mother; she takes him to her sweet-smelling bosom, δακρυόεν γελάσασα [smiling through her tears]. This stirs Hector's feeling for her, and putting his arm round his wife he speaks her name and comforts her. Then he puts his helmet on again. She does as her husband says and goes home, where the women fill the whole house with weeping because they are sure he will not return from that fight. Thus they mourn for him while he yet breathes.

Throughout this passage no little of the charm is due to the epithets: κορυθαίολος Ἕκτωρ [Hector of the flashing helm], οὗ παιδὸς ὀρέξατο φαίδιμος Ἕκτωρ [glorious Hector held out his arms for his child], ἐϋζώνοιο τιθήνης [his girdled nurse], λόφον ἱππιοχαίτην [horsehair plume], πατήρ τε φίλος καὶ πότνια μήτηρ [his dear father and lady mother], κόρυθα παμφανόωσαν [blazing casque], φίλον υἱὸν [darling child], ἀλόχοιο φίλης [beloved partner of his bed], κηώδει κόλπῳ [sweet-smelling bosom] (which I have already mentioned), and κόρυθα ἵππουριν [helmet with crest of horsehair].

It is this gift which is chiefly responsible for the fact that no one has ever had enough of Homer, but is led on by continual delight as he reads.

These are the emotions that Horace is talking about in the lines:

A play wherein the characters seem real,
Though little charm there be, no depth or skill,
Will pleasure give, and hold the people in their seats,
Far more than lines of substance empty,
Trifles melodious but thin.

Cicero has a number of famous accounts of this sort, like the one in the *Second Philippic* about Antony: 'In a carriage rode the tribune of the people, before him advanced the lictors, their fasces crowned with laurel, and in their midst carried in an open litter was an actress' (and so on – you know the passage well enough). There are others in the same speech, like the one where he brings a love letter to his mistress with a hood pulled over his head, or takes part in the running at the Lupercalia in spite of being consul.

Such accounts please when not only the actions but the gestures of the

* * * * *

10 epithets] *Iliad* 6.466ff
21 Horace] *Ars poetica* 319–22
29 Cicero] *Philippics* 2.58, 77, 84

LB I 108F

ᴅᴇꜱ· ᴇʀᴀꜱᴍɪ

ROTERODAMI, DE DVPLICI COPIA
Verborum ac Rerum Commentarij
duo multa accessione, nouisᷢ
formulis locupletati.

BASILEAE IN OFFICINA FROBENIANA

M. D. XXXIIII

Cum gratia & priuilegio Cęsareo

Title page of final authorized edition of *De copia*
Basel: Froben August 1534
Royal Library, Copenhagen

characters are described, as in this passage from *In Pisonem*: 'They were so cleverly and artistically written out that the treasury clerk who entered them, after writing up the accounts, scratched his head with his left hand and muttered to himself, "The accounts are clear enough, but the money's nowhere to be seen"'; or this one: 'You reply, with one eyebrow shooting up to your hair and the other coming down to your chin, that you have no taste for cruelty.'

Such details also serve to make what we are saying sound credible, since things put in that are not essential to the story have an air of ingenuousness. Quintilian admires this passage in Cicero's *Pro Milone*: 'Milo stayed in the Senate that day until the end of the session, went home, changed his sandals and clothes, waited – as one does – while his wife was getting ready ...'

There are also figures of speech relevant to this question of providing enjoyment. These can be discovered easily enough in the handbooks of rhetoric, and could not be discussed by us except at great length.

Allusions also give pleasure, but only to a person who recognizes them. They should therefore be introduced in the appropriate place.

Epilogue

And so the speaker who prefers that famous Laconic brevity must first of all do as Attic orators do, and eschew all introductory paragraphs and emotion-rousing passages. He must set out his matter in simple and summary form, and not use every argument, but only the leading ones, and these should not be deployed over a wide area, but brought up in close formation, so that the line of reasoning is carried more or less in single words, in case anyone should wish to set it out in extenso. He must be content merely to give information, and refrain from expansions, asseverations, similes, illustrative examples, maxims, acclamations, anecdotes, fables, allusions, and witty remarks, unless any of these is so essential that it would be a crime to leave it out. He must shun all figures that would make his speech sonorous, splendid, vehement, elaborate, or delightful. He must not treat the same material over and over again in different forms, and must express each idea in a single telling word, so that much more is understood than is actually heard, and one thing can be inferred from another.

* * * * *

1 *In Pisonem*] 61
5 this one] *In Pisonem* 14
10 Quintilian] 4.2.57; *Pro Milone* 28

On the other hand, the speaker who is pursuing the abundant style
will endeavour to expand his various sections in all the ways I have indicated.

A fault to be avoided on both sides

Both speakers however must take care not to fall into the related fault by
excessive straining after effect. The lover of brevity must not merely try to
say as little as possible, but to say the best things as briefly as possible. If he
fancies the Homeric phrase παῦρα μέν [briefly indeed], he should also
fancy what immediately follows, ἀλλὰ μάλα λιγέως [but very clearly]. If he
admires οὐ πολύμυθος [the man of few words], he should not forget what
comes next: οὐδ᾽ ἀφαμαρτοεπής [but never a wasted one]. Nothing befits
brevity better than elegance and appropriateness. If we find simplicity in
addition, the fault of obscurity, which very often accompanies the pursuit
of brevity, will be easily avoided. This same speaker must also take care that
his speech does not freeze into ineffectiveness while he is avoiding all
warmth of emotion. He will therefore have to set things before the eyes of
his audience in such a way that they silently and of themselves plant their
stings in the mind of the hearer, and he will have to season the whole with
Attic elegance.

It is of prime importance not to leave out essential things because of a
passion for brevity.

The practitioner of *copia* on the other hand must exercise choice in
vocabulary, subject-matter, expression. He must have no silly ideas, no
irrelevant examples, no flat maxims, no excessively long digressions at
inappropriate points, no strained and far-fetched figures of speech. He
must above all take due account of order and arrangement lest a mass of
unorganized material throw the whole speech into confusion and disorder.
Everywhere boredom must be relieved by variety, delight, laughter. Variety depends in particular on the use of figures, and so does delight; laughter
on the principles laid down by Cicero.

Neither should one neglect the possibilities of variety appropriate to
the various divisions. Accordingly it will be useful to have a good many
different opening formulae ready to hand. There are various ways of narrat-

* * * * *

11 Homeric phrase] These four all occur in *Iliad* 3.214–15.
20 plant their stings] Cf Cicero *De oratore* 3.138.
33 Cicero] See 654:17n.

LB I 110A

ing facts, and different methods of argument; neither are the emotions of one kind only, though you must read about these in the handbooks of rhetoric.

I would also advise you not to try to express yourself with equal fullness at all points, as some things are simply unproductive. So leaving aside the things that do not naturally lend themselves to fullness of expression, choose the most fertile and easily handled topics, unless of course one wants to try one's hand or demonstrate one's cleverness on occasion, and make an elephant out of a fly, as the saying goes. Thus Favorinus eulogized fever, Synesius baldness, myself folly (in my *Moriae encomium*), and I also extolled Aldus' anchor in the *Adagia*. In any case youth when training may be pardoned for letting the tree grow rather wild. But where it is no light-hearted matter but a grave and dangerous issue, the orator who has any sense will use discretion, and apportion his eloquence to suit the requirements of his case.

Peroration

I did have an example of a theme first handled concisely and then expanded and broadly treated, but I have not put it in lest the addition should prove too heavy a burden. The material may be found in the book dedicated to the illustrious young prince, William, duke of Cleves, and called *De pueris statim ac liberaliter instituendis.*

* * * * *

9 saying] *Adagia* I ix 69: 'Elephantum ex musca facis'

9 Favorinus] Sophist of the second century AD; none of his works are extant; the information is derived from Aulus Gellius 17.12.

10 Synesius] Orator and philosopher of the fourth century AD, who was converted to Christianity and became bishop of Ptolemais in Libya; he wrote several rhetorical pieces, including *Calvitii encomium*.

10 *Moriae encomium*] Published 1511

11 *Adagia*] II i 1: 'Festina lente'

18 Peroration] This peroration belongs to the final expanded form of *De copia* published by Froben in August 1534; the material referred to was published in 1529 as *De pueris instituendis* (text ed J.C. Margolin in ASD I-2 3–78). A further reason given by Erasmus for not including it in *De copia* as he originally intended was that the man to whom he had entrusted the manuscript in Rome for copying (William Thale: see Ep 244:7n) returned it incomplete (see Allen Ep 2189, the dedicatory letter to *De pueris instituendis*).

23 William] He was eighteen years old when this reference to him was printed.

ON THE METHOD OF STUDY

De ratione studii
ac legendi interpretandique auctores

translated and annotated by
BRIAN MCGREGOR

Praecipitat omnia 'He writes everything in a hurry': the celebrated self-critique, in the *Ciceronianus*,[1] of his literary style should not delude us into supposing that the thoughts which flowed with such apparent ease from the pen of Erasmus were the facile effusions of a shallow mind. The germination of the educational programme which finds its mature expression in *De ratione studii* can be traced back to Erasmus' letters of the years 1496–8, which he spent in Paris, where he was obliged to earn his living by giving lessons to Christian and Heinrich Northoff, the sons of a merchant from Lübeck, and to two Englishmen, Thomas Grey and Robert Fisher.[2] Several of the precepts and writers recommended to the attention of teacher and pupil in *De ratione studii* make their first appearance in these letters – and often in the order and language of the later work. We may assume, therefore, that Erasmus readily accepted the opportunity afforded by his correspondence in 1511 with John Colet, dean of St Paul's and founder of St Paul's School, of setting down in fuller detail, both for pattern and incitement, his views on the method of study which the student of the classics should follow.

De ratione studii ac legendi interpretandique auctores liber, to give the work its full title, was first printed in an abridged form by G. Biermans at Paris for Jean Granjon, and published there in October 1511 in a volume which also included a collection of letters by the Italian humanist Agostino Dati. This version of the text omits passages quoted in the correspondence with Colet of September 1511. As these passages were to appear in the 1512 and subsequent authorized editions, it is almost certain that Granjon's edition was brought out without Erasmus' consent. The edition of 1512, incorporating the material from the Colet correspondence, was published by Josse Bade in Paris (July), then by Thierry Martens in Louvain (September). It is upon these and subsequent editions authorized by Erasmus, in particular the revised August 1514 edition of Matthias Schürer published in Strasbourg, that the attempt to reconstruct the author's autograph is based.[3]

The style of *De ratione studii*, like that of Erasmus' other educational treatises, is characteristically *tumultuarius* 'breathless,' yet lucid and straightforward in its syntax. Among typical features of his Latinity we may

* * * * *

1 LB I 1013E
2 See Epp 54, 56, 58, 61, 62, 63, 64, 66 and their introductions. For Ep 66, which served as a preface to *De ratione studii*, see below 665.
3 On the history of the text see J.-C. Margolin's introduction to his critical edition, ASD I-2 83–109. The abridged version (1511) is printed in ASD I-2 147–51. The present translation is based on the ASD text, which is that of the August 1514 (Strasbourg: Schürer) edition.

note the following examples: a penchant for the use of diminutives, for example, *chartula, pauculi, flosculi, narratiuncula, notula*; a preference for the Silver Latin *ceu* 'as' or 'like'; the use of *modo ut* for *dummodo, simul et* for *simul ac*; frequent use of *siquidem* for 'since'; *sed* as a variant of *et*, in the style of Sallust; a readiness to employ the rare word drawn from his wide knowledge of the full range of Latin literature, for example, *balbuties, caecutire*, and his use of the Roman legal term *postliminio*; the use of the impersonal third person singular of the passive, for example, *si id hominis ingenio negatum est*; the occasional pun implicit in the word *infans* – both 'inarticulate baby' and 'incompetent orator.' Erasmus' attitude towards the language is summarized in his advice to the young to take Terence as a standard because he is 'closest to everyday speech.'[4] He is concerned above all with preserving the vitality of Latin as a living language. Like Lorenzo Valla, he is prepared to exploit the full range of the language to achieve this end.

The content as well as the style of *De ratione studii* is heavily indebted to the *Institutio oratoria* of Quintilian, but Erasmus, unlike Quintilian, is confronted by a crucial issue: the relation of Christian to classical culture.[5] Erasmus shares the humanist objective of re-creating the past in its totality, or as far as the ravages of time permit. To see the past as it really was, to absorb its categories of thought, to appreciate its artistic canons, requires the closest critical attention to its literary and material remains. We may refine our pleasure in reading the various authors of antiquity by applying the techniques of analysis and comparison as laid down by Quintilian and endorsed by Erasmus, yet there remain for the Christian reader grave moral dangers in the subject-matter of much of pagan literature. We may note Erasmus' passing remark on the need to censor certain passages in Plautus if he is to be used by the young. The exegesis[6] of the second *Eclogue* of Virgil with its reliance on extensive allegorical interpretation is an explicit example of the same concern: the moral dangers inherent in classical literature when imbibed without the prophylactic of Christian theology. Similar sentiments are to be found in St Basil, writing on the value of Greek literature in the fourth century AD. In the twentieth century we find the problem formulated in the following remarks by one whose concern for the classical tradition and whose commitment to Christianity were as profound as Erasmus': 'In ages like our own ... it is the

* * * * *

4 See below 669:10n.
5 On this issue see *Antibarbari* in CWE 23 passim.
6 Below 683:25ff

more necessary for Christian readers to scrutinise their reading, especially of works of imagination, with explicit ethical and theological standards. The "greatness" of literature cannot be determined solely by literary standards; though we must remember that whether it is literature or not can be determined only by literary standards.'[7] The reader's response to such a proposition will, in part, determine his evaluation of *De ratione studii*.

B MCG

* * * * *

7 T.S. Eliot 'Religion and Literature' in *Selected Essays* 3rd ed (London 1951) 388

My sweetest [Thale] you have indeed foreseen with skill, and now state
with truth and dignity, that it matters enormously what plan and order one
applies to each action; and that the importance of this consideration, great
as it is in all activities, is particularly so in literary studies. Do we not ob-   5
serve that skill makes easily possible the lifting of huge weights, which otherwise no degree of force could move? Similarly, in warfare it does not matter
so much how large your forces are, or how massive your attack, as how good
your dispositions are and what order you maintain in the battle. And those
who are familiar with short cuts reach their destination much sooner than   10
those who take the river-bank or the shoreline as their guide, as Plautus
remarks. You ask me accordingly to lay down for you an ordered course of
study so that, following it like Theseus' thread, you may be able to find your
way in the labyrinths of letters. I shall certainly be happy to obey, as far
as in me lies, the wish of a friend so dear to me that I could not possibly   15
deny him any request, much less one so useful and honourable as this.

    ... This, my dear Leucophaeus, is what I had to write to you for the
moment on the method of study. Use it, if you like it; but if you do not,
at least take my diligent efforts in good part. Only go on as you have begun,
and confer lustre on your distinguished birth by equal prowess in letters.   20
Farewell.

    [London, 15 March]

    * * * * *

1 Erasmus ... to his friend] Ep 66 (Paris? 1497?). First printed as the preface to *De
ratione studii*, which was originally composed for Thomas Grey, as is indicated
by the name Leucophaeus (line 17), a Greek translation of 'grey' (cf Ep 221:39).
It was apparently among the papers entrusted to William Thale in Ferrara in
1509 (cf Ep 30:17n). Thale, on returning to Paris, had it printed, substituting
his own name for Grey's in the preface. He did not, however, have sufficient
knowledge of Greek to detect the significance of Leucophaeus and so left it
unchanged. When Erasmus published *De ratione studii* in an authorized
edition, together with the *De copia* (Paris: J. Bade, 15 July 1512), he replaced
Thale's name with that of Pierre Vitré and changed Leucophaeus to 'mi Petre.'
Pierre Vitré (Latin, Viterius) was a close friend of Grey and may have succeeded Erasmus as his tutor (cf Ep 58:204n).
11 Plautus] Cf *Poenulus* 627–8; *Adagia* II vii 81.
14 labyrinths] Cf *Adagia* II x 51.

ON THE METHOD OF STUDY

In principle, knowledge as a whole seems to be of two kinds, of things and
of words. Knowledge of words comes earlier, but that of things is the more   5
important. But some, the 'uninitiated' as the saying goes, while they hurry
on to learn about things, neglect a concern for language and, striving after a
false economy, incur a very heavy loss. For since things are learnt only by
the sounds we attach to them, a person who is not skilled in the force of
language is, of necessity, short-sighted, deluded, and unbalanced in his   10
judgment of things as well. Finally you may observe that none are more
given to constant quibbling over the minutiae of language than those who
boast that they pass over mere words and concentrate on the matter itself.
Accordingly the best in each category must be learnt at once and, moreover,
learnt from the best teachers. For what could be more foolish than to learn at 15
great effort something that you are subsequently compelled to 'unlearn' at
even greater? Nothing to be sure is acquired more easily than what is right
and true. But once bad habits get a grip on a character, it is remarkable how
they cannot be eradicated.

* * * * *

4 of things and of words] To sophisticated readers this phrase would have
recalled a more complex subject than pedagogy or curricula. 'Things and
words' suggests or describes a topic that had been debated by philosophers
for centuries: the question of universals, the reality of genera and species. The
question descended from Plato (*Cratylus* and *Republic*) and Aristotle (his
writings on logic and the *Metaphysics*) through Porphyry (*Isagoge*), Augustine
(cf *De doctrina christiana* 1.2, 2.1–3) and Boethius (on Porphyry's *Isagoge*) to
Abelard and his successors.
In *De duplici copia verborum ac rerum*, where Erasmus is concerned not with
metaphysics or formal logic but with effectiveness and variety in communication, with rhetoric, he discusses both abundance of expression (book I) and
abundance of subject-matter (book II). The opening sentence of *De ratione
studii* reminds us that things and words, objects (of thought or experience) and
language, comprise the whole of knowledge. Hence it is not surprising that *De
ratione studii* contains echoes of *De copia* and allusions to it.
References to *De copia* in the notes are to the translation in this volume.
6 'uninitiated'] Literally 'with unwashed feet' (Erasmus quotes the Greek in the
text), a proverbial expression used to characterize precipitate or immature
action; *Adagia* I ix 54. Erasmus traces the derivation of the expression from the
religious practice of washing and purifying things to be used in sacred
ceremonies. The religious tone of the metaphor with its implicit stress on
piety as a prerequisite for the Christian pupil's approach to learning is characteristic of the author's philosophy of education and helps set the tenor of the
programme he now proceeds to outline.
14 learnt at once] Quintilian 2.3.2

Grammar, therefore, claims primacy of place and at the outset boys must be instructed in two – Greek, of course, and Latin. This is not only because almost everything worth learning is set forth in these two languages, but in addition because each is so cognate to the other that both can be more quickly assimilated when they are taken in conjunction than one without the other, or at least Latin without Greek. Quintilian prefers us to begin with Greek, with the proviso that, once it has been acquired, Latin is to follow after a short time. To be sure he cautions that equal care must be devoted to each. 'And in this way,' he says, 'neither should hinder the other.' Accordingly the rudiments of both languages must be assimilated, and without delay, and from a really good teacher. If the teacher is not available, then (as the next best thing) the best authors must certainly be used. Personally, I should like them to be very limited in number but carefully chosen. Among the Greek grammarians everyone assigns first place to Theodorus Gaza; Constantine Lascaris, in my opinion, rightly lays claim to second place. Among the ancient Latinists there is Diomedes; among the more recent I see little to choose, save that Niccolò Perotti appears the most painstaking, but this side of pedantry. But just as I admit that examples of the above sort are necessary, so I should like them to be very few, provided that they are of the best. Nor have I ever agreed with the common run of teachers who, in inculcating these authors, hold boys back for several years.

* * * * *

6 Quintilian] 1.1.12. In *The Governour* (1531) Sir Thomas Elyot advised that Greek and Latin be taken up at the same time, but the ordinary practice in Renaissance schools was to begin with Latin.

15 Theodorus Gaza] A Greek scholar (c 1400–78) who taught for many years in Italy. His Greek grammar was published at Venice in 1495. Erasmus translated two books of this (Louvain 1516, 1518; text in LB I 117–64; and see Ep 428 and Allen Ep 771).

15 Lascaris] 1434–1501. One of the Greek exiles who came to Italy after the fall of Constantinople in 1453, he taught Greek at Milan and Naples. His Greek grammar appeared in 1476; it was the first book printed in Greek type. On the role of Theodorus, Lascaris, and other Greeks in early Italian humanism see *New Cambridge Modern History* I (1957) 95–126; L.D. Reynolds and N.G. Wilson *Scribes and Scholars* (Oxford 1968).

16 Diomedes] Grammarian of the fourth century AD

17 Niccolò Perotti] 1430–80. Famous philologist and secretary to Cardinal Bessarion, and thus a member of the literary circle which included Theodorus Gaza and Lascaris. He was the author of the *Rudimenta grammatices* (Rome 1473), the first modern Latin grammar. On the significance of the Greek exiles in Italy in the early Renaissance and of Bessarion's circle in particular see D.J. Geanakoplos *Greek Scholars in Venice* (Cambridge, Mass 1962).

Characters in Terence's *Eunuchus*
From *Terentius, cum directorio vocabulorum, sententiarum, artis comice, glosa …*
comentariis … (Strasbourg: Grüniger 1499), fol XXVIII[v]
In 1532 Erasmus wrote, in the preface to an edition, that of all authors Terence is the
best, as well as the most enjoyable, for learning clear and correct Latin style
(Allen Ep 2584:70–2).
Reproduced by permission of the Thomas Fisher Rare Book Library,
University of Toronto

For a true ability to speak correctly is best fostered both by conversing and consorting with those who speak correctly and by the habitual reading of the best stylists. Among the latter the first to be imbibed should be those whose diction, apart from its refinement, will also entice learners by a certain charm of subject-matter. In this category I would assign first place to 5 Lucian, second to Demosthenes, and third to Herodotus; again, among the poets, first place to Aristophanes, second to Homer, third to Euripides. For Menander, to whom I would have given even the first place, is not extant. Again, among Latin writers who is more valuable as a standard of language than Terence? He is pure, concise, and closest to everyday speech and then, 10 by the very nature of his subject-matter, is also congenial to the young. Should someone think that a few, selected comedies of Plautus, free from impropriety, should be added to the above, I would personally not demur. Second place will go to Virgil, third to Horace, fourth to Cicero, and fifth to Caesar. If someone thinks that Sallust should be included, I would not offer 15 much objection. These, then, I believe to be sufficient for a knowledge of each language. For I have no time for those who, in thumbing through any author you can think of with this end in view, waste an entire lifetime, considering in effect a person a mere beginner who has missed any work – however minor. 20

Having, therefore, developed a pure, if not ornate, skill in language, we must next direct the mind towards an understanding of things. Of course some considerable knowledge of things as well as of words is acquired in passing, from these writers whom we read in order to refine our language, but traditionally almost all knowledge of things is to be sought in 25 the Greek authors. For in short, whence can one draw a draught so pure, so easy, and so delightful as from the very fountain-head? But perhaps it would be more appropriate for me to indicate elsewhere the order in which the branches of knowledge should be learnt and from which masters in particular. Let us meanwhile return to the studies of early youth. 30

In order, then, that you may acquire an earlier and fuller enrichment

* * * * *

6 Lucian] On Erasmus' interest in Lucian see *De copia* 603:17n. His translations of Lucian and Euripides are reprinted in ASD I.

8 Menander] Most of his work has perished, but Erasmus would have been aware of his high reputation through his reading of ancient authors and critics, by whom some of the poet's lines were preserved.

10 Terence] Always a favourite with Erasmus who, according to Beatus Rhenanus, knew him by heart (Allen I 55:84, 70:540–1). He produced an edition in 1532; in the prefatory letter to this he praises Terence very warmly as a standard of diction and an author for boys (Allen Ep 2584:70ff).

31 enrichment] *copia*

from the writers from whom, I have said, a treasury of language is to be sought, I believe that you should diligently study Lorenzo Valla, the extremely elegant arbiter of elegant Latin. Aided by his precepts you will notice much for yourself; for I would not like you to follow Valla's precepts slavishly in everything. It will be an additional aid if you learn off the 5 grammatical figures set out by Donatus and Diomedes; memorize the rules of poetry and all its patterns; have at your fingertips the chief points of rhetoric, namely propositions, the grounds of proof, figures of speech, amplifications, and the rules governing transitions. For these are conducive not only to criticism but also to imitation. 10

Informed then by all this you will carefully observe when reading writers whether any striking word occurs, if diction is archaic or novel, if some argument shows brilliant invention or has been skilfully adapted from elsewhere, if there is any brilliance in the style, if there is any adage, historical parallel, or maxim worth committing to memory. Such a passage 15 should be indicated by some appropriate mark. For not only must a variety of marks be employed but appropriate ones at that, so that they will immediately indicate their purpose. If someone should decide that dialectic be added to the above I shall not gainsay him much, provided that he learn his dialectic from Aristotle and not from that prolix breed, the sophists. 20

* * * * *

2 Lorenzo Valla] 1407–57. Italian humanist whose *Elegantiae linguae latinae* sought to restore contemporary Latin to the purity of classical usage. First published in 1471, it had already run to over sixty editions before 1550. See F. Buisson *Répertoire des ouvrages pédagogiques du XVIe siècle* (Paris 1886). For Valla himself see G. Mancini *Vita di Lorenzo Valla* (Florence 1891). On Erasmus' epitome of Valla's *Elegantiae* see Ep 23:108n. A critical edition of this *Epitome* is included in ASD I-4 191–351.

6 Donatus] Notably in his *Commentarius in Terentium*. Aelius Donatus was a Latin grammarian of the fourth century AD and author of an *Ars grammatica*. His literary survival was to a large extent the result of his being incorporated into the medieval scheme of personification of the Seven Liberal Arts as the exemplar of Grammar (for which he vies with Priscian).

6 Diomedes] Above 667:16n

7 chief points of rhetoric] On these terms see *De copia* above: propositions 595–605, 650–3; grounds of proof (commonplaces) 605ff, 637ff; figures 333–42; amplifications 437, 507; transitions 410, 648ff.

14 adage … parallel] Erasmus collected these in his *Adagia* and *Parabolae*.

15 maxim] *De copia* 627:11 ff, 630:7ff.

20 the sophists] The sophists emerge in Greece during the fifth century BC to meet the needs of the politically ambitious in the nascent democracies where vote-winning through persuasive oratory was essential to gaining political power. It was the sophists' claim to be able to teach men the art of expressing their ideas in the most plausible manner, without entering into any ethical

Nor, again, should he rest at that point and (to quote Gellius) pass into old age by the rocks of the Sirens.

But meanwhile, bear in mind that the best master of style is the pen and you must therefore give it plenty of practice in poetry, prose, and every sort of literary material. We must not neglect memory, the storehouse of our reading. Although I do not deny that memory is aided by 'places' and 'images,' nevertheless the best memory is based on three things above all: understanding, system, and care. For memory largely consists in having thoroughly understood something. Then system sees to it that we can recall by an act of recovery even what we have once forgotten. Furthermore, care is of the highest importance, not only here but in all things. That being so you must repeatedly re-read very carefully what you want to remember. Next, we must regularly tax ourselves with its recall so that if something happens to elude us it can be reinstated. The following is a small point but one well worth making. It will be of considerable help if you take things which it is necessary but rather difficult to remember – place-names in geography for instance, metrical feet, grammatical figures, genealogies, and so forth – and have them written as briefly and attractively as possible on charts and hung up on the walls of a room where they are generally conspicuous even to those engaged on something else. In the same way you will write some brief but pithy sayings such as aphorisms, proverbs, and maxims at the beginning and at the end of your books; others you will inscribe on rings or drinking cups; others you will paint on doors and walls or even in the glass of a window so that what may aid learning is constantly before the eye. For, although these measures seem trivial in themselves when taken singly, yet taken together they make a profitable addition to the

* * * * *

discussion of the nature of the ideas, which accounted for their notoriety (see the *Clouds* of Aristophanes) and also for their initial success. Later sophists often became absorbed in pointless debates on matters of style. Hence Erasmus' gibe about their prolixity.

1 Gellius] 16.8.17

3 best master of style] Quintilian 10.3.1, from Cicero *De oratore* 1.150 and 257

6 'places' and 'images'] The places and images impressed on the memory as an aid to instant recall were the key to the ancient art of 'artificial memory.' See H. Caplan's edition (Loeb Classical Library) of *Ad Herennium* 3.16.28–40. For a detailed account of artificial memory and Renaissance attitudes towards it see Frances A. Yates *The Art of Memory* (London 1966). As his remarks in *De ratione studii* show, Erasmus was sceptical about its claims. See also his *Ars notoria* (Thompson *Colloquies* 458–61).

23 paint on doors and walls] As is done in the house of Eusebius in *Convivium religiosum* (Thompson *Colloquies* 46–78).

treasury of knowledge – a factor not to be passed over by someone striving
to be enriched by these resources. Finally, if you should often be teaching
others also, then that will lead not only to one of our objectives, but to all of
them at once. For there is no better means of grasping what you understand
and what you do not. Sometimes new ideas occur to one in preparing a   5
lesson, and everything is more firmly fixed in the mind when teaching.

On the method of teaching pupils

10

But I see that you want me to make some observations on the method of
teaching as well. Very well, let Vitré's wish be granted, although I see that
Quintilian has left a very thorough treatment of these matters, so that it
would seem the height of impertinence to write about a subject he has
already dealt with. Well then: he who wishes to instruct someone will be   15
careful from the beginning to teach only the best, but he who is to teach
what is best most correctly must, it follows, be omniscient; or, since this is
denied to human understanding, he should at least know the fundamentals
of each discipline. In this I shall not be content with the usual ten or twelve
authors but will demand the proverbial 'encyclopaedia' so that even some-   20
one who is preparing to teach a very little is very widely read. He must,
therefore, range through the entire spectrum of writers so that he reads, in
particular, all the best, but does not fail to sample any author, no matter
how pedestrian. And in order to enhance the value of that exercise, he
should have at the ready some commonplace book of systems and topics, so   25
that wherever something noteworthy occurs he may write it down in the
appropriate column. I have indicated how this ought to be done in the

* * * * *

  1 striving to be enriched] Cf Hesiod *Works and Days* 24. Erasmus quotes the
    Greek.
12 Vitré's] For the little that is known of Pierre Vitré (Viterius), to whom *De*
    ratione studii is dedicated, see Ep 66 introduction.
13 Quintilian] Bks 1 and 2
20 proverbial 'encyclopaedia'] As the immediately prior remarks indicate, Eras-
    mus is thinking not of encyclopaedic knowledge in a modern sense but rather
    of the ἐγκύκλιος παιδεία or traditional range of subjects which constituted a
    general education for the ancients. In the Middle Ages this scheme became
    standardized in the Seven Liberal Arts, comprising the trivium (grammar,
    rhetoric, dialectic) and the quadrivium (geometry, arithmetic, astronomy,
    and music).
26 in the appropriate column] Erasmus is here advocating the use of the 'com-
    monplace book,' in which Courage, Danger, Economy, and so forth were each

second part of my *De copia*. But if someone suffers from a lack of time or books, Pliny alone will furnish an immense amount of information, Macrobius and Athanaeus much, and Gellius a variety of things. First and foremost, however, recourse must be had to the sources themselves, that is, to the Greeks and the ancients. Plato, Aristotle, and his pupil Theophrastus will serve as the best teachers of philosophy, and then there is Plotinus who combines both these schools. Among theological writers, after the Scriptures, no one writes better than Origen, no one more subtly or attractively than Chrysostom, no one more devoutly than Basil. Among the Latin Fathers, two at least are outstanding in this field: Ambrose who is wonderfully rich in metaphors, and Jerome who is immensely learned in the sacred Scriptures. If you lack the time to dwell on them individually, I nonetheless recommend that they should all be savoured. But for the present it is not my intention to compile a comprehensive list. Certainly in an exposition of the poets, who are accustomed to flavour their compositions with knowledge drawn from every quarter, you must command a good supply of mythology, and from whom is it better to seek this than Homer, the father of all myth? But the *Metamorphoses* and *Fasti* of Ovid, although written in Latin, are of no small importance. Geography too, which is useful in history, not to mention poetry, must also be mastered. This is dealt with most succinctly by Pomponius Mela, most eruditely by Ptolemy, and most comprehensively by Pliny. For Strabo does not write on this exclusively. Here the main object is to have observed which of the vernacular words for mountains, rivers, regions, and cities correspond to the ancient. A similar care must be

* * * * *

allocated a page to which were added apposite texts gleaned from one's reading.

1 second part of my *De copia*] See 635–48.

2 Pliny] the Elder Pliny, author of the *Naturalis historia*

8 Origen ... Chrysostom] See Allen Epp 1844; 1558:171ff; 1800:81ff.

9 Basil] St Basil (c 330–79 AD) had also written on Greek literature for the young, and this work provides some interesting insights into Erasmus' concerns in *De ratione studii*. See N.G. Wilson ed *St Basil on the Value of Greek Literature* (London 1975).

10 Ambrose] Allen Ep 1855

11 sacred Scriptures] Erasmus may intend here the apocryphal as well as canonical scriptures. Jerome gave attention to both; he introduced the term 'Apocrypha.'

21 Pomponius Mela] He wrote, in Latin, a geographical survey of the world (first century AD).

22 Strabo] A Greek scholar (c 64 BC–21 AD) who wrote on both history and geography, but his *Geography* alone has survived.

LB I 523B / ASD I-2 120

shown for the names of trees, plants, animals, tools, clothes, and precious
stones, of which, incredible as it sounds, the common run of teachers
knows absolutely nothing. A list of these objects can be collected from the
different authors who have written on agriculture, military science, ar-
chitecture, cooking, minerals, plants, and the nature of animals. Although   5
Julius Pollux has professedly written on things and their names, I only wish
the distinctions he draws had matched in accuracy the richness of his
material. It can also be drawn, in part, from etymologies and partly from
these languages which preserve to this very day the clear traces of the
ancient, pure language. I have in mind the Greek of Constantinople, and   10
also Italian and Spanish, for French has degenerated further than the rest.
We must hold fast to the knowledge of antiquity which is culled not only
from ancient authors but also from old coins, inscriptions, and stones. The
genealogy of the gods must also be learnt, since stories from every source
are full of them. After Hesiod, Boccaccio dealt with the genealogy, with   15
more elegance than one would expect from the age in which he lived.
Astronomy must not be passed over, especially that of Hyginus, since
the poets liberally sprinkle their creations with it. The nature and essence

* * * * *

  6 Julius Pollux] He compiled (second century AD) an *Onomasticon* or thesaurus
     in Greek but included also quotations covering a wide range of topics, as
     Erasmus mentions. See Ep 260:52–6.
13 coins, inscriptions] For the study of coins and inscriptions during the Renais-
     sance see R. Weiss *The Renaissance Discovery of Classical Antiquity* (Oxford
     1969) chaps 11, 12, and the corresponding bibliographies. A celebrated exam-
     ple of the use of coins as historical evidence, and one which Erasmus would
     certainly have in mind, is to be found in Lorenzo Valla's *De falso credita et
     ementita Constantini donatione declamatio* (1440), where it was argued that the
     absence of any reference to the Donation of Constantine on papal coins or
     medals was a forceful *argumentum ex silentio* that no such gift took place. See
     the Teubner text of the *Donatio* ed W. Schwahn (Leipzig 1928) 9.32. For the
     relationship between the revival of classical literature and the revival of the
     visual arts in general as seen by the humanists themselves see the preface to
     the *Elegantiae* of Lorenzo Valla mentioned above.
15 Boccaccio] In his *De genealogia deorum gentilium* (c 1472), an encyclopaedic
     work which sought to bring together the diffuse but interlocking relation-
     ships of the deities and heroes of classical antiquity, and as such became a
     bridge between the mythology of the Middle Ages and that of the Renais-
     sance. See J. Seznec *The Survival of the Pagan Gods* trans Barbara F. Sessions
     (New York 1953) passim.
17 Hyginus] The reference is to the *Poeticon astronomicon libri IV* (*editio princeps*
     Ferrara 1475) attributed to one Hyginus, to whose name editors, apparently
     without any manuscript authority, prefixed the additional designation C.
     Julius (the celebrated freedman of Augustus who had become head of the

of everything must be grasped, especially since it is from this source that they are accustomed to draw their similes, epithets, comparisons, images, metaphors, and other rhetorical devices of that kind. Above all, however, history must be grasped. Its application is very widespread and not confined to the poets. Or again, if a man wishes to expound Prudentius, the one really stylish poet among Christian authors, he must also be skilled in the secrets of Scripture. In short, there is no branch of knowledge, whether military, agricultural, musical, or architectural, which is not useful for those who have undertaken an exposition of the ancient poets or orators. But I see that you have been frowning for some time. Truly, you say, you place an immense burden on a mere elementary teacher. Agreed, but I place it on one person so as to remove it from as many as possible. I would have one man read it all, rather than have everyone read everything.

Now Quintilian has dealt thoroughly with the correct formation of boys' spoken language and with the method akin to play or sport by which the shape of the letters should be imparted. After the first elements have been imparted I should personally prefer a boy to be encouraged to practise speaking right from the start. For since young children can pronounce any language, however barbarous, within months, is there any reason why the same thing should not occur in Greek or Latin? But there is no scope for this in a large crowd of boys and it requires the private company of a teacher. Still, even in a school the teacher will be careful to speak as correctly as possible, whether conversing with several boys or with one alone. He should explain things in passing and encourage them to imitate him. He should, on occasion, compliment them when they express themselves particularly well or correct them when they go wrong. Such a practice will produce in them also the habit of speaking with greater care and precision and a more attentive regard for the teacher when he is speaking. It will be an additional aid if, as an incentive, a quasi-legal code of rewards and punishments be devised so that the boys themselves correct one another. Furthermore the teacher should choose some of the more advanced pupils to sum up an argument. It will be time well spent to lay down some

* * * * *

Palatine library). The crudities and barbarisms of the work are such that no scholar now believes that in its present shape it could be attributed to a man renowned for his erudition.

2 similes ... metaphors] On similes see *De copia* 337:8ff, 587:10, 616:9–10, 635:21ff, 641:5ff; on epithets 579:15ff, 590:23ff; on comparisons 579:12–14, 593:6ff, 616:6ff, 624:22ff, 630:6ff, 635:19ff; on parallels 621:1; on images 623:18ff, 642:22ff; on metaphors 333:1ff, 335:1ff. See also General Index.

5 Prudentius] Erasmus wrote commentaries on two of his poems (LB V 1338–58).
14 Quintilian] 1.1.11, 24–6

guidelines for boys as to the sort of speech they should employ at play, in company, and at meal times. These ought to be well informed, yet easy and agreeable. In addition my industrious, learned, and acute teacher will not shun collecting all the precepts of the grammarians, selecting the simplest and briefest as far as this is possible and arranging them in the most 5 suitable order.

After those have been imparted the boys should, without delay, be directed to the study of an author who is most suitable for the purpose, and to the habit of speaking and writing. At this stage the teacher will carefully drive home the points previously made, together with their examples, to 10 which he will add some of his own, preparing even now as it were for more advanced studies. From this point they should be trained in topics. In these one should avoid above all the common mistake of having topics vacuous in content or dull in form; they should have a certain point or charm which is not too remote from youthful capabilities, so that while they are concentrat- 15 ing on something else, they will learn material relevant to higher studies. He should, therefore, have a theme or memorable historical episode to set before the boys. For instance: the rash self-confidence of Marcellus under- mined the Roman state; the prudent delaying tactics of Fabius restored it. Although here there is also an underlying general principle that over-hasty 20 schemes seldom turn out well. Likewise: it would be difficult to decide who was the sillier, Crates who threw his gold into the sea, or Midas who held it to be the supreme good. In similar vein: the unrestrained eloquence of Demosthenes and Cicero was their undoing. Again: no praise can match the merits of King Codrus, who considered that the citizens' safety should 25 be redeemed at the cost of his own life. But it would be no great trouble to collect a number of examples of this type from the historians, in particular Valerius Maximus. Or he should employ mythology, for example: Hercules won immortality for himself by vanquishing monsters; or the Muses take special delight in springs and groves and shun the smoky cities. Or he 30

* * * * *

1 guidelines] As is done in the earliest *formulae* in the *Colloquies* (555ff), and cf *De civilitate* 1530 (LB I 1033–44).

10 examples] See *De copia* 606:26ff.

14 a certain point or charm] See *De copia* 627:11ff on *sententiae* or maxims.

18 Marcellus] Marcus Claudius Marcellus (third century BC), a famous Roman general who fought against the Gauls and later in the First Punic War

19 delaying tactics of Fabius] Quintus Fabius Maximus, who earned his title of 'cunctator' (the delayer) by his policy, when dictator of Rome, of constantly harassing Hannibal without engaging him in a set battle. He forms one of the subjects of Plutarch's *Lives*.

25 Codrus] Last of the legendary kings of Athens, who is said to have sacrificed himself for his country when invasion threatened it from the Peloponnesians

should make use of a fable; for example: the lark was correct to teach that one should not entrust to a friend business which one can finish by oneself. Likewise: everyone sees the wallet which hangs in front of him, while nobody sees the one he carries behind him. So too: the fox showed cunning in preferring to retain the flies which were by this time almost sated, rather than to shake them off and allow on him those which were ravenous and thirsty to suck what remained of his blood. Or he should employ the apophthegm; for example: that he who preferred a man for himself rather than for his money was far out of step with the common values of our age. Or again: Socrates rightly condemned those who do not eat to live but live to eat; Cato was quite right in disapproving of those whose palate is more refined than their intellect. Or the proverb, such as: let the cobbler stick to his last; and it is not for everyone to sail to Corinth. Since I have published so many adages it should not be difficult to come by examples. Or he should employ the aphorism: for instance, nothing costs more than what is got by begging; and flattery begets friendship, truth hatred; and distant friends are no friends. Other themes may be suggested by the special properties of something, such as: the magnet draws iron to itself, naphtha fire. Likewise: such is the nature of the palm tree that, when weighted down, far from sinking to the ground, it strives upwards and raises itself up higher. So too the astonishing ability of the cuttle-fish which changes its colour to merge with the sea-bed in order to evade the fisherman's net. Or consider that striking figure of speech, climax: riches beget luxury, luxury excess, excess cruelty, cruelty widespread hatred, hatred destruction. Or the simile: just as iron is worn away by use, yet if not used it is eaten away by rust, so ability is consumed by over-working, yet if not exercised it is further atrophied by disuse and neglect. Or the metaphor, for example: fire should not be fought with fire, nor oil poured on troubled waters. Or chiasmus,

* * * * *

1 the lark] Aulus Gellius 2.29

3 wallet] Cf Catullus 22.21 and Phaedrus 4.10.1.

8 apophthegm] Erasmus published a collection of apophthegms, in eight books, in 1531 (LB IV 93–380).

10 Socrates] Cf *Apophthegmata* (LB IV 160C).

11 Cato] *Apophthegmata* (LB IV 260–2 passim)

12 cobbler] *Adagia* I vi 16

13 sail to Corinth] *Adagia* I iv 1; see *De copia* 295:10n. This and the adage in the preceding line were favourites of Erasmus.

15 got by begging] See *De copia* 444:4n.

16 flattery begets friendship] Cf Terence *Andria* 68.

16 truth hatred] *Adagia* II ix 53

16 distant friends are no friends] *Adagia* II iii 86

18 magnet … palm … cuttle-fish] *Adagia* I vii 56, I iii 4, II iii 91

such as: it is not because I am exceptionally fond of you that I consider you
to be such a person, but because I consider you to be such a person that I am
exceptionally fond of you. Or rhetorical division, for example: he is too
stupid to be capable of silence, too childish to be capable of speech. He is
too ingenuous to be capable of lying, too dignified to wish to lie. But it is   5
sufficient on my part merely to have pointed the way. Or he should use
some choice turn of phrase, of which no example is necessary. There is
nothing to prevent several apt literary devices such as the aphorism, the
historical example, the proverb, and figurative language from occurring in
the same speech. Accordingly, the teacher, who should be well versed in   10
the best authorities, will compile a small widely chosen anthology of this
sort and will present such selections, or will even adapt them to a form
suitable to boys' abilities.

After the boy has acquired some degree of skill in speaking by these
methods, he should then, if it seems opportune, be referred to the more   15
advanced stages of grammar, which should be imparted by some scheme of
arrangement and systematization, in such a way that in the first place the
simplest are set out, and briefly at that. Then, as the learners' talents
mature, so will it be necessary to introduce all the more advanced rules in
order. The model for such a system may be taken from the Grammar of   20
Theodorus Gaza. I should not, however, like them to be detained overlong
on this but to be referred, next, to weightier authorities, especially if they
have already grasped that outline of rhetoric of which I have spoken,
together with figures of speech and the forms of poetry. Meanwhile they
should be trained in more difficult exercises also, in the selection and   25
teaching of which they will require a diligent and well-informed teacher. If
he should be of moderate ability but also modest, he will not object to
seeking these exercises from someone more learned. The form of the exercises can generally be as follows. At one time he should set out the
subject-matter of a short but expressive letter in the vernacular which has to   30
be construed in Latin or Greek or both. On another occasion he should set a
fable, on another a short but meaningful narrative, on another an aphorism
composed of four parts, with a comparison between each of the two parts or
with an accompanying reason attached to each. At one time the adducing of
proofs should be dealt with in its five parts, at another the dilemma in two,   35

* * * * *

21 Theodorus] See above 667:15n.
30 letter] On letter-writing see Erasmus' *De conscribendis epistolis* 1521, 1522 (LB I
   345–484; ASD I-2 157–579).
32 aphorism ... of four parts] *De copia* 628:1–7
35 five parts] *Ad Herennium* 2.18.28

at another what is called *expolitio* or refinement should be developed in its
seven parts. Sometimes, as a prelude to rhetoric, the pupils should deal
with one of the parts separately. Aphthonius has written rhetorical exercises of this sort. Sometimes they ought to deal with praise, censure,
mythology, simile, comparison; sometimes with a figure of speech, or 5
description, division, impersonation, rhetorical question and answer, signification. They should be regularly instructed to turn verse into prose and
at different times to put prose into verse. From time to time they should
imitate in vocabulary and style a letter of Pliny or Cicero. Sometimes they
should express, again and again, the same proposition in different words 10
and style. Sometimes they should vary the expression of the same proposition in Greek and Latin, in verse and prose. Sometimes they should express
the same proposition in five or six kinds of metre which the teacher has
prescribed. Sometimes they should recast the same proposition in as many
forms and figures as possible. And it is a highly beneficial exercise to 15
translate from the Greek. Accordingly it is desirable for the pupils to receive
the most frequent and careful training in this exercise. For as soon as the
mind is trained to grasp meanings, then the vigour and peculiarity of each
language is thoroughly appreciated and points of similarity and variance
between ourselves and the Greeks are grasped. Finally, to capture the 20
peculiar tone of the Greek one must deploy all the resources of the Latin
language. If this seems difficult for boys to begin with, it will become easier
through practice, and the wit and application of the teacher will remove a
good part of the burden from the boys by supplying what he considers to be
beyond their capacity. 25

Meanwhile the reading of good authors should be constantly interspersed with those exercises so that the pupils always have material for
imitation. Nevertheless the teacher, after setting an exercise, ought to
provide as well a good supply of vocabulary and figures of speech. Under

* * * * *

1 *expolitio*] *De copia* 630:7ff; and see *Ad Herennium* 4.42.54.
3 Aphthonius] Rhetorician (fourth century AD) whose progymnasmata or exercises were used as a school text in the sixteenth century
5 simile, comparison] See 675:2n.
6 division] Distribution: *Ad Herennium* 4.35.47; cf 4.40.52; *De copia* 427:17ff.
6 impersonation] *Sermocinatio* (dialogue) in *Ad Herennium* 4.52.65 but combined by Quintilian 9.2.29–32 with *prosopopoeia* (impersonation)
6 question and answer] *De copia* 347:30ff, but see also ASD I-2 131:5n.
6 signification] 'Description of something by indicating the signs that accompany it' (*De copia* 332:18)
7 turn verse into prose] See *De copia* 303:21–4.
26 reading] Quintilian 1.8.1–12; 2.5.1–17

this heading they should also be encouraged to strive to discover those for
themselves, so that once the bare bones of an argument have been set out,
each may discover by his own efforts what will be appropriate to the
treatment, adornment, and enrichment of the theme. And in this I shall
require diligent attention to selection and variety on the part of the learned   5
teacher; meanwhile I shall give a sample of what I mean. He will regularly
set out the argument of the persuasive, dissuasive, exhortatory, dehorta-
tory, narrative, congratulatory, expostulatory, commendatory, and con-
solatory letter. He will point out the nature of each type, some features and
set-phrases they have in common, and, once the argument has been set out,   10
their peculiarities as well. The same method will apply to an exercise in the
different kinds of formal oratory, for instance, if he should order them to
revile Julius Caesar or to praise Socrates in the demonstrative genre.
Likewise, in the persuasory genre: that the best should be learnt at once;
that happiness does not consist in riches; that a mother should nourish her   15
offspring with her own milk; that one should or should not attend to Greek
letters; that a man should or should not marry; or that one should or should
not travel abroad. So too, in the judicial genre, that Marcus Horatius did not
deserve punishment. But of course a man who has assumed the role of a
teacher will not disdain to indicate to those entering the arena for the first   20
time, first, in how many propositions that argument can be treated. Furthermore he will show the order of the propositions and how one follows
from another. Next, the number of reasons by which each proposition
should be supported, and the number of proofs of each reason. Then he will
indicate sources for the circumstances and grounds of proof. Then, with   25
what sort of similes, contrasts, examples, analogies, aphorisms, proverbs,
myths, and fables each part may be enhanced. He should also point out the
use of rhetorical figures and where striking examples may be employed
which may render the speech more pointed or more rotund, of greater

* * * * *

2 once ... the theme] A succinct statement of the purposes of *De copia*

3 by his own efforts] *Adagia* i vi 19

7 argument] *De conscribendis epistolis* provides analysis and examples of these
types of letters.

14 the best should be learnt at once] So Ep 56:32

16 her own milk] A theme to which Erasmus returned more than once; for
example in *Puerpera* (Thompson *Colloquies* 272–85)

17 marry] See *De copia* 598:9n.

18 travel abroad] Or 'go on pilgrimage'

18 Marcus Horatius] Livy 1.26. The example of Horatius, tried and acquitted for
the killing of his unpatriotic sister, is a favourite with Quintilian: 3.6.76, 4.2.7,
7.4.8.

clarity or appeal. Should amplification be called for somewhere, he should explain the method underlying it, whether by means of commonplaces or by those methods which Quintilian has divided into four types. Should any appeals to emotion be called for he will advise how these too are to be expressed. He should of course set out the principles governing connection 5 and what form the best transition would take: from the opening section to the main outline, from the main outline to the division, from the division to the proofs, from proposition to proposition, from reason to reason, from the proofs to the epilogue or peroration. He should also point out some formulae by which they may be able to launch smoothly into the exordium or 10 even the peroration. Finally he should, if it is possible, point out some passages in authors where they may be able to take something for imitation because of its relevance to the task in hand. When all that has been performed seven or eight times, then they will begin 'to swim without cork,' to quote Horace, and it will be sufficient to supply the bare subject of the 15 exercise, and no longer necessary, as with infants, to be constantly putting predigested food into their mouths.

Nor am I averse to that type of exercise which I see was employed by the ancients: I refer to the selection of themes from Homer, Sophocles, Euripides, Virgil, or even the ancient historians on occasion. For instance: 20 Menelaus should reclaim Helen before the Trojan assembly: or Phoenix should persuade Achilles to return to the battle: or Ulysses should urge the Trojans to give back Helen rather than endure the war. Several rhetorical exercises of Libanius and Aristides exist along these lines. Again: that a

* * * * *

1 amplification] *De copia* 437:7–11, 507:9–15, 592 ff. Cf Quintilian 8.4.1 ff.

3 four types] See Quintilian 3.6.80 ff; 8.4.3.

6 transition] *De copia* chap 53 (above 410)

14 'to swim without cork'] That is, need no further assistance. Horace *Satires* 1.4.120; *Adagia* I viii 42

16 infants] An Erasmian pun. *Infans* is taken in its literal sense of 'inarticulate child' and in this context 'incompetent orator.' Cf Cicero *De oratore* 2.162. The analogy between teacher and midwife goes back to Socrates.

24 Libanius] Greek rhetorician (fourth century AD) from Antioch whose school at Constantinople was patronized by the emperor Julian. Erasmus translated three declamations by Libanius in 1503; they were published at Louvain in 1519 (text in ASD I-1 175–92). He dedicated them to Nicolas Ruistre, bishop of Arras and chancellor of the University of Louvain. The presentation copy of these translations, in Erasmus' hand, is in the library of Trinity College, Cambridge. See Ep 177.

24 Aristides] Aelius Aristides, a second-century Greek rhetorician who wrote letters and speeches in imitation of the best Attic style. The *editio princeps* of Aristides was published in 1517 by Giunta at Florence, but Erasmus had been

LB I 526C / ASD I-2 134

friend should urge Cicero not to accept the terms offered by Antony, an argument which is found in Seneca; or that Phalaris should persuade the priests of Delphi to consecrate the bronze bull to their god. The letters which circulate under the name of Phalaris and Brutus are relevant here. In correcting, the teacher will praise any felicity of invention, treatment, or 5 imitation, and will censure any omission, misplacement, excess or slackness, obscurity, or even an infelicity of expression. He will show how it can be corrected and will insist that his pupils acquire the habit of correcting. He will, in particular, stimulate the pupils' spirits by starting with comparison among them, thereby arousing a state of mutual rivalry. 10

Now in reading authors I should not like you to follow the practice of today's common run of teachers who, through some perverse ambition, attempt to treat every passage as a text for exhaustive disquisition, but would like you to confine yourself to those points alone which are relevant to the interpretation of the passage under consideration – unless the occa- 15 sional digression seems appropriate to enhance their enjoyment. If you ask me about the method of this also, then the following seems to me to be the best approach. In the first place the teacher should give a brief appreciation of the writer on whom he proposes to lecture, in order to win over his audience. Then he should point out the pleasure and benefit to be derived 20 from his argument. Next, if (as is frequently the case) the tenor of the argument should offer a variety of applications, he should explain these and distinguish between them. For example, take a comedy of Terence. Before

* * * * *

given access to a manuscript in preparing his *Adagia*: 'Many learned men of their own accord offered me authors not yet published.' (See *Adagia* LB II 405C–D.)

2 Seneca] The Elder Seneca. Cf Suasoria 6, which gives the various arguments for and against. For this suasory or deliberative type of speech in which the theme is set and then the arguments for and against are put forward, see Quintilian 2.4.24. A famous Elizabethan example is Hamlet's 'To be or not to be' soliloquy.
De copia 597:26ff contains suggestions for a suasoria on Antony's offer to Cicero.

2 Phalaris] Tyrant of Acragas in Sicily during the sixth century BC who was said to have roasted his victims in a bronze bull; *Adagia* I x 86

3 letters ... Brutus] Letters thought to have been written by Phalaris were shown by Richard Bentley (1697) to be forgeries. Authenticity of two of the letters by Marcus Junius Brutus in his correspondence with Cicero has been questioned (cf Loeb Classical Library edition of *Ad familiares* 3.616–19).

11 reading] See above 679:26ff.

16 digression] *De copia* 589:7ff.

23 Terence] See above 669:10n.

translating this he should first of all discuss briefly the author's circumstances, his talent, the elegance of his language. Then he should mention how much enjoyment and instruction may be had from reading comedy; next the significance of that form of literature, its origins, the number
of types of comedy and its laws. Next he should explain as clearly and   5
concisely as possible the gist of the plot. He should be careful to point out
the type of metre. Then he should make a simple arrangement of these
points and then explain each one in greater detail. In this respect he should
carefully draw their attention to any purple passage, archaism, neologism,
Graecism, any obscure or verbose expression, any abrupt or confused   10
order, any etymology, derivation, or composition worth knowing, any
point of orthography, figure of speech, or rhetorical passages, or embellishment or corruption. Next he should compare parallel passages in authors, bringing out differences and similarities – what has been imitated,
what merely echoed, where the source is different, where common, inas-   15
much as the majority of Latin works have their origin in Greek. Finally he
should turn to philosophy and skilfully bring out the moral implication of
the poets' stories, or employ them as patterns, for example, the story of
Pylades and Orestes to show the excellence of friendship; that of Tantalus
the curse of avarice. Here Eustathius, the commentator on Homer, will be a   20
substantial aid to the teacher. And so it will come about (assuming mental
agility on the teacher's part) that if some passage is encountered which may
corrupt the young, far from its harming their morals it may in fact confer
some benefit, namely by concentrating their attention, partly on annotation
of the passage, partly on loftier thoughts. If, for instance, someone were   25
going to read Virgil's second *Eclogue*, he should prepare or rather protect
the minds of his audience with a suitable preface along the following lines:
friendship can exist only among similar people, for similarity promotes

* * * * *

4 significance of that form] See *De copia* 591:9n.
11 composition] Ways of linking phrases; *De copia* chap 30 (345:1ff)
17 moral implication of ... stories] A topic that offered endless opportunities to
   Renaissance authors. See *De copia* 610:16ff.
19 Tantalus] *Adagia* I vi 22 and II vi 14
20 Eustathius] A twelfth-century archbishop of Thessalonica who wrote very full
   commentaries on the *Iliad* and *Odyssey* (*editio princeps* Rome 1542–50) which
   were important for preserving the scholia and commentaries of earlier scholars.
26 Virgil's second *Eclogue*] On the moral interpretation of pagan literature for a
   Christian audience and brief discussion of Erasmus' attitude towards it see
   Bolgar, esp 337–40; CWE 23 xxix–xxxii; and above 663–4.
28 friendship] Adagia I i 2

A ORAT ABDVCERE.Orat vt abducat.figuratū eſt:vt donat habere, id eſt donat vt habeat.
ET FACIET.Noluit dicere,& faciam:ne quē amabat offenderet,ſi ſe velle alteri dare munus
diceret quod ei parauerat.
Huc ades ô formoſe puer:tibi lilia plenis
Ecce ferunt nymphæ calathis:tibi candida Nais
Pallentes violas,& ſumma papauera carpens,
Narciſſum,& florem iungit bene olentis anethi.
Tum caſia,atque aliis intexens ſuauibus herbis,
Mollia luteola pingit vacinia caltha.
Ipſe ego cana legam tenera lanugine mala,
Caſtaneáſque nuces,mea quas Amaryllis amabat.
Addam cerea pruna,& honos erit huic quoque pomo.
Et vos ô lauri carpam,& te proxima myrte:
Sic poſitæ quoniam ſuaueis miſcetis odores.

D HVC ADES O FORMOSE PVER,tibi lilia plenis Ecce ferunt nymphæ calathis. Tantum ho‑
noris habet puero: vt ei dicat etiam numina obſecutura. Sane calathus, græcū eſt: nam latine
quaſillum dicitur.Cicero in philippicis, An non inter quaſilla pendet aurum ʳ CANDIDA
NAIS ,Vel pulchra,vel dea. Nam dii vmbris contrarii ſunt,quas nigras eſſe conſtat. hinc eſt,
Candidus inſuetum miratur limen olympi. PALLENTES VIOLAS.Amantium tinĉtas
colore.Horatius,Et tinĉtus viola pallor amantium. Vnde non præter affeĉtionem amantis,eos
flores nymphas dicit offerre,qui ſunt amantibus ſimiles.PAPAVERA CARPENS, NAR‑
E CISSVM ET FLOREM BENE OLENTIS ANETHI.Sane Papauer,Narciſſus,Ane‑
thus,pulcherrimi pueri fuerunt: qui in flores ſuorum nominum verſi ſunt:quos ei offerendo,
quaſi admonet nequid etiam tale aliquid vnquam ex amore patiatur. TVM CASIA. Herba
ſuauiſſimi odoris:vt ſequentia indicant: quã Græci caſiam dicunt.Et ſic diĉtum eſt Tum caſia,
atque aliis intexēs ſuauibus herbis:vt in Salluſtio,Leonem,atque alias feras. MOLLIA LV‑
TEOLA PINGIT VACINIA CALTHA.Mollia vacinia pingit,id eſt componit de caltha
luteola.Nam niſi LVTEOLA,ſeptimus ſit caſus,non ſtat verius.Mollia autem,taĉtus plumei
F ſcilicet.Hoc dicens,ex colorum diuerſitate quærit ornatum. CANA LEGAM TENERA
LANVGINE MALA.Mala dicit cydonea: quæ lanuginis plena ſunt:ſed non præter obliqui‑
tatem.Nam in AEneide diximus,apud Cretenſes,infamiæ genus iuuenibus fuerat, non ama‑
tos fuiſſe.Et verecunde rem inhoneſtam ſupprimit:quam Thocritus aperte commemorat .
CASTANEÁSQVE NVCES.Bene ſpeciem addidit:dicens caſtaneas.Nam NVCES,genera‑
liter dicuntur omnia teĉta corio dutiore:vt auellanæ,amygdalæ,iuglandes,caſtaneæ.ſicut con‑
tra dicuntur poma,omnia molliora. MEA QVAS AMARYLLIS AMABAT.Ne cas vi‑
les exiſtimes, quas Amaryllis eſt amare dignata,nam apud illam in ingenti fuerunt honore.
G CEREA PRVNA. Aut cerei coloris:aut molia .Horatius, Cerea Telephi laudát brachia .
HONOS ERIT HVIC QVOQVE POMO.Si à te dileĉtum fuerit:ſicut caſtaneæ in honore
fuerunt amatæ Amaryllidi. O LAVRI.Licet Horatius dixerit,Depone ſub lauru mea:me
lius tamen eſt iuxta ſecundam formã infleĉtere: nam melius ſonat . PROXIMA MYRTE.
Vel vicina lauro: vel ad odorem proxima. poteſt enim vtrunque intelligi . SIC POSITAE
QVONIAM SVAVES MISCETIS ODORES.Quoniã permiſtione veſtra ſuauē odorē creatis
Ruſticus es Corydon,nec munera curat Alexis:
Nec ſi muneribus certes, concedat Iolas.
Eheu quid volui miſero mihi? floribus auſtrum
Perditus,& liquidis immiſi fontibus apros.
Quem fugis ah demens?habitarunt dii quoque ſyluas,
Dardaniuſque Paris. Pallas quas condidit arces,

Virgil's second *Eclogue*, lines 45–55,
followed by the relevant passages from the greatest of ancient commentaries
on Virgil, that of Servius, in a handsome folio edition
Paris: R. Stephanus 1532
In *De ratione studii* Erasmus suggests how the master should prepare his pupils for
reading the second *Eclogue*. See pages 683–7.
Reproduced by permission of the Thomas Fisher Rare Book Library,
University of Toronto

mutual good will, while dissimilarity on the other hand is the parent of hatred and distrust; moreover, the greater, the truer, the more deeply rooted the similarity, the firmer and closer will be the friendship. That of course is the essence of so many proverbs in literature. For example: the good attend the banquets of the good without having to be invited; again, like takes pleasure in like; equal delights equal; look for a wife who is your equal; God always brings like to like; jackdaw always associates with jackdaw; like lips, like lettuce; equals congregate most easily with equals; an elderly man marries an elderly woman; one stammerer best understands another; the cricket is dear to the cricket, the ant to the ant, the Cretan to the Aeginetan. Conversely, the many proverbs on dissimilarity amount to nothing else than that, among people of different station, way of life, or interests, either friendship is totally absent, or, if present, does not become firmly established and is quickly broken. And for that reason the ignoramus detests the scholar, the layman the priest, the rustic the courtier, the young man the old. In the same category comes the hatred of the Epicurean for the Stoic, the philosopher for the lawyer, the poet for the theologian, the stammerer for the eloquent. For this reason the friendship of the twin brothers Amphion and Zethus almost dissolved, because the one was devoted to the lyre, the other enjoyed tilling the fields; and it would in fact have dissolved had not Amphion thrown away his lyre and given in to his brother's interest. For the same reason the friendship of Castor and Pollux was fragile, even going so far as attempted parricide, although each had been born from the same egg – in this sense they could not have been truer twins – all because the one was a boxer, the other devoted to horses. Hence, too, the incompatability of Remus and Romulus, because the one was sombre and austere in character, the other more easy-going; and for this reason his name was changed from Romus to Romulus. Because they were

* * * * *

1 dissimilarity] See *Amicitia* (Thompson *Colloquies* 516–27), which deals with antipathies as well as sympathies in nature.

4 For example ... Aeginetan] For these examples, in the order in which they are quoted in the text, see *Adagia* I x 35; I ii 21; I ii 20; I viii 1; I ii 22; I ii 23; I x 71; I ii 20; I ii 62; I ix 77; I ii 24; I ii 27.

21 Amphion] The twin brother of Zethus and son of Zeus and Antiope who, as joint ruler with his brother, built the walls of Thebes. Like Orpheus, his skill on the lyre was legendary and he is said to have drawn the stones for his walls into place by the power of his music.

22 Castor and Pollux] Also termed Dioscuri; they were the twin sons of Zeus by Leda; famous for their bravery and fighting prowess. In later legend they were associated with the constellation Gemini.

28 name was changed] Servius on *Aeneid* 1.273 records that the name of Romus was changed to Romulus (a diminutive form).

drawn to different types of life, Cain and Abel were anathema to one
another. The deepest form of love coincides with the deepest resemblance,
and so it has been portrayed by the poets. For instance, as soon as Narcissus, who had previously shunned every form of friendship, had caught
sight of his own reflection on the glassy surface of a pool, he immediately   5
began to burn with an all-consuming passion. For what is more like ourselves than our own reflection? Thus when the learned is drawn to the
learned, the sober to the sober, the modest to the modest, the honest to the
honest, each is drawn to nothing other than his own character as reflected in
another person, that is, to himself in another form. But if such a likeness is   10
rooted in the goods of the soul – the only true goods – that is, piety, justice,
and temperance, then the resulting friendship is based on those qualities
by which it was promoted, that is, it is honest, true, sincere, firm, and
eternal. On the other hand, he will point out that if it is based on the
transience of earthly things or even on baseness, then no true, pleasant, or   15
lasting friendship is possible. Accordingly he should show how Plato
conceived of two types of Venus, the one celestial, the other terrestrial;
similarly of two types of Cupid, corresponding to their respective mothers.
The celestial Venus brings true forms to birth and her son implants true and
honourable affections. Among the good, love is always mutual, while   20
among the low it is common for one to love, the other to hate, one to pursue,
the other to flee. That occurs generally because of a dissimilarity in temperament and outlook. The Cupid of the poets is the cultured expression of
this: sometimes piercing one person with a golden dart, another with a
leaden one, thus making the former love, the latter recoil from it, and   25
nothing can be more wretched than this form of 'friendship.' It is, then, a
symbolic picture of such an ill-formed friendship which Virgil is presenting
in this Eclogue. Corydon is from the countryside, Alexis from the city.
Corydon is a shepherd, Alexis a courtier. Corydon is unsophisticated (for
Virgil calls his songs artless), while Alexis is widely read. Corydon is   30
advanced in years, Alexis in his early manhood. Corydon is ugly, Alexis
handsome. In short, they differ in every respect. The prudent man should
therefore choose a friend in tune with his own character, if he wants the
affection to be mutual. If, then, he prefaces his remarks in this way, and

* * * * *

3 Narcissus] Ovid *Metamorphoses* 3.407ff

17 two types of Venus] Cf Plato *Symposium* 180D–E. For a discussion of the 'twin
Venuses' and their importance in Renaissance Neoplatonism see Erwin
Panofsky 'The Neoplatonic Movement in Florence and North Italy' in his
Studies in Iconology (New York 1939). They are the subject of Titian's famous
painting 'Sacred and Profane Love.'

34 he] The teacher

thereupon shows the passages which indicate the mistaken and boorish affections of Corydon, I believe the minds of his audience will suffer no ill effects, unless someone comes to the work who has already been corrupted. For such a person will have brought his infection with him and will not have acquired it from this activity. I have dealt with this particular example at some length so that each person may more easily come by similar means of exposition for himself in other cases.

Now in approaching each work the teacher should indicate the nature of the argument in the particular genre, and what should be most closely observed in it. For instance, the essence of the epigram lies in its pointed brevity. Then he will deal with the theory of wit which Quintilian and Cicero present, pointing out that this literary form takes particular delight in rhetorical exclamations, cleverly thrown in at the end, and thereby startling the reader into remembering their point. In tragedy, he will point out that particular attention should be paid to the emotions aroused, and especially, indeed, to the more profound. He will show briefly how these effects are achieved. Then he will deal with the arguments of the speakers as if they were set pieces of rhetoric. Finally, he should deal with the representation of place, time, and sometimes action, and the occurrence of heated exchanges, which may be worked out in couplets, single lines, or half-lines. In comedy, he should show in particular that decorum and the portrayal of our common life must be observed, and that the emotions are more subdued: that is, engaging, rather than passionate. He should show that decorum especially is studied, not only in its universal aspect, I mean that youths should fall in love, that pimps should perjure themselves, that the prostitute should allure, the old man scold, the slave deceive, the soldier boast, and so on, but also in the particular delineation of different characters as developed by the poet. For example, in the *Andria* Terence introduces two old men of widely different temperament. Simo is forthright, rather irritable, yet not stupid or dishonest. On the other hand, Chremes is polite and always calm, self-controlled on every occasion, resolving all

* * * * *

11 theory of wit] Quintilian 6.3.1ff; Cicero *De oratore* 2.217ff; *De officiis* 1.103–4. Cf *De copia* 654:16ff.

13 rhetorical exclamations] Quintilian's 'acclamation' (8.5.11); *De copia* 629:6ff

18 respresentation of place, time] *De copia* 587:13–589:4

21 decorum] Erasmus is sensitive to decorum in dress and speech (*De civilitate* passim; Thompson *Colloquies* 210–16, 445–6; *Ecclesiastes* LB V 966F–7A) but does not treat at length the nature of artistic decorum. The fundamental exposition of decorum is Cicero *De officiis* 1.93–101, where 'propriety,' 'appropriateness' (the definition of decorum) is said to be identical with what is morally right: 'quod decet, honestum est; et quod honestum est, decet' (1.94).

Master and pupils

When praising Colet in his dedicatory letter to *De copia* (Ep 260) Erasmus expresses
the common sixteenth-century conviction about the importance of having youth
'absorb Christian principles together with an excellent literary education from their
earliest years.' Tudor schoolmasters were regularly required to teach the catechism.
This illustration from a 1593 edition of Alexander Nowell's *Catechism or Institution of
Christian Religion* (London: Windet) shows the master rewarding a proficient pupil.
Folger Shakespeare Library

differences as far as he can, gentle but hardly simple-minded. Likewise he
introduces two young men of divergent natures: Pamphilus, wise for his
years, and very resourceful, but rather blunt, so that you recognize him as a
true son of his father, Simo. Set against him is Charinus who is childish,
inept, and resourceless. Again, two slaves of different character: Davus,   5
crafty, packed with guile, unshakably optimistic; Byrria is the exact opposite, totally lacking in initiative, a constant source of despair to his master.
Likewise in the *Adelphi*: Micio is gentle and gay even when scolding, while
even the sweetness of Demea has a touch of bitterness to it. Again, take
Aeschinus who, because he is city-bred and has the trust of Micio, will   10
attempt anything, but you still appreciate the basic decency of the man who
is dutiful towards his brother, faithful to his sweetheart. On the other hand,
Ctesipho is rather boorish and timid because of his inexperience in those
things. Syrus is wily and daring, constantly confounding truth and falsehood, so that in drunkenness alone is his deceit revealed; while Dromo is   15
dull and obtuse. But it is not my purpose here to develop these points; it is
sufficient for the present to have pointed the way. In the *Eclogues* the
teacher should remind them that the setting is the Golden Age with its
portrayal of the fabulous antique way of life. Consequently, he should
point out that in such a context all the aphorisms, similes and comparisons 20
are drawn from pastoral life; that the characters' emotions are simple and
they delight in songs, aphorisms, and proverbs, and are susceptible to
signs and portents. In the same way he will be careful to remind pupils of
the essential nature of epic poetry, history, the dialogue, the fable, satire,
the ode, and the other literary genres. Then he will not shirk from pointing 25
out the merits or even the faults of particular authors in particular passages,
in order that the young may become accustomed, even at so early an age, to
employing what is, in everything, of paramount importance – judgment. In
this matter, apart from his own expertise and native wit, the teacher will

* * * * *

15 Dromo] Erasmus' memory of *Adelphi* seems to be at fault here. Dromo is
referred to by Syrus at line 376 but does not appear in the play. The character
sketch in lines 14–16 above does not fit the only other slave (Syrus) with a role
in the play.
17 *Eclogues*] On Theocritean and Virgilian pastoral, its influence on Renaissance
pastoral poetry, and Renaissance conceptions of pastoral see E.R. Curtius
European Literature and the Latin Middle Ages trans Willard R. Trask (New York
1953) chap 10 183–202; W. Leonard Grant *Neo-Latin Literature and the Pastoral*
(Chapel Hill 1965); T.G. Rosenmeyer *The Green Cabinet: Theocritus and the
European Pastoral Lyric* (Berkeley 1969); Fred J. Nichols 'The Development of
Neo-Latin Theory of the Pastoral in the Sixteenth Century' *Humanistica
Lovaniensia* 18 (1969) 95–114.

LB I 528E / ASD I-2 143

obtain additional help in Cicero's short treatise *De claris oratoribus* and in the literary criticism of Quintilian, Seneca, and Antonio Campano, not forgetting the ancient interpreters; Donatus in particular was concerned with this.

Relevant to this is the theory underlying the literary form: why, for 5 example, did Cicero feign fear in his defence of Milo; and what lies behind Virgil's eulogistic portrayal of Turnus, the enemy of Aeneas; and why, in Lucian, does the disowned doctor, far from striking his stepmother, actually praise her and is more hostile towards the father than the stepmother? But here again the scope is vast. Yet someone will criticize all this as 10 involving too much hard work. For my part, I want a learned teacher, one trained by long experience. Given such a person, the boys will acquire such knowledge, even easily. But if such a programme proves rather arduous to begin with, progress and practice will make it easier. Unless I am mistaken, it is the best one; and it is fitting to accustom them to the best from the start, 15 although these points are not to be inculcated in their entirety on every occasion – otherwise boredom is likely to overwhelm the pupils – but rather the more important should be inculcated as they occur. Nor, of course, should the teacher take less care in testing what he has imparted than in putting it across. This is far and away the heaviest burden on the teacher, 20 but is most useful to his pupils. It is not merely the bare outlines of the lesson which he should test but the substance of the points which must be

* * * * *

1 *De claris oratoribus*] The *Brutus*, a treatise by Cicero on famous orators. On Roman rhetorical history and Cicero's attitude towards it see the edition of *Brutus* by A.E. Douglas (Oxford 1966) introduction.

2 Seneca] The Elder Seneca, compiler of the *Controversiae* and *Suasoriae*

2 Antonio Campano] 1429–77. Friend of Pius II, who made him bishop of Cotrone (Crotone) and later of Teramo. He translated Plutarch and Aesop and wrote amorous poetry. Erasmus calls him 'a man born for jesting and wit' (Ep 61:153–4). See *Io Antonii Campani epistolae et poemata* ed J.B. Mencken (Leipzig 1707); Flavio Di Bernardo *Giannantonio Campano* (Rome 1975).

3 Donatus] Above 670:6n

6 Cicero] *Pro Milone* 1.1

7 Virgil's] *Aeneid* 7–12

8 Lucian] In his *Abdicatus*, which Erasmus had translated in 1506 (ASD I-1 398–409), a son who had been disowned and studied medicine cures his father of insanity; then he is taken back into the family. Later, when his stepmother becomes insane, he refuses to cure her and is consequently disowned again. (Erasmus does not deal with the question of whether the son's references to his stepmother are ironical.)

20 the teacher] On the importance of having teachers who are both learned and humane see Ep 56. For glimpses of schoolmasters who perhaps fell short of this ideal see Thompson *Colloquies* 22–4, 44–5.

known – that is what they should be used to reproducing faithfully. The difficulty should not deter them from this, as it is surmounted even in the space of a month. I have never approved of youths writing down every word they hear, for this practice leads them to neglect the cultivation of the memory, allowing for the fact that some may want to make a few brief notes of certain things, but that only until such time as the memory has been strengthened and they no longer desire the prop of the written word.

Finally, such weight do I attach to the correct method of teaching, provided that the teacher is conscientious and learned, that I would not hesitate to hazard this promise: given youths who are not totally incompetent intellectually, I would with less trouble, and within fewer years, bring them to a creditable degree of eloquence in each language than those notorious instructors who force their charges into their own stammering form, or rather lack, of expression. Having, therefore, received a thorough grounding in primary school, a boy may then with confidence turn his attention to higher studies; and whatever direction this takes, he will readily demonstrate how important it was that he received his first instruction from the best teachers. I am setting these precepts down for you for the present, my dearest Pierre, as my views on the method of studying. Do make use of them, if you think fit; if not, at least take the pains I have bestowed on it in good part, since you are so true to me. Only forge ahead as you have begun: apply yourself zealously to the cause of learning, and adorn your native France, so illustrious in other spheres, with ennobling studies as well. Farewell.

* * * * *

10 this promise] See Colet's comment on this passage in Ep 230:10–16.
15 with confidence] Literally 'with good birds,' that is, favourable auspices; *Adagia* I i 75

ERASMUS' CATALOGUES

OF HIS WORKS

Already I hear some of my friends from time to time grumbling about the
division of my entire works into volumes. Whether there is anything in my   5
writings that is worthy of posterity, be it for others to decide; at least, if they
do descend to our successors, I could wish I had some loyal and scholarly
Tiro to do for me when I am dead what he did for Cicero his master. And
yet, in case anyone thinks it worth trying, why, I will show him the most
convenient way to do it.   10
    In the first volume can be put everything that concerns literature and
education, for example:
De copia, two books
Ratio conscribendi epistolas
Ratio studiorum, addressed to Pierre Vitré   15
Theodorus' *Grammar*, two books, in my version
Syntaxis
All my versions from Lucian, the titles of which are *Saturnalia, Cronosolon*
    or *Leges Saturnaliciae, Epistolae Saturnales, De luctu, Icaromenippus,*
    Toxaris, Pseudomantis, Somnium sive Gallus, Timon, Abdicatus, Tyran-   20
    nicida, De mercede conductis in aulis potentum, sundry dialogues
    (*Cnemonis et Damippi, Zenophantae et Callidemi* [*dae*], *Menippi et Tan-*
    tali, Menippi et Mercurii, Menippi et Amphilochi et Trophonii, Charontis
    et Menippi, Cratetis ac Diogenis, Nirei ac Thersitae, Diogenis ac Mausoli,
    Simyli ac Polystrati, Veneris et Cupidinis, Martis ac Mercurii, Mercurii et 25
    Maiae, Veneris et Cupidinis, Doridis et Galateae, Diogenis et Alexandri,
    Menippi et Chironis, Menippi et Cerberi), *Hercules Gallicus, Eunuchus,*
    De sacrificiis, Lapithae, De astrologia. I should not wish the prefaces to
    these to be omitted, which make clear to whom each is dedicated.
A short declamation rendered from the Greek of Libanius, with several   30
    themes also translated
A declamation against a tyrannicide, in answer to Lucian's

* * * * *

1 Catalogue] From the letter to Johann von Botzheim (printed in Allen I
    38:12–42:10; the entire letter will appear in CWE as Ep 1341A). The main part of
    the letter is dated 30 January 1523. This list of writings was added to the second
    edition, September 1524. See Allen I 1 introduction. Translated by R.A.B.
    Mynors
28 *De astrologia*] Erasmus omits *Longaevi*, on which see Allen I 8:8n, VIII xxi, and
    ASD I–1 372–3.

Laus medicinae
Similia, one book
Colloquia, one book
Euripides, version of *Hecuba* and *Iphigenia*
Miscellaneous poems, on other than religious subjects, for those I have kept   5
 for their appropriate section
Commentarius in Nucem Ovidii
  The second volume can be dedicated to the *Adagia*, which make a
whole volume by themselves; and the subject-matter is not far from the
main theme of volume one.   10
  The third should be allotted to my *Epistolae*, for in these too there is
much that is relevant to practice in composition; for most of them are trifles
which I wrote as an adolescent or at least as a young man. These I will revise,
and add a certain number, perhaps also removing some. To this class I
should wish a number of preliminary dedications to be added, which   15
printers often either omit or alter according to their fancy. Such, for example, are the prefaces to the works of St Hilary and St Cyprian, to the Greek
Lexicon, the letter to Jean Desmarez prefixed to my *Panegyricus ad Philippum*, the preface added to my *De principe* intended for Charles' brother
Ferdinand, and anything else that may seem to deserve preservation.   20
  Volume four may be given to works which contribute to the building
of character. To this class belong:
Most of the Lucian, though I have given it a place in the first volume
All my versions from Plutarch, the titles of which are *De discrimine adulatoris*
 et amici, Quo pacto possit utilitas capi ex inimico, De tuenda bona val-   25
 etudine, Principi maxime philosophandum, An graviores sint animi morbi
 quam corporis, De cupiditate divitiarum, Num recte dictum ab Epicuro
 λάθε βιώσας
Moriae encomium, a small book full of humour, but it teaches serious les-
 sons, so do not be surprised to find it in this section.   30
Panegyricus, a speech of welcome to Philip, father of the emperor Charles,
 on his return from Spain
Institutio principis christiani, addressed to the emperor Charles
Isocrates de regno, addressed to him likewise
Consolatio de morte filii   35
Querimonia pacis
Dialogus Charontis et Alastoris
Carmen de senectute, addressed to Copp the physician
Paraenesis to Adolf, heer van Veere, who was then a child
De morte subita, to Joost van Gavere   40
This is the place for Cicero's *Officia*, revised by me and supplied with

summaries and notes. Why should one not also add the *Catunculus*,
the *Mimi Publiani*, and other things of the sort?

The fifth volume can be allocated to works of religious instruction.
Among these are:

Enchiridion militis christiani

Letter to Paul Volz, abbot of Hügshofen

Methodus verae theologiae, from the edition of 1523 published by Michael
   Hillen

Paraclesis

Exomologesis

Commentarii in Psalmos primum et secundum

Paraphrasis in Psalmum tertium, dedicated to Viandalus

Commentarius in Epistolam ad Romanos

Paraphrasis in Precationem Dominicam

Commentarius in duos hymnos Prudentii

Concio de puero Iesu

Concio de misericordia Domini

Comparatio virginitatis et martyrii, to the nuns of Cologne

Expostulatio Iesu, in verse

Casa natalitia

Michaelis encomium

Liturgia virginis Lauretanae

Three prayers, two to the Virgin Mother and one to Jesus

The sixth volume shall be assigned to the New Testament as rendered
by me, with my notes on it; a work which I have already revised and
enriched for the fourth time. Anyone who does not like large books can
divide this into two volumes.

The seventh is for the Paraphrases on the whole New Testament,
exclusive of the Apocalypse. These too can be divided into two volumes, if
anyone so pleases.

Let the eighth volume be occupied by the Defences. These too (alack
the day!) will make a whole volume. Their titles are as follows, and I pray
there may be nothing to add:

Ad Iacobum Fabrum Stapulensem, one book

Ad Eduardum Leum, two books

Ad Iacobum Latomum de Linguis

Adversus Nicolaum Ecmondanum de loco Pauli ad Corinthios: 'Omnes quidem
   resurgemus'

Adversus quorundam clamores de hoc quod verteram: 'In principio erat sermo'

Ad Ioannem Briardum Atensem pro Encomio matrimonii

Ad taxationes Stunicae in Novum Testamentum

Adversus libellum Impietatum et Blasphemiarum eiusdem, of which the first
   words are: *Vix mihi delitigata*
Appendix adversus eiusdem libellum, entitled πρόδρομος. First words: *Dum
   haec excuderentur*
Adversus conclusiones eiusdem. First words: *Reddidit mihi tuus*   5
Adversus Sanctium Caranzam theologum de tribus locis ab illo notatis. First
   words: *Post longas et inutiles rixas*. Here let my own words only be
   reprinted, omitting what was included from Stunica and Sanctius in
   the first edition.
Epistola ad R.P. Christophorum, episcopum Basiliensem, de delectu ciborum ac   10
   caeteris
Epistola ad Marcum Laurinum contra rumorem, of which the first words are:
   Nae tu plurimum debes
Epistola ad Martinum Dorpium de Novo Testamento, which hitherto has been
   appended to the *Moria*   15
Apologiae, prefixed to the New Testament
Spongia adversus Ulricum Huttenum
Liber antibarbarorum
De libero arbitrio διατριβή
   Volume nine shall be dedicated to the *Letters* of Jerome, on which I   20
have expended so much labour that I can without impudence add this work
to my own list; though Hilary too cost me a lot of work, and so did Cyprian.
Of Quintus Curtius I will say nothing; in Seneca I can claim nothing for
myself, except that in that field I lost much labour by trusting to the
promises of my friends. If Christ grants me life and strength enough to   25
finish my Commentaries on the Epistle to the Romans, they will occupy
volume ten.

1530 CATALOGUE   30

List of all the works of Erasmus of Rotterdam

SERIES OF BOOKS THAT CONCERN LITERATURE AND EDUCATION   35
De copia, two books [260]
Ratio conscribendi epistolas [71; 117; 1284]

   * * * * *

   30 Catalogue] From the letter of 15 March 1530 to Hector Boece; Ep 2283. Num-
      bers within brackets refer to letters which give information on the history of
      the works.

Ratio studiorum, addressed to Pierre Vitré [56; 66]
De pueris statim ac liberaliter instituendis, 1529 [2189]
De recte pronunciando [1949]
Ciceronianus [1948]
De civilibus puerorum moribus [2282]   5
Theodorus' *Grammar,* two books, in my version [428; 771]
Syntaxis [341]
All translations from Lucian; the titles are:
—   *Saturnalia* [261]
—   *Epistolae Saturnales*   10
—   *Cronosolon* or *Leges Saturnaliciae*
—   *De luctu*
—   *Icaromenippus*
—   *Toxaris* [187]
—   *Pseudomantis* [199]   15
—   *Somnium sive Gallus* [193]
—   *Timon* [192]
—   *Abdicatus*
—   *Tyrannicida*
—   *De mercede conductis in aulis potentum* [197]   20
—   Sundry dialogues [205]:

Cnemonis et Damippi	*Simyli ac Polystrati*
Zenophantae et Callidemi[dae]	*Veneris et Cupidinis*
Menippi et Tantali	*Martis ac Mercurii*
Menippi et Mercurii	*Mercurii et Maiae* 25
Menippi et Amphilochi et Trophonii	*Veneris et Cupidinis*
Charontis et Menippi	*Doridis et Galateae*
Cratetis ac Diogenis	*Diogenis et Alexandri*
Nirei ac Thersitae	*Menippi et Chironis*
Diogenis ac Mausoli	*Menippi et Cerberi* 30

—   *Hercules Gallicus*
—   *Eunuchus*
—   *De sacrificiis*
—   *Lapithae* [550]
—   *De astrologia* [267]   35
—   I should not wish the prefaces to these to be omitted, which make
     clear to whom each is dedicated.
A short declamation rendered from the Greek of Libanius, with several
     themes also translated [177]
A declamation against a tyrannicide, in answer to Lucian's [191]   40
Laus medicinae [799]

Encomium matrimonii, 1529 [604:10]
Similia, one book [312]
Colloquia, one book but frequently enlarged; latest edition 1529
      [130:92; 909; 1041; 1262; 1476]
Hecuba and *Iphigenia* of Euripides translated [188; 198; 208]
Miscellaneous poems, on other than religious subjects, for those I have kept
      for their appropriate section
Commentarius in Nucem Ovidii [1402]
Prooemia Galeni translated, addressed to the physician Antoninus [1698]

SECOND SERIES
Opus adagiorum, often revised and enlarged, most recently in 1528
      [126; 211; 269; 1204; 1659; 2022–3]

THIRD SERIES
Volumen epistolarum, enlarged by more than a third, 1529 [2203]

FOURTH SERIES, ON MORAL QUESTIONS
Translations from Plutarch:
—   *De discrimine adulatoris et amici*, addressed to the king of England
      [272; 657]
—   *Quomodo possit utilitas capi ex inimico* [284; 297; 658]
—   *De tuenda bona valetudine* [268]
—   *Principi maxime philosophandum*
—   *An graviores sint animi morbi quam corporis*
—   *De cupiditate divitiarum*
—   *Num recte dictum sit ab Epicuro* λάθε βιώσας
—   *De inutili verecundia* [1663]
Moriae encomium [222]
Panegyricus, a speech of welcome to Philip, father of the emperor Charles,
      on his return from Spain [179; 180]
Institutio principis christiani, addressed to the emperor Charles [393; 853]
Isocratis de regno, to the same [677]
Consolatio de morte filii
Querimonia pacis [603]
Carmen de senectute, to the physician Copp
Lingua [1593]
Cato, and other things [298; 676; 1725]
Officia Ciceronis, successfully revised, 1528 [152; 1013; 1994A]
Opera Senecae oratoris, diligently revised, 1528 [2091]
Xenophontis Tyrannus, translated, 1530 [2273]

FIFTH SERIES, WORKS OF RELIGIOUS INSTRUCTION
Enchiridion militis christiani [164; 858]
De contemptu mundi [1194]
Methodus verae theologiae [745; 1365]
Paraclesis [1253:22]   5
Exomologesis, enlarged 1529 [1426]
Commentarii in Psalmos primum et secundum [327; 1304]
De matrimonio christiano, addressed to the renowned queen of England,
       Catherine [1727]
Vidua christiana, addressed to Mary, sometime queen of Hungary and sister   10
       of the emperor Charles [2100]
Paraphrasis in Psalmum tertium [1427]
Concio in Psalmum quartum [1535]
Concio in Psalmum octuagesimum quintum [2017]
Concio in Psalmum vigesimum secundum [2266]   15
Paraphrasis in Precationem Dominicam [1393]
Commentarii in duos hymnos Prudentii [1404]
Concio de puero Iesu [175]
Libellus concionalis de misericordia Domini, addressed to Christopher,
       sometime bishop of Basel [1474]   20
Comparatio virginis et martyris, addressed to the Maccabeitic nuns of
       Cologne [1346; 1475]
Expostulatio Iesu, in verse
Casa natalitia, in verse [47]
Michaelis archangeli encomium, in verse   25
Virginis matris paean [93:101]
Ad eandem obsecratio [93:101]
Precatio ad Iesum servatorem
Liturgia virginis Lauretanae cum concione [1391; 1573]
Consolatio, addressed to the nuns of St Clare, in England [1925]   30
De bello Turcico, 1530 [2285]

SIXTH SERIES
Novum Testamentum cum annotationibus, fourth edition revised and
       enlarged 1527 [1571:19; 1789]   35
Paraphrasis in Novum Testamentum, 1524 [1255; 1400; 1381; 1333; 1414]

SEVENTH SERIES
Translations from Chrysostom:
—   *Adversus Iudaeos*, five homilies [1800]   40
—   *De Lazaro et divite*, four homilies

— *De visione Esaiae*, five homilies
— *De Philogonio martyre*, one
— *In Epistolam ad Philippenses*, two homilies [1734]
— *De orando Deum*, two homilies [1563]
— *In Acta apostolorum*, four homilies [1801]   5
— *Commentarium in totam Epistolam ad Galatas* [1841]
— *In secundam ad Corinthios*, ten homilies
Translations from Athanasius:
— *Epistolae de Spiritu sancto duae* [1790]
— *Epistola contra Eusebium de Niceno synodo*   10
— *Apologeticus adversus eos qui calumniabantur quod in persequutione
   fugisset*
— *De passione Domini*, one homily
— *De eo quod scriptum est*, 'Euntes in castellum quod contra vos est,' etc
— *De virginum instituto*   15
— *De peccato in Spiritum sanctum*
— *De Spiritu sancto liber illi inscriptus*
Translated from Origen:
— *Fragmentum in Matthaeum* [1844]
Translated from Basil: 20
— *Principium Esaiae* [229]

EIGHTH SERIES, CONTAINING THE DEFENCES
Ad Iacobum Fabrum Stapulensem de Eloim [597:32]
Ad Eduardum Leum, two books [1037; 1100]   25
Ad Iacobum Latomum de Linguis, one book [934:3]
Adversus Nicolaum Ecmondanum de loco Pauli 'Omnes quidem resurgemus,'
   etc [1126:129]
Adversus quorundam clamores quod verteram, 'In principio erat sermo,'
   one book [1072]   30
*Ad Ioannem Briardum Atensem, quondam Lovaniensis Academiae cancellarium,
   pro Encomio matrimonii*, one book [670]
Ad taxationes Stunicae in Novum Testamentum [1428]
Adversus libellum Blasphemiarum eiusdem [App xv]
Appendix adversus eiusdem Πρόδρομον   35
Ad Sanctium Caranzam theologum de tribus locis ab illo notatis [1277:22]
De delectu ciborum, addressed to Christopher, bishop of Basel [1274.14]
Ad Martinum Dorpium theologum Epistola, which hitherto has been
   appended to the *Moria* [337]
       * * * * *

   34 App xv] See Allen iv 620ff.

Spongia adversus Ulrichum Huttenum [1378; 1389]
Liber antibarbarorum, one book, for the second and third perished through
      the dishonesty of certain men [30:16; 1110]
Adversus Petrum Sutorem Cartusianum, one book [1591]
De libero arbitrio diatribe sive collatio, one book [1419]   5
Adversus Martini Lutheri Servum arbitrium Hyperaspistes, two books
      [1667; 1853]
*Adversus Natalem Beddam theologum Parisiensem Elenchus, Divinationes et
      Supputationes* [1664]
Ad epistolam Alberti Pii Carporum principis, one book [1634]   10
Adversus calumnias monachorum Hispaniensium, 1529 [1877; 1879; 1967]
*Ad quendam Franciscanum qui notarat aliquot loca in annotationes meas ad
      Romanos*, one book [1823]
Contra Pseudevangelicos Epistola una, 1530 [2219:11]

                                                                                15

NINTH SERIES
Totus Hieronymus cum scholiis, revised anew, 1526 [1465; 1451; 1453; 1504]
Cyprianus, often revised; added to it in the last edition 1529 was *Liber de
      duplici martyrio*, hitherto unpublished, 1529 [1000]
Hilarius, revised with great effort, 1523 [1334]   20
Irenaeus, revised anew from the oldest manuscripts 1528 [1738; 2007]
Ambrosius, in part revised by me 1527 [1855]
I edited two new short works of Ambrose, *Apologia David* and *Interpellatio
      David*, 1529. [2190; 2076]
Lactantius de opificio Dei, revised with scholia [2103]   25
Omnia opera divi Augustini, revised with infinite toil 1529 [2157]
Algerus de Eucharistia, revised [2284]

WORKS FREQUENTLY CITED

SHORT-TITLE FORMS
FOR ERASMUS' WORKS

INDEXES

WORKS FREQUENTLY CITED

This list provides bibliographical information for publications referred to in short-title form in introductions and notes. For Erasmus' writings see the short-title list following (pages 706–9).

Allen	P.S. Allen, H.M. Allen, and H.W. Garrod eds *Opus epistolarum Des. Erasmi Roterodami* (Oxford 1906–47) 11 vols, plus index volume by B. Flower and E. Rosenbaum (Oxford 1958). Letters are cited by epistle and line numbers; see CWE 23 xi n.
Allen *Age of Erasmus*	P.S. Allen *The Age of Erasmus* (Oxford 1914)
Allen *Lectures*	P.S. Allen *Erasmus: Lectures and Wayfaring Sketches* (Oxford 1934)
ASD	*Opera omnia Desiderii Erasmi Roterodami* (Amsterdam 1969–)
Baldwin	T.W. Baldwin *William Shakspere's Small Latine and Lesse Greeke* (Urbana 1944) 2 vols
Bennett	H.S. Bennett *English Books & Readers 1475 to 1557* (Cambridge 1952)
Bierlaire	Franz Bierlaire *La familia d'Erasme: Contribution à l'histoire de l'humanisme* (Paris 1968)
Bolgar	R.R. Bolgar *The Classical Heritage and Its Beneficiaries* (Cambridge 1954)
Colloquia Erasmiana Turonensia	J.C. Margolin ed *Colloquia Erasmiana Turonensia* (Paris and Toronto 1972) 2 vols
CWE	*Collected Works of Erasmus* (Toronto 1974–)
Dorne	Falconer Madan ed 'Day-Book of John Dorne, Bookseller in Oxford, A.D. 1520' Oxford Historical Society *Collectanea* I ed C.R.L. Fletcher (Oxford 1885) 71–177; *Collectanea* II ed Montagu Burrows (Oxford 1890) 453–78
Hyma	Albert Hyma *The Youth of Erasmus* (Ann Arbor 1930)
Keil	H. Keil ed *Grammatici Latini* (Leipzig 1855–80) 8 vols
Kohls	E.W. Kohls *Die Theologie des Erasmus* (Basel 1966) 2 vols
LB	J. Leclerc ed *Desiderii Erasmi Roterodami opera omnia* (Leiden 1703–6) 10 vols

Leach   A.F. Leach ed *Educational Charters and Documents 598 to 1909* (Cambridge 1911)

Lupton   J.H. Lupton *A Life of John Colet* (London 1887; 2nd ed 1909; repr Hamden, Conn 1961)

Marginalia   G.C. Moore Smith ed *Gabriel Harvey's Marginalia* (Stratford-upon-Avon 1913)

Migne PL   J.P. Migne ed *Patrologiae cursus completus ... series latina* (Paris 1844–64) 221 vols

Nelson   William Nelson ed *A Fifteenth Century School Book* (Oxford 1956)

Opuscula   Wallace K. Ferguson ed *Erasmi opuscula: A Supplement to the Opera omnia* (The Hague 1933)

Phillips *'Adages'* Margaret Mann Phillips ed and trans *The 'Adages' of Erasmus: A Study with Translations* (Cambridge 1964)

Reedijk   C. Reedijk ed *The Poems of Desiderius Erasmus* (Leiden 1956)

Rix   Herbert David Rix 'The Editions of Erasmus' *De copia*' *Studies in Philology* 43 (1946) 595–618

Rogers   Elizabeth Frances Rogers ed *The Correspondence of Sir Thomas More* (Princeton 1947)

Rollins and Baker Hyder E. Rollins and Herschel Baker eds *The Renaissance in England* (Boston 1954)

Scrinium Erasmianum J. Coppens ed *Scrinium Erasmianum* (Leiden 1969) 2 vols

Thompson *Colloquies* Craig R. Thompson ed and trans *The Colloquies of Erasmus* (Chicago and London 1965)

Tracy   James D. Tracy 'The 1489 and 1494 Versions of Erasmus' Antibarbarorum liber' *Humanistica Lovaniensia* 20 (1971) 81–120

Vander Haeghen F. Vander Haeghen ed *Bibliotheca Erasmiana, Repertoire des œuvres d'Erasme* (Ghent 1893; repr Nieuwkoop 1961)

Woodward   W.H. Woodward *Desiderius Erasmus Concerning the Aim and Method of Education* (Cambridge 1904; repr New York 1964)

SHORT-TITLE FORMS FOR ERASMUS' WORKS

Acta contra Lutherum: Acta academiae Lovaniensis contra Lutherum
Adagia: Adagiorum chiliades 1508 (Adagiorum collectanea for the primitive form,
    when required)
Admonitio adversus mendacium: Admonitio adversus mendacium et obtrec-
    tationem
Annotationes de haereticis: Annotationes in leges pontificias et caesareas de
    haereticis
Annotationes in Novum Testamentum
Antibarbari: Antibarbarorum liber
Apologia ad Fabrum: Apologia ad Iacobum Fabrum Stapulensem
Apologia ad Caranzam: Apologia ad Sanctium Caranzam
Apologia adversus Petrum Sutorem: Apologia adversus debacchationes Petri
    Sutoris
Apologia adversus monachos: Apologia adversus monachos quosdam hispanos
Apologia adversus rhapsodias Alberti Pii
Apologia contra Latomi dialogum: Apologia contra Iacobi Latomi dialogum de
    tribus linguis
Apologia contra Stunicam: Apologia contra Lopidem Stunicam
Apologia de 'In principio erat sermo'
Apologia de laude matrimonii: Apologia pro declamatione de laude matrimonii
Apologia de loco 'omnes quidem': Apologia de loco 'Omnes quidem resurgemus'
Apologiae duae
Apologiae omnes
Apologia invectivis Lei: Apologia qua respondet duabus invectivis Eduardi Lei
Apologia monasticae religionis
Apophthegmata
Argumenta: Argumenta in omnes epistolas apostolicas nova
Axiomata pro causa Lutheri: Axiomata pro causa Martini Lutheri

Carmina
Catalogus lucubrationum
Cato
Christiani hominis institutum
Ciceronianus: Dialogus Ciceronianus
Colloquia
Compendium rhetorices
Compendium vitae
Conflictus: Conflictus Thaliae et barbariei

De bello turcico: Consultatio de bello turcico
De civilitate: De civilitate morum puerilium
De conscribendis epistolis
De constructione: De constructione octo partium orationis
De contemptu mundi
De copia: De duplici copia verborum ac rerum
Declamatio de morte

Declamationes
Declamatiuncula
Declamatiunculae
Declarationes ad censuras Lutetiae: Declarationes ad censuras Lutetiae vulgatas
De concordia: De sarcienda ecclesiae concordia
De immensa Dei misericordia: Concio de immensa Dei misericordia
De libero arbitrio: De libero arbitrio diatribe
De praeparatione: De praeparatione ad mortem
De pronuntiatione: De recta latini graecique sermonis pronuntiatione
De pueris instituendis: De pueris statim ac liberaliter instituendis
De puero Iesu: Concio de puero Iesu
De puritate tabernaculi
De ratione studii
Detectio praestigiarum: Detectio praestigiarum cuiusdam libelli germanice scripti
De tedio Iesu: Disputatiuncula de tedio, pavore, tristicia Iesu
Dilutio: Dilutio eorum quae Iodocus Clithoveus scripsit adversus declamationem
     suasoriam matrimonii

Ecclesiastes: Ecclesiastes sive de ratione concionandi
Enchiridion: Enchiridion militis christiani
Encomium matrimonii
Encomium medicinae: Declamatio in laudem artis medicae
Epigrammata
Epistola ad fratres: Epistola ad fratres Inferioris Germaniae
Epistola consolatoria: Epistola consolatoria in adversis
Epistola contra pseudevangelicos: Epistola contra quosdam qui se falso iactant
     evangelicos
Epistola de apologia Cursii: Epistola de apologia Petri Cursii
Epistola de esu carnium: Epistola apologetica ad Christophorum episcopum
     Basiliensem de interdicto esu carnium
Epistola de modestia: Epistola de modestia profitendi linguas
Exomologesis: Exomologesis sive modus confitendi
Explanatio symboli: Explanatio symboli apostolorum sive catechismus

Formulae: Conficiendarum epistolarum formulae

Gaza: Theodori Gazae grammaticae institutionis libri duo

Hyperaspistes

Institutio christiani matrimonii
Institutio principis christiani

Julius exclusus: Dialogus Julius exclusus e coelis

Liber quo respondet annotationibus Lei: Liber quo respondet annotationibus
     Eduardi Lei

Lingua
Liturgia Virginis Matris: Virginis Matris apud Lauretum cultae liturgia
Lucubrationes
Lucubratiunculae

Methodus
Modus orandi Deum
Moria: Moriae encomium, or Moria

Novum instrumentum
Novum Testamentum

Obsecratio ad Virginem Mariam: Obsecratio sive oratio ad Virginem Mariam in
    rebus adversis
Oratio de pace: Oratio de pace et discordia
Oratio de virtute: Oratio de virtute amplectenda
Oratio funebris: Oratio funebris Berthae de Heyen

Paean Virgini Matri: Paean Virgini Matri dicendus
Panegyricus: Panegyricus ad Philippum Austriae ducem
Parabolae: Parabolae sive similia
Paraclesis
Paraphrasis in Elegantias Vallae: Paraphrasis in Elegantias Laurentii Vallae
Paraphrases in Novum Testamentum
Paraphrasis in Matthaeum: Paraphrasis in Matthaeum, etc.
Peregrinatio apostolorum: Peregrinatio apostolorum Petri et Pauli
Precatio ad Virginis filium Iesum
Precatio dominica
Precationes
Precatio pro pace ecclesiae: Precatio ad Iesum pro pace ecclesiae
Progymnasmata: Progymnasmata quaedam primae adolescentiae Erasmi
Psalmi: Psalmi (Enarrationes sive commentarii in psalmos)
Purgatio adversus epistolam Lutheri: Purgatio adversus epistolam non sobriam
    Lutheri

Querela pacis

Ratio verae theologiae
Responsio ad annotationes Lei: Responsio ad annotationes Eduardi Lei
Responsio ad annotationem Stunicae: Responsio ad annotationem Iacobi Lopis
    Stunicae
Responsio ad collationes: Responsio ad collationes cuiusdam iuvenis gerontodidas-
    cali
Responsio ad disputationem de divortio: Responsio ad disputationem cuiusdam
    Phimostomi de divortio
Responsio ad epistolam apologeticam: Responsio ad fratres Germaniae Inferioris ad
    epistolam apologeticam incerto autore proditam
Responsio ad epistolam Pii: Responsio ad epistolam paraeneticam Alberti Pii

Responsio adversus febricitantis libellum: Responsio adversus febricitantis cuius-
    dam libellum
Responsio contra Egranum: Responsio apologetica contra Sylvium Egranum

Spongia: Spongia adversus aspergines Hutteni
Supputatio: Supputatio calumniarum Natalis Bedae
Syntaxis (De constructione)

Vidua christiana
Virginis et martyris comparatio
Vita Hieronymi: Vita divi Hieronymi Stridonensis

Index of Classical Sources in *Parabolae*

Aelian *De natura animalium* (1.25) 240;
(2.16) 240; (4.36) 241; (5.40) 240;
(10.29) 241; (10.47) 240; (17.10) 241
Aristotle
Historia animalium (8.28[605b31])
241n
Politica (2.3[1262a20]) 239
Problemata (1[859a–66b].3) 271,
(14–15) 270, (27) 271, (35) 271, (53)
271, (54) 271; (3[870a–6a].3) 271, (10)
271, (16) 271, (18) 272, (21) 272,
(5[880b–5b].8) 272, (10) 272, (25) 272;
(7[886a–7b].1) 272, (4) 272;
(12[906a–7b].2) 272, (5) 272, (9) 272;
(13[907b–9a].2) 272–3, (4) 273, (9)
273; (15[910b–13a].1) 273, (5) 273;
(19[(917a–23a].5) 273, (14) 273, (16)
273, (50) 273; (20[922a–7a].28) 273;
(26[940a–7b].9) 273, (25) 274, (39)
274; (31[957a–60a].2) 274, (25) 274;
(34[963b–4b].7) 274; (35[964b–5a].1)
274; (38[966b–7b].1) 274, (11) 274

Cicero
De officiis (1.113) 214
Epistulae ad Atticum (2.1.1) 244
Columella *Res rustica* (6.35) 240

Demosthenes
De corona (298) 218
De pace (5.12) 218

Homer *Odyssey* (4.221 ff) 238; (9.196 ff)
264; (10.510) 266; (12.327) 276

Justinian *Digest* (3.2.4) 245

Lucian *Nigrinus* (8) 218; (11) 218; (32)
218; (37) 218; (38) 233

Pliny *Naturalis historia*
– book 2 (4) 241; (5) 241; (10) 242; (11)
242; (14) 241, 242; (28) 242; (32)
242–3; (34) 242–3; (39) 242; (45) 242;
(54) 242; (89) 243; (92–3) 242; (94) 242;
(99) 242; (101) 242; (107) 243; (109)
243; (113) 243; (127) 243; (135) 243;
(135–6) 243; (137) 243; (140–1) 243;
(142) 243; (145) 243; (146) 243; (182–3)
247; (219) 245; (221) 245; (222) 245;
(223) 245; (224) 246; (226) 246; (228)
246; (230) 246; (233) 246, 246–7; (234)
246; (235) 246; (236) 246
– book 3 (9–10) 247; (152) 247
– book 7 (8) 247; (12) 247; (14–15) 247;
(15) 247; (16) 247; (16–18) 247, 247–8;
(28) 248; (30) 248; (34) 248; (41) 248;
(45) 248; (57) 248; (125) 220; (213) 248
– book 8 (28) 248–9; (34) 249; (40) 240,
249; (45) 249; (48) 249; (52) 249; (54)
249; (62) 240; (66) 240; (68) 249; (69)
249; (71) 249; (77–8) 250; (78) 250 (84)
234, 250; (85) 241, 250; (86) 250; (87)

In this index the classical reference is given first, in parentheses, followed by the
page number in CWE 23 or 24. For subject references, names not in this index,
Erasmus' comments on authors, and all other matters consult the General Index.

Index of Classical and Early Christian Sources in *De copia*

Aelian *De natura animalium* 585
Aeschylus *Oresteia* 613
Aesop *Fables* 297; (4) 585, 632; (40) 639;
  (124) 634; (162) 632
Ambrose, St *Life of St Agnes* 650
Anthologia palatina (9.47) 629; (9.331)
  612; (16.275) 643n
Apion 615
Apuleius
  Apology (9) 332n; (10) 332n; (22) 591;
  (70) 317n; (73) 317n
  Florida (3) 316n; (7) 571; (9) 573, 583;
  (23 [*De deo Socratis* prologue]) 297,
  633
  Metamorphoses (2.4) 386n; (5.1–2)
  587; (5.29) 321n; (10.16) 319
Aristophanes
  Birds (1353–7) 615
  Frogs 643; (293) 388n, 643; (1150 ff)
  299
  Plutus 389n, 582; (1154 ff) 642
  Wasps (1241) 338
Aristotle
  Categories (1) 307n; (10) 342n
  Historia animalium 585n; (9.13) 615
  Rhetoric (1.11) 654n; (2.1–17) 584,
  654; (2.20 ff) 607
  Topica 606n
Asconius Pedianus
  Commentarium in Cornel. (68) 517n

Oratio … in toga candida (73) 517n
Augustine, St *De civitate Dei* (1.14)
  613; (2.27) 376; (3.17) 521n
Ausonius *Epigrams* (33.3) 582, 643n

Boethius
  Aristotle's *Categories*, translation of
  307n
  Aristotle's *Topica*, translation of
  606n
  Cicero's *Topica*, commentary on
  606n
  Consolatio philosophiae 318; (1.1) 583

Caesar
  Bellum civile (1.27.2) 468n; (2.27.2)
  432; (3.51.4) 544; (3.59 ff) 644n
  Bellum Gallicum (1.16.4) 570; (1.36.1)
  552; (4.37.3) 475; (6.31.1) 429; (7.20.1)
  448
Cato
  De re rustica (2.1) 377; (65.1) 517;
  (161.2) 517
  Disticha Catonis (4.42) 311
Catullus (3.2) 401; (5.3) 443; (22) 430;
  (23.12) 388n; (25.13) 532; (29.11–12)
  432; (33.8) 443n; (49.6–7) 372; (58.5)
  315; (64.139) 495; (67.28) 341; (68.16)
  336; (68.28) 502; (74.3) 315; (107.6)
  502

In this index the classical or early Christian reference is given first, in parentheses,
followed by the page number in cwe 23 or 24. For subject references, names not in
this index, Erasmus' comments on authors, and all other matters consult the General
Index.

General Index

Aalst 125
abbots, accused of preferring ignorant monks 25, 32, 80
Abel 686
Abelard 666n
abominatio 347
abundance of expression. *See copia*
abusio. *See* catachresis
Academic school of Greek philosophy 56, 68, 429
Academy of Plato 19, 39, 69, 102
Accius, Roman tragic poet 228
acclamation (epiphonema) 609, 629, 687n
Achelous, river god overcome by Hercules 341, 611
Achilles 19, 50, 145, 180n, 331, 389n, 390, 581, 590, 610, 618, 623, 681; how he must be depicted 584
Acidula, a spring 246
Acragas (Agrigento) in Sicily 226, 228n, 331n, 391n, 682n
Acursius (Francesco Accorso), jurist 98n
adiuratio 347
admiratio 347
Adrian de Castello, Italian churchman resident in England 581
Adriatic 341, 386
adversative statements 368–9
adversity, behaviour in 197, 205, 216, 237, 245, 266
advice, bad, consequences of 228–9
Aeacus, grandfather of Achilles 331
Aeginetan 685

Aemathia (Thessaly) 312
Aemilius Paulus, famous Roman general 37
Aeneas 118, 331, 394n, 645, 690
Aeschines, pupil of Socrates 624
Aeschinus, character in Terence 689
Aeschylus, ridiculed by Aristophanes 299
Aesculapius 201, 640
Aesop: his fables attributed to Hesiod by Quintilian 631–2; best of fabulists 631–2; mentioned 166n, 224, 690n
Aesopus, celebrated Roman actor 103n, 104, 391n
Aesopus, M. Clodius, son of the actor, who squandered a fortune 103, 104, 391
affection: dangerous when feigned 251; harmful if excessive 252, 255
Africa 138n, 227, 243, 408, 409
Africans: whether trustworthy 415; mentioned 608
Agamemnon lxviii, 27, 218, 227, 585
Agathon, friend of Socrates 640
Ages of Gold, Silver, and Iron 582
Agricola, Rodolphus (Huisman) 8, 30n; 'a man of more than human stature' 289
Agrigento. *See* Acragas
Agrippa, as name 248
Agrippa, Marcus 248
Ajax 50, 389, 585
Alba 325
Albania 247

272; 'the teacher of life' 591, 625; must be studied 675

Hoffman, Manfred xxivn

Holland 3, 14, 23

Holofernes xliv

Holy Spirit, as source of eloquence and learning 10, 45n, 114, 115, 116, 117, 118, 120, 121

Homer: as school author xliv, 669, 681; moral allegory in his poetry xlvi, 611n, 612–13; excels both in fullness and compression 298; supremacy of 496; unrivalled in descriptive power 577, 580, 581, 654; rich in epithets 579, 642–3, 646, 655; use of figures 623; skill in dialogue 649; skill in expression of emotion 654; 'father of all myth' 673; mentioned 27, 37, 43, 105n, 145n, 152, 156n, 178, 202, 232, 238, 321, 331, 359, 610, 613, 625n

homoiologia. *See* sameness of colour

homoioseis 124. *See also* parallel

homonyms 307

honour 242, 249

honours, dangerous if too sudden 243

Hoogstraten, Jacobus van, inquisitor 11

Horace: as school author xliv, 669; description in 580; fable of country mouse 633; mentioned 2, 21, 22, 31, 36, 42, 47n, 73, 83, 100, 103n, 114, 117n, 308, 332, 681

Horatius, Marcus, legendary Roman hero 618, 653, 680

Horman, William, vulgaria by xxxivn, xxxvin

Hortensia, Roman matron famed for an oration 371n

Hortensius, orator and jurist, rival of Cicero 320, 629–30; master of plain style 496

Hugo of Saint-Cher 239n

humanism, humanists xx–xxii, xxvii, xxxiii–xxxiv, xxxviii, xlivn, xlv, lvii, 8; Christian 10

humour 249; Cicero on 654

Hungary lx

Hutton, James lxix

Hydra, monster overcome by Hercules 36, 390

Hyginus 674

Hyma, Albert 5, 11, 12

Hypanis, river in Scythia 243

hyperbole 344, 385

Hyperbolus, Athenian demagogue 625

hypocrisy 230, 272

hypothesis 593

hypotyposis 577–9

Hyrcania 162

Icarus 22, 390; story of, a moral allegory 611

Idaean Daktyls 188n

Ilissus 3

Ilium 298

illness. *See* disease

illustrative examples. *See* examples

image. *See* likeness

'images' to aid memory 671

imitation xli–xlii, 670

imperative 439

impersonation 679. *See also* prosopopoeia

inconsistency 241, 245, 249

indefinites 398, 402

Index librorum prohibitorum (1559, 1564), and Erasmus lvi

India 32, 109, 235, 248

Indians li, lxvii, 222, 253, 268, 581

induction 623–4

inference 593–4

innovations 316–20, 337–9

inscriptions. *See* coins

insignia of rank, no proof of merit 262

instability of mind 258

instruction. *See* education

intellection. *See* synecdoche

intemperance 213

intensification 373–5, 377–8, 378–9

interpretation (as rhetorical term) 320

interrogatio 347

inventions (fictions) 634–5

Ionian mode 574

Ionian sea 143n

Petronius, criticized for mixing prose with verse 318

Pettie, George lxvin

Pfeiffer, Rudolf lviin, 5, 74n

Phaedo, friend of Socrates 640

Phaedra, wife of Theseus 645

Phaedria, character in Terence 584, 645

Phaedrus, fabulist 47n, 677n

Phaedrus, friend of Socrates 119, 640

Phaethon 44, 386n; story of, an allegory 611

Phalaris, tyrant of Acragas 228, 331, 385, 391; spurious letters of 585, 682

Pharsalus, battle of 321, 594

Philargus 542

Philip of Macedon 161n, 202

Philiscus (Philistus), denigrator of Virgil 69

Philiscus. *See* Fieschi

Philistines xxx

Philistus. *See* Philiscus, denigrator of Virgil

Phillips, Margaret Mann xxvi, xxxiiin, xlin

philosophers: and Christianity 24, 102; virtues and weaknesses of 55, 56, 64, 68; Augustine on 97; mentioned 168, 178, 179, 180, 187, 189, 194, 207, 209, 210, 211, 216, 233, 247, 260, 269

Philosophia Christi xvi, xxivn

philosophy: use and misuse of 96–7, 162, 175, 198, 216, 217, 218, 219, 220, 223, 230, 233, 236, 264; power and pursuit of 102, 135, 139, 150, 151, 164, 184, 185, 187, 209, 210, 211, 212, 238, 245, 246, 250, 265; and poetry 181, 183–4, 625; features of 585; 'banisher of vice' 591; best teachers of 673

Philostratus, description by 581

Philotis, character in Terence 584

Philoxenus (of Cythera?), Greek poet 106

Philoxenus (of Leucas), Greek poet 181

Phintias 20n

Phocion, Athenian general 188, 200, 391, 585

Phoenix, tutor and friend of Achilles 585, 681

Phormio, character in Terence 389, 584

Phrygia 138n, 218, 230; home of Aesop 632

Phrygian mode 574

Phrygians, wise after the event 554

physics 95

Pindar 206; admired by Quintilian 301

Pirithous (Peirithous) 19, 20n

Pisano, Bartolomeo 90

Pisistratus 585

Pittacus of Mitylene, philosopher 229, 614

Pius II, pope 690n

Pius IV, pope, index of (1564) lvi

'places' to aid memory 71

plagiarists 260

Platina, Bartolomeo 106

Plato xxii, xxviin, xlviii, lxviii; and *Antibarbari* 3; compared with Cicero 380; wisest of philosophers 590, 591; doctrine on community of wives 652; as teacher of philosophy 673; on universals 666; on love 686; mentioned 16, 24, 27n, 32, 40, 55, 58, 68n, 101, 102, 106, 119, 139, 183, 186, 205, 206, 208, 324, 392n, 438, 459, 585, 586

– works: *Apology* 29n, 65n; *Charmides* xxviin; *Cratylus* 666n; *Demodocus* 33; *Laws* 51, 158; *Menexenus* 68n; *Phaedrus* 39, 99, 119; *Protagoras* 29; *Republic* 16n, 51, 141n, 205n, 666n; *Symposium* 686n

Platonists and Christianity xxxi; Augustine on 97

Plautus: as school author xliv, 669; characterization in, contrasted with Terence 584; mentioned 77, 305, 308, 333n, 339n, 385n, 663, 665

This book

was designed by

ANTJE LINGNER

based on the series design by

ALLAN FLEMING

and was printed by

University

of Toronto

Press